from the publishers of **Which?**

The Good Food Guide 1979

D1344430

Edited by Christopher Driver

Founded in 1951 by Raymond Postgate

Consumers' Association and Hodder & Stoughton

The Good Food Guide 1979 is published by
Consumers' Association and Hodder & Stoughton
on behalf of The Good Food Club Ltd.,
14 Buckingham Street, WC2N 6DS
© The Good Food Club Ltd. 1979

Maps
© The Good Food Club Ltd.

The Good Food Guide is published annually.
This is a new edition, brought up to date
throughout, and with a new Preface. Please do not
rely on an out-of-date Guide. Since many of the
places in the last edition are no longer recommended
(some have closed or changed hands),
disappointments may well result.

Other publications from The Good Food Guide:
The Good Food Guide Dinner Party Book
The Good Cook's Guide

Design by Banks & Miles

Cover design by Ron Newman & Associates

Printed and bound in England by
Hazell Watson & Viney Ltd,
Aylesbury, Buckinghamshire

CONTENTS

HOW TO USE
THE GUIDE

CLASSIFICATION Generally speaking, British hotels and restaurants
are too diverse for precise classification. Descriptions
are indispensable. But over the years, the *Guide*
has found that most restaurants and hotels fall
naturally into one of the following categories:

Credit This category sets the tone for all entries in the
Guide. It indicates careful, honest cooking, of
whatever national style, that is appropriate to the
resources of the place. It also embraces wide
variations of character and – be it freely admitted –
quality. *Guide*-users will know that before they visit
a restaurant, they are wise to read all the lines in
an entry, and sometimes between them as well.
Many different people's thoughts and experiences
are represented in what is written, and we
therefore like to print as many approvers' names as
there is room for (provided the people concerned
give their consent on the report forms).

Pass These places are signified by a short description
with details printed underneath the text instead of
approvers' names. These are hotels and restaurants
which are seldom worth seeking out for the sake of
their food, drink and service alone, but they are
often welcome places to discover, either in a parched
terrain or as alternatives to more expensive places.
Please remember that we need reports on these
places just as badly as we need them on others.
This year's pass can be next year's credit – or
drop-out.

Italic entries In both these categories, italic type is used to
denote a new, newly organised, or otherwise
disputable place on which a satisfactory verdict
cannot be reached by the time we go to press. We
are particularly anxious for members' reports on
these.

Distinction Restaurants and hotels may earn one or more of the following *Good Food Guide* distinctions. The 'pestle', the 'tureen', the 'bottle', the 'glass' – and the value-for-money underlinings – set marks for restaurateurs to aim for and Good Food Club members to judge by.

A pestle-and-mortar symbol denotes unusual skill, imagination and energy in a chef or team. Good Food Club members will bestow this label grudgingly. Sound materials, judicious menu-building, and a good technique should be looked for, as well as indefinable, indispensable flair, and more than ordinary reliability.

A tureen is confined to hotels. It signifies at once a well-kept table and a house where it is a pleasure to stay for more than a weekend. This category recognises those hoteliers, especially in parts of the country popular for holidays, who are conspicuous for the trouble they take to please their guests, and whose kitchens can produce – perhaps not every night, but often – a dish or a meal of 'pestle-and-mortar' standard.

A bottle denotes a wine list and service out of the usual run. Here again, it is best to be cautious. Skill is above all shown in the compilation of a well-balanced and annotated list, suitable to the pocket and preferences of discriminating customers, and in cellaring and service. (Service alone can easily subtract pounds from the real value of mature claret or burgundy, and a smoky atmosphere can render the wine almost worthless.) For this distinction to be awarded, a current list must be submitted before the *Guide* goes to press.

A glass symbol picks out places whose resources of skill, space, or capital are not equal to the demands of a 'bottle', but which make a serious effort, in a complicated market, to pick out wines of character, even among the cheaper bottles that are all most people can afford to drink. The glass symbol is also sometimes used for places whose wine lists, taken in isolation, might deserve a 'bottle', but which suffer from one or other of the shortcomings discussed in the previous paragraph.

BEER Our criteria for describing the various kinds of beer are outlined in our pub section on p. 441.

CARAFE WINES The Weights and Measures (Sale of Wine) Order 1976 restricts carafe wines to sealed bottles or open vessels holding one of the following quantities: 25 cl, 50 cl, 75 cl, one litre, 10 fl oz (half a pint), or 20 fl oz. The place must tell you, if you ask, which measure is being used, but in almost all cases where the information has been supplied on our questionnaire we have ourselves specified not only the measure but also the origin or brand of such wine.

RESTAURANTS Unless otherwise stated, a restaurant is open all the week and all the year and is licensed. Meal times refer to first and last orders.

Cost of a meal for one
Tdh £2·50 (meal £3·70)
Alc £4·50 (meal £6·80)

The first table d'hôte figure is the cost of a set meal as notified to us by the restaurant in autumn 1978. The first à la carte figure is our estimated cost of three middle-priced courses from the menu. The meal price (in brackets) in both cases is the food price for one person, with 'extras' (cover, service, VAT), plus coffee and half the cheapest bottle of wine. Without wine, the cost will be over £1 less. (In oriental or health-food restaurants, we have substituted the kind of food and drink customarily ordered.) 'VAT inc' and 'service inc' mean that an inn's policy is to incorporate these charges in its food prices.

Value Prices underlined in the left-hand column like this: Tdh D £5·50 (meal £7·25) are those which represent, in our judgment, unusual value for money, taking wine as well as food prices into account. They are not necessarily the cheapest restaurants in the *Guide*. (See list on page 520.)

Access for the disabled ♿ means that doorways are over 31½ ins wide and passages 35½ ins; that there are no more than the stated number of steps leading to the restaurant; and 'w.c.' means that the lavatories are accessible to wheelchairs – (m) and/or (f). This information has been provided by the restaurants. Please let us know of any inaccuracies.

HOTELS   Bed and breakfast and full board prices are those quoted to us by hoteliers; where possible we have given minimum off-season and maximum in-season prices for one person sharing a double room.

Dogs   In hotels, 'no dogs in public rooms' may mean that dogs are allowed in bedrooms. Enquire.

Fire cert   This phrase (see regulations in the Fire Precautions 'Hotels and Boarding Houses' Order, 1972) means that a hotel was granted a Fire Certificate before we went to press.

ABBREVIATIONS

a.c.	appellation contrôlée	*Chr*	Christmas	*inc*	inclusive
alc	à la carte	*cl*	centilitre	*L*	lunch
App	approvers	*D*	dinner	*min*	minimum
B&B	bed and breakfast	*d/r*	dining-room	*n.v.*	non-vintage
c.b.	château-bottled	*exc*	except	*p.d.*	per day
Ch.	Château	*fl oz*	fluid ounces	*p.w.*	per week
		HT	high-tea	*res*	residents
				rest	restaurant
				tdh	table d'hôte

TELEPHONE   For major cities which have a basic STD code and several all-figure subsidiary exchanges, a dash separates the code from the local number. Thus the telephone number of the Midland Hotel in Manchester is 061-236 3333. For other places listed in the book, the name of the exchange is given, not the STD code, which sometimes varies according to the whereabouts of the caller.

MAPS   Any town or village in which there is a *Guide* entry is printed in black on the maps at the end of the book. 'Credit' recommendations are in bold capitals; 'pass' entries are in small letters; hotels are indicated by a triangle; distinctions have a bolder outline. A tankard indicates a pub, a glass a wine bar (both in italic type – see map key).

REPORTS   Please send in reports as soon as you can during the year, but particularly before September 30, 1979, in time for the next *Guide*. Report forms are at the back of the book. When you have filled them in, send them without a stamp to Freepost, The Good Food Guide, 14 Buckingham Street, London WC2N 6BR, and we will gladly send you more.

DISTINCTIONS

LONDON

Chez Nico, SE22

Connaught, W1

Le Gavroche, SW1

La Giralda, Pinner

Ma Cuisine, SW3

Oslo Court, NW8

Tante Claire, SW3

ENGLAND

Alresford, Hants
O'Rorkes

Ambleside, Cumbria
Rothay Manor

Bath, Avon
Popjoys

Bray, Berks
Waterside Inn

Burham, Kent
Toastmaster's Inn

Cheltenham, Glos
Food for Thought

Chesterton, Oxon
Kinchs

Chittlehamholt, Devon
Highbullen Hotel

Christchurch, Hants
Splinters

Cleeve Hill, Glos
Malvern View Hotel

Colyton, Devon
Old Bakehouse

Dartmouth, Devon
Carved Angel

Dedham, Essex
Le Talbooth

Gittisham, Devon
Combe House

Glastonbury, Somerset
No 3 Dining Rooms

Grasmere, Cumbria
White Moss House

Great Dunmow, Essex
The Starr

Gulworthy, Devon
Horn of Plenty

Halesworth, Suffolk
Bassett's

Harrogate, N. Yorks
Number Six

Helford, Cornwall
Riverside

Hintlesham, Suffolk
Hintlesham Hall

Horton, Northants
French Partridge

Isle of Wight
Peacock Vane

Kenilworth, Warwicks
Restaurant Bosquet

Kintbury, Berks
Dundas Arms

Manchester
Midland Hotel French Restaurant

Moulton, N. Yorks
Black Bull

Northleach, Glos
Old Woolhouse

Oxford, Oxon
Restaurant Elizabeth

Pool-in-Wharfedale, W. Yorks
Pool Court

Poundisford, Somerset
Well House

St Martin in Meneage, Cornwall
Boskenna

Salisbury, Wilts
Crane's

South Petherton, Somerset
Oaklands

Thornbury, Avon
Thornbury Castle

Ullswater, Cumbria
Sharrow Bay Country House
   Hotel

Windermere, Cumbria
Miller Howe

Woolverton, Somerset
Woolverton House Hotel

Wye, Kent
Wife of Bath

Eddleston, Peeblesshire
Cringletie House

Glasgow
Central Hotel
Malmaison Restaurant

Gullane, E. Lothian
La Potinière

Inverness, Inverness-shire
Dunain Park

Nairn, Nairnshire
Clifton Hotel

Perth, Perthshire
Timothy's

Selkirk, Selkirkshire
Philipburn House Hotel

Uphall, W. Lothian
Houstoun House

WALES

Llandewi Skirrid, Gwent
Walnut Tree Inn

CHANNEL ISLANDS

Sark
Hotel Petit Champ

SCOTLAND

Achiltibuie, Ross & Cromarty
Summer Isles Hotel

Ballater, Aberdeenshire
Tullich Lodge

Beattock, Dumfriesshire
Old Brig Inn

Cupar, Fife
Timothy's

IRELAND

Cork, Co Cork
Arbutus Lodge

Mallow, Co Cork
Longueville House

Oughterard, Co Galway
Currarevagh House

Shanagarry, Co Cork
Ballymaloe House

PREFACE

Ten years ago, to the month, Raymond Postgate said farewell on this page to members of the Good Food Club. (Characteristically, he used the Latin word *valete*.) Postgate's editorship of the book he founded had been a long one; he minded the nation's stomach for twenty years, ever since a series of magazine articles from his hand gathered round him a group of people who cared passionately – and at that time, unfashionably – about what they and others ate and drank in restaurants and hotels. By the act of buying this book and reporting on your own experiences you are yourself part of this group, now tens of thousands strong.

This remains the essence of the matter. No one is infallible. The *Guide*'s present editor and chief inspector can both remember occasions when their own experience, good or bad, of particular places has turned out to be freakish and unrepresentative. There have also been times, be it said, when they have felt obliged to back their own judgement against the majority view expressed by the reports on file, but these are the exceptions. The real strength of this book is that every single entry represents a random sample of meals eaten by unrecognised, unobtrusive people who claim no free meals, special service, recompense or reward. We know of but one other restaurant guide in the world that conducts itself successfully on this principle, accepting neither advertising nor sponsorship however disinterested, and that book, *Where to Eat in Canada*, was modelled on the *Good Food Guide*. The *Guide* is one of the few bits of the co-operative movement that actually works, though co-operators, and progressives generally, tend to purse their lips and shake their heads over a book that professes such ideals and applies them to the pursuit of pleasure – worse still, the pleasures of the table.

At the same time, the *Guide* has never been particularly popular at the other end of the political or commercial spectrum either. Indeed, the book's dependence on ordinary restaurant customers for much of its information and evaluation explains why some highly articulate sections of the catering trade resent and fear what is written about them. They always have done. In the second (1952) 'ition, Postgate wrote about the correspondence he had received publication of the first: 'One innkeeper, thinking he found a hint of criticism in a highly laudatory entry, had the nerve to send a solicitor's letter. And other letters showed that there are still hoteliers in this land who do not think they are the servants of the public, but dictators to it.'

Well, there still are. If anything, arrogance and self-satisfaction among caterers have become more noticeable because of the trade's successes. After all, over the 30-year period since the gestation of the first *Good Food Guide*, Britain has emerged as a country in which an international tourist, if catholic in his tastes and highly selective in his choice of addresses, can eat as well as he can anywhere but in the most favoured regions of France. Much of this advance has been achieved by amateurs or immigrants in the teeth of accountants, food synthesisers and other commercials who exist to slice the customer as thin as they slice their own roasts; but still, the bridgehead has been secured. Again, even the past ten years have seen at least a proportion of English pubs, formerly sacred to the unaccompanied drinking man, become for the first time in centuries places where uncomplicated home-cooked food can also be obtained during normal eating hours, and consumed on the premises by men, women, and children.

But for all the *Guide*'s own efforts in this and other directions, and for all the national obsession with cooking and kitchens celebrated by glossy magazines and colour supplements, it is very doubtful whether a larger proportion of the people who are now to be found in expensive restaurants know more about good eating and drinking, or are more prepared to make a fuss to obtain what they are paying for, than did their counterparts in Postgate's generation. As a result, up and down the country there are hundreds, even thousands, of restaurateurs who have come to believe their own order books, convincing themselves that Brillat-Savarin himself would be humbled if he could taste the confections that issue from their kitchens. One such person, whose restaurants in the West End of London would risk being reported to a Society for the Prevention of Cruelty to Food if they operated in a less indulgent milieu, sent a letter during 1978 to suggest that there could not be much wrong with places that had been established for over 100 years and were turning over upwards of £1m. per annum. 'It seems to me quite absurd that we are not included in your *Guide*.' Quite so, and *The Mousetrap* is the best play in London. But mind how you laugh, for even some of the genuinely superior places that appear in the following pages are not immune from the same conviction of total righteousness. Often it arises simply for want of day-to-day, night-to-night tasting at the service door, and criticism from the dining-room. The professional chef of one place where I ate last summer would have been understandably hurt to be told that he would have a first-rate restaurant if he would keep sugar out of his main courses and salted butter out of his puddings, but it would have been fair comment – and that was one of the better places. On another occasion last year a country innkeeper wrote in patronising tones, and not for the first time, to enquire why he was persistently excluded from the *Guide*. As it happened, his establishment had been inspected the previous week. (He was not to know this, of course, lacking in the *Guide*'s case what another hotelier revealingly described to *Caterer and Hotelkeeper* as 'the good relationship we have built up over the years with AA and Ronay inspectors'.) Not only was the food pretty disgusting ('lobster soup "in the French manner" looked and tasted like wallpaper paste crossed with parsley sauce . . . cheesecake coated the mouth') but an'old have-your-cake-and-eat-it trick was being tried with the service: 'Gratuities are left to grateful customers' appeared on the menu; 10 per cent was added to the bill.

Guide inspectors, by the way, whether voluntary or part-time professional, do not declare themselves before, during or after the meals, for reasons which should now be obvious: they may need to visit the same place again another year, for their service happily tends to spread over a decade or two. They are recruited primarily from the ranks of ordinary Good Food Club members, on the strength of a succession of reports which give evidence that they know what they are talking about. On the whole, the further from London you live, the better your chances of being drawn into this inner circle of information-gathering. Details of a competition designed to widen the circle without weakening it will be announced in the *Guide*'s 'half-term' newsletter, sent in June to all purchasers of the book whose names are recorded in this office.

Perhaps enough has been said by implication, both in this and in previous prefaces, to indicate to readers new and old what we all think the book is about. But there is one area of misunderstanding that has persisted from Postgate's time into mine, and deserves a separate note. It is sometimes said or written that the *Guide* leaves out places because they are expensive, and admits others because they are cheap, with the supposedly ludicrous result that one or two major British cities are represented in these pages by a Bangladeshi take-away rather than by one of those places where Sir Carolus Pianissimo will do you bed, breakfast and evening meal for forty quid or so.

There is no reason to suppose that the average reader of this book, or the average member of the British public, or even the average foreign visitor, is entirely uninterested in the price he or she pays for meals out. However, whether you are able, or inclined, to spend £5 or £15 or even a sheikhly £50 a head on a restaurant meal is up to you. All the *Guide* can do from its collective experience is to indicate, within the constraints imposed by the information you supply and the resources the sales of our book provide for inspection, where in any of these categories good food can be found at a price fair for its quality. In this approach, the separate philosophies of the *Guide* and Consumers' Association (our publishers since 1963) converge. Obviously, from him who charges most, the most is expected, and there is no need for us to apologise for excluding London places that ask Gavroche-like prices without achieving Gavroche-like professionalism and dependability. Likewise, the accidental location of very different types of hotel or restaurant in our pages or on our maps implies no direct comparison between one and the other: *Motoring Which?* does not blame a Cortina for not being a Rolls-Royce, nor vice versa, and neither do we. But we do attempt to point out the virtues and defects of the catering equivalents within their own range of ambition and possibility. Indeed, Good Food Club members, like the best critics of all the arts, are often most severe on the places whose technique and principles they admire most.

This, I believe, is what serious restaurateurs and serious customers both want. There are other books for people to use if they want the gaps on the map filled by nearly-good, or would-be-good, or occasionally-good restaurants and hotels. The *Guide*'s reputation has been earned by declining to admit such places, unless they are useful enough to be summarily described, or new enough to be given the term of probation that is usually implied in these pages by italic type. In this restless search for sincerity and technical competence combined, it matters little what genre a restaurant represents, or in what price bracket it lies: some of the dearest are among the most disgraceful, but equally, there are hundreds of cynically run Chinese and Indian places, over-adapted to various levels of the British market, and customers do well to avoid them, even if the financial penalty incurred by them is in most cases relatively small.

There are well over 1,000 addresses in this book, taking restaurants, hotels, pubs and wine bars together. Such are the vicissitudes of catering, and the time-limits of publishing (even this kind, which enables us to incorporate information only six weeks old when the book goes on sale) that already there may be a dozen places that ought not to be in, and a dozen more that should replace them. Tell us. Tell us not just in September, when the final date for reports to the 1980 *Guide* falls due, but as soon as possible after your meal, so that inspections can be properly and economically planned later in the year. Use the forms at the back of the book if you like, or ask for others when you write. Send them without a stamp to Freepost, The Good Food Guide, 14 Buckingham Street, London WC2N 6BR; and as Postgate used to say with gusto at this point, good eating.

Christopher Driver

A SURVEYOR'S REPORT ON 'HOUSE' WINES

by Edmund Penning-Rowsell

As many travellers have noticed, it usually costs more to drink fine French wines in France than it does in Britain. This is because the great majority of such wines bypass the retail market altogether and go straight to restaurants, where they are normally marked up by about 300 per cent. (People paying their own bills content themselves with humbler, more local bottles.) In Britain, the restaurant mark-up is lower, usually about 100 per cent, though there are several places in this book that keep it as low as 50 per cent, or substitute a flat-rate mark-up that makes the dearer bottles better value. There are also a few restaurateurs, almost all of them French, who cheerfully put 200 per cent on every bottle, as though they had never left home. British restaurant customers – not all of them on expense accounts – can often be observed drinking the leading wines, or at least the middle-ranking ones, in the places that stock them. But wine of this quality is so accessible in this country that most of it is drunk far more cheaply in private homes, and it is bottles from the lower end of the wine scale that are found on most tables in most restaurants.

This is clearly sensible, for save in exceptional circumstances and settings, who would want to drink high-priced classed-growth clarets or *grand cru* burgundies, where bouquet and flavour may be contaminated by cigarette or cigar smoke from the next table? And in any case how can one know the state in which they have been kept, and not least, how long they have been mulling in the restaurant dispense? So for reasons of cost or caution, it is branded *vins courants* – I refuse to use the deprecatory term said to have originated either in Australia or the Flanders *estaminets* of World War One – that are most frequently drunk in the restaurants the *Guide* lists. They are usually identified by name if the restaurant has supplied the information (which may or may not be given on wine lists).

Relatively inexpensive as most of these wines are, is their quality reasonably good and are they good value for money? To test this, the *Guide* staff picked out some of the bottles most frequently chosen by restaurateurs as their carafe wine for 1979,

bought them (11 reds and 10 whites) at retail shops, and invited
ten people to taste them. As this was not a competition, the wines
were not tasted blind, and none of the men and women tasting was
in the wine trade. They included the Editor, the Chief Inspector
and myself, and other independent judges. All were sufficiently
acquainted with wine to know what they were about when
confronted with a restaurant wine list, but this does not mean that
they were unacquainted with, or uninterested in, the cheaper
bottles obtainable.

The evaluation of a wine's quality must always be to some extent
subjective. Marking by numbers imposes a certain discipline,
though this is diminished if the range is too wide. Here a rather
tight range of 1–5 was adopted, closely linked to word-evaluations.
1 indicated 'very poor', 2 'poor', 3 'acceptable', 4 'good', 5 'very
good'. Some of the tasters found this a little restricting, and gave
half marks. It was realised, of course, that the markings reflected
the 'ordinaire' style of the wines. We were not comparing them with
classed-growth clarets or fine white wines, but with the best that
could reasonably be expected for the money.

The results were disappointing, although, of course, there were
variations of opinion. Only three wines – two red and one white –
were judged 'very good' by anyone, and only the white example
received more than a single vote at this level. Yet twelve were
marked as 'very poor', and eight of these were white. The most
universally disliked wine was the red Choix du Roy which received
seven '1's. It lacked colour, had an 'off' nose, and was variously
described as 'thin', 'sour', 'vinegary' and as having 'no body'. (When
a wine drew particularly adverse comments, a second bottle was
opened, but was found to be no different.)

Not one of the twenty-one wines escaped a 'poor' rating from
at least one taster, and the white Litre Vin collected this verdict
from five of the ten tasters, and also received two 'very poor's.
Comments ranged from 'bitter rather than fruity, watery' to
'sulphury'. The most favourable mark for this wine was $3\frac{1}{2}$
(acceptable-good), with the comment 'grapey nose, dry, clean,
rather flat taste'. However, two white wines received an even lower
overall rating: the Solitaire and the white Choix du Roy, with an
average vote of 1.9. Judgements of the Solitaire included
'coloured' – a sign of oxidation for a white wine – and 'dirty nose,
dirty taste'. One taster, however, marked it as 4 (good), with the
comment 'more golden than others so far. Sweetness continues into
taste, but with slight roughness.' Notes on the white Choix du Roy
were even more critical, including 'mild vomit on the nose', 'sick

	AVERAGE
WHITE	(OUT OF 5)
Plonque Blanc Sec, Balls Bros France 1 litre £1·85	2.5
Choix du Roy, Balls Bros France 1 litre £1·70	1.9
Nicolas Blanc Sec, Morgan Furze France 70 cl £1·42	2.8
Solitaire, Grierson Blumenthal France 70 cl £1·19	1.9
Litre Vin SIVIMIPI (Independent Wine Buyers' Consortium)	
France 1 litre £1·79	2.15
Toujours, Stowells of Chelsea France 1 litre £1·87	2.15
Carafino, Morgan Furze Hungary 1 litre £1·62	3.55
Monte Campo, Clode Baker & Wyld Italy 1 litre £1·79	2.95
Franchette dry white, Cullens Argentine 70 cl £1·22	2.5
Hirondelle, Hedges & Butler Italy 70 cl £1·39	2.9

RED	
College Claret, Dolamore France 73 cl £1·94	3.5
Plonque Rouge, Balls Bros France 1 litre £1·85	2.9
Choix du Roy, Balls Bros France 1 litre £1·70	1.4
Nicolas Vieux Ceps, Grants of St James's France 70 cl £1·42	3.35
Solitaire, Grierson Blumenthal France 70 cl £1·19	2.65
Litre Vin SIVIMIPI (Independent Wine Buyers' Consortium)	
France 1 litre £1·79	2.35
Toujours, Stowells of Chelsea France 1 litre £1·87	2.65
Carafino, Morgan Furze Spain 1 litre £1·62	2.9
Monte Campo, Clode Baker & Wyld Italy 1 litre £1·79	2.95
Franchette, Cullens Argentine 70 cl £1·22	2.45
Hirondelle, Hedges & Butler Italy 70 cl £1·39	2.2

nose' to 'non-taste or flavour'. It mustered no higher than three 'acceptable' (3) votes.

Turning, thankfully, to the other end of the scale, the red wine judged best was Dolamore's College Claret, deliberately put in as a 'marker' of an independent wine merchant's house wine, and not a brand. It was also an Appellation Contrôlée wine, which the others did not profess to be. It had 'a genuine claret nose', 'a smell and taste of real claret; though edgy at finish, would respond to keeping.' Another comment was 'young but promising'. Some of the bitterness that others noted would probably diminish with a further year in the bottle – which all too few basic Bordeaux rouges receive. Had it not been for this immaturity it would certainly have received a higher overall mark than 3.5, slightly above the Nicolas Vieux Ceps, the best-liked of the brands, which was, of course, a good deal cheaper. Indeed the relatively high price of the College Claret was commented on by more than one taster, but 'you get what you pay for . . .'

The most favourable comment on the Vieux Ceps was 'deep

colour, nice nose, good body; good for an ordinary wine'. Others were 'has character and fruit', 'smooth, drinkable'. Its most severe critic said it was 'short', a criticism made of many of the wines sampled, but one cannot expect too much of this class of wine, designed to be drunk at once. It was the only red wine, except for the College Claret, to achieve a '5' (very good) mark from any taster.

The best white wine was judged to be the Carafino, which now comes from Hungary. It received two '5' (very good) ratings – the only white wine to do so, and an overall average of 3.55. It had 'a good nose, with slight sweetness; fairly full, round, well-balanced wine'. Another was 'more sweetness than the others. I would have thought this more generally acceptable.' Less complimentary was 'a fairly rich gluey nose, verging on the medium-sweet side of dry'. Not everyone likes the rather full-bodied style of Hungarian white wines, and one taster marked the Carafino down as a wine too sweet to drink through a meal.

The relatively low standard of the whites was demonstrated by the fact that the one receiving the second highest marks, the Monte Campo, received an overall average below 3 (acceptable), although it managed to achieve four '4's (good). One taster commented 'mediciny, not too sweet, but a very palling taste' and marked it '1'; but another said 'grape markedly different and pleasing; dry – one would enjoy it with fish'; and a third wrote 'flowery nose and flavour; light, fruity'.

No doubt these variations in individual reaction to the wines would be reflected among restaurant customers, and it was generally agreed that many of the wines would taste better with food – or at least, that their mediocre qualities would be masked. However, disappointment was general. One taster wrote: 'I found the tasting rather depressing.' Another said of the reds, 'This lot were pretty dire.' A third found the College Claret hardly a basis for comparison with southern French, Italian, Argentine and Spanish reds. 'How much pleasanter even a cheap authentic claret is than some of these blends from, probably, more than one region.' This is surely true, although if one is paying a normal restaurant mark-up, the difference in cost becomes even more marked.

But may one not conclude from all this that even quite sophisticated restaurant customers are far less critical of the wines provided than of the food? It is understandable that many who are prepared to pay quite handsomely for food, particularly for dishes that they are unable or unlikely to produce at home, draw back from buying expensive wines, whose mark-up is more obvious than it is for the food. But it is less clear why some people are prepared to settle in restaurants for wines, whether named or anonymous, that are actually worse than the cheapest they consume at home.

The problems of the suppliers of brand wines may be recognised. The market is extremely competitive. Hence the switch of source from time to time for some brands; although, excluding the avowed claret, it is interesting to note that, in the tasting, six of the ten red and white restaurant 'pops' in each case came from France. Indeed the label of Plonque Blanc Sec described it as a *'vin de pays provenant des propriétés du Bordelais'*. Where do these Bordelais have their second wine home? And the Plonque Rouge proclaimed that it was *'provenant des régions les plus célèbres de France'*, which might promote some argument round the table as to which these were, and for what they are chiefly celebrated.

It is not easy, either, for the brand suppliers to ensure consistency for what is often a huge through-put of mass-produced blended wine – though Nicolas have a good reputation for this. Some of the more recent entrants into the business, notably the chain stores Marks & Spencer and Sainsbury, have also usually surmounted this problem; though to be fair, the quantities involved are not comparable with those handled by the biggest groups. One taster's footnote to the white wines sampled read; 'I have tasted better at the price, for example Sainsbury's Anjou Blanc at £1·40, which people seem to like.' Marks & Spencer have gone for quality rather than low price, and members proposing to visit unlicensed restaurants might well consider stopping off at a chain store rather than an off-licence.

The main responsibility for providing reasonably drinkable inexpensive table wines must, however, rest with the restaurants themselves. Their best sources are the traditional wine merchants who offer inexpensive house wines, whether a.c. – like the College claret – or non-a.c., such as Averys Clochemerle, or Berry Bros' Vin Rouge de Table. For unless and until the EEC succeeds in reducing our duties on wine, and with wine prices still rising at source, restaurant-goers are likely to rely increasingly on the cheap end of the wine list, which, this tasting showed, is being less than adequately served.

VINTAGE CHART

The ratings given on this and other vintage charts have not been handed down like Tablets of the Law, but are intended to be helpful on hurried occasions, as when one is handed a wine list by an impatient wine waiter. In particular two caveats must be made. First, clarets are derived from the largest fine-wine region in the world, and consequently they can vary greatly. In some years the Médocs are better than the St Emilions, or vice versa. Then the Loire, Rhône and Rhine are long rivers, with considerable variations in types of wine and weather patterns among the vineyard districts adjacent to their banks. Secondly, a high rating does not necessarily imply a vintage ready to drink. Among claret years, for example, 1970 is certainly a better year than 1971, but the latter is now more ready to drink. Moreover, because an old vintage enjoys a high marking, this does not imply that it is still at its best: both 1959 and 1964 clarets are now tending to show their age.

| YEAR | BORDEAUX | | BURGUNDY | | | RHONE | | |
	CLARET	SAUTERNES	RED	WHITE	LOIRE	RED	GERMANY	ENGLAND
1955	5	5	5	5	4	5	4	—
1956	1	—	—	—	—	—	—	—
1957	2	3	5	4	—	5	2	—
1958	3	4	—	—	—	—	—	—
1959	6	6	6	5	6	6	6–7	—
1960	3	2	—	—	—	3	2	—
1961	7	4	6	5	4	7	4	—
1962	4	4	3	7	—	5	3	—
1963	1	—	—	—	—	—	—	—
1964	4–5	3	5	5	4	5	5	—
1965	1	—	—	—	—	—	—	—
1966	6	4	6	6	4	5	4	—
1967	4	7	4	4	3	5	3	—
1968	1–2	—	—	—	—	—	—	—
1969	2	3	5	5	5	5	6	—
1970	6*	6	4	4	6	5	4	5
1971	5	5	6	6	5	6	7	6
1972	2*	2*	5	3–4	3	6–7*	3	—
1973	3*	3*	3	6	6	3*	4	5
1974	4*	1*	3*	3	3	3*	3	2
1975	6*	6*	2*	4	6–7	3–4*	7	3
1976	6*	5*	6*	6*	6	6*	7*	4
1977	—	—	2	3	—	4	3	2
1978	—	—	—	—	—	—	—	—

7 = very good
1 = poor
* = recommended for future rather than current drinking

Rhine and moselle have been combined since in no case do they differ by more than half a point.

In port and champagne, vintages are declared in good years only. The best include:

Port: 1945, 1948, 1955, 1958, 1960, 1963*, 1966*, 1967*, 1970*, 1975*
Champagne: 1961, 1964, 1966, 1969, 1970, 1971, 1973

GREATER LONDON

PREFACE

There are many Londons, in food and drink as in other pursuits, and everyone is apt to think that his or her own London is the one that matters. Between people who lunch in Hackney and those who dine in Hampstead, or between people who reckon to spend £20 a head on a French meal and others who stick at £5 for a Chinese one, there is no automatic communication. But both groups expect, fairly enough, that the *Good Food Guide* will at least try to serve their interests. Indeed, the extraordinary degree and quality of reader participation that this book enjoys, coupled with the natural inclinations of the full-time staff, result in a catholicity of taste that would be surprising in a single individual.

At the same time, the section that follows – and this year, the coloured London pages begin the book rather than being tucked away towards the end – does not claim to be a comprehensive guide to eating and drinking in the capital. It seldom mentions informal or tiny places or unlicensed places for meals, snacks, and takeaways, though in the intervals of following up Good Food Club members' restaurant nominations, most of us have taken pleasure – to stray no further than Soho – in smoked fish at **Hamburger Products**, 'duck plates' at **Lee Ho Fook** in Macclesfield Street, char siu buns from the **Kowloon**, salt beef at **Carroll's**, pizza at **Pizza Express**, croissants at **Chez Valérie** and patisserie at **Madame Bertaux**.

Moreover, for every restaurant and hotel that appears here, there are half a dozen others of which we have reports on file, sometimes to their credit, sometimes not. Even the places that an inspector has found on balance careless, or poor value, or an unpleasant environment for an evening, often have *something* to be said in their favour: perhaps there is a single dish that they do rather well; perhaps they are so well served and well spaced that people in search of a private conversation will tolerate food that does not rise above acceptability; perhaps they possess illustrious wine lists at prices markedly lower than the same bottles would be in Paris or New York.

In other words, if you can define your own needs or wants in certain ways, various places in the *Guide* and perhaps a few outside it begin to form functional groupings that can be taken in parallel with the *Guide*'s own indices of restaurants listed by national genre, value for money, Sunday opening, and so on. For instance, in the years before talk of our national economic decline was endorsed even by prime ministers, the **Savoy**, the **Mirabelle**, the **Café Royal** and one or two other famously grand places were virtually automatic choices for this book. No longer, but even so, not everything about them has changed. Optimists may even hold that micro-chip technology will ultimately restore the dependability of the **Mirabelle**'s cooking and the **Savoy**'s service. But for the time being these are places that belong to the rather large London genre which can offer a rich man excellent food and drink, in surroundings of some dignity, provided he does not permit them to interfere very much with the fine raw materials they buy. The **Guinea Grill** and **La Bussola** (in this year's *Guide*) partially fit this category too, and something of the same logic permits a Londoner to suggest **Simpson's** to a foreigner who must have roast sirloin of beef or saddle of mutton, and is willing to close off his senses and sensibilities to various other aspects of his meal and its service.

Again, for a person who would like at lunch-time to choose from a good variety of displayed cold food and eat it in varying degrees of comfort, there is something in common between **Le Perroquet** at the **Berkeley Hotel**, **Maudie's** at the **Drury Lane Hotel**, **Justin de Blank**, and the **Cork and Bottle** wine bar (all in the *Guide*). This category ought to be much larger. In the old *Guide* days it would have included the **Norway Food Centre**, but members seem to have fallen out of love with it. Sooner or later, no doubt, some oriental entrepreneur will assemble, perhaps in Soho or near the new British Museum when it is built, a range of Chinese and Indonesian dishes that lend themselves to buffet service, and invite a good architect to create an environment in which they can be enjoyed.

Wine-lovers, for their part, will know that their own choice may have to be made between the discomfort, low wine prices, and limited food of **Davy's** or other wine bars (in the *Guide*) and the comfort, long prices, and routine 'international' food of the **Dorchester**, the **Ritz**, the **Charing Cross**, the **Intercontinental** and other hotels old or new, which realise the advantages that storage space and capital resources confer on their wine buyers. Mere restaurants, as Edmund Penning-Rowsell points out in his annual commentary (page 15), are seldom satisfactory places in which to drink important wines.

AFTER DARK Map 12

144–145 Upper Street,
N.1
01-226 4218

Closed Sun; Sat L;
Apr 13; Dec 25 & 26;
Jan 1
Must book weekends
Meals 12–2.30, 7–12

Alc £4·60 (meal £7·10)

Seats 50 (parties 30)
&. rest
Air-conditioning
Am Ex, Diners

Bare brick and cork may do as much for Mexican make-believe as the spicing does in Richard Smith's 'very dark' restaurant. There are plants and goldfish too, and sincere, often successful attempts at guacamole, 'lemony and fresh-tasting, as though there were real chillies in it', tacos and tamales. Old Mexico hands also know just how hard it is to find edible Mexican food in Mexico, so the chilli sauces, veal chop in green tomato and almond sauce (£2·95), red snapper, quince paste, and tequila cocktails are well worth encouraging. But a few deplorable or bland main courses and sweets, or ill-cooked rice, have also been reported, so do not regard the place as Montezuma's gift to Islington, but as an experiment worth continued assessment. Wines from £2·30 in 1978. Good coffee. Ethnic and other music. No dogs. More reports, please.

AJIMURA Map 15

51–53 Shelton Street,
W.C.2
01-240 0178

Susumi Okada's 'least intimidating London Japanese restaurant for a novice' has a helpful menu and cooperative staff. Even so, this style of eating demands practice and plenty of time, and is not for the ravenous. Sit at the counter and try the lunchtime grilled mackerel set menu (£2·50) – slices of fish, a bowl of shrimps, miso soup, morsels of sweetish omelette, sticky rice (often tepid and under-salted) and a fruit salad. A la carte, fisherman's grill (£3) has been liked. Drink tea, Carlsberg (35p) or saké (85p the flask). Japanese records.

Closed Sun; Sat L;
Dec 24 & 31; public hols
Meals 12–2.30, 6–11

Tdh from £2·50
Alc £4·65 (meal £6·25)

VAT inc

Service 10% D
Seats 50 (parties 20)
No dogs
Access, Barclay

ALONSO'S Map 16

32 Queenstown Road,
S.W.8
01-720 7079

Closed Sun; Sat L; public
hols
Must book
Meals 12.30–2.30,
7.30–11.30

Tdh L £4·50 (meal
£7·50), D from £7 (meal
£10·35)

When the bell is rung the closed outer door is opened on 'the expensive murmur of all those we've-made-our-packet voices' and the view expands into a series of small rooms with dull yellow baize or bare brick walls, subdued lighting, and well-set, flowery tables. The owner, Alonso Velasco-Galvez, cooks himself, and offers set lunches and dinners, in rich and strange Franco-Spanish combinations of colour, texture and taste. No dish, in fact, is run-of-the-mill except the rather plainer vegetables and some of the sweets. Bread is hot, herbed and garlic-buttered (its crust could well be crisper); the champagne and Camembert soup is rich and smooth; and a trio of attractively garnished

Seats 60 (parties 45)
♿ rest
No dogs
Am Ex, Diners

smoked fish mousses, in three colours, seem well differentiated in flavours. According to one pair of diners the first-course masterpiece is pâté de foie gras (so to speak) with 'a Seville orange sauce, and sweet-and-sour sculptured radish, spring onion, twist of orange, Brussels sprout leaflets and pale jade lettuce'. Main dishes praised include 'relish of the gods': fillet of beef in puff pastry 'with a delicious, slightly sweet sauce', Alonso's version of coulibiac, chicken with sweetbread mousse and lobster sauce, and veal with Mozzarella, cream and (sometimes over-toasted) almonds. Service is excellent and unobtrusive. The wines are mainly French, but red Marqués de Riscal '71 is a bargain £4; French house wines £2·80 the litre. Recorded music.

App: A. J. Murison, A. Aird, Dr S. R. Soldin, Carol Steiger, M.F., and others

L'AMICO   Map 16

Dean Bradley House,
44 Horseferry Road,
S.W.1
01-222 4680

Honourable friends from the Palace of Westminster have found a new *amico* in this well-served Italian restaurant within division bell distance (some may remember it as the Old Russia). The cooking is creditable, by accounts of the house tagliatelle 'with a well-balanced sauce of cream and strips of ham', and mussels in a light broth (£1·75). Veal, duckling with cherry sauce, and the fresh vegetables are also praised. But venison at a test meal was 'tough and bland', salad vinegary, sweets dull. There are sound Italian wines under £4.

Closed Sat; Sun; public hols
Must book
Meals 12–2.45, 6.30–11

Alc £6 (meal £9·25)

VAT inc
Service 12½%
Cover 45p

Seats 80 (parties 40)
Air-conditioning
No dogs
Access, Am Ex, Barclay, Diners, Euro

LES AMOUREUX   Map 13

156 Merton Hall Road,
S.W.19
01-543 0567

Closed Sun; L Mon &
Sat; Aug & Jan; most
public hols
Must book D & weekends
Meals 12.30–2, 7.30–10

Alc £4·40 (meal £6·80)

VAT inc
Service 10%
Cover 30p

The name excuses the close quarters and pink pretty-prettiness, perhaps, and the volume of reports since last year's début suggests that Nigel Thomson (who cooks) and his wife Angela Scott-Forbes are one of Wimbledon's favourite mixed doubles. It is evident, indeed, that demand in the spring brought the vegetable cooking, especially, to the point of collapse. Other little expedients or misjudged temperatures are noted too. But ideas and execution are alike lively, and there is no lack of dishes to cite: among first courses, noodles with mushrooms or cream cheese, cauliflower in a mustardy dressing, crab bisque, mackerel in various ways, calf's liver or kidneys, and garlicky snails in choux pastry envelopes; then good quality

Seats 48
♿ rest (1 step)
Access, Am Ex, Barclay

roast lamb, pork calvados ('the liquor added too late'), sauté of rabbit with olives, stuffed neck of duck, civet de lièvre 'very rich and dark, including the liver', navarin of lamb, and veal in tarragon sauce. Rhubarb with meringue and Pernod does not always quite work, but rum and walnut cake is well made, as is crème brûlée, and loganberry tart had 'good shortcrust pastry with lots of fruit'. Coffee is 'middling'. Red Beaujolais or white Bordeaux are £2·25, and Côtes du Rhône or Gros Plant also seem appropriate. Recorded music. Smoke is a nuisance, and service (apart from the owner's) sometimes descends to 'failed au pair' level.

App: R. A. & J. M. Williams, Richard Gibson, P.C., J. S. Evans, R. B. Coyle, T. F. Main, and others

ANARKALI   Map 13

303–305 King Street, W.6
01-748 1760 *and* 6911

People find it pleasant, even 'joyful' to eat in Mr Raj's 'once sumptuous, now well-worn' two-tier restaurant, where spices in the dishes taste freshly ground and thoughtfully combined. For an enlightening contrast, try chicken tikka, sheek kebab and reshmee kebab as first courses; then mutton bhuna, Madras prawn, or Persian pulao. The dhal is pretty good, too. Only gulab jamun for sweet. Carlsberg lager is 35p, Dortmunder 40p, and Nicolas wines £3·70 the litre. No children under five. Recorded sitars.

Must book D & weekends
Meals 12–3, 6–11.45

Alc meal £4·90

Seats 80 (parties 20)

No dogs
Access, Am Ex, Barclay, Diners

ANNA'S PLACE   Map 12

69 Barnsbury Street, N.1
01-607 7172

Closed L; Sun; Mon;
3 weeks Easter; Aug;
2 weeks Chr
Must book
D only, 7–10.30

Alc £6·05 (meal £9·25)

Cover 25p
Seats 24
No dogs

'What a magician,' says an inspector (not normally fond of catering conjurors) about Anna Hegarty's minute, packed, Swedish-inspirational dining-room, which she shares with her brother Eric Norrgren. 'She could have slid effortlessly into an alto role in Bergman's *Magic Flute*', and she can cook too, to judge by her crab bisque (£1·10) – the shells grilled to bring out the flavour, faisan normande (£4·25), 'just high enough to be interesting, with a creamy sauce featuring calvados and currants', hasselbacks potatis (25p), 'brown and crunchy on their ribbed tops', and white cabbage with bay leaf and orange rind. In other opinions, gravlax and filet de veau Maxim (£3·55) confirm this talent, and Eric's chocolate cake has a rich fragility unfamiliar in the genre, at least in London. Other dishes well worth trying include Swedish herring, of course, the fried Camembert with gooseberry jam and parsley to which the *Guide* has wedded Anna's clients, crêpe florentine for vegetarians, pierogi (which is a kind of Cornish pasty with mackerel, egg, and rice), and little chocolate tarts. Wines begin at £2·45 for French ordinaires but £5 secures sound '71 claret – 'and altogether they earn their long Christmas, Easter and summer breaks.' Too close quarters for smoking, though.

App: W.S., A.H., Henry Potts, M.S., and others

ARIRANG   Map 15

31–32 Poland Street, W.1
01-437 6633 *and* 9662

Closed Sun L; Apr 15 &
16; Dec 25, 26 & 31;
Jan 1
Must book
Meals 12–3, 6–11

Tdh L from £2, D from
£5·50
Alc meal £5·35

Service 10%
Seats 65 (parties 35)
 rest
Air-conditioning
No dogs
Access, Am Ex, Barclay,
Diners

Korea's muscle has already been felt by shipbuilders, steelmen, and other dying imperial breeds, and now the Wee family have jumped straight into north Soho with a fighting manifesto: 'Korean cuisine is less greasy than the Chinese and more spicy than the Japanese.' Inspection of their gracefully served grey-green grotto suggested that there was actually some truth in this assertion, and there are several contented accounts of original dishes picked at random from the long menu: kosaree (marinated bracken stalks: now there's a nascent industry for Scotland and Wales, but better take oriental advice first), tuenjang chige (soya bean cake with green chillies in soup), yuk kwe (raw sliced beef with a sweet gingery sauce and fresh pear, £2·50), bulgogi (marinated beef), barbecued beef spare ribs, and good prawn or squid dishes too: batter-fried saywoo tiu gim (£2) and chilli-hot ojingo pokum (£2·50). There is a choice between sticky Japanese-style and separate Chinese-style rice, and between plates and forks or rice-bowl and chopsticks. (Chinese places please imitate.) There are wines (not bad ones) from £2·50, ginseng gin of course at £1·50 a measure, and saké. Korean recorded music. More reports, please, on the set meals too, and on the Wees' new venture in Knightsbridge.

ARK   Map 13

122 Palace Gardens
Terrace, W.8
01-229 4024

Casual bistro, simply furnished. Enter two by two for shipshape cooking on the reasonably priced à la carte menus (more choice and a bit dearer at night). Warm praise for spinach quiche, lapin bonne femme, raie au beurre noir, entrecôte marchand de vin and pot au chocolat. French house wine £2·65 the litre, 50p the glass. Pilsner Urquell beer. No music.

Closed Sun L; 4 days	Alc L £3·60 (meal £5·70),	Service 10% (parties)
Chr & Easter; L May 7 &	D £4·30 (meal £6·45)	Seats 62
28; Aug 27; Jan 1		Am Ex, Barclay
Meals 12–3, 6.30–11.30	VAT inc	

See p. 108 for London pubs and wine bars.

ARLECCHINO   Map 13

8 Hillgate Street, W.8
01-229 2027

Both street and restaurant are small scale, the decor is forgettable, and the music bland, but the cooking can excel – fresh basil in aubergine siciliana, 'delicious, gooey' Mozzarella impannata, unusually apposite sauces for saltimbocca and lambs' kidneys. Good, fresh vegetables, too. Better give the sweets a miss. House Chianti is £2·35 for 72 cl, 45p the glass.

Closed Sun (winter);
Apr 16; Dec 25 & 26;
Jan 1
Must book D
Meals 12–3, 6–12
(6.30–11.30 Sun)

Alc £4·25 (meal £7·25)

Cover 35p
Seats 50

♿ rest
Air-conditioning
Access, Am Ex, Barclay,
Diners

AZIZ   Map 13

116 King Street, W.6
01-748 1826

Closed Dec 25 & 26
Must book D & weekends
Meals 12–3, 6–11.45

Alc meal £4·20

Seats 52
No dogs
Am Ex, Barclay, Diners

Mr Aziz (who cooks) has survived pretty well the challenge implicit in the way he rates himself, and the service in this 'civilised' little place is attentive without being overbearing. (Aziz himself is busy frying onion bhajias and coating his reshmee kebabs with 'a mysterious net-like substance we were told was egg'.) Nan and poppadums are good, chutneys interesting. Other dishes praised include lamb tikka (80p), chicken tandoori (80p), dry bhindi, bhindi gosht (£1·40), chicken bhuna and Persian lamb pulao; note too the owner's own preferences for shellfish patias (which are hot) and dry patwal, among others. There are wines, and lager. Recorded music.

*App: Diana Chapman, M. G. Mark, Pam Holmes,
L. M. Luscombe, and others*

BAGATELLE   Map 13

5 Langton Street,
W.10
01-351 4185

'English diners seem to treat this potted palm and bentwood restaurant with a quasi-religious respect,' says a French admirer of their modestly helped duck and lamb. Small errors at a test meal spoilt the effect of crab mousse (£1·35), tender entrecôte de veau Orloff (£3·05) with correct pommes lyonnaise, and 'liquorous' cold soufflé Grand Marnier (for one thing, neither main dish was hot enough). The French cheeses are good, and note Jacques Andreu's turbot à l'oseille. 'Light and pleasant' house wines (£3·40) are poor value by the glass (90p).

Closed Sun; Apr 13 &
16; Dec 24, 25 & 26;
Jan 1
Must book D
Meals 12–2, 7–11.30

Alc £6·10 (meal £9·45)

VAT inc
Cover 40p
Seats 50

♿ rest (1 step)
No dogs
Access, Am Ex, Barclay,
Diners, Euro

LA BAITA Map 12

200 Haverstock Hill,
N.W.3
01-794 4126

Livio Becce manages and Bruno Ferrari cooks for
this offshoot of La Lupa down-town. Haverstock
Hill residents or frequenters are thankful for small
mercies: mushrooms sauté with green peppers (85p),
'tender and flavourful' osso buco (£2·50) with
well-cooked rice, escalope Cordon Bleu, and their
own suggestion, sole Adriatica (£3·35), for a splash.
The cover charge includes olives. Italian-bottled
wine begins at £2·60. Recorded music – 'they didn't
even notice when it stuck in its groove.'

Closed L Dec 25 & 26	VAT inc	♿ rest
Must book D	Service 10%	Car park
Meals 12–2.30, 6–11.30	Cover 30p	No dogs
	Children's helpings	Access, Am Ex, Barclay,
Alc £4·75 (meal £7·25)	Seats 70	Diners, Euro

BALZAC BISTRO Map 13

39 Bulwer Street, W.12
01-743 6787

Lorenzo Vucciol, the chef-patron of this 'dark,
deep-red, but well-spaced' bistro at the Shepherd's
Bush end of Wood Lane, has drawn warm accounts
of his soupe de poissons, mussels, champignons
farcis, 'garlicky frogs' legs in tomato sauce', lapin
en cocotte, 'succulent guinea-fowl', steak au poivre
vert, and especially the côte de boeuf 'cooked rare
for two, and far better than many steaks I've had
elsewhere'. Vegetables (apart from red cabbage) and
sweets were comparatively poor when tested, and
there is no note of cheeses. The French red
ordinaire is 'pretty sharp'.

Closed Sun; L Apr 13;	Tdh £3·75 & £5·25 (meal	Cover 35p
L Dec 24 & 31	£6·85 & £8·60)	Seats 65 (parties 30)
Must book L		Access, Am Ex, Barclay,
Meals 12–2.30, 7–11		Diners, Euro

BANGKOK Map 14

9 Bute Street, S.W.7
01-584 8529

'Why did the Bunnags cross the road?' asks someone,
but perhaps the new place feels more spacious to
them if not to their customers. Anyway, that apart,
the Thai-Cantonese cooking is as good as ever. Their
best dishes, they say, are piquant chicken soup,
spare ribs, fried chicken with garlic, and Thai rice
noodle. Members add the satay pork with chilli, and
beef in oyster sauce. Jasmine tea (40p), sometimes
stingily served. Morgan Furze wines. No music.

Closed Mon; public hols;	Alc (min £2·80) meal	Service 10%
Dec 24 & 31	£4·80	Seats 60
Must book D		No dogs
Meals 12.15–2.15, 6.30–11	VAT inc	

IL BARBINO   Map 13

32 Kensington Church
Street, W.8
01-937 8752

Tiny, cramped restaurant with white walls and pink cloths. Long printed à la carte menu, but about eight daily main dishes (vegetables included in the price). The antipasto were a reasonably fresh selection when tried, fish soup was virtuous, ravioli bolognese adequate, pollo sorpresa and veal escalope worth ordering. Sweets were poor, though, and coffee tepid. House Valpolicella or Soave is £2·60 for 70 cl, 65p the glass. Pot-boiling classics on tape.

Closed Sun; Sat L;
Dec 25 & 26; Jan 1;
L public hol Mons
Must book
Meals 12–3, 6.30–12

Alc (min £3) £5·50
(meal £8·40)

VAT inc
Service 13%

Cover 35p
Children's helpings
Seats 50
Air-conditioning
Access, Am Ex, Barclay,
Diners, Euro

LA BARCA   Map 16

80–81 Lower Marsh,
S.E.1
01-928 2226 and
261 9221

Closed Sun; Apr 13 & 16;
May 28; Aug 27;
Dec 25 & 26
Must book D
Meals 12.30–3, 7–12

Alc £5·20 (meal £7·70)

VAT inc
Service 10%
Cover 30p
Seats 82
[&] rest
Access, Am Ex, Barclay,
Diners, Euro

A chef from the Meridiana has opened up here, with irresistible claims, since it is so handy for the South Bank and Waterloo. The cooking is not as thick and floury as it is in so many Italian places and spaghetti La Barca (with seafood, £1·40), creamy lasagne, trenette al pesto, penne all'arrabbiata, hot stuffed aubergines, Mozzarella salad, 'sharp and lemony' piccatina al limone (£1·80), 'excellent calves' liver with sage and butter', 'very fresh trout in white wine' and 'light and generous zabaglione' sound better than the usual version found even north of the Thames, but gritty parsley and poor gâteau St Honoré are also mentioned. The teasing waiters ('would you like some non-fattening cream?') seem not to lapse into over-familiarity. Wines begin at £2·40, but there is better value around £3·30. Recorded music. No dogs.

App: Philippa Hayward, P.S.A.W., Thomas Ward, H.W., and others

Most places will accept cheques only when they are accompanied by a cheque card or adequate identification. Information about which credit cards are accepted is correct when printed, but occasionally restaurants add to or subtract from the list without notice.

The Guide News Supplement will be sent out as usual, in June, to everyone who buys the book directly from Consumers' Association and to all bookshop purchasers who return the card interleaved with their copy. Let us know of any changes that affect entries in the book, or of any new places you think should be looked at.

AL BEN ACCOLTO   Map 14

58 Fulham Road, S.W.3
01-589 0876

The lighting is 'weird', the floor tiled, the pictures diverse, the staff busy, the clientele loyal, and food – well, 'could do better' is the verdict after a test meal that included very agreeable cucumber mousse with sour cream, pollastrina alla tarragone (£1·95), mixed salad in an oily-mustardy dressing, and good coffee; but also 'ill-conceived' fried aubergines with squid, tender fillet of pork with tinned peach in the sauce, mediocre spinach and fennel as vegetables, and prentice versions of crème brûlée and profiteroles. Wines from £2·40 for 72 cl of house Chianti.

Closed Sun; public hols	Alc £5·15 (meal £8·45)	Seats 50
Must book		♿ rest (1 step)
Meals 12.30–2.30, 7–11.30	Cover 40p	No dogs
		Access, Am Ex, Diners

BEOTYS   Map 15

79 St Martin's Lane,
W.C.2
01-836 8768

Owned by the same family for over thirty years, in and out of the *Guide* for twenty, this starched but amiably served restaurant still provides a sense of occasion without breaking the bank, and they can time a pre- or post-theatre meal perfectly. People still prefer the Greek-Cypriot dishes: 'piquant' taramosalata, kalamarakia, arnakia melitzanes, moussaka, peasant salad with Feta cheese, honeyed pastries and Turkish delight with the coffee. 'Cyprus burgundy' is £2·40 for 26 oz, 65p the glass; Bacchus red or Kolossi dry white at £2·80 are acceptable, too. No music.

Closed Sun; public hols	Alc £4·30 (meal £7·30)	Air-conditioning
Must book		No dogs
Meals 12–2.30, 5.30–11.30	Cover 30p	Access, Am Ex, Barclay,
	Seats 100	Diners, Euro

BERKELEY HOTEL   Map 14

Wilton Place, S.W.1
01-235 6000

Closed Sun (Perroquet);
Sat (rest)
Must book
Meals 12.30–3, 7–11.30

Alc £8·35 (meal £12·40),
buffet L (Perroquet)
from £3·50 (meal £6·20)

VAT inc

Decoratively, the bar (which also offers salted almonds rather than peanuts) is more restrained than Le Perroquet downstairs and the 'lilac and polystyrene' main dining-room. Where you choose to eat depends on age, mood, or income group: Le Perroquet at lunch-time offers a competent range of salads made by Cordon Bleu girls, and develops a little dancing in the evenings; the restaurant proper, served with the usual London-hotel mixture of traditional courtesy and juvenile impertinence, expresses its schizophrenia in joyous franglais ('mousse de haddock', 'chump chop poêlé chez soi') and apparently sees no incongruity between what

Service 15%
Cover 40p
Seats 100 (parties 30)
Car park
No dogs
Access card
152 rooms (all with bath)
Prices on application

it does well and what it does badly. On the one hand agreeable hors d'oeuvre, with extra morsels personally chosen by the maître if he likes the look of or knows you, and 'rather good' Paris-Brest and savarin au rhum on the sweets trolley; on the other, good meat and game but 'suspiciously brown' sauces, and 'barely edible' chips and spinach at a test meal. The wines are 'almost as good as they should be at the price charged': Ch. de Pez '70, c.b., £7·95; Ch. Paveil-de-Luze '71, £6·85. 'It is worth going to hear the doorman enquire: "Would Madam be requiring any form of transportation?", as though he could summon a double-decker with a wave of a gloved hand.' Wear a tie. Details are approximate.

App: Mrs Caroline Laidlaw, Robert Muller, J.S., R.McR., and others

BEWICK'S Map 14

87–89 Walton Street,
S.W.3
01-584 6711

Closed Sun; public hols
Must book
Meals 12.30–2.15, 7.30–11

Tdh L £4 (meal £7·45)
Alc £7·05 (meal £11·05)

Cover 50p
Seats 50 (parties 18)
Air-conditioning
No dogs
Access, Am Ex, Barclay,
Diners, Euro

Viscount Newport's soigné French restaurant, with James Skelton as manager and Jean Vella as chef, faltered a little last spring, and reports spoke of erratic helpings ('about sufficient for a small child' is a doctor's not very jolly verdict), rising prices, and variable cooking. But later in the year the boned and stuffed gigot d'agneau (a speciality, £3) was once again 'first-class and most tender' rather than 'overdone' or 'oleaginous', and the beignets au fromage (80p) recovered from 'heavy' to 'so light I ate all six.' A useful alternative to this popular first course is the mousse de concombre. Accolades also descend upon good soups and pâtés, the boudins noirs, and 'superb' filets de sole Bercy (£3·10). Vegetables are 'really fresh'. As for the sweets, one visitor thought the chocolate mousse (90p) alone made his meal worthwhile. Menus change roughly every month, and the lunch *carte* is an abbreviated version of dinner's, though you may like to try the set lunch at £4·50 (cover included), with a choice of three starters and main dishes. A nice touch is thé (40p, two tea-bags): one member had a pot with his dinner. House wines (French) are £2·85, and a glass of white is 70p. Temptations lie in the wide range of clarets: note Ch. Durfort-Vivens (£5) and Ch. Malescot-St-Exupéry (£7, or £3·75 a half) if you care to risk a '72. White wines start at £2·95 with a Bordeaux Sauvignon '76. Vintage ports will be decanted, given notice. 'Tolerable' music, all styles.

App: Roy Mathias, Gavin Dunnett, Mrs T. Laidlaw, F.O.C., R. David Hall, and others

If you think you are suffering from food-poisoning after eating in a restaurant, report this immediately to the local Public Health Authority (and write to us).

BLOOM'S   Map 12

90 Whitechapel High
Street, E.1
01-247 6001 *and* 6835

Closed Fri D; Sat;
Jewish hols
Open 11.30–9.30
(Fri 11.30–2 [winter]
11.30–3 [summer])

Alc £4·20 (meal £4·90)

VAT inc
Children's helpings
Seats 130
Air-conditioning
Car park
No dogs
Unlicensed

The Bloom that flowers in the desert of east
London never wants for customers, especially at
Sunday lunch-time, when even the mightiest have to
queue. 'A previous *Guide* said that Bloom's had to
stand comparison with Momma's cooking. In our
case it is Bube's cooking, and Bube was a fine cook,
especially of chopped and fried fish. Bloom's stands
up well.' This irreverent grandson started with
stuffed miltz ('next to the spleen,' the waiter may
say), continued with a large plate of salt beef,
tsimmes, and potato latke, and ended with lockshen
pudding, an archetypal Bloom's meal that leaves
room for nothing, but nothing, unless it be lemon
tea. Chopped liver (65p), kreplach soup, sweetbreads
in a stock-rich sauce, blintzes, baked klops, salt
tongue and other alternatives are also discussed in
people's memories of this brilliantly lit, offhand,
sometimes sloppy restaurant. (To be fair, the
customers are often sloppier than the waiters.) No
music. Remember it is a take-away place too: even
the new green pickles are better than other people's.
Unlicensed, but no corkage.

*App: C.W., G. S. Carr, Alan Firth, W. M. Thomas,
J.S., M.B., and others*

LA BRASSERIE   Map 14

272 Brompton Road,
S.W.7
01-584 1668 *and*
581 3089

Down a peg even since last year in one visitor's
opinion – 'a third-class brasserie, with rude,
forgetful service' – but, as we said then, the all-day
provision of hard-to-damage authentic dishes (soupe
à l'oignon, andouillette grillée, boudin noir, tripe) is
worth knowing about. 'Delicious rognons au Pernod
with mushy rice.' They let you sit undisturbed over
the good Cafetière coffee – except at peak time. The
Spanish house wine at £2·45 the bottle is a
one-glass drink, some say. Bar snacks. International
newspapers. No music, but the gossip is a diary
editor's delight.

Closed Dec 24 D;
Dec 25 & 26
Open 8 a.m.–11.30 p.m.
(D 7–11.30)

Alc £4·45 (meal £7·15)

VAT inc
Service 12½%
Cover 30p

Seats 75
♿ rest
Air-conditioning
No dogs
Barclay, Diners

BUBB'S   Map 12

329 Central Market,
E.C.1
01-236 2435

Francis Bureau is back in the kitchen at Peter and
Catherine Bubb's Smithfield Market refuge for its
fourth appearance in these pages, and if its City and
Fleet customers (who have no comparable places)

Closed Sat; Sun; Aug;
Dec 24 & 31; public hols
Must book
Meals 12.15–2, 7.30–9.30

Alc £5·65 (meal £8·75)

Service 12%
Seats 36
No dogs
Access, Barclay, Diners

could stagger their visits between lunch and dinner, everyone's life would be easier. True, the entrance vestibule and stairs do their best to put guests off, but book early for lunch nevertheless. The hard chairs and dark paint do not matter; the charm resides in the hot but delicate fish pâté (the accompanying hollandaise had 'broken' on the hot plate at a test meal), the grilled sardines anointed with aïoli, the mussels in white wine, the fish soup, and simpler tomato Jeannette. Then there may be 'very fresh salmon trout' or veal cutlet in wine and grape sauce (a speciality), or very rich pantoufle de volaille, or well-flavoured lamb or beef (as might be expected in this locality): 'lamb cutlets done in pastry with flageolet beans were superb,' a diner reports. Sweetbreads, cailles aux myrtilles, and côte de boeuf aux avocats are also worth considering. Be careful about vegetables: they do not always warn you what goes with what, and pommes boulangère or dauphine are good but naturally rich. There will be a good French cheese or two, and competent crème caramel or Mont Blanc (chocolate mousse disappointed an inspector, who recommended the imported blackcurrant sorbet instead). Kirs are made dry, wines begin at £2·50 for French ordinaire, and there are one or two modest '71 or '73 clarets at £5 or so. No music, but plenty of noise – and Mr Bubb might help his young waiters more, a Brussels visitor thinks.

App: Mr & Mrs G. T. Ferrero, Steven Curson, A.T.H., M.R.J., J. D. B. Wood, and many others

BUMBLES   Map 16

16 Buckingham Palace
Road, S.W.1
01-828 2903

Popular, ground-floor-and-downstairs little place, handy for Victoria. Dinner menu is an 'unwieldy scroll' with blackboard extras. Inventive cooking pleases many: leek soup, gazpacho, courgettes in wine with toasted almond sauce, salmon steak, beef casserole, pork brochette with saffron rice. Fish pâté disappointed an admirer on one occasion. Valbois (Gironde) red or white is £2·80 the bottle. Friendly waitresses. Recorded music.

Closed Sun; Sat L;
Dec 24 D; public hols
Must book
Meals 12–2.15, 6–10.30
(6.30 Sat)

Alc (min L £2, D £3·50)
£4·55 (meal £7)

VAT inc
Service 10% (Sat)
Children's helpings
(under 10)

Seats 64 (parties 30)
⟨&⟩ rest (1 step)
Air-conditioning
Access, Am Ex, Barclay,
Diners

See p. 120 for the restaurant-goer's legal rights, and p. 118 for information on hygiene in restaurants.

LA BUSSOLA Map 15

42 St Martin's Lane,
W.C.2
01-240 1518 *and* 1148

This spacious, well-padded basement (Spaghetti Houses' pride and joy) fills certain precise needs. Outside these, members have voted it poor value for money in 1978, for the reliably excellent materials are not always as expertly cooked as they were. So if you want a discreet Italian lunch or a pre-theatre supper, or a late dinner with live music (which bumps up the price much further), don your jacket and tie, and consider antipasto and 'pink, delicious' liver with fresh sage (£4) or rosticciata (£3·50), 'superb vegetables and raspberries', and Cafetière coffee. Otherwise, wait till they have improved the first courses, the sweets, and the service (charged or suggested at a rate now revealed).

Closed Sun; Sat L;
Dec 25–26; Jan 1;
L public hols
Must book weekends
Meals 12–2.30, 6–1.30

Tdh D (6–8) £7·50
(meal £12·55)
Alc £11·45 (meal £18·20)

VAT inc
Service 14%

Cover L 50p; Tdh D £1;
Alc D £2; Sat £2·50
Seats 185
Air-conditioning
No dogs
Access, Am Ex, Barclay,
Diners, Euro

CALABASH Map 15

38 King Street, W.C.2
01-836 1976

Rather stark but comfortable and well-spaced basement in the Africa Centre, now 'slightly up-marketed', but still erratic, with lukewarm food and service, cold plates, a fallible bread supply and variable cooking. But people who strike lucky return for pumpkin soup, chicken groundnut stew, egusi (beef stew with melon seeds, dried shrimps and peppers, £1·30), hot, crisp, fried plantain and nicely seasoned jollof rice. Pineapple fritters are the only cooked pudding. Carafe is La Bastiche, £1·60 the half-litre, 45p the glass. Recorded music, said to be African, but sometimes Viva España.

Closed Sun; Sat L;
public hols
Must book
Meals 12.15–2.30, 6.15–10

Alc £3·35 (meal £5·45)

VAT inc
Service 10%

Cover 15p
Seats 48 (parties 100)
No dogs
Am Ex, Diners

CAPABILITY BROWN Map 12

351 West End Lane,
N.W.6
01-794 3234

Closed L (exc Sun);
Sun D; L Apr 13;
L Dec 31; public hols
Must book

It is possible to know almost too much about the movements of chefs. Ann Tebboth's green-and-white, plant-strewn restaurant on the Hampstead foothills was one of 1978's success stories, and every guide-book likes a good new place. But Lawrence Elbert, late of the Connaught, goes to California this April and is to be succeeded by his sous-chef. Although David Smart is from the same stable, a second trial of the

Meals 12.30–2.30 (Sun),
7–11.30

Tdh Sun L from £3·95
(meal £6·50)
Alc £5·95 (meal £10)

Service 12½%
Cover 50p D
Seats 44
No dogs
Access, Barclay

ambitious à la carte menu on a 'chef's night off' in the autumn made it clear what a tightrope the place was already walking: petit savarin de brochet (£1·45), 'so delicate, light, and buttery' on the first occasion, had become 'solid and puddingy, and the garnish of spinach purée overcooked'. Main course, grapefruit sorbet, and petits fours showed a similar falling-off. So fingers must be crossed for the pâté de poisson (£1·25), truite de rivière Marie (£2·75), piccata de veau Monsieur Davie (£3·65), and foie de veau aux citrons verts (£2·95) that are still listed as specialities. Still, give or take a few inaccuracies or miscalculations, these and several other dishes (not forgetting minceur *essays such as ballotine de poulet purée de cresson, and banane en papillote with a fruit purée) were undeniably delicious in 1978. Service was 'pretty and enthusiastic'. Wines (from £2·80 for Chianti or Verdicchio) are just about adequate (though not knowledgeably chosen or listed). If readers, and owners, can limit their expectation to what can reasonably be achieved, fears may be liars. More reports, please.*

CAPITAL HOTEL RESTAURANT   Map 14

Basil Street, S.W.3
01-589 5171

Must book
Meals 12.30–2, 6.30–10.30

Alc £8·90 (meal £14·60)

Service 15%
Cover 50p
Children's helpings
Seats 30 (parties 20)
Air-conditioning
Car park (12)
No dogs in public rooms
Access, Am Ex, Barclay,
Diners, Euro
56 rooms (all with bath)
Room only, from £25
Breakfast from £3·25
Fire cert

Crown princes seldom succeed easily, and reports at the turn of last year (just too late to catch the 1978 *Guide*) conveyed this message about Brian Turner, whom David Levin, owner of this clinically modern hotel near Harrods, promoted when his previous chef left. But as the year wore on, and Mr Turner learnt what exacting standards at least a proportion of his customers brought to their meals in this suavely served dining-room, Mr Levin's reputation as a good picker began to revive. There are still matters to mend. The famous mousseline de coquille St Jacques would be better given a rest, for it is not what it was (though the accompanying sea-urchin sauce may be). The puddings are sometimes over-sweet or disappointing (the sublime sorbet à la Fine Champagne, served between courses, is not counted in this category). They do overcook meat on occasion. Sometimes the service declines into an arrogance that its competence does not quite justify, though 'salted butter was replaced on request' and 'by extra-sensory perception the head waiter knew I would want Brie and brought a particularly fine one.' Masterly dishes are common: chicken or sweetbread vol-au-vents, oeufs Pascal, fresh sardines dijonnaise, pâté with poivrons à l'huile, and gravadlax among first courses; the pinkly roast carré d'agneau 'with a delicious herbes de Provence stuffing' (£9 for two), 'admirably cooked' quenelles de brochet sauce armoricaine, filleted salmon trout meunière with buttered mange-touts, luscious médaillons de veau biscayenne, côte de boeuf, and other things. A member who took a great deal of trouble to get a private dinner right was amply rewarded by the occasion. There is nothing to drink under £3·85 (Piesporter '77) but some prices might easily be markedly higher than they are: Ch. Meyney '67, c.b., and Savigny-les-Beaune Les Lavières '72, (Bouchard Père et Fils) are listed under £7 on the menu sent, and on the main list, Ch. Pape-Clément '67, c.b., is £8·75. Leave the first-growths – especially the '62s, perhaps – to those who will not mind either their prices or their weaknesses. No music. Wear a jacket for preference. Pipes discouraged.

App: J. R. Tyrie, H. Berger, F. Clive de Paula,
J. H. Briggs, C. J. Fyffe, R. Duffy, J.R., and others

CARLO'S PLACE   Map 13

855 Fulham Road,
S.W.6
01-736 4507

Closed L; Mon; mid-July
to mid-Aug; public hols
Must book
D only, 7–11

Alc £5·15 (meal £7·75)

VAT inc
Cover 35p
Seats 48 (parties 14)
♿ rest
Air-conditioning

Carlo Ferrari has evidently had a busy year in these, rooms whose red cloths, coloured lights and festoons of stove pipes recall a fairground roundabout. People have emerged hot-foot (because the kitchen lies below) from the small back room, and the service may overlook you there, or be generally too busy to tender useful advice about the dishes of the day (often the best choice). But Jean Delahaye's cooking maintains a creditable standard, from the crêpe with ham, cream and almonds, 'mild fish soup', and 'imaginative salad of avocado, chicken, apples and almonds' that may begin a meal, to sweetbreads meunière (£3·10), 'exceptional beef casserole in red wine', crisply roasted duckling, carré d'agneau au poivre, and duck pie. Vegetables are not bad considering the pressures, and salad was good when tried. Chocolate and walnut pie, and meringue with fresh grapes, are mentioned among sweets, and the coffee is strong. Espigou red or Entre-Deux-Mers white wines are £2·50, and there are a few other bottles of no great moment. No music.

App: Sybil Eysenck, Richard Orgill, V. F. Irish,
C.R.B., A.M., M.W., and others

CARLTON TOWER CHELSEA ROOM   Map 14

Cadogan Place, S.W.1
01-235 5411

Closed Apr 16; Dec 24 D;
Dec 26
Must book
Meals 12.30–2.45, 7–11.15
(10.45 Sat, 10.15 Sun)

Alc £14·25 (meal £18·35)

Construction of a lovable hotel seems beyond the powers of late-20th-century London, but the space and tree-top view from almost everywhere in this dining-room make some inspectors wonder why they spend so much time in rabbit-hutch restaurants. They know very well, though, that they are only found here because Bernard Gaume cooks, and they sizzle in the pan when they discover – on Sunday nights especially, it seems – that their livers are at the mercy of a salt-loving deputy. Red cockerels on the menu direct guests to M Gaume's own specialities,

Service inc
Seats 50
Air-conditioning
Car park
No dogs in public rooms
Access, Am Ex, Barclay,
Diners, Euro
296 rooms (all with bath)
Room only, from about
£33
Fire cert

though some other dishes too belong to the style of *cuisine* rather unhelpfully called *nouvelle*. Freshness and immediacy, rather than novelty for novelty's sake, are what counts in the escalopes of goose liver, either tossed in butter with chervil (£6·50 as a first course), or with raw spinach salad; or in the hot oysters, crab soup with a garlic and saffron mayonnaise (£2), ris de veau cressonnière, filets de turbot, homard et concombres, ('fresh and firm fish and an excellent sauce of wine, cream and butter', £7·50), and 'very delicate and ungreasy' steak de canard à l'armagnac et truffes (£6·50). Mange-tout peas and haricots verts seem the favourite vegetables. But sometimes equally promising dishes such as potted duckling with truffles, or safari de poisson au safran, taste oddly heavy and dull, given the skill behind scenes. Puddings are not a feature, apart from soufflé glacé à l'ananas (£2) and it is probably wisest to choose the fine fresh fruit, though 'chestnut mousse with chocolate and cream was good.' The service, supervised by Jean Quéro, is polite without being unusually expert or sharp-eyed. The menu features wines chosen by Paul Bocuse, but even he cannot make '77 Brouilly taste like '76, so study the wine list too. Ch. La Lagune (Ludon) '69, c.b., repaid an inspector's £8·50, he says. Montpellier red, or basic Sancerre, are £5·20 a litre. A pianist plays. Wear a jacket and tie. Don't confuse this restaurant with the Rib Room, which fulfils a function, but not the same one.

App: Jennifer Rhodes, Dolores Williamson, J.R., R.F.V., Alasdair Aird, C.P.D., and others

---

CARRIER'S Map 12

2 Camden Passage, N.1
01-226 5353

Closed Sun; public hols
Must book
Meals 12.30–2.30,
7.30–11.30

Tdh L from £9 (meal
£13·20), D from £11
(meal £15·60)

Service 12½%
Seats 82 (parties 25)
⌖ rest (1 step)
Air-conditioning
Am Ex card

'One of London's glories,' says a magazine as glossy as the restaurant. Well, no. Even this year, after better performances than Robert Carrier's international clientele have lately been accustomed to at his Islington headquarters, more than one experienced diner begins his report: 'Now I know why Carrier's was dropped from the *Guide* while others thought it could do no wrong.' Still, the impresario of this theatrical interior (he thinks it resembles a 19th-century French country inn) keeps his nerve and his staff. Gunther Schlender and Terence Boyce cook in what passes in the 20th century for the grand manner, and the service is 'almost very good; a slight feeling of suppressed frenzy, but suppressed anyway'. The breads are good (though they use a different kind for toast). So is the butter. Menus are table d'hôte and offer some seasonal variation, but it was a particularly good one that began with 'elegantly arranged and fishy-tasting rillettes of eel' and advanced to flaked trout in lettuce packets with a 'buttery, winey, eggy sauce that must have had infinite calories and tasted divine'. Watercress soup, aspic of vegetables, 'delicious terrine of pigeon', seafood salad flavoured with saffron, and 'light and crumbly Roquefort quiche' are also praised at this stage. Délices de Gruyère, though they taste of nutmeg and the right cheese, do not exactly float. Lamb or beef done over an open fire with various herb or garlic butters is a conservative choice thereafter; liver with avocado slices, or guinea-fowl with limes and green peppercorns, or brochette of sweetbreads and kidneys, are more original, or, at least, characteristic of the house. Blander flavours also occur: 'The envelope of veal tasted like a manila one – cooked.' Sweets have always been among London's better ones (not that the competition is intense in the metropolitan acceptance world) and 'well-balanced' lemon posset, 'sumptuous' chocolate mousse and 'a tour de force of an iced soufflé Grand Marnier' are all noted. They keep much good wine but do not understand it, says a professional who found the clarets too young, the wine glasses curved outwards, and decanting the exception rather than the rule. However, the house Sauvignon Côtes de Duras at £2·50 for 50 cl is always soothing, Ch. Latour Blanche '70, c.b., was well forward (being a St Emilion) at £7·25, and the small Loire and Rhône sections at a similar price are well judged. The woman who pointed out to one cigar-smoker that he had only bought the air-space over his own table lived to tell the tale. No music.

App: Barbara Schall, A.M.P., R.McR., A.T.H., E.P-R., and others

---

CARROLL'S   Map 15

32 Great Windmill Street, W.1 01-437 7383	Mark Segal's cafe with counter stools and a few tables remembers when the Windmill was the Windmill, and still has famous customers for Vincent Proto's crisply fried latkes, chopped liver (50p), gefilte fish, 'good and tender hot salt beef or tongue (£1·70)' and 'fat little frankfurters with unusually fresh green pickles and pale and fresh sauerkraut: excellent.' Lemon pancake was 'immaculately done' on one occasion, and 'disappointing' on another. There is a choice between strong or weak lemon tea.

Closed Oct 1; Dec 25 Open noon–11.30	Alc meal £4	Air-conditioning No dogs
	Seats 30	Unlicensed

See p. 108 for London pubs and wine bars.

CERVANTES Map 3

105 Brighton Road,
Coulsdon, Surrey
01-660 0907 *and* 3721

Closed Sun; Apr 13;
Dec 26; Jan 1
Must book
Meals 12–2.30, 7–11.30

Tdh £4·25 (meal £6·80)
Alc £6·55 (meal £10·10)

VAT inc
Service 12½%
Cover 30p alc D
(60p Fri & Sat)
Seats 100 (parties 60)
♿ rest; w.c.
No dogs
Access, Am Ex, Barclay,
Diners

'Cervantes is a rather unreal establishment,' writes
one critic of this restaurant, but a fairer comment
would be 'improbable in Coulsdon', for Tony Lopez
the owner and Manuel Fidalgo the chef are as
Spanish as quince cheese. Food in the ground-floor
'Gran Restaurant' is frenchified, but in the wine
cellar below, Spanish food and wine have fewer
pretensions, and here an inspector enjoyed a 'very
tasty' spinach, nut and raisin pancake, veal in
tomato and garlic, and moderately good cheese, on
a set menu. The coffee (a 'bottomless cup') was
35p extra. Specially praised are the champignons
à l'espagnole (£1·10), the hors d'oeuvre 'chariot'
with two different fish pâtés (£1·40), red mullet,
fresh crab ('spot on'), a chicken Wellington
'chock-full of rich stuffing' (an end-of-term treat
for pupil and parent alike), and a huge veal chop
with baked peppers and chips (£3·90). Most people
seem to skip the sweets and rest content with the
caramelised fresh fruit served with the coffee.
Recorded music at lunch varies in strength; at night
one visitor describes 'two elderly, very cool and
very black musicians performing on electric guitar
and organ in a Palm Court style'. Dancing on
Fridays and Saturdays doubles the usual cover
charge. House wines are £3·60 a bottle, and the
modest list of mainly French and Spanish wines
ranges from £3·95 to £11·50 for a '72 Givry – which
seems excessive. Pressurised beers.

*App: A.F., Dr John D. Levi, Ellis Blackmore,
Joan Clowes, and others*

CHAGLAYAN KEBAB HOUSE Map 12

86 Brent Street, N.W.4
01-202 8575

'Don't despise Ata Chaglayan's little place,
rope-decorated like a monster macramé, just because
it is within striking distance of the Hendon Odeon.
His tahini is potent, his shish kebab maison is pink,
juicy and tender, and his ekmek kataif with honey
and almonds is melting and delicious – he said I'd
have to go to Istanbul for another. Turkish coffee
and loukoum are also excellent of their kind.'
Kleftiko (£1·70), the spicy lamb sausage that
appears in karisik kebab (£2·50), pilaff rice, and
other sweets are praised too. 'Sunday night opening
seems irregular.'

Closed Sun L; Apr 15 &
16; Dec 24, 25 & 26;
Jan 1
Must book D & weekends
Meals 12–2.30, 6–12

Alc £3·50 (meal £6·05)

Cover 10p
Seats 35

♿ rest (1 step); w.c.
No dogs
Access, Am Ex, Barclay,
Diners, Euro

CHAOPRAYA   Map 15

22 St Christopher's Place,
W.1
01-486 0777

Thai places have lodged themselves in members'
affections before now, and though this shy place has
alienated a few by patchy cooking in its first year,
inspectors and others who have enjoyed the 'light
and crisp fried wun-tun', fried squid with garlic and
pepper, prawns in hot peppers and lemon grass,
broccoli in oyster sauce, and kanom sai sai
('coconut cream with a molasses-like core in carefully
stitched leaves', 50p) wish Mr Nilawongse well.
Perhaps the menu, at least in the evening, should
be shorter. Wines from £2·75; 'ecclesiastical' tea.
Smartish surroundings on two floors, but rather
elementary loos. Thai music.

Closed Sun; public hols
Meals 12–3, 6.30–11

Alc meal £4·85

Service 10%

Seats 120
No dogs
Access, Am Ex

CHATEAUBRIAND   Map 12

48 Belsize Lane, N.W.3
01-435 4882

Sergio Latorraca's long-popular meatery has had a
thorough-going refit, but no one demands any
change in the way they buy and cook their
chateaubriand béarnaise, carré d'agneau, steak au
poivre and so on. Take a first course (champignons
à la mode du chef, perhaps) rather than a sweet,
unless it be crêpes Grand Marnier. Parties should be
careful how they order vegetables, but the service
is careful enough, and the house burgundy well
chosen. Recorded music.

Closed L; Sun; Dec 25,
26 & 27
Must book
D only, 7–12

Alc £5·70 (meal £8·20)

VAT inc

Service 12½%
Cover 20p
Seats 40

LE CHEF   Map 12

41 Connaught Street, W.2
01-262 5945

Closed Sun; Mon; Sat L;
Aug; public hols
Must book
Meals 12.30–2.30, 7–11.30

Tdh L £4·25 (meal
£6·20), Sat D £5 (meal
£7·10)

Alc £4·65 (meal £7·30)

Service 10%

A letter from the National Heart Hospital – doctor,
not patient – reports a two-stone weight gain within
two months of buying the 1978 *Guide*. Two visits in
quick succession to Alan King's informal, crowded,
Left-Bankish restaurant were included in this
pacemaker's work-out, and it is the kind of place
that others, too, visit and revisit, not least because
they can afford it. It is no use expecting everything
to be refined or grease-free, but the ever-popular
rusty-red fish soup with rouille gives a strong sense
that it started in the fishmonger up the street,
which is what matters. Champignons farcis or en
croustade are alternatives (the pâté is unremarkable
and the tomato salad inevitably uses the wrong
tomatoes). Main dishes are more diverse: 'tender

Cover 25p alc
Children's helpings
Seats 50
♿ rest (2 steps)
No dogs
Access, Euro

stewed kidneys in wine and cream', 'succulent and crisp canard aux olives', even navarin de mouton (*not* d'agneau) to remind an inspector of a half-forgotten taste. Vegetables may 'spring a surprise' too: 'sensational salsify'; 'delicious navets à la crème'. Poulet basquaise (£2·30) is another suggestion. The set meals for weekday lunch and Saturday dinner remain normally excellent value ('a huge hunk of grilled cod once appeared as a first course.') The tarte maison is dependable, and so are the cheeses – 'they must have a whole herd of goats working full time for them.' The coffee is *filtre*. The Costières du Gard ordinaire is no better than can be expected for £2 in a restaurant, but occasionally other finds appear: Ch. Archevesque '70 at £4·50 seemed worth it in 1978, but the current wine list is not to hand. Recorded French music.

App: by too many members to list

CHEZ FRANÇOIS   Map 3

5a Avenue Parade,
Bush Hill Park, N.21
01-360 4247

We confused François Salmon's two restaurants last time – *this* is the eight-year-old one, with the same chef as when it opened. If you can endure heat, smoke, noise and some uncomfortable seating, you should enjoy the cheerfully casual atmosphere and genuine bistro cooking, from an infrequently changed menu with blackboard additions. Try pâté, fresh sardines, tomates Versailles (£1·10), braised tongue, 'extremely garlicky' chicken Kiev (£2·40), and côtelettes d'agneau niçoise (£2·30), with unexceptional vegetables and sweets. House wine, £2·50 the bottle. French recorded music.

Closed L (exc Sun); Sun D; Mon; 3 weeks Aug; Dec 25 & 26 Must book	Meals 12–3 (Sun), 6.30–11.30	VAT inc Seats 40
	Alc £5·55 (meal £7·80)	

CHEZ MOI   Map 13

3 Addison Avenue, W.11
01-603 8267

Closed L; Sun; 3 weeks
Aug; 3 weeks from Chr;
public hols
Must book
D only, 7–11.30

Alc £8·35 (meal £13·10)

Cover 45p
Seats 54 (parties 18)

The name of this small, chic restaurant could well be changed to Chez Nous, for Richard Walton, chef, Colin Smith and Roland Peacock have owned it as partners for more than ten years. It is discreetly luxurious and service is excellent, but the 'Lilliputian' tables are too close for comfort, and smoke naturally obtrudes. Prices, too, make New Yorkers feel at home (main dishes range here from £2·35 to £6·75, vegetables excluded) though rarely do you meet quality and originality going so smoothly hand-in-hand. Apart from 'après Moi le déluge' reports of 'tough' pigeon, 'nearly raw' kidneys and 'greasy' entrecôte, there is only praise for such delicate creations as the oeuf poché Christophe – a cold poached egg on smoked salmon, coated with a mousse of smoked cods' roe (£2.25) – and the chicken liver and prune pâté (£1·05) at the start; and as main courses the ballotine de petit poussin (£3·85), and lamb in various forms, either roast pink and stuffed with mint and garlic, or en brochette on brown rice with apricots. Try, this year, Mr Walton's Devon crab claws in a creamy lobster sauce (£4·95). Vegetables are fresh, appetising, and well-buttered, and salad dressings can be had with or without garlic. Chef-made sorbets or ice-cream, petits pots de chocolat, a gateau or fruit salad are the conservative dessert choices. Cheeses are unreliable. Coffee is strong and cups replenished. Wine by the glass costs as much as 95p, and in carafe £3·85, or £2·15 a half, but £10 or more brings out distinguished clarets and burgundies (subject to deletions on the wine list), and vintage ports are £1·35 a glass. No music.

App: A.M., Kenneth Cleveland, B.J.P., C.F.

♿ CHEZ NICO   Map 16

148 Lordship Lane,
East Dulwich, S.E.22
01-693 8266

Closed L; Sun; Mon
(exc May 7); 3 weeks
summer; 10 days Chr
Must book
D only, 7–10

Alc (min £4·80) £7
(meal £10·75)

Service 10%
Cover 30p
Seats 40
♿ rest (1 step)
No dogs

Once in a while it is necessary to be blunt: over the past five years this has probably been the best and certainly the most imaginative *chef-patron* restaurant in London. The near-silence about it in some other quarters has been deafening, but then, Nico Ladenis does not suffer fools gladly. In this office it has always been an easy entry to write because experienced *Guide* inspectors and people they have never met react in concert. 'Smoked salmon pâté with sorrel was the lightest, smoothest, most delicate thing you could hold down on a plate, pink with a central layer of green, the colour picked up by a decorative slice of kiwi fruit.' 'I had quail pâté with a few toasted almonds and a puree that might almost have been caramelised apple but was actually onion marmalade à la Guérard with a little cassis: the combination set up all kinds of subsidiary flavours and nuances.' 'This year we came to London from Paris rather than Washington, but Nico's coq au vin jaune flanqué de morilles (£5·50 at 24 hours' notice) held its own with anything we ate in one- and two-rosette restaurants there.' (First courses are included in main dish prices.) 'I lost a third of my stomach last year and a prime reason for my delight in being restored to health is that it allows me once again to eat here – this time the filet de boeuf au poivre à la façon du Moulin, with a superbly balanced raisin and green peppercorn sauce, and simple but perfectly cooked haricots verts and courgettes on a separate plate.' (It is fair to add that an inspector who had this last dish in October found the flavours, with the garlic in the beans, altogether too swashbuckling, as though in sympathy with Nico's piratical beard.) After all this it is difficult to avoid falling into a list of other notabilities to look out for: poached mackerel fillets with a dazzlingly heretical sauce combining tomatoes and raspberries, 'flawless calf's liver with a caramelly port-based sauce and an ethereally light lettuce puree', fillets of veal with apple and calvados (just to learn what other restaurants up and down the land are parodying) – and, of course, the puddings. Nico (reacting to sweet-toothed members who have claimed that his desserts are a grade below the rest) is actually proposing to compose more complex codettas to his meals than his marquise fondant au chocolat, sauce au café; or his liquorous ice-creams that are as innocent of mere milk as his sauces are of flour; or for that matter his assemblages of fresh fruit. Cheeses are good too. Wines are fully adequate to the menu (from only £2·90 for Corbières and Rhône house wines). Ch. Léoville-Poyferré '69, c.b., is £8·50, Muscadet '76, £4·70. There is a wide range of eaux de vie and marcs. No music. 'A pestle of course, and for my money, a Croix de Guerre to Dinah-Jane for defending rare meat and other French causes without provoking, as Nico would, a nightly nuclear exchange.' No pipes.

App: by too many members to list

CHUEN-CHENG-KU   Map 15

17 Wardour Street, W.1
01-734 3281 *and*
437 1398

Closed Dec 28
Meals 11 a.m.–midnight

Alc (min L £2, D £3)
meal £4·30

VAT inc
Service 10%
Seats 250
♿ rest
No dogs

This two-floor restaurant in south Soho, with the chandelier upstairs surviving from who-knows-what earlier incarnation, is not one of your fly-by-night places, and numerous reports, mostly favourable, indicate its volume of business and claim on affections. The rate of turnover is your best protection against the squalors of cooking, service, or surroundings that are occasionally reported, and it is best if you know what you want. For most people this is the dim-sum (not served after 6 p.m.) which include at 40p each, char siu cheung fun (Chinese cannelloni), wafer king prawn, yam croquettes, steamed roast duck dumpling, and other recondite pleasures. Casually ordered main dishes are to some extent pot luck; successful ones have included crab with ginger and black bean, duck with chilli and black bean (£1·70), whole (or half) fish (usually grey mullet) with pork and ginger, with minor additions such as sweetcorn with crab sauce, broccoli or Chinese cabbage, or wun-tun soup. Egg tarts, sweet water-chestnut paste, or milk with almonds are soothing finishes. A member who spoke to the head waiter in advance and put a large party in his hands at a stated price did very well; junior service is more hit-or-miss. A good place for children, especially at Sunday lunch. No music.

App: Carol Steiger, P.S., William & Barbara Moyes, A.J.H., Lawrence Brown, and others

---

COLOMBINA   Map 15

4–5 Duke of York Street, S.W.1
01-930 8279

The more owners and names change (last in the 1977 *Guide* as Casa Mario), the more this useful trattoria between Fortnum's and the London Library remains substantially the same, with the usual Italian dishes ('good barbecued spare ribs') plus, on occasion, less usual variants: Mozzarella with oranges and fennel, or wind-dried beef from the Dolomites, as first courses; deftly fried batons of cod, or veal escalope with prawns and white rum as dishes of the day; and even – for the Italian-Welsh community perhaps – 'traifol moda nostra' as a sweet. Espresso coffee. 'Fragrant' Chianti Classico Rocca delle Marie '76 (£3·20).

Closed Sun; Dec 27 & 31; public hols
Must book L
Meals 12–3, 6–11

Alc £4·25 (meal £6·85)

Cover 35p D
Seats 85

♿ rest (1 step)
No dogs
Access, Am Ex, Barclay, Diners

LE CONNAISSEUR   Map 12

10a Golders Green Road, N.W.11
01-455 4882

Closed Sun; Sat L;
3 weeks summer; public hols (exc Jan 1)
Must book D
Meals 12–2.30, 7–11

Alc £8·15 (meal £12·80)

VAT inc
Service 15%
Cover 50p
Seats 36 (parties 30)
No dogs
Access, Am Ex, Barclay, Diners, Euro

'One of the nicest sensations is to sit down in a serious restaurant knowing that whatever you choose the result will please. I got a strong whiff of this feeling here and was not disappointed.' True, this and other correspondents have confined themselves fairly strictly to the short list of specialities on Herbert Berger's menu, and the 'come-on' of this first-floor restaurant a step away from Golder's Green tube depends wholly on its *maître/patron* Mario Martinelli, whose service is 'expert and concerned'. The room, lined with prints of notorious beauties, is small ('though they accommodated a large party at very short notice') and tables are not crowded, which goes far to excuse the price. The best first courses are the beignets de champignons 'wonderfully crisp, filled with a garlic, olive and parsley mixture, and served with a real tartare', 'creamily delicate' pumpkin soup (95p), moules marinière when offered, and (an ideal prelude to a light fishy main dish) brioche à la moelle with a dark, satiny madeira sauce. Main course specialities include suprême de turbot au Champagne (£3·95) and – despite last year's criticisms – médaillons de veau au saumon fumé. Carré d'agneau en croûte, though the périgourdine sauce is on the sweet side, is excellent, as are the coeur de filet, and coquilles St Jacques Côte d'Azur (£3·95) – 'the best scallops since Au Roy Gourmet in Paris, in a delicate tomato and cream sauce, accompanied by crunchy mange-tout peas and unusually crisp, very buttery sauté potatoes.' Tarte aux fraises, the restaurant's own mousse (not to be confused with crème) brûlée, well-made soufflés glacés, and the petits fours which justify the price of the Cafetière coffee, are all praised. Wine prices (from £3·95) may terrify, but Mr Martinelli's advice is worth taking. Pernand-Vergelesses '76 (Maufoux) at £7·10, Ch. Chasse-Spleen '70, c.b., at £8·80, and halves of sweet Ch. La Tour Blanche '55, c.b., at £4·50, have pleased people. No music.

App: Sir Michael Hanley, Adrian Levine, D. M. Gaythwaite, M.B-J., and others

---

🥄 🍷 🍾 CONNAUGHT Map 15

Carlos Place, W.1
01-499 7070

Closed (Grill Room) weekends & public hols
Must book
Meals 12.30–1.30, 6.30–10

Tdh (Rest) from £9·30 (meal £16·35), D from £9·80 (meal £16·55)
Alc (Grill Room) £14·85 (meal £19·25)

VAT inc
Service 15%
Seats 80 (parties 20)
🔲 rest (3 steps)
No dogs
Access, Euro
89 rooms (all with bath)
Prices on application
Fire cert

It takes all tastes – though alas, not all income brackets – to make a Connaught customer ('client' is probably the hotel's own word). There is plenty for the student of human nature between these panelled walls, according to the sociological lady who contemplates a thesis on 'pecking orders in Connaught servants' and the writer who goes to watch 'Socialist ministers gorge themselves on red-blooded grouse'. The quiet excellence of the service at its best cannot now be depended upon, especially at the younger end, and the kitchen has its weaknesses too, some of them perhaps traditional and therefore ineradicable. Every now and then these faults combine to make a disappointing meal. But the place remains by far the most familial and gracious of London hotels. The graces include an uncommonly able French chef, Michel Bourdin. Whether in the Restaurant (where you pay by the cost of the main dish) or in the adjoining Grill (which is à la carte) the dishes that extend him, or which he is likely to have overseen, should be considered first. There are a few specialities which have to be ordered in advance. One such, oeuf en surprise Connaught, was 'perfect of its kind, a large cocotte containing an egg *à point* in the midst of a cheese soufflé, enrobed with lobster-rich sauce and browned'. Zéphir de filets de sole (quenelles with two sauces, one white wine and the other lobster) was equally dazzling. Numerous other subtleties are reported: mosaïque de saumon, pâté de turbot (perhaps a little too delicate for its sauce), terrine Connaught, croustade d'oeufs de caille Maintenon, poularde de Bresse, and the house's potato specialities, pommes Carlos (sliced and baked) and 'zephyr-like' pommes soufflées. A test meal included as a daily dish the shining brown oxtail, done with chestnuts and neatly turned vegetables. But that day it was a curious lapse of dining-room management that put on the steaming trolley not the indestructible oxtail but the coulibiac of fish whose crisp pastry was inevitably ruined. The roast crumbed lamb 'du Kent' (as they put it) can also suffer in timing and texture this way. The puddings are bizarre by contemporary taste (outside aristocratic nurseries) but perhaps none the worse for that: one does not lightly embark on bread-and-butter pudding elsewhere once one has tasted this one, trifle is a superior version, and there is even an account of a '*trompe l'oeil* fried egg in chocolate and meringue'. Cheeses may be inexcusably poor in view of the fine clarets and burgundies – not to mention ports – that are here kept and properly served at gentlemanly rather than *parvenu* prices: Ch. Haut-Bailly '61 (c.b.) at £19·50, and Romanée-St-Vivant '70 (Louis Latour) at £16. Chassagne-Montrachet '73 (Joseph Drouhin), £10 the bottle, £5·20 the half, would flatter some of the delicate fish dishes. Excellent breakfasts. No music. No pipes. 'No jeans' – fancy them having to say that.

App: by too many members to list

LA CROISETTE   Map 13

168 Ifield Road, S.W.10
01-373 3694

Closed Mon; Tue L
Must book
Meals 12.30–2.30, 8–11.30

Tdh £9 (meal £12·35)

VAT inc
Service 15%
Seats 35
No dogs
Am Ex card

Albert Bracci and Pierre Martin's set fish feast here is up to £9 basic now (the à la carte version is confined to their Le Suquet, *q.v.*, which shares the import costs of fresher, more various seafood than Billingsgate provides). It is amazing what people will put up with to nourish their brains in the style Jeeves approves. 'Every abusive comment I've read about the service seems true. When you book they only speak French. They offer a small, rather poor, complimentary Kir when you arrive. Shoddy music surrounds you during the many hours you sit at table (the plateau de fruits de mer alone takes about an hour). Vegetables and other things are apt to come late or not at all.' Still, others have found the waiters 'quite jolly if your French is up to it'; and the 'notably fishy, well-dressed salade niçoise', fish soup, 'delicious crab and crevettes grises', 'sea bass cooked to perfection over fennel', glazed salmon, acceptable fruit tarts, and more than acceptable coffee, bring people back. They keep sound white wines, from Métaireau Muscadet or Gros Plant to still champagne, between £5 and £10.

App: Steven Brook, V. Westerman, and others

Unless otherwise stated, a restaurant is open all week and all year and is licensed.

CYPRIANA KEBAB HOUSE   Map 15

11 Rathbone Street, W.1
01-636 1057

Nick Soteriou's restaurant is an unfailing resource for benighted or exhausted regulars, and hummus, yoghourt and cucumber, mixed kebab or 'best of all, the lamb casserole with okra or beans and a separately ordered salad' keep the food in moderate favour, though the taramosalata, mezedes, pastries and coffee are easily surpassed elsewhere. Wines from £2·80 the bottle.

Closed Sun; Sat L;
2 weeks summer; public
hols
Must book
Meals 12–3, 6–12

Alc £2·95 (meal £5·05)

VAT inc
Seats 50

⟨⟩ rest (3 steps)
No dogs
Barclay, Diners

DA CARLO   Map 12

102 Kilburn Square,
Kilburn High Road,
N.W.6
01-328 4930

Closed Sun; public hols
Must book weekends
Meals 12.15–2.30,
6.30–11.30

Alc £4·20 (meal £7·15)

Service 10%
Cover 30p
Children's helpings
(under 5)
Seats 65
⟨⟩ rest
No dogs
Access, Am Ex, Barclay,
Diners

Hardly anybody finds this ristorante by accident, for it is tucked away on the first floor of a shopping block on the corner of Brondesbury Road. This gives it a vaguely clubby atmosphere, and only repetitive music spoils its cool blue elegance. Emilio is cooking now, and has settled in well, to judge by a test meal after the change, with a fresh-tasting seafood salad (95p), penne alla Carlo – 'richly sauced with tomato, cream, and plenty of garlic' (75p), 'nicely moist' fried breast of chicken parmigiana (£1·60), and carefully fried courgettes. Butter was good, grissini and rolls crisp, and other dishes approved by various people include spaghetti alle vongole (£1·05), scaloppine zingara with peppers, ham and mushrooms (£1·65), saltimbocca, and steaks. Frogs' legs are also a speciality, as is sole with artichokes. The vegetables included are usually adequate. A limited range of sweets is displayed on the centre table, and crème caramel was the thickened sort when tried, but they will make zabaglione or crêpes Suzette if asked early enough – the service sometimes flags late at night. Straccali Chianti is £2·45, and even the best Italian wines stocked are under £4.

App: Roy Mathias, Ron Salmon, C.J.D., J. & P.S., Charles Shepherd, and others

The Guide News Supplement will be sent out as usual, in June, to everyone who buys the book directly from Consumers' Association and to all bookshop purchasers who return the card interleaved with their copy. Let us know of any changes that affect entries in the book, or of any new places you think should be looked at.

See p. 108 for London pubs and wine bars.

DANWICH SHOP Map 13

48 Union Street,
Kingston-upon-Thames
01-546 6349

'Only a snack bar', but a particular one, whose menu-by-numbers offers proper mayonnaise for the prawn sandwich, and pink meat for the beef one, 'with delicious cole-slaw'. Take-away prices range from 30p for a Havarti cheese Danwich to 75p for a smoked eel one; note there are also off-sales of gravlax and dill sauce. 'A pity the drinks are limited to coffee or tinned orange juice.' Recorded classical music. No smoking between 12 and 2.

Closed D; Sun; public hols
Open 9.30–5.30 (6 Sat)

Alc meal £1·40

VAT & service inc

Seats 10
No dogs
Unlicensed

DAPHNE'S Map 14

112 Draycott Avenue,
S.W.3
01-589 4257 *and*
584 6883

Closed L; Sun; public
hols
Must book
D only, 7.30–12

Alc £6·60 (meal £10·75)

Cover 50p
Seats 65 (parties 16)
♿ rest (2 steps); w.c.
Air-conditioning
No dogs
Access, Am Ex, Barclay,
Diners, Euro

Daphne dates, like Dornford Yates, but with an evocative, expensive air that makes her – that is, Julian Tennant's restaurant – one of the dining trade's imperishables. Survival is the name of the game, thinks one customer who was offered half an avocado with a few curried prawns at £1·55, but at least by grumbling (how many do?) he got a graceful apology and a substitute first course, 'and the rest of the meal was excellent.' Another member who started with saumon fumé farci (£2·65) also felt that he would have done better to plunge *in medias res* with 'the very model of an entrecôte béarnaise' (£3·70). So try watercress soup, perhaps, cold or hot, which someone has had to work on, and then rely on Pierre Brebbia's skills as a *rôtisseur* – of carré d'agneau paloise (£3·40) for example, 'with an exquisitely light minty hollandaise', or grouse: 'We asked for one very bloody, one medium bloody and one well done, and we were all delighted.' Coquilles St Jacques Mornay (£3·50) and chicken Kiev (£2·90) are old favourites, and 'good fresh vegetables included, imaginatively, bean sprouts.' They specialise in sweet soufflés, and 'a light sleeper was offered jasmine tea.' Wines begin at £3·50 for Provencal red or white, and gentlemanly claret at £6 or so (Ch. Haut-Bergey '67, c.b., a Graves). A half-bottle of Ch. Loupiac-Gaudiet is £2.30.

App: J.C., C.F.O., Lord Shuttleworth, J.M.

DIDIER Map 12

5 Warwick Place, W.9
01-286 7484

There are some who have felt that Dodd and all his diddy men would serve them more expeditiously and efficiently than the team here, both before and after Pagan Gregory's apparent departure, but Sue Miles is still tending the stove in this neatly arranged

Closed Sat; Sun; last
3 weeks Aug; most
public hols
Must book D
Meals 12.30–2.30, 7–10.15

Alc £4·15 (meal £7·65)

Service 10%
Cover 40p
Children's helpings
Seats 25 (parties 30)
 rest (1 step)
No dogs
Am Ex card

Little Venice backwater, and even those who grumble about the service find the place amiable and the cooking good. The menu (varied slightly between lunch and dinner) is very short. Main dishes may be the best, and 'the trust they put in lambs' kidneys with mustard sauce (£2·65) is not misplaced'; casseroled fillet steak in red wine, an inspector says, was also nicely flavoured and extremely tender, with good Anna potatoes and braised chicory. Cold stuffed veal with tuna sauce (£2·60) and baked pigeon with oranges are other favourites. Mushroom soup, gazpacho, sauté chicken livers, and smoked herring are possible first courses, and among the few sweets, crème brûlée was 'very lovely, a perfect creamy consistency and a top that crazed properly when tapped'. 'Fromage blanc with passion-fruit was a very delicate idea.' French ordinaire is £3, and the Georges Duboeuf generic burgundies at £4–£6 are perhaps the best choices thereafter. They keep port and dessert wine by the glass, and tea as well as coffee. No music.

App: Roy Mathias, C.H.C., Iwan Williams, R.B.J., Peter J. Holder, J.G., and others

---

DIWANA BHEL POORI HOUSE   Map 12

---

(1) 121 Drummond Street
N.W.1
01-387 5556
(2) 50 Westbourne Grove
W.2
01-221 0721

Closed Dec 25
Open noon–10.30 p.m.

Alc meal £2·30

VAT inc
Seats 50
No dogs
Unlicensed
Access, Diners

These are two of the best-value eating-places in London, provided you can forgo meat and fish and enjoy highly spiced Gujerati vegetable dishes – vigorous, not discreet; discrete, not mushed up. The **Westbourne Grove** branch is more comfortable, with cedar-wood hangings and 'curvy-backed' chairs; some think the spicing is blander than at the **Drummond Street** one. Whichever place suits you there is a choice between a 'thali' (a compartmented steel tray, usually including four savoury dishes and one sweet) and somewhat more interesting things à la carte, notably the crisp potato-stuffed pancake called dosa de luxe, eaten with coconut chutney; samosas, crisp 'bhel poori' shells with various sauces and a strong fresh coriander taste, 'rather solid' iddly sambar (rice-flour dumpling with curry sauce), and sweets among which members seem to prefer the creamy, cardamon-flavoured shrikhand. 'Sweet masala pan' for long chewing is 10p. Unless you take your own drink, which they do not mind, ask for fresh orange juice or yoghourty lassi (salt or sweet) or – if you fancy 'a raspberry milk shake with noodles in it' – Kashmiri falooda (45p). It is hard to spend more than £3 a head.

App: S. I. Cohen, A.H., J.C., P.S., Peter Shier, and others

DIWAN-I-AM Map 15

161 Whitfield Street, W.1
01-387 0293

'Scruffy but not really off-putting' surroundings do not keep the faithful from this North Indian restaurant's good tandoori chicken, nan, various curried dishes, including khali dhal 'made with black lentils, and very special', and syrupy sweets. The pilau rice and vegetables are less successful. Some wines; Dortmunder on tap. Courteous service. Recorded Indian music. A few tables outside on sunny days – 'pity it's the wrong end of Whitfield Street.'

Closed Dec 25	Alc meal £4·10	🔊 rest
Must book D & weekends		No dogs
Meals 12–3, 5.50–	Service 10%	Access, Am Ex, Barclay,
midnight	Seats 98	Diners, Euro

DRAGON GATE Map 15

7 Gerrard Street, W.1
01-734 5154

Closed Dec 25 & 26
Meals noon–11.15

Alc meal £3·80

Seats 80 (parties 40)
🔊 rest
Unlicensed
Am Ex, Diners

'Sets you sweating like a ship's engineer in the first stages of malaria' is one inspector's warning of the shrimps with hot garlic sauce (£1·90) at Mr Liu's modest, draughty Szechuan place. (Silver Jubilee Investments Ltd's expansion into 1 Gerrard Place was still only a promise when we went to press.) Another visitor was 'charmed by the delicate, slightly sweetened taste, the kick of sesame oil, and the coarsely ground Szechuan pepper' in the tripe with chilli sauce – but not by the curt service. 'Homeside bean-curd' (£1·30), and aubergine with a 'hot-and-sour, brown, gingery and shiny' fish sauce are also worth stoking up on if you are to emerge, like all the best dragons, breathing fire. Licence and other details uncertain. More reports, please, on both places.

Please report to us on atmosphere, decor and – if you stayed – standard of accommodation, as well as on food, drink and prices (send bill if possible).

Prices of meals underlined are those which we consider represent unusual value for money. They are not necessarily the cheapest places in the Guide.

Inspections are carried out anonymously. Persons who pretend to be able to secure, arrange or prevent an entry in the Guide are impostors and their names or descriptions should be reported to us.

We rewrite every entry each year, and depend on fresh, detailed reports to confirm the old, as well as to include the new. The further from London you are, the more important this is.

Wine prices shown are for a 'standard' bottle of the wine concerned, unless another measure is stated.

DRURY LANE HOTEL
MAUDIE'S RESTAURANT   Map 15

10 Drury Lane, W.C.2
01-836 6666

Blessed be the London hotel that has got even part of one meal approximately right, and in this neat restaurant, where you look at the Blessed Osbert Lancaster's cartoons and snarl because they have left the captions off the blow-ups, the source of merit is the lunchtime cold buffet (basis of the £3 set meal) which, when tested, included nicely Italianate aubergine parmigiana, salami with peppercorns, mackerel vinaigrette, smoked trout, squid and other pleasantries. Hot dishes have been found less happy, but Schnitzel Holstein was well fried, an inspector says. Georges Maréchal wines begin at £3·60, but you would have been better off with the Rubesco '73 they had for Italian week. Service 'not very bright'. Recorded music. More reports, please.

Closed Dec 25 & 26
Must book
Meals 12.30–2.30, 6–11
(Sun 12.30–2, 6.30–9.30)

Tdh buffet L from £3
(meal £5·50), L from £5·25
(meal £9·10), D from
£6·25 (meal £10·20)

VAT inc
Seats 85 (parties 80)
♿ rest (3 steps)

Air-conditioning
Car park (6)
No dogs in d/r
Access, Am Ex, Barclay,
Diners, Euro
128 rooms (all with bath)
Prices on application

DUE FRANCO   Map 12

207 Liverpool Road, N.1
01-607 4112

Some Italians try ever so hard to conceal their basic competence behind a screen of songs, snatches, and peppermillinery: Franco is one of them. But he and Giuseppe, who cooks, run a lively, locally popular place, and their cannelloni, saltimbocca, and involtini Casa Nostra (£2·25) are tasty, vegetables for main dishes or seafood salad fresh, and zabaglione frothily adequate. Escalope Mont Blanc and médaillon beurre noir are other specialities. Arithmetic is not their strong point, but service is well-timed. Settesoli red wine is £2·85. Recorded music.

Closed Sun; Sat L; public
hols
Must book
Meals 12–2.30, 6–11.30

Alc £5·30 (meal £8·25)

VAT inc

Cover 35p
Seats 40 (parties 30)
No dogs
Am Ex, Barclay, Diners

EATONS   Map 14

49 Elizabeth Street,
S.W.1
01-730 0074

There is a staple, wisely short à la carte menu, with supplements changed weekly, at this simple, fresh-looking restaurant (convenient for the Victoria terminals) which is managed by Shayne Pope and Dieter Vagts. As before, Santosh Bakshi, 'the ovoid

Closed Sat; Sun; public
hols; 3 weeks Aug;
Dec 24 & 31
Must book
Meals 12–2, 7–11.15

Alc £5·15 (meal £8·05)

Service inc
Cover 30p
Seats 40 (parties 14)
 [&] rest (2 steps)
No dogs
Access, Am Ex, Diners

bloke', cooks. Tables feel a little cramped especially
when the place is full, but service remains smiling
and one or other of the owners is always on parade.
As for the food, 'it is the sort of place one can with
confidence recommend to anyone,' says a regular,
and few disagree with his verdict; the secret may
well be that not too much is attempted, and prices
are kept reasonable. Smoked salmon blinis with sour
cream (£1·20) remain the favourite first course,
with the spinach and the cauliflower soups as
runners up. Main courses specially praised are
escalope of pork filled with red cabbage and raisins
(£2·20), chicken suprême in a white wine and cream
sauce with asparagus, and lamb and kidneys
provençale. 'The vegetables are always fresh and
accurately cooked.' Many feel the sweets have
improved since last year's criticisms, and single out
a 'light creamy cheesecake', 'moist mocha gateau',
and tarts based on fresh fruit in season; but 'cheeses
are a blank spot.' The French house wines,
especially the reds, are acceptable (£3·30 a litre, 55p
a glass), and there is also an unassuming wine list.

App: W.H., R. W. D. Orders, C.D.,
M. Essayan, Roy Mathias, and others

EFES KEBAB HOUSE   Map 15

---

80 Great Tichfield Street,
W.1
01-636 1953

Closed Sun; public hols
Must book
Open noon–11.30 p.m.

Alc £4 (meal £6·55)

Seats 30 (parties 30)
 [&] rest
Access, Am Ex, Barclay

Mr Kesimli's restaurant has become one of the most
popular north of Oxford Street ('pocket bleeps at
the next table reminded us how near we were to the
Middlesex Hospital'), and it is wise to book unless
you are just taking away doner kebab, which here
turns over as fast as it turns round. 'The face-lift
has not spoilt things, or raised prices', though 'the
music sounds like tom-toms for hungry cannibals.'
Service is brisk, even brusque unless they know you.
The cooking is not just ethnic but imaginative
within its limits: chicken in walnut sauce is a popular
first course, as is the 'superb muska börek' (fried
cheese pastries). Lamb's liver, stuffed vegetables or
dolmades are other choices, and there may follow
'highly spiced and authentic' anteb koftesi, or ulcer
filetosu (beef, lamb and chicken) with 'green chillies
that must have been blanched because I could eat
them without hitting the roof.' Salads are well
presented. Sweets are of a sound standard, but fruit
may be the best finish, apart from the Turkish
coffee. 'The muscular Gunesi red is better than the
thin and characterless house wine.'

App: F. Jaeger, A. & R. Piepe, A. F. Bedford,
G.T.C., Mrs J. Stephenson, Dr & Mrs T. S. Worthy,
and others

L'EPICURE Map 15

28 Frith Street, W.1
01-437 2829 *and* 734 2667

Closed Sun; Sat L; public
hols; Dec 24
Must book
Meals 12–2.30, 6–11.15

Alc £6·05 (meal £9·70)

Cover 40p
Seats 50 (parties 20)
♿ rest (1 step)
No dogs
Access, Am Ex, Barclay,
Diners, Euro

French cooking is best left to the French, as one
commentator remarks, and with Greek chefs working
(now) for an English owner it is no use expecting
everything on the vast international menu to be as
it should be. But after a bereavement or a bankruptcy
you may find that this chip off the old Soho, with
fishtail gas-jets outside signalling the leaping
tableside flames within, possesses a wistful appeal.
Besides, 'they asked me how I wanted my omelette,
soft, medium or firm.' Other visitors able to recall
temps perdu say that crevettes Alfonso (cooked with
mushrooms in a sherry sauce, on toast), chicken
diable and sole Colbert are as they were. Kidneys
too are well done, and house specialities include
champignons Dordogne and (on the lamp of course)
steak maison (£3·50). It is interesting to see venison
sausages with red cabbage and Greek pot-roasted
lamb on a day's menu, but the taramosalata is on
the bland side. If you want a sweet, crêpes Suzette
suggest themselves (at £1·10), and they offer
savouries too. The house French ordinaire is £2·75;
Ch. Laville Haut-Brion '73, c.b., £7·10, Aloxe-Corton
Les Boutières '71, £8. No music. Sometimes they
will let you 'split' a meal either side of a theatre.

App: Michael Meyer, A.L., J.C., S.T.

L'ETOILE Map 15

30 Charlotte Street, W.1
01-636 7189 *and* 1496

Closed Sat; Sun; 3 weeks
Aug; Dec 24 & 31;
public hols
Must book
Meals 12.30–2.30, 6.30–10

Alc £9·15 (meal £13·45)

VAT inc
Service 12½%
Cover 60p
Seats 50
No dogs
Am Ex, Diners

One day no doubt Chris Vavlides' L'Etoile will
follow the way of both restaurants and stars and
sink into a black hole, but the moment is not yet.
Judgements vary from 'this is the place by which
all others are judged' (after 25 years' regular
patronage), to 'the food is still better than the
administration' and 'it is unfair to judge it by the
very highest standards.' Another summary, 'the
service, the hors d'oeuvre and the cheese are among
the best in London and other items are quite
decent', actually does less than justice to Jorge
Ribeiro's main dishes, especially his ris de veau
braisé aux champignons (£4·85), rognons de veau
sautés au vin rouge (£2·95), tripe, and calf's head.
Escalope Zingara, filets mignons de chevreuil,
grilled Dover soles, and grouse in season are also
worth attention. But it is primarily the dressed
crab, loup de mer, and turbot monégasque (£2·55)
that people would remember if the word 'étoile'
were hurled at them on the psychoanalyst's couch.
Salad and fruit salad are better than vegetables and
confected puddings. The place would be, as someone
says, 'ideal for a wine-lovers' celebration' (and has
been so used by at least one member since Postgate
dined with him, and cervelles panées were 7s 6d,

53

not £2·95) − if only tobacco-lovers did not celebrate too. The clarets at about £8 (Ch. Troplong-Mondot '64, Ch. Cantemerle '67), the Louis Latour white burgundies at similar prices, or Morgon '76 and Hermitage Rochefine '73 at £5 or so, and the marcs or vintage ports they keep by the glass, all help to explain people's loyalties. No music.

App: Christopher Forman, Peter Liechti, T.S., Geoffrey Finsberg, and others

---

FINGALS   Map 13

690 Fulham Road, S.W.6
01-736 1195

Closed Sun; Sat L;
Dec 24 & 31; public hols
Must book D
Meals 12.30–2.30, 8–11.40

Alc L £2·45 (meal £4·40),
D £4·50 (meal £7·30)

Cover 25p D
Seats 32
♿ rest
Barclaycard

'The first impression is that you are walking into someone's front room' − and in fact you are, because Richard Johnston lives over the shop. The style changes between lunch and dinner: at lunch-time Tina Boland cooks a simple hot dish or two, with gnocchi or quiche and interesting salads, and 'amber sludge' treacle tart (they have borrowed the Guide's *Times description) if you want a sweet; at night, Alexander Somkowicz cooks and the menu becomes more bistro-ish, with soups, lamb cutlets, boeuf bourguignonne or (he suggests) veal Zingara (£2·70). Spanish Yecla red (£2.10) or Provencal red and white wines (£2·85) are most people's choices, and Mr Johnston has a developed taste in spirits. Recorded 'modern' music. More reports from informality-lovers, please − for the latest evening visitor reports 'intermittently competent' cooking, spoilt by ill-kempt and lackadaisical service.*

FOGAREIRO   Map 12

16 Hendon Lane, N.3
01-346 0315

Closed Sun; Apr 13 & 16;
Aug 27; Dec 25 & 26;
Jan 1
Must book D
Meals 12–2.30, 7–11.30

Tdh L £3·95 (meal £6·50)
Alc £6·05 (meal £9·45)

VAT inc (tdh L)
Cover 35p
Seats 50
No dogs
Access, Am Ex, Barclay,
Diners, Euro

Senhor Augusto Costa's Portuguese restaurant near Finchley Central tube (and but a step away from the house where the *Guide* itself was born) is a welcome addition to the short list of good Iberian eating-places in London. He and his wife Maria, with their chef Celestino Pavao, list international as well as Portuguese dishes, but members find the latter, especially the fishy ones, at once authentic and refined, and have been happy to eat them with Portuguese wines rather than the dearer French ones. The kitchen attempts too much perhaps, for on one evening 'everything we had seemed mistimed and overcooked.' Still, the day's 'catch' of halibut, brill or bass may well be shown you in the raw, with lobsters 'alive, alive, oh!' An expatriate visitor hails piri-piri prawns with nostalgic pleasure, and at a test meal, the seafood pancake 'totally belied expectations by the absolute freshness of the fruits de mer, lightness of the pancake and brandied-ness of the sauce'. Halibut steak in cider 'was not overcooked, and had a julienne of carrots and cucumber on top and a well-made cream and cider sauce.' Try also the bouillabaisse, and the brochette

de fruits de mer Fogareiro (£3·20) – which the chef
recommends. From the charcoal grill there are
steaks and cutlets for the less adventurous, and
juliana preta e branca (£2·65) is a beef and veal
speciality with green and red peppers. Vegetables
and fruit here are carefully chosen and always fresh.
Red, white and pink Portuguese wines cost £2·75 to
£3·25, and clarets and burgundies from £3·10 to a
generous £15·95 for '61 Ch. Latour. Rüdesheimer
and Oppenheimer whites would go well with rich
fish dishes. House wines are 55p a glass. Service is
considerate, decor traditional, and air-conditioning
is promised for this year, not before time.

*App: R. P. Crofton, J. C., Penny Sack, C.P.D.,
and others*

FOOD FOR THOUGHT Map 15

31 Neal Street, W.C.2
01-836 0239

*'Nothing wholier-than-thou about the Damants' place:
just vastly better cooking than leguminous London
expects.' Good smells; cramped wooden tables; queues.
Siriporn Duncan and Veronica Thompson's favourite
dishes are scalloped vegetables (80p), stir-fry courgettes
with wine sauce (80p), wild apricot and pineapple
sponge (50p), and the home-made wholemeal bread;
but inspectors who suggest, for two people,
three half-portions of the day's savouries and a shared
pudding also delighted in the discrete flavours of the
leek and aduki bean casserole, soy bean gumbo,
savoury rice, and others things (the short menu
changes daily). Unlicensed. Drink tea or coffee or take
your own bottles (no corkage charged).*

Closed Sat; Sun; public hols	Alc meal £2·45	Seats 30 Air-conditioning
Open 12–8	VAT & service inc	Unlicensed

LA FRINGALE Map 14

4 Hollywood Road,
S.W.10
01-351 1011

For a cosy, not too quick late supper in or about
the Fulham Road, people still like M Busquets'
narrow, relaxed bistro, which does not attempt more
than it can perform: 'well-seasoned' vegetable soups,
sound chicken liver pâté, 'slightly pink' liver
berlinoise, cutlets with not very garlicky mayonnaise,
fillet of beef in red wine sauce, and so on. Vegetables
and sweets are merely moderate. The house
burgundy is a modest £2·10. 'Family pictures, a
mahogany bar, and velvet banquettes', though an
inspector would have liked cleaner table linen too.

Closed L; Sun; public hols	Alc £4·10 (meal £6·80)	Seats 55 (parties 25) ♿ rest (1 step)
Must book	Cover 30p	No dogs
D only, 7–11.45		Barclay, Diners

GANPATH Map 12

372 Gray's Inn Road,
W.C.1
01-278 1938

Small, calm South Indian place hard by King's
Cross. Manager-chef was at the India Club. Try
masala dosai (crisp, potato-filled pancake, 60p) with
coconut chutney, iddly (light, rice-flour dumplings,
30p) with hot lentil sauce (sambar) and tender
bhuna gosht, gulab jamun or almond cake for sweet,
and lassi to drink. There is Stella Artois, too, at 35p.
Indian records. Air-conditioning planned.

Closed Sun; Dec 25 & 26;
public hols (exc May 7)
Must book D
Meals 12–3, 6–10.15
(10.45 Fri & Sat)

Tdh L £1·10
Alc (min £1) meal £3·10

Seats 36

♿ rest
No dogs
Access card

GATAMELATA Map 13

343 Kensington High
Street, W.8
01-603 3613

Closed Sun; Sat L;
Apr 13 & 16; D Dec 24;
Dec 25 & 26; Jan 1
Must book D & weekends
Meals 12–2.45, 7–11.30

Tdh £4·15 (meal £6·85)
Alc £6·05 (meal £9·45)

VAT inc
Service 12½%
Cover 45p
Seats 40
Air-conditioning
Access, Am Ex, Barclay,
Diners, Euro

This branch of the Soho Rugantino (q.v.) went
rather quiet last summer, but seems to be flourishing
still. Instead of 'si' or 'yes', 'fantastico!' cry the
waiters accepting your order, and sometimes it is
even true. An inspector who asked for a mixed plate
from the hors d'oeuvre trolley got vegetables à la
grecque, marinated trout, whitebait, aubergine with
Mozzarella and tomato, and seafood salad in
generous helpings – 'all delicious'. Another first
course, the spinach croquette (£1·10) is fresh spinach
rolled into a ball with smoked ham, chicken or veal,
and herbs, coated with breadcrumbs, fried crisp and
served dripping with garlic butter. Thumbs down,
though, for tinned tomatoes with veal piccata, for a
too-hastily assembled fegato alla veneziana – 'and
for the state of the cutlery,' adds an American. Most
main dishes are in the £2–£4 range, but the set
meals at £4·15 should be worth a trial. Wines are
from the Belloni stable, with Valpolicella and Soave
as red and white house wines at £2·95 a litre, 65p
the glass. No music.

App: A.L., J.R., A. A. Ryner, G.R.W–G.

☜ ♢ LE GAVROCHE Map 14

61–63 Lower Sloane
Street, S.W.1
01-730 2820 *and* 5983

Closed L; Sun; public
hols
Must book
D only, 7–12

Alc £15·10 (meal £22·70)

'The silver lining to a recent visit by American
clients turned out to be the most gruelling
gastronomic assault course I have ever undertaken
in the United Kingdom. It began – and should have
ended – here.' In other words, the Roux brothers'
senior restaurant ranks high in this book because it
sets the mark at which hardly any restaurants in
Britain – even in the most expensive London
hotels – bother to aim. Sensible Britons realise that
without their American (and French) clients the

VAT inc
Service 15%
Cover £1·20
Seats 47
Am Ex, Diners

Gavroche, and indeed haute cuisine of any kind, would not exist here, though if we can afford Concorde, £30 a head from time to time on mousseline de brochet, the two-stage duck, and sablé aux fraises does not seem excessive. What does seem excessive are the occasions, not infrequent in 1978, when pretensions are not lived up to: one diner had an undignified haggle to obtain a remotely adequate reduction on the bill when the staff actually forgot to bring the second instalment of caneton Gavroche. Besides, even the Roux brothers 'ought to remind themselves from time to time that caneton St Martin at Barrier in Tours is an incomparably finer dish.' However, a test meal late in the autumn showed the restaurant at its formidable best. Feuilleté de bécasse Néné (a first course, £6·80) was 'a perfect round pie, cylindrical, deep gold and glossy, the flakiest and most delicate pastry imaginable. Inside were chunks of tender meat and forcemeat and a rich brown sauce, pitched precisely between the bland and the alarmingly gamey.' Or try, perhaps – though naturally not at the same meal – breasts of pigeon, boned, crumbed and fried with a stuffing of partridge and duck livers, 'the most delicious pigeon I remember'; or nouilles aux fruits de mer. Vegetables seem to be better than salads. But if you want three courses, be careful to order appropriately. (Pot au feu, very well worth a try, is a fairly gentle main dish.) It would be a pity, in any case, to miss such peaks of the *pâtissier*'s art as the charlotte aux poires J. Millet (£3·60) served at a test meal. The list of clarets is unrivalled in London, and if you want to pay £105 for Ch. Latour '18 or nearly £200 for the '45, they will let you. But they do keep tolerable Alsace or '76 Beaujolais or other quaffing wines under £7·50 too, and you may need them: 'I was horrified to see them encouraging pests with an enormous mountain of different boxes of cigars.' (Others say that breathing is easier than it used to be.) But no lapse of taste is surprising from French caterers who will take a well-dressed (but tieless) guest and drape him in someone else's old school tie, kept for the purpose, before they will consent to feed him. Details are approximate.

App: Carol Steiger, D. M. Gaythwaite, W.B., R.M., Dr John Fell, and others

GAY HUSSAR   Map 15

2 Greek Street, W.1
01-437 0973

Closed Sun; public hols
Must book

Victor Sassie's Soho restaurant has had the key of the *Guide* door for 21 years now, and Raymond Postgate's 1957 entry is still valid: 'It is one of the few places where you will find Central European dishes properly done and where it is worthwhile

Meals 12.30–2, 5.30–11.30

Tdh L from £4 (meal £7·35)

Alc £6·05 (meal £9·15)

Cover 25p
Seats 30
♿ rest (1 step)
Air-conditioning
No dogs

consulting the proprietor about your meal.' True, the six shilling set lunch is now £4–£4·50, and some of the cooking is good only in the sense that Schweik was a good soldier. But a regular visitor in 1978 who calls it 'one of the best values in London' has widespread support. It is a jovial, well-padded place, even when there is no room to move, Victor is urgent with his advice, and the waiters bustle or argue. Diners of all nationalities and more than one political persuasion are nowadays to be seen, and most find their appetites sated before the third course. Wild cherry soup pleases many, though it is a sweetish start to the meal; alternatives might be the Bulgar salata or gull's egg. There is a vast à la carte menu of goulashes, ragouts, schnitzels and stuffed pancakes. Almost anything with red cabbage is good, especially roast goose or widgeon, but the dumplings with ox tongue in a 'tangy' sauce are 'rather solid' and may turn up again, as a sweet flavoured with cheese and lemon, in plum sauce. At lunch-time resist suggestions to take a Hungarian cocktail or peach brandy aperitif before wine and follow on with Hubertus liqueur, or the gypsies will get you. House wines: red Hungarian Cabernet or Balatoni Riesling white at £1·80 a half-litre or 55p a glass are liked, and there are plenty more to choose from. Smoking discouraged. No music.

App: David Potter, Jonas Kristjansson, Ron Salmon, Prof Ian Oswald, Michael Meyer, and many others

GEETA   Map 12

59 Willesden Lane, N.W.6
01-624 1713

The Vijay's chef and accountant have migrated to this 'clean and comfortable' place nearby, with a catholic 'Madonna to Siva' decor. There are more meat dishes than South Indians expect, but it is best to take the vegetable specials, such as the 'tennis-ball' dahi vadia (20p each) with spicy salt yoghourt, masala dosai (pancake with coconut chutney, 65p) and coconut rice with mustard seed and curry leaves in it. However, a chicken special 'in a creamy lentil sauce with strong cardamom flavour' was delicious and unusual, spinach bhaji admirably fresh and spiced. Ladoo (30p) is worth trying for those who like their cardamom as a sweet flavour too. Wine would be foolish; lager is 55p a pint. More reports, please.

Closed Dec 25 & 26
Must book weekends
Meals 12–3, 6–11 (12 Fri, Sat)

Alc (min £1) meal £3·35

Seats 42

♿ rest; w.c.
No dogs
Barclaycard

Unless otherwise stated, a restaurant is open all week and all year and is licensed.

♥ LA GIRALDA Map 3

66 Pinner Green,
Pinner, Middx
(Rickmansworth Road
between Cuckoo Hill and
Elm Park Road)
01-868 3429

Closed Dec 25
Must book
Meals 12–2.30, 6–10.30

Tdh L £2 (meal £3·85),
D £3·75 (meal £5·75)

Alc L (min £2) £2·80
(meal £4·80)

Service 10%
Seats 90 (parties 40)
♿ rest; w.c.
No dogs
Access, Am Ex, Barclay,
Diners

Every London suburb needs a David Brown, though if he were cloned, the letters would obviously not arrive so thick and fast from Watford, Ealing, Perivale and Pooterland generally about this unassuming, disconcertingly resonant shopping-parade restaurant, whose modestly priced Hispano-English cooking, and even better value Spanish wines, earned it a medal or two in the last edition. However, a good restaurateur needs to keep at least two steps ahead of the opposition, and a few gathering clouds in 1978 – including a test lunch of awesome proportions – suggested that Mr Brown and his chefs (Derek Knight and Julio Alonso) were becoming victims of their own success: 'With 150 covers a night, plus lunches, we need Superwaiter to cope,' was one admission made to a beleaguered customer. Of course, plenty of bad solutions present themselves: they could raise prices or mechanise the cooking. (Some dishes at the test meal had that production-line taste already, and an extension, the Velasquez room, has since been opened.) But, for instance, the beguiling Spanish wines deserve more robust Spanish flavours in the food, and this might thin down the crowds a little – though 'an English individual steak and kidney pie with plenty of tender beef and a lovely crust', or 'generous grilled steak very tender and done precisely as ordered' already offer plenty of relief to the nervous. Plain fish dishes are anyway better than paella here. 'Composed' entrees and puddings – seafood pancake, stuffed peppers, chicken Seville (stuffed with pâté £1·60), escalope of veal with mushrooms and oregano, profiteroles, Mont Blanc – are variably praised. Cheesecake is 'unbaked' – an odd taste, inspectors thought. The wines, from £2·20 for red or white Rioja, remain a revelation even now that others are beginning to catch up with the merits of Spanish wines. Gran Viña Sol '75 (white) at £4·20, Ardanza of Tondonia '70 (red) at £4 or so, and sweet white Diamante '75 at £3·50 will serve as an introduction. A guitarist may play Villa Lobos at night: sit next to him if you prefer the music to the clatter and hubbub. Pay your bill by 7.30 if you want £1 discount.

App: by too many members to list

Inspections are carried out anonymously. Persons who pretend to be able to secure, arrange or prevent an entry in the Guide are impostors and their names or descriptions should be reported to us.

Meal times refer to first and last orders.

IL GIRASOLE   Map 14

126 Fulham Road, S.W.3
01-370 6656

Light, airy ristorante, but the waiters 'with gold crosses nestling in their chest hairs' could be sunnier (and should perhaps keep an abacus handy too). Cooking is variable – regulars seem better satisfied than casual callers. The antipasto, tagliatelle Don Maria, cannelloni, spaghetti vongole and pollo alla fiorentina (with garlic sauce) are approved. Fair choice of Italian wines, but we have not seen a list. Tables outside. Italian records.

Closed Mon L; Apr 15 & 16; Dec 25

Must book D & weekends
Meals 12.15–3, 7–11

Alc £5·35 (meal £8·10)

Cover 30p
Seats 60

 ⌖ rest (1 step)
No dogs
Am Ex, Barclay, Diners

GOAN INDIAN   Map 12

16 York Way, N.1
01-837 7517

'Basic' King's Cross cafe, boasting 'the only Goan cooking in Europe', which means mackerel stuffed with sweet-sour spices, sorpotel (pork and liver with spices), Bombay pomfret curry (flat fish with coconut cream and herbs), and doce (lentils, coconut and sugar) as a sweet. But 'Goan-style vegetables bhaji' was too much like 'over-stewed cabbage' for one westerner, and chicken dishes can be gristly and tough. Carlsberg on tap. Slow service. Take-away. Indian records.

Closed Sun; Apr 13; Dec 25

Must book
Open noon–midnight

Alc meal £2·60

VAT inc
Seats 36

⌖ rest (1 step)
No dogs
Access, Am Ex, Diners

GOODY'S KOSHER RESTAURANT   Map 15

55 Berwick Street, W.1
01-437 6050

Closed Oct 1; Dec 25 & 26; Dec 31 D; Jan 1
Must book L; D weekends
Meals 12–2.45, 5.45–9.45

Tdh L £1·95 (meal £3·35)
Alc £4·85 (meal £7·35)

VAT inc
Cover 30p
Seats 50 (parties 30)
⌖ rest
No dogs
Access, Am Ex, Barclay, Diners, Euro

Strategically sited for Oxford Street shoppers, as well as vendors and merchants, Goody's offers heimische cooking in more genteel surroundings than its kosher cousins in Whitechapel do. The welcome is smooth, and the table linen pink, but the old Jewish favourites have a familiar ring. Many of the regulars never stray from salt beef (£2·05), or heimische fish (£3·10), but an inspector also liked the chicken neck with tsimmes, crisp and tastily stuffed, followed by three large tender slices of first-class tongue, unadulterated by the usual highly seasoned sauce. Avoid the calf's foot jelly unless you like brawn. The set lunch may disappoint. Vegetables are not always fresh but red cabbage is sweetly spicy, if overcooked for some tastes. Lockshen pudding (50p) is nicely concocted with fine noodles, orange peel and spices. Israeli wines are mostly sweetish and something of an acquired taste; the house Italian is £2·50. More reports, please.

LE GOURMET   Map 14

312 Kings Road, S.W.3
01-352 4483

More frolicking than galloping among the dark and 'slightly eerie' Victoriana here, where mere women tend to be relegated to the basement. 'Many of our regulars call it "home", ' says the proprietor. Well, an inspector did not feel exactly *chez lui* with his too-tomatoey beef Stroganoff and soggy strawberry cheesecake. But creamy spaghetti carbonara, gazpacho, steak and kidney pie, and the eggy 'Kings Road pudding' may redeem matters. Italian house wine is £3 the litre, 45p the glass. Recorded classics.

Closed L (exc Sun);
public hols (exc Apr 13);
Dec 24
Must book D
Meals 12–3 (Sun),
6.30–11.45

Tdh Sun L £4 (meal £6·20)
Alc £4·80 (meal £7·90)

VAT & service inc
Service 12½%
Cover 30p D

Seats 36 (parties 30)
▣ rest
Air-conditioning
No dogs
Access, Am Ex, Barclay,
Diners

GOURMET RENDEZVOUS   Map 12

263 Finchley Road,
N.W.3
01-435 0755

Closed Dec 25
Meals 12–2.30, 5.30–12

Tdh L 90p, D from £2·80
Alc meal £3·75

Service 10%
Seats 42
No dogs
Access, Am Ex, Barclay,
Diners, Euro

Mr Tsui's smilingly served and spruce little restaurant is all the better (and cheaper), some think, for not being related to the other Rendezvous Pekinese restaurants in London. The chefs are called Lau and Fung now, and the Szechuan accent at a test meal was confined to the pickled cabbage with pork (even the soup made with the same materials was dull). On the whole, the set meals seem to offer the more zestful tastes, to judge by 'delicious' king prawns with green pepper and garlic, and 'slightly too sweet but also good' chicken with cashew nuts and yellow-bean sauce. Sweet-sour pork, so often scamped, was well cooked, and crispy duck adequate, though many will need to order extra pancakes at the outset. Egg-fried rice was better than either plain or 'special'. If you want a few extra dishes, try the Pekinese dumplings, sesame shrimp toasts (crisply fried in good oil, and enough for four people's preliminary nibbles, £1·80), deep-fried shredded beef in chilli and, as a change from toffee bananas, the 'hot and crisp' mashed red-bean pancake (£1 – 'and worth the wait'). Alas, Mr Tsui seems to have taken the *Guide*'s question about music as an invitation to instal some, and one customer says he was the victim of a more serious linguistic misunderstanding over payment of a bill.

App: John & Terry Banks, M.C.C., A.W., M.E.D.

The Guide accepts no advertising. Nor does it allow restaurateurs to use its name on brochures, menus, or in any form of advertisement. If you see any instances of this, please report them to us.

GRAHAME'S SEA FARE   Map 15

38 Poland Street, W.1
01-437 3788

Fish and chips with a difference, for Robert de Haan's much-beset little place is 'best called heimische', and you may begin with gefilte fish (60p) or chopped egg with the good caraway bread, and proceed to sweet-and-sour halibut or plaice with (rather plump) chips, or grilled haddock – 'though I found the scaly skin disagreeable.' 'Grandmother in the Bronx does better with strudel and cheesecake but lemon tea is good.' Muscadet is £3·20. No music.

Closed Sun; Mon D; public hols (exc Apr 13 L); Jewish hols Meals 12–12.45, 5.30–8.45 (Sat 6–8.45)

Alc £4·30 (meal £7·10)

VAT inc
Cover 30p D & weekends

Children's helpings
Seats 78
 ♿ rest
No dogs

GRANARY   Map 15

39 Albemarle Street, W.1
01-493 2978

'A good place for a light quick meal in an expensive district' about sums up Jon Shah's busy ground floor and basement, which Margaret McDonald runs from the kitchen range. They do their own cooking, but if you want to try their favourite dishes (chicken Coronation, lamb with lemon and mint, or beef burgundy, all £1·30), it is best to go early in a session before they have been kept warm too long. Pork and plums, meringue sweets, strawberry japonaise and lemon soufflé (55p) are also worth looking out for. Wine or lager, both 45p the glass.

Closed Sun; Sat D; Dec 24 & 31; public hols Open 10–6.50 (10–2.30 Sat)

Alc (min £1 L) meal £3·25

VAT & service inc
Seats 98

♿ rest (1 step)
Air-conditioning
No dogs
No cheques L

GRAND INDIAN   Map 15

6 New Row, W.C.2
01-240 0785

Mr Khalique's theatre-land restaurant has a firm following in spite of long waits in dim corners and the odd mistake on the bill. Nan, parathas, the rice and other extras are usually impeccable, and 'my favourite dishes are always good and always slightly different – a good sign.' Try, perhaps, samosa or chicken tikka, then the mild, creamy mutton korma, yoghourty chicken bhoona or palate-searing Bangalore phal followed by a soothing gulab jamun. French ordinaire is £2·85. Lager. Indian records.

Closed Dec 25 Meals 12–3, 5.30–11.30

Alc meal £3·65

VAT inc
Service 10%
Seats 44

No dogs
Access, Am Ex, Barclay, Diners, Euro

THE GRANGE   Map 15

39 King Street, W.C.2
01-240 2939

Closed Sun; Sat L;
Dec 24; public hols
Must book
Meals 12.30–2.30,
7.30–11.30

Tdh from £7·10 (meal
£7·80)

VAT inc
Seats 65 (parties 25)
Air-conditioning
Am Ex card

'A place to show foreign visitors that English cuisine is not always to be passed by,' writes a culinary patriot, and although prices creep inexorably upwards most people agree that the Grange's set menus still offer good value. All include a half-bottle of wine and unlimited coffee, although the cheapest version deprives you of a pudding. Good vegetables can still be bought in Covent Garden even though the wholesale market has gone, and crudités here are always impeccably selected and the cooked vegetables imaginative. The French beans are favourites. Fishy dishes are good too, including an 'irresistible' shrimp, apple and celery cocktail, gravlax with dill and mustard sauce, and the ever-popular poached salmon trout hollandaise or mayonnaise. Meat eaters may prefer the 'delicate pinkish cutlets' of lamb Shrewsbury, the beef Wellington, or the julienne of veal or pork, which are subtly sauced variations on a beef Stroganoff. For pudding, Geoffrey Sharp's chef, Jurgens Boldt, recommends the Atholl brose (a house favourite for ten years now), and few can resist the miniature crème brûlée. The wines listed on the menu are mostly well chosen, especially Saumur and Côtes de Bourg, although you can pay a surcharge for domaine-bottled Chablis or St Julien if you prefer. Service is efficient, if occasionally impersonal, and the David Hicks decor wears well. Popularity, though, breeds the usual complaints of crowded tables and involuntary, if often beguiling, eavesdrops. No music.

App: Geoffrey Finsberg, Ivor Hall, Joan Chenhalls, J. L. Finney, Ellis Blackmore, S.R., and many others

LA GRENOUILLE   Map 13

515 Battersea Park Road,
S.W.11
01-228 2869 *and* 5385

Closed L; Sun; Dec 24,
25 & 26; Jan 1
Must book
D only, 7.30–12

Alc £5·20 (meal £8·75)

Service 12½%
Cover 35p
Seats 45 (parties 18)
  rest
Air-conditioning

The Grenouille is now a two-floor restaurant, and its success is such that 'three unfortunates waited from 8.30 to 11 for a table and were seen drinking enviously in the wine bar opposite.' 'You have to like green to eat here: the table-linen is pale peppermint and the cushions froggy.' M Gautier, who also owns a wine-importing company, and his manager Yves Muzart, see to the front of the house. Jack Combe produces French food in the kitchens, and reports are almost unanimous about its authentically robust flavours – notably the fish soup with croûtons, and the crisp sardines from the charcoal grill. Cassoulet au confit d'oie (£3), truite aux amandes, and tripes lauragaises (£3) have been praised, and to end with, the open French lemon or pear tarts from their own bakery are a good choice.

Access, Am Ex, Barclay,
Diners, Euro

M Gautier's wine list has numerous reds and whites
from the South of France at £3–£4·70, some
excellent Beaujolais from named villages, four good
Loires, a sprinkling of higher priced burgundies and
clarets and, unusually, a whole page of armagnacs
and cognacs, ending up with calvados. House wine
is £2·50. No music.

*App: C. S., Bel & Kevin Horlock, J. P. Kiszely,
E.L.F., D.P., and others*

GUINEA GRILL   Map 15

30 Bruton Place, W.1
01-629 5613

Closed Sun; Sat L; public
hols; Dec 24 & 31
Must book
Meals 12.30–2.30, 7–11

Alc £12·85 (meal £19)

Cover 50p
Seats 120
Air-conditioning
No dogs
Access, Am Ex, Barclay,
Diners, Euro

*'Aujourd'hui c'est le produit qui compte,' pronounces
Bocuse, which is perhaps why London's rich wisely
forgo cooking much of the time, and plank down their
twenty guineas a time for smoked salmon, asparagus,
steaks and lamb cutlets that they can depend upon.
Antonio Albuquerque in the kitchen and the suavest
team of Spanish pirates you ever saw in a dining-room,
supervise this transfer of gold from New World
vice-presidents to the Guinea's Scottish-sounding
owner. There is no menu, and no prices, until the
itemised bill at the end, so you make your choice from
the display of food in the raw. (Artichokes, kidneys
and sausages are other possibilities, and the sausages,
with 'splendid hot steak pies', also appear in the much
cheaper saloon bar at lunch-time and in the evenings.)
They keep the right wines, if at the wrong prices, but
swallow your pride and encourage them by drinking
the Young's bitter on hand-pump – or Marqués de
Riscal '71, perhaps, at a very decent £4. No music.
More reports, please.*

HARD ROCK CAFE   Map 15

150 Old Park Lane, W.1
01-629 0382

'A down-town, Southern-cum-Mid-Western, funky,
American roadside diner' is manager Prab
Nallamilli's description of this, well, hamburger
joint. Small wonder someone else describes the
atmosphere as 'inimitable' . . . Open all week, with
an always-present but fast-moving queue, and the
loudest music in town (challenges unwelcome). The
burgers ('4 oz, with crisp fries, salad and sesame bun
£1·55') are good, and they do filet mignon (£3·80),
chili, and various pies and sundaes. Fast, friendly
service. House wine, cocktails, and American beers.

Closed Dec 24–26	Alc £2·80 (meal £4·80)	Seats 130
Open noon–12.30 a.m.		♿ rest
(1 a.m. Fri & Sat)	VAT inc	No dogs

Do not risk using an out-of-date Guide. A new edition
will be published early in 1980.

HARRY MORGAN Map 12

31 St Johns Wood
High St, N.W.8
01-722 1869

'London-Jewish middle-of-the-road cooking' here,
with sound kreplach and kneidlach soup, 'smoothly
golden' cold fried gefilte fish with fine-textured flesh,
and an apfelstrudel or lockshen pudding like
Momma's. But tsimmes and chopped liver were
below par when tried, and note the 10p charged for
matzos and chraine. Belloni wines. Good lemon tea.
No music.

Closed Mon; Fri D;
public hols (exc Apr 15)
Meals 12–2.45, 6–9.45

Alc (min weekends £1·50)
£4·25 (meal £6·75)

Service 10%

Seats 40
Access, Am Ex, Barclay,
Diners, Euro

HATHAWAYS Map 13

13 Battersea Rise, S.W.11
01-228 3384

Closed L; Sun; public
hols (exc Apr 13)
Must book
D only, 7–10.15

Alc £4·70 (meal £7·45)

VAT inc
Cover 35p
Children's helpings
Seats 34
Air-conditioning
No dogs
Access, Am Ex, Diners

Kathie and Carl Scheiding have made firm friends
at their homely rose-pink Battersea restaurant (ring
the front door bell to gain entrance). The room is
small but air-conditioned; only one member has
complained of feeling cramped – but she had to put
up with loud wine-talk from the next table. Menus
change monthly, and are imaginative, with rich,
high-calorie, spicy, alcoholic and fruity Canadian,
old English and central European dishes happily
mingling. The chowders (meat and fish) and the
individually baked meat pies and fresh vegetables
seem to be favourites with members: 'country
cabbage (with chopped bacon) delicious', and
'ratatouille and new potatoes rolled in butter and
parsley very good'. There is special praise for boned
chicken with a crab stuffing and prawn sauce,
served on rice, and lamb's kidneys with juniper
berries and gin ('all three ingredients in abundance,
especially the gin'). All main dish prices (£3–£3·75)
include salad, potatoes and two vegetables. Less is
heard about sweets, but sometimes they are called
'stodgy'; try pears in burnt cream, perhaps, or the
hot pie, 'always home-made, always good, always
full of calories'. There are a few 'specially selected
clarets', such as a '71 Ch. Palmer at £9·25, but
prices of the thirty or so others seem on the high
side, and to print against each 'vintage as available'
tells the customer nothing at all. House wines
(Spanish) are £2·65 a bottle and 40p a glass. No
music.

*App: David Potter, Nancy Asvat, Neil Fairlamb,
Pam Holmes, Hilda Woolf, V. G. Saunders, and others*

For the explanation of 🔹 denoting accessibility for the disabled,
see 'How to use the Guide', p. 4.

HOLY COW   Map 13

38 Kensington High
Street, W.8
01-937 2005

In the former premises of Chez Ciccio and Medusa
this tandoori restaurant offers snacks or cheapish
lunches, and more leisurely dinners. 'A hundred per
cent good experience,' wrote one couple after
working their way through the Holy Cow special
(£2·95), including sag paneer with home-made curd
cheese, tarka dhal, hot, fresh nan and pistachio
kulfi, all helped down with cool lassi. Licensed.
Service is unrushed and helpful. Indian records.

Must book D & weekends	Service 10%	♿ rest
Meals 12–2.45, 6–12	Cover 25p	Air-conditioning
	Children's helpings	No dogs
Tdh from £2·75	(under 10)	Access, Am Ex, Barclay,
Alc meal £4·90	Seats 85 (parties 80)	Diners, Euro

HOSTARIA ROMANA   Map 15

70 Dean Street, W.1
01-734 2869

Michelangelo Mansi's bustling trattoria is fun to be
in. ('The waiter twice dropped a huge peppermill on
us.') Standards in cooking seldom waver either up or
down, and this is one place where a prawn cocktail
is worth trying. Tuna-fish salad, tagliatelle, lamb
with rosemary, veal stew in cream and wine,
sweetbreads and the sauté potatoes are good too,
though if you want other vegetables to be well
cooked, order them separately. Puddings are lavish.
Settesoli red wine is £2·20. Italian records.

Closed Apr 15; May 7;	VAT inc	Seats 160 (parties 35)
Aug 27; Dec 25	Service 10%	♿ rest (1 step)
Must book L & weekends	Cover 30p	Air-conditioning
Meals 12–2.30, 6–11.30	Children's helpings	No dogs
	(under 8)	Access, Am Ex, Barclay,
Alc £4·25 (meal £6·55)		Diners, Euro

HUNG FOO   Map 13

6 West Hill, S.W.18
01-870 0177

'An oasis in Wandsworth', this Pekinese restaurant
on the South Circular is about to be extended, so
let us know of changes. Praise for 'well-prepared
dishes, most with distinctive flavours'. Some are
bland (beef in oyster sauce, chicken and pineapple),
but most are as they should be: grilled dumplings
(85p), duck with bamboo shoots and Chinese
mushrooms (£1·40). Vegetables are crisp and fried
rice 'a cut above most'. The waiters are friendly and
articulate. Drink tea or, perhaps, Wan Fu at £3;
corkage £1 if you take your own. Recorded music.

Closed Sun L; Dec 25 &	Tdh L from 75p,	Service 10%
26	D from £3	Seats 45
Must book D & weekends	Alc meal £4·15	♿ rest; w.c. (m)
Meals 12–2.30, 5.30–12		No dogs

TRATTORIA IMPERIA   Map 15

19 Charing Cross Road,
W.C.2
01-930 8364

Still a useful place on the short list of sound ones near Trafalgar Square. But some of the élan left with Gino in 1978, and inspectors since have had satisfactory rather than inspired tagliatelle, mixed antipasto (£1·55), fegato veneziana, petto di pollo alla crema, and other dishes. Vegetables have not been so well cooked either lately, and zabaglione turned out to be sweet rather than Marsala-rich. Espresso coffee. 'The usual animation at close quarters.' The ordinaire is Settesoli, £2·65 for 75 cl. No dogs.

Closed Sun; public hols
Must book
Meals 12–2.45, 6–11.30

Alc £5·05 (meal £8·35)

Cover 35p
Seats 46

   rest
Air-conditioning
Access, Am Ex, Barclay,
Diners

JASON'S   Map 16

50 Battersea Park Road,
S.W.11
01-622 6998

'Only the food and the music are Greek-Cypriot' – the rest is trendy but subdued Fulham-style. 'And cheaper than Greece,' adds someone else. The mezedes (£3 a head, minimum two people) remains an excellent introduction to the genre: creamy taramosalata, moist hummus, minty tsatsiki (not enough garlic), fresh garides (under-salted, though). Moussaka, afelia, sheftalia, shashlik too, with good pitta but nasty English coffee (Turkish is 5p more). Most people keep to the Demestica house wine, red or white (£2·55 the bottle, 50p the glass), and there is a Greek rosé – Roditis. Lager. Taped bouzouki.

Closed L; Sun; most
public hols
Must book
D only, 6.30–midnight

Alc £3·35 (meal £5·95)

Cover 12p

Seats 55 (parties 35)
   rest
No dogs

JUSTIN DE BLANK   Map 15

54 Duke Street, W.1
01-629 3174

'I looked for a handy, inexpensive place off Oxford Street. Was surprised to find this self-service cafe with philosophical remarks on the wall.' Modest helpings, but the food is 'good to look at, wholesome to eat', especially the homely soups, fine breads and pastries, spare ribs with fluffy, well-seasoned rice, blanquette de veau, 'irresistible' fruit brûlée, and loganberry mousse. The house wine is drinkable, but we have seen no list. Smoking is 'discouraged but not forbidden', and the air-conditioning, seems to cool the food. No music. Take-away also.

Closed Sun; Sat D;
public hols
Open 9–3.30, 4.30–9.30
No bookings

Alc meal £4·30

VAT inc

Seats 60
Air-conditioning
No dogs

KERZENSTUBERL   Map 15

9 St Christopher's Place,
W.1
01-486 3196 *and* 8103

Ilse and Herbert Rauscher put so much into their Austrian *Volkslieder* and customer-jollying that some sad mistakes are let out of the kitchen: leaden knödel and tough apfelstrudel pastry at a test and other meals. Sometimes, too, guests' conviviality runs away with itself. But when tried, freshly fried gebackenes champignons, herring salad with good sour cream sauce, red cabbage, and jam pancakes, said rather more for Klaus Stange's cooking. As for main courses, try kessel goulash (£2·25) or Bauernschmaus (£3·95), with Austrian wines from £3·95 a litre for Blauer Burgunder red or Grüner Veltliner white, and wish the pair stiff Austrian competition in the West End one day.

Closed Sun; Sat L;
mid-Aug to mid-Sept;
Dec 24; public hols
Must book
Meals 12–2.15, 6.15–11

Alc £5·50 (meal £9·60)

Service L 10%, D 12½%
Cover L 45p, D 55p
Children's helpings
Seats 48

  rest (2 steps)
Air-conditioning
No dogs
Access, Am Ex, Barclay,
Diners

KEW RENDEZVOUS   Map 13

110 Kew Road, Richmond
01-940 1334 *and* 948 4343

Closed Dec 25 & 26
Must book D & weekends
Open noon–11.15 p.m.

Tdh from £4
Alc meal £4·95

Service 15%
Seats 120 (parties 50)
Air-conditioning
No dogs
Access, Am Ex, Barclay,
Diners

Remember you should be in Richmond not Kew to find this branch of Mr Young's spreading water-chestnut tree, and note the service charge (for which, admittedly, the waiters work hard). Mr Wong's cooking is sometimes 'inappropriately bland' for the Pekinese style of food in this award-winning building. But his quick-fried slices of lamb with leeks and garlic, and equally garlicky mixed diced fish are called 'a magnificent surprise', and on the whole the other dishes hold their standard well: crab-meat and corn soup (60p), seaweed and dried scallops, barbecued spare ribs (£1·30), sesame prawn toasts (£1·30), prawns or deep fried shredded beef with chilli, sliced sole in wine sauce, chicken and cashew nuts in yellow bean sauce (£1·60), and the rest. Unless you eat this style often enough to be bored, or are on your own, the set meals may well suffice. Colcombet red wine is £3·20, Hirondelle white £2·80. No music.

*App: V. Westerman, H.P.D., A. J. Monkcom,
J. D. B. Wood, J. S. & F. Waters, and others*

'Must book' is the restaurant's information, not ours. The context of the entry usually indicates how much or how little it matters, but a preliminary telephone call averts frustrated journeys. Always telephone if a booking has to be cancelled: a small place may suffer severely if this is not done, and customers are also the losers in the end.

KOLOSSI GRILL   Map 12

56–58 Rosebery Avenue,
E.C.1
01-278 5758

A leisurely, amiable, family-run Greek place, handy for Sadler's Wells. Rather cramped, 'and you are liable to be smoked out by the newspaper and post office salariat.' Dishes liked include hummus, taramosalata (60p), avgolemono (35p), 'well-marinated' meat in various guises: kleftiko ('tender lamb with fatty but delicious roast potatoes, and a nice cabbage salad', £1·45); lunza pilaf ('rather overcooked pork', with coriander and wine, £1·55); spare ribs, or spring chicken. Sweets flag often, and aperitifs are stiff (financially). Good Greek coffee, and Greek wines from £2·75. No music. No jeans.

Closed Sun; public hols
Meals 12–3, 5–11

Alc £2·80 (meal £4·85)

VAT inc

Seats 50
 ⅍ rest
No dogs

KOWLOON   Map 15

21 Gerrard Street, W.1
01-437 1694

Bears with buns are to be found in this little cafe. That is, the manners of the waiters, at least to Europeans, leave something to be desired, but the freshly made savoury char siu buns or equally light vanilla cream and other sweet buns are infinitely desirable (25p). So are the 'crisp and wobbly egg custard tarts', and, if you sit down rather than take away, the wun-tun soup may be made before your eyes by a cheerful chef with a cleaver. Expect for company Chinese drinking tea-bag tea with milk and sugar.

Must book
Open noon–midnight

Tdh L £2·20

Alc meal from £1·60

VAT inc

Service 10%
Seats 150
Access card

LACY'S   Map 15

26–28 Whitfield Street,
W.1
01-636 2411 and 2323

Closed Sun; Sat L;
public hols (exc Jan 1);
Dec 24; Dec 31 L
Must book
Meals 12.30–2.30, 7.30–11

Tdh L from £6 (meal
£9·05)
Alc £8·35 (meal £13·25)

Margaret Costa and her chef-husband Bill Lacy – not to mention the *Guide* itself – have never forgotten the year when there were over sixty reports on their north Soho basement and the entry had to be divided into 'Lacy's is lovely . . . is lousy' sections. Life has been quieter lately, but this year again opinions tend to polarise. 'In an uncertain age, Lacy's remains a sure thing. On two visits, cold cucumber and avocado soups would have been a credit to any restaurant, cornet of smoked salmon with trout mousse was excellent; best end of lamb with apricot sauce and medallions of veal with mushrooms were thoroughly professional; the vegetables on the much-criticised platter were

Cover 60p alc
Seats 65
No dogs
Access, Am Ex, Barclay,
Diners, Euro

uneven, but at least the green ones were good; and peppermint chocolate mousse was almost as good as I remembered it. Service was very attentive, as always, though they should not sell cigars in this ill-ventilated room.' However, another – equally representative – report speaks of 'a nasty meal. The cockles in cockles and soft roes were so steeped in brine that the head waiter agreed they were inedible, then charged full price for the dish because I had enjoyed the roe. Rack of lamb and cutlets were barely seasoned and coated in almost identical oversweet sauces. We did not order coffee, neither was any served, yet we were charged £1·60 for it.' Even the same dishes get equally contradictory verdicts, as though continuity in the kitchen were insecure: one man's 'delicious' fish mousse is another's 'whitish paste with a Fanny Cradock element in the decoration'. The middle ground is scarcely tenanted, except by an inspector whose lunch could fairly be called 'good in most parts'. In other words, the more things change the more they remain the same. Mrs Lacy (a vital collaborator on the *Guide* in its early days) encourages this verdict by referring on the back of her 1978 menu to the distinction conferred on her restaurant in 1972, as though forgetting what she used to think about this kind of advertising. Turbot poché sauce mousseline and hot fruit brûlée are her own nominations. Drink with caution, because the house's pay-as-you-go system for most wines leans heavily on the honesty and tact of the waiters. Coffee and bread are both good. The owners' friendliness to customers, known or unknown, is often generous, but obviously, time can only be spared for a minority, and some of it might be better spent on getting the whole production together. No music.

App: Stephen Brook, A.A.D., A.L., C.W.B., and others

LANGAN'S BRASSERIE   Map 15

Stratton Street, W.1
01-493 6437

Closed Sun; Sat L;
Dec 23–26; Dec 31 L;
Jan 1 & 2; public hols
Must book
Meals 12.30–2.30, 7–11.30
(8–12.30 Sat)

Alc £6·85 (meal £10·05)

VAT inc
Service 12½%

The Peter Langan Principle, according to which restaurants tend to be promoted one grade above their level of competence, is borne out by the relative success of this relatively unambitious – but cavernous, animated, and picture-hung – restaurant opposite the Ritz. The attempt to keep Odin's (dropped again this year) steady on parade at the next level up must be such a strain: here everyone (but especially the proprietor) can relax, gossip, drink, eye each other, and think of that earnest fellow Richard Shepherd in the kitchen, actually working. In visiting and reporting, take note of the time of day: in the early evening, for instance, the waiters may spurn you as a person of no

Cover 50p
Seats 170
🔲 rest (1 step)
Air-conditioning
Am Ex, Diners

importance, but you may get better food, more quickly served. The best first courses, they think – and so on the whole do we – are the coeur d'artichaut farci à la Nissarda ('fresh, with a lovely duxelles stuffing and a perfect hollandaise'), spinach soufflé with anchovy sauce (£1·50), croustade of quails' eggs, and duck pâté with armagnac. Then Bratwurst or choucroute of course, to make it feel like Alsace, and grills of turbot or bass or salmon, or entrecôte béarnaise, or 'beautifully underdone calf's liver'. Complex main dishes and puddings (sauté potatoes too) are inadvisable, even if correctly described on the menu, and dressings tend to be vinegary. They invite you to admire their ice-creams and 'sculpted' cheese trolley. Wines, from £2·60 for red burgundy or white Bordeaux, keep Mr Langan's interest; Beaujolais, Rhône and Spanish Panadés (Torres) should perhaps catch your eye. Unpredictable, often good, live music starts at about 10 p.m.

App: M. Y. Palmer, S. C. Whittle, H.W., J.M., Pembroke Duttson, C. Stevenson, C.P.D., and others

---

LEBANESE RESTAURANT   Map 12

---

60 Edgware Road, W.2
01-723 9130 *and* 262 9585

Must book (summer)
Meals 12.30–midnight

Alc £5·10 (meal £8·70)

Cover 50p
Seats 60
🔲 rest
Air-conditioning
No dogs
Access, Am Ex, Barclay,
Diners, Euro

On the whole, members' experience of London Lebanese restaurants has been unhappy, but both advice and trial suggest that this suavely decorated place, frequented mostly by Arabs, is at any rate worth a year's experiment with its fatayer (spinach pastries, 85p), cold dressed brains, kibbeh nayeh (raw lamb steak tartare-style, £1·25 as a first course), and – from a substantial charcoal-grill repertoire – the house suggestions of lahm meshwi kebab (£2·65) and shawarma (£2·95). Ouzi (stuffed whole lamb) is also a speciality, and as in Greek places one may order meze for a party, to be served with the ouzo-like arak (70p a glass). Samke harrah is baked fish with nuts, coriander and tangerine juice, and there may be a dish of the day 'if feel like cooking', says Mr Abouzaki the chef, ominously enough. The cover charge brings various crudités at the start. Among the sweets katayef was particularly good when tested – 'light, crisp shreds, with a slightly cheesy vanilla cream inside.' Italian Cabernet wine is £2·95. Lebanese Ch. Musar red in various vintages ranges from £7·95 to £19·95 (the '59). National music. More reports, please.

LEITH'S   Map 12

---

92 Kensington Park
Road, W.11
01-229 4481

Prue Leith's restaurant began as a considerable landmark in north Kensington, for both food and Nathan Silver's interior design, and celebrates its tenth *Guide* appearance in equally good fettle,

Closed L; Dec 24, 25 & 26
Must book
D only, 7.30–12

Tdh £9·50 (meal £13·80)

Service 15%
Seats 95 (parties 30)
 ♻ rest (2 steps)
Air-conditioning
No dogs
Access, Am Ex, Barclay,
Diners, Euro

which is no mean achievement in '70s London. Last year, business was good, as Miss Leith did not mind admitting, and the service got above itself from time to time – 'no wonder, since my guest saw a departing diner tip the cloakroom attendant £5.' But Max Markarian has lasted much longer in the kitchen than most of his predecessors, and it shows. There are some who find the formula – lush hors d'oeuvre trolley/main course/lush sweets trolley – rather limiting, bearing the price in mind, but professionalism and consistency is the other side of that coin, and a test meal put the place well to the front of the league it has chosen. Of the cold first courses, avocado mousse was 'surprisingly interesting', trout mousse in a wrapping of smoked salmon excellently flavoured, and mackerel in tomato 'very fresh and good'. Two slightly underdone quails were set off by a skilful calvados cream sauce, scallop quenelles by an equally delicious 'pinky-orange' lobster one, and the accompanying Kenya beans and lemony courgettes were well cooked too. Other perennially popular main courses include Leith's duckling (though it does not do much for the wine), the juniper hare to which Jean Reynaud (a chef turned restaurant manager) attaches his name, ribs of beef béarnaise, and Miss Leith's own likings: Stilton soup 'more interesting than vichyssoise', deep-fried chicken with ginger and Gruyère stuffing, or lemon sole stuffed with salmon and a spinach mousse. Puddings on the trolley, like the first courses, are made by Leith's lithe young ladies (it is a pity that mobility on wheels – for the puddings, not the ladies – precludes the pleasure of seeing everything spread out). Chocolate mousse, ginger syllabub, blackcurrant sorbet, and the rest are well made, but something hot with a different texture – beignets de fromage are often offered – may be welcome at this stage. 'Tea and coffee were served with glazed fruits.' The house wines are fairly priced at under £3·50 for Bourgogne Aligoté '76 (Duboeuf) and Côtes du Rhône '73, nor were Ch. Nenin '67 (£8) and other more important clarets and ports unduly dear in 1978. Miss Leith has a few caprices: 'We serve nothing that I don't like to eat myself . . . I can never understand how restaurateurs can dare take someone's money and tell him not to smoke.' But the postscript on the bills that extracts 15% from the customer without asking for it is a miracle of ingenuity. No music.

App: Pat & Jeremy Temple, M.H.N., Z. & J.R., D. M. Gaythwaite, J.M., H.C.S., and others

---

If you think you are suffering from food-poisoning after eating in a restaurant, report this immediately to the local Public Health Authority (and write to us).

LEMON TREE   Map 13

8 High Street, S.W.19
01-947 6477

Closed Mon; Dec 25 & 26
Must book D
Meals 12–2.30, 7–11

Alc £4·25 (meal £6·80)

VAT inc
Cover 30p
Seats 55 (parties 20)
♿ rest
No dogs
Am Ex, Diners

Some of the answers to last year's requests for more reports on Michele d'Aversa's restaurant were lemons, and there are a few signs that Gian Battista's cooking – not to mention the lay-out of the place itself – had been projected into a league for which they were not prepared: 'Nobody would call me a fussy man, but I do expect my food seasoned'; and 'we were expected to drink our aperitifs standing up.' Yet there were obvious points in favour. For various people these have included the reasonable prices, a baveuse omelette au fromage, laitances à l'indienne, champignons au four, 'tender and meaty pigeon', poularde St Herbon, paupiettes de boeuf, gigot catalane, noisettes d'agneau village, 'luscious' chocolate and orange mousse, and other things. So it is a pity that vegetables and coffee are often poor, and many dishes not authentic enough for people who know better. It might be wise to keep good cheese and fruit on hand. Tables are also too close for those who find Wimbledonians 'not reticent', and for amiable but unskilled waitresses. Sangiovese or Trebbiano ordinaires are £2·65 a bottle. No music. More reports, please, in the hope that a promising place can outlive its growing pains.

LEONARDO   Map 14

397 Kings Road, S.W.10
01-352 4146 and 4287

A new, bustling, Italian restaurant in a modern block between Chelsea Community Centre and Worlds End reminds one member of 'all the cheek and panache of Meridiana in the early days'. But the food has been patchy to date, with good crespolini and fresh but bland pasta, very good calf's liver, interesting skewered scampi with Mozzarella, lemon and mint (which works – just), and too-sweet Marsala, both for saltimbocca sauce and zabaglione. Vegetables poor; coffee adequate. Few sweets. The house wine is Valpolicella or Soave, £2·45 for 72 cl, 55p the glass. The poor ventilation has spoiled some people's evenings. No music. Small dogs allowed. More reports, please.

Closed Sun; Apr 13;
public hol Mons (exc
Aug 27 D); Dec 25 & 26;
Jan 1
Must book

Meals 12.30–2.45,
7.15–11.45

Alc £4·70 (meal £7·35)

VAT inc
Cover 35p
Seats 70
Access, Am Ex, Barclay,
Diners, Euro

Numbers are given for private parties only if they can be accommodated in a room separate from the main dining-room; when there are several such rooms, the capacity of the largest is given. Some restaurants will take party bookings at times when they are normally closed.

LICHFIELD'S Map 13

Lichfield Terrace,
Sheen Road, Richmond
01-940 5236

Closed L; Mon; Dec 25 &
26
Must book
D only, 7–11

Alc £7·25 (meal £10·20)

VAT inc
Cover 40p
Children's helpings
Seats 40
♿ rest (1 step)
No dogs
Access, Am Ex, Barclay

Stephen Bull won two years in the *Guide* as
proprietor of the Meadowsweet at Llanrwst (*q.v.*),
and on present form Wales's loss seems England's
gain (though his place is not all that far from
Twickenham). This is a very clean, quiet restaurant
in a row of shops near Lichfield Gardens, with the
owner and Roger Davis, late of the Tate, (*q.v.*),
doing the cooking. The menu is frequently
changed: 'There is an emphasis on the food *I* like,'
says Mr Bull frankly, 'which could loosely be
described as classic European.' Certainly local
residents agree with him about such first courses as
spaghetti al pesto, scallop quenelles with mousseline
sauce (£1·80), and roulades au fromage ('two very
thin pancakes stuffed with a light cheese soufflé
mixture covered with cheese sauce and served hot
from the grill,' £1·20). The crispy roast duck with
fresh lime compote (£4·50) and medallions of lamb
with mint-flavoured hollandaise (£3·75) are both
praised as main dishes; try also the chefs'
recommendation of turbot soufflé with mousseline
sabayon sauce (£3·75). Vegetables do not lose their
freshness in the cooking. Sweets such as chef-made
passion-fruit sorbet or St Emilion au chocolat are
just as attractive. Coffee is good, and service
unobtrusive. Wines, alas, are nearly all over £4, but
are well-chosen and tended. The house Riojas
(white and red), at £3 a 26 fl oz carafe or 60p a
glass, are quite acceptable. It was all half the price
in Llanrwst, some may say, but it was probably
not as good. No music.

*App: A.M., C. R. Handley, Mrs M. Popham, P.H.,
W.J.A.D., G. K. Wray*

LIGHT OF INDIA Map 13

284/286 King Street, W.6
01-741 1903 *and* 748 2579

Mr Ganguly's place hit a bad patch during and after
last year's extension: indeed, 'I found a piece of the
alterations in the curry.' Service still varies 'all the
way from the obsequious to the imperious'. However,
lately the samosas, nargis kebab and reshmee kebab
have recovered some of the old crisp egginess, and
other tandoori dishes – chicken tikka or tandoori,
seekh kebab – are also praised, along with tarka
dhal, nan and poppadums. Try also prawn patia
(£1·45), chicken dhansak (£2·50), and mughlai dishes
at £18 for four and a day's notice. Very dear wines;
drink Carlsberg or Dortmunder lager.

Closed Dec 25 & 26
Must book wekends
Meals 12–3, 6–12

Alc meal £4

Service 10%
Seats 110 (parties 50)

♿ rest; w.c.
No dogs
Access, Am Ex, Barclay,
Diners, Euro

LITTLE AKROPOLIS   Map 15

10 Charlotte Street, W.1
01-636 8198

Closed Sun; Sat L;
public hols
Must book
Meals 12–2.30, 6–10.30

Alc (min £3·60) £6·35
(meal £9·95)

VAT inc
Cover 35p
Seats 32 (parties 20)
 🔔 rest (1 step)
Air-conditioning
No dogs
Access, Am Ex, Barclay,
Diners, Euro

Niki Ktori's 30-year-old restaurant, behind its
miniature shrubbery, is Cypriot without being
ashamed of it (unless you regard the 'international'
bits of the menu as a smoke-screen). It is also
genially and gently served, with starched linen on
the tables. This period charm makes the fishy,
unextended taste of the taramosalata and the
nuttiness of the aubergine puree (both 80p) a
pleasant surprise. Kalamaria are another good first
course, and though lamb chops may come either
pink or red, they are 'large, plump, and
garlic-scented from the charcoal grill'. The
pot-roast kleftiko (£3·15), aromatic with juices and
mushrooms under the lid of the oven-glass dish, is
equally good, or you may try moussaka, kebabs or
pilaffs at the same price. Salad is a much better buy
than vegetables. Baklava and halva are good of
their kind, and the rose-petal jam pancakes (80p)
are 'delicate, crisp, fragrant, and red hot'. Loukoum
is 'all rose water and nuts', and good Greek coffee
is poured from its long-handled copper pot.
Demestica, Bacchus, Castel Danielis and Corinth
wines are all £4. Recorded Greek music.

App: P. Findlater, Dolores Williamson, and others

LOCKETS   Map 16

Marsham Court,
Marsham Street, S.W.1
01-834 9552

Parliaments come and go, and so do the chefs that
cook for them at this Berkmann restaurant poised
near Westminster. The food is seldom subtle, but
when tested most of it was sound: good bread and
anchovy butter on the tables, Stilton soup (95p),
mousse of Arbroath smokies (£1·55) 'for which the
advertised malt whisky would have done little even
if it had been detectable', sweetbreads and
mushrooms in port, and 'good old-fashioned tripe
and onions' an each-way bet on the Lancashire
marginals. Good potatoes and broccoli; poor
cheesecake and coffee; excellent wines from £2·75
(Georges Duboeuf '75 burgundies; Ch. Pape-Clément
'66, c.b., £10). No music.

Closed Sat; Sun; Dec 24;
public hols
Must book L
Meals 12.15–2.45, 6.30–11

Tdh D £5·50 (meal £8·10)

Alc £7·05 (meal £10·35)

VAT inc
Cover 50p alc
Children's helpings
(under 6)

Seats 100 (parties 30)
 🔔 rest
Air-conditioning
No dogs L
Access, Am Ex, Barclay,
Diners

Unless otherwise stated, a restaurant is open all week
and all year and is licensed.

113 Walton Street,
S.W.3
01-584 7585

Closed Sat; Sun; Dec 24;
public hols
Must book
Meals 12.30–2, 7.30–11

Alc £7 (meal £10·80)

VAT inc
Cover 45p
Children's helpings
(under 5)
Seats 30
♿ rest; w.c.
No dogs
Am Ex card

'The great virtue of Guy and Lucette Mouilleron is that they are there, and care.' That, with their love of true French tastes, makes this one of the most sought-after *restaurants* (*trop*) *intimes* in London, and the pressure on their places, especially for dinner, makes it hard to understand why they are actually prepared to sell anti-social cigars to customers who would do everyone a favour if they took their money elsewhere. (At least pipes are banned.) M Mouilleron's style of cooking, like all styles that matter, is based on the market. The printed menu is conservative in the sense that well-achieved specialities – the pâté d'anguille à la mousse de cresson, the noisettes d'agneau pastourelle – survive from year to year, but the window and the menu are daily enlivened by more topical offerings: a buttery-crisp leek quiche hot from the oven, a garlic-sprightly dish of jambon de Bourgogne, a freshly poached trout, a tarte aux fraises des bois. Filet de truite Ninotte (£2·95), on a bed of tomato concassé with a flourless saffron sauce, courts both eye and palate; so does the mousseline de St Jacques à l'orange. Meat main courses are darker in tone (though not overcooked), and too often the sauces are unacceptably salty to an English palate. But the lamb and the poularde, especially, are of the highest quality, and 'breast of duck, lightly grilled, with béarnaise sauce and delicious pieces of kohlrabi' surpassed an eager visitor's expectations. Salsify, nutmeggy spinach, braised endive and other vegetables are often mentioned. 'Hot, plain-baked avocado with lamb must have been chosen with an eye to colour rather than taste.' Mousse brûlée remains perhaps the best of the sweets (£1·10), though it is at least amusing to meet a Frenchman's version of bread-and-butter pudding, as though it were Boulez re-interpreting Elgar. The coffee is excellent, and 60p does not seem too much in view of the home-made chocolates that arrive with it. They have also found or make good bread rolls. Wines (from £3·50 for Corbières) are adequate without being thrilling: there are some useful half-bottles now, and £5–£7 secures a choice of Savennières or Pinot d'Alsace or St Véran '76 (Duboeuf), or decent claret (Ch. Chambeaud '67) and less dependable '77 Beaujolais. As befits a Béarnais, the armagnacs from £1·50 a glass are 'revelatory': try Miguel Clément in a promisingly unspectacular bottle. Skilful service. No music.

App: Roy Mathias, M.W.K.G., William Moyes, C.P.D., B.K., Mrs T. Laidlaw, S.S., and others

MANDARIN Map 12

279c Finchley Road,
N.W.3
01-794 6119

Closed Sun L; 2 days Chr
Must book weekends
Meals 12–2.15, 6–11.15

Tdh D £3·75
Alc (min £1·20)
meal £4·10

Service 10%
Seats 48
No dogs

Unlike his near-neighbour, the Gourmet Rendezvous (q.v.), Mr Koh offers his speciality dishes with a Szechuan accent à la carte rather than in set banquets, and it is best to take these, says an inspector who found the cooking of 'deliciously crisp and fresh' prawn toasts (£1·80) and 'underseasoned but elegant' stir-fried squid with vegetables 'uncannily swift'. Hot-and-sour cabbage (£1·10) in a gingery dressing makes a nice cold hors d'oeuvre, and hot prawns with cashew nuts (£2·40) had fresh prawns and a good kick to the (over-thickened) sauce. Others also approve the crispy beef, 'very salty' jin jiang chicken with pancakes (£1·80), crispy duck, and toffee apples. The girls who serve in the simple little restaurant are pleasant enough – but try to make yourself clear to them. There are wines. No music.

App: Diana Chapman, Mark Morreau, C.J.D., R.C.R.

MANDEER Map 15

21 Hanway Place, W.1
01-323 0660 and 0651

This Gujerati vegetarian restaurant near Centre Point has suffered a sharp decline since last year's entry, with complaints of tired or lukewarm food and too much starch in the fillings. At a test meal the (well-filled) samosas were not as fresh as they should have been and shrikhand lacked cardamom. But vadi and onion balls were 'substantial – almost meaty, with a good, thick sauce', nan was nice and puffy, and the bhindi (okra) was mustardy and good. Carlsberg lager. Helpful service. Indian records. More reports, please, in case the chef changes again.

Closed Sun; public hols
Must book weekends
Meals 12–3, 6–10.30

Tdh from £2·75
Alc meal £2·80

VAT inc

Service 10%
Seats 75 (parties 100)
No dogs
Access, Am Ex, Diners, Euro

The Guide News Supplement will be sent out as usual, in June, to everyone who buys the book directly from Consumers' Association and to all bookshop purchasers who return the card interleaved with their copy. Let us know of any changes that affect entries in the book, or of any new places you think should be looked at.

'Must book' is the restaurant's information, not ours. The context of the entry usually indicates how much or how little it matters, but a preliminary telephone call averts frustrated journeys. Always telephone if a booking has to be cancelled: a small place may suffer severely if this is not done, and customers are also the losers in the end.

MANZI'S   Map 15

1–2 Leicester Street,
W.C.2
01-437 4864

Fish restaurant-with-rooms on the fringes of Soho,
family-run for generations. Some like the short
menu on the bustling ground floor, others the
Cabin Room aloft (now with taped music instead of
pianist, it seems). Sauces are not their forte (even if
the parsley sauce for stewed eel has supporters), so
keep to plain, grilled fish – fresh sardines, Dover
sole, trout, with crisp chips. But salads are variable,
and more serious lapses ('dry halibut') do occur. The
(bought-in) strawberry tart is 'as decadent as ever'.
Manzi's carafe (white burgundy) is still a good buy
at £2·50. Service is sometimes brisk, sometimes
sloppy. No under-fives.

Closed Sun L; L Apr 13;
Dec 25 & 26; L Jan 1
Must book
Meals 12–2.45, 5.30–11.40

Alc £5 (meal £7·05),
(Cabin Room) £7·40
(meal £10·25)

VAT inc
Service 10% (Cabin
Room D)
Cover 35p (Cabin Room)
Seats 70 & 45

No dogs
Access, Am Ex, Barclay,
Diners
14 rooms (12 with
shower)
B&B from £5
Fire cert

MATA HARI   Map 12

34–38 Eversholt Street,
N.W.1
01-388 0131

Closed Mon; Dec 25 & 26
Must book D
Meals 12–3, 6–11.30
(12 Fri & Sat)

Tdh about £5
Alc meal £5

Service 12½%
Seats 160 (parties 75)
  rest (2 steps)
No dogs
Access, Am Ex, Diners,
Euro

*This large, comfortable, well-spaced Indonesian
restaurant beside Euston station made a tentative
appearance in the last Guide, and members are still
wondering which way it is going to jump. A test meal
last time suggested that the owners and chef had it in
them to make it one of London's best 'ethnic' places, and
several subsequent visitors have been equally fortunate
with the fairly mild but pleasant Sumatran rendang
(curried beef with coconut), grule kambing (lamb),
sayur lemak (vegetable soup with chillies and
coconut), and other dishes. Even the rijsttaffel set
meals, which might be expected to betray creeping
anglicisation first, have included good satay with
peanutty sauces, delicate pancakes, and good coconut
or chilli-hot sauces with prawns, chicken and
vegetables. But knowledgeable visitors who went in
search of the tastes of blachan, tamarind, and lemon
grass mostly failed to find them in, for instance, ikan
masak tanco (95p), rojak, and goreng teri, and for
that matter the rendang too. Drink tea or lager. Please
continue to report.*

MAXIM   Map 13

155 Northfield Avenue,
W.13
01-567 1719

It has taken the Chows a year longer than they
hoped to expand their dimly lit restaurant, but
work should be complete by the time this is
published, they say. One customer hopes to see

Closed Sun L;
Dec 25 & 26
Must book D & weekends
Meals 12–2.30, 6–12

Tdh from £2·60
Alc meal £4

Service 10%
Seats 70 (parties 30)
⟨&⟩ rest (1 step)
Air-conditioning
No dogs
Access, Am Ex, Diners

efficient table-heaters included in the refit, but autumn visitors have continued to find the cooking and friendliness 'above the usual Pekinese run', with some items in the banquets 'as good as I've had in Hong Kong'. The dearest, eleven-course meal at £5·60 a head yielded 'meaty and tender spare ribs'; 'crisp and not too sweet' fried seaweed; handsomely arranged hors d'oeuvre with finely sliced beef, tongue, sausage and baby sweetcorn, all well-dressed; first-rate crispy duck; 'particularly succulent' whole shelled prawns; and lightly cooked toffee apples at the end. 'The standard chicken and beef dishes were less interesting.' The take-away service seems as popular as the table. Modest wine list, but probably best to drink tea. Recorded music.

App: John Carne, Madeleine Rae, H.C.W., A.A.R., and others

MAXWELL'S   Map 12

76 Heath Street, N.W.8
01-794 5450

Multi-level art-deco hamburger cafe, with a games room for pool and video battles. Very pleasant service, decent hamburgers (from 4 oz, £1·20), including imaginative salad and chips or baked potato). Try also corn on the cob, salt beef, charcoal-grilled chicken (£1·70), chili (£1·40), or a 12-oz T-bone steak (£2·90). Sweets are the cheesecake or sundae sort. House wines, £2·30 the bottle; various American beers – and Fosters. Loud music, 'but not as killing as at the Hard Rock' (*q.v.*).

Closed Dec 25 & 26
Meals 12.30–3, 6–12
(noon–12.30 a.m. Fri &
Sun; 1 a.m. Sat)

Alc (min £1 after 7 p.m.)   Seats 130 (parties 30)
£2·60 (meal £4·70)

MON PLAISIR   Map 15

21 Monmouth Street,
W.C.2
01-836 7243

Closed Sat; Sun; Dec 24 &
31; public hols
Must book
Meals 12–2, 6–11

Tdh L £3 (meal £5·55)
Alc £4·55 (meal £7·70)

Cover 30p alc
Seats 45 (parties 20)
⟨&⟩ rest (1 step)
No dogs

'Flying by the seat of its pants' (last year's expression) apparently puzzled Alain Lhermitte, so he had better be spared any more Battle of Britain language. But members remain divided about this minute, sought-after, atmospherically French bistro which some of them have been visiting for twenty years. 'Very good food, well cooked' . . . 'helpful and charming service' . . . 'beautiful soup and quail' . . . 'rare entrecôte with herby tomato sauce' represent one side; 'lukewarm soup' . . . 'limp, dull sardines, all two of them' . . . 'boeuf bourguignonne an undistinguished stew with hard potatoes' . . . 'lack-lustre, khaki-coloured spinach' represent another. Regular or familiar faces know that Ernst Stark can cook, and admire pink steaks, good allumettes, tarte normande, and the often excellent

French cheeses, but they wonder whether the memories of today's first-timers are as rewarding as their own once were. Adequate house wine; or try Ch. de Crock '71 c.b., at £5·50, perhaps. Service is variable.

App: Dr R. Neville, J.B.R., A.L., and others

MONTPELIANO   Map 14

13 Montpelier Street, S.W.7
01-589 0032

Closed Sun; Dec 24 L; Dec 31; most public hols
Must book
Meals 12.30–3, 7–12

Alc £5·60 (meal £9·20)

Cover 40p
Seats 75 (parties 26)

A change of management in the cool green bowers of the Montpeliano has raised prices but not depressed the kitchen. This is still one of the better places for faintly esoteric Italian dishes. But more than one member remarks the addition of bottled mussels to otherwise good seafood salad, so that inferior vinegar drowns the flavour of the clams, squid or prawns. It is an odd lapse, since the menu usually includes fresh cozze marinara, in a tasty lemon and parsley sauce. If carbohydrate holds no terrors, the pasta, particularly the fettuccine al pesto (£1·20), is probably better than the risotto, although both may arrive at the table rather less than hot. Main dishes are interesting and where else, an inspector wonders, could you find sweetbreads, brains, quail, liver, kidneys, wild duck and grouse all on one menu? At a test meal the quail were pot-roast with a mushroom and wine sauce marred only by too much rosemary – a national foible that both Franco and his predecessor must have imbibed with their mothers' milk. The quail come with 'fat and fluffy' Italian rice and the vegetables (included) are usually well done. Veal Montpeliano (£3·50) is combined with Mozzarella, a sharp tomato sauce and more garlic and rosemary. Zabaglione (90p) is a house recommendation, but some think the crêpe Montpeliano not as delicious as it was: perhaps a less wobbly hand now controls the liqueur bottle. The Italian house wines are reasonable at £2·80. Coffee comes in individual filters, so you pay more for more. Service is usually good and 'totally un-matey, thank goodness', although one regular is fascinated by the bandit-style three-day stubble some of the waiters affect. The tables could with advantage be prised further apart. No music.

App: Michael Copp, D. N. Whyte, A.P., T. W. E. Fortescue Hitchins, A.H., D.B.

'VAT inc' means that an inn's policy is to incorporate VAT in its food prices.

Most places will accept cheques only when they are accompanied by a cheque card or adequate identification. Information about which credit cards are accepted is correct when printed, but occasionally restaurants add to or subtract from the list without notice.

MR BUNBURY'S Map 3

1154 London Road,
S.W.16
01-764 3939

Cheap and cheerful bistro with dim lighting, rickety chairs, sliding cushions, and friendly service. The menu, changed quarterly, offers predictable pâté, Bunbury pie, 'plenty of tender meat in a rich gravy, but rather tired pastry' (£1·95), or creamy boeuf Stroganoff (£2·65), or baked salmon (£2·95). Rice is well cooked and salads come with a jug of mustardy vinaigrette. Finish with crème caramel or 'nice cheesy cheesecake'. Good coffee with refills, and tolerable house wine, £2·60 for 73 cl. Lunches are new this year. 'The recorded music wasn't too loud and obtrusive, though some of our fellow-diners were.'

Closed Sun; Sat L; public hols (exc Dec 25) Must book weekends Meals 12–2, 7–11.30	Tdh L £2·25 (meal £4·25) Alc £5·05 (meal £7·30) VAT inc Service 10% L	Children's helpings (under 10) Seats 38 ♿ rest (1 step) No dogs Access, Barclay

M'SIEUR FROG Map 12

31a Essex Road, N.1
01-226 3495

Closed L; Sun; Apr 16;
Aug; Dec 24, 25, 26 &
31; Jan 1
Must book
D only, 7–11.30

Alc £6·25 (meal £8·80)

VAT inc
Seats 51

Again a new chef chez Frog, but continuity of style in the kitchen is preserved by Howard Rawlinson's brother-in-law, who has been sous-chef since this Islington restaurant opened. Larger tables and more comfortable chairs have been installed in the dining-room, which is presided over by the Rawlinsons themselves, giving a warm welcome to the north London garlic establishment that forms their regular custom. After unfortunate experiences early last year – mostly with 'floury' sauces – visitors' reports picked up in tone and praised 'delicious' cuisses de grenouille, filet de porc aux abricots, côtelettes d'agneau Joséphine (spread with veal forcemeat and coated with cheese) and veal casserole. The cheeses are unusually good for a place of this kind, but opinions vary on the coffee (40p). Menus change 'every six weeks or so' and the owners suggest their lapin rôti à la crème (£2·85) and caneton rôti aux abricots (£3·25) as good choices this year. French house wines from the Rhône (£2·75 a bottle or 60p a glass) are liked; the wine list has about 20 other wines from £2·85 to £10. No music.

App: Ron Salmon, Myra S. Kaffel, and others

Since each restaurant has a separate file in the Guide office, please use a separate form or sheet of paper for each report. Additional forms may be obtained free (no stamp required) from The Good Food Guide, Freepost, 14 Buckingham Street, London WC2N 6BR.

NEW RASA SAYANG   Map 15

3 Leicester Place,
Leicester Square, W.C.2
01-437 4556

Closed Dec 24 & 25
Must book D
Open noon–11.30 p.m.
(12.30 a.m. Fri & Sat)

Alc meal £3·75

VAT inc
Seats 100 (parties 30)
Air-conditioning
No dogs

*Robert Kee manages here, so the lime-green,
ex-Lime-Grove-style set for a 'been to Borneo' TV
documentary may come as no surprise. Sjamsir
Alamsjah, the chef, moved across to the new place
from the old Rasa Sayang (still open). The demands
are heavier, and the year's visitors are not sure that
the cooking has really settled down, but the quality of
Mr Alamsjah's cardamom-flavoured minced chicken
satay, Singapore laksa (rice vermicelli in spicy fish
and coconut soup, £1·10) ikan asam pedas (mackerel
cutlets in tamarind sauce, 95p), Padang fried chicken,
and pergedel (potato cakes, 60p each) gave plenty to
admire, even at higher prices. Beef rendang and kalio
kentar (£1·05) are also good, they think (and are
explained on the menu). Rojak (the universal South
East Asian peanutty fruit and vegetable salad) was
'sloppily composed' when tested. Kue dada, fritters,
and other banana or coconut-based sweets are worth
trying, or drink chendol (50p) if you want a
technicolour-dream-coat experience. There are wines
from £2·95, or lager. More reports, please, not
forgetting the old Bateman Street place, which was
mediocre when last tested but has been redecorated and
may survive, à la Poon's (q.v.).*

NONTAS   Map 12

16 Camden High Street,
N.W.1
01-387 4579

Messrs Chrysaphiades and Vassilaka's restuarant
lost its place last year but has got the message,
according to members who have found the atmosphere
agreeable and the Greek home cooking – especially
the meze – better than the norm in this very Greek
district. Hummus, tahini, fried squid, cheese pâté,
grilled haloumi, marinated mullet, sheftalia (spicy
sausages), dolmades, afelia, kebabs, indeed the whole
menu apart from the sweets (do not stray from
yoghourt and honey) can be safely suggested to a
party. The usual Cypriot wines or retsina are £2·40.
Recorded music. Details approximate.

Closed Sun; public hols
(exc May 7)
Must book

Meals 12–2.45, 6–11.45

Alc £2·45 (meal £4·55)

Seats 54
 ♿ rest
No dogs
Access, Diners

PLEASE keep sending in reports, as soon as possible after each meal.
Closing date for the 1980 Guide is September 30, 1979, but reports are even
more useful earlier in the year, especially for the remoter areas and new places.

'Meal' indicates the cost of a meal for one, including food,
coffee, half the cheapest bottle of wine, cover, service, and **VAT** (see
'How to use the Guide', p. 4).

OLIVER'S CAFE   Map 13

10 Russell Gardens, W.14
01-603 7645

'Not exactly a cafe', if you notice the stripped brick, paintings, and candles rather than the 'loud taped music' and 'amiable women who share the waiting'. 'Slight changes' – mostly just more flavour to lasagne, roast veal with herbs, and so on – 'would make it much better', for chicken liver pâté, moules marinière, grilled, crumbed sole, vegetables and salads, are quite well done; the Iberian chef-patron also suggests chicken Kiev or roast ribs of beef (£2·15). 'Mint crisp is the best sweet', though there are various cheesecakes to choose from, and the espresso coffee and modest corkage charge (there is no licence) make it all seem good value.

Closed Dec 25
Open noon–10 p.m.

Alc £3·75 (meal £4·70)

Service 10%

Seats 80
No dogs
Unlicensed

♥ OSLO COURT   Map 12

Prince Albert Road,
N.W.8
01-722 8795

Closed Sun; Mon; Sat L;
2 weeks Easter; 3 weeks
Aug/Sept; Dec 26–Jan 1
Must book D
Meals 12.30–2, 6.30–10

Alc £8·20 (meal £12·25)

VAT inc
Cover 50p
Seats 70
 ⌖ rest (3 steps)
Air-conditioning
No dogs

The Katnic family's restaurant lies at the foot of a block of flats, approached from Charlbert Street. If you could forget the prices, the plush, the cut glass, and the staff-to-customer ratio, the sense that a village celebration somewhere in Herzegovina had simply been transferred to St John's Wood would begin to grow on you. The Cockney phrase 'everything regardless' also applies. But Rajko in the kitchen and June in the dining-room do go to immense and productive trouble, from the side dishes of smoked fish pâté that accompany the crudités at the start of a meal, to the Turkish delight and Polish pastries that may be handed round when you are sighing at the finish. The cooking is best described as Balkan transcendental. Mr Katnic's repertoire ranges from stuffed cabbage to bouillabaisse, and he is particularly enterprising with fish, to judge from detailed descriptions of his onions stuffed with a mixture of bass and salmon trout, served hot with a 'very delicate' egg and lemon sauce; or king prawns Istria; or stuffed ink-fish; or trout with a persillade, served with a salad of brown beans and sorrel; or 'triumphant' salmon trout in pastry with fennel, mushrooms and Pernod. Duck Bosnaka (£4·50) with livery stuffing and a cherry sauce, remains a popular speciality, and veal San Stefan (£9 for two) – again in pastry, with a core of pureed crayfish, and 'heavenly' tarragon sauce – is no mean dish. Mange-tout peas and potato cakes justify the vegetable extras. Wise men and women end with something fruity – perhaps hot raspberries, or strawberries salamandered with brown sugar and served with home-made lemon ice-cream, or fresh mango. The wines are not the least surprising aspect of this restaurant, and although the tables are too close, air-conditioning, coupled with a little tactful exhortation from June Katnic, has made it somewhat easier to enjoy the extraordinary range of clarets, including four '61s in half-bottle as well as, say, Ch. Cos d'Estournel '67 at £10. The white burgundies are on the mature side (which can be rewarding, but not always). But so are the red ones: Bonnes-Mares '66 (Clair-Däu) £11·50. House Mâcon is £3·75. A half-bottle of '57 Ch. d'Yquem is £22. No music.

App: Ron Salmon, John Bennett, C.C., S.H.B., H.P., M.R., and others

---

OSTERIA LARIANA   Map 15

49 Frith Street, W.1 01-734 5183	Modest little Italian restaurant, run by Giovanni Dalmasso and his family. The place is comfortable, the service pleasant, and members have been well satisfied with their meals: 'moist and livery pâté' (75p); 'calf's liver – always good here, as are the vegetables'; 'plump and juicy' quails in white wine sauce (£2·85); 'lemony and non-fatty' piccata alla limone (£1·65). Coffee may be 'over-cooked'. Italian wines, with the house one £2·30 the bottle. 'Noisy' recorded music, turned down on request.

Closed Sun; last 3 weeks Aug; public hols Must book L	Meals 12–3, 6–11.30 Tdh L £1·80 (meal £3·25) Alc £4·05 (meal £6·40)	VAT inc Cover 20p alc Seats 30 No dogs

---

OVEN D'OR   Map 3

4 a Crescent Way, Orpington, Kent Farnborough (Kent) 52170 Closed Sun; Sat L; Aug 6–27; 1st week Jan; public hols (exc Dec 25 L) Must book D & weekends Meals 12.30–2, 7–10 Tdh L £3 (meal £5·75) Alc £6·20 (meal £9·35) VAT inc Service 12½% Seats 30 (parties 10) No dogs Access, Am Ex, Barclay, Diners	*'In spite of the silly name, M Grenier's place takes itself seriously' and bluff Orpingtonians are taking it seriously too, for suburban Kent is unused to French restaurants of some ambition. (In 1979, the Oven will move upstairs, and Le Troquet – a Rhône name for a bistro – will open in the present room.) The chef, Ono Kunihiko, moves easily among specialities that include petit pâté chaud (£1·90) and pintadeau aux champignons (£6·85 for two). A test meal involving dishes of the same style – crêpes jurassienne, filled with ham and Gruyère, and duck in wine and cream sauce – was satisfactory; and smoked haddock mousse (£1·10) at the beginning and poires aux groseilles (two pears cooked in red wine and perched on sharp blackcurrants in a meringue nest, 80p) were even better. Salmon in pastry has also been successful. There are many well-known Bordeaux and burgundy wines at ludicrous prices, perhaps to encourage people to drink up the Languedoc wine lake at under £4 for the house wines. Côte Rôtie '64 or '74 is £7·50 or so. Recorded 'dinner music'. More reports, please.*

I PAPARAZZI   Map 15

52–54 Dean Street, W.1
01-437 3916 *and* 1703

Closed public hols
Must book
Meals 12–3, 5.45–11.45

Alc (min £1·50) £3·90
(meal £6·70)

Cover 30p
Seats 105 (parties 40)
♿ rest
Air-conditioning
No dogs
Access, Am Ex, Barclay,
Diners, Euro

Even Fleet Street *paparazzi* sometimes make mistakes like Corrado and Alvaro, who sent us a wrong telephone number last year. Happily, members have still responded to the request for further information at the foot of that provisional entry. Less happily, they find the cooking too, though genuinely Italian in many ways, subject to similar lapses of accuracy: 'dry gamberini', 'much too buttery eel', 'the chef seemed to think parsley would do for both basil in the pasta and rosemary with the bass.' Still, Mr Michele's agnolotti or fettuccine alla panna ('superb'), 'herby calamari', chicken livers fried and garlicked ('very good value', 95p), sgombro Saracena (smoked mackerel reposing on avocado mayonnaise), charcoaled liver or rib of beef, and other dishes, show what can be done if care is taken. Coda vaccinara (oxtail Roman-style, £1·95) is one of the standing daily specialities: there may be others to enquire about, and 'it pays to keep the initiative with the waiters.' 'I don't go for the "bella signora" style of service much,' says another critic. Linen is starched, and since most communicators are late for lunch, eat early. No music, at least.

App: Ron Salmon, A.L., J.H., L.W., C.G., Howard Gee, and others

PEKING CASTLE   Map 3

379 High Road, Wembley
01-902 3605

'Better than the usual anglicised suburban takeaway,' admits one suburbanite after a patchy meal at this Pekinese place near the Conference Centre, but others who think the set meals here fair value (£3·25 a head for two or more) single out 'excellent' hot-and-sour soup, crispy duck, well-cooked rice, 'very hot' prawns in chilli, chicken with almond and yellow-bean sauce, and toffee apples or bananas which 'go down well at the end of the meal'. Good jasmine tea. No music.

Closed Dec 25 & 26
Must book D & weekends
Meals 12–2.30, 6–12

Alc meal £4

Seats 50

♿ rest (1 step)
No dogs
Access, Am Ex, Barclay

The Guide accepts no advertising. Nor does it allow restaurateurs to use its name on brochures, menus, or in any form of advertisement. If you see any instances of this, please report them to us.

Please report to us on atmosphere, decor and – if you stayed – standard of accommodation, as well as on food, drink and prices (send bill if possible).

PEKING HOUSE   Map 12

454 Edgware Road, W.2
01-262 8910

Martin Wang's restaurant, with Mr Chik and Mr Kao in the kitchen, has branched out from Westbourne Grove to this place near enough to Little Venice not to have to depend on the Edgware Road custom for their 'timidly flavoured but interesting' Szechuan sesame chicken (£1·30) and fried dumplings. Cornfloury sauces – a pity with nice crunchy green peppers or beans – are regretted, but food is served very hot and the decor is attractive. Try also wine-cooked fish slices (£1·50) and beef with oyster sauce (£2). Recorded music. More reports, please.

Closed Sun; Apr 16;
Dec 24, 25 & 26
Must book D & weekends

Meals 12–2.30, 6–11.30

Alc meal £3·50

Service 10%
Seats 50
No dogs
Am Ex, Barclay

PILGRIM'S   Map 12

175 Archway Road, N.6
01-340 3344

Tiny, candlelit, Carib-and-Hib evening restaurant in a converted post-office on this 'much juggernauted' highway. George Fuller and Fitzroy Pilgrim pride themselves on personal buying and serving, and are confident enough to cook in full view of their customers. One party's meal included 'conventional, well-made' celery soup, very good turkey and walnut pie, 'adequate' egg florentine, and duck à l'orange. Salads are crisp. But 'pâté' was potted meat at best and the baked potatoes tasted 'kept'. Petit pot au chocolat and nutty ice-cream are usually sound, coffee drinkable. Wines are few and unremarkable; carafe is Arc de Triomphe at £2·25. 'Romantic' records.

Closed L; Sun; Mon;
Dec 25 & 26
Must book
D only, 7–11
(11.30 Fri & Sat)

Alc £3·95 (meal £6·15)

VAT inc
Service 10%
Cover 20p

Children's helpings
(under 10)
Seats 30
♿ rest
Air-conditioning
No dogs

Entries for places with distinctions carry symbols (pestle, tureen, bottle, glass). Credits are fully written entries, with approvers' names below the text. Passes are telegraphic entries (useful in the area) with details under the text. Provisional entries are in italics (see 'How to use the Guide', p. 4).

Prices of meals underlined are those which we consider represent unusual value for money. They are not necessarily the cheapest places in the Guide.

See p. 120 for the restaurant-goer's legal rights, and p. 118 for information on hygiene in restaurants.

PLUMMERS   Map 15

10a James Street, W.C.2
01-240 2534

Martin Plummer's former vegetable warehouse is something of a hybrid. Plastic cloths, casual service and obtrusive records evoke a hamburger joint, but 'low-key elegance' and a vein of invention raise it above the genre. The hamburgers are fair value, and Californian chili is 'hot in both senses'. Spare ribs were disappointing when tried. Liver and bacon, or a large veal chop, make good dishes of the day. Fair vegetables. Apple pie sounds nicer than the jammy cheesecake. French ordinaire is £2·65 for 26 fl oz, and there is Heineken lager too. 'Quite good coffee.' A few tables outside.

Closed Sun; Sat L;
Dec 25 & 26; Dec 31 L;
L public hols
Must book

Meals 12–3.30, 5–11.45

Alc £4·05 (meal £6·45)

VAT inc

Service 12½%
Seats 50 (parties 20)
Air-conditioning
Access, Am Ex, Barclay,
Diners

POISSONNERIE DE L'AVENUE   Map 14

82 Sloane Avenue, S.W.3
01-589 2457 *and* 5774

Closed Sun; Dec 24 & 31;
public hols
Must book D & weekends
Meals 12.30–2.45, 7–11.30

Alc £6·45 (meal £10·05)

VAT inc
Service 12½%
Cover 50p
Seats 80 (parties L 26)
Air-conditioning
No dogs
Access, Am Ex, Barclay

Sound, medium-price fish restaurants in London (or anywhere) are uncommon, and though expansion into the house next door, decorated in the same wooden beam and panelling style, has not solved all Peter Rosignoli's problems or made his waiters less inclined to hustle customers out to make room for more, the cooking often has a verve that more gracious places lack. A country mouse reports happily of an orgy involving 'exquisite scallops in Pernod, a treatment I have just discovered, buttery and garlicky stuffed clams, pale apricot mussels in a delicious sauce, and lovely flaking turbot with a hollandaise just the right side of curdling.' A town mouse 'took the raw mushrooms with chives, having never eaten raw mushrooms before', and found the grilled turbot (£3·85) also very fine, 'though was it really grilled?' Fish soups, brill in spinach sauce, raie au beurre noir, paupiettes of mullet in a saffron sauce ('the saffron hardly tasted through the *fumet*') and other dishes are praised, though not surprisingly the place has its bad days too. The simple sweets and coffee also have generally true flavours. The house Sauvignon is £3·30, Muscadet £4, Sancerre £6, Montrachet £8, listed (to us at least) without vintages. No music. The tables are too close, so you had better like tobacco (yours or other people's).

App: Michael Copp, J.S.W., S.M., Hilda Woolf, Helen Macintosh, and others

1979 prices are as estimated by restaurateurs in the autumn of 1978.

27 Lisle Street, W.C.2
01-437 1528

Closed Dec 24, 25 & 26
Must book D & weekends
Open noon–11.30

Tdh £2
Alc (min 80p) meal £3·70

Seats 40 (parties 20)
No dogs
Unlicensed

A series of overpriced, under-flavoured experiences at posh Poon's in Covent Garden have driven members back to louche Poon's in Soho, and though a few have been disconcerted by the cramped, communal tables (unless your party fills one) and brusquerie, there is seldom much doubt of Liu Hai Ting's cooking, or of the winter-time 'wind-dried sausages and duck' that are Shirley Poon's chief speciality here. Other suggestions include stewed eel with crispy belly pork (much missed when it is off), stewed meatballs with Chinese mushrooms, deep-fried crispy sweet-and-sour wun-tun, oil soak squid (£1·50), and roasted duck (£1·40). A test meal also yielded interesting fried bean curd, barbecued pork with bitter cucumber, and 'tangy, crunchy' fried beef with green pepper and salted black beans. If there is time or a party for a day's advance ordering, stewed duck with mixed seafood, or stuffed boneless duck, may be considered, and 'deep-fried fresh milk' too, on which one kindly pianist supplies a comment because 'I can never resist a good title, and I liked the way it appeared, logically enough, under "beef dishes". The effect is of plaques of thickened custard deep-fried in batter, eaten with sugar (or with salt, I suppose): not bad in a weird way.' Other peculiarities to notice include the ceiling fan which scatters cigarette ash if you are unlucky, and the 'alarming' steps down to the loos. No music, and a happy *année de pèlerinage* to all.

App: Robert Muller, S.M., Reynell Grissell, P.S., Hilda Woolf, Kevin O'Mahoney, and many others

231 Ebury Street, S.W.1
01-730 7763

Members have a love-hate relationship with the Poule, who can peck when she chooses, leaves crumbs on the carpet, and goes rather broody about her prices. The blackboard menu tells little and the waiters recite other dishes. However, terrine with sticky dark rye bread is generous, and fresh mushroom soup (better than the 'rather greasy' onion), quiche, lapin aux pruneaux, poulet chasseur and raspberry tart are also praised. Vegetables are unambitious ('luckily I like petits pois for all seasons') and meat may be carelessly trimmed. You pay for what you drink from French magnums (or 30p for a glass). French recorded music.

Closed Sun; public hols
Must book
Meals 12.30–2.30, 7–11.15

Tdh L £3·65 (meal £6·90)
Alc £6·60 (meal £10·50)

Service 12½%

Cover L 30p, D 45p
Seats 40 (parties 16)
🔲 rest (1 step)
Am Ex, Barclay, Diners

PRINCE OF INDIA   Map 13

75 The Broadway, S.W.19
01-542 8834

A comfortable, dim restaurant offering generous helpings of mostly well-cooked food: chicken tikka massalum (£1·60) tastes nicely of yoghourt; onion bhajia has 'beautifully crisp outsides though rather soggy interiors'; chicken dhansak (£1·30) has plenty of lentils; prawn patia (£1·30) is 'generous, hot and sweet'; lamb dopiaza is 'oniony but rather greasy'; chicken Madras is too sweet. Generally friendly service. Water comes with ice and is worth asking for, since the mineral water on each table costs 55p. Various bottled beers at 35p; wine 55p the glass. Recorded music.

Closed Dec 25 & 26	VAT inc	Seats 56 (parties 30)
Must book D & weekends	Service 10%	🔌 rest
Meals 12–2.45, 6–11.30	Children's helpings	No dogs
	(under 12)	Access, Am Ex, Barclay,
Alc £3·30		Diners

RED LION CHINESE   Map 13

18 Red Lion Street,
Richmond, Surrey
01-940 2371 *and* 948 1961

The Chens' Pekinese place round the corner from Marks and Spencer has a firm following for crispy duck, but mixed reports of stingy prawn dishes, 'sparse' sweet-and-sour pork, and soggy rice. However, the 'grand hors d'oeuvre' (smoked fish, pickled cabbage, beef and fried seaweed) makes an excellent start to a meal; hot-and-sour soup is well flavoured; chicken and almonds in yellow-bean sauce, mixed vegetables and spare ribs are all as expected; and toffee apples (though cold on one occasion) make a good finish. Carafino is £1·60 the half-litre. Friendly service. Recorded music.

Must book D	Alc (meal £4·05)	🔌 rest
Meals 12–2.15, 6–11.15		Air-conditioning
	Service 10%	No dogs
Tdh £2·50	Seats 44 (parties 40)	Access, Barclay, Diners

THE REFECTORY   Map 13

6 Church Walk,
Richmond, Surrey
01-940 6264

Closed Mon; D Sun–Wed;
public hols
Must book
Meals 12–2.30, 7.30–8.45

Tdh D £4·65 (meal £6·50)
Alc L (min 75p) £2·75
(meal £3·80)

Churchyard restaurants are still uncommon, and the Kingsleys' setting in Georgian parish rooms is suitably English. Indeed, it sets a much-needed example to its Anglican neighbours by sharing responsibility between the sexes: she cooks, he cherishes an interesting range of English and Commonwealth wines. A repertoire of pies and casseroles, rather than roasts and other unforgiving dishes, helps to keep standards up and prices down, though an inspector found, as before, 'a tendency to overcook and undersalt'. Leek soup, smoked haddock in cheese sauce, mushrooms in garlic mayonnaise;

VAT inc
Children's helpings
Seats 54
♿ rest (1 step)

then cidered pork, spiced lamb with apricots, or chicken with honey and orange: these are the kind of dishes to expect on menus. 'We also like beef casserole, and fidget or fisherman's pies.' Leeks in cream sauce, mashed parsnips, and other vegetables indicate trouble taken with them. If you find cheesecake dense, as you may, consider ginger syllabub or chocolate nutcake. 'Prince Albert's pudding is another find.' A Spanish vintner found the Broadwater '77 (£3·45) from Framlingham *'flojo y huele de azufre'*; the *Guide* tester was more taken with it. Even Mr Kingsley has his doubts about the Felstar '77 red, but McWilliam's Cabernet Shiraz '70 from New South Wales is a fair £4·05. No music.

App: I. D. Usher, Edwina Culver, M.A., O.M., Joyce & David Johnson

---

RICHMOND RENDEZVOUS   Map 13

Richmond, Surrey
(1) 1 Paradise Road
01-940 5114
(2) 1 Wakefield Road
01-940 6869

One of the longest-serving of Mr Young's chain, this Pekinese restaurant still gets bouquets for its banquets (from £3·90): spare ribs, 'chilli beef', good crispy duck, diced chicken with almond in yellow-bean sauce, sliced sole in wine sauce and 'tasty' mixed vegetables. 'It was comfortable in the Wakefield Road annexe but offhand service and a bill dispute suggest need for care.' Hirondelle £2·40. Stella Artois lager. No music.

Closed Dec 25 & 26
Must book D & weekends
Meals noon—11.15

Tdh from £3·90

Alc (min £2) meal £5·15

Service 12%
Seats (1) 45
(2) 100 (parties 20)

Air-conditioning
No dogs
Access, Am Ex, Barclay, Diners

RIVE GAUCHE   Map 13

541b King's Road,
S.W.6
01-736 7644

Closed L (exc Sun);
1 week Easter;
1 week Chr;
public hols
Must book D
Meals 12–2.30 (Sun),
7–11.45

Tdh £3·95 & £5·95 (meal
£7·15 & £9·40)

VAT inc
Service 12½%
Cover 45p

'Cuisine du sud' announces this engaging if close-packed restaurant at the *ouest* end of the King's Road. M Caelle and his anonymous French chef seem to mean it, and the garlic bread (40p on top of the cover charge) is 'an offer you can't refuse,' says an inspector who also enjoyed 'very fresh and well-cooked' sardines provençale and lamb kebabs flavoured with herbs and onion. Canard à l'aixoise, too, with lemon, honey and a little cognac, was 'generous and delicious' in an agrodolce sauce. Another, more frequent, visitor likes the 'French family business' air, the strong flavours (lapin moutarde is another speciality), and forgives the 'table neighbours discussing sexual politics at the top of their voices'. So perhaps the teething problems noticeable at first have been overcome. Of the two menus, at different prices, the cheaper one offers minimal choice. Puddings are adequate, no more, and the microwave (presumably) left a baked Bramley*

Seats 55
♿ rest (1 step)

'looking as if it had just left a greengrocer's stall'. The Provencal house wine at £2·95 is decent, and if you fancy Fitou or Bandol they will cost you £3·95 or £6·75 respectively, which might alarm them down in Aix. Recorded music. More reports, please.

RIVER BISTRO   Map 13

15 Barnes High Street,
S.W.13
01-876 1471

A friendly little bistro 'with Mme Rivolta much in evidence'. 'Capable girls' serve fairly standard bistro fare: escargots (£1·15), smooth, livery pâté maison (70p), stuffed aubergines, an anglicised salade niçoise, escalope à la crème (£2·35), chateaubriand (£7·50 for two), 'excellent' scampi provençale, and ever-popular profiteroles. Duck and chicken may come as pink as beef and lamb, some sweets are bought in, and the cheese may run out before the end of the evening, but vegetables are 'well and imaginatively cooked'. House wine £2·45 the carafe, 55p the glass. Recorded music.

Closed L; Sun; Apr 13;
3 weeks Aug/Sept;
4 days Chr
Must book

D only, 7–11.30

Alc £5·10 (meal £7·85)

VAT inc

Service 12½%
Cover 25p
Seats 40 (parties 40)
♿ rest
Barclaycard

ROWLEY'S   Map 15

113 Jermyn Street, S.W.1
01-930 2707

Malcolm Livingston moved on early last year, but reports still flutter down in favour (mostly) of this handsome Edwardian chamber, once the home of Wall the sausage king, whose owners also run the Princess Louise pub in Holborn (*q.v.*) and another ('markedly inferior') Rowley's in Baker Street. Amiable service softens the sausage-machine effect of a fast throughput and a formula meal: good bread and salad, then entrecôte done as you like with a patent spicy butter, followed by 'good sweets: say, trifle and pears in wine, and a rhubarb fool'. Cheeses are sound, if often limited (though Paxton and Whitfield are only a few doors away). Cafetière coffee. They charge by measure for house Bordeaux or Soave at £5·30 a magnum, but if you drink a mere glass it may cost you dear. Songs to a guitar at night.

Closed Dec 25
Meals 12.30–2.30,
6.30–11.30

Tdh £4·75 (meal £7·55)

Service 12½%
Cover 15p

Seats 70
♿ rest
No dogs
Access, Am Ex, Barclay,
Diners, Euro

Inspections are carried out anonymously. Persons who pretend to be able to secure, arrange or prevent an entry in the Guide are impostors and their names or descriptions should be reported to us.

ROYAL GARDEN HOTEL
BULLDOG CHOPHOUSE   Map 13

Kensington High Street,
W.8
01-937 8000

Vinyl-padded, club-like adjunct to this well-known hotel, where tourists puzzle over coy menu terms (Crusader's Pear; Traitors' Gate, £9·95 for two). Useful even so for a dogged attempt at some English dishes: pea soup, mixed grill (good in parts), excellent roast beef and horseradish sauce, sherry trifle. The mead is Petit Château (£3·80 for 70 cl).

Closed Sat L	VAT & service inc	Access, Am Ex, Barclay,
Meals 12.30–2.30,	Children's helpings	Diners
6.30–10.30 (Sun 7)	Seats 80	Room only, from £34
	Car park	Breakfast from £2·50
Alc £6·80 (meal £9·25)	No dogs in public rooms	Fire cert

RUGANTINO   Map 15

26 Romilly Street, W.1
01-437 5302

This bustling, crowded trattoria has disappointed too many this time, and 'useful' seems the kindest description. But if you keep to the simpler things – liver with sage and butter, the tuna and bean hors d'oeuvre, 'lovely cheesy aubergine', kidneys with wine and mushrooms – you can fare worse in this district. Vegetables are variable, sweets dull, coffee poor. Reports needed on the set meal. House wine is £2·95 a litre. Friendly service. Recorded music.

Closed Sun; Sat L; public	Tdh £4·35 (meal £6·55)	Seats 46 (parties 28)
hols (exc Apr 13);	Alc £5·80 (meal £9·20)	⟨⟩ rest; w.c.
Dec 24 L		Air-conditioning
Must book L	VAT inc	No dogs
Meals 12–2.45, 6–11.30	Service 12½%	Access, Am Ex, Barclay,
	Cover 45p alc	Diners, Euro

ST MORITZ RESTAURANT   Map 15

161 Wardour Street, W.1
01-734 3324

The spickness, paraphernalia, customers and tunes make you believe in the Swissness of Mr Loetscher's place, and so did the texture and flavour of inspectors' fondue neuchâteloise (£4·80 for two). Assiette des Grisons (air-dried beef, £1·95) makes a good prelude. Try too, perhaps, Peter Biber's fondue bourguignonne (£8·80 for two), or emincés zurichoise (£2·25) with rösti potatoes. Drink white wine with cheese fondue ('red will knot your stomach') but Swiss bottles begin at £6; Arc de Triomphe is £2·50. Take coffee rather than a sweet.

Closed L Sat & Sun;	Alc (min £2) £5·55	Cover 30p
Dec 25; Jan 1; L public	(meal £8·80)	Seats 38
hols		No dogs
Must book D & weekends	Service 10%	Access, Am Ex, Barclay,
Meals 12–2.30, 6–1.30 a.m.		Diners

SALAMIS   Map 14

204 Fulham Road, S.W.10
01-352 9827

Ernest Victory's restrained, efficiently run restaurant, 'established for 25 years', has a seldom-changed menu ('international with Greek additions') and a firm following. His best dishes, he thinks, are the fresh sardines, whole lamb with herbs, fillet of veal with peppers, and the 'golden finale' pancake. Others would add calamares and the fresh vegetables. Morgan Furze wines. No pipes.

Closed Sun; public hols
Must book
Meals 12.30–2.30, 6.30–12

Tdh £2·50 (meal £4·95)

Alc £4·50 (meal £7·35)

Service 10%
Cover 15p
Children's helpings

Seats 40
🔒 rest (1 step)
No dogs
Access, Am Ex, Barclay, Diners

SANDRO'S   Map 12

114 Crawford Street, W.1
01-935 5736

Closed Sun; Sat L;
public hols
Must book
Meals 12–2.45, 6.30–11.15

Alc £6·30 (meal £10·20)

Service 12½%
Cover 30p
Seats 45
🔒 rest
No dogs
Am Ex, Barclay, Diners

Bruno Peruzzi manages this narrow and resonant restaurant for Antonio Valeri of Tonino's (q.v.) and the kitchen has a new chef, Marcantonio. Names matter here, for these are two very personal restaurants: 'I like the way they choose meat and cook it as you want it, without swamping delicate liver in sauces.' 'The fettuccine Tonino (£1·10) are delicious but best to order when the boss is at hand to supervise the operation.' 'Antipasti are good but watch that they don't show you the trolley and then wheel it away to make their own choice.' There are no major changes, though 'the batter for courgettes is heavier now and salads are smaller.' Anyway, try the liver with sage, veal perhaps, or carré d'agnello (£3·90), and end with strawberries in Strega (for most seasons). Wines from £2·78; Valpolicella Amarone £5. No music.

App: V. Westerman, Donald May, A.W., and others

SAN FREDIANO   Map 14

62 Fulham Road, S.W.3
01-584 8375

No raptures about the San Fred, but it is an animated place, especially at night, and 'there were nice fresh shrimps to eat with drinks, and the pasta with fresh sage – or chopped liver – tasted home-made.' Crespolini (95p) are advocated too, and they are proud of their veal dishes. 'But chicken Cordon Bleu was only moderate, with a mediocre tomato sauce.' Valpolicella or Soave are £2·35.

Closed Sun; public hols
Must book
Meals 12.30–2.30, 7.15–11.30

Alc £4·20 (meal £6·70)

VAT inc
Cover 40p
Seats 85

🔒 rest (1 step)
Air-conditioning
No dogs
Access, Am Ex, Barclay, Diners, Euro

SAN LORENZO   Map 14
SAN LORENZO FUORIPORTA   Map 13

(1) 22 Beauchamp Place,
S.W.3
01-584 1074
(2) Worple Road Mews,
S.W.19
01-946 8463

Both San Lorenzos are predicated upon what passes in Britain for *la dolce vita*. The **Wimbledon** one (approach it from the mews, not through the picture window on Wimbledon Hill Road) is ideally designed for a hot summer with 'the scent of garlic and rosemary on the air'. With the doors shut, the packed tables, the smoke, and the service can be maddening unless the kitchen has paid more attention than it sometimes does to your grilled sardines, brains, petti di pollo farciti, veal with aubergines and Mozzarella (£3·20), and zabaglione. In **Knightsbridge**, too, customers know they are there to be seen rather than served ('the rain was dripping through the skylight five feet from Anthony Quinn'), and cooking is similarly patchy: at a test meal, excellent raw vegetables for bland bagna cauda, tasty calamari with black rice (£1·50), dry wood-pigeon with off-putting polenta (£4·50), and the 'most agreeable' house pancake, cold, with maraschino flavours in the creamy stuffing. 'Drink Nuragus house white at £2·80'; order better red, perhaps.

Closed (1) Sun; 1 week
Chr; public hols;
(2) Dec 24; public hols
Must book
Meals (1) 1–2.30, 8–11.30;
(2) 12.30–3, 7.30–11

Alc £7·90 (meal £11·25)

VAT inc
Service 12½%
Cover 35p

Seats (1) 100 (parties 30)
(2) 50 (parties 35)
No dogs
(2) Access, Am Ex,
Barclay, Diners, Euro

SATAY HOUSE   Map 12

13 Sale Place, W.2
01-723 6763

Dim light and plastic tablecloths, but the chairs (and the chef) are new since last year's entry. The cooking remains 'proper Malaysian' and pleases most comers, though 'too much peanut' is the main criticism. The set meals (including rijsttaffel) offer good variety. Dishes mentioned this time include the satay, pergedel (potato patties), rendang (beef in dry coconut and spice paste), pajri nanas (pineapple and dried prawns), and acar (mixed pickled vegetables). The puddings are based on rice or sago, and condensed milk may come with the coffee. House wine is £2·90, 60p the glass. Tiger beer. Two tables outside. Malaysian records.

Closed Dec 25 L
Must book D
Meals 12–3, 6–11.15

Tdh £3·50
Alc meal £3

Service 10%

Seats 32
♿ rest
No dogs
Access, Am Ex, Barclay

See p. 108 for London pubs and wine bars.

SAVVAS KEBAB HOUSE   Map 13

7 Ladbroke Road, W.11
01-727 9720

Un-smart 'Greek home-cooking' near Notting Hill Gate tube, where soups, grills and salads are the best buy: avgolemono is properly made, spit-roasted souvla 'very Greek, very overdone, very delicious'. Few sweets. Cypriot carafe £2·20, 40p the glass. Tables outside. Greek records.

Closed Sun; public hols
(exc Apr 13)
Must book weekends

Meals 12–3, 5–11.30
(noon–11.30 Sat)

Alc £2·40 (meal £4·15)

VAT inc
Seats 35 (parties 40)
♿ rest (1 step)
No dogs

LA SCALA   Map 15

35 Southampton Street,
W.C.2
01-240 1030

Welcoming trattoria, useful in the Covent Garden theatreland where fast service and reasonable prices are at a premium. Soups and sauces may be floury, but calves' kidneys, osso buco, veal with lemon sauce, the deep-fried aubergines or courgettes, and zabaglione are applauded. Trolley gateaux are standard offerings. Sangiovese £2 for 72 cl. Italian bottled beer. Close-packed tables make smoking anti-social. Recorded music.

Closed Sun; Sat L; public
hols
Must book
Meals 12–2.30, 5.30–11

Alc (min £1) £5·40 (meal
£7·80)

VAT inc
Cover 30p

Seats 50 (parties 25)
♿ rest (2 steps)
No dogs
Access, Am Ex, Barclay,
Diners

SEA SHELL FISH BAR   Map 12

35 Lisson Grove, N.W.1
01-723 8703

This popular fish and chip shop has the snags you would expect: a queue, cramped quarters, and sometimes a faster turnover of customers than table-wipers can cope with. (It also has 'magic realism' pictures on the walls.) But to eat here, or take away, there is 'devastatingly fresh fish, served red-hot, in a light, crisp batter'. Quantities are generous, and what's on depends on the market, but in 1978 'small' halibut ('a massive portion') was £1·80, plaice on the bone £1·80, Dover sole from £2·60. Chips are included – and good. Avoid the sauces and puddings. Glass of lemon tea, 20p. Unlicensed.

Closed Sun; Mon; public
hols
No bookings
Meals 12–2, 5.30–11

Alc £2·45

VAT & service inc

Seats 60
No dogs
Unlicensed

Meal times refer to first and last orders.

SHALIMAR   Map 12

229 Finchley Road, N.W.8 01-794 8344	*So many restaurateurs clamour for attention in the Finchley Road that it is worth recording the character an inspector gives Mr Bhadti's well-established place (related to the Maharani in Westbourne Grove). 'He buys good meat and the spicing is both subtle and individual. Try mild and rich chicken masala or moghlai (£1·80), spicier and drier lamb dopiaza (£1·40), nargisi kofta – a kind of Bengali Scotch egg; among vegetables, channa masaladar (90p) or muttar paneer.' Service is polite. Music ('Bombay Symphony Orchestra'). More reports, please.*
Closed Dec 25 Meals 12–3, 6–12 (1 Sat & Sun)	Alc (min £2) meal £4·05 Service 10%	Seats 70 No dogs Access, Am Ex, Barclay, Diners, Euro

SIENA   Map 12

17–19 Highbury Corner, N.5 01-607 3976	Some think Rossi and Biagioni's cafe-restaurant marginal, even for Ballspondia; some have been more gratified to find 'hot, cheesy and meaty' lasagne ('even the small version at 90p seemed large to me'), chicken or scaloppina in white wine sauces, trout with almonds, freshly and correctly made zabaglione, and good communication between proprietor and staff. Espresso is 'short and powerful'. But it is not a place in which to order roast pheasant with gravy. Italian wines from £2·60. Recorded music.
Closed Sun; public hols Must book Meals noon–10 p.m.	Alc L £3·05 (meal £5·60), D (min £3·50) £5 (meal £8·30) VAT inc	Seats 65 (parties 20) ♿ rest No dogs Barclaycard

SINGAPORE   Map 15

62 Marylebone Lane, W.1 01-486 2004	Simple but adequate restaurant near the Wigmore Hall. The Malaysian and Singapore specialities are the best thing. Try laksa – a soup with a 'coconutty taste', rojak (salad), fried sa ho fun 'with nice bouncy fish-cakes'. Few sweets. Good tea (15p). A short wine list. No music.
Closed Dec 24, 25 & 26 Must book L Meals 12–2.45, 6–10.45	Tdh L £1·60, D £4 Alc meal £4·45 VAT inc	Service 10% Seats 100 (parties 60) ♿ rest No dogs Am Ex, Diners

1979 prices are as estimated by restaurateurs in the autumn of 1978.

SOPNA TANDOORI   Map 3

175 High Street,
Hampton Hill
01-979 2977

Shafique Ullah serves this 'not very ethnic' area
well in his 'discreet' little tandoori restaurant. The
'mixed grill' includes tastes of tandoori chicken and
king prawn, lamb tikka, sheek kebab and a salad
for £2·50. Samosas and the bhajias are praised, and
people like the dhal and even the rice. Draught
Carlsberg. Corrida £3 the litre. 'Polished' service.
Recorded Indian classics. No dogs.

Closed Dec 25 & 26
Must book D & weekends
Meals 12.30–2.45, 6–11.45

Alc meal £4·30

Seats 50

♿ rest; w.c.
Access, Am Ex, Barclay,
Diners, Euro

STANDARD INDIAN   Map 12

21–23 Westbourne Grove,
W.2
01-727 4818 *and* 229 0600

Closed Dec 25
Must book D & weekends
Meals 12–3, 6–12

Alc (min £2) meal £4·60

VAT inc
Service 10%
Seats 120
♿ rest
No dogs
Access, Am Ex, Barclay,
Diners, Euro

Ramlal Bedhan's normally reliable Standard had a
below-standard chit from September visitors, both
for cooking and service, and neither the seating, the
lighting nor anything else does much to assuage any
sense of discontent. But perhaps it was the long
cool summer, for at a test meal later in the warm
autumn 'our waiter was sweetness itself, and the
dishes he talked up were almost all successes.' Nan
was heavy and poor, but lamb tikka suggested that
the tandoor was still operational, and the house
speciality butter chicken (£2·10), had a good
sauce, with tomatoes and nuts. Shahi korma –
lamb in a mild sauce with silver leaf decoration,
sag meat, channa masaladar, and the relishes are
among other items praised, and the sweets –
rasgulla (55p) and rus malai – are not bad, though
they need their sauces. Notre Dame ordinaires are
£2·60 for just under a litre. No music.

*App: Pam & Keith Holmes, C.W.B., P.S., P.B.,
P. Hayward*

SULTAN'S DELIGHT   Map 12

301 Upper Street, N.1
01-226 8346

'In good Turkish style' all the cooking is done in the
front window, so the fug is noticeable, but meze for
a party of three upwards (from 70p a dish) and
'spicy Adana' (or other) kebabs with rice attract
some critical customers. 'Sweets of moderate quality
are claimed to be made on the premises.' Italian
carafe wine is £2·50 a litre but it may be worth
paying £3·10 for Turkish Kavaklidere. No dogs.

Closed Sun L; Apr 15;
Dec 25 & 26
Must book weekends
Meals 12–2.30, 6–12.30

Tdh L £1·75 (meal £3·65)
Alc £3·30 (meal £5·35)

VAT inc
Service 10%

Children's helpings
Seats 80 (parties 20)
♿ rest (1 step)
Access, Am Ex, Barclay,
Diners

LE SUQUET   Map 14

104 Draycott Avenue,
S.W.3
01-581 1785

Closed Mon; Tue L;
Dec 24 & 31; public hols
Must book
Meals 12–2.30, 7.30–11.30

Alc £7·70 (meal £12)

VAT inc
Service 15%
Cover 50p
Seats 35
No dogs
Am Ex card

The occupational disease of French chefs in London is arrogance, and they are not innocent of it in this relation of La Croisette (*q.v.*), according to several visitors who have found the sloppiness of some dishes or practices hard to understand in the light of the excellence also achieved. Service, too, is only reliably considerate to those who are firm or knowledgeable. Encounter with wizened winkles and a faintly ammoniac crab on the justly famous plateau de fruits de mer (£5·50) sent one visitor on the next occasion to filet de rouget sauce mireille, 'absolutely delicious, the sauce being very delicately flavoured with fresh tarragon'. Equally refined, too, are the coquilles safran (£2·50), and more robust appetites may choose the 'pink, brown and shell-tasting' fish soup with rouille (£1·80), or the bass grilled on fennel twigs. They do not seem to mind what order you eat things in. Sweets are moderate – oeufs à la neige, perhaps, or a pear tart – and the presence of French cheeses cannot be depended upon. Coffee is good. Drink the Métaireau Muscadet, or Gros Plant, or Provencal Estandon at £4·85. The Dufy-decorated bar is upstairs. There is just enough room, but the ladies' loo is 'fit only for midgets'.

App: Richard Lawrence, C.P.D., P.C.H., and others

SWEETINGS   Map 12

39 Queen Victoria Street,
E.C.4
01-248 3062

Atmospheric Victorian 'ordinary' near Mansion House tube. Go early or expect a wait to sit up at counters or down at table. The sea-tasting oysters (now £2·25 for six) must reach even the most jaded City palate. Take your fish plain – poached or grilled turbot or halibut – for sauces are a mistake. Expect little in the way of sweets. The house Muscadet is £3·50 – pour your own and confess. Smokers can be a problem.

Closed D; Sat; Sun;
Dec 24 & 31; public hols

L only, 12–2.30

Alc £5·50 (meal £8·25)

Seats 32
♿ rest (3 steps)

We rewrite every entry each year, and depend on fresh, detailed reports to confirm the old, as well as to include the new. The further from London you are, the more important this is.

Wine prices shown are for a 'standard' bottle of the wine concerned, unless another measure is stated.

'VAT inc' means that an inn's policy is to incorporate VAT in its food prices.

SWISS CENTRE RESTAURANT   Map 15

2 New Coventry Street,
W.1
01-734 1291

In no way can a book like ours monitor close on a million meals a year in this canton of restaurants, but its uses remain: superb croissants (cheaper in the Centre's retail shop, of course) and decent coffee in the Imbiss (entrance on Wardour Street); comfort, bookings, and competent cooking in the Chesa; and in the Rendezvous, Locanda or Taverna that lie between these extremes, sound salads and cold dishes, pink liver if you ask, satisfying composite dishes such as Basler bebbi topf (£2·62, service included, VAT added by cashier), and sometimes disappointing gateaux. Côtes du Roussillon Villages is £3·30, the better Swiss wines barely worth the premium ('try the Feldschlossen beer,' says someone). If you cross the service or management in any way, they may make you feel as though you had jumped a red light in Berne. Somewhere they keep a small no-smoking section.

Closed Dec 25
Must book (Chesa)
Open 11.30 a.m.–
midnight

Alc £4·75 (meal £7·05),
(Chesa) £6·55 (meal £9)

Service inc

Seats 364
Air-conditioning
No dogs
Access, Am Ex, Barclay,
Diners

⌣ TANTE CLAIRE   Map 14

68 Royal Hospital Road,
S.W.3
01-352 6045

Closed Sat; Sun; 2 weeks
Aug; 1 week Jan; public
hols
Must book
Meals 12.30–2, 7–11

Tdh L £7 (meal £10·35)
Alc (min £6) £8·65
(meal £13·05)

VAT inc
Cover 65p
Seats 35
No dogs
Am Ex card

'Son of Gavroche' (q.v.) is a slightly ambivalent recommendation, but Pierre Koffmann's smaller-scale enterprise, in this long narrow room lined with Klimt prints, shows welcome signs of developing its own personality to put beside the high professionalism of the cooking. Very few chefs in London come within sighting distance of Mr Koffmann's andouillette de la mer au vinaigre de Cassis, (£2·30), the speciality that began a test dinner: 'Roughly speaking, it was a slice of turbot rolled round a fish mousse with strips of smoked salmon, accompanied by a buttery, fumet-based sauce that had a judicious sprinkling of sharp blackcurrants as well as the reduced vinegar.' Among other dishes described almost as lovingly in reports there are the tarte aux poireaux, 'very ducky' terrine de canard en croûte with pistachios (£1·60), scallops on a bed of spinach, bar au fenouil in crêpe-lined pastry, a delicate ragoût de volaille 'Madame Cadeillan' (with exquisite little vegetables included in the dish, £4·50), and pied de cochon to remind us of our humble origins. Foie de veau au citron vert (£4·80) is another speciality. The chief problems at present are that dishes are sometimes crossed off the menu disconcertingly, or arrive too cool. The service is cool too, but that is the style,

and it is basically benign. There are also some
delectable puddings: order early if you want the
feuilleté of pear because it takes half an hour.
Marquise au chocolat (£1·95) is 'not as rich as you
might think'; oeuf à la neige au coulis de fruit
(£1·50) 'scrumptious', with caramel toffee dribbled
over meringue and a substratum of raspberry puree.
The coffee is good, the petits fours not always as
crisp as they should be. The wines are adequate:
Montagny Ch. de la Saule '75 (Thévenin) suits the
fish dishes well, but you may need to spend twice
as much on claret or red burgundy. They may offer
'a little cocktail we make' with sparkling white wine
and armagnac at £1·70 a glass. (The draught from
the opened door blows the smoke towards the back,
remember.) No music. They now offer a set lunch –
reports welcome.

*App: E.M., Ian Hay Davison, J.M., C.P.D.,
M.E.D., and others*

TARABYA Map 16

107 Loampit Vale, S.E.13 01-691 1503	This kebab house 'lacks atmosphere', though the ethnic music may represent effort, and evenings liven up later. The food makes up for much – passable taramosalata and hummus with good bread, usually excellent kebabs (the mixed one is the best value) and home-made 'high density' keshkul (with custard, honey and coconut). The Turkish house wine at £2·55 is drinkable; others are around £3·25. Take-away service. Reports, please, on Mr Uzum's new place in Market Parade, Sidcup, Kent.

Closed L; Dec 26 & 31 D only, 6–1 a.m.	Children's helpings (under 12)	Air-conditioning No dogs Access, Barclay
Alc £3·85 (meal £6·35)	Seats 50	

A TASTE OF HONEY Map 13

2 Kensington Park Road, W.11 01-727 4146 *and* 229 6731	*Half-moon-shaped 'cottagey' first-floor restaurant 'with a wholesome feel' and more vegetarian dishes expected since the closure of 'Naturally' last year. Well, Mrs Dean took over the cooking as we went to press, so not too much can be made either way of mundane toast, dull pâté and 'watery' crab mousse, or good home-made soup (75p), trout with fennel, lamb with apricot and walnuts, and gooseberry and ginger fool. Licensed now, but no details. No under-eights. Recorded music. More reports, please.*

Closed Sun; public hols; Dec 27 Must book weekends	Meals 12–3, 6.30–11.30	Cover 40p Seats 45
	Alc (min L £2·50, D £3) £5·45 (meal £8·90)	No dogs Am Ex, Diners

TATE GALLERY RESTAURANT   Map 16

Millbank, S.W.1
01-834 6754

Closed D; Sun; Apr 13;
Dec 24, 25, 26 & 31;
Jan 1
Must book
L only, 12–3

Alc (min £1) £6·25 (meal
£9·45)

Cover 35p
Children's helpings
(under 11)
Seats 120
♿ rest (side entrance);
w.c.
Air-conditioning
No dogs

The best news about Tom Machen's 'light, airy, relaxed and informal' lunchtime restaurant in the Rex Whistler room of the Tate Gallery is also the reason for its appearance in italics this year: the chef changed in September and the food appeared to improve. Earlier, though most meals, including a test one, displayed some good or imaginative things, much was intolerable, especially at the price. Again, several people have had dry salmon, either hot or cold. 'Soft cauliflower in vinegar does not make a first course.' So is all now well once again for the wine-lovers who throng this place for the sake of the best-bought, best-priced bottles in London, set off by 'English historical' food? Well, a previous chef, Michael Driver, has returned, and later, 'poached salmon trout was not dry at all', 'a chunky terrine, yoghourt and cucumber soup, veal kidneys in puff pastry, and profiteroles were all well up to standard,' and so far, so reassuring. But it will be a pity if Mr Driver simply takes up where he left off. As an inspector remarks, 'Some of the recipes belong to a time when the flavour of meat was much stronger than it is now, and the wild honeys used were less sweet than refined sugar.' In other words, some dishes have always made odd partners for Grands Echézeaux (domaine-bottled at Romanée-Conti) '73 at £7·80, or château-bottled Ch. Meyney '61 at £6·50 or Ch. Lagrange '67 in magnum at £8·30. White wines, though not quite as good, are headed by Le Montrachet '72 (domaine Jacques Prieur) at £10·95, and the sweet Ch. Lafaurie-Peyraguey '66 or '69 at £2·80 is about half what many restaurants would charge for a half-bottle. Ports begin (in age, not price) with Graham '24, madeiras with Solera Malmsey 1808. The house wines are a '72 claret at £2·30 and Mâcon Villages '75 at £2·30, and various wine critics now have a page on the list on which to nominate their own favourites. No music. If you want a non-smoking table, mention it when you book and help the charming, competent and considerate waitresses to enforce the restriction where it applies. More reports, please.

Unless otherwise stated, a restaurant is open all week
and all year and is licensed.

The Guide accepts no advertising. Nor does it allow restaurateurs to use
its name on brochures, menus, or in any form of advertisement. If you
see any instances of this, please report them to us.

Numbers are given for private parties only if they can be accommodated
in a room separate from the main dining-room; when there are several such
rooms, the capacity of the largest is given. Some restaurants will take
party bookings at times when they are normally closed.

THROGMORTON RESTAURANT
OAK ROOM Map 12

27 Throgmorton Street,
E.C.2
01-588 5165

Handy for the Stock Exchange and the Bank, and as solid as either, after 78 years, this oak-panelled Lyons' basement 'down splendid marble stairs', has motherly waitresses, a simple menu and modest prices, 'every hour on the hour' at lunch-time. Regulars – and others – enjoy the generously served thick roast beef and trimmings (£2·45), roast pork (£1·75) or steak and kidney pie (£1·80). Soup, vegetables and cheeses are uninspired. Bertorelli ices. Spanish house wine is £2·65 the bottle. Bar snacks and IPA from the cask in the Bar Sinister. No music, Wear a jacket and tie (pin-stripes are nice).

Closed D; Sat; Sun; public hols	Tdh £2·30 (meal £4·50)	Seats 370
	Alc (min £1·40) £3·75	Air-conditioning
Must book	(meal £6·10)	No dogs
L only, 11.45–3		Access, Am Ex, Barclay,
(Mon–Fri)	VAT inc	Diners, Euro
	Cover 20p	

TONINO'S Map 12

12 Glentworth Street,
N.W.1
01-935 4220

Closed Sun; public hols
Must book
Meals 12–2.45, 6.30–11.15

Alc £5·20 (meal £9·50)

Service 12½%
Cover 35p
Seats 35 (parties 27)
No dogs
Am Ex, Barclay, Diners

Antonio Valeri's little room near Baker Street tube '*looks* like a restaurant' with its tiled floor, oil paintings, red cloths and white china: 'You get a sense of high morale, confirmed by the freshness of the prawns on the hors d'oeuvre trolley and the fruit dishes on the sweets one. The home-made fettuccine, fresh from copper saucepan to soup plate, is creamy, cheesy, and truly delicious', and at a test meal scampi Casanova (£3·90) and veal al limone were also cooked with a light touch. Spinach was 'fresh, buttery, and nutmeggy'. Pasquale Triunfo's spaghetti al cartoccio is also worth trying. Sweets, apart from strawberries Romanoff perhaps, are less remarkable. Service can be slow but is 'anxious to please, and good at picking up the mood of an evening's customers'. Wines begin at £2·70 for Valpolicella or Soave.

App: Jonas Kristjansson, R.S., A. Ross, J.J.S.W.

LA TOQUE BLANCHE Map 13

21 Abingdon Road, W.8
01-937 5832

Closed Sat; Sun; Aug;
public hols; Dec 24 & 31
Must book D
Meals 12.30–1.45, 7–10.45

M Giovagnoli's small, crowded, but skilfully laid-out and formally decorated restaurant derives at least half its reputation from the courteous professionalism of the service. Yet the cooking, too, has claimed its place here for the best part of a generation, and this year is no exception to judge by accounts of 'rich and substantial' soupe de poissons with the usual

Alc £6·80 (meal £10·50)

VAT inc
Cover 40p
Seats 40
♿ rest
No dogs
Am Ex, Diners

trimmings, competent – but at a test meal, not hot enough – crêpes aux fruits de mer (£3), entrecôte bourguignonne cooked precisely as requested, ballotine de volaille with good spinach (though 'rather so-so haricots verts'), generally admired langoustines, or truites flambées; good salads and, for London, exceptionally good French cheeses. If you must have a sweet, sorbet au cassis or a hot pancake is probably the wisest choice. Wines begin at £3·60, and they will serve a glass as an aperitif; the older Bordeaux or burgundies at much longer prices are usually decanted. But before you order one, reflect that 'at least half the customers smoke.' (Lunch is calmer.) 'Quiet' recorded music.

App: R. H. Williams, Christopher Forman, I.M., A.M., K. W. Daley, and others

UNCLE PANG Map 12

30 Temple Fortune
Parade,
Finchley Road, N.W.11
01-455 9444 *and*
458 3558

Closed Dec 24, 25 & 26
Must book
Meals 12–2.30, 6–11

Alc meal £4·25

Service 10%
Seats 60
♿ rest; w.c.
Air-conditioning
No dogs
Am Ex, Barclay, Diners

Hunger pangs are easily satisfied at bonhomous Mr Pang's, for the cooking in this quite chic restaurant is rich by Cantonese standards. The keynote dish is perhaps the interesting speciality 'deep-fried boned duck plastered with minced king prawn' (£2·80). The chicken roll (£1·20) also needs a strong digestion. But there are other and perhaps better ideas: 'very pretty' stir-fried squid with 'crunchy haricots verts of dazzling brightness'; spare ribs with plum sauce (though the barbecued version is also a good one); 'interesting things with bean curd'; and 'fatty, coarse-grained, but tender flank of beef casseroled in a gravy pregnant with the spice called "five fragrances"'. Crab with ginger and spring onion (£3·30), or steamed fish, should also be considered. Fried chicken in lemon sauce was poorly cooked when tried, 'memorable only for a tomato-coloured lemon slice garnish'. Service is 'unusually earnest', and gives you a choice of bowls or plates. The sweets are standard, and one visitor substituted for them one of the exotic cocktails: Chinese Passion (gin, brandy, passion-fruit juice, ice and a lime wedge, £1·40). More reports, please, especially because a second branch opened as we went to press: Pangs, 215 Sutherland Avenue, W.9 (tel. 01-289 0970).

PLEASE keep sending in reports, as soon as possible after each meal. Closing date for the 1980 Guide is 30th September 1979, but reports are even more useful earlier in the year, especially for the remoter areas and new places.

Do not risk using an out-of-date Guide. A new edition will be published early in 1980.

Wine prices shown are for a 'standard' bottle of the wine concerned, unless another measure is stated.

UPPER CRUST Map 14

9 William Street, S.W.1
01-235 8444

'Where else in Belgravia can you eat for under £5 (just) and eat English?' . . . 'Where else can you eat three courses composed entirely of Yorkshire pudding?' Sit downstairs (quieter – no music) at this 'rustic-modern' pie-shop (the turkey, celery and cranberry is a good one). Kedgeree, though inauthentic, is tasty, and pickled brisket or bangers and mash arouse nostalgia. The cover charge includes excellent bread and butter and variable vegetables. House red burgundy is 'drinkable' – a pity they keep no ale or cider.

Closed Dec 25 & 26
Must book
Meals 11.30–3, 6–11.15

Alc (min £1·95) £4·60
(meal £7)

Cover 60p
VAT inc
Service 10%
Seats 85 (parties 40)
 ⅃ rest (1 step)

Air-conditioning
No dogs
Access, Am Ex, Barclay, Diners

VALCHERA'S Map 13

30 The Quadrant,
Richmond, Surrey
01-940 0648

'Still the Edwardian touch' with gold patterned walls, old-fashioned glass and mirrors, starched linen, and heavy, plated cruets. The waiters bustle ('avuncular verging on snappish'), but get the food hot to table. On a long menu, people like the minestrone, fresh sardines, osso buco (£2·25), scaloppine alla Marsala (£2) and tournedos Rossini. Doubters mention 'curry-hot' ratatouille, dull and rather fatty veal chop rosemary (£2·20) and the mashed potato (though cauliflower, spinach and haricots verts are sometimes sensitively cooked). Monte Bianco comes with strawberries and almonds (95p) and pineapple is well sprinkled with kirsch. House Italian wine £3·10 the litre. No music.

Closed Sun; public hols
Must book
Meals 12.15–2.30,
6.30–10.30

Tdh L about £2·20 (meal £4·70)
Alc £5·40 (meal £8·90)

Cover L 25p, D 30p

Children's helpings (under 12)
Seats 75 (parties 35)
 ⅃ rest
Access, Barclay, Diners

VASCO AND PIERO'S PAVILION Map 15

Poland Street/Oxford
Street, W.1
01-437 8774

Closed Sun; Sat L;
Dec 25–Jan 1; public hols
Must book L
Meals 12–3, 6–11

Hungry film-goers need only climb the stairs to find this 'utterly congenial' blue-and-gold pavilion above the Academy Cinema, although Vasco and Piero draw their net among a wider public. The welcome is decorously warm and even the restaurant cat, playing a supporting role on occasion, seems fastidiously well bred. The cooking is consistently careful. The tenerelli stuffed with spinach and ricotta (£1) are good enough for a main course in

Alc £6 (meal £8·70)

VAT inc
Cover 40p
Children's helpings
Seats 45
No dogs
Access, Am Ex, Barclay,
Diners

one visitor's eyes, and the aubergine parmigiana (£1) is tasty if not quite cheesy enough for some. Pasta-lovers note the seafood lasagne and taglierini con crema e funghi, and among main dishes, the grilled veal chops and kidneys piccanti (£2·50) are both steady box-office draws. A test meal also produced turbot in a good wine and cream sauce (£3·60), and a slightly sharp chicken with lemon and sage (£2·20). The zuppa inglese is properly italiana, light and alcoholic, with cream, chocolate, and egg custard, and two visitors who dislike tinned peaches were delighted to find fresh ones used with Amaretti and zabaglione sauce. The list of Italian wines is short but interesting and their advice about the less familiar names is worth listening to. A recommended Ghemme '72 at £5 was so memorable that the recipient intends to try the '61 at £8 next time. The house Montepulciano and Trebbiano are £2·20 for a half-litre carafe. Good and unlimited coffee is 35p. A classical guitarist plays in the evening.

App: G.C., Michael Copp, J.C., Jane Moore, A.H.

VILLA BIANCA   Map 12

1 Perrins Court, N.W.3
01-435 3131

Ferrari and Costa's chic trattoria near the Ham and High has bowed to its critics and turned its upstairs restaurant into a bar. More leisure for chefs and waiters has done everyone good, it seems. Parma ham and melon, scampi in tomato and cream sauce, rigatoni with shellfish, chicken provinciale, 'saltimbocca alla romana and pollo sorpresa always well done', and crisply fried zucchini, all give pleasure. Uccelletti Perrins Court (chopped steak with port and walnuts) is also admired. Strawberries or chocolate gateau seem the most popular sweets. 'Tables are close and they like a quick turnover but it was not all that noisy.' Chianti Straccali is £2·60.

Closed L (most public hols)
Must book
Meals 12–2.30, 6.30–11.30

Alc (min £3) £6·50
(meal £9·80)

VAT inc
Service 12½%
Cover 50p

Children's helpings (Sun)
Seats 65 (parties 28)
Air-conditioning
No dogs
Access, Am Ex, Barclay,
Diners, Euro

WALTONS   Map 14

121 Walton Street, S.W.3
01-584 0204

Closed Sun D; Dec 24;
public hols
Must book D
Meals 12.30–2.30,
7.30–11.30

'Softly, softly, catchee monkey' has always been the PR approach of this mirrored, primrose-and-grey silk restaurant (designed by Michael Smith). Only the hard-hearted will resist the blandishments of a young chef (Murdo MacSween) 'discovered by Egon Ronay cooking in a residential home for the elderly in Ayrshire', or find fault with the 'bland three-fish mousse' that one inspector criticises, for previous

Tdh L £5·50 (meal £9·45), D from £9 (meal £18·15)

Service 15%
Seats 60 (parties 10)
Air-conditioning
No dogs
Am Ex, Barclay, Diners

chefs, too, affected the London-clinical style of cooking, with unexpectedly sharp stabs of the English 18th century ('vinegary pickled walnuts did nothing for the madeira sauce with collops in the pan'). Anyway, Ayrshire OAPs' loss is Hampstead Garden Suburb's gain, for since the change of management that automatically took Walton's out of the *Guide* last time, standards have been well maintained, at both set and à la carte meals. Soups are excellent, whether the cream of celery or cauliflower at lunch, or the chilled Stilton with walnuts that is a second-course option in the four-course dinner (priced by the main course). Spinach pâté, and vegetable tartlet – 'crisp and frilly short pastry with a filling of fresh vegetables in good mayonnaise' – are successful hors d'oeuvre, along with the good bread, butter and house-traditional sandwiches of pumpernickel and cream cheese, coloured to resemble liquorice allsorts. 'Quenelles of carp were barely tethered to the plate, and the lobster sauce with them was delicate.' Rack of lamb and beef Wellington (for two) are deservedly popular dishes; porc aux pruneaux is classically cooked, and vegetables at a test meal could hardly be improved ('very dark green cabbage, excellent peas à la française, and new potatoes with bacon, served on heated side-plates'). Vacherins are variable, sorbets more consistent, coffee excellent. The house wines, at £4·25, come from the Rhône, the Loire, the Rhine, Bordeaux and Champagne, and though there are prohibitive wines listed, from a run of Ch. Pétrus to '45 Ch. d'Yquem at £80, there is good drinking at £10 or so: Meursault Goutte d'Or '76 (Abel Garnier); Ch. Meyney '67; Ch. Climens '70. Warre '60 port is £1·75 the glass. Service is attentive and good. No music – and no dress rules, to give them credit.

App: John Rowlands, N.S., A.T.H., I.C., and others

WARUNG JAVA TIMUR   Map 12

---

45 Praed Street, W.2
01-402 6492

Mrs Chaudhry's 'Halal Javanese' place has no more outward charm than the most run-of-the-mill fish and chip shop, but in thirty years as a Londoner she has not forgotten how to cook sate ayam or kambing (chicken, 97p, or lamb, £1·08), bakmie ayam (fried chicken noodles, 92p), 'coconutty' kare ayam, and a 'rice mixture' called nasi rames (£1·19). A peanutty and chilli-hot salad makes a useful contrast. Skip sweets. Take-away service. Unlicensed; 'no alcohol on premises.'

Closed Wed; some
Moslem hols
No bookings
Open noon–6.45 p.m.

Alc meal £3

VAT inc
Children's helpings

Seats 30
No dogs
Unlicensed
No cheques

WEI HAI WEI· Map 13

7 The Broadway,
White Hart Lane,
S.W.13
01-876 1165

Decor and lighting discourage lingering, which may help to explain the popular take-away service, but the Pekinese banquets on the spot are sound for the price, according to a test and other meals that yielded good dried seaweed, rather bland spare ribs and soup, good crispy duck or pork with pancakes, 'rather sweet sweet-sour pork and rather salt chicken and cashew nuts', and 'woolly toffee apples with excellent batter', all served very hot on clean tables. Hirondelle £2·50.

Closed L (Mon–Thur);
Dec 25 & 26; Jan 1
Must book weekends

Meals 12.15–2.30,
6.15–11.15

Alc meal £3·90

Service 10%
Seats 40
♿ rest
No dogs

WILLIAM F Map 14

140 Fulham Road, S.W.10
01-373 5534

Closed L; Sun; 5 days Chr
Must book
D only, 6.30–11.30

Alc £5 (meal £7·15)

VAT inc
Seats 36
♿ rest (1 step)

William F(uller) cooks, with Anthony Jones, in this loose-box bistro, and several good and regular judges have thought the place a cut above last year's short entry, quite apart from glimpses of a famous actor supping full – not with horrors, but with croustade de lotte thermidor (95p) and selle de chevreuil en papillote (£3·75). The bread, délice d'avocat, courgettes à la farce de lièvre, noisettes d'agneau béarnaise (£2·45), and paupiettes de porc dijonnaise, are also reported with pleasure; pork mousse with figs may be too bland or sweet for some. The 'wickedly rich' chocolate fudge, or cake soaked in cognac, may be the best sweets, unless orange and grapefruit salad with cinnamon seems advisable. Touraine red or Côtes de Duras Sauvignon are £3·15.

App: Lauretta Harris, P. & K.H., James Collins, H.W.

WOLFE'S Map 15

34 Park Lane, W.1
01-499 6897

Plushy – almost staid – hamburger restaurant near Hyde Park Corner. The high quality of beef in the 'wolfburgers' (6 oz, £1·45, with the usual relishes, salads and bun) may surprise visiting Texans. Try potato pancakes ('fried crisp, really tasty') with apple sauce are a treat, too, and there are plain steaks, soles, and even egg and chips ('child's platter', 75p). Skip sweets. No wine under £3·50 (85p the large glass). Friendly service. Subdued pop music.

Closed Dec 25 & 26
Open 11.30 a.m.–
midnight

Alc £3·10 (meal £4·95)

VAT inc
Seats 60
♿ rest (1 step)

Air-conditioning
No dogs
Access, Am Ex, Barclay,
Diners, Euro

LONDON PUBS AND WINE BARS

BAKER AND OVEN   Map 12

10 Paddington Street,
W.1
01-935 5072
12–3
Closed D; weekends;
public hols

'Cheering, intelligently decorated' lunchtime cellar
wine bar attached to a pub/restaurant. 'Strong on
soups, goulash, steak and kidney pies', with other
nominations for quiches and mousses (smoked trout),
as well as 'excellent French bread and good coffee'.
Spanish house wine, £2·25 the carafe, 45p the 5 oz
glass. Blanc de Loire (Stodart & Taylor) £2·55. Port
and sherry. Other drinks from the ground-floor pub.
No music. Five outside tables.

BALLS BROTHERS   Map 12

142 Strand, W.C.2
01-836 0156
11–3, 5.30–7.30
Closed weekends; public
hols

A rather pubby wine bar (part of a City chain) with
restaurant attached. Simple, competent,
unambitious food at lunch, and till 7.30 for
pre-theatre snacks: ham on the bone (£1·65 with
salad), roast beef (£1·50), pâté (85p), veal, ham and
egg pie (85p) and sandwiches made freshly to order,
as well as a daily hot dish ('Italian-tasting' rigatoni,
85p) and healthy cheeses. Interesting wines: try the
Bow Lane Reserve Amontillado (40p) or Sercial
madeira (35p), before enticing bottles or halves (Ch.
Cos Labory '67, £4·70; Oppenheimer Krotenbrunnen
Spätlese '76, £4·70). No opinions on downstairs
restaurant (lunch only, 12–3). No music.

BOOS   Map 12

1 Glentworth Street,
N.W.1
01-935 3827
11–3, 5.30–8
Closed weekends;
2 weeks Sept

The Roses have taken over Michael Gould's wine
bar, 'but the quiet style is the same (at least in the
evening) and they have developed the faintly Pall
Mall atmosphere.' A dozen sandwiches on brown
bread (from 40p) are impressive ('unmistakably
home-cooked ham'), and there are also pâté, quiche,
taramosalata and cheeses. Cheesecake 'even better
than my mother's' (35p), and Rombouts coffee.
Good aperitifs (Palo Cortado 55p, Gaudin Chambéry
35p); house wines by glass, half-litre or bottle
(Rhône Domaine de la Borie, 50p); several
interesting bottles: Ch. La Lagune '70, £4·95;
Beaune Les Marconnets '72 (Albert Morot), £5·85.
No music. No dogs.

Hours given are opening times. Food may not be served over the whole period.

Wine bars are represented by a wine glass on the maps, pubs by a tankard.

BRAHMS AND LISZT   Map 15

19 Russell Street, W.C.2
01-240 3661
11.30–3, 5.30–11
Closed Sun; public hols

Wine liszt on tables, menu on blackboard and optional waitress service (10% if you take the option) at this trendy, two-floor Covent Garden place, throbbing with 'jazz/funk specially imported from America'. Quiche and salad at £1·50 sounds dear but ingredients are sound, presentation thoughtful. Other choices might be tuna fish mousse (hot or cold), crudités, meat-loaf and salad, and in winter hot dishes such as bobotie or teriyaki. The fresh pineapple Pavlova is still a winner. A few unexceptional wines by the glass, thirty bottles from £2·40 (Blanc de Blancs). Sherry, madeira, port. A few tables outside.

BRAYS PLACE   Map 14

198 Fulham Road, S.W.10
01-352 0251
11–3, 5.30–11
(Sun 7–10.30)

'On that lively piece of Fulham Road that masquerades as Chelsea', Judy Bray's buzzing, overheated bar offers a couple of hot dishes (smoked haddock kedgeree, turkey Stroganoff), all £1·30, as well as various salads, pâtés, pies and cheeses. To say nothing of Kinsale oysters at 50p each, £2 the half-dozen. Unambitious wines by glass, half-pint or bottle (Valpolicella, £2·55 the bottle, 52p the glass); house claret £2·40. They cater for film and TV crews – bad luck if their location is your local.

COATES   Map 12

(1) 109 Old Broad Street, E.C.2
01-588 5138
11.30–3, 5.30–7
Closed weekends; public hols

(2) 45 London Wall, E.C.2
01-628 5861
11.30–3, 5–7
Closed weekends; public hols

With a single exception, the food (lunch only) in these two City pinstripers' bars (not far away from each other) has to be regarded as a vehicle for the excellent Corney & Barrow wines, which can all (or nearly all) be drunk here at a modest corkage charge. The exception is the fruit cake ('chock-a-block with currants') at the Old Broad Street branch, which goes beautifully with a glass of tawny port or Bual madeira. Table wines by the glass vary from week to week. The smoked fish, roast joints, and bread or baked potato are adequate, no more. Often standing room only.

CORK AND BOTTLE   Map 15

44–46 Cranbourn Street, W.C.2
01-734 7807
11–3, 5.30–11
Closed Sun; public hols

The Hewitsons' understandably popular basement bar – now with an offshoot in W.1 (Shampers, q.v.) – still provides shoppers and theatre-goers with well-thought-out bar food and well-chosen wine at fair prices: mushrooms provençale (65p) are fresh-tasting and good, salads are crisp and wholesome ('they are not afraid of caraway and other marked flavours'), meat-loaf with tomato sauce seems 'just like mother's'. Blackboard wine list: a dozen or so by the glass (65p–75p) and three special lists – German, bin-ends and champagnes (see Shampers). Classical guitarist at night.

CORTS   Map 12

84–86 Chancery Lane,
W.C.2
01-405 3349
11–3, 5.30–8
Closed weekends;
public hols

'A dark green room full of City men', where it is wise to book even for a snack lunch (12–3). 'Limited menu, typical wine bar stuff, competently done': potted shrimps (95p), soup (40p), various quiches and pies, 'good, underdone roast beef' (£1·50), a few hot dishes, cakes and cheeses. 'Good coffee and bread.' Wine by the glass from 45p (£2·30 the bottle). Various others in bottle (no halves) and sherry, port and madeira by glass (45p) or double (90p). 'Efficient and amiable service.' (Reports welcome on the Old Bailey branch too.)

CROWN   Map 12

Aberdeen Place, N.W.8
01-289 1102
11–3, 5.30–11

Marble walls and plaster ceilings in this large, imposing pub, known as Crocker's Folly because Mr Crocker built it in the 19th century in the vain hope that Marylebone station would be sited there. Unobtrusive live pop music in one bar. Bar snacks (exc Sun): choice of pâté, cold meats, rolls, cheesecake; home-made flans at lunch-time. Fuller's London Pride, Samuel Smith's bitter, Bass, and others (pump). Wine. Juke-box; fruit machine; bar billiards; darts. Tables outside.

CROWN & SCEPTRE   Map 15

86 Great Tichfield Street,
W.1
01-636 7940
11–3, 5.30–11

A Bass Charrington pub, with blue velvet banquettes, etched glass, and almost enough space for its many BBC and garment-trade regulars. Daily hot dishes often include shepherd's pie and baked beans 85p, carbonnade of beef with vegetables 95p, chicken and mushroom pie 95p. Also quiches, cheeses (nice sesame bread), pork pies and salads. Bass and IPA on hand-pump. Wine. Blackthorn cider. Juke-box; fruit machine; darts. Seats on the pavement in summer.

DAVY'S WINE BARS

Boot and Flogger
(Map 16)
10–20 Redcross Way,
S.E.1
01-407 1184
11–3, 5.30–8.30
Closed weekends;
public hols

Bottlescrue (Map 12)
Bath House,
Holborn Viaduct, E.C.1
01-248 2157
11.30–3, 5–8
Closed weekends;
public hols

Most of the Davy's wine bars have at least one friend among our reprobate members, for as people are not slow to point out, where else in London can you stroll at half-past two in the afternoon into an elementary but flavoury wood-and-candle setting and order a bottle of fine burgundy or claret at not too much over retail price, and eat with it something sound (if cold and predictable): a dish of prawns or smoked fish, a plate of rare beef or competent (not inspired) game pie, or a generous helping of Brie or Stilton? This account is slightly sentimentalised, for the menu in most of the bars is in fact boringly limited, and hardly changes from year to year, while excursions into fripperies such as trifle or coffee are generally inadvisable. Nor do all the bars reliably offer food to be had in the early evening,

**Davy's Wine Vaults
(Map 16)**
165 Greenwich High
Road, S.E.10
01-858 7204
11.30–3, 5.30–10.30
(Fri 11; Sat 12–3, 7–11)
Closed Sun; public hols

when theatre-goers and marriage-rockers might
welcome it. But the Boot and Flogger, for example,
offers a choice between Savigny-les-Beaune '73
(Bouchard Père et Fils £5·60) and Ch. Malescot-St
Exupéry '71 (£6·30) and dozens of others, large
glasses of mostly well-chosen house wines at 65p,
sherries and madeiras at 50p, and about a hundred
legendary ports for decanting, going back to Taylor
'70 (1870) at £95 or '12 at £28, or a half-bottle of
Fonseca '60 at £6·50 if you don't dare spend the
house-keeping. No music.

Grapeshots (Map 12)
2/3 Artillery Passage, E.1
01-247 8215
11–2.30, 5–7
Closed weekends;
public hols

Gyngleboy (Map 12)
27 Spring Street, W.2
01-723 3351
11–3, 5.30–10.30
Closed weekends;
public hols

Skinkers (Map 16)
40–42 Tooley Street, S.E.1
01-407 9189
11–3, 5–8.30
Closed weekends;
public hols

EBURY WINE BAR   Map 14

139 Ebury Street, S.W.1
01-730 5447
11–3, 5.30–11
(Sun 12–2.30, 7–10.30)
Closed 4 days Chr

Popular bar (book for meals on weekdays) near
Victoria coach station and air terminal. You perch
on bar stools or sit at table, in 'dark wood
surroundings'. Longish menu of soups, smoked fish,
two daily casseroles or other hot dishes (from £2·30
with veg), 'delicious spinach quiche', grills, salads,
'well-prepared and displayed cold table' (about £1·70).
'Impressive' wine list plus blackboard items, and
monthly 'special offer' on champagne. House red is
45p the glass, eleven others around 50p–60p, forty
sensibly chosen bottles, including Pilton Manor '76.
Sherry, port, four madeiras, Chambéry, Kir.
Children allowed in restaurant area at evenings and
weekends. Booking necessary for the restaurant.
Live music at night. (Reports also welcome on their
newest venture, Draycotts, at 114 Draycott Avenue,
S.W.3.)

FIVE LAMPS   Map 12

3 St Katherine's Row,
E.C.3
01-488 1587
11.30–3, 5.30–7.30
Closed weekends;
public hols

From Crutched Friars, look for French Ordinary
Court, or from Fenchurch Street, look for St Olave's
church, to find Mr Valente's dark, crowded cellar
where you book and sit down, or eat round the walls
off wine-cases and barrels (food 12–3 only). Cold
buffet – from £1·25 for smoked chicken to £2·50 for
smoked salmon, with 'rather vinegary' seafood St
Laurent, salads (40p), jacket potato (30p), cheese,
trifle. Mainly Corney & Barrow wines: not many by
the glass (house red is Côte de Blaye, white Blanc
de Blancs) but good bottles: 'Ch. Rauly '73 a
big-nosed Bergerac.' Sherry 40p, port 45p (80p for
'63 Croft). No music.

See p. 441 for 'How to use the pub section'.

FLASK   Map 12

Flask Walk, N.W.3
(off Hampstead High
Street)
01-435 4580
11–3, 5.30–11

Handsome and popular old pub, with a 'basic'
public and a more comfortable saloon bar. 'Chips
with everything' at lunch-time – and what chips –
'best in the country,' claims a Northern expert.
Sandwiches in the evening; home-made sausage rolls
Sat L; no food Sun. Young's mild, bitter and special
(pump), Winter Warmer from the cask. Wine.
Dominoes. Patio.

FREEMASONS ARMS   Map 12

32 Downshire Hill, N.W.3
01-435 4498
11–3, 5.30–11

Large 1930s pub on the edge of Hampstead Heath.
Snacks (12–2.30, 5.30–10, exc Sun D) and hot dishes
(Mon–Fri 12.30–2) at the Buttery Bar: home-made
ham and veal pie 85p, cheese and potato pie 75p,
curry £1, salads, sausages, ploughman's. Bass and
Charrington Crown bitter (pump); others pressurised.
Wine. Fruit machine; pool table; darts; Old English
skittles. Garden and forecourt.

JIMMIE'S   Map 13

Kensington Palace
Barracks,
Kensington Church
Street, W.8
01-937 9988
12–3, 5.30–11
(Sun 12–2, 7–10.30)
Closed Dec 25 & 26

'Terribly English in a debby and barracksy way' –
a cheerful, dark, ramshackle place where the main
snag is the semi-self-service ('hard work at night
when it's crowded'). Huge steaks and chops
(£1·55–£2·60), sausages and hamburgers – all
displayed impressively while they wait, and then
charcoal-grilled. Daily roast joint (£1·30, including
vegetables), cheeses, approximate Bakewell tart.
House wine is 35p the glass (40p at night), four
others, and sparklers at 60p. About thirty bottles,
£2·40–£7·20, and a few 'fine wines'. Folk or modern
music live at night.

JUST WILLIAMS   Map 13

6a Battersea Rise,
S.W.11
01-223 6890
12–3, 5.30–11
(Sun 12–2, 7–10.30)
Closed Dec 25, 26, 27 &
28; Jan 1

'Rather basic, sometimes draughty' corner spot near
Clapham Common, with five backgammon boards,
hot port, and live guitarists or singers for trendies.
Pleasant service of blackboard food: chicken à la
crème, seafood crêpes, liver provençale (all with rice
or potatoes, salad or vegetable, £1·50), various
salads, pâtés and cheeses; 'nice squidgy chocolate
cake'. About forty wines, many by the glass: house
wine (43p); Côtes de Provence (63p); Chianti Classico
(55p). List lacks vintages. Guitarists on Tue and
Fri evenings; pop tapes otherwise. Tables on the
terrace.

The Guide News Supplement will be sent out as usual, in June, to everyone
who buys the book directly from the Consumers' Association and to all
bookshop purchasers who return the card interleaved with their copy. Let
us know of any changes that affect entries in the book, or of any new places
you think should be looked at.

LAMB AND FLAG   Map 15

33 Rose Street, W.C.2
(off Garrick Street)
01-836 4108
11–3, 5.30–11

Licensed in the reign of Elizabeth I and later frequented by the likes of Dryden and Dickens; in a small, cobbled, gas-lit alley. Bar food at all times: home-made game pie with salads £1, fourteen English cheeses 50p–75p, variety of pâtés, including one home-made; hot daily dishes such as Kentish pie and Exeter stew. Courage Directors (pump); others pressurised. Wine. Darts. Drinking outside.

LOOSE BOX   Map 14

136 Brompton Road,
S.W.3
01-584 9280
12–3, 5.30–11
Closed Sun; Easter; Chr

Spacious and pleasant Searcy's wine bar on several floors, opposite Harrods. Stalls and counters, and some more elegant ground-floor tables, with buffet food, both hot and cold: casseroles, sausage and mash, quiches, salmon, turkey, salads, and good cheeses ('heavenly runny Brie') with decent French bread. A dozen wines by the glass (from 32p for Spanish red), ports and sherries and various reliable bottles: La Borie, n.v., £2·10; Chorey les Beaune '73, £5·50. Roof garden for summer fun. No music. 'Customers and staff quite Sloane Ranger, apart from the barker who gets rid of you at closing time.'

MOTCOMBS   Map 14

26 Motcomb Street,
S.W.1
01-235 6382
12–3, 5.30–11 (Sat 6–11)
Closed Sun

Smart decor and clientele in this plush restaurant/wine bar – 'if you eat a full meal, you're certainly reminded by the bill that you're dining in Belgravia.' Stay at ground level, then, for snacks (pâtés, quiches, cheeses, crisp salads) and ungreedily priced wines (chosen by Harry Waugh): Bordeaux or burgundy at £3 the bottle, 50p the glass; Dão red, £3·95; Sancerre '76 (Moreux-Tissier), £5·65. Various aperitifs, port and Buck's Fizz (60p). Live music in the restaurant.

ORANGE TREE   Map 13

45 Kew Road, Richmond,
Surrey
01-940 0944
10.30–2.30, 5.30–10.30
(11 Fri, Sat)

Crowds of people from all walks of life and ages in this Edwardian-type pub, with its own theatre. Self-service food in the cellar bar (12.15–2.15, 6–10; 6–8 Sat): salads with pork chops £1·40, lasagne £1·30, beef in beer £1·40, lamb and aubergine curry £1·30. Menu changes daily. Three-course L £1·40, D £1·60. Young's bitter, special bitter, mild and Winter Warmer (pump). Wine. Darts. Tables on forecourt.

Hours given are opening times. Food may not be served over the whole period.

Inspections are carried out anonymously. Persons who pretend to be able to secure, arrange or prevent an entry in the Guide are impostors and their names or descriptions should be reported to us.

PLANTHOUSE   Map 15

10 Old Compton Street,
W.1
01-734 3748
11.30–3, 5.30–10.30
Closed Sat L; Sun;
public hols

Light and leafy basement wine bar beneath – and
owned by – Trattoria Bacco 70. Limited menu:
pâtés, cheeses, ham, and various salads; occasional
hot dishes (braised chicken in a tomato sauce, £1·20;
stuffed aubergines or courgettes, 75p). House wine
40p the glass, £2·20 the bottle. Various other bottles
(sadly, no halves): Barbera £3·10, Pinot Grigio £3·25.
Service 'scatty but pleasant'.

PRINCESS LOUISE   Map 12

208 High Holborn, W.C.1
01-405 8816
11–3, 5.30–11
(Sat 6.30)

Large horseshoe bar on the ground floor serving
lunchtime bar snacks (Mon–Fri only; 12p–70p):
sausages, pasties, pizza, curry, pâté, cheese. Apples
and Pears wine bar on the first floor has wider
choice, including Danish sandwiches, soup,
cheesecake and salads. Fuller's ESB, Brakspear's
bitter and special bitter, Ruddle's bitter and County
ale, Samuel Smith's bitter, Courage Directors,
Young's special bitter (pump). Wine. Fruit machine.

RUSSKIES WINE CELLAR   Map 13

6 Wellington Terrace,
Bayswater Road, W.2
01-229 9128
11.30–3, 5.30–11
(Sun 7–10.30)
Closed Sun L;
Dec 25 & 26

Basement opposite 'Millionaire's Row' with languid
service and room to relax among the Edwardian
clutter. Food is 'passable' only – homey soups,
variable quiches, middling-to-good pâtés, crisp
salads, dull gateaux. Hot dish is micro-waved daily.
Main interest is in the wines (though the list could
be better annotated) with Tres Torres (45p the
glass, £2·60 the bottle) and Australian Rejina
Riesling (40p, £2·30) among the house offerings, a
good choice of other Australian bottles at around £4,
and even a fizzy Russian at £6. Soft jazz.

SHAMPERS   Map 15

4 Kingly Street, W.1
01-437 1692
11–3, 5.30–11
Closed Sun; Sat D;
public hols

New offshoot of the Cork and Bottle (q.v.) sharing
its bar menu and wine list, but offering waitress
service in the basement – mainly casseroles:
chicken in champagne, navarin of lamb, pork in
barbecue sauce. Salads are unusually fresh and
wholesome, sweets mediocre. Champagne comes at
£5·50 the bottle (Perrier Jouet), £1 the *flute* (6 oz),
and in various concoctions (with framboise, with
cassis . . .) at around 68p. Other wines about 75p.
Port, sherry. 'No-smoking' sign near the counter.

THATCHED HOUSE   Map 13

115 Dalling Road, W.6
01-748 6174
11–3, 5.30–11

Not a blade of thatch in sight. A well-run, homely
pub which often gets crowded. Bar lunches (exc
Sun): lamb cutlets, pork chops, gammon, scampi,
plaice, cod. 'Superb' sandwiches and rolls at all
times. Young's bitter, special bitter and Winter
Warmer (pump). Wine. Fruit machine; darts;
cribbage; dominoes. Tables outside.

THROGMORTON RESTAURANT   Map 12

See main *Guide*

WHITE SWAN   Map 3

Riverside
Twickenham, Middx
01-892 2166
10.30–2.30, 5.30–10.30
(11 Fri, Sat)

A 'pubby pub' with open fires, and some food 'up to French standards' – moules marinière rather than haggis, presumably? Usual pâtés, smoked fish, steak and kidney pudding, as well as hummus with pitta, fish pie (90p) and 'an occasional pud'. (No food Sun L exc tdh, £2). Sandwiches in the evening, to order. Watney's pressurised beers; fined bitter (pump). Wine. Children. Fruit machine; darts; cards; dominoes. Outside gents'.

Restaurants, pubs and wine bars open on Sunday

Anarkali, W6
Arirang, W1 (D)
Ark, W8 (D)
Arlecchino, W8 (summer)
Aziz, W6
La Baita, NW3
Bangkok, SW7
Bloom's, E1
La Brasserie, SW7
Brays Place, SW10 (D)
Capability Brown, NW6 (L)
Capital Hotel Restaurant, SW3
Carlo's Place, SW6 (D)
Carlton Tower Chelsea Room, SW1
Carroll's Restaurant, W1
Chaglayan Kebab House, NW4 (D)
Chez François, N21 (L)
Chuen-Cheng-Ku, W1
Connaught, W1 (Restaurant)
La Croisette, SW10
Crown, NW8
Crown & Sceptre, W1
Diwana Bhel Poori House, NW1 & W2
Diwan-I-Am, W1
Drury Lane Hotel, Maudie's, WC2
Dragon Gate, W1
Ebury Wine Bar, SW1
Flask, NW3
Freemason's Arms, NW3
Geeta, NW6
La Giralda, Pinner
Il Girasole, SW3
Goody's Kosher Restaurant, W1
Le Gourmet, SW3
Gourmet Rendezvous, NW3
Grand Indian, WC2

Hard Rock Cafe, W1
Harry Morgan, NW8
Holy Cow, W8
Hostaria Romana, W1
Hung Foo, SW18 (D)
Jimmie's, W8
Kew Rendezvous, Richmond
Kowloon, W1
Lamb and Flag, WC2
Lebanese Restaurant, W2
Leith's, W11 (D)
Lemon Tree, SW19
Lichfield's, Richmond (D)
Light of India, W6
Mandarin, NW3 (D)
Manzi's, WC2 (D)
Mata Hari, NW1
Maxim, W13 (D)
Maxwell's, NW3
New Rasa Sayang, WC2
Oliver's Cafe, W14
Orange Tree, Richmond
I Paparazzi, W1
Peking Castle, Wembley
Poon's & Co., WC2
Prince of India, SW19
Princess Louise, WC2
Red Lion Chinese, Richmond
The Refectory, Richmond (L)
Richmond Rendezvous, Richmond (L)
Rive Gauche, SW6
Rowley's, SW1
Royal Garden Hotel, W8
Russkies Wine Cellar, W2 (D)
St Moritz, W1 (D)
San Lorenzo Fuoriporta, SW19

Satay House, W2
Shalimar, NW3
Singapore, W1
Sopna Tandoori, Hampton Hill
Standard Indian, W2
Sultan's Delight, N1 (D)
Le Suquet, SW3
Swiss Centre Restaurant, W1

Tarabya, SE13 (D)
Uncle Pang, NW11
Upper Crust, SW1
Villa Bianca, NW3
Walton's, SW3 (D)
Wei Hai Wei, SW13
Wolfe's, W1

Restaurants classified by the predominant nationality or style of their cuisine

African
Calabash, WC2

American/hamburgers
Hard Rock Cafe, W1
Maxwell's, NW3
Wolfe's, W1

Austrian & Swiss
Kerzenstüberl, W1
St Moritz, W1
Swiss Centre, W1

British (see also Franco-British)
The Grange, WC2
Guinea Grill, W1
Lockets, SW1
Royal Garden Hotel, W8
Tate Gallery, SW1
Throgmorton Restaurant, EC2
Upper Crust, SW1

Chinese
Cantonese
Chuen-Cheng-Ku, W1
Jade Garden, W1
Kowloon, W1
Poon's & Co., W1
Uncle Pang, NW11

Pekinese & Szechuan
Dragon Gate, W1
Gourmet Rendezvous, NW3
Hung Foo, SW18
Kew Rendezvous, Richmond
Mandarin, NW3
Maxim, W13
Peking Castle, Wembley
Peking House, W2
Red Lion, Richmond
Richmond Rendezvous, Richmond
Wei Hai Wei, SW13

Fish
La Croisette, SW10
Fogareiro, N3
Grahame's Sea Fare, W1
Manzi's, WC2
Poissonnerie de l'Avenue, SW3
Seashell Fish Bar, NW1
Le Suquet, SW3
Sweetings, EC4

Franco-British
Berkeley Hotel, SW1
Connaught Hotel, W1
Lacy's, W1
Leith's, W11
Mr Bunbury's, SW16
Walton's, SW3

Franco-Italian
Lemon Tree, SW19

French (see also Franco-British)
Les Amoureux, SW19
Ark, W8
Bagatelle, W10
Balzac Bistro, W12
Bewick's, SW3
La Brasserie, SW7
Bubb's, EC1
Capability Brown, NW6
Capital Hotel, SW3
Carlo's Place, SW6
Carlton Tower Chelsea Room, SW1
Chateaubriand, NW3
Le Chef, W2
Chez François, N21
Chez Moi, W11
Chez Nico, SE22
Le Connaisseur, NW11
La Croisette, SW10
Daphne's, SW3
Didier, W9

L'Epicure, W1
L'Etoile, W1
La Fringale, SW10
Le Gavroche, SW1
Le Gourmet, SW3
La Grenouille, SW11
Langan's Brasserie, W1
Ma Cuisine, SW3
Mon Plaisir, WC2
M'sieur Frog, N1
Oven d'Or, Orpington
Poissonnerie de l'Avenue, SW3
La Poule au Pot, SW1
River Bistro, SW13
Rive Gauche, SW6
Le Suquet, SW3
Tante Claire, SW3
La Toque Blanche, W8

Hungarian

Gay Hussar, W1

Indo-Pakistani

Anarkali, W6
Aziz, W6
Diwana Bhel Poori House, NW1 & W2
Diwan-I-Am, W1
Ganpath, WC1
Geeta, NW6
Goan, N1
Grand Indian, WC2
Holy Cow, W8
Light of India, W6
Mandeer, W1
Prince of India, SW19
Shalimar, NW3
Sopna Tandoori, Hampton Hill
Standard Indian, W2

Italian (see also Franco-Italian)

Amico, SW1
Arlecchino, W8
La Baita, NW3
Il Barbino, W8
La Barca, SE1
Al Ben Accolto, SW3
La Bussola, WC2
Colombina, SW1
Da Carlo, NW6
Due Franco, N1
Gatamelata, W8
Il Girasole, SW3
Hostaria Romana, W1
Trattoria Imperia, WC2
Leonardo, SW10

Montpeliano, SW7
Osteria Lariana, W1
I Paparazzi, W1
Rugantino, W1
Sandro's, W1
San Frediano, SW3
San Lorenzo, SW3
San Lorenzo Fuoriporta, SW19
La Scala, WC2
Siena, W5
Tonino's, NW1
Valchera's, Richmond
Vasco and Piero's Pavilion, W1
Villa Bianca, NW3

Japanese

Ajimura, WC2

Jewish

Bloom's, E1 (Kosher)
Carroll's, W1
Goody's, W1 (Kosher)
Grahame's Sea Fare, W1 (Kosher)
Harry Morgan, NW8

Mexican

After Dark, N1

Middle Eastern

Beotys, WC2
Chaglayan Kebab House, NW4
Cypriana Kebab House, W1
Efes Kebab House, W1
Jason's, SW11
Kolossi Grill, EC1
Lebanese, W2
Little Akropolis, W1
Nontas, NW1
Salamis, SW10
Savvas Kebab House, W11
Sultan's Delight, N1
Tarabya, SE13

Portuguese & Spanish

Fogareiro, N3
La Giralda, Pinner

Scandinavian

Anna's Place, N1
Danwich Shop, Kingston-upon-Thames

South-East Asian

Arirang, W1
Bangkok, SW7

Chaopraya, W1
Mata Hari, NW1
New Rasa Sayang, WC2
Satay House, W2
Singapore, W1
Warung Java Timur, W2

Vegetarian/Wholefood
Diwana Bhel Poori House, NW1 & W2
Food for Thought, WC2
Granary, W1
Mandeer, W1
A Taste of Honey, W11

Restaurants open after midnight (*time of last orders in brackets*)

Arlecchino, W8 (12 exc Sun)
Il Barbino, W8 (12)
La Barca, SE1 (12)
La Bussola, WC2 (1.30)
Chaglayan Kebab House, NW4 (12)
Chateaubriand, NW3 (12)
Chuen-Cheng-Ku, W1 (12)
Cypriana Kebab House, W1 (12)
Daphne's, SW3 (12)
Diwan-I-Am, W1 (12)
Le Gavroche, SW1 (12)
Geeta, NW6 (12 Fri & Sat)
Goan, N1 (12)
Gourmet Rendezvous, NW3 (12)
La Grenouille, SW11 (12)
Hard Rock, W1 (12.30, 1 Fri & Sat)
Holy Cow, W8 (12)
Hung Fu, SW18 (12)
Jason's, SW11 (12)
Kowloon, W1 (12)

Langan's Brasserie, W1 (12.30 Sat)
Lebanese, W2 (12)
Leith's, W11 (12)
Light of India, W6 (12)
Mata Hari, NW1 (12 Fri & Sat)
Maxim, W13 (12)
Maxwell's, NW3 (12, 12.30 Fri & Sun, 1 Sat)
Montpeliano, SW7 (12)
New Rasa Sayang, WC2 (12.30 Fri & Sat)
Peking Castle, Wembley (12)
St Moritz, W1 (1.30)
Salamis, SW10 (12)
Shalimar, NW3 (12, 1 Sat & Sun)
Standard Indian, W2 (12)
Sultan's Delight, N1 (1)
Swiss Centre Restaurant, W1 (12)
Tarabya, SE13 (1)
Wolfe's, W1 (12)

DINERS' GUIDE
TO CATERING HYGIENE

Restaurants, and the food they produce, must be clean. A restaurant
kitchen handles such a lot of food in a year that there is bound to
be a risk of some cross-contamination. Sound practice cannot
always be relied upon, and because, unfortunately, good food and
clean food cannot always be equated, even in these pages restaurants
sometimes appear whose conduct is open to criticism on public
health grounds. *Guide* inspectors are not trained as Environmental
Health Officers, and, to preserve their own anonymity, they usually
ask to see kitchens only if other customers are also invited to do
so. But an alert consumer can often sense what is happening behind
the scenes by knowing what to look for elsewhere. For instance:

1. How does the place look from outside? Is the menu grubby, are the
windows and curtains uncleaned? Is there garbage about, or food deliveries
waiting for attention? Is the ventilator grille greasy and dirty? Inside, are
there tell-tale signs of rodents about – a gnawed food packet, or holes in the
skirting-board?

2. What are the table-cloths and settings like? Does the restaurant smell clean? Is the dining-room floor clean at the approaches to the kitchen? If they do not bother with what the customer sees, would you expect them to bother with what he does not see?

3. Notice the lavatories. Provision for the staff is unlikely to be better than it is for customers, and negligence in this area probably indicates the management's attitude to hygiene in general.

4. Watch the personal habits of the staff. Are cuts and sores covered with waterproof dressings? Incidentally, smoking while handling open food (including drinks) is a legal as well as a social offence.

5. Is open food exposed for long at room temperature, or where it can be breathed over? Do the cooked meat and fish on an hors d'oeuvre table, or the creamy puddings on a sweets trolley, look at though they had lasted the weekend? Is reheated food hot through? (Poor temperature control is a principal cause of food-poisoning, because it encourages organisms to multiply.)

If conclusions so far are unfavourable, you are not – unless you are a *Guide* inspector – obliged to take the risk of eating a meal. Just drop us a line. But if, in spite of favourable appearances, you still decide afterwards that you have been poisoned, you should if possible take the following steps:

1. Whether or not you have been to a doctor, get in touch promptly with the Environmental Health Department of the restaurant's Local Authority (or your own Department if you ate in a distant town – they will pass the information on). If you can provide a specimen of the food or its after-effects, so much the better.

2. Check with other members of the party, if any, to pin down the source of the trouble (which items on the menu did everyone affected eat?) and the time at which symptoms appeared.

3. If you feel strong enough, tell the restaurant proprietor and, in any event, the *Guide*.

4. Remember that the meal to blame may not be the last one you ate. Some forms of food-poisoning wreak their vengeance quickly, but most organisms take anything from a few hours to two days or more.

5. Be particularly careful for a few days afterwards about the way you prepare food for other people: consult your doctor.

Remember that Environmental Health Officers are just as concerned to advise and educate restaurateurs as to prosecute them and that by reporting a case of suspected food-poisoning you may spare many others from similar suffering.

[For your civil rights as a restaurant customer, see the Diners' Guide to restaurant law, p. 120.]

This check-list has been prepared with the help of the Public Health Advisory Service. PHAS is a charitable organisation which provides free advice on matters of public health.

DINERS' GUIDE
TO RESTAURANT LAW

A restaurant does not have to accept your booking, or serve you, even if there is obviously space. But it is illegal for them to refuse to serve you on the grounds of your colour, sex, race, or ethnic origin. And if a restaurant which is part of a hotel (not a private hotel) refuses food and drink to a traveller, the proprietor could be prosecuted and made to pay damages.

Booking a table at a restaurant obliges you to turn up and obliges them to provide a table. Either side may sue for breach of contract if the booking is not honoured. Strictly speaking, even if you later telephone to cancel the booking (as you certainly should if you change your plans) you can be made to pay something, though most restaurateurs will be grateful just to be told. If you fail to show up altogether, the restaurateur can ask for compensation for his expense in keeping your table, and for his business loss.

You have no redress in respect of items which are on the menu, but which turn out to be 'off' when you come to order.

The menu must be accurate in describing the food and drink served. Any wrong description should be reported to the Trading Standards Department of the local authority (as well as being taken up with the manager), with a view to action under the Trade Descriptions Act. If a restaurant is convicted under this Act, the court may award compensation to anyone who suffered from the misdescription.

The quantity specified in what you are invited to order must be provided (so oeufs en cocotte should mean at least two). But in practice this rule has hitherto applied to beer and little else in a restaurant. Now it also applies to wine sold in carafes. For the new rules, see 'How to use the *Guide*', page 4.

The meals served in a restaurant must be edible and composed of ingredients which conform to strict and well-defined standards. Failure in this regard is a criminal offence under the Food and Drugs Act. The local Environmental Health Officer deals with this.

If you are ill through eating bad food, the restaurant could be fined for infringing the Food and Drugs Act, and must compensate you for the pain, suffering, loss of earnings and other expenses you incur. Smoking by staff in the kitchen, breaches of the rules about hygiene, and failures in kitchen cleanliness, are also forbidden. (See also our hygiene article on page 118.)

The food, drink and service provided by a restaurant must be reasonable, according to the standards you might expect from the type of place it is. A serious disparity between what you reasonably expected and what you actually received entitles you to compensation for breach of contract. In theory you are entitled to recover this compensation by deducting a fair sum from the restaurant's bill for food or service. If *in extremis* you do this, do not be put off by any threat to call the police, or even by any contrary advice that a policeman who is called may give. Deducting from the bill is a civil matter, and so has nothing to do with the police, unless a breach of the peace is involved. This you will naturally do your best to avoid, for instance, by providing a verifiable name and address, but you are entitled to quote, and to stand fast on, your rights in this situation. If things look very difficult, you could pay up, making it clear that you do so 'under protest' and 'without prejudice'. You would then have to sue to get the money back.

Always check a restaurant bill for accuracy. If it is correct, you must pay it there and then, in cash. The restaurant is not obliged to accept a cheque or payment by credit card, although it can, of course, do so if it wants to.

If a service charge is prominently mentioned on the menu, you must pay it, if the service was satisfactory. You may assume that it is imposed in lieu of expecting a tip. If the service is seriously deficient, you can recoup the compensation you are entitled to for this by refusing to pay some or all of the service charge. You are never obliged to leave a tip, as such – don't feel pressured by social niceties into paying one. What happens if you withhold it is not a matter of law. Not unless you are actually assaulted. But that is another matter.

David Tench

GLOSSARY

A rough-and-ready description of some of the dishes frequently encountered on restaurant menus and in the pages of the *Guide*.

Amer	American	Fr	French	Mid East	Middle Eastern
Arab	Arabian	Ger	German	Pek	Pekinese
Aust	Austrian	Gk	Greek	Rus	Russian
Austral	Australian	Indo	Indo-Pakistani	Scot	Scottish
Canton	Cantonese	Ital	Italian	Span	Spanish
Eng	English	Jap	Japanese	Swed	Swedish
Flem	Flemish	Mex	Mexican	Sw	Swiss

agrodolce (Ital) sweet-sour sauce, usually accompanying game or duck, which may contain pine nuts, sultanas, bitter chocolate and redcurrant jelly as well as the obligatory wine (or vinegar) and sugar (or honey)

aïoli (Fr) garlic mayonnaise

amandine (Fr) almonds as garnish (e.g. pommes amandine)

aranci caramelizzati (Ital) oranges, cooked whole in syrup, garnished with caramelised peel

Argenteuil (Fr) with an asparagus sauce or garnish (often served with eggs or chicken)

armoricaine (Fr) (américaine) ingredients include tomato, herbs, white wine, brandy and the coral (if the dish includes lobster)

Atholl brose (Scot) originally a thick drink made from oatmeal, water, honey and whisky. Modern versions are normally a syllabub-like sweet containing cream

avgolemono (Gk) chicken or fish broth with rice, eggs and lemon

baklava (Gk) thin pastry (filo) layered with nuts and spices, with a honey-and-lemon syrup poured over

béarnaise, sauce (Fr) an egg and butter sauce flavoured with vinegar and tarragon

béchamel, sauce (Fr) white sauce

beef Wellington see boeuf en croûte

biriani (Indo) elaborate dish of spiced saffron rice cooked with pieces of meat, chicken or prawns (dry)

blanquette (Fr) a 'white' stew, usually of veal, the sauce thickened with cream and egg yolks

boeuf en croûte (Fr) beef fillet cooked whole, seasoned with duxelles (q.v.), baked in puff pastry, served with a rich sauce, e.g. Madeira

boeuf Stroganoff (Fr) thin strips of fillet or sirloin steak, sour cream and onions (mushrooms and tomato puree may be added)

boeuf tartare (Fr) finely minced steak, served raw, garnished with a raw egg yolk, onion and capers

bordelaise (Fr) cooked in or served with a red wine sauce, often with beef marrow

borshch (Rus) beetroot soup (often garnished with sour cream)

boulangère (Fr) garnish of onions and potatoes cooked at the same time as a joint

boulangère, pommes (Fr) potatoes cooked in the oven with onions, dripping and stock

bourguignonne, à la (Fr) cooked with burgundy, onions and mushrooms

brandade de morue (Fr) cream of salt cod with milk, olive oil, garlic, served hot with croûtes (q.v.) or cold as an hors d'oeuvre

bretonne, à la (Fr) (of meat) served with haricot beans, sometimes as a puree; (of scallops) served in the shell with cream sauce and breadcrumbs

cacciatore (Ital) sauce includes tomatoes, herbs, onion and garlic

Café de Paris (Fr) garnish of truffles, asparagus, mushrooms, prawns, oysters, and lobster sauce

carbonara, alla (Ital) beaten eggs and chopped ham or bacon, used as a sauce for pasta

carbonnade flamande (Flem) beef cooked in beer, often with bread on top to form a crust

carbonnade nîmoise (Fr) mutton or lamb cooked slowly in a casserole with vegetables

ceviche (Mex) fillets of white fish – often scallops or sole – 'cooked' by marinating in lime juice with onions and seasonings

chasseur (Fr) sauce or dish which contains white wine, shallots, mushrooms and tomatoes

chateaubriand (Fr) thick centre cut of beef fillet (usually cooked for two)

chocolat turinois (Fr) sweet made from chestnuts, butter and chocolate

Choron (Fr) garnish (for tournedos) of artichoke bottoms filled with peas and pommes noisette (q.v.)

Choron, sauce (Fr) tomato-flavour sauce béarnaise (q.v.)

coq au vin (Fr) casseroled fowl in a rich, wine-based sauce

coquilles St Jacques (Fr) scallops

coulibiac (Rus) (koulibiak) a type of fish cake in pastry (usually salmon)

couscous (Arab) ground wheat (semolina) with vegetables, spiced, and usually served with mutton

crème pâtissière (Fr) confectioner's custard made of flour, eggs and milk, used as a filling for eclairs, profiteroles and fruit tarts (crème St Honoré has beaten egg whites added – see gâteau St Honoré)

créole (Fr Carib) ingredients include rice, peppers, tomatoes

crêpes Suzette (Fr) thin pancakes, flamed at table, in a sauce of butter, orange, lemon, curaçao and brandy

crespolini (Ital) spinach-filled pancakes and cheese in a béchamel sauce

croûte, croûton (Fr) bread, fried or toasted, used as base or garnish (see brandade de morue, tournedos Rossini, gazpacho)

croûte, en cooked in pastry case (see boeuf en croûte)

Cullen skink (Scot) fish soup made from smoked haddock, milk, onion and potato (named after a Morayshire village)

Dacquoise (Fr) layered meringues, often made with ground almonds, with cream, butter cream and/or fruit between the layers

darne (Fr) thick slice of a large fish

daube (Fr) slowly braised meat in an enriched wine stock with herbs
    à l'avignonnaise: made with mutton
      provençale: with tomatoes, garlic and olives

dauphine, pommes (Fr) duchesse potato mixture combined with unsweetened choux paste, formed into cork-like shapes, crumbed and deep fried

dauphinoise, gratin (Fr) sliced potatoes cooked in the oven with milk or cream, and garlic or cheese

dhal (Indo) lentils

dhansak (Indo) a Parsee curry of lamb or chicken cooked in dhal (q.v.)

dijonnaise (Fr) (sauce) containing Dijon mustard (sometimes mayonnaise-like)

dim-sum (Canton) light snacks, mostly savoury, and mostly served in the bamboo baskets in which they are steamed

dolmades (Gk) vine leaves stuffed with meat, rice and herbs

dopiaza (Indo) onion-based korma (q.v.) (wet)

duxelles (Fr) minced mushrooms, shallots, herbs, cooked in butter, used for seasoning (see boeuf en croûte)

Dugléré (Fr) (fish) poached in white wine, with cream and tomatoes added to the sauce

émincés (Fr) sliced or chopped left-over roast or braised meat, reheated in a sauce or gravy

émincés de veau zurichoise (Fr) sliced veal in a wine and cream sauce

escalope (Fr) thin slice of meat (usually veal, sometimes pork) cut from the leg or fillet (see saltimbocca, veal Cordon Bleu, and wiener Schnitzel)

estouffade (Fr) similar to daube (q.v.), though the meat is marinated and fried before braising

fish plaki (Gk) baked in a mixture of tomatoes, onions, garlic, parsley, wine and lemon juice

florentine (Fr) ingredients or garnish include spinach

fondue (Sw) melted cheese, wine and kirsch, served in a communal pot into which are dipped chunks of crusty bread on long forks

fondue bourguignonne (Sw) cubes of fillet steak are cooked by each diner in oil at the table and eaten with a selection of sauces

fritto misto (Ital) batter-fried morsels, either of vegetables and delicate meats, or of fish (di mare or di pesce)

gâteau St Honoré (Fr) choux paste balls, filled with a light crème pâtissière (q.v.) and caramel coated, piled on a pastry base

gazpacho (Span) cold soup, made from raw tomatoes, onions, garlic, cucumber, olive oil, garnished with croûtons and chopped vegetables

golubcy (Rus) stuffed cabbage

gougère (Fr) choux paste enriched with eggs and diced Gruyère cheese, eaten hot or cold as an hors d'oeuvre

gratin, au (Fr) (with) a browned topping of crumbs and butter or cheese

gratinée lyonnaise (Fr) consommé, enriched with egg and port, topped with bread and grated cheese, and browned in the oven

gravlax (Swed) (gravadlax) marinated or pickled salmon, dill flavoured, and usually served with a sweetish mustard sauce

grecque, à la (Fr) garnish of (hot) savoury rice and tomato sauce; method of marinating and cooking vegetables (artichokes, mushrooms) in white wine, water, oil, spices and herbs (served cold)

guacamole (Mex) a puree of avocado, oil, garlic and hot peppers, served as a dip for raw vegetables or savoury biscuits

hollandaise sauce (Fr) an egg, butter and lemon juice sauce

huevos a la flamenca (Span) eggs baked on a bed of onions, tomatoes and other vegetables, garnished with chorizo (garlic sausage), ham and pimento

hummus (Mid East) (homous) a paste of chick peas, lemon juice, mint, garlic, sesame and olive oil, used as a dip for bread or vegetables

jambalaya (Amer) a pilaff (q.v.) with ham, shrimps, peppers and spices

Kiev, chicken suprême (q.v.) stuffed with garlic butter, crumbed and fried

Kir (Fr) (vin blanc cassis) chilled white wine flavoured with blackcurrant liqueur

kofta (Indo) meat or vegetable balls, plain or stuffed, served dry or in a curry sauce

korma (Indo) mild meat curry, braised in yoghourt or cream (wet)

kromeski (Rus) (cromesquis) cutlets made from finely minced meat, deep fried in batter or egg and breadcrumbs

kulfi (Indo) ice-cream, often flavoured with pistachios or almonds

lamb Shrewsbury (Eng) lamb cutlets with mushrooms and a brown sauce flavoured with Worcestershire sauce and redcurrant jelly

lassi (Indo) yoghourt-based drink, either sweet or salt

lobster thermidor (Fr) served chopped in a shell, with a béchamel (q.v.) and wine sauce, cheese and crumbs on top

macédoine (Fr) mixture of diced fruit or vegetables, the latter often bound with mayonnaise (q.v.) or white sauce

madrilène (Fr) (consommé or other dish) flavoured with tomato juice

marchand de vin (Fr) in a wine sauce

Marengo, poulet (Fr) chicken sauté with tomatoes, mushrooms, garlic, eggs and crawfish, finished with brandy

meunière (Fr) method of cooking fish, lightly floured, in butter (which is used as a sauce with lemon juice and parsley)

mille-feuille (Fr) layers of puff pastry and cream, crème pâtissière (*q.v.*), and/or fruit or jam

monosodium glutamate (MSG) white crystalline food additive, supposedly (but not really) tasteless, which accentuates the flavour of a dish

Montmorency (Fr) ingredients or garnish include cherries

Mornay (Fr) cheese sauce

moules marinière (Fr) mussels cooked in white wine with shallots

moussaka (Mid East) layered aubergines or potatoes and minced beef or lamb, with tomato sauce, and béchamel sauce (*q.v.*) or an egg custard on top

nan (Indo) bread cooked in a clay oven (see tandoori)

Nantua (Fr) sauce made from béchamel (*q.v.*), crawfish puree, cayenne and cream

noisettes (Fr) lamb: cutlets from the best end, boned and tied
                   veal: miniature escalopes (*q.v.*) (sometimes called médaillons)
                   pork: cut from the chump end of the loin, boned

noisette, pommes (Fr) garnish of small potato balls, browned in butter

normande (Fr) in a fish dish the ingredients include shrimps, mussels, mushrooms; with meat, cider and calvados; with puddings, apples

osso buco (Ital) shin of veal, with its marrow, cooked in white wine, tomatoes, garlic, parsley and lemon rind. The Milanese version is served with saffron-flavoured risotto

paella (Span) a mixture of fish, shellfish, onions, tomatoes, saffron, garlic, rice, usually chicken or chicken livers, pimento, peas (named after the dish in which it is cooked)

paloise, sauce (Fr) similar to béarnaise (*q.v.*) with mint instead of tarragon

papillote, en (Fr) cooked in a packet of greaseproof paper or foil

Parmentier (Fr) ingredients include potatoes

Parmentier, pommes (Fr) ½″ cubes of potato, cooked in clarified butter

pavé (Fr) (literally paving-stone) cold dish, either savoury (mousse with jelly coating) or sweet (sponge layered and coated with butter cream) made in a square or rectangular mould

Pavlova (Austral) a soft meringue case filled with fruit and cream

périgourdine (Fr) ingredients include truffles and sometimes pâté

pesto (Ital) a sauce for pasta (or other things) made from fresh basil, garlic, Parmesan cheese, pine nuts and olive oil

pilaff (Fr) (pilaf, pilau) rice cooked in stock, often flavoured and coloured with saffron, with meat, vegetables or fish added (pulao: Indo)

pipérade (Basque) a mixture of eggs, onions, green peppers and tomatoes, with the texture of scrambled eggs

pistou, soupe au (Fr) soup with vegetables and thick vermicelli, flavoured with a liaison of pounded garlic, basil, tomatoes and oil

pitta (Mid East) round or oval bread, only slightly leavened, with a pocket in the centre. Served in strips with hummus and taramosalata (*q.v.*) or halved and filled with kebabs and salad

pizzaiola (Ital) highly seasoned sauce, with tomatoes and garlic

poivre vert (Fr) unripe green peppercorns, softer and with a milder flavour than ripe black or white ones

polenta (Ital) yellow maize flour, boiled, or cooked in other ways

pollo sorpresa (Ital) Italian version of chicken Kiev (*q.v.*) (pollo: chicken)

pommes soufflées (Fr) thin, square slices of potato, fried in deep fat till partly cooked, removed and plunged into hotter fat so that they puff up

portugaise (Fr) ingredients include tomato

profiteroles (Fr) little balls of choux paste, usually filled with cream or ice-cream and often served with chocolate sauce, hot or cold

provençale (Fr) ingredients include oil, tomatoes and garlic

quenelles (Fr) light oval dumplings of fish (e.g. 'brochet' – pike), veal or chicken forcemeat, bound with eggs or bread, poached, served with a cream sauce (often sauce Nantua, q.v.)

quiche Lorraine (Fr) a savoury tart of bacon, cream and eggs

rasgulla (Indo) curd cheese balls in rose-water syrup

ratatouille (Fr) a stew of aubergines, courgettes, tomatoes, green and red peppers and onions, served hot or cold

rémoulade (Fr) mayonnaise sauce with mustard, chopped capers, parsley, herbs, and sometimes gherkins and anchovy essence

rillettes (Fr) potted pork, seasoned with herbs or spices

risi e bisi (Ital) green peas and rice, cooked with ham and Parmesan cheese – Venetian dish

rogan gosht (Indo) Kashmiri lamb curry, aromatic rather than fiery

rösti (Sw) grated potato, mixed with onions and seasoning, and fried as a cake

rouille (Fr) creamy sauce, flavoured strongly with garlic and chillies, traditionally served with (or in) fish soups

sabayon (Fr) French version of zabaglione (q.v.) substitutes white wine for the Marsala, and uses whites as well as yolks of the eggs

salmis (Fr) duck or game, roasted, jointed and served in a strongly flavoured sauce made with stock from the carcase. Usually garnished with croûtons

salpicon (Fr) (savoury): cubed meats and/or vegetables, bound with a brown or white sauce, used to fill pastry cases, canapés, etc., or to make rissoles or stuffings; (sweet): fresh or candied fruits soaked in liqueur

saltimbocca (Ital) 'jump into the mouth', veal escalopes (q.v.) cooked with ham, sage and Marsala

sashimi (Jap) sliced raw fish (tunny, mackerel, bream, salmon, etc.), served with soy sauce, grated horseradish and sliced ginger

saupiquet (Fr) piquant cream sauce served with ham or game

scaloppe, scaloppine (Ital) escalopes (q.v.)

shashlik (Mid East) lamb, mushrooms and onions, marinated and grilled on skewers (similar to kebabs)

shrikhand (Indo) curd cheese or yoghourt sweet, spiked with lemon and cardamom

smitane (Fr) (smetana, Rus) in a sour-cream and onion sauce

smokies (Scot) Scottish oak-smoked haddock, traditionally from Arbroath

sorpotel (Goan) spicy red curry of pork and other meats

soubise (Fr) a puree of onions and either béchamel (q.v.) or rice, used as a sauce for mutton or a stuffing for meat

steak Diane (Fr) fillet steak often cooked at table, usually with mushrooms, onions, Worcestershire sauce, flamed in brandy

stracciatella (Ital) chicken broth into which egg and grated Parmesan have been beaten

suédoise (Fr) (sweet): jellied fruit (apricot, plum) puree, usually served with cream or custard; (savoury): mayonnaise with apple puree and scraped horseradish

sugo (di carne) (Ital) standard Italian meat and tomato sauce to serve with pasta

sukiyaki (Jap) thinly sliced steak cooked at table with soy sauce, green onions, beancurd, transparent noodles, bamboo shoots. Served with a raw egg for dipping

suprême (Fr) the breast and wing of chicken (or other bird) removed raw in one piece from the carcase

sushi (Jap) morsels of vinegared rice with raw fish, dried kelp or egg, flavoured with ginger and horseradish

syllabub (Eng) traditionally made by milking a cow into a pan of white wine, this cold sweet is now usually cream with sugar, lemon, and white wine or sherry added

tandoori chicken (Indo) marinated in yoghourt, lemon juice, garlic and spices, cooked in a tandoor (clay oven) or over a charcoal grill

taramosalata (Gk) grey mullet roe or smoked cod's roe, pounded to a paste with garlic, lemon juice and olive oil, served with hot toast, or bread (pitta, q.v.). It is often 'lightened' with mashed potato, breadcrumbs, cream, or cream cheese

tempura (Jap) batter-fried morsels of fish and vegetables

toffee apples (Pek) apple segments, cooked in batter, coated with a caramel glaze, plunged into iced water to crisp the glaze

tournedos Rossini (Fr) a thick slice of beef fillet, sauté in butter, topped with pâté, set on a croûte (q.v.), and covered with Madeira sauce

Turbigo (Fr) (usually fried kidneys) served with mushrooms and chipolatas and a tomato-and-wine sauce

vacherin (Fr) rounds of meringue layered with cream, fruit, and sometimes liqueur and ice-cream

vallée d'Auge (Fr) ingredients include calvados, apples and cream

veal Cordon Bleu (Fr) veal escalopes (q.v.), sandwiched with ham and Gruyère cheese, crumbed and fried

Véronique (Fr) garnish of white grapes (commonly served with sole or chicken)

vichyssoise (Amer) a cream soup made from leeks, potatoes and chicken stock, served hot or cold

vigneronne (Fr) ingredients or garnish include grapes

Walewska (Fr) garnish of Mornay sauce (q.v.), lobster and truffles (for poached fish)

wiener Schnitzel (Aust) veal or pork escalopes (q.v.), crumbed and fried, served with lemon and (sometimes) anchovies or capers (Schnitzel Holstein has a fried egg on top)

wun-tun (Canton) (won ton) thin wrappers of dough ('Chinese ravioli'), filled with minced pork, shrimp, vegetables or dates; served either as dumplings (dim-sum, q.v.), in soup, or deep fried

zabaglione (Ital) (zabaione) a frothy sweet made from egg yolks, sugar and Marsala, usually served warm

zarzuela (Span) mixed fish stew cooked with wine, onions, garlic and tomatoes, served with rice or boiled potatoes

zingara (Fr) garnish (usually for escalopes) of ham, tongue, mushrooms and truffles in a demi-glace sauce flavoured with tomato and tarragon

Closures and changes of management

Readers who notice the disappearance of a place from the *Guide*'s pages often ask why. For obvious reasons, we cannot tell them about individual cases. But it has been found helpful to list here places that have been dropped for reasons unconnected with members' comments or silences: closure, conflagration, material changes in management or kitchen team that took place too late for adequate investigation.

London
Busby's, SW3
Lavender Hill Restaurant, SW11
Naturally, W11
Spread Eagle, SE10

England
Ampthill, Beds
King's Arms
Bath, Avon
Priory Hotel
Birtle, Gtr Manchester
Normandie Restaurant and Hotel
Brixham, Devon
Randall's Restaurant Français
Chardstock, Devon
Tytherleigh Arms
Chichester, W. Sussex
Clinchs' Salad House
Clanfield, Oxon
Plough Hotel
Dufton, Cumbria
Sycamore House
Faringdon, Oxon
Bell Hotel
Fawley, Bucks
Walnut Tree
Hatch Beauchamp, Somerset
Farthings
Henley-on-Thames, Oxon
Le Radier
Hexham, Northumberland
Abbey Flags
Holmes Chapel, Cheshire
Yellow Broom
Leeds, W. Yorks
Rules
Limpley Stoke, Wiltshire
Tearles
Northampton, Northants
Vineyard
Ottery St Mary, Devon
Wheelhouse Restaurant
Oxford, Oxon
Tudor Cottage
Piddletrenthide, Dorset
Old Bakehouse

Rushlake Green, E. Sussex
Priory Hotel
Selsey, W. Sussex
Thatched House
Stratford-upon-Avon, Warwicks
Buccaneer Restaurant Wayside Hotel
Truro, Cornwall
Bear Essential
Walton-on-Thames, Surrey
Bruno's
Wickham, Hants
Old House Hotel
Woodland, Devon
Rising Sun
York, N. Yorks
Aardvark

Wales
Aberporth, Dyfed
Penrallt Hotel
Fishguard, Dyfed
Hoppy's
Maenan, Gwynedd
Plas Maenan Hotel

Scotland
Anstruther, Fife
The Cellar
Edinburgh
Duncan's Land
Humbie, E. Lothian
Johnstounburn House
Kilchoan, Argyll
Kilchoan Hotel
Moffat, Dumfriesshire
Beechwood Country House Hotel
Struy, Inverness-shire
Mauld Bridge House (Kristine's
    Kitchen)

Republic of Ireland
Curracloe, Co Wexford
Esker Lodge

Northern Ireland
Ballinamallard, Co Fermanagh
Brooklands Hotel

ENGLAND

The Elms
on A443
Great Witley 666

Must book
Meals 12.30–2, 7.30–9.30

Tdh L £3·80 (meal £5·50),
D from £6·40 (meal £9)
Alc L £6·15 (meal £8·30)

VAT inc
Cover 20p alc L
Seats 50 (parties 60)
♿ rest; w.c.
Car park
No dogs in d/r
Access, Am Ex, Barclay,
Diners, Euro
20 rooms (all with bath)
B&B £13·50–£14·50
Full board £24·50–£26
Fire cert

Last year this 'splendid old house' overlooking the
Teme Valley was about to celebrate its silver wedding
with the *Guide* when the relationship was ruptured
– on this side, but not wantonly and inadvisedly,
for commercial success under Donald Crosthwaite's
ownership seemed to have stretched Mrs Schädler's
cooking and the dining-room service as thin as
strudel dough. Not surprisingly, numerous
conscience-stricken regulars have come to its aid this
year, and, happily, inspectors' meals too have had
something of the old flair and friendliness along
with the new luxury. 'Main courses on both nights
were worthy of note: roast guinea-fowl with a cream
cheese and walnut stuffing, and duck with lemon
and tarragon sauce.' 'A good sludgy gazpacho with
all the trimmings was followed by really fresh
haddock in a fishy, winey, cheesy sauce.' Most meals
are still table d'hôte (priced by the main course at
dinner), and begin well with brown or white hot
rolls with herb butter. First courses still often offer
fresh pears in curry cream sauce, or Stilton and port
mousse, or prawns aïoli, and main courses remarked
include lamb duxelles ('too fatty and too much, but
nice'), saddle of lamb with artichoke hearts and
tomato, chicken Richelieu, and pork in beer (nor are
they too proud to keep beer to drink with it).
Vegetables have improved, and salads are praised
too. Some say the *bombes* have lost their *surprise*,
some say the opposite, but at a test meal lemon
soufflé was 'a really good one', and there are
caramel or apricot variants on the same recipe, or
mulberry mousse or gâteau St Honoré. Drinking
begins at about £2·50, and the clarets remain
formidable, with two '73s at about £4, and various
finer wines (Chx. Talbot, Haut-Brion, and Latour,
all château-bottled) in the '68 vintage at prices
which reflect its riskiness. The Rully '76 (Clos de
Belle Croix) at £5·95 is also admired. The lunchtime
bar buffet (six days a week) is substantial. No music.

*App: Michael Copp, N.R., H.L., P. E. Carter,
P.H.B., David Fearnley, T.C., and many others*

PLEASE keep sending in reports, as soon as possible after each meal.
Closing date for the 1980 Guide is September 30, 1979, but reports are even
more useful earlier in the year, especially for the remoter areas and new places.

AISLABY North Yorkshire Map 8

Blacksmith's Arms
Aislaby
on A170
2 m NW of Pickering
Pickering 72182

An inn since Elizabeth I's time, with an attractive bar in the old smithy, well-spaced tables, tomato plants on the window-ledges and 'a competent air'. Mr Murray, the chef-proprietor, enjoys turning local produce into meals 'with a French flavour': fish or game soup, avocado mousse with prawns (85p), tender duck with a good sauce made from fresh cherries (£3·90), pigeon braisé aux olives (£2·50), tranche d'agneau à la poitevine (£3·75). Prices include carefully cooked vegetables. 'Sweets satisfactory but not memorable.' Lunch is a simpler meal with soups, pâté, quiche, pot au feu (£1·60), cold game pie with orange salad (£1·80), and fruit salad, ice-cream or cheese. Short wine list, with French house wines, £2·20 for 75 cl. Recorded music.

Closed Tue; Jan 1
Must book (summer)
Meals 12–2, 7.30–9.30

Alc L £2·65 (meal £4·45),
D £5·10 (meal £7·15)

VAT inc

Children's helpings
Seats 45
 🔾 rest
Car park
No dogs

ALDBOROUGH Norfolk Map 6

Old Red Lion
off A140
6 m S of Cromer
Hanworth 451

The Plumes' 16th-century house a few miles from the sea, beside a 'best-kept village green', is run like an officers' mess in the East where Standards Have To Be Kept Up. This may slow up your dining or speed your parting, but the set meals offer a generous choice of local crab, fish, and duckling, and the *carte* supplements these with good steaks in various ways (rump steak chasseur, £3·30). Praise also for the hot rolls, a sole offered at the plaice price when plaice was not available, and 'pork in breadcrumbs, topped with onions and a hint of soy'. Sweets are creamy or ice-creamy. Routine wines; by the glass 50p. Recorded music. Smoking in the lounge area only. Carlsberg on tap, and light lunches in the bar (baked crab and fried parsley, £1·30).

Closed Mon
Must book
Meals 12–1.30, 7–9.30

Tdh L £3·50 (meal £6·20),
D £4·50 (meal £7·40)

Alc (min as tdh) £6
(meal £9·15)

Children's helpings
(under 10)

Seats 40 (parties 20)
 🔾 rest (2 steps); w.c.
Car park
No dogs

'Must book' is the restaurant's information, not ours. The context of the entry usually indicates how much or how little it matters, but a preliminary telephone call averts frustrated journeys. Always telephone if a booking has to be cancelled: a small place may suffer severely if this is not done, and customers are also the losers in the end.

ALDERLEY EDGE Cheshire   Map 5

Le Rabelais
75 London Road
Alderley Edge 584848

Closed Sun; Sat L;
Aug 19–Sept 17; Dec 25;
Jan 1; L public hols
Must book D
Meals 12–2, 7–11

Alc £5·40 (meal £8·80)

Seats 42
No dogs
Access, Diners

Patrick and Sally Guilbaud emphasise the 'legal, medical, political, religious and philosophical' preoccupations of Rabelais rather than the ones everyone else thinks of. The chastity of the decor in their upstairs room, and their uncompromisingly aromatic food, are likewise a challenge to be accepted gratefully. A test meal, after nominations received from near and far, was mostly very successful, especially the soupe aux moules (£1·20) 'that arrived under a skull-cap of very light flaky pastry', the sausage en brioche with madeira sauce (£1·70), and the brochette d'agneau (£3) 'with a butter, thyme and garlic sauce that demanded to be mopped up with bread to the last drop'. Among vegetables (which are included) 'ratatouille was short on both aubergines and salt, but creamed turnips were a dream.' Other dishes people like include blanquette de veau, tournedos Richelieu (£3·95), profiteroles, and brioche Lorraine (with crème pâtissière, sultanas and crème fraîche, 80p). Coffee is good; well-chosen wines from Rodney Densem include Provence red and white at £3·65 and Ch. Cos Labory '73 at £6·60. Recorded music. Wear a tie. More reports, please.

ALRESFORD Hampshire   Map 2

O'Rorkes
♥
34 Pound Hill
Alresford 2293

Closed L; Sun; 2 weeks
July/Aug; Dec 25 & 26
Must book
D only, 7–9.30

Tdh from £6 (meal £9·05)

VAT inc
Seats 36 (parties 12)
Car park
Access card

Travelling west, you meet Brian O'Rorke's unassuming restaurant on the right-hand side, up a slip road from the A31 just past New Alresford square. After 14 years (in these pages), most members know how to find it, even if admiration is more qualified than it once was. A few chills in the room or on the plate, and 'tough chunks of meat for kebabs or spicy Moroccan lamb' have to be set against Michael Harvey's fine pike quenelles, salmon with sauce Messine, veal with ham and cheese, and duck with ginger and orange. However, there are also regular visitors who can seldom fault what is offered, even the steaks, and one of the critics of the lamb was well content to begin with asparagus béarnaise and end with chocolate mousse and peach with zabaglione. 'You could help yourself to as much of a fine Stilton as you wanted, and there were Bath Olivers too.' Their vinous allegiance now lies with Averys and others: the list is short, but offers Chianti Classico '74 at £3·20, Savigny Lavières '72 at £4·90, and youngish claret. You may drink half a bottle for half the price plus 30p. Josephine Fulford ('a woman of rugged beauty') plays the harpsichord on Wednesdays, and plays well, but a member who found her there on a Thursday was disconcerted.

App: A.B. & J. M. King, S.J., S.K.J., H.R., and others

ALSTON Cumbria   Map 8

High Fell
on A686
1½ m S of Alston
Alston 597

The Chipmans' comfortable 17th-century hill farm now takes guests, who seem content with mushrooms Patrice (70p), a 'belting' soupe de poisson (60p), trout cooked in vin rosé, or canard à l'anglaise (with ratatouille, peas and potatoes . . .), apricot bavarois or crème brûlée. Vegetables may come from the garden. About ten wines, with Italian Ambra at £2·30 for 75 cl. 'Light classical' recorded music. More reports, please, as they settle in.

Must book D & weekends
Meals 12.30–2, 7.30–9.30

Alc £5·65 (meal £8·60)

Children's helpings
Seats 20
Car park
No dogs

7 rooms (2 with bath, 1 with shower)
B&B from £5·50

AMBLESIDE Cumbria   Map 7

Apple Pie Eating House
Rydal Road
Ambleside 3679

It is hard to keep apple-pie order in this bakery-cum-tea-shop, because a scrum forms at the counter much of the day. You queue to eat there or take away the sensibly limited range of food: sandwiches (four kinds of bread), ploughman's, quiche, shepherd's or meat pie with salad (80p), 'herbily roast chicken', apple pie and cream (40p), and 'proper custard tarts'. Unlicensed, but the coffee is freshly ground and the lemon tea reviving on a hot day.

Closed Nov–Easter
No bookings

Open 9–5·30

Alc meal £1·40

Seats 65
Unlicensed

Rothay Manor

Rothay Bridge
Ambleside 3605

Closed Jan & Feb
Must book D & Sun L
Meals 12.30–2, 7.30–9

Tdh buffet L £2·50 (meal £3·95), Sun buffet L £3·50 (meal £5·05), D from £8 (meal £10)

VAT inc
Children's helpings
Seats 40
⟨⟩ rest (1 step); w.c. (m)
Air-conditioning
Car park

There is a warmer tone than for some years past in accounts of this handsome and thoughtfully furnished Georgian house and garden, which is peaceful even though the one-way system at this edge of the town makes access difficult. People seem reconciled to the occasional dish that 'reads better than it tastes' by Bronwen Nixon and her sons' evident desire to stretch themselves in what they attempt. 'They could not get the goose livers so had to buy the geese' for a special winter Périgourdine meal. (The continuation was consommé cerfeuil, truite au beurre blanc, dinde aux cèpes, Roquefort and goat cheeses, and cremets myrtille, all with appropriate wines.) Most residents find the breakfasts a dependably excellent meal, with 'fresh orange juice, hot croissants, and a Cumberland platter. At dinner, soups are almost always good, and other first courses praised include trout mousse, apple and Stilton savoury, cheese pudding, and chicken liver pâté. Main dishes tend to be rich, and though every now and then they are overcooked

No dogs in public rooms
Am Ex, Diners
12 rooms (8 with bath,
1 with shower)
B&B £15–£15·50
Fire cert

or under-helped, there are accounts of first-rate braised wood pigeon with herbs and redcurrant jelly. Poussin Auvergne, duck à l'orange, and well-cooked vegetables – including crunchy cabbage, and peppers in batter – are also noted. 'Desserts always included a tart made with a "fruit of the day",' and at a test meal, though grape brûlée was 'rather runny', orange soufflé, Sachertorte and Cumberland rum nicky were all good. The wines are consistently interesting and reasonable (besides, you may drink half a bottle of anything for 3/5 of the full price). Among reds under £4, note Australian San Carlo '71 claret, Marqués de Riscal '71, Gamay de l'Ardèche, and Barolo '73. Most good Bordeaux are over £5 now, but Ch. Haut-Claverie '70, a Sauternes, is £4·30. The German list is also inviting. No smoking in the dining-room, either. No music. Dress 'reasonably'.

App: R. T. Davies, M. C. T. Brookes, S.W.,
A. T. Langton, C. J. Richardson, and many others

Sheila's Cottage
The Slack
Ambleside 3079

A pleasant Westmorland cottage, where you eat in the sitting-room, with attentive service. Sensibly short English menu: celery and chicken soup (35p), liver pâté with Cumberland sauce (70p), various oven-to-table dishes ('ham and Gruyère cheese', £2·50), Cumberland sausage with apple and onion sauce (£2·50), good crisp salads. 'An affection for tinned asparagus, and rather heavy-handed apricot streusel'. Strong coffee; Swiss Apfelsaft. Unlicensed as yet. More reports, please.

Closed Sun; Jan & Feb;
Dec 25 & 26
Meals 12–2, 6.30–8.30

Alc £4·10 (meal £5·20)

Children's helpings
(under 10)

Seats 40
No dogs
Unlicensed

ARDINGLY West Sussex   Map 3

Camelot
86–88 High Street
Ardingly 892503

Ideas surpass execution in the Scholefields' neatly kept shopping-parade place, for seasoning is unreliable. Sweets depend too much on liquor or meringue. But the set 'Taste of England' dinner and French *carte* make a good contrast, and both are usually well cooked, say visitors. An inspector, likewise, admired accurate oeufs en cocotte, and the sauce for sole Véronique, although he wished the grapes had been skinned and pipped. Chantesec is £3 a litre; other wines well chosen. 'Faint' music.

Closed Mon; Sun D;
D Dec 25 & 26
Must book
Meals 12–1.30, 7–9.30
(10 Fri & Sat)

Tdh L £2·75 (meal £5·40),
D £3·85 (meal £6·85)
Alc £6·45 (meal £10·15)

Cover 30p alc
Children's helpings

Seats 38
♿ rest (3 steps)
No dogs
Access, Am Ex, Barclay,
Diners

The Cottage
Bakewell 2488

Closed Tue
Must book
Meals by arrangement

Tdh L £3·50 (meal £5·60),
D £4·50 (meal £6·70)

VAT inc
Seats 20
[symbol] rest (1 step); w.c.
No dogs
Access, Am Ex, Barclay

The responsibilities of batting (virtually) for an entire county in last year's *Guide* did not daunt Mrs Rhodes – how could they, with that name? – but since she does almost all the work herself in this little cottage, the dinners have forced her to 'cut down' on lunches and teas. Predictably, her severest critic is another tyke, who disliked the pewter wine goblets and the long wait for the communal start to the meal, and found shoulder of lamb with rice stuffing 'rather greasy'. Even so, the borshch, the cauliflower, and the cinnamon cream cheese pancakes gave pleasure, and others praise, for instance, blinis, cheese mousse with prawns, beef with mushroom and onions, almond cream pie, and strawberry and hazelnut gateau. The coffee is Cona now. From the few wines, drink the Dãos perhaps at £3–£4, unless you care to risk Vino Veritas at £2·40. You share a table unless you are a four. No music. 'A few imitators would be a delight in Derbyshire.'

App: W. G. White, Vernon F. Moore, M.W., F.G.A.

The Lornies
on A24
10 m N of Worthing
Ashington 892575

Ancient timbering and ingle-nooks help make the Lornies' farmhouse restaurant attractive. The short menu, though seldom changed, is freshly cooked to order, and members have enjoyed spinach and watercress soup, chicken liver pâté, seafood Saratine ('mixed seafoods in a rich cream sauce and rice', £3·50), and steak and chicken in various ways. Carefully cooked vegetables, mainly ice-cream-based sweets. Berry Bros wines from £2·40 – no carafes. No music.

Closed L (exc by
arrangement); Sun; Mon;
Dec 25 & 26; Jan 1
Must book

D only, 7.15–9.15

Alc £4·90 (meal £7·65)

Children's helpings

Seats 20
[symbol] rest (1 step)
Car park
No dogs

The Guide News Supplement will be sent out as usual, in June, to everyone who buys the book directly from Consumers' Association and to all bookshop purchasers who return the card interleaved with their copy. Let us know of any changes that affect entries in the book, or of any new places you think should be looked at.

Towns shown in black on our maps contain at least one recommended restaurant or pub (see map key). The dot denotes the location of the town or village, not the restaurant. Where necessary, we give directions to the restaurant in the entry. If you can, help us to improve them.

AUSTWICK North Yorkshire Map 8

Game Cock Inn
½ m off A65
17 m E of Lancaster
Clapham 226

Mary Howarth's fortieth year at this little inn in Dales pot-holing country finds the house still well kept and the simple, no-choice meals well cooked: roast beef, duck or chicken, then fruit tarts or trifle. Service may be hard-pressed at weekends. Breakfasts are enormous and weekday bar snacks popular (above all the home-made meat pies, 55p). Yates & Jackson wines and beers. No music.

Closed L Mon–Sat (exc bar); Tue (exc res); Dec 24, 25, 26 & 31
Must book
Meals 12.30–1.30 (bar exc Sun), 7–8 (8.30 Sat)

Tdh Sun L from £2·85 (meal £4·25), D from £4·50 (meal £6·05)
VAT inc
Children's helpings (under 14)
Seats 24 (parties 10)

♿ rest
Car park
No dogs in d/r
3 rooms
B&B £7–£8
D, B&B £11–£13
Fire cert

BADWELL ASH Suffolk Map 6

Singing Chef
8 m NW of Stowmarket
between A45 & A143
Walsham-le-Willows 314

Closed L; Sun; Tue; Apr 16; May 28; Aug 27
Must book
D only, 7.30–11

Alc £4·90 (meal £7·90)

Service 10%
Cover 25p
Children's helpings (under 10)
Seats 30
♿ rest
Car park
No dogs

It feels a long way from anywhere to Badwell Ash, but old admirers of Kenneth Toyé's genuine French cooking (and at times singing) find themselves equal to the journey to the open-plan ground floor of his house. (Remember that except on Fridays and Saturdays, you must be a party of six or more, and that you are encouraged to order by telephone.) Some who like the Suffolk produce he uses find the Suffolk service maladroit, and the contrasts unnerving: 'We were expected to look on the lamb when it was red but the girl who commended it that way turned out to be a vegetarian.' Anchoïade or pissaladière could do with more anchovies. But quiche, oeufs mimosa, boeuf gardiane, 'pork with apples and delicious crackling', local vegetables, and crisp side salads 'with elderflowers scattered in with the lettuce' are all praised. Try too bohémienne (an aubergine dish, 85p), lamb tagine (£2·85) and omelette soufflée flambée (£1·50 for two). Profiteroles vary, crème caramel is correct in the genre, and tarte Tatin is a very fair version. Wines (from £2·50 for Cantonelle, apparently a Tolly Cobbold tipple) are modest, but 'Ch. Beaumont de Bolivar '71 at £3·50 drank well.' There are French *chansons* on record too, and 'baby-minding in a private room'.

App: G. S. Carr, T.A.G., B.J.B.

'Meal' indicates the cost of a meal for one, including food, coffee, half the cheapest bottle of wine, cover, service, and VAT (see 'How to use the Guide', p. 4).

Peppermill
11 South Bar
Banbury 3610

Closed Sun; Sat L;
2 weeks Aug;
Dec 25 & 26
Must book
Meals 12–2, 6.30–10.30
(11 Fri & Sat)

Tdh L from £1 (meal
£1·85)
Alc £4·30 (meal £6·35)

VAT inc
Children's helpings
Seats 32
♿ rest
No dogs

The two-course set lunch seems more of an
achievement for the price than the dinners, but
either way people have enjoyed their meals at Peter
and Denise Smith's 'young and good-natured'
natural brick restaurant. At midday 'soup was poor
but quiche and scampi were generous, and 50p extra
for sweets brought delicious bitter chocolate mousse
with a hint of orange.' In the evening there are
both fixed and seasonal menus now. Quiches are
variable, and smoked mackerel is best without a
sauce unless carefully filleted first. But chicken
Kiev (or a variant with tomato and mushroom as
stuffing), daubes of pork and lamb (£2·75), and the
vegetables included (Anna potatoes and good
courgettes at a test meal) are all praised. Finish,
perhaps, with planter's ice-box cake or crème brûlée.
French ordinaires are £2·30 and there are a few
other wines. 'Topless' recorded music, says an
acoustically-minded inspector.

App: R. T. Davies, J. M. Stabler, D.M., and others

BANBURY see also pub section

Chez Maurice
5¼ m W of Salisbury
Wilton 2240

Closed Sun D; Dec 26;
Jan 1
Must book D
Meals 12–1.30, 7–9.30

Tdh L from £3 (meal
£4·50), D £6·50 (meal
£8·35)
Alc (min £3) £6·70
(meal £9)

VAT inc
Service 10%
Seats 35 (parties 20)
♿ rest; w.c.
Car park
No dogs
Barclay, Diners

Mme Ricaud prickled slightly at last year's
sympathetic comment about empty tables at this
modern-looking restaurant (which lies at a junction
where motorists between Salisbury and Shaftesbury
take a dog-leg turn). 'We do not employ staff and
would rather do 20 covers properly than 30–40
badly.' Her reward for this devotion is a member's
remark that her 'precise, considerate and unobtrusive
service lifted a sound meal into an experience.'
Not all reports are quite as enthusiastic, and if you
eat à la carte and drink liberally the experience will
be costly. But Maurice Ricaud's soups, bread rolls,
duck pâté, well-assembled hors d'oeuvre, and more
substantial rump steak with herbs, civet of venison,
and barbecued spare ribs of veal – 'a dish of the day
served with pommes dauphine' – are all admired.
For sweet there may be meringue glacée or pot au
café crème. Lobster cold or hot, and rouelle de gigot
d'agneau et rognons au romarin (£3·20) are
specialities. Granvillons ordinaires are £3·50 for
white and £3·40 for red per litre, and around £5
there is attractive Alsace or '76 Beaujolais. Recorded
music. No children under nine.

*App: J. P. Berryman, Neil Fairlamb,
H. K. Heseltine, and others*

BARNARD CASTLE Durham   Map 8

Blagraves House
The Bank
Teesdale 37668

A handsome old house, said to have been patronised by Richard III and Oliver Cromwell, among many. Open fires, heavy beams, and courteous service encourage enjoyment of Josie Davidson's cooking: generous helpings of loin of pork with a peach and brandy sauce 'and smashing crackling' or trout in a cream, prawn and mushroom sauce, with Whitby crab or home-made soup before and rich (too rich?) sweets after. Vegetables are fresh and imaginatively cooked. Litre Vin carafes £2·90 for 70 cl; Ch. Giscours '73, c.b., £7·20. No music.

Closed L; Sun; Apr 13; Dec 24, 25 & 26; Jan 1 Must book

D only, 7.15–9.15

Alc £5·85 (meal £9·05)

Seats 40 (parties 24)
No dogs

BARNSTAPLE Devon   Map 1

Lynwood House
on A377
Barnstaple 3695

Closed Sun D; Sat L; L Apr 13 & 16; L May 7 & 28; L Aug 27
Must book
Meals 12–2, 7–10

Tdh Sun L from £3·50
Alc L £4 (meal £6·55), D £5·90 (meal £8·65)

VAT inc
Children's helpings
Seats 50 (parties 18)
♿ rest
Car park
No dogs
Access, Am Ex, Barclay, Diners

For one reason or another, North Devon has been visited by teams of metropolitan carpetbaggers this year, and these three well-set linked rooms in green and gold make their debut here. Years ago, John Roberts, then a catering lecturer, married his best pupil, who keeps her herb garden as proficiently as her kitchen, to judge from the fumet in which the hot sea trout at a test meal had been poached. Fish is a speciality, and other visitors report equally good crab vol-au-vent, platter of seafood, and sole in wine sauce. From the Sunday buffet, the roast joints and cold beef loaf are praised, along with a baked potato 'with good butter', and imaginative, well-dressed salads. Cheesecake afterwards 'seemed to have a touch of ginger as well as lemon zest', and crème caramel, praline trifle, and oranges in grenadine are also mentioned. Coffee, when tested, was tasteless, but the accompanying chocolate truffles redeemed that stage of the meal. Carillon ordinaires are £3·90 a litre but in 1978 there were also plenty of interesting choices under £4, with Ch. Lagravière '73, c.b., a red Graves, £5·90. There are bar snacks. Recorded music. They would like, but do not quite dare, to restrict smoking, and as for children, 'age is not important, manners are.'

App: Jeffrey Lomas, Janet Tomalin, A. J. Bates, C.H.C., K. & J.F., and others

Meal times refer to first and last orders.

Bed and breakfast prices have been quoted to us by hoteliers; where possible, we have given minimum off-season and maximum in-season prices for one person sharing a double room.

BASINGSTOKE Hampshire Map 2

Franco's Ristorante
22 Hampstead House
Basingstoke 50754

Cheerful shopping-centre place, with competent service, crisp linen and crusty rolls. Praise for the chef-made pasta, crespelle alla fiorentina (90p), minestrone, veal or chicken in generous portions with creamy sauces, and caramel oranges. Take salad rather than green vegetables. House wine £1·90 the bottle. Well-behaved children and jeans welcome, sleeveless vests not. Recorded music.

Closed Sun; Mon L;
Apr 13 & 16; Dec 25 & 26
Must book D Fri & Sat
Meals 12–2.30, 7–11.30
(10 Mon)

Alc £5·20 (meal £7·20)

VAT inc
Service 10%
Cover 20p

Seats 80 (parties 25)
♿ rest
No dogs
Access, Barclay, Diners

BASLOW Derbyshire Map 5

Cavendish Hotel
on A619
3 m NE of Bakewell
Baslow 2311

Must book D & weekends
Meals 12.30–2, 7–10

Tdh L £4 (meal £7),
Sun L £5 (meal £8·15)
Alc £6·15 (meal £9·55)

Children's helpings
Seats 50 (parties 12)
♿ rest
Car park
No dogs in d/r
Am Ex, Barclay
13 rooms (all with bath)
Room only, £10

The Cavendish (formerly the Peacock) has not appeared here since 1957, when high tea was 6s. 6d. (32½p): former habitués would recognise neither the hotel, the cooking nor the prices since Eric Marsh took its structure and image in hand three years ago. No shy violet he, but as a substitute for staying in Chatsworth, inspectors and others have found the place acceptable, with 'a restful view over the estate, splendid rooms, and slightly upstart but stylish food: Ascot soup (lobster and mushroom), ribs of lamb with almonds, honey and thyme, and the Devonshires' grouse at £6·50 if you wanted it.' More brown-booted set lunches (no choice during the week) are also praised: 'The tomato soup and the brown rolls had both been made in the kitchen, and beef or a huge piece of halibut were served with fresh vegetables and a tomato with chives and yoghourt.' Nicholas Buckingham also proposes toad-in-the-hole (£3). Sweets have been less mentioned by members so far. There are substantial bar meals at lunch. Bass in cask is adumbrated, and a Mansfield firm supplies Galipette red wine at £2·85, Mâcon-Lugny '75 (Gruber) at £4·25, and Ch. d'Angludet '71 at £6·15. No music. More reports, please.

BATH Avon Map 2

Ballingers
Pierrepont Place
Bath 64545

Closed Sun; D Mon &
Tue; Dec 25 & 26;
D Dec 24 & 31; Jan 1
Must book D
Meals 12–2, 6.30–8.15

Brother and sister (Jean Mears and Allen Ballinger, who cooks) have opened this pair of basement rooms (one non-smoking) with pictures, a fire in winter, 'not a piece of plastic in sight', and nothing plastic about the food either, to judge by accounts of simple, well-treated materials. A test meal yielded 'a pork pie that would have satisfied William Pitt's dying wish'. Soups and smoked mackerel mousse are also praised, salads are made freshly and dressed well, quiches are 'made with farm eggs and cream and served warm' and

Alc £2·70 (meal £4·10)

VAT inc

Seats 38 (parties 20)

other English puddings, notably Mrs Siddons' and treacle tart, also tempt. But they do need better wine and beer. Smaller helpings for children under twelve. Classical records. More reports, please.

The Laden Table
7 Edgar Buildings,
George Street
Bath 64356

Closed Sun; Mon; Sat L;
Dec 24; public hols
Must book
Meals 12.30–1.30, 7.30–9

Tdh D from £6·25 (meal £9·35)
Alc L (min £3·50) £6·30 (meal £9·05)

VAT inc
Seats 20
No dogs
Access, Barclay

'A low-key little restaurant, with a tranquil atmosphere and keen attention to detail, both in table setting and in food.' 'Over-flavoured, over-creamed, and over-priced: no wonder there was plenty of room.' When inspectors differ so radically, the weight of members' opinion really comes into its own, and on the whole everyone likes Tony Gulliford's cooking, which is nicely introduced by 'nuts, biscuits and olives served with drinks, and current magazines on the tables'. Prawns with piquant sauce (and finger-bowl with napkins, £1·20) or grilled sardines make good first courses if the fishmonger has called, and even a critic admires the pastry of quiche Lorraine, though he was surprised to find so much onion in it. Poached salmon with lemon and caper sauce, jugged hare (£4), 'crisp, pink' best end of lamb with pimentos, and generous if not really very characterful guinea-fowl are admired as main courses. Vegetables may be limited, but well cooked. Peach and almond tart would be your best chance of avoiding cream – if they did not pour it over before it reached the table. Coffee and mints are a stiff 45p. The Averys and other wines (from about £3) are unexciting and details not supplied: 'chambré Fino and over-chilled Muscadet' are reported. No music. No children under 14. No jeans. No pipes.

App: Mrs Shirley Scott, Michael Latham, J. A. Sankey, F.I., H.L.P., and others

---

Lyons Bistro
12 Argyle Street
Bath 63625

Closed L Sat & Sun;
Dec 25 & 26; Jan 1
Must book D
Meals 12.30–2.15, 7–11.30

Tdh L £2·25 (meal £5·20)
Alc £4·15 (meal £7·15)

Children's helpings
Seats 42 (parties 30)
♿ rest
Air-conditioning
No dogs
Access card

Geof Lane has been doing well enough to be planning an approach to his cellar from Argyle Street instead of Grove Street or Riverside Walk, and a lounge upstairs for waits and snacks. 'It still feels like waiting for Harry Lime' downstairs, and laundry bills are not allowed to run out of control, but as bistro cooking goes, this earns its full entry for 'really quite fishy' fish soup with 'scorching' garlic bread, onion soup, crumbed and fried mushrooms in Camembert, 'separate and crisp' whitebait, sauté kidneys with ginger and Cointreau 'cooked to the right tenderness, and plenty of them', tasty moussaka, and scallops in peppers and brandy sauce. 'Banana fritters weren't fritters but tasted well.' Toujours ordinaires are £3 a litre and the beer is 'Euro-fizz'. Brisk service; recorded music; no under-tens after 8.30 p.m.

App: M.G. & V.A. Hart, J. D. Mitchell, S. M. Drage, E. Jenkins, Jonathan Wright, F.I., and others

Popjoys

🍷

Beau Nash House
Sawclose
Bath 60494

Closed L (Nov–Mar); Sun;
Mon L; 1 week Chr
Must book
Meals 12–2, 6.45–10.30

Tdh D (Sat) £8·75
(meal £12·65)
Alc £7·45 (meal £11·85)

Service 12½%
Seats 50 (parties 34)
🔽 rest; w.c.
No dogs
Access, Am Ex, Euro

The trouble with having pestles-and-mortars and other distinctions in a book such as this is that in any given year, a few restaurants win or lose by narrow margins. Except for the naming of Judith Rymer as co-chef, there has been no visible change in the régime of Kenneth Bell's partner, Stephen Ross. Allow time for the one-way maze to the car park nearby, ring the bell, and you are in an elegant and well-served, if crowded, room, faced with a short à la carte menu that – like Thornbury Castle's (*q.v.*) – is not as heavy as it once was. Second helpings may be sought without embarrassment, so grumbles of meagreness may be discounted. Almost all reports remark on at least one, often more, dish of high invention and achievement: 'a light and deliciously striped terrine of sole and salmon (£1·95) with a rind of crêpes, accompanied by superb mayonnaise and an appropriate salad of walnuts, celery and apples'; 'exquisitely crisp and light beignets soufflés'; 'judiciously seasoned fish soup with light, soft quenelles'; 'eye-opening' turbot *minceur*; entrecôte *saignant*, with delicious aubergines'; masterly rum bavarois, praline ice and hazelnut meringue gateau; even good bread. Gigot en aillade (£4·25) is one of the kitchen's favourites. However, a test meal failed to yield main courses that were more than mildly creditable, and though various earlier criticisms did not survive inspection, gratin dauphinoise potatoes, served with most main dishes, are too liquid on occasion. 'Pernod is better in a glass,' says someone else of the chicken dish that features it. Coffee may be taken upstairs in the salon; the fig blend seems unpopular. The wines, though always likely to be marred by smokers here, are excellent and reasonable, with six house ones from £3·35 by bottle, half or glass, recent reinforcements from the south (Gaillac, Fitou and so on), accessible '73 clarets, mature Châteauneuf-du-Pape and Hermitage, four marcs at £1 a glass and two '45 ports at £20 a bottle. No music.

App: Jill Welbourne, Anne Hardy, Nancy Eddy,
C.F., B.J.P., J.M.B., and others

Woods

9–13 Alfred Street
Bath 314812

Closed Sun D; Dec 24,
25 & 26
Must book D & weekends
Meals 12–2, 7.30–11

The pickings for an up-market caterer in Bath have tempted Hugh Corbett in from Broadway and Ian MacKenzie (who also runs Lamb's in Moreton-in-Marsh, q.v.) to this leafy, well-set restaurant near the Circus. 'I was served by a "resting" teacher and surrounded by prosperous youngsters entertaining their parents and in-laws,' says one tart observer of current moeurs, who also found it hard to believe, after two visits, that the same kitchen was producing both the

Tdh D £5·25 (meal £7·60)
Alc L £2·75 (meal £4·75)

VAT inc
Service 10%
Seats 100
♿ rest (2 steps)
Am Ex, Barclay, Diners

*careful dinners and the rather slap-happy lunches. A
test dinner was indeed mostly successful, with
'alluringly presented crudités, good mayonnaise, and
mustardy vinaigrette', followed by 'outstanding'
second courses: bourride, and chicken livers with bacon
in a brandy sauce. Veal Wood's style – a thick boned
chop in a rich sauce with sultanas – was well cooked,
but lamb should have been better trimmed and the
scabby new potatoes scraped. Quenelles of pike, and
escalope of veal with chestnut and grape stuffing, are
also worth noting. The choice of puddings is not large.
The wine list is grotesque for a restaurant of these
ambitions, and mean with information about the
bottles – few and dear – that it contains: keep to the
French-bottled Baronnette red and white ordinaires,
which are palatable. No music. More reports, please.*

BATH see also wine bar section

BEAMINSTER Dorset   Map 2

Pickwick's
The Square
Beaminster 862094

Closed L; Sun; Mon;
1st two weeks Oct;
Dec 24 & 25
Must book
D only, 7–10

Tdh £5·50 (meal £8·80)

Service 10%
Children's helpings
(under 10)
Seats 30 (parties 20)
♿ rest
Air-conditioning
No dogs
Access, Barclay, Diners

Bibliophiles who remember Stevens Cox's
mullioned shop in the old market town now find
Bill Mulligan selling unlimited editions of half-birds
(guinea-fowl or duck) with rich sauces. There are
fewer criticisms of excessive helpings this year,
though the sweet tooth may remain: 'We both had
rack of lamb with redcurrant jelly, port and
oranges.' However, an old India hand found the
chicken breast tandoori, marinated in lemon and
yoghourt, 'up to oriental standards', whatever kind
of oven it was cooked in. Fish is delivered daily;
boeuf en croûte and vegetarian or diet meals may
be ordered in advance. Begin perhaps with
mushrooms either à la grecque or stuffed with pâté
and baked. Jill Mulligan does the desserts –
'gooseberry mousse followed by madeira rounded off
the evening excellently.' Most wines, from £3 for
ordinaire, come from Eldridge Pope: the Gigondas
'72 praised last time at £3·65 is now £6 in the '77
vintage, and there is better value in the Loires,
Alsaces, or even Ch. Smith-Haut-Lafitte '73, c.b., at
£6·50. No music. Smoking discouraged.

App: E.K.D., F.J., and others

BEESTON Cheshire   Map 5

Wild Boar Motor Lodge
L'Aperitif Restaurant
on A49
S of Beeston Station
Bunbury 260309

'It is difficult to reach a balanced judgement about
a place that is not itself balanced,' says one couple,
fairly enough, since for years Mr R. I. Roberts has
been his own as well as the *Guide's* worst enemy,
turning away lucrative customers if he does not like
the way they talk, look, or dress. Another brief
description of his house, Tudor to the power of ten,

Closed Sun D
Must book D & Sun L

Tdh Sun L £4 (meal £7)
Alc £7·35 (meal £10·55)

VAT & service inc
Cover 45p
Seats 100 (parties 50)
Car park
30 rooms (all with bath)
Room only, about £9·50
Breakfast from £1·50

is 'a well-thought-out short-order bar, with extortionate wines'. That may be fair for the Huntsman grill, where people have been served 'large helpings of good materials, admirably cooked, with despatch', but the Aperitif restaurant is self-confident, serious, and expensive (though not so dear at Sunday lunch). Sometimes balance goes awry in the kitchen too: 'We would hardly have guessed that the soup (75p) was mushroom, whereas the salt in boeuf Stroganoff (£4·95, including vegetables) and the curry powder in suprême de volaille Edouard VII (£4·80) had been added with a rather heavy hand.' Vegetables, meringues, fruit, the fine blue and white Cheshire cheeses, and petits fours do the impresario credit, though 'it seems mean to add 25p for cream – albeit superb Jersey – with coffee without anyone asking whether it is wanted.' There is little of significance to drink under £10, though the price softens a little with the reflection that it includes VAT and service. The taped music is a trial. The motel rooms attached are well kept and equipped. Wear a tie. Prices are for 1978.

App: B.H.T., R. Neville, H.D. & A.L.R.

BERKHAMSTED Hertfordshire   Map 3

Christl's
118a High Street
Berkhamsted 73707

'Christl's lithe orderliness adds a unique flavour to the restaurant', a 'rather spartan' place. But even on her days off her staff produce very competent meals: smoked haddock in a tomato and cheese sauce; leeks in mayonnaise; chicken Yassa, a West African dish (£3·50); 'excellent pepper steak' (£4·50); 'light and spicy' Chinese prawns in chilli sauce; 'super' chocolate cake, 'rather stodgy' cheesecake. Vegetables are well cooked, and coffee 'actually tastes like coffee'. Attentive service. Various wines. No music.

Closed Sun L; Dec 24 & 25; L Dec 26 & 31; L Jan 1 Must book L & weekends Meals 12–2, 7–10 (10.30 Sat)	Alc £6 (meal £8·65) VAT inc Service 10%	Seats 52 (parties 30) Air-conditioning Car park No dogs Barclaycard

---

Fiorentina
21–23 Lower Kings Road
Berkhamsted 3003

Closed Sun; Mon;
Dec 25 & 26; Jan 1
Must book D
Meals 12–2, 7–9.30

Two houses with shop fronts have been joined together to make this British-owned restaurant with an Italian chef (Vincenzo Iannone) who knows his trade, by contented accounts of tagliatelle Alfredo, 'biteable' spaghetti napoletana, fresh lasagne verdi al forno (£2·25), and paglia e fieno (green and white strips of 'grass and hay' pasta with a cream sauce). Chicken, whether cacciatora or in the Cordon Bleu style, has been well cooked, and bistecca Fiorentina accurately

Alc £4·05 (meal £6·65)

Service 10% D
Seats 65
🔵 rest
Access, Am Ex, Barclay,
Diners

done. Vegetables, apart from aubergine fritters, are less interesting. Look for the day's dish on the blackboard, perhaps osso buco (£2·05). Sangiovese or Trebbiano ordinaires are £2·65 and Chianti Classico £4·25. Recorded music. No ban on children 'because some five-year-olds behave better than some adults.' More reports, please.

BIDDENDEN Kent   Map 3

Ye Maydes
High Street
Biddenden 291306

Handsome 13th-century inn with ingle-nooks, candles and crotchet in a half-timbered and wavy-roofed village. Concerned service from the Daniels (new since the place last appeared here). They offer a simple set lunch or more ambitious dishes from the *carte*: borshch, turbotin Dugléré, chicken stuffed with prawns and garlic (£3·60), roast duck with 'jammy' cherry and gooseberry sauce (£3·80). Seasonal vegetables. Sweets are sometimes amateurish. French Goustome wine, £1·60 the half-litre. No music. Children's helpings.

Closed Mon; Sun D;
Dec 25 & 26; Jan 1
Must book
Meals 12.15–1.45,
7.30–9.30

Tdh L £3·30 (meal £5·75)
Alc (min L £2·10,
D £3·30), £5·45 (meal
£8·15)

VAT inc
Seats 54 (parties 21)
🔵 rest; w.c. (f)
No dogs
Access card

BIDDENDEN see also pub section

BILBROOK Somerset   Map 1

Dragon House Hotel
on A39
6 m E of Minehead
Washford 215

There is a gracious air, in spite of the traffic, to Mr Walker's Jacobean house and garden, and most correspondents like it, in spite of the erratic, if often excellent, cooking usually reported. Inspectors and others this year have had good pea and oxtail soup, smoked trout pâté, sweetbreads and steaks with good vegetables, 'superior' lemon mousse and 'fruity' diplomat pudding. There is little need to consult the *carte*, unless in pursuit of a rather gross Wienerschnitzel. But the points against, in a test meal, were serious enough for exclusion to be mooted: a poor frying medium, watery soup, and a steamed taste and texture to roast duck. Breakfasts are creditable; wines (apart from a few bin-ends, and sufficient half-bottles) unremarkable. Service is feminine and competent. No music. Details are approximate.

Must book
Meals 12.30–2, 7.30–9.30

Tdh L £3 (meal £5·40),
D £4·25 (meal £6·90)

Alc £6·30 (meal £9·30)

Service 10%
Children's helpings

🔵 rest (1 step)
Car park
No dogs in public rooms
B&B from £8

143

Bow Window
116 High Street
8 m SW of Stowmarket
Bildeston 740748

'An attractive red restaurant in the black-beamy genre', where Mary Cox and her staff serve interesting dinners with great care and some originality. Praise for meaty soups, prawn bouchées (80p), a brown rice paella with pork, chicken and prawns (£2·80), crisp, well-seasoned vegetables, syllabub and ice-cream gateau. The speciality sirloin stuffed with chestnuts and mushrooms (£3·30) needs better meat, and Pavlova may turn out to be just meringue. 'Splendid' home-made bread and 'endless' coffee. Reasonably priced wines, with Notre Dame carafes at £2·75 for 75 cl. Mostly classical recorded music.

Closed L; Sun; Mon	Alc £4·85 (meal £7·75)	🔂 rest (2 steps)
Must book		No dogs
D only, 7.30–9.30	Seats 40	Access, Barclay

Blue Lamp
2 Robin Hood Lane,
Hall Green
on A34
at Robin Hood
roundabout
021-745 5445

A converted police station near the Robin Hood roundabout seems a jumping-off point to anything. Prices are Robin Hood, table space cell-like, staff friendly but uninformed, the chef Swiss-trained, the menu Interpol. Sentence yourself to generous pastrami on rye or Swiss smoked meats (both 85p) rather than prawns in burnt butter at £2·50. Take into account also the arresting steaks (Côte d'Ivoire: 'sirloin steak cooked in orange liqueur, with lobster, paw-paw, bananas, coconut, peanuts, peppers and cream', £5·50), frogs' legs, trout, sole, scampi. Vegetables (85p) fresh apart from the piped potato decorations. Good mille-feuille, Black Forest gateau, strawberry syllabub. French house wine, £2·75 the bottle. The band plays on record. Heavy fines at the end. On probation: evidence welcome.

Closed Sat L; Sun D;	Tdh L from £2·10 (meal	Seats 38 (parties 20)
Apr 16; Dec 25, 26 & 31;	£5·40), D £4·50 (meal	🔂 rest; w.c.
Jan 1	£7·50)	Car park
Must book	Alc £6·40 (meal £9·80)	No dogs
Meals 12.30–2, 7.30–10.30		Access, Am Ex, Barclay,
	Service 12½%	Diners, Euro
	Children's helpings	
	(under 10, Sun L)	

La Capanna
Hurst Street
021-622 2287

Renovations – and a huge 'capodimonte' fresco 'of vintagers squaring up to each other in a grape cart' – seem to have pepped things up in this cheerful and crowded ristorante. Home-made pasta, vitello tonnato (£1), pollo cacciatora (£1·90), and beef and veal in various ways have pleased customers. Soup and coffee may not be served hot enough. Zabaglione comes from the mixing bowl – 'about six glasses full'. Other helpings are generous too. Service is friendly but leisurely. Italian house wines, £2·50 the bottle. No music.

Closed Sun; public hol Mons; Dec 25 & 26; Jan 1
Must book D & weekends
Meals 12.15–2.30, 6.15–11.15

Alc £5·15 (meal £8·10)

Cover 20p
Children's helpings (under 6)

Seats 60 (parties 25)
 rest (1 step)
Car park D
No dogs
Am Ex, Diners

La Galette
68-69 The Green,
King's Norton
021-459 4995

Closed Sun; Sat L;
public hol Mons
Must book weekends
Meals 12–2.30, 7–11

Tdh L £1·75 (meal £2·95)
Alc £4·50 (meal £7·60)

Children's helpings
Seats 32
 rest (1 step)
No dogs

'Midland Red 147 bus half-hourly from New Street takes about 20 minutes virtually to the door,' says an inspector who knew his Birmingham once so did not expect to eat agreeably, as he did in Mr Benavente's olive-green restaurant. The bar is 'poky and ill-stocked, and Tio Pepe tepid in its little flute', but after that, pleasure is expressed in the onion soup, 'generous entrecôte Café de Paris, cooked saignant with anchovy-buttery juices', pork brochette, good courgettes provençale and jacket potatoes. Frogs' legs (£1·50) and boeuf Stroganoff (£3·15) are other dishes to try. The house galette is sufficiently interesting, with apples, sultanas, chopped hazelnuts and spices in a shortcake pastry. 'The coffee subsided to Brum level.' La Vie de France ordinaire is £3·35 a litre and though the list is short and poor, half-bottles are present. Recorded music. More reports, please.*

Giovanni's
27 Poplar Road,
Kings Heath
021-443 2391

A pleasant though crowded small restaurant, run by the Buttos. Occasional delay or confusion over bookings is forgiven by those who appreciate the bargain set lunch (smoked mackerel, veal milanese and sherry trifle, say, £2·60), the crisply cooked vegetables, the Gorgonzola, the coffee and the flowers. Pasta is over-peppery for some. Italian house wine, £2·60 the litre. Recorded music.

Closed Mon (exc Dec 31 D); Sun D;
Apr 15; Aug 11–25;
Dec 25 & 26; Jan 1
Must book
Meals 12–2, 7–10.30

Tdh L £2·60 (meal £3·90)
Alc £5·80 (meal £7·65)

VAT & service inc
Cover 30p alc
Children's helpings L

Seats 43
 rest (1 step)
No dogs
Access, Barclay, Diners

Jonathans'
16 Wolverhampton Road,
Quinton
021-429 3757

Closed Sun; Mon; Sat L;
1 week Easter; 3 weeks Aug
Must book
Meals 12–2.30, 7–9.30

No one would expect the Guide to resist a place that lists tripes-à-la-mode twice on a relatively short à la carte menu (once as a first course, 90p; once as a main, £3·60 including vegetables). But the two Johns here, Baker and Bedford (the latter cooks also), have other claims on members' attention. Their Victorian mahogany and disarming atmosphere are 'reinforced by a formidable house servant dressed up as if to dispense brimstone and treacle' rather than their delicious salmon soup, jugged steak, portmanteau'd

Alc £5·80 (meal £8·80)

VAT inc
Seats 30
No dogs
Barclay, Diners

lamb chops, chicken with apples and cider, and enterprising vegetables: 'carrots with fennel, mushrooms with coriander, cucumber with almonds, spinach in apricot sauce.' Sweets praised include apricot and almond fool, syllabub (naturally) and 'strongly alcoholic whim-wham'. 'The wines, like the menus, are constantly changing', and they add a fixed charge, not a percentage, to each bottle, so since the Loire ordinaires are a relatively modest £2·50 you do even better with Ch. Meyney '67 at £4·60 or Ch. Brane-Cantenac '73 at £6·80. Recorded music. Parking is easy at night and there is a 'Victorian yard' for outdoor eating. More reports, please.

BIRMINGHAM West Midlands   Map 5

Michelle
182–184 High Street,
Harborne
021-426 4133

Closed Sun; public hols;
Dec 24
Must book
Meals 12–2, 7–10

Tdh L £1·50 (meal £2·40),
D from £3·60 (meal £7·55)
Alc £6·20 (meal £8·80)

VAT inc
Seats 42

Back in Harborne after several years' sojourn in Smethwick, Michelle Vale is now running both a restaurant and an attached delicatessen. They feed each other, early accounts suggest, because the quiches and salads and French cheeses look and taste fresh: moreover, the patronne *and her assistants in the kitchen do not overplay their hands, offering a very simple and cheap set lunch (potage, a made-up dish with a sauce, and tarte aux pommes, perhaps); and set and à la carte meals at various prices in the evening. Both are approved, though it is wise to ask exactly how main dishes are cooked since the service is unpolished and listings sometimes rather approximate. Basic wines from £1·66 for 50 cl of Valpierre. Recorded chansons. Children's helpings. No dogs. More reports, please.*

Le Provençal
1 Albany Road,
Harborne
021-426 2444

Closed Sun; L Mon &
Sat; most public hols
Must book
Meals 12–1.30, 7–10
(10.30 Fri & Sat)

Alc £4·35 (meal £6·05)

Seats 50 (parties 25)
⌖ rest (3 steps)
Access, Barclay, Diners

The rest of the Harborne revival has not yet caught up with René Ernst and Geoffrey Rhodes, say admirers of their soupe de poissons with croûtons and rouille, home-made chicken pâté, steak au poivre, 'really good ratatouille', and rösti potatoes ('at least if you like them burnt, as I do'). Veal zurichoise is more debatable for the price, it seems, but it is always worth trying the specialities of the week, such as 'prawns in sauce' (their description, £2·80) or canard aux petits oignons. However, in neither sweet nor cheese departments is M Ernst the local market-leader. Coffee is good. The atmosphere is relaxed, with an extra room open upstairs at weekends, but 'the service may get sloppy when they know you.' Vins du patron (from Provence) are £2·80. No dogs. Recorded music.

App: Eric Deeson, W.P., Henry Potts

Please report to us on atmosphere, decor and – if you stayed –
standard of accommodation, as well as on food, drink and prices
(send bill if possible).

VAT & service inc
Seats 45 (parties 30)
Access, Am Ex, Barclay,
Diners
5 rooms (4 with bath)
B&B from £13
Car park

and soufflé omelettes with rum (£2 extra for two on the set dinner menus which are priced inclusively at present by the cost of the main course). Averys Clochemerle red and Bordeaux dry white are £3·20; Ch. Cantemerle '67, c.b., is £9·75. No music. Dress smartly. Leave under-14s (and dogs) at home, they suggest. More reports, please – and since they were publicly claiming a Guide *entry two months before they had it, better watch their step.*

BISHOP WILTON Humberside   Map 6

Fleece Inn
5 m E of Stamford Bridge
between A166 & A1079
Bishop Wilton 251

The village is pretty, and you are stabled in a stall for the elaborate weekend dinners (£4·25) in this free house. Simpler weekday dinners (£2·75) and lunches are served at three tables off the bar. Local produce is at its best simply treated (vegetable soup, pâté, chicken, steaks, and fruity puddings). Seasonings, sauces and temperatures need a steadier hand. Attentive service. Les Celliers wine 35p the glass. Bar snacks include open sandwiches, stuffed pancakes, and steak and chips, with Samuel Smith's bitter on hand pump. Taped music.

Closed Mon L;
L Dec 25 & 26
Must book D & weekends
Meals 12–1.30 (bar),
7.30–10

Tdh Sun L £1·95 (meal
£3·80), D £2·75 (meal
£4·60), Fri & Sat D £4·25
(meal £6·10)

VAT & service inc

Seats 14 & 38 (parties 35)
rest (1 step); w.c.
Car park
No dogs
4 rooms
B&B £4

BLACKPOOL Lancashire   Map 5

Danish Kitchen
95 Church Street
Blackpool 24291

This spruce white and pine self-service restaurant (behind the Vernon Humpage shoe shop) has branches elsewhere in the north. Here it rescues tourists, entertainers and other people who find most Blackpool food 'something to be endured'. The same menu lasts all day with no minimum charge. Freshly made soups, open sandwiches (from 40p), salads, quiches, pizzas, omelettes, pastries and gateaux (from 35p). Coffee (16p) actually dropped in price with the world market. Chanson house wine is £1·80 for 50 cl. 'Friendly and helpful staff' share the profits. No music. 'The only rule is decent behaviour.,

Closed D; Sun; Dec 25 &
26
Open 9.15–5.15

Alc meal £1·45

VAT & service inc
Children's helpings

Seats 104
rest (1 step)
Air-conditioning

Numbers are given for private parties only if they can be accommodated in a room separate from the main dining-room; when there are several such rooms, the capacity of the largest is given. Some restaurants will take party bookings at times when they are normally closed.

La Casita
Bridgwater Road
3 m SE of Weston-super-
Mare
(M5 exit 22)
Bleadon 812326

Garry Waite's tiny restaurant expresses its 'Spanish accent' more in lace, crystal and attentive service than in cooking. Praise for moules marinière, fried calamares (95p), guinea-fowl, steak in a bacon and mushroom sauce (£3·45), potato and cheese puffs, and the cheeses. Sweets are ordinary. Wine list reveals little, but Ch. Batailley '70 is £5·25, El Marqués £1·50 for 50 cl. Taped music *da capo*.

Closed Tue; Dec 26
Must book
Meals 12.30–2, 7.30–11

Alc £6 (meal £8·50)

VAT inc
Seats 24 (parties 24)

♿ rest (2 steps)
Car park
No dogs

Lower Brook House
on B4479
3½ m NW of
Moreton-in-Marsh
Blockley 286

Closed Sun D; Mon L;
Dec 24 D; Dec 25–Jan 19
Must book D & Sun L
Meals 12.30–2, 7.30–9
(9.30 Fri & Sat)

Tdh Sun L (res) & tdh D
(res) £4 (meal £6·85),
tdh D (non-res) £5·50
(meal £9·55)

VAT inc
Children's helpings
Seats 34
♿ rest (2 steps)
Car park
No dogs
Access card
6 rooms (4 with bath)
B&B £9
Fire cert

The village, and the house, are famously picturesque with natural stone walls, though partitions in the house are flimsier. The Greenstocks are capable of advertising 'midday munchies', not only on the gate, but across the tee-shirted corbels of the girls who serve. The food has lapses too, but 'at least my avocado with Stilton and grapes was an interesting failure', and at the same meal, veal with cheese and mushroom sauce, a puree of garlicky peas, and 'luscious apricot meringue pie and honey mousse' were all liked. The same was true of 'well-fried, dry and crisp' cheese beignets and trout with hot shrimps, when expertly assayed. 'Creamy baked tomatoes', lamb cutlets with cheese and spinach sauce, and chocolate praline puddings are other favourites of the kitchen team for the three-course set meals at different prices. Mr Greenstock himself cooks breakfast very capably. Litre Vin carafes are £2·95 (a litre), and the wines are well chosen: Mâcon-Lugny Les Genièvres (Louis Latour) '76, £4·80; Gigondas '73 (Meffre) £4·75; local Three Choirs white '76 at £4·25, and interesting bin-ends. 'How nice to buy a glass of Muscat de Beaumes de Venise for 40p.' No music. No infants, nor under-sevens at dinner.

App: D. Saunders, R. W. E. Wiersum, D.W.D., Joan Chenhalls, A. B. X. Fenwick, H.L., and others

La Locanda
Fox Lane
Norwich 713787

Family-run Italian place with standard menu and competent cooking. Praise for fresh crab, lasagne al forno (pasta is offered as first or main course, at about £1 and £2 respectively), scaloppine di vitello provenzale, with properly cooked vegetables, and

fresh fruit salad to finish. The set lunch might
include soup or sardines, Glaven trout, chicken
cacciatora or savoury omelette, with gateaux or
ice-cream (£2·25). Italian house wine, £2·85 the
bottle. Recorded music. No jeans. No children under
eight in the evening.

Closed Sun; Sat L; part of May & Sept; Dec 24; public hols	Tdh L £2·25 (meal £4·45) Alc (min L £2·50, D £3·50), £5·65 (meal £8·15)	Children's helpings L (under 10) Seats 40 (parties 20)
Must book D & weekends Meals 12.30–1.45, 7.30–10.45	VAT inc	Car park No dogs Access, Am Ex, Barclay

---

BODIAM East Sussex   Map 3

Curlew
on A229
2½ m S of Hawkhurst
Hurst Green 272

Closed Mon; Sun D;
Dec 25
Must book D
Meals 12.30–1.30,
7.30–9.15

Tdh L £3·25 (meal £4·95)
Alc £7·35 (meal £9·45)

VAT & service inc
Cover 40p D
Seats 18
Car park
No dogs in d/r
Access, Am Ex, Barclay,
Diners, Euro

*'Before you are half-way into the place, there are
notices in three languages telling you how marvellous
they are,' says a world-weary inspector of Tom
Geary's white-boarded, conventionally furnished inn
one mile from Bodiam's sublime castle. Mr Geary is
an enthusiastic chef (who irrupts, tousled, into the
dining-room from time to time), and people have
expressed themselves well content with his roulade des
gourmands (£1·20), fillets of sole in a barquette of
pastry with asparagus ('looked delightful and tasted
gorgeous', £5·25), roast beef for Sunday lunch,
Stilton, and Black Forest gateau. Main dish prices
include vegetables. But ambition o'erleaps itself with
his crevettes géants Moska – 'any taste the prawns and
the saffron rice may have had were overpowered by
rosemary spikes in the oily sauce poured over it.'
Vegetables, blackcurrant cheesecake and other items
further betrayed an incipient preoccupation with looks
at the expense of taste. Harvey's Sussex bitter is on
hand pump, though it was out of condition when tried.
The House French ordinaire at £2·75 is more
promising, and though claret and burgundy prices are
in some cases immoderate, £5·50 is not too bad for
Viña Pomal '55, nor £11 for Croft '66 port. There is
a self-service buffet in the bar except on Sunday
evenings and Mondays. No music. No children under
12 except at Sunday lunch. More reports, please – on
the set lunch too.*

BONCHURCH see ISLE OF WIGHT

BOROUGHBRIDGE North Yorkshire   Map 8

Fountain House
St James Square
Boroughbridge 2241

Closed L (exc Sun);
Sun D; Mon; public hols

*Too much rests on Peter Carwardine as owner-chef for
the five-course dinners in this rambling old house's
well-set dining-room to be wholly reliable, and not for
nothing did he borrow an adjective from last year's
entry and offer 'an anglicised and delicious moussaka'
on one of his menus (which normally have about six*

Must book
Meals 12.30–2 (Sun),
7.30–10

Tdh Sun L £4 (meal
£6·10), D £6·50 (meal
£8·85)

VAT inc
Seats 45 (parties 20)
⅄ rest (3 steps)
No dogs

*choices of main course, and numerous first courses and
sweets). Still, both the cooking and service are
professional enough, and appreciative accounts of a
rich mousse of duckling and port 'on one of those lovely
Victorian cabbage-leaf plates', cassoulet de sole aux
champignons, with a creamy white wine sauce and a
crisp pastry lid, and 'almost bitter' grapefruit and
Pernod sorbet, save the place from its critics. Wines are
young for the most part and far from cheap: settle for
one of the Chanson generic burgundies, perhaps, at
£4·45. No music. More reports, please, for not many
members seem to have reached Boroughbridge this year.*

BORROWDALE Cumbria   Map 7

Leathes Head House
on B5289
3½ m S of Keswick
Borrowdale 247

Closed L; early Nov to
Apr 1
Must book
D only, 7.30–8.15

Tdh £6·50 (meal £7·65)

VAT & service inc
Seats 30
⅄ rest (3 steps); w.c.
Car park
No dogs in public rooms
12 rooms (3 with bath)
B&B £10
D, B&B £16
(min 2 nights)
Fire cert

The Hills did not have an easy passage in their first
Guide entries, but their grown-up daughter's service
now softens the faint prickliness that goes with a
house like a new pin and a firm ban on children
under nine, and a fair judge now finds the
family's self-confidence amply justified. The
surrounding acres are peaceful and everyone seems
to have enjoyed the cooking (by Mrs Hill and Kevin
Wright) from the substantial country breakfasts to
the five-course dinners 'which seemed to get better
each evening'. They might be better still if soups
were 'started from scratch', as someone puts it,
and if other short-cuts unworthy of the kitchen
were ruthlessly avoided, even at the expense of the
extra course. But avocado and grapefruit salad, or
chicken and veal terrine, make good beginnings,
and main dishes praised include roast (but moist)
guinea-fowl, boned cherry-stuffed quail, veal in
cream sauce with rice, and lamb's liver with
Dubonnet and orange, always with a good choice of
vegetables ('featherlight chips and tender broad
beans'). Diners obviously build up to the varied
cheeses and the sweets, such as 'dark and delicious'
summer pudding, crème brûlée with grapes, charlotte
russe Grand Marnier, sherry trifle and brandy-snaps.
The wines (from £2·35) are probably adequate for
most guests, though even a mild criticism of a
'fizzing' Muscadet caught Mr Hill on the wrong foot.
Heritage bitter is pressurised. 'Generous' packed
lunches are provided. No music. No smoking at
table. Conventional dress requested.

*App: E. D. Barraclough, Mrs A. Simons, L.J.R.,
T. P. Walter, M.F., D. A. Murdoch, and others*

Most places will accept cheques only when they are accompanied by a
cheque card or adequate identification. Information about which credit cards
are accepted is correct when printed, but occasionally restaurants add to or
subtract from the list without notice.

BOURNEMOUTH Dorset Map 2

Crust
Exeter Road,
The Square
Bournemouth 21430

Closed Sun (Jan–Easter);
Dec 25 & 26
Must book
Meals 12–2.30, 6.30–11
(11.30 Sat)

Alc £4·95 (meal £7·25)

VAT inc
Service 10%
Children's helpings
Seats 60
 rest
Car park (4)
No dogs
Access, Am Ex, Barclay,
Diners, Euro

Bournemouth in general, and this restaurant in particular, has had bad luck with the *Guide* since Patrick Markby left, but after uncertain beginnings Paul Harper and his young team have returned Crust to 'godsend' status. Though surrounded by *bis motoribus* in this location, people eat comfortably with a view of good pictures and the kitchen itself. 'I had not expected much of mushroom soup but it arrived fragrant, with lightly cooked caps on top and a vital touch of soy sauce. Prawns in garlic butter, though, were hardly worth the shelling, first-aid kit, and bathtub needed.' Another visitor admires above even the saddle of lamb and the local fish 'a place that knows how to buy vegetables and cook them'. Casseroles of venison, oxtail, and Moroccan lamb are noted too, and Mr Harper recommends his own chicken yakitori (£2·40) and cured loin of pork with Cumberland sauce. Sweets include lemon and treacle tart, or raspberry sorbet with Cassis (75p). Wines are well chosen from various sources, beginning with Loire Gamay or Gros Plant sur lie '75 at about £3. A musician found the service 'almost alarmingly friendly: they served the Gewürztraminer as though it came from Tutankhamen's tomb and let us stay long past closing time.' Recorded music was fortunately too quiet for him to notice it.

App: Shirley Winn, B.J.P., Paul Daneman, J. Pluck, T. M. Clark, and others

The Stable
3–4 Granville Place,
Yelverton Road
Bournemouth 22651

The names of the Bournemouth places this time suggest that the town has an unsuspected yearning for the simple life: however, as Crust (q.v.) is to the bus station, Robert Towle's new place is to an earlier stage of the borough's transport system (harness from the old borough stables adorn the walls). Lunches have alas already been dropped, but in the evening, tureens of creamy vegetable soup, 'fresh-roasted turkey with buttered parsnips', and competent boeuf bourguignonne have raised hopes. 'Dried-out vegetables and mediocre sweets' lowered them again for a Bank Holiday Saturday visitor. More reports, please.

Closed L; Sun; Dec 25	Children's helpings	Car park (6)
Must book	(under 10)	No dogs
D only, 7–11	Seats 42 (parties 20)	Am Ex, Barclay, Diners
	Air-conditioning	
Alc £4·75 (meal £7·50)		

Please report to us on atmosphere, decor and – if you stayed –
standard of accommodation, as well as on food, drink and prices
(send bill if possible).

Rose Tree Restaurant
Riverside
Bourton-on-the-Water
20635

Closed Mon (exc L public
hols); Sun D; D Dec
25 & 26; 3 weeks Jan
Must book D
Meals 12.30–2, 7.30–10

Tdh L £3·25 (meal £5·55),

Sun L £3·95 (meal £6·35)

Alc £5·80 (meal £8·40)

VAT inc
Service 10%
Children's helpings
(Sun L)
Seats 28 (parties 20)
 ♻ rest (1 step)
No dogs

The Rose Tree was dropped when the McAllisters
left, and it is encouraging to hear from many
members that the new resident proprietors of this
Queen Anne house by the Windrush are cooking far
better food than can be expected in a village
normally awash with coach parties. A set lunch for
four, including kipper pâté, chicken livers in bacon
with garlic bread, guinea-fowl and roast beef, and
puddings from the trolley, cost £6 a head all in
with one bottle of claret, and was the more enjoyed
because of the relaxed atmosphere. Crab crêpes,
paupiettes de sole, and turbot are also praised, and
another couple making their second dinner visit
report agreeable crudités, 'hot and spicy' rognons de
veau as a first course (£1·25), crisp duck, and
well-cooked strips of beef in a cream sauce with
rice, and good coffee soufflé and banana and caramel
meringue. Chocolate roulade, by contrast, was
'rather dry and tasteless', but 'home-made
loganberry ice-cream' (75p), and passion-fruit
charlotte with calvados sound interesting. The
house wines are Libertine red (Gamay) and white
(Mâcon) from Lionel Bruck at £3·25, and Mr
Gaynor is pleased with his La Terrasse of the
unfashionable '74 vintage at £3·60, not to mention
white Three Choirs '76 from Newent at £3·75. Ch.
Meyney '67 and '70 were both under £6 in 1978.
Recorded classical music. 'Try not to smoke in the
restaurant.' Snacks can be taken in the riverside
garden. Toddlers 'welcome by prior arrangement'.

*App: Kathy Martin, Mrs S. Tamlyn, Michael
Latham, K. V. Baillie Hill, J. & J.W., and others*

Porthole Eating House
3 Ash Street
Windermere 2793

Gianni Berton's 17th-century cottage bistro is
usually bursting at the seams. His English chef's
cooking is helped out by his wife's gateaux and
bread – and mother-in-law launders the table linen.
A very 'standard' menu is enlivened by daily
specials (unpriced): fish salad, spaghetti all'aglio,
fresh lobster or salmon, and well-cooked vegetables.
Long and dazzling wine list (Ch. Mouton Rothschild
'59, £20, and no fewer than 30 English ones); house
wine £3·40 a litre. Recorded music.

Closed L; Tue;
Dec & Jan
Must book
D only, 7–10.30

Alc (min £3·50) £5·10
(meal £8·20)

Children's helpings

Seats 38 (parties 20 out
of season)
No dogs

1979 prices are as estimated by restaurateurs in the autumn of 1978.

BRADFORD West Yorkshire   Map 5

Bradford College
Pine Room
Great Horton Road
Bradford 34844 (ext 318)

A sunny room at the top of the college offers bargain lunches (and dinner on Thursdays) during term-time with well-supervised staff. The atmosphere makes up for the random element – 'my two crêpes were obviously made by different hands' – and an inspector was encouraged by pretty 'though rather bland' hors d'oeuvre varié, crisply fried fish with good chips, competent aubergine provençale and cauliflower, 'custard with too much vanilla', and freshly made coffee. Various wines by the glass from 35p; Notre Dame litres, £2·50. Telephone at least two days in advance, between 11.30 and 3.

Closed Sat; Sun; D (exc Thur); vacations	Tdh L £1·20 (meal £2), D £2·50 (meal £3·30)	Cover 10p L Seats 64 (parties 24)
Must book	Alc £1 (meal £1·95)	♿ rest (lift)
Meals 12.15–1, 7–7.30 (Thur)	VAT & service inc	Car park No dogs

The Cottage
869 Thornton Road,
Thornton
Bradford 832752

Several people still feel upstaged by this 'classy barn' of a cottage, though others think the set dinner, or quieter lunch à la carte, worth the crowds and occasional defects. A four-course test meal produced 'fresh and tasty' fruits de mer, a well-made vegetable soup, plump grilled chicken rather swamped in its 'lyonnaise' garnish, patchy vegetables, and profiteroles with spun sugar. To say nothing of the coffee and carnation. Service is competent. Wines are dear, and those listed are not always available. House Bordeaux is £4·45 a bottle. No music. 'Jacket and tie preferred.' No dogs.

Closed Tue; Sat L; Dec 25 D	Tdh D £6·45 (meal £9·95) Alc L £5·45 (meal £8·85)	Service 10% Seats 80 (parties 25)
Must book D		Car park
Meals 12–2.15, 7–10.15	VAT inc	Access, Am Ex, Barclay

Last Pizza Show
50 Great Horton Road
Bradford 28173

Mario Benericetti aims for 'a Romagna atmosphere with Romagnola music' – no easy task in Bradford, opposite the Deutsche Evangelische Kirche, just down the hill from Delius's birthplace. But this is a cheerful open-plan place on two floors, with bamboo chairs and red tasselled lamps. The huge pizzas (a dozen varieties, from £1) and the lasagne (95p) are praised. Veal Marsala (£2·60 with sprouts and crisp chips) was a creditable dish of the day. Herbing could be more vigorous – and who needs steak Diane? Home-made ice-cream and a choice of Cona or espresso coffee make acceptable endings. Italian house wine, £2·50 for 75 cl; Chianti Classico is £4.

Closed Sun L; Dec 25; L public hol Mons	Alc £3·95 (meal £6)	Service 10% (parties) Seats 60
Meals 12–2, 6–11.30	VAT inc	No dogs

BRAMPTON Cumbria   Map 8

Farlam Hall
on A689
2½ m E of Brampton
Hallbankgate 234

Closed L (exc Sun); Feb;
Dec 25–31
Must book
Meals 12.30–1.15 (Sun),
7–7.45

Tdh D £5 (meal £7·25)
Alc Sun L (min £2·50)
£3·55 (meal £5·65)

VAT inc
Seats 50
⅃ rest (2 steps)
Car park
No dogs in d/r
Access card
11 rooms (2 with bath,
2 with shower)
B&B from £8·50
Fire cert

John Wesley preached and George Stephenson slept
in the Quinions' 17th-century farmhouse in rolling
country at the west end of Hadrian's Wall, and first
impressions of a warm welcome 'even survived
insistent pressure to choose from the dinner menu
while we still had luggage in our hands after a long
drive' (note the unusually tight dinner-time). The
food itself was good, though, by this and other
accounts. 'Herbed potato soup came with delicious
hot wholewheat rolls (and I make my own at
home).' Grilled trout tasted farmed rather than
free-range, but 'salmon caught that morning' was
excellent, wood pigeon was tasty, and baked
potatoes, along with an immense platter of lightly
cooked vegetables including a whole cauliflower in
white sauce, 'appealed even to a vegetable-hater.'
Mr Quinion values his Stilton and sage Derby well
enough to like serving them before the chocolate,
pear and brandy gateau or damson cheesecake, and
there is coffee by the fire afterwards. Breakfasts are
equally substantial. Wines, from £2·50, are modest,
though there are a few nice Rhine wines at £5 or so,
one of them red. No music.

*App: Dr & Mrs P. W. Love, M. J. Cleave,
M.M.G.J., Diane Kopscick, and others*

BRAY Berkshire   Map 3

Waterside Inn

Ferry Road
Maidenhead 20691 *and*
22941

Closed Mon; Sun D
(winter); 2 weeks Jan
Must book
Meals 12.30–2, 7.30–10.30

Alc £12·25 (meal £15·70)

VAT & service inc
Children's helpings
Seats 80
⅃ rest; w.c.
Car park
No dogs
Access, Barclay

The precise point at which the *accueil* of a
restaurant and the technical or diplomatic skills of
its service affect the taste of the food are debated
by serious diners much as doctors debate the
existence of psychosomatic disorders. Last time, too
many members felt that they did not receive in the
Roux brothers' elaborate river-house the automatic
consideration and counsel they expect at two-rosette
restaurants in France itself, and bang went a
'pestle'. It is idle to pretend that this problem –
which MM Roux may or may not recognise to be a
problem – is entirely solved, or could be, without a
language laboratory on the premises. 'A January
visit provided a warm welcome (there were just
eight diners all evening), impeccable service, and
one of the best meals eaten this side of Lasserre.
Especially notable were pink slices of saddle of hare
in a pungent, creamy sauce, and mouth-watering
sablé of pears with raspberry puree. In June, it took
three staff to establish that we did have a booking
and longer than that to get a smile out of anybody.'
It is a tribute to the accomplishment of the kitchen
that rather worse treatment on Gold Cup Day –
'with celebrities from Lester Piggott to Mr
Teasy-Weasy sprinkled round the dining-room' –

left a family party not too discontented to pay almost £100 for four (even so, the total was still left 'accusingly blank' on the credit card voucher) for such dishes as the feuilleté d'asperges (£3·50), duck with curaçao (£12·80 for two), truite saumonée à la Champagne ('an exceptional fish dish, delicate flesh surrounding a superb fish mousse in a sauce with a true flavour of the wine', £15·20 for two), crunchy haricots verts with shallots (£1·50) and peach in champagne sauce, or mille-feuille aux framboises (both £2·50). London-bottled Meursault '70 on that occasion cost £12·30 and 'comparatively well-valued' Ch. Malartic-Lagravière '67, £12·70. Other notes include 'heavenly crab des îles'; 'masterpieces such as the boudin blanc and the terrine de homard (£5·10, but never mind)'; gigot au Pauillac, garnished with an apricot stuffed with cream cheese, 'perhaps the best lamb dish any restaurant has given me'; and a Christmas Day lunch with Albert Roux presiding sunnily over the goose 'aux trois purées', turkey 'with real cranberries' and le pouding anglais. Note that VAT, 15 per cent service and cover are now included in bills, so you get your Malvern water, canapés, and petits fours with coffee free, so to speak. Details are approximate and the prices those for 1978, for MM Roux are less communicative than their customers.

App: A. B. X. Fenwick, Francesca Swann, David Hammond, A.M.P., Christopher Forman, and others

---

BRIDGNORTH Salop Map 5

Bambers
65 St Mary's Street,
Bridgnorth High Town
Bridgnorth 3139

'Comfortable, down-at-heel and purple' bistro with Victoriana and bright young things for decor – and good service. Vaguely French provincial menu, short and often changed: stuffed peppers, stuffed shoulder of lamb (£3·10, including good vegetables), salad, and chocolate meringue sponge succeed; ratatouille and cheeses may not. Litre Vin house wine is £2·75 for 83 cl. Recorded music.

Closed L; Sun; Mon;
Sept; Dec 25 & 26; Jan 1
Must book
D only, 7–9.30
(10 Fri & Sat)

Alc (min £2) £4·75
(meal £7·05)

VAT inc
Seats 46

🔲 rest (2 steps)
Air-conditioning
No dogs

Parlors Hall Hotel
Mill Street,
Low Town
Bridgnorth 2604

A welcoming hotel, part 15th-century, with a handsome dining-room in the Victorian music room. Simple set meals (good soups, generous roast beef, 'first-class' vegetables, and milk puddings or fruit tarts), with roasts and grills à la carte (duckling with black cherry and port sauce, £4·25). Attentive service. Bouchard Aîné burgundies (from

£2·60 the bottle, 40p the glass). Recorded music; occasional dancing. Bar snacks and Banks's bitter and mild on hand pump.

Closed Sun D; Sat L;	Tdh £3 (meal £4·65)	♿ rest
Dec 25 D; Dec 26;	Alc £5·20 (meal £6·85)	Car park
Dec 31 L; Jan 1		No dogs in public rooms
Meals 12.30–2 (2.30 Sun),	VAT & service inc	Access, Am Ex
7–10	Children's helpings	12 rooms (2 with bath)
	Seats 56 (parties 120)	B&B £8·50

BRIGHTON & HOVE East Sussex   Map 3

(1) Athenian Restaurant
12 Preston Street
Brighton 28662

'Mr Chris' provides a solicitous welcome in this modest, well-served taverna, where the Greek-Cypriot dishes are the most popular: hummus or taramosalata, moussaka ('more aubergine would have been nice') or lamb kebabs with roast potatoes and salad (£2·20); fresh fruit or rather English puddings; Turkish coffee and Turkish delight. Cypriot wines, £1·50 for 50 cl, 40p the glass. 'Mostly Greek' recorded music. Children treated kindly.

Closed Dec 25 & 26	Alc £4·15 (meal £6·50)	♿ rest
Must book weekends		Air-conditioning
Meals 12–2.30, 5.30–1 a.m.	Cover 20p	Access, Am Ex, Barclay,
	Children's helpings	Diners, Euro
Tdh L £2 (meal £3·80),	Seats 50	
D £3 (meal £5)		

---

(2) Bannister's
77 St George's Road
Brighton 687382

Closed Sun; Mon; 3 weeks
Jan/Feb; Dec 25 & 26
Must book
Meals 12–2, 7–11

Tdh L £3·50 (meal £5·35)
Alc £5·65 (meal £8·75)

VAT inc (tdh L)
Cover 25p (Sat D)
Seats 24
Air-conditioning
No dogs
Am Ex card

The cooking of the Roes under another name (the former owner's) is smelling almost as sweet in this upstairs-downstairs restaurant (the stair gallops must be very slimming for Maureen Roe, who serves). Geoffrey, who cooks, formerly catered for St John's in Cambridge, which helps to explain accounts of freshman successes here such as melon with crème de menthe, haddock mousse, scallop and artichoke soup, crépinettes de crabe armoricaine, 'tasty with fresh-caught crab, and almost large enough for a main course' (£1·30), chicken suprême with pâté and a madeira sauce, and 'slightly pink' carré d'agneau aux herbes de Provence. The Roes specialise, they say, in whatever is in season. Fresh gooseberry or rhubarb fools, or peaches poached in wine, are also praised, and the 'taste of Britain' lunch looks worth a try. But not everything went smoothly in the first six months ('semolina-like sauce on paupiettes de veau') and they discourage smoking less firmly than their predecessors did. Nor can they aspire to the St John's cellar, but do their best with interesting French regional house wines under £3, '76 Beaujolais and Rhônes from Vincent Denis, or white burgundy from Louis Latour, at about £6, and Ch. Lyonnat '66, c.b., at £7·75. Indian records are sometimes played. More reports, please.

BRIGHTON & HOVE
(Not to scale)

(3) Café de Flore
10 Upper Market Street,
Hove
Brighton 739546

Closed L; Sun; Mon;
Sept 16–Oct 2; Dec 25 &
26; Jan 1
Must book
D only, 7.30–10 (11 Fri &
Sat)

Alc £4·70 (meal £7·25)

Seats 24 (parties 12)
No dogs
Am Ex card

*Tom and Dolores McGuinness define their market
neatly as 'lemon sole rather than Dover, wood-pigeon
rather than pheasant': that is what comes of an
accountant's training (his) and an affection for
cuisine bourgeoise (hers). The place is small enough
for them to control as though it were the dining-room at
home, and inspectors and others report very capable
onion soup, pâté, and smoked salmon mousse as first
courses; then fresh fish from Brighton market, rack of
lamb 'cooked exactly to medium rare', 'delicately
flavoured' escalope de porc Café de Flore (with cider,
calvados and Dijon mustard, £2·60) and other specials
depending on landings (loup de mer or St Pierre) or
season (chevreuil en croûte). 'Sweet-sour shallots and
carrots in a puree made interesting vegetables.' Sweets
are kept simple, 'but home-made chocolate trifle is
popular, albeit not French.' Nothing has been heard
about cheeses. Borderive ordinaires are £2·20, and
though the Richard Martin wines will rise at least ten
per cent in 1979, in 1978 there were sound Loire
whites or Bordeaux reds under £4. Recorded music.
More reports, please.*

---

(4) Eaton Restaurant
Eaton Gardens,
Hove
Brighton 738921

'A conventional restaurant providing conventional
food for conventional people' is one summary of
Forfars the Bakers' 'plush, suburban place'. So when
a doctor suffered a vaso-vagal attack, there were two
consultants at the adjacent table to see to him.
Fewer surprises in the cooking, but 'modest

competence' with whitebait, mushroom quiche, 'roast duckling with crisp skin', steaks, and some interesting vegetables – salsify, for example. Raspberries and cream and strawberry soufflé are among the sweets praised. From the *carte* the chef recommends coq aux morilles (£4·25) and truite aux amandes (£2·90). House wine is £4 the litre. Pleasant and efficient service. Recorded music. No pipes.

Closed Sun D; Apr 13; Dec 25	Alc £6·30 (meal £8·90)	Air-conditioning Car park
Must book	VAT inc	No dogs
Meals 12.30–2.30, 6.30–9.45	Service 10% Children's helpings (under 10)	Cheques by arrangement Access, Am Ex, Barclay, Diners, Euro
Tdh L £4·25 (meal £6·75), D £5 (meal £7·60)	Seats 100 (parties 80)	

BRIGHTON & HOVE East Sussex   Map 3

(5) Al Forno
36 East Street
Brighton 24905

Crowded, table-sharing trattoria near the Lanes. Simplest dishes are best: pizzas (about 20 of them), pasta (lasagne alla casalinga, £1), salad and ice-cream. 'Primitive' Italian house wine £2·30 for 72 cl. Friendly service, 'nice to children too'. When the smoke and noise get too much, in summer at least there are outside tables.

Closed Mon; Sun L; Apr 13; Dec 25 & 26; Jan 1	Alc £3·35 (meal £5·15)	Service 10% Seats 55
Meals 12.30–2.30, 6.30–11.30	VAT inc	Access, Am Ex

(6) Le Grandgousier
15 Western Street
Brighton 772005

'Rather like dining in a train, but with better food and no jolts', is one verdict on this little French restaurant where you eat a set meal at long tables, helping yourself *ad lib* to the crudités with aïoli, salamis and terrine which make up the first three 'courses'. Thus armoured, you may face a 'less than spectacular main course' with equanimity, and anyway there follow 'superb' Brie and sorbets or mousses. Half a bottle of house wine is included in the price; excesses cost £3·20 the bottle; impressive list of old armagnacs. Enthusiastic, non-English-speaking waiters. French recorded music. If only British Rail had the sense to shop carefully and serve most train food uncooked . . .

Closed Sun; Sat L; Aug 27; Dec 25, 26 & 31; Jan 1	Meals 12.30–1.30, 7.30–9 (10.30 Fri & Sat)	VAT inc Service 12% Seats 38
Must book D weekends	Tdh £5·25 (meal £6·20)	No dogs Access, Am Ex, Barclay

(7) Hove Manor Restaurant
Hove Street,
Hove
Brighton 730850

Not manorial at all, but a small shopping-parade restaurant near the sea, below the Hove Manor flats. The owners and their chef are Spanish, the decor grandiloquent, and the service very smooth. 'Generous' fresh crab cocktail, huevos a la portugesa (70p), 'fresh-tasting' gazpacho, sole fillets in lobster and prawn sauce (£4), tournedos chasseur ('rather an anonymous sauce'), profiteroles or crème caramel. The main dish price includes several vegetables. The set meals offer a wide choice, but at lunch most people choose the joint on the huge silver carving-trolley. Routine wines; French house wine £2·95 the bottle. Recorded music. Dress nicely. Smaller helpings for children under five.

Closed Mon (exc May 7);
Sun D
Must book
Meals 12.15–2, 7–10

Tdh L £3 (meal £5·65),
D £3·75 (meal £6·50)
Alc (min £3) £4·75
(meal £7·70)

Seats 35
Air-conditioning
No dogs
Access, Am Ex, Barclay,
Diners, Euro

---

(8) Lawrence Restaurant
40 Waterloo Street,
Hove
Brighton 772922

Closed L; Sun (exc before
public hol Mons); Tue;
Dec 25 & 26; Jan 1
Must book
D only, 7–9.30

Alc £4·70 (meal £6·65)

VAT inc
Service 10%
Children's helpings
(under 10)
Seats 20
♿ rest
No dogs
Am Ex, Barclay

Gerald and Susan Campion – as always, wherever they are – get interesting customers in this tiny restaurant where they cope with little outside help. Whether because it is Brighton or because the place is small enough for it to be a serious matter, they also get at least their share of boors who book and fail to show up. There is no cover charge even for the bread, butter, salami and olives that greet people as they sit down, and there may follow 'ham and pea soup garnished with cream and almond slivers', or 'delicious fried cheese croquettes', or 'butter-fried scallops beyond criticism', or one of the owners' own favourites, salade périgourdine (walnuts, hot slices of ham and omelette, and vinaigrette, 90p). Local fish is naturally good, whether raie au beurre noir ('the best I have tasted') or brill with a fresh sorrel or normande sauce. Loin of pork with fresh orange and ginger sauce (£3) and roast duckling with veal and walnut stuffing and a port sauce (£3·25) are other proprietorial ideas. Vegetables are well cooked and included in the main-course price, though Mr Campion may have to keep them pending while he does other things. 'Marvellous meringues' or 'delicate home-made frozen praline in cream' make a good finish. Good wine at a modest price is kept: 'We stock nothing that we do not know well and drink ourselves.' That means Gaillac red or Coupage white at £2·30 and £2·15 (50p a glass) at one end, and at the other, Aloxe-Corton '72 (Morgan Furze) or Ch. Chasse-Spleen '71, c.b., at a mere £5 and £6 respectively. No music, and 'unfortunately' (their word) no ban on smoking.

*App: Vivian Liff, Alan Sayer, Roy Mathias,
Julian Corbluth, B. C. Sloman, P.A.L., and others*

161

(9) Peking
9 Western Road,
Hove
Brighton 722090

Closed L Dec 25 & 26
Must book
Meals 12–2.45, 5.30–11.45

Alc (min £2) meal £4·15

Cover 10p
Seats 40
  rest
No dogs
Access, Am Ex, Barclay

John Man's cooking is everyman's taste this year behind the ordinary façade that hides a *House & Garden* decor and what he describes as 'crispy white napery'. 'Over the last 18 months we've never had a bad meal here and sometimes a memorable one,' say regulars who advise beginning with sesame prawns and aromatic duck with pancakes and plum sauce. That, with hot-and-sour soup, is conventional enough for the genre, but other dishes to note include assorted hors d'oeuvre (£1·15), fish soup Shanghai-style (60p), deep-fried shredded beef with chilli, prawns in chilli sauce (£1·35), sliced duck with pineapple, and Mr Man's own nominations, Szechuan pork (£1·15) and grilled sole Peking-style. The service is courteous and English-speaking. 'The music, though infinitely preferable to anything ethnic, could well be spared.' Wines, from £2·75 for Côtes du Luberon red and £3 for Sauvignon white, are sensibly chosen for a place of this kind and even Gewürztraminer '76 is no more than £3·75.

App: A. M. Reid, Robert Cahn, S.W., M.B., A.M.R., P. J. Hubbard Ford, and others

(10) La Pergola
41 Castle Street
Brighton 28653

Vito Vallone has transformed a French restaurant into a resolutely Italian one. The pace is relaxed, the lighting low and Vito cooks within view. The menu is sensibly short, with a few specialities and a dish of the day (duck cooked with fresh peaches and red wine, £2·95). People like the 'tour of Italy in twelve months' which brings a set five-course dinner (£4·75) from an Italian city: Naples offered antipasto, spaghetti alle vongole or zuppa di pesce; fritto misto, steak or veal; Dolcelatte with port; and a sweet. Reasonably priced Italian wines; house wine £3·10 the litre. Recorded music.

Closed Sun; Dec 25 & 26
Meals 12.30–2, 7–11

Tdh D £4·75 (meal £7·05)
Alc £4·55 (meal £6·60)

VAT inc
Service 10%
Cover 20p (alc D)
Children's helpings
(under 8)

Seats 30 (parties 20)
  rest (2 steps)
No dogs
Access, Am Ex, Barclay

BRIGHTON see also pub section

Gorny
13 Cotham Road South
Bristol 426444

Several people have written about Michael Gorny's single-handed place since last year's tentative entry, some with praise and some with good advice. A narrow range, gummy sauces, poor steaks, and over-age Stilton are mentioned. But black olives with drinks, smoked haddock ramekin, pork normande, and marinated rare beef as first courses; then 'very rich' roast duck with cream and cranberries (£3·10 including fresh and lightly cooked vegetables) and at the end chocolate mousse with stem ginger or iced Tia Maria soufflé are all praised. Overdue decoration has been done. No children under school age. Recorded music 'mostly classical'.

Closed L; Sun; Mon; Apr 13; Aug; 1 week Chr
Must book weekends
D only, 7–11

Alc £4·45 (meal £7·40)
Children's helpings
(under 12)

Seats 28
No dogs

Restaurant du Gourmet
43 Whiteladies Road
Bristol 36230

Closed L; Sun; Mon; Apr 13; Dec 25 & 26; Jan 1
Must book
D only, 6.30–12

Alc £5·45 (meal £8·50)

Service 10%
Seats 86 (parties 25)
♿ rest (3 steps); w.c.
Air-conditioning
No dogs
Am Ex, Barclay, Diners

People tend to judge Serge and Lucien's restaurant by high standards after their regime's seven years in these pages. 'Much was good but too many little things were not, and the opulent new bar has attracted a noisy set who are indulged at the expense of the cooking.' True, one lady was given 'a superb meal of French onion soup, salmon poached in wine and served with cream sauce and asparagus, a judiciously prepared tomato and cucumber salad, and strawberries with Grand Marnier'. Hot lobster, coquilles St Jacques and sole are also praised, though basic tastes may sometimes be obscured by excess garnish or an over-strong sauce. Steak au poivre or côte de veau parisienne (£2.75) are the house's favourite meat dishes. But 'crêpe Cévenole – two pancakes with "chestnut filling" – were not hot enough and came suspiciously soon, while the filling was a sticky, over-sweet, fruit and chestnut sauce.' The coffee was 'unlimited but rather too weak'. Voisier ordinaires are £2·70 a litre, and the Averys wines are appealing, with Mâcon-Lugny '76, £3·70, Ch. Taillefer '59, £7, and half-bottles of sweet Cérons £1·90. Recorded music. 'A pipe was tolerated – pity.'

App: N. P. Bray, M. Slater, P.S., D. Godden

Michael's
129 Hotwell Road
Bristol 26190

Closed L (exc Sun [Sept–May] & Dec 25); Mon (exc L May 7); Sun D; Jan 1; Chr Day D
Must book weekends
Meals 1.30–3.30 (Sun only, Sept–May), 6.30–11.30 (12 Sat)

Alc £5·30 (meal £7·80)

The menu and billhead decoration at this floridly furnished restaurant are in character. But 'you can take Aunt Edna there' and provided Michael McGowan himself is cooking, the food is capable of excellence. He has taken the odd leaf from another Michel's (*Cuisine Minceur*) book, and early admirers of the restaurant lately praise aubergine caviare, and 'very splendid' ducks' legs in sweet and sour sauce. Grilled guinea-fowl with limes (£7·75 for two) is another possibility in this section. Curried mussels, artichokes with 'superb béarnaise', crab pancake, quail, roast pheasant, lamb kebabs, and various other dishes, with interesting salads or (normally) well-cooked vegetables, all confirm people's affections. 'Gem squash, a rarity, tasted

VAT inc
Service 10%
Seats 55
 ♿ rest (1 step)

delicious with lemon and pepper.' An inspector who
called on an off-day for food also had a tiff with
Averys Clochemerle Blanc at just under £2 a half-
litre, but Ch. Haut-Bages-Monpelou '70 seems fair
at £4·75. Home-made chocolate or brown bread
ice-creams are 'well out of the ordinary'. They try to
confine smoking and the taped music to the bar.
Dogs and children must alike be well-mannered.
Service may be slow.

*App: Keith Wedmore, R. A. Farrand, Peter Searle,
J. Latham, J.B., T.S., and others*

BRISTOL Avon   Map 2

Parks
51 Park Street
Bristol 28016

A listed Georgian house full of potted plants,
mahogany and mirrors, open usefully long hours,
and popular with students as well as 'middle-aged
ladies lunching on Pimm's and pancakes'. Buckwheat
flour makes the Breton crêpes rather solid, but the
chicken liver in red wine version was approved when
tested (though it lacked salt like almost all dishes).
Garlic bread and pie-crust were both flabby, so try
simple sandwiches and salads ('crisp and fresh, with
a choice of four dressings') with American-style
'desserts' (passion cake, fudge brownies). Helpings
are generous, and the coffee is good. House wine
(from Dolamore) is £2 the bottle; Ch. Lynch-Bages
'69 is £5·95. Recorded music, 'sometimes Noel
Coward and chamber pieces'.

Closed Dec 24, 25 & 26; Dec 31 L	Open 11 a.m.–11 p.m.	VAT inc Children's helpings
No bookings	Alc £2·85 (meal £4·40)	Seats 80

Rajdoot
83 Park Street
Bristol 28033

Tales from the Rajdoot are seldom exciting, except
for vignettes of people dropping in after the Wine
Fair or before attending a wife in the labour ward.
When they can be descried in the Malabar Caves
light, tikkas, tandoori chicken (£2·90), lamb pasanda
and rogan gosht (£1·50), poppadums and the set
meals are worth ordering if you do not mind mild
spicing and a premium for the setting. But at the
price, pilau rice, dhal, sweets and coffee should be
less humdrum. Wines from £2·90; lager. Indian
records.

Closed L Sun & public hols (exc Apr 13); Dec 25 & 26	Tdh L £2·40, D from £4·30	Cover 25p Seats 58
Must book D	Alc (min £2·50) meal £5·50	♿ rest (2 steps) No dogs
Meals 12–2.15, 6.30–11.30	VAT inc Service 10%	Access, Am Ex, Barclay, Diners, Euro

---

BRISTOL see also wine bar section

BRIXHAM Devon   Map 1

Flynn's Inn
39 Fore Street
Brixham 4468

Closed Sun; D Mon,
Tue & Thur (Sept–
Easter); Aug 27 L;
Dec 25 & 26; Jan 1
Must book D & weekends
Meals 11.30–2.30,
7.30–10 (11 Sat)

Tdh D from £3·50 (meal
£7·40)
Alc buffet L £1·70 (meal
£2·65)

VAT inc L
Children's helpings
Seats 60
♿ rest (2 steps); w.c.
Access, Barclay

Flynn's in the kitchen, which is what counts, and locals as well as tourists say that the atmosphere of his casual restaurant in Brixham's main street is 'rather like entering a bath after a hard day at the office, warm and soothing'. Lunches are brisker, in other words buffet-style. But at dinner (table d'hôte, based on the price of the main course) you relax into your booth, hope for good company, and enjoy salade niçoise, poisson provençale with scallops and prawns in a cream sauce (£4·25), limandes à la bretonne 'whose butter sauce with shallots, prawns and capers even pleased my wife who prefers her fish plain', biftek au poivre vert, croustillon montagnard (beef pieces in a sauce with anchovies and cheese, £3·50) and other similarly robust dishes, which include potatoes and vegetables or salad. Fruit or cheese may be the best finish. Les Frères ordinaires are £1·75 for 50 cl and there is little else. Dogs are only allowed at lunchtime. Recorded 'sottish' music – or perhaps 'softish' – it is hard to tell from Mr Flynn's writing.

App: G. R. Oversby-Powers, F.M.B., E.R.

BROADSTAIRS Kent   Map 3

Marchesi Restaurant
18 Albion Street
Thanet 62481

After 95 years in the hands of the same family, the Rogers' spruce sea-view restaurant seems secure enough, and indeed they have perkily bought the next-door hotel from Trust Houses Forte, and this has left a cadet chef in charge in the original restaurant. One regular visitor says 'you could do well with hors d'oeuvre (£1·65) alone', and local plaice or other fish, and meringue glacé are also well done. But more reports on the French ambitions are needed. Valpolicella or Soave are £2·50, or try Sicilian Corvo. No music.

Closed Dec 25 & 26
Must book L & Sat D
Meals 12–2, 6.30–10

Tdh L £3·50 (meal £5·85),
D £4·50 (meal £6·95)

Alc £6·30 (meal £8·90)

VAT inc
Service 10%
Cover 25p
Children's helpings tdh

Seats 70 (parties 60)
♿ rest (3 steps)
Car park
Access, Am Ex, Barclay,
Diners, Euro

BROADWAY Hereford & Worcester   Map 2

Hunter's Lodge
High Street
Broadway 3247

Closed Mon; Sun D;
Dec 26; Jan
Must book

The reappearance of this well-equipped old house in the Guide after a long gap would be less tentative, perhaps, if Kurt Friedli – a Swiss chef with 'high recommendations and experience at Aviemore' – had fed and served a lunchtime inspector as well as (by various accounts) he has fed diners. Lunch and dinner are both à la carte, though at different prices, and

Meals 12.30–2, 7.30–10

Alc L £3·50 (meal £6·05),
D £7·35 (meal £10·90)

Children's helpings
Seats 56 (parties 50)
⅘ rest (2 steps)
Access, Am Ex, Barclay,
Diners

menus sound interesting, from bar nibbles of 'sage leaves in batter' to 'delightful paupiettes de truite with dill and sour cream sauce as a first course', and guinea-fowl with weinkraut, poached salmon hollandaise, and 'duck or gloriously grilled sole' to follow. Soups and vegetables are genuine. By Swiss standards sweets are mediocre and the service amateurish. French ordinaires are £2·80, and Ch. Fombrauge '73, c.b., £5·80 on the Edward Sheldon list. There are bar lunches with Carlsberg on tap and various bottled beers. No music. Car park. No dogs. More reports, please.

BUCKFASTLEIGH Devon   Map 1

As we went to press, the restaurant recommended here changed hands.

BUNGAY Suffolk   Map 6

Browne's
20 Earsham Street
Bungay 2545

A small Georgian house in a small market town, 'run by two men and one waitress', trading as 'Known Earlier Years Limited'. The menu, on a gilt-framed blackboard, is changed to suit seasonal produce. You might find, and enjoy, oeufs aïoli (on a bed of rice, walnuts and sultanas, 85p), poached apple filled with smoked haddock, peppers and mayonnaise (85p), prawns with garlic butter, seafood scallop in a champagne sauce (£3·95, including vegetables), veal provençale (£3·60), casseroled grouse with juniper berries, brandy and cream (£2·95), pot au chocolat (65p) or apple pie with almonds, sultanas and honey. French house wine, £2·45 the bottle, and some other interesting wines. Recorded classical music. More reports, please.

Closed L; D Sun; Thur;
public hol Mons; Dec 25,
26 & 31; Jan 1
Must book
D only, from 7.30

Alc £4·95 (meal £7·45)

Children's helpings
Seats 24

⅘ rest (1 step)
Car park
No dogs
Access, Barclay, Diners

BURGESS HILL West Sussex   Map 3

La Padella
2 Keymer Road
Burgess Hill 3521

Closed Sun; Wed L;
Dec 25 & 26
Must book

Meals 12–2.30, 7–11.30
Alc (min D £2·50) £5·35
(meal £8·25)

Seats 40
 ♿ rest
No dogs
Access, Am Ex, Barclay

Members already seem well suited at this former gents' outfitters, for it has been fitted out as a restaurant (opposite the station) by the Renzullis, late of La Cucina in Lewes. A couple who heard the news on the county's academic grapevine found the cannelloni 'just as I had remembered it'. Can this mean 'bland, boring, and tepid in the middle' (an inspector's experience)? But the fishy hors d'oeuvre, sole with prawn and lobster sauce, and scampi, have been praised, and the rest of a test dinner settled at somewhere near London trattoria standard, with moderate cooking and service 'on the plate'. Meat dishes in the padella (Eng. pan) include veal escalope with clams, and chicken with bananas and asparagus (£1·65). At 48 hours' notice there is sucking-pig. Finish with oranges in caramel, or 'an enormous glass of zabaglione'. Sangiovese or Trebbiano wines are £2·50, but the house Chianti at £3·40 is perhaps a better buy. Recorded music. More reports, please.

BURHAM Kent   Map 3

Toastmaster's Inn

Church Street
4½ m NW of Maidstone
Medway 61299

Closed Sun; Mon; 2 weeks
Sept; Dec 25 & 26
Must book
Meals 12–2, 7–10

Alc £6·85 (meal £10·95)

Service 10%
Children's helpings
Seats 35
♿ rest (1 step); w.c.
Car park
No dogs in d/r
Barclaycard

Snodland, the nearest town, 'sounds like Enid Blyton and looks like 1984', but Burham is rural enough for Gregory Ward's inn to have signed up most of the village to grow herbs for Tim Dalglish and Paul Duvall (who cook) and to provide cellarage for the encyclopaedic wine collection. The bar food, with well-chosen current wine or Bob Luck's cider or an enviable range of real ales, is warmly praised for quality and value by one visitor whose family ate beef and vegetable pie, chicken Kiev with yellow rice and curry sauce, and juicy rare cold beef, with chips all round. The dinners, as always, are less well-adapted to what is likely to be drunk with them, and devilled beefsteak, when tried, was good meat overcooked, oversalted, and over-devilled. But moules marinière or clams au gratin, champignons en chapelure or savoury apple and celery cheesecake are all acceptable first courses, and rack of Romney Marsh lamb with sauce paloise (£4·95 with vegetables) was well cooked at a test meal, though criticised for toughness at another. Even turnips have made a friend, and the owner smokes his own fish and meat. Puddings may include pond pudding ('what a sinker') in winter, or summer pudding in summer, but it is the range of English and French cheeses that will take the eye of anyone lingering over his choice from a wine list that is remarkable now even in half-bottles, let alone full, with for example, Ch. Malescot-St Exupéry, c.b., £7 in the '62 vintage and £9 in the '61. Anyone with an unlimited purse, and with time for notice to be given, may then browse among clarets or burgundies

167

of the '28 or '34 vintages, or hocks of the '49 or '59 ones: sweet whites from Loire or Bordeaux are equally comprehensive, and from these or similar sources there is plenty of interesting drinking under or just over £5: Muscat d'Alsace '76 (Hugel) £4·40; Ch. Maucaillou '73, c.b., £5·75. Less familiar wine areas are also represented. No music. No pipes or cigars – 'though they were tolerated on my last two visits, unfortunately.'

App: Michael Mowbray Silver, M.A.S., R. I. Cowan, and others

BURNHAM MARKET Norfolk   Map 6

Fishes'
Market Place
on B1155
Burnham Market 588

Closed Mon (mid-Sept to
mid-July); Sun D
(Oct–June); Dec 25 & 26
Must book summer &
weekends
Meals 12.15–2, 7–9.30
(9 in winter)

Tdh L weekdays £2·50
(meal £4·55), Sun L £3·50
(meal £5·65)
Alc £5·20 (meal £7·60)

VAT inc
Children's helpings
Seats 48 (parties 20)
 ♿ rest (1 step)
No dogs
Am Ex card

Gillian Cape's converted shop, homely to a fault, has oddities that do not end with the placing of its apostrophe. Real cooking is done, so service stutters badly at busy times, and some recipes, for sweets especially, were clearly unsound when tested on the spot, and the variation from day to day that is to be expected in a fish restaurant does not all arise from the vagaries of the market. The best things are the crab soup (75p), their own smoked fish, the poached trout (sea or river) with bananas and almonds, or lemon and orange, and the salmon fish-cakes, which may be had with crab sauce but may taste better without this distraction. More elaborate dishes may cloy, and sugar spoils some sauces. Salads are good, with 'very pretty' apple, sliced orange, unskinned peaches and walnuts (60p) at a test meal. This meal, however, did not confirm last year's 'glass' distinction since several bins on the interesting and fairly priced wine-list turned out to be empty, and white wines have arrived far too cold. Chain-smokers are also tolerated, although they may be asked to move to an adjoining room. However, Mrs Cape is aware of most of these problems, and the numerous people who have enjoyed their meals are prepared to be tolerant in this part of East Anglia. No music. Abbot Ale in cask.

App: Amanda Weston, P. L. Joslin, Robin A. Hood, Pat & Jeremy Temple, Mr & Mrs S. Alexander

---

Hoste Arms
The Green
Burnham Market 257

Closed L (exc bar);
Thur; Dec 25 D; Feb
Must book
Meals 12–1.45 (bar),
7–9.30

Sir William Hoste was a sea captain who, like his contemporary Nelson, went to school at North Walsham. The young Carneys, who have taken the hotel over but are not at present offering rooms, do the old fellow credit, members say, with the lunchtime buffet they lay out (in July and August only, £1·95, pudding and coffee extra) in the long room upstairs, with 'sweet Suffolk ham, quiches, rolled shoulder of mutton, good salads, Stilton, and coffee, and other things'. At night, too, their determination to keep the menu small and

Alc D £4·25 (meal £6·75)

Cover 10p
Children's helpings
(under 10)
Seats 26
Car park
No dogs
No rooms

seasonal, and to cook vegetables properly, has evoked warm praise for 'original hors d'oeuvre, including stuffed aubergines', 'fresh and excellent grilled turbot' and 'delicious chocolate ginger cake'. Sesame chicken (£2·40), veal Milanese, Persian lamb, and local wild duck are other favourite dishes. Hungarian red or Yugoslav white wines are £2·20 and there are a few others, along with pressurised beers. There are bar snacks all year round. They do not double-book tables. Recorded classical music. More reports, please.

BURNHAM-ON-CROUCH Essex   Map 3

Contented Sole
80 High Street
Maldon 782139

Closed Mon; Sun D;
Dec 22–Feb 1
Must book
Meals 12.15–2, 7–9.30

Tdh L £2·25 (meal £4·25),
Sun £3·50 (meal £5·60)
Alc £6·40 (meal £8·70)

Service inc
Children's helpings
Seats 70 (parties 30)
♿ rest (1 step)

Mr R. T. Walton has been chef-patron of this civilised and efficiently served restaurant for many years, and members have lately been wondering why they ever let it fall out of the *Guide*. At least, one of them had to go to another part of the country to realise the merits of the house speciality, crêpe de fruits de mer – 'a light pancake full of shrimps, scallop, salmon, white fish and (I am sure) lobster, topped with a cheese sauce and browned under the grill.' First courses warmly praised include fresh asparagus in season (£1·50) 'served with a fork under the plate to tilt the butter towards the tips', gravadlax, moules marinière (£1·25), champignons farcis frits (95p) and baked celery in ham. Apart from the sole itself (£4·65 in the 'grillé du chef' version), chicken Kiev and beef en croûte deserve remark, as do the Sunday roast beef, and on the set lunches, fried codling 'caught by the waiters'. Among sweets, look for crème brûlée, banana fritters with apricot sauce, or glace Grand Marnier. The Grierson-Blumenthal wines, from Arc de Triomphe ordinaires at £2·65 upwards, do not excite: one of the '75 moselles at about £5, or '76 Gewürztraminer and '73 clarets at about £4, looked the best choice in 1978. No music.

App: A. B. Goad, Ramon Evans, P.A., E.S., Jean Wilding, and others

---

CADNAM Hampshire   Map 2

Le Chanteclerc
Romsey Road
on A31
Cadnam 3271

Closed Sun; Mon; Apr 13;
2 weeks Aug; 2 weeks
from Chr
Must book D
Meals 12–1.45, 7–9.45

Alc £6·90 (meal £9·75)

Take exit 1 from the M27 to find the Denats' restaurant behind a BP garage at the London end of Cadnam. Already there are plenty of Jags on the gravel (which ought to make their owners more punctual than they are, according to Mme Denat). M Denat has also chosen (on the evidence of a test meal) to offer a long and highly priced à la carte menu at the expense of the distinctive tastes he can achieve when he tries: duck pâté was 'bland to a degree', and though lobster thermidor (£5·75) was expert enough, cauliflower cheese and dauphinoise potatoes did nothing for it. Other favourites are the

VAT inc
Seats 50 (parties 20)
♿ rest (2 steps)
Car park
No dogs
Access, Barclay

steaks and the avocado with shrimps, but the
tartelettes Escoffier with chicken livers, grapes and
brandy sauce (£1·35), and in season perdrix au
choux (£5·15), sound more promising. 'Grouse on a
day's menu was too fresh though, and it was
perched on mediocre bread.' The best sweet is the
pancake, filled with raspberry puree and flamed.
French ordinaires are £3·15 a litre, and other prices
on the list are still awaited. No music.

App: G. A. Wright, R.M., F.L., and others

CALDBECK Cumbria   Map 7

Parkend Restaurant
on B5299
1½ m W of Caldbeck
Caldbeck 442

Closed Mon; Dec 24;
D Dec 25 & 26;
Dec 31 L; Jan; Feb;
Must book D
Meals 12–2, 7–9

Tdh D from £5·25

(meal £6·35)

Alc £4·45 (meal £5·80)

VAT & service inc
Children's helpings
Seats 30
♿ rest
Car park
No dogs in d/r
Access card

The Arnesens' return to catering, with their
daughter Joyce in the kitchen of this
well-furnished 17th-century stone farmhouse, was
hailed last year as a useful refuge for all pockets at
the northern edge of the Lakes, and so it has
turned out – though remember they have only a
restaurant licence, not a pub one. 'See Wainwright
Book 5', they say, for the walks on High Pike
(2,157 ft) and if you are down by lunchtime there
is à la carte service of anything from a snack to a
full meal in bar or restaurant. Home-made onion
soup and rolls (40p), a mélange of cream cheese and
grapefruit, gammon with spiced apricots, potatoes
and salad (£2·10), Cumberland sausage with apple
sauce, and fruit fool or Cumberland rum nicky
(70p) seem nicely calculated for this kind of need.
Similar dishes form the *carte* in the evening, when
there is also a choiceless (but well-chosen) set meal
of four or five courses with coffee. Mushrooms in
garlic butter, cream or carrot soup with chervil,
grilled salmon steak with green sauce, raspberry
bombe, and English cheeses make up one version
reported to us; another is 'generous' Highland
prawn cocotte, lamb's liver with Dubonnet and
orange, and 'gorgeous' rum and chocolate pavé. To
drink there is Heritage pressurised bitter, Argentine
red or white wine at £2·20 (£1·45 for 50 cl, 30p a
10 cl glass), and about thirty others: Ch. du Colombier
'73, £3·60. No music. No children under eight in the
restaurant at night. Smoking 'not encouraged'.

*App: T. P. Walter, Gordon K. Johns, A. W. Wyatt,
J.K.L.*

CAMBRIDGE Cambridgeshire   Map 3

Peking
21 Burleigh Street
Cambridge 54755

Closed Mon; Dec 25 & 26
Must book D

Mr Mao is a cookery book writer (in Chinese) as
well as owner of this unusually suave restaurant,
cosy downstairs, red-white-and-gold upstairs. The
cooking is normally excellent, from a pre-ordered
Peking roast duck which even a Chinese visitor was
moved to admire, to generous if dearish prawn

Meals 12–2.15, 6–10.45

Tdh L from 75p (one course)
Alc meal £4·50

Service 10%
Seats 64
Air-conditioning
No dogs

toasts with sesame seeds (£2·20 for two), 'fresh and lightly grilled' sole Peking-style (£2·30), diced chicken with lemon (£1·70) and other dishes on the regular *carte*. It was the more surprising to hear from a former admirer that a complaint on the spot about half-cold spare ribs led to a scene that would have disgraced the Gang of Four. There was nothing wrong with the spare ribs or indeed anything else at a subsequent test meal, so perhaps a waiter had a brainstorm. Dishes of which the kitchen is proud include sliced beef with leeks and garlic (lamb is also done this way), toufoo (bean curd) with minced meat in hot pepper sauce (£1·50), fried crispy chicken wing (£1·30), and fried mixed vegetables. They know more about east-of-Suez long drinks than about wine. No music.

App: P.J.F., P.K. & G.H.W., and others

CAMBRIDGE see also pub section

CANTERBURY Kent   Map 3

Roma Antica
9 Longport
Canterbury 63326

Closed Sun; public hols (exc Apr 13)
Must book
Meals 12–2.30, 6.30–10.30

Tdh L £2·20 (meal £4·35)
Alc £5·25 (meal £8·30)

Service 10%
Cover 30p D
Seats 55
♿ rest (3 steps); w.c.
No dogs
Access, Am Ex, Barclay, Diners, Euro

Graham and Serafino's long, narrow (but quite well-spaced) trattoria is *antica* in *Guide* terms now, but its standards hold up very well, according to various visitors and inspectors who have tried the 'hot, fresh and light' cannelloni al forno, 'tasty' crostino alla Toscana (£1·30), and insalata di calamaretti 'with just the right touch of lemon juice and black pepper'. Main dishes too are skilfully cooked, by accounts of veal cutlet en papillote, with an artichoke heart in the parcel, 'crisp, dry and hot pollo sorpresa', and costantine d'abbacchio all'uccelletto (lamb chops braised in wine with a herby tomato sauce and 'real white beans', £2·20). Vegetables are 'less brilliant', brought automatically (but charged for) and served on to the 'rather small' plates. Taleggio cheese, oranges in syrup, peaches in red wine, and 'surprisingly digestible zuppa inglese' are praised, and 'the only fault with the zabaglione is the din they make beating it.' (Remember the kitchen closes early at lunchtime, though.) Cordevino or Soave wines are a reasonable £2·20 and there are good Italian bottles beyond these. Recorded music. Smaller helpings for under-sixes.

App: P. L. Leonard, Hilda Woolf, J. & Z.R.

Since each restaurant has a separate file in the Guide office, please use a separate form or sheet of paper for each report. Additional forms may be obtained free (no stamp required) from The Good Food Guide, Freepost, 14 Buckingham Street, London WC2N 6BR.

Aynsome Manor Hotel
off A590 (M6 exit 36)
2 m NW of
Grange-over-Sands
Cartmel 276

Closed L (exc Sun);
Sun D (exc res);
Dec 24, 25 & 26
Must book
Meals 1 (Sun), 7–8.30

Tdh Sun L £4·50 (meal
£6·60), D £6·50 (meal
£8·80)

VAT inc
Seats 30
♿ rest
Access card
16 rooms (9 with bath,
2 with shower)
D, B&B from £9
Fire cert

'The hotel's brochure reads like an ad-man's holiday,' says one guest, 'but for once it was mostly true' (as well as being decent, legal, etc., etc.). Half the energetic Williams family were away, so 'unmemorable' main courses and some service strains could be forgiven. But at other times, by all accounts, the cheerful welcome and open fires at this peaceful manor (once occupied by 'founder's kin' of Cartmel Priory) lead to reliable dinners with home-made soups, lamb Doria 'not pink but acceptable', a 'profuse' cold table, and most inviting sweets. There are pressurised beers, and Nicolas ordinaires are £3·50 a litre, which may be an invitation to try the Chanson and Louis Latour burgundies from Youdell (a markedly better choice than claret here, and be warned that Ch. Haut-Brion '66 at £20 or so is still not ready even if you can afford it). Recorded music. Smaller helpings for under-twelves, and supper in their rooms for under-fives. No dogs in public rooms.

*App: D. A. Slade, C. J. Richardson, D. R. &
A. J. Linnell, H. K. Heseltine, A. T. Langton*

CARTMEL see also pub section

CAULDON LOWE Staffordshire   Map 5

Jean Pierre
Waterhouses
between A52 & A523
7 m SE of Leek
Waterhouses 338

Closed Sun; Sat L;
July 14; Dec 25; Jan 1
Must book
Meals 12–1.30, 7.30–9.30

Alc £5·95 (meal £8·15)

Service inc
Seats 20
♿ rest (2 steps)
Air-conditioning
Car park
No dogs

When the Normandie at Birtle became too small for both of them, Yves Champeau took his flocks and herds northwards, and Jean-Pierre took the barren territory to the south. Telephoned by the *Guide*, his reply roughly ran: 'If Mr Christopher Driver want to see 'ow to run a leetel pub dining-room, 'e come 'ere an' 'e will see.' But others had already reported 'Normandie food, if anything better and fresher, served with more warmth'. 'We can report good onion soup and avocado julienne, large helpings of salmon with sorrel sauce, wild duck with gooseberries (£3·65 with vegetables), spinach with cream and nutmeg, and even a massive home-made ice-cream with nuts, sitting in a Grand Marnier moat.' Terrine, frogs' legs, poussin aux cèpes et girolles, crêpes flambées and – if M Champeau has time – a sweet soufflé, are no less alluring on this menu, which offers some half a dozen choices in each course. French ordinaire is £1·95 for half a litre and there are a good thirty others. Service can be slow. No music. No pipes. No children under seven.

*App: G. O. Smedley, R.N.H., Katherine Muir,
E.L.F., R.V.M., and others*

CAWSAND BAY Cornwall   Map 1

Criterion Hotel
Garrett Street
Plymouth 822244

Friendly, cottagey hotel overlooking Plymouth Sound. The Shimells run it zestfully, serve a set dinner only, and close in the winter. Few complain about the limited choice when given crab soup or flan, perhaps, bouillabaisse, brill with aubergines, pork Périgord, orange-glazed leg of lamb, kidneys Turbigo, fresh vegetables, brandy-snaps with clotted cream, fruit Pavlovas and pies. Collier wines, from £2·40 for litres of French Brigatin. Cold lunches for residents only. Recorded music. No smoking till the coffee stage. Babies and children over 12 welcome, but the cliff edge rules out the years between.

Closed L (exc res);	Tdh £5 (meal £6·80)	7 rooms (2 with shower)
Sept 30–May 3		B&B £8–£10
Must book	VAT inc	D, B&B £12–£15
D only, 7.30	Seats 30	(min 3 days)
	No dogs	Fire cert

CHAGFORD Devon   Map 1

Gidleigh Park Hotel
2 m W of Chagford
Chagford 2225 *and* 3289

Closed L (exc res)
Must book
D only, 7.30–9

Tdh £8 (meal £9·50)

VAT & service inc
Seats 30 (parties 12)
♿ rest
Car park
No dogs
11 rooms (all with bath)
B&B £15

One has learnt to dread the phrase 'new to catering' when it is used about aspirants to these pages, especially ones who see fit to begin by taking over an Edwardian merchant's Tudor folly on the edge of Dartmoor, and by stocking it with fine but modestly priced wines on their overdraft. However, Kay and Paul Henderson are Americans, and between them they seem to know plenty about both cooking and business. Her onion 'tart' wrapped in cabbage leaf with tomato sauce, and slices of salmon sauté with a red wine sauce, stood up very well by comparison with the elaborate £20 dinner-with-wines cooked the next day by the guest kitchen team from a serious restaurant in Paris. Both residents and casual diners who have later reported on their meals (innocent of choice until the sweet stage) describe well-judged touches of cuisine nouvelle or minceur in the terrine of eggs, spinach and mushroom, veal kidneys with juniper, and gâteau marjolaine. Duck breasts with green peppercorns and poulet au vinaigre are Mrs Henderson's own favourites. Visiting teams for gourmet weekends have included Kenneth Lo with a Chinese programme. The hotel has been made more than comfortable, and the wine list owes much to Harry Waugh, David Wolfe and Tom Machen. You pay for what you drink (at £3·25 a bottle) of white Mâcon Villages '75 or '72 Margaux, but the temptation of '76 Fleurie (Thévenin) or Clos Fourtet '70 or fine '71 burgundies at a pound or two more is unlikely to be denied. Sauternes, Australian, and Californian wines are also well represented. No music. No children under ten. More reports, please. Approach the hotel from Chagford, not Gidleigh village.

CHELTENHAM Gloucestershire   Map 2

Aubergine

Belgrave House,
Imperial Square
Cheltenham 31402

Closed Sun; Mon L;
Apr 13; Dec 24 D;
Dec 25 & 26; Jan 1 L
Must book D
Meals 12–1.45, 7–10

Alc £6·60 (meal £9·50)

VAT inc
Service 10%
Seats 40 (parties 20)
♿ rest (rear); w.c.
No dogs
Am Ex, Diners

Inaki Beguiristain's portrait photography and old
cameras make a beguiling decor for this well-set (but
dimly lit) basement restaurant. For some – including
two separate inspectors – this promise has been
fulfilled by skilful cooking of, for instance,
cauliflower soup, prawns in garlic butter, fried
salmon steak with lemon butter (£3·90), venison
chop with a slightly orangey cream and brandy
sauce, and lamb's kidneys with croûtons (£2·75).
Potatoes, pears in wine, and home-made ices are
praised too. The thick Jersey cream helps any dish
it appears with. But the 'civilised, well-spoken girls'
who serve are less expert than the chef-patron, and
shortcomings that occur – 'taste of raw onions in
avocado and Stilton mousse', 'oily onion soup and
tough pheasant' – are serious offences at the prices
charged, especially when 'throughout the meal no
one asked if we were happy.' ('Exotic' omelettes
appear at lunchtime, as do salads and casseroles.)
Rioja '73 red or '76 white are £3·78 and £3·36 a litre
respectively, and mark-ups discourage further
exploration of the modest list. Recorded music at
dinner.

App: J.W., D.J. & R.S. Boyd, H.L., and others

Food for Thought

🍷

10 Grosvenor Street
Cheltenham 29836

Closed L; Sun; Mon;
Dec 25 & 26; Jan 1;
Cheltenham Gold Cup
week
Must book
D only, 7.30–9

Tdh £6·60 (meal £9·50)

Seats 20
♿ rest
Air-conditioning
No dogs

Christopher Wickens (who manages, and buys the
wine) and Joanna Jane Mahon (who cooks) do
indeed think about your feeding, and everyone likes
the atmosphere of their cosy place down an ominous
alleyway. ('Cosiness extends to storing spirits in the
ladies' loo,' reports an inspector.) The food seems to
lean very little on the freezer, and among first
courses, the soups, pâté, stuffed mushrooms, prawns
in aïoli, and cold curried peach are all liked.
'Crumbly, garlic-baked sprats' is another possibility.
Lemon chicken, 'a good casserole of beef and crunchy
cauliflower', 'four little pork cutlets wrapped in
bacon and served with baby leeks', and braised
pigeon ('not perfectly tender, but the sauce was
superb') are among the main dishes people praise on
the elegantly laid-out set menus, which usually offer
three or four choices in each course. Lamb and mint
kebabs with a piquant sauce, and kidneys in batter
with mustard sauce, are kitchen favourites.
'Beautiful moist brown bread' accompanies meals,
and a pause is often tactfully suggested before
embarking on meringue with cream and
blackcurrants or frangipane tart, perhaps with a
glass of Muscat de Beaumes de Venise. The house

French red or white wines are £2·95. Mr Wickens buys from good merchants, describes his bottles infectiously, and prices them fairly, with Gewürztraminer '74 as well as Saumur Blanc or English Three Choirs under £4 in 1978, and Louis Latour's Mâcon-Lugny '76, or Ch. Coufran '71, or a domaine-bottled, if fairly anonymous, '66 red burgundy, all under £5. There are off-sales too. Recorded music. 'Anti-smoking hints on the menu.'

App: J.R.D., J. & J.H., L.M.L.,
C. R. Bartholomew, A.A.B.C., and others

CHELTENHAM see also wine bar section

CHENIES Buckinghamshire **Map 3**

Bedford Arms
on B485 (off A404)
4 m W of Rickmansworth
Chorleywood 3301

Attractive Thistle hotel (overlooking the Chiltern meadows) with repro Elizabethan interiors. Generous helpings of, for example, assiette de crudités, avocado with prawns Marie Rose, steaks (either chateaubriand at £9·50 for two, or tournedos with various sauces at about £5), chicken Kiev or roast beef. Yorkshire pudding and sauce béarnaise could be improved, but vegetables are generally well cooked. Few can manage a sweet, though they at least look better than the cheeses: 'not only the plastic wrappings,' a visitor reports, 'but even "bargain offer" supermarket stickers.' 'Excellent service by mature staff.' Some fine wines (Ch. de Camensac '70, £5·60). Christopher's Corbières, £2·60. Bar snacks (sandwiches at weekends, wider choice on weekdays) and S&N pressurised beers. No music.

Closed Dec 25 D
Must book
Meals 12.30–2, 7.30–10

Tdh Sun L £5·25 (meal £8·15)
Alc £8 (meal £11·40)

Children's helpings
Seats 42 (parties 25)
♿ rest; w.c.
Car park
No dogs in d/r

Access, Am Ex, Barclay, Diners, Euro
10 rooms (all with bath)
Room only, from £13
Fire cert

CHESTER Cheshire **Map 5**

Jean's Kitchen
1 Newtown Close,
St Anne Street
Chester 24239

When Jean's in her red-checked kitchen 'on the corner of a council estate in a shopping precinct', all's well with the cooking, and the Relais Routier plaque signals a French pattern of set meal: egg salad, pâté or home-made soup; then scaloppe milanese, lamb cutlets, mixed grill, or chicken in mushroom and wine sauce, with vegetables; apple pie and ice-cream or cheese to finish. The carte and the clientele for it are a step up: expect Argentine-style steaks as well as occasional 'feasts'. But you play routier's roulette, for

not all five cooks are as talented as Jean, it seems.
Spanish house wine, £1·40 for ⅓ litre. No dogs. A move
is on the cards: more reports, please.

Closed Sun; Dec 25;
L public hols
Must book
Meals 12–2.15, 5.30–10.30
(public hols 6–11)

Tdh (until 7 p.m.) £2·50
(meal £3·45), (after 7)
from £3·90 (meal £5·35)
Alc £4·70 (meal £6·20)

VAT inc

Service inc L
Children's helpings £1
(until 7 p.m.)
Seats 35
⌷ rest
Access card

CHESTERTON Oxfordshire   Map 2

Kinchs

on A4095
3 m SW of Bicester
Bicester 41444

Closed L (exc Sun); Mon;
Sun D; Dec 25 & 26;
Jan 1
Must book
Meals 12–1.45 (Sun),
7–9.45

Tdh Sun L £5·25 (meal
£7·95), D £4·75 & £6·60
(meal £7·40 & £9·45)

VAT inc
Service 10%
Children's helpings
(under 8)
Seats 40 (parties 14)
⌷ rest (2 steps)
Car park
No dogs
Access, Am Ex, Barclay,
Diners

'You eat off wood, by candlelight, in a place the height of a barn'; and but for the feminine service, rather conscious atmosphere, and Christopher Greatorex's more individual food, it would feel like a rusticated High Table. After years of 'struggle' Mr Greatorex felt more visited and appreciated by customers last year. Poor meals do occur, for much is attempted in the kitchen, and the flavours of pâtés, terrines, mousses and such are more often rebuked for sweetness or blandness than for excess vigour. But one normally critical couple's reservations were dispelled by their four-course meal. (Except on Saturdays, there is also a simpler three-course version.) 'Wholemeal bread and cold water on the tables make a good impression, and our dinner included tasty coriander mushrooms and well-made soups of onion or leek and potato. For main course, six crayfish were lined up with their eyes on their white wine and cream sauce, both potatoes and white cabbage were interestingly treated, salad was enterprising, and although crème brûlée was slightly too thin for perfection, there was an admirable orange and almond cake.' Others have done equally well with mussel pancake or quenelles of pike. Mr Greatorex himself thinks his best dishes to be salmon trout baked in sorrel leaves, fillet of lamb in pastry with basil, or poussin with garlic and herbs. Puddings are kept fairly simple. Rhône red or Bordeaux white wines are £2·95, and at a slightly higher level the house white burgundy (£3·95) and Gamay de l'Ardèche are much liked. The list as a whole is well diversified and serious, with plenty of Loires and Rhônes and honeyed white Bordeaux to back up fine clarets that begin with Ch. Roland la Garde '73 at £4·75 and rise by way of Ch. Fombrauge '70, c.b., to half-bottles of Ch. Léoville-Lascases '61 at £9·95. Courage best bitter is in cask. Some consideration is expected from smokers. Musical or Elizabethan evenings are sometimes held, but otherwise no music.

App: P. H. Skelton, Geoffrey & Jenifer Rowntree, M.S.W., S.P., E.A.W.

CHICHESTER West Sussex   Map 3

Little London Restaurant
38 Little London
off East Street
Chichester 84899

Closed Sun; Mon; Dec 25,
26 & 27; Jan 1
Must book
Meals 12–2, 7–10 (later
after theatre)

Tdh L from £2·40 (meal
£5·05)
Alc £7·10 (meal £9·95),
(Savourie) £2·90 (meal
£4·60)

VAT inc
Cover L 20p, D 50p
(75p after theatre)
Seats 40 (parties 14)
♿ rest; w.c.
No dogs

There must be something seriously amiss with dolls'
houses in West Sussex, for last year's description of
Philip Stroud's intricately designed and miniaturised
house of restaurants seems to have upset several of his
customers: perhaps, in Chichester, the comparison
should have been with royal or at least ennobled
nurseries. Quite apart from this, there are happily
more reports than usual, especially dinner ones, and
though the prices belong to Big rather than Little
London (and only the host's menu carries them), an
exacting visitor finds the cooking imaginative and
the service 'excellent'. 'Chicken livers sauté (and
cooked as I requested) with halves of peeled and
pipped white grapes, and served on a croûte, made
a dish of real distinction, and escalope of veal with
orange in a ginger and madeira sauce was also
delicious.' Someone understands fish too, by accounts
of goujons of plaice with orange mayonnaise, smoked
haddock rémoulade, crab mousse, and matelote
rouge. But on one occasion 'halibut in wine sauce
was overcooked and cold lobster (at over £8) dry.'
Duck, steaks, noisettes of lamb and other dishes are
praised too, and fillet of lamb in pastry has also
appeared as a day's dish in the cheaper Savourie
upstairs, which offers counter-service of soups,
salads, sweets, and wines. Vegetables generally are
worthy but variable – 'runner beans were grossly
oversalt, marrow delicately sauced.' The creamy or
fruity cakes are well made. Wine prices may make
you glad that the house claret and Beaujolais are
sound, but 'good estate-bottled Sancerre '77
(£5·30)' is also mentioned. 'A pity "no pipes" does
not extend to cigars and for that matter cigarettes.'
No young children, or over-casual dress in the
restaurant. Details are approximate.

*App: Sally & Neville Goodman, Pat & Jeremy Temple,
I. C. Lucas, R.B.J., E.C., C.K., and many others*

CHITTLEHAMHOLT Devon   Map 1

Highbullen Hotel

off B3226
5 m SW of South Molton
Chittlehamholt 248

Closed L (non-res)
Must book
Meals 1–2 (Sun), 7.30–9

Tdh Sun L £5 (inc wine),
D £6 (meal £7·75)

Tastes change, and after a dozen years the Neils'
Victorian house on a remote plateau is both admired
and criticised for qualities different from the ones
that first commended it. Food, furnishing, and
heating standards have risen elsewhere. But so have
prices, and the Mercedes and Porsches parked
outside suggest that it is not only the new poor who
appreciate the value given here at table, in the
cellar, and in the way the hotel is equipped indoors
and out (a deer park is about to be added, and
outdoor swimming in warm water retains its appeal).
Breakfasts are admired, with 'hot toast handed
round in a wicker basket'. At dinner, most first

177

VAT & service inc
Seats 60
♿ rest
Car park
No dogs
25 rooms (all with bath)
B&B £10
D, B&B £15
Fire cert

courses and sweets are cold, 'apart from a fresh
vegetable soup I enjoyed immensely', reports an
inspector whose austerely helped main courses of
lamb and pork alsacienne (with sauerkraut) were
also well cooked. Guacamole, mushrooms arménienne
and poulet Mère Michel remain perennial favourites,
but 'believe it or not, there have been a couple of
new sweets: home-made blackcurrant ice-cream and
fresh plum jelly' (though visitors are glad that
apricot and hazelnut meringue, and chocolate and
chestnut turinois with Devonshire cream, have not
been swept away to make room for them). Cheeses
may be ruined by refrigeration. The long wine list
covers all main regions, and is especially
distinguished in clarets: a half of Ch. Lynch-Bages
'61 (c.b.) is £6; Ch. Cantemerle '67 (c.b.) is £7·50
the bottle; Ch. Coutet '72 (c.b.) is £2·60 the
half-bottle. French house wine (Paul Beaudet) is
£3·50 the litre. No music. No children under 13.

*App: Stephen & Judy Parish, Dr & Mrs J. S.
Courtney-Pratt, Anna Dickie & Peter Kann*

CHRISTCHURCH Hampshire   Map 2

Splinters

♢

12 Church Street
Bournemouth 483454

Closed L; Sun;
Dec 25 & 26
Must book
D only, 6.30–10.30

Alc £5·50 (meal £8·10)

VAT inc
Seats 34
♿ rest; w.c.
No dogs

The Carters, Peter Hornsby, and Juanita Franke
run this relaxed little restaurant, with wine boxes
and a white cat here and there among the pine
booths, a Victorian polyphon fighting it out
sometimes with Monday night bell-ringing from the
Priory, and candles competing with diners' tobacco
to make early evening meals advisable. The
seriousness of both food and wine is the more of a
surprise. Soups, omelette, or 'a coarse, dense,
well-flavoured terrine aux herbes' may be the best
first courses if you are proceeding to fish – and the
quality of the sauces for turbot Mornay (a dish of
the day) and filets de sole Barfleur (£3·95) at a test
meal made this an excellent idea. However, others
report equally well-cooked suprême de volaille
Célestine (£2·50) and tournedos périgourdine among
specialities, and accurately treated courgettes and
sauté potatoes too. A ripe Brie and well-balanced
lemon syllabub are variously praised, and in buying
wine – which he does in large quantities for this and
the firm's other restaurants in Lymington and
Winchester (*q.v.*) – John Carter also considers both
sweet and savoury tastes, with good sweet Quarts
de Chaume or Ch. Coutet '73 (£6·20, £3·10 the half)
as well as half-bottles of Ch. Léoville-Lascases '57
(£4) and forty other clarets or red burgundies.
There are sound whites from Loire, Rhône or Mosel
at £5 or so. The house wines are Gros Plant or
Minervois (£2·95 in 1978). No children after 9 p.m.

App: K. B. Bushen, E.K.D., Hazel Ricketts, and others

CLAUGHTON Lancashire   Map 8

Old Rectory
on A683
6 m NE of Lancaster
Hornby 21455 *and* 21560

Closed Mon; Sun D;
Dec 25 & 26; Jan 1
Must book
Meals 12.30–1.45, 7–9

Tdh L £3 (meal £4·95)
Alc £5·85 (meal £8·10)

VAT inc
Children's helpings
(under 10)
Seats 38
♻ rest; w.c.
Car park
No dogs in public rooms
5 rooms (2 with bath)
B&B £8

The lunches, especially on Sundays, are the best
value at the Martins' substantial Lune valley house
and stream-girt garden, which has remained in the
book, not without some dissent, for a decade now.
Fortunately, local taste seems not to mind
beginning meals with, say, a mixture of cottage
cheese, chives and tinned peaches, and ending with
very sweet, very creamy chocolate or meringue
confections. But visitors from near and far like the
considerate and informative staff, and the
straightforward cooking of simple vegetable or onion
soups, chicken pie 'with an excellent crust and
well-cooked vegetables', and roast lamb with
redcurrant and orange sauce. Main dishes at a test
dinner were similarly satisfactory, though noisettes
of lamb should have been more carefully trimmed.
Roast beef and Yorkshire is a speciality, as is rice
pudding, if you or your pancreas cannot take
Fostontiche. Wines, from £2·20, are mostly
innocent of vintages, or just innocent, so Ch.
Léoville-Lascases or Aloxe-Corton at £6·50 may or
may not be bargains. Pressurised beers. Recorded
music. A comfortable overnight stop.

App: Michael Meyer, B.G., J. & K.L., and others

CLEEVE HILL Gloucestershire   Map 2

Malvern View Hotel
♢
on A46
4 m NE of Cheltenham
Bishops Cleeve 2017

Closed L; Sun D (exc
res); 3 weeks Chr
Must book
D only, 7.30–9.30

Tdh £6·50 (meal £8·65)

VAT & service inc
Seats 42 (parties 20)
Car park
No dogs
7 rooms (5 with bath,
2 with shower)
B&B £10
Fire cert

Apart from one June evening when dinner seemed
to have lost its savour, people seem well content
with their meals and short stays at Mr and Mrs
Sparks's stone-built Victorian hotel at the foot of
grassy Cleeve Hill. The deep browns, candles, silver
and glass in the dining-room look inviting, and led
one guest to an equally deep brown dish of venison
in port with juniper berries, preceded by smokies in
white wine and cream. Impeccable taramosalata
with black olives, escargots Malvern View (in a
pastry parcel), avocado with crab, and, for that
matter, melon – 'a whole one' – are other first
courses praised, and 'my carré d'agneau en croûte,
with tender and moist lamb rolled round rosemary
in crisp flaky pastry, would have been served for
two in many restaurants.' Quails with black cherries
may be better than guinea-fowl with calvados and
cream; the vegetables and salads offered seem
imaginative and carefully prepared. There are
several notes of residents' Sunday dinners, with
generous slices of roast beef and cold salmon. 'The
list of puddings did not actually set the pulses
racing,' says one member of the 'sugary fancy', but
gateau and banana Brazil have been found agreeably
light, and cheeses are good. So are the cooked
breakfasts. The atmosphere, sedate as you would

179

expect on the outskirts of Cheltenham, is not overbearing, and though wine prices are firm and a poor bottle of Gevrey-Chambertin '70 is reported, the cellar is imposing, especially in claret and vintage port, with Ch. Cos d'Estournel '67 (£10), double magnums of Ch. Nenin '70 (£33), and Croft '63 (£12·50). No music. No children under six. Ties 'preferred'.

App: P. E. Goodhead, P. R. Mortimer, M. C. T. Brookes, Mr & Mrs W. A. Southall, G. Froyd

---

COATHAM MUNDEVILLE Durham   Map 8

Hall Garth Hotel
off A1(M) at junction
with A167
4 m N of Darlington
Aycliffe 312818

Closed Sun D (exc res)
Must book
Meals 12–1.30, 7.15–9.15

Tdh L from £4·50 (meal £6·65), D from £5·75 (meal £8·15)

Children's helpings
(under 8)
Seats 52
 rest
Car park
No dogs
11 rooms (6 with bath, 1 with shower)
B&B from £8

Ernest Williamson and Janice Crocker have established themselves more firmly now in this decorous Georgian house, and hold out hopes of 'sorrel, spinach and Swiss chard' from the vast walled garden. Enough meals have miscarried during the year for some to feel still that their former pub restaurant must have been easier to control and its turnover faster. Mr Williamson's enthusiasm may then irritate. But most visitors write warmly about Mrs Crocker's pâtés of game or smoked haddock, prawns in Alabama sauce, potted mushrooms with brandy, and 'unusual, spicy and delicious' chicken soup with Martini as beginnings to the set menus, which usually offer four or five choices in each course. Beef and wine pie and roast spring lamb with 'oh, joy, properly roast potatoes' similarly impressed a passing inspector. Others praise halibut in wine sauce or roast mallard, and poule-au-pot or baked pork with mushroom stuffing are kitchen favourites. The sweets range from treacle lick 'as at Hesleden' to 'perfectly poached pear Bénédictine', 'refreshingly different' Muscatel sorbet and raspberry charlotte, and 'luscious' crème brûlée and chestnut cream with apricot brandy. Wines, though more are listed than seem always to be available, are carefully chosen and fairly priced, from £1·50 for 50 cl of Valgardello ordinaire. The Yapp white Loires at £3–£4 in 1978, or superior Condrieu and Château Grillet at £8–£9, stand out. Oddly, three of the nine clarets are '64: the Ch. Giscours of that year at £8 contrasts with the '73 at £6·75. No music. No smoking in the dining-room. Rooms are comfortable, including at least one with a four-poster, and breakfasts good.

App: N. C. Heavisides, C. R. Handley, W. A. Henderson, R. E. Heffer, E.L.F., J. M. Butterfield, and others

---

Do not risk using an out-of-date Guide. A new edition will be published early in 1980.

COCKERMOUTH Cumbria   Map 7

Old Court House
2 Main Street
Cockermouth 823871

Closed Sun; Dec 24,
25 & 26
Must book D
Meals 11.30–2, 7–9

Tdh D £5·50 (meal £6·95)
Alc L about £3·30

VAT & service inc
Children's helpings
Seats 30
 ⑤ rest
No dogs

'The smoking, fat cigars and all, in this intimate room was an abomination,' writes one member, who noticed a waiter light up too. However, that apart, both this and other correspondents praise Rüdiger Geissler's cooking and his staff's service in what was once the lock-up by the Cocker, 'approached by a boardwalk over the foaming stream'. Lunch is first come, first served, but in the evening they like to phase bookings. Dishes, listed in German but patiently translated on the set menu, are rich without being pretentious, and hot food is hot. Vegetable soup with herbs and cream, scallops in white wine sauce with a Parmesan 'crust', fillet steak with cream, brandy, peppers and onions, fresh vegetables, and syllabub with sherry and lemon made one good dinner. Sweets as a whole are limited, but among main dishes look out for the pork dish called Schweingeschnetzeltes badische art, or roast duckling with Weinkraut. The lunch menu offers light snacks or a full meal (open sandwiches are about 60p). The ordinaire is Hirondelle, and more interesting wines are sometimes added to the German standards on the list: Zeltinger Himmelreich Auslese '75, £5. No music.

App: G. McIntosh, R. F. Kojecky, M.T.B., and others

COLCHESTER Essex   Map 3

The Barn
Williams Walk
off East Stockwell Street
Colchester 67867

Colchester's old 'Dutch quarter' is lucky in this graceful tile-and-timber barn and the housewives who run it for the Brightmores of Bistro Nine (*q.v.*). Open all day, they offer croissants (15p), stuffed peppers, roast Parmesan chicken (95p), good bread and cheeses, fools or home-baked fruit pies, Dundee cake and other delights. Help-yourself system, but conscientious assistance. Charbonnier house wine, £2·70 the litre, or Adnams' bottled pale ale. Coffee, various teas, and squeezed orange juice. No music.

Closed D; Sun; Mon;
Dec 25 & 26
Open 10–5.30

Alc £2·30 (meal £3·15)

VAT inc

Seats 70
⑤ rest
No dogs

Bistro Nine
9 North Hill
Colchester 76466

Closed Sun; Mon; 2 weeks
June; 1 week Chr
Must book D & weekends
Meals 12–1.45, 7–10.45

'There is a strong sense that someone is enjoying himself in the kitchen,' writes one member, and although there is also a sense that Marcus Butcher and Penny Bruton tend to expect or inflict a sweet tooth, or develop vaulting ambitions, this kind of gusto befits the Brightmores' church-pew bistro. Vegetable soup with their good wholemeal bread, aubergine dip, and strawberry cream meringue

Alc £4·10 (meal £6·80)

Children's helpings
Seats 75 (parties 35)
♿ rest (3 steps); w.c.
No dogs
Access, Barclay

made such a good snack lunch for one man that he went back the very same evening for 'green' or mackerel pâtés, duck and apple pancakes, gammon with apricot stuffing (more like chutney) and brown bread ice-cream – a failure because the caramelised crumbs in it tasted stale. The freshness of salads is praised, though, and criticism of 'gooey' moussaka is set off by good steaks, jacket potatoes, and New Orleans beef. Favourite dishes include paglia e fieno (£1·95), American pie (£2·45) and lamb and redcurrant pancakes (£2·95). Rhubarb crumble was 'generous with fruit, judicious with ginger'. Coffee is praised. Charbonnier carafes are £2·80 a litre and the few other wines, though likely to rise by £1 a bottle in 1979, include dry white Ch. Doisy-Daëne '76 at £3. No music, to musicians' relief.

App: P. & L. M. Luscombe, A. V. Wraight, V. R. Sladden, W.B., Ian Jewel, and others

---

COLCHESTER Essex   Map 3

Wm. Scragg's
2 North Hill
Colchester 41111

Closed Sun; public hols
Must book D
Meals 12–2.15, 7–10.30

Alc £6·70 (meal £9·20)

VAT inc
Service 10%
Children's helpings
Seats 50 (parties 30)
No dogs
Access, Barclay

Inspectors' early view that Alice Percival (now helped by Hilary Hicks) had few rivals in East Anglia as a fish cook has been confirmed by the year's accounts of Thorogood's neatly laid-out and kept-up wine bar and restaurant, lodged in a restored house that fetched £135 in the year of the Great Reform Bill. Since the tastes are true and not disguised, even in rich versions such as sole Wm. Scragg's (£3·30) and salmon cutlet with shrimp and lemon sauce, much depends on the day's materials: 'You notice if it is a bad week for scallops, but the grilled soles that followed were superb.' Oysters 'mid-way in price between Orford and the West End' are prime, as Colchester should expect, and crab with good mayonnaise, or fish pie, are other good choices. Begin with prawns and grapes in wine (£1·15), perhaps, and end with apricot brûlée or home-made ices. Abbot ale is 36p a pint, Bordeaux Sauvignon 58p a glass, and under £4 there is Uerziger Schwarzlay '75 or Touraine Cabernet (if you take the optional chicken dish, or simply like red wine with fish). Recorded music.

App: P. L. Joslin, Pat & Jeremy Temple, Susan Tamlyn, H.L., and others

---

For the explanation of ♿ denoting accessibility for the disabled, see 'How to use the Guide', p. 4.

Prices of meals underlined are those which we consider represent unusual value for money. They are not necessarily the cheapest places in the Guide.

COLYTON Devon   Map 2

Old Bakehouse

♥

Colyton 52518

Closed L; Sun D (exc
res); Nov–Feb
Must book
D only, 7–9

Alc £5·75 (meal £9·10)

Service 10%
Children's helpings
Seats 28 (parties 16)
& rest (1 step)
Car park
No dogs
7 rooms (1 with bath)
B&B £7·50–£8·50
D, B&B £88–£95 p.w.
Fire cert

'We booked a summer week in a town we had never heard of merely because we liked the sound of the Old Bakehouse in the last two *Guides*,' writes a Lancastrian who was not disappointed by Susan Keen's cooking: 'I have never eaten at that standard before so consistently and so reasonably.' Others emphasise that full hotel services (other than breakfast) must not be expected in the Keens' 17th-century 'restaurant with rooms', but the atmosphere is thoughtful, even if one Londoner also calls it 'awfully English'. The food, by contrast, is consciously French provincial, above all in the occasional regional dinners. The list of Mrs Keen's preferred dishes transports one to the homeland of Boulestin and Escoffier: oeufs farcis périgourdine (served with home-made tomato sauce, £1·50), walnut soup, gayettes de Charente-Maritime, dodine de volaille and daube des Causses (£3·95). Salmon trout in champagne and brochet façon de Quincy (£4·40) show that other regions are not neglected, and guests mention herring calaisienne, scallops in brandy cream and onions (£1·50) and salade aveyronnaise (90p) among first courses; then perhaps duck albigeoise or chicken Célestine. But if you are hesitating between, say, stuffed sea bream or plaice deauvillaise and tranche d'agneau or escalope de veau cauchoise, take the fish every time. 'Vegetables, (included in the main course price) were always fresh and cooked in an original way' – perhaps too original, given so many rich and copious sauces elsewhere and rich sweets too: good style in cooking implies restraint. But, 'I was converted to meringue dishes by the hazelnut meringue gateau, layered once with apricots and nuts and once with raspberries.' Cheeses are good but may need more variation, for the wines improve steadily. Mr Keen has wisely withdrawn some '66 clarets for later consumption, and can afford to, while Ch. Cantenac-Brown '61 is still there at £10·50, with two other '61s in half-bottle. There are some important burgundies too, and more basic drinking is interestingly provided for, with Cabernet or Sauvignon open wines at £3, Gros Plant '76 or Fitou or Pécharmant among many under £4, and Muscat de Frontignan or Ch. Suduiraut '70 under £5 for dessert. 'No smoking, hurrah, in the dining-room, and no music, bravo.'

*App: L. S. Luff, Mrs J. Ellis, Barbara Greetham,
W. M. Bunker, B. P. McTernan, Roger Baresel,
and many others*

'VAT inc' means that an inn's policy is to incorporate VAT in its food prices.

COMBEINTEIGNHEAD Devon   Map 1

Netherton House Hotel
3 m E of Newton Abbot
off B3195
Shaldon 3251

The Godfreys have run their family home as a hotel for some years, but only recently have 'outsiders' been able to have meals here. Twenty wooded acres on the River Teign provide ample peace and exercise (swimming-pool, tennis courts, croquet lawn) as well as much of the fruit and vegetables which appear on the sensibly short menus. Praise for potato and onion soup, Swiss delights (deep-fried cheese balls with tartare sauce), tender duckling, local salmon, or Lancashire hot-pot, with mostly competent vegetables. 'Splendid' country-house sweets: almond tart, German chocolate cake, lemon syllabub, fruit salad. Argentine house wine, £2·30 for 26 fl oz. Friendly staff. Recorded music. Wear a jacket and tie in the evening.

Closed L (exc res and Sun in winter); Sun D; Jan; Feb
Must book
Meals 12.15–1.30 (res & Sun in winter), 7.15–9

Tdh Sun L £4·50 (meal £6·20), D £6·50 (meal £8·40)

VAT & service inc
Seats 40
♿ rest

No dogs in public rooms
Barclaycard
10 rooms (6 with bath, 1 with shower)
B&B £10–£14
D, B&B £13–£16·65
Fire cert

COMPTON Surrey   Map 3

Withies Inn
off B3000
4 m SW of Guildford
Godalming 21158

Gaston Magnin's ancient and well-kept inn, with tables under the willows for outside eating, achieved some local notoriety not long ago as the place that turned away the late Bing Crosby because he had not booked. As an index of prosperity the tale is not misleading, and if you take the more straightforward dishes from the charcoal grill (from £3·55), or perhaps half a crisply roasted duck with orange salad, you may think it deserved. Besides, vichyssoise was good, and 'home-made lobster soup' (75p) at a test meal did indeed seem to depend on the numerous lobsters that leave the kitchen in other guises. Sauces incline to be sweet, and oddly enough the same could be said of pastry for a lunchtime steak, kidney and mushroom pie (£1·75). But the pie was otherwise good, and the house 'crispy potatoes' and fresh green beans excellent. Sweets and coffee are less admired. The Nicolas carafes are £2·50 a litre, and there are about 60 other wines, mostly on the young side except for Ch. Pichon-Lalande '69 at £10, an odd choice perhaps. There are bar snacks at bar times, and pressurised beers. Recorded music. No under-fives, but older children are nicely treated.

Closed Sun D
Must book
Meals from 12.30 (Sun 12 and 2); 7.30 and 9

Alc (min £2·50) £4·60 (meal £8·15)

Service 10%
Cover 25p (Sun L late sitting 50p)
Seats 38
Car park
No dogs
Am Ex, Access, Barclay, Diners

App: M. R. Wills, C.H.C., David & Pamela Newth, D.S., J.S. Evans, D. H. Brett, and others

184

CONINGSBY Lincolnshire   Map 6

Ratty's
43 High Street
Coningsby 42285

'Opposite the church with the one-handed clock', the Tuckers' restaurant (converted from two small barns) is friendly, 'if slightly crowded', and the service is 'civilised and relaxed'. Their produce is fresh and people like the prawns in cream sauce, garlic mussels, tournedos Marcus (£3·80 including vegetables and salad), 'delicious' grilled salmon (with mediocre hollandaise) and veal or chicken in various ways. Warm praise for brown bread ice-cream with brandy, and the cheesecake. Italian house wine, £2 for 75 cl, 40p the glass. 'Subdued' recorded music.

Closed L; Sun; Mon;
1 week Easter; 2 weeks
Aug; 5 days Chr; Jan 1;
last week Feb
Must book

D only, 7.30–9.15

Alc £4·95 (meal £6·95)

VAT inc

Children's helpings
Seats 38
 ♿ rest (1 step)
Car park
No dogs

COOKHAM Berkshire   Map 3

Le Radier
19 Station Hill Parade
Bourne End 25775

Closed L; Sun
Must book
D only, 7–9.30

Alc £5·20 (meal £7·85)

Service inc
Seats 25
Car park
No dogs

There are few more English painters than Stanley Spencer, but French cooking is becoming a secondary (or perhaps primary) draw in Cookham, for Lucien Voisin has moved his family restaurant from Henley to this shopping-parade place with a flat above. 'Probably the best find we've ever made from the *Guide*,' says a member who pursued the Voisins from the one place to the other for the sake of their avocado and crab terrine and noisettes d'agneau en chemise 'of butter-like tenderness', served with tarragon sauce. Pancakes are consistently good, both sweet and savoury, and people who have begun with pipérade or coquilles St Jacques or quenelles de brochet with sauce américaine or 'succulently contrasted' snails with red wine, grapes and croûtons, have been even better pleased. The mustardy sauces for main-course chicken or beef and the apple-and-calvados one for veal are all praised highly, and sole fillets stuffed with a light spinach mousse and garnished with a prawn sauce and juicy prawns prompts admiration for the way distinct tastes emerged from a harmonious whole. 'Courgettes were exquisitely cooked, but the sauté potatoes were rather flabby and dull by comparison.' Sweets, as often in this genre of cooking, are less inspired, though not perfunctory. The coffee is good. Madame Voisin serves hospitably. Wines come from Bordeaux Direct Ltd, whose Bergerac white or red, or Chusclan rosé, cost about £3·50 in 1978. Recorded music.

App: M.S., R. L. Vardy, R.A.R.H., Frederick Williams, T.M.F., Vincent & Pat Tseng, D.B.

Ramblers of Corbridge
18 Front Street
Corbridge 2424

Closed L Oct–Easter
(exc Dec); Sun; Mon;
Dec 25 & 26; Jan 1
Must book D
Meals 12–2, 7–10

Alc L £3·15 (meal £5·30),
D £5·15 (meal £7·70)

Children's helpings L
Seats 55
⟨&⟩ rest (2 steps)
No dogs
Access, Barclay

The Herrmanns' 'charming roughstone conversion' of
their house in a quiet street makes a good
resting-place on a long journey north or south. The
Guide's letter this year caught Heinrich between
menus, so who knows whether 1979 readers will find
his aprikosen gebratenes Schweinekotelett (£3·10) or
Lammkeulenschnitte athenische art? But these,
along with crab soup, cheese profiteroles, soups,
melon in mango chutney sauce, roast duck, apricot
and almond flan and black cherry cheesecake (80p)
have been much enjoyed by 1978 visitors, as well
as 'pleasant and helpful service'. 'Coffee, alas, was
weak and not very hot.' Don Cortez ordinaires are
£2·10, and a German white carafe wine is promised;
Ch. Haut Bel Air is £3·45, and there are pressurised
beers. Recorded music.

*App: E. D. Barraclough, M.R-H., E.L.F., M.G.,
and others*

Corse Lawn House
on B4211
5 m SW of Tewkesbury
Tirley 479

Closed Mon; Sun D;
Must book D
Meals 12.30–2, 7–10

Tdh L £3 (meal £5·60)
Alc £6·70 (meal £9·70)

VAT inc
Service 10%
Children's helpings
Seats 45 (parties 35)
⟨&⟩ rest; w.c.
Access, Am Ex, Barclay,
Diners

*Between Michael Ross's departure from this brick
house 'reached by a pot-holed track round the village
green', and the arrival of the Hines from Three Cocks
(q.v.), there was an interregnum that may have been
unhelpful; at least, a test lunch here in the summer
found the restaurant empty and the cooking well below
Mrs Hine's best, with bland sauces, 'positively
dreadful' vegetables, and jaded sweets. Happily other
inspectors' experiences of dinners with 'exquisite'
hot shrimps en croustade and lobster and scallop
pancakes have been better, and peach Romanoff and
the coffee have also been praised, but faultless meals
remain elusive. Try, they suggest, guinea-fowl
normande or médaillons de porc poivre vert (both
£3·75), and coffee chiffon flan (95p) – and report, of
course. House red Bordeaux or white Mâcon from
Mason Cattley are £3·20 and Denis Hine
recommends his Muscadet '76 at £3·60. Ch.
Cantemerle '67 is £9·50. No music. No dogs.*

Barbara's Kitchen
10 m SE of Helston
St Keverne 281

'Just an ordinary bungalow in the village', but one
with an all-female staff, friendly and efficient service
and no microwave oven. The dinner menus, both
table d'hôte and à la carte, are sensibly unelaborate.
You might be lucky enough to find sardines in
garlic butter (75p), lemon sole with cream sauce
(£2·95), halibut with prawn sauce, lamb sauté
Parmentier, or chicken bordelaise; as helpings are
not gross, you will be able to try the trolley sweets

or cheeses. French house wine is £3·20 the litre. Some would consign both smoke and music to the sea winds. No under-sixes.

Closed L; Dec 25	Tdh £3·50 (meal £6)	Service 10%
Must book	Alc £5·25 (meal £7·90)	Seats 36
D only, 7–10		♿ rest (1 step)
	VAT inc	No dogs

CRACKINGTON HAVEN Cornwall   Map 1

Coombe Barton Hotel
off A39
11 m SW of Bude
St Gennys 345

Friendly, family-run hotel in a rocky bay, with decent cooking. The set dinner menu reads well and changes daily: mackerel and horseradish pâté, crab quiche, grapefruit with Pernod, 'melting' beef olives with 'fresh and well-cooked vegetables', grilled salmon, liver with Dubonnet and orange, with 'lingeringly tangy' gooseberry and elderflower sorbet, tarte Tatin or Royal Mint gateau to finish. The home-made bread and rolls appear in lunchtime bar snacks too, as well as pasties and St Austell's pressurised bitter and other beers. Good breakfasts. Wine by the glass 45p. No music. No children under five.

Closed L (exc bar);	VAT inc	No dogs in public rooms
Nov 1–Mar 1	Seats 40	11 rooms
Must book	♿ rest (3 steps)	B&B £7
D only, 7–9.30	Air-conditioning	D, B&B £11
	Car park	Fire cert
Tdh from £4·50 (meal £6·70)		

CRAWLEY Hampshire   Map 2

Fox and Hounds
5 m NW of Winchester
Sparsholt 285

'A good brick-built pub, friendly and warm on two miserable spring days,' says one weekday bar-luncher *en passant* from Paris who found Mrs Marsden's soups, 'especially the watercress', excellent, quiche good, desserts fair and coffee indifferent. In the dining-room, Sparsholt smokies, 'delicious poached salmon, very fresh Dover sole' and 'first-rate meat from John Robinson in Stockbridge' are also reported. Berry Bros French house wine (£3·40 a litre) or Pompey Royal beer on hand pumps. No music.

Closed Mon; Sun D;	Tdh Sun L £4 (meal £5·90)	Seats 35
Dec 25 & 26	Alc £6 (meal £8)	♿ rest; w.c.
Must book		Car park
Meals 12.30–2, 7.30–10	VAT & service inc	No dogs in d/r

See p. 120 for the restaurant-goer's legal rights, and p. 118 for information on hygiene in restaurants.

Cranks
Shinners Bridge
Totnes 862388

The 'eat, drink, shop and relax' complex at Shinners Bridge is very Dartington, and Cranks has the virtues (and vices) of the same style elsewhere: hand-thrown crockery, and a wholesome heaviness about the food that makes you wonder how the staff rein in their waistlines. When tried, onion soup was thick and grossly salt, cashew nut baked custard creditable; but try too, they say, mushroom pie, buckwheat and rice savoury, nut rissoles, or apple cake with clotted cream (28p). A glass of elderflower wine (40p) or their own carrot juice or lemonade may distract you from ordinary wines and beers. Recorded classical music. Four (only) non-smoking tables.

Closed D; Sun L; public
hols
Open 10–5

Alc (min L 70p) meal
£3·15

VAT & service inc

Seats 70
Car park
No dogs

Carved Angel

2 South Embankment
Dartmouth 2465

Closed Mon; Sun D;
Dec 24, 25 & 26; Jan
Must book D
Meals 12.30–1.45,
6.45–10.30

Alc £8 (meal £10·75)

VAT & service inc
Children's helpings
Seats 40 (parties 15)
rest (3 steps)
No dogs

On his menu lately Tom Jaine has been quoting Oliver Edwards: 'I consider supper as a turnpike through which one must pass, in order to get to bed.' Self-deprecation can hardly go further. For most people whose travels luckily take them within striking range of the graceful restaurant that lies behind this quayside picture window, bed and breakfast is merely a turnpike through which one must pass in order to taste Joyce Molyneux's lunches and dinners. Some such people this year say they have been so dazzled by the Angel that, as Watts puts it, 'Praise sits silent on our tongues.' But others begin at the beginning with 'the generosity and love of simple flavours' manifest here. Generosity appears in the abundant (but not overfacing) quantities, the superb black olives and cheese straws, the three kinds of bread, the fudge and almond biscuits with coffee, and the extra tureen of fish soup 'that was too good to pass over (with garlic croûtons and rouille, £1·25)'. For simple flavours, think perhaps of local fresh prawns or glistening white turbot with aïoli, or mussels in hot butter, garlic and parsley, or oeuf mollet with watercress mousseline, or of the buttered salsify and puree of celeriac that may accompany more complex main dishes: brill with lobster sauce, 'thick and delicious casserole of oxtail and grapes', or casserole of veal with sorrel (£4). Salmon in pastry with currants and ginger remains a perennial speciality and the 'mild lamb curry with its condiments' (£4) is worth trying. Crème brûlée, sorbets, and summer pudding (£1) are models of their kind: 'It is not easy to pack such a weight of five fruits into this pudding, simple as it seems'; 'raspberry sauce with oeufs à la neige tasted absolutely fresh even in April.' If prices for food and especially wine seem high, recall that 'service is included and a very substantial tip was politely refused.' Ch. Gloria '70 or Ch. Meyney '67, both château-bottled and £8, are therefore fair enough, and the Averys burgundies are dependable for an occasion (Bonnes-Mares '69 in magnum, £25). There are also nice sweet wines by half-bottle or glass. A hair in the soup, a dry fillet of mackerel once and a chilly room one winter night 'that deterred us from waiting for the hot chocolate soufflé' about exhaust the criticisms, for the service seems settled in now. No music.

App: by too many members to list

Taylor's
8 The Quay
Dartmouth 2748

Closed Tue; mid-Jan to mid-Feb; Dec 26
Must book D
Meals 12–2.30, 7–10.30

Tdh from £4·60
(meal £7·60)
Alc £6·05 (meal £9·35)

Seats 40
No dogs
Access, Am Ex, Barclay, Diners

Diana Taylor clearly has no qualms about being the alternative restaurant on Dartmouth Quay, and perhaps her choice of a black-draped Bedouin tent with lone camel mural and imperfectly cured goatskins, and service 'apparently by resting mummers', is the best possible solution to the problem. Anyway, people have been content here, whether with dinner in the tent, or with 'unfailingly splendid soup and brown bread', and freshly cooked mackerel, sardines in garlic butter, or liver, in the less daunting bar, with its log fire and view of the Dart. At night, 'I ordered avocado with banana and honey in the spirit of research, but the result, with a syrupy yet sharp sauce, was far better than I expected, and enormous crabs were then presented, the bodies filled with the soft meat in an excellent creamy sauce, and the detached claws accompanied by lobster picks and finger bowls.' Other oddities on which Aircraftsman Shaw's comments might have been worth hearing include lemon sole with lychees and oregano, or with toasted almonds and ginger wine (£4·35, including vegetables). Vegetarian curry and risotto are also offered (£3·70). There are one or two savouries as well as the sweets (75p), and mint tea (25p) as well as coffee. Sidi Larbi (of course) is £3 and careful ordering may be necessary before embarking on clarets from £4·50. Disappointingly conventional recorded music. More reports, please.

DEDDINGTON Oxfordshire   Map 2

Holcombe Hotel
High Street
Deddington 274

Closed Sun D; Dec 25 & 26
Must book

One or two bar meals, and a Saturday set lunch, seem to have fallen well below *Guide* standard, but no one seems to feel this about the dinners at the Daniels' unassuming but hospitable hotel. The weekend bargain breaks are popular, though on Friday (fondue) night the atmosphere in the 'mainly red' dining-room becomes rather heavy-laden. Zrazy

Meals 12.15–2, 7.30–9.30

Tdh L £2·50 (meal £4·80),
Sun L £3·25 (meal £5·60)
Alc L £4 (meal £6·45),
D £6·10 (meal £8·90)

VAT inc
Children's helpings
Seats 60 (parties 20)
 ♿ rest
Car park
No dogs in d/r
Access, Barclay, Diners,
Euro
12 rooms (1 with bath,
1 with shower)
B&B £7–£9

Nelson (beef fillet with kümmel, mushrooms,
cucumber and cream, £3·75) is another of Mrs
Daniel's specialities, and a test meal that included
'hot and delicious' aubergine au gratin, and trout
'Pernolais' with a Pernod cream sauce, was
uniformly satisfactory. Vegetables, too, were
enterprising and well cooked, with fennel, ratatouille,
and potatoes 'with very edible skins'. Sweets are
about standard for their creamy genre, though
Jamaican rum banana at the test meal for once had
enough rum, and others speak well of caramelised
grapes in brandy, and pineapple cheesecake. Monte
Campo ordinaires are £3·40 a litre, Dolamore's
College range of wines £3·40 a bottle, and Ch.
Meyney '67, £6·70. Recorded music. No children
under eight after 8 p.m.

*App: M. S. Hicks, D. G. Foot, G. A. Wright,
A.J.H., J. & J.W., and others*

DEDHAM Essex   Map 3

Le Talbooth

⚟

Gun Hill
off A12
7 m NE of Colchester
at Stratford St Mary
Colchester 323150

Closed Dec 24, 25 & 26
Must book
Meals 12.30–2, 7.30–9

Alc £7·75 (meal £10·85)

VAT inc
Service 10%
Children's helpings
Seats 80 (parties 50)
Car park
No dogs
Access card
10 rooms (9 with bath,
1 with shower)
B&B £15–£22·50
Fire cert

A quarter-century sits easily on Gerald Milsom's
embonpoint, and while the attributions of Constable
paintings waver, there is no doubt who owns and
runs this flowery black-and-white house by the
Stour, and its luxurious residential lodge (Maison
Talbooth) half a mile away across the A12, where
breakfasts are models of their kind, and baths big
enough for two, say people who expect this of any
maison. Prices are firm enough for the highest
standards to be expected, or appreciation might be
less grudging: 'all right on the whole and outstanding in parts' is a common verdict. At least the
peaks are more evident under Samuel Chalmers than
they used to be. Members have variously noticed
'those delicately marinated herrings, and delicious
spinach soup', 'a subtle horseradish sauce with a
fresh and juicy smoked trout', and a casserolette de
sole en feuilleté with mushrooms and asparagus
(£4·95, including vegetables) 'which few places could
have bettered'. Other soups (including lobster,
artichoke, watercress, and duck), sea bass marinated
in Pernod and lemon juice, breast of pheasant,
saddle of lamb, and 'a magnificent apple pie and
cream' (to represent Mr Milsom's Taste of England
responsibilities) are also praised. Vegetables are
mostly local, but more erratic. Sweets may need
more attention too: lemon sorbet is admired but
good judges have called the chocolate and praline
charlotte 'bland and boring'. The home-made bread
at the outset and fudge at the end are welcome.
Service sometimes lacks experience or English
('water was poured into my half-full wine glass in
spite of a timely warning'). The wine list starts at
£3·20 and has few gaps, except in half-bottles. The

Alsace and moselle whites for the fine fish at about
£8, the '66 and '70 clarets (slow developers all) in
the £8–£12 range, and the vintage ports, all deserve
notice. No music. Reports also welcome on Mr
Milsom's newest venture, The Pier at Harwich.

*App: Ron Salmon, Norman Punt, W.B., M.P.,
Henry Fawcett, and others*

DEDHAM see also pub section

DERBY Derbyshire   Map 5

Ben Bowers
13–15 Chapel Street
Derby 365988 *and* 367688

A relative of the Nottingham Ben Bowers (*q.v.*), this
restaurant complex (opposite a multi-storey car
park) also offers bar snacks and a help-yourself
buffet in the Blessington Carriage at ground level,
with Ansells pressurised beers. Upstairs there is a
sedate set lunch and some dishes from the *carte*, but
at night you eat round the world in 80 minutes with,
perhaps, taramosalata or barbecued spare ribs
(85p), Highland fillet (cooked in Glayva and cream,
£4·10), or a Scandinavian seafood platter (£3·40),
with sweets or Stilton to land on. 'Worth the trip
for the garlic bread alone.' Various house wines from
£3·62 the litre. Random music, live or recorded.

Closed Sun D; Sat L; Dec 25 & 26; L most public hols	Tdh L £2·75 (meal £5) Alc £4·85 (meal £7·30)	Seats 70 (parties 30) Air-conditioning No dogs
Must book D & weekends Meals 12–2, 7–11	VAT inc Children's helpings (under 10)	Access, Am Ex, Barclay, Diners, Euro

---

Cathedral Restaurant
22 Irongate
Derby 368732

*On the first floor of a listed building overlooking the
Cathedral gardens, this little restaurant has walls and
floors 'at crazy angles' and almost equally crazy
fish-net-and-shell decor. The à la carte menu tries too
hard perhaps, and the set lunch not hard enough. But
there is guarded praise for prawns in a hot garlic sauce
('though I'd prefer more garlic, less Tabasco') £1·35;
tender fillet steak similarly treated, and fillet kebab in a
rather bland sauce. The vegetables (80p) have merit:
'lightly cooked carrots, cauliflower, cabbage, aubergine,
leeks, sprouts and two kinds of potato.' No details of
sweets, but the coffee is good. Italian house wine, £2·75
the litre. 'Recorded evergreens', that is, spinach music.
Dress 'smartly'. More reports, please.*

Closed Sun; Thur D; May 28 L; Aug 27; Dec 26; 2 weeks Jan/Feb	Tdh L £1·85 & £2·75 (meal £4 & £5·05), D (exc Sat) from £2·75 (meal	VAT inc tdh D Children's helpings (under 8)
Must book Meals 12–2, 7–10.15	£5·50) Alc (min £2·50) £5·80 (meal £8·65)	Seats 40 (parties 12) No dogs Barclaycard

DERBY Derbyshire   Map 5

Ristorante San Remo
5 Sadler Gate
Derby 41752

Luigi Negro's old house in the pedestrian precinct
has 'rather spartan accommodation'. But prices are
modest and the service charming and efficient.
There is a simple set lunch (tagliatelle, grilled trout,
treacle sponge) and a more elaborate *carte*: a chicken
liver pâté with burgundy, Marsala and brandy;
beef fillet San Remo (£3·50); chicken Sophia Loren
(£2·75); veal alla crema (£3); or kidneys siciliana
(£3). (Prices are approximate.) Italian house wine, £2
for 25 fl oz. 'Popular, pleasant' recorded music.
Children's helpings.

Closed Sun; Mon D;	Tdh L £2 (meal £3·85)	Seats 45
3 weeks July/Aug;	Alc (min D £2) £5·25	No dogs
public hols (exc Apr 13)	(meal £7·95)	Diners card
Must book		
Meals 12–2, 7–10	Cover 25p alc	

DEREHAM (EAST) Norfolk   Map 6

Phoenix Hotel
Church Street
Dereham 2276

A comfortable Trust House ('excellent breakfasts')
with better staff than most. Set meals still seem
best value, offering a sensibly limited choice of
soups, roasts or grills 'with appropriate vegetables',
and the occasional good sweet. The *carte* aspires
higher, from snails Rockefeller to Phoenix sword
(beef, flamed in brandy and served with a mustard,
cider and cream sauce, £4·75). Arc de Triomphe
ordinaire, £2·80 for 26 fl oz. Adnams' Abbot ale on
hand pump and weekday lunchtime snacks in the
Otter Bar. Live and recorded 'middle of the road'
music, with dancing on winter Saturdays.

Must book	Alc £6·55 (meal £8·35)	Car park
Meals 12.30–2.15, 7.30–10		No dogs in d/r
(Sun 9.30, Fri & Sat	VAT & service inc	Access, Am Ex, Barclay,
10.30)	Children's helpings	Diners, Euro
	Seats 80 (parties 150)	28 rooms (17 with bath)
Tdh L from £3·50 (meal	🔓 rest (2 steps)	B&B £9–£10
£4·90), D from £4 (meal		Fire cert
£5·40)		

DEVIZES Wiltshire   Map 2

Sidmouth Arms
Sidmouth Street
Devizes 4664

*Five nights a week Alain Noizet cooks 'for the bons
vivants of Devizes.' He shops daily, and the results are
good stock-based soups, a cold table of about 30 dishes
– 'watch out, you can easily fill yourself up on that
alone', individual steak and kidney pies, 'young and
sweet' rack of lamb, lemon sole, sirloin steak (plain,
or with garlic butter, or a butter and lemon sauce, or
brandy, peppercorns and cream). Lightly cooked
vegetables; 'the cooking of potatoes is not impressive.'*

Adequate sweets and cheeses. Edwin Giddings wines;
Litre Vin £3 the litre. Engaging and friendly staff.
Recorded music. More reports, please. Smaller helpings
for under-tens.

Closed L; Sun; Mon;
Dec 25 & 26
Must book weekends

D only, 7–10.30 (11 Fri &
Sat)

Seats 40
No dogs

Tdh £4 (meal £6·90)

DREWSTEIGNTON Devon   Map 1

Castle Drogo
3 m SW of A30
between Exeter and
Okehampton
Chagford 3306

Lutyens designed the Drewe family's castle (now
owned by the National Trust), from the lion over
the entrance to the huge pestle-and-mortar in the
scullery. The food is scrupulous in the modern
restaurant too. Try morning coffee and afternoon
cream teas with home-baking, or light and tasty
lunches: home-made soups, local pasties, toasted
sandwiches, 'really fresh salads', healthy cheeses
and light fruity puddings. Local housewives and
students serve. Wine by the glass (45p in 1978),
local cider by the pint mug. No smoking. No music.
No dogs.

Closed D; Nov 1–
Mar 31; Apr 13
Open 12–5.30 (L 12–2)

Alc £2·05 (meal £2·75)

VAT & service inc
Children's helpings

Seats 45 (parties 45)
⑤ rest; w.c.
Car park

DURHAM Durham   Map 8

Undercroft
The College
Cathedral Cloisters

'It takes at least half a day to get round the
Cathedral and its treasures', so how prescient of the
Dean to have arranged with Milburn Bakers to
provide nourishment in the monks' dormitory before
and after: morning coffee and afternoon tea as well
as light, self-service lunches: soup, quiches, salads, a
hot dish in winter (lasagne is popular). A choice of
six wines by the glass, 45p. Service is pleasant and
youthful. No music, and they underline 'no dancing',
to which cathedrals were once more hospitable than
they are now.

Closed D; Sun; public hols
Open 10–5 (L 12–2)

Alc £1·80 (meal £2·45)

VAT & service inc

Seats 84
⑤ rest (ramp); w.c.
No dogs

EARLS COLNE Essex   Map 3

Draper's House
53 High Street
Earls Colne 2484

After seven years, the Higbys' clientele at their
affable, 'granny's parlour-like' restaurant is mostly
local and regular, whether personal or business.
Visitors from further afield are doubtful; but eat up
your cottage cheese and walnut pâté, local pink
trout, beef dishes (including winter steak and kidney

pudding), fresh vegetables, steamed syrup pudding, and home-made meringue speciality, and steer clear, perhaps, of more pretentious fare. The bar and cellar are well-stocked: a pity to take Spanish at £3·10 a litre when there are proper clarets (including Ch. Bel Orme '61) under £5. Recorded music.

Closed Sun; Mon; Sat L; Apr 13; Dec 26; Jan 1 Must book Meals 12–2, 7.15–9 (9.30 Fri & Sat)	Tdh L £2·50 (meal £4·80) Alc £5·70 (meal £8·60) Service 10% Children's helpings	Seats 50 (parties 36) Car park No dogs Access, Barclay, Diners, Euro

EASTBOURNE East Sussex Map 3

Bistro Byron
6 Crown Street,
Old Town
Eastbourne 20171

Closed L; Sun; public
hol Mons; Dec 25 & 26
Must book
D only, 7.30–10.30

Alc £5·50 (meal £7·90)

VAT inc
Cover 20p
Children's helpings
Seats 22 (parties 10)
No dogs
Barclaycard

Simon and Marian Scrutton's tiny and 'newly dressed up' restaurant is not easy to find ('ask a policeman,' advises a Londoner). But another Londoner is grateful to the *Guide* for saving him 'from having to eat another meal in one of the town's grander hotels'. Mr Scrutton's individual cooking gives you time to consume plenty of his desirable black olives and bread rolls, but it is worth the wait for 'exquisite pancakes with cheese and spinach, salmon sometimes, and other fillings', charcuterie with his own mayonnaise, 'superb crab île de Bréhat (£2·85), with better sprouts than I get from my own allotment', well-cooked red cabbage, and 'very fresh salads'. Other specialities include calmars à l'étuvée (£1·20 as a first course), escalope de veau à la crème et aux champignons, and rond de gigot aux herbes de Provence (£2·45). 'There was nothing scrimped in the peach fool', and profiteroles were 'delicious beyond words'. Sometimes, too, there are 'soirées périgourdine', and Mrs Scrutton's front of house presence is obviously part of the attraction. The wines (from £2·45 for ordinaire) are modest: Beaujolais '76 (Louis Latour) £4·80; French-bottled Duché de Longueville cider £1·45. No cigars or pipes before 10 p.m. No music unless overheard from the kitchen.

App: R. J. Cherry, A.F., A. M. Reid, Roy Mathias, M.E-F., Moira Carlisle, and others

Porthole
8 Cornfield Terrace
Eastbourne 20767

A sorry lunch and a cold restaurant in February, and later reports of tepid food, long waits, or ill-cooked sweets, take Mr Puplett's cosy restaurant down a peg this year, but after four years' appearance here there are still many enthusiasts for soup, pâté, prawn pancakes, halibut, plaice on the bone and other fishy specialities. With notice, the Spanish and English chefs will make vegetarian dishes, or a bouillabaisse. You get a free glass of Le Cellier ordinaire with the set lunch; Cuvée St Pierre burgundy is £3, and there are several English wines at about £4. Recorded music; bar lunches; no smoking downstairs. *(See also Seaford: Masthead.)*

Closed D Dec 25 & 26 Must book Meals 12–2, 6.30–10.30 Tdh L from £2·30 (meal £3·60)	Alc (min L £2·20, D £4) £6·25 (meal £8·85) VAT inc Service 10%	Seats 36 ⑤ rest Air-conditioning No dogs Access, Barclay, Diners

---

EAST GRINSTEAD West Sussex   Map 3

Gravetye Manor
5 m SW of East
Grinstead
off B2110 at sign West
Hoathly
Sharpthorne 810567

Must book
Meals 12.30–1.45,
7.30–8.45

Alc £9·45 (meal £13·85)

VAT inc
Service 12½%
Cover 30p
Seats 40 (parties 16)
⑤ rest (bar entrance)
Car park
No dogs in d/r or
bedrooms
14 rooms (12 with bath,
2 with shower)
Room only, from £10·50
Breakfast from £1·75

Peter Herbert's panelled, creeper-clad Elizabethan manor and famous garden epitomises the stockbroker belt, but has been secure of its place here for a dozen years while Karl Löderer, now at Storrington (q.v.), was in the kitchen conjuring up the lost enchantments of the Austro-Hungarian empire. Michael Quinn, a young chef with a James Galway beard who has skipped to Gravetye via some notable stepping-stones, has inherited several of the Viennese pops, from the champignons farcis frits (£1·20) to the médaillons de chevreuil, and is gradually slimming them down. Visitors in the autumn reported that avocado with smoked salmon mousse and dill sauce seemed a poor substitute for gravlax, and that sauces were blander and details less assured than of yore. 'Red cabbage was positively nasty'; game underhung. Salzburger Nockerln have gone and crêpe fraisalia (another Löderer sweet) tasted like an understudy's. But there were good things noticed too: the mustardy mayonnaise served with crudités at the beginning, the capable cooking of the bisque de homard (90p) and the venison, 'delicately flavoured' aiguillettes de caneton au poivre vert (£5·25), and melon sorbet. The central tables are too crowded, but service is good. Coffee is too weak. The wines are justly famous, in almost all departments, from Gewürztraminer '71 at £6·80, through Beaune Clos des Ursules '73 (Louis Jadot) at £9·40, to Wehlener Sonnenuhr Spätlese (J. J. Prüm) at £8·40. No pipes or cigars in the dining-room. No children under seven in the hotel. Please report fully and often, while the tureen and bottle distinctions previously earned are suspended.

EAST HORSLEY Surrey   Map 3

Tudor Rose
15 Bishopsmead Parade
East Horsley 4484

Closed Mon; Sun D;
Dec 1–Jan 15
Must book
Meals 12–2.15 (2.45 Sun),
7–10 (10.30 Sat)

Lunchers and diners chez Chapman are prone to vehemence, pro or con, and it is some tribute to the pulling power of Mrs Chapman's modestly priced cooking in this suburban shopping parade that booked and punctual customers who have once been abruptly turned away still sometimes come back for more. However, 'just book in good time and eat early, and once you are in, Mr Chapman will do his utmost for you,' says one regular customer. There is

Tdh L £1·85 (meal £3·85),
Sun L £2·85 (meal £4·95)
Alc £3·95 (meal £6·65)

VAT inc tdh
Children's helpings
Seats 27
No dogs
Access, Am Ex, Barclay,
Diners, Euro

every reason in this district to record delighted
accounts of 'creamy-cheesy Stilton soup, rare lamb
cutlets and melting duck, the freshest of vegetables,
and sharp, smooth, moist apricot mousse'. Veal with
Marsala and cream sauce (£2·50), roast beef for
Sunday lunch, and chocolate rum and walnut
gateaux (45p) are other house favourites. There are
about thirty wines, and pressurised ale. No music.
Wear a tie. Note the prolonged end-of-year closure
while the Chapmans are visiting relatives in Australia.

*App: Alan C. Sayer, W. Frankland, M.J.D.,
K.E.R., and others*

EAST MOLESEY Surrey   Map 3

The Lantern
20 Bridge Road
01-979 1531

Closed L; Sun; Apr 13 &
16; May 7 & 28;
Aug 27; Chr week
Must book
D only, 7–11

Tdh £6·35 (meal £9·55)
Alc £6·80 (meal £10·05)

VAT inc
Service 10%
Cover 35p
Children's helpings
Seats 45 (parties 20)
🔂 rest (2 steps)
No dogs
Access, Am Ex, Barclay,
Diners

In his seventh *Guide* year, whether Peter
Morphew's discreet little restaurant is as good as
the Hampton Court trade allows it to be, or whether
some things are its own fault, remains a question.
There is an account of 'sardines in a most delicate
mustard sauce, melting mignons de boeuf with
another excellent sauce, carefully chosen and
cooked vegetables, and magnificent sweets';
but another special meal described was apparently
'underseasoned all the way from the leek soup and
salmon in pastry to the chateaubriand béarnaise.'
Still, local admirers interested in cooking find Mr
Morphew consistently inventive in his regional
French dinners, and he thinks himself that his
bourride provençale (£3·10), saucisses alsacienne
(£1·35) and carré d'agneau persillé (£7·25 for two)
are among his best dishes. A critical visitor from
further afield during 'Orléannais' week enjoyed the
meal as a whole, finding the pâté too cold and too
compacted, and the sauce for roast guinea-fowl
unsatisfactory, but the prawn tartlet, courgettes and
mushrooms, and chocolate mousse very rewarding.
The wines (from £3·05 for French-bottled ordinaire)
are called 'bewildering, outlandish and dear', but
not all those epithets are deserved, and there are
some halves too. Not that it matters much when a
man is 'allowed to come in smoking a cigar and put
it down only four times during his meal – once for
each course and once to light another.' Music has
'crept in' too – the *mot juste* for Sinatra?

*App: Brian Singleton, F. & E. A. Jaeger, T.S., and
others*

If you think you are suffering from food-poisoning after eating in a restaurant,
report this immediately to the local Public Health Authority (and write to us).

Wine prices shown are for a 'standard' bottle of the wine concerned, unless
another measure is stated.

EAST RUNTON Norfolk   Map 6

Meadow Cottage
on A149
1 m W of Cromer
Cromer 513988

The Baums are serving simple food at modest prices in what was once the dairy of their 18th-century cottage. Liver and bacon, plaice and chips, cottage pie or salads at lunch-time (children's dishes, 40p) give way to burgundy and brandy pâté, Glaven trout with toasted almonds (£2·65), chicken Marengo (£2·40) or steak Mowbray (prices include fresh vegetables) at night. Friendly service. They hope to be licensed early in 1979; no corkage. Recorded music.

Closed Mon (Sept–Apr);
Sun D; Dec 25 & 26
Must book D & weekends
Meals 12–1.45, 7–9.15

Alc L £1·65 (meal £2·05),
D £3·55 (meal £4·15)

VAT inc
Children's helpings

Seats 26 (parties 12)
♿ rest (1 step)
Car park (3)
No dogs
Unlicensed

EASTRY Kent   Map 3

Coach and Horses
Lower Street
Eastry 692

Closed Tue
Must book
Meals 12.30–1.30, 7.30–10

Alc £5·15 (meal £8·20)

Service 10%
Seats 18
♿ rest
Car park
No dogs

All that is needed for a good meal in the Longs' tranquil little dining-room (formerly a pub) is forethought, since they like you to choose in advance from the printed menu they send. The flavours of freshly roasted birds and freshly picked garden vegetables that this system allows more than make up for the inconvenience, people report, and a half duck with apples, prunes and calvados (£3·30) was 'picked clean to the bones'. Fishy first courses, such as the house version of sole in white wine sauce with almonds, or sea supreme (in puff pastry, £1·50) or scallops 'fresh and cooked for just the right length of time' are popular, and other main dishes described included tender coq au vin, boeuf bourguignonne or Stroganoff, and poulet à la crème. 'Suprême of chicken wrapped in smoked salmon and pastry, with a parsley sauce, seemed too fussy to be worth it.' Rum chocolate truffle (75p) is Mrs Long's favourite sweet. Wines, from £3 for house claret, include some promising (if under-described) French-bottled burgundies (Morey-St-Denis '66, £8). No music.

App: G. Thorpe, R.H.D.J., W.H., and others

ELY Cambridgeshire   Map 6

Old Fire Engine House
25 St Mary's Green
Ely 2582

Closed Sun; July 30–
Aug 12; Dec 24–Jan 7;
public hols

With hindsight, last year's entry ought to have been in italics, for the illness of key staff during 1978, and Mrs Ford's remarriage to Michael Jarman (they both do some of the cooking) created an element of pot-luck at her farmhouse-style parlour. The food is in the same style, being natural and mostly English; you enter through the kitchen, sit on benches, and

Must book
Meals 12.30–2, 7.30–9

Alc L £3·60 (meal £5·60),
D £4·50 (meal £6·55)

VAT inc
Children's helpings
Seats 30 (parties 20)
Car park

look at flowers on the tables and water-colours on the walls (or eat outside under the apple trees). Though some tepid or tough dishes are best forgotten, there are generally compensating virtues in the same meals, such as the mushroom soup, the pâtés, or the syllabub, and luckier visitors report 'very tender' pork chop braised in cider, or roast partridge 'hung just right', beef in beer, trout in garlic and cognac cream sauce, 'accurately cooked fresh vegetables left in their earthenware dish for second helpings', and 'delicious apple or gooseberry pies with plenty of cream, or help yourself from a whole Stilton.' Jugged hare or Muscovy duck are other specialities. Pedrotti red wine is £2·75 a litre, and Alsace Muscat or Gewürztraminer '76, or Ch. Cissac '72, are all under £5. The bitter is Adnams' and the cider Aspall, and they do bar lunches 'when not too busy'. No music.

App: H. L. Horne, B.W., Geoffrey Finsberg, F.J.P., and others

EXETER Devon   Map 1

Grael Wholefoods
15 North Street
Exeter 37782

A barely furnished yoga-to-yoghourt place, part of the Centre for Human Communication. Here they communicate competently as well as humanly, and provide vegetarian food (to eat here or take away) made from virtuous ingredients: lettuce soup, oatmeal cheese roast, wholemeal pizza (75p), Tibetan barley bread and vegetables (95p), piroshki, various salads and exceptionally rich cakes (chocolate fudge seems the favourite). Curry, and dandelion coffee, are more debatable. Unlicensed; corkage 20p; Sainsbury's opposite. No smoking upstairs. Recorded music.

Closed D; Sun; Mon;
Apr 13; Dec 25 & 26;
Jan 1
Meals 12.15–2.30, 4–5.30

Alc meal £2·30

VAT inc
Children's helpings
(under 10)

   rest
Unlicensed
Access, Barclay

EXETER see also pub section

FADMOOR North Yorkshire   Map 8

Plough Inn
on A170
2½ m N of
Kirkbymoorside
Kirkbymoorside 31515

This is the seventh *Guide* appearance of the Browns' whitewashed village-green inn, and for one local inspector 'this is one place which seems actually to have been improved by success.' True, one visitor was disappointed to find that he could not even drink there, let alone eat, at midday, and another wished the menu had changed since his last visit – but Kath Brown would alter more if her customers

Closed L weekdays; Mon;
Sun D; Dec 25; 10 days
Feb & Oct
Must book
Meals 12–1.30 (Sat &
Sun bar only), 7.30–8.30

Tdh D from £3·95 (meal
£5·85)

VAT & service inc
Seats 28 (parties 14)
Car park
No dogs in d/r
No rooms

allowed her to, and since she was off the next week
on a cookery course in Dieppe she cannot be accused
of resting on her bay-leaves. Perhaps if Dieppe had
been Marseilles her aïoli with prawns would be more
emphatic, but a subsequent visitor found it hard to
quarrel with her soupe de poisson normande (50p
extra), chicken with ceps (£4·30), and blackcurrant
sorbet. Other favourites include the almondy
Waterbury soup, mushrooms en cocotte, pheasant
with apples (in another Norman sauce, perhaps),
accompanied by château potatoes, mushroom
fritters, sprouts with parsley sauce, and the usual
cole-slaw as well. Mrs Brown herself would add her
suprême de volaille à l'estragon, 'authentic coq au
vin', redcurrant water-ice, and bombe favorite. The
weekend bar snacks with Cameron's Strongarm ale
(on pumps) are substantial, with their home-made
bread and perhaps a Malaysian chicken curry 'as in
the *Good Cook's Guide*'. Wines are modestly priced
for what they are, with plenty of choice around
£3, and Ch. Rauzan-Gassies '67, c.b., £6·45. But in
proportion there are rather too many '69 clarets. No
music. No children 'under eight or unable to eat a
full meal of this kind'. The atmosphere, though
smoky, alas, is otherwise welcoming.

*App: A. Taylor, W.M., Mr & Mrs P. M. Paxton,
P.O'R.S., D.C.M., and others*

FALMOUTH Cornwall   Map 1

Continental
29 High Street
Falmouth 313003

A rather stuffy cellar restaurant, tolerant of
children, with a relaxed atmosphere. The menu
'reads' like standard flambé-steak-and-scampi,
but the food is freshly cooked. Praise for pâté (70p),
savoury pancake (with chicken and mushrooms,
75p), steak Diane (£2·85), and the sauces with fish.
Wines from various sources, including several good
Spanish at reasonable prices (Marqués de Riscal red
'71, £3·70); French house wine £2·90 for 70 cl.
Good service. Recorded music.

Closed L; Sun; two weeks
Nov; Dec 25 & 26; Jan 1
Must book
D only, 7–10

Alc £4·70 (meal £7·15)

VAT inc

Children's helpings
(under 7)
Seats 30
No dogs
Diners card

FALMOUTH see also pub section

FARLAM see BRAMPTON

See p. 440 for the pub section, and p. 505 for the wine bars.

Old Parsonage
on A37
7½ m N of Shepton Mallet
Temple Cloud 52211

Closed Mon; Sun D;
Apr 13 & 15; Dec 25 &
26; Jan 1
Must book
Meals 12.30–1.30, 7–9.30

Alc £6·45 (meal £9·65)

Service 10%
Children's helpings
Seats 16 (parties 14)
♿ rest (1 step); w.c.
Car park
No dogs
3 rooms (1 with bath)
B&B £10
Fire cert

The Gofton-Watsons' house in an unremarkable
village has many old-fashioned virtues, including
the furniture and the personal service given by
the proprietor ('it even extended to washing the
windows of a guest's mud-stained car'). For this an
element of fuss-pottery can be readily forgiven, and
'I was young once,' he says in extending his
hospitality to members' children. But be punctual.
Ann Oakes cooks, and Mrs Gofton-Watson
deputises capably when an unruly horse has put the
prima cavallerizza out of commission. Inspectors
and others express high pleasure in their pâté,
mushrooms in garlic, fresh prawns with mushrooms
in wine and cream (£1·50), large and deftly cooked
Dover soles coated with parsley butter (£5·25),
salmon hollandaise, breast of guinea-fowl sauté
with pineapple, or with tarragon sauce, fillet of
pork with spiced apricots (£4·50), and equally
well-cooked vegetables (included in the main course
price). Pheasant in wine is another occasional dish.
Not everyone gets as far as a sweet but 'I wish I
knew how they get that intensity into gooseberry
ice.' Elderflowers, perhaps? Breakfasts are warmly
praised. Solitaire carafes are £2·35; we have not seen
the full list this year, but Muscat de Beaumes de
Venise is 80p a glass, and suppliers of wines are
sound. No music.

*App: S. Hulland, Roy Greenfield, M.T.B., M.R.,
G.R.P., and others*

Boote House
3 m SE of Great Dunmow
Great Dunmow 820279

Closed L; Sun; Mon;
2 weeks Aug; Dec 25 &
26; 2 weeks Jan

Must book
D only, 7–9.30

Alc £6·55 (meal £9)

VAT inc
Service 10%
Seats 50 (parties 36)
♿ rest (2 steps)
No dogs
Am Ex, Diners

Jack Graham runs a very personal restaurant in this
reticent 16th-century house, and after twenty years
word of mouth suffices to sell it. Word of mouth
(Mr Graham's) also suffices for a menu. Please
commit your opinions to paper, for locals know it
too well to report often, but inspection reveals, as
usual, well-meant, often skilful cooking of very
substantial meals: woe unto him or her who begins
with Chinese meatballs wrapped in noodle paste,
with rice and sweet-sour sauce, then eats roast pork
ribs in wine sauce with mushrooms, and finishes
with Morello cherry pancakes. Though sauces may
be on the heavy side, lasagne, duckling with fresh
orange, and poached bream with prawn sauce (both
£4·25 with vegetables) are among dishes that have
tasted well, and a plain or slightly lemony
cauliflower is a mercy. 'Blackcurrants Romanoff was
refreshingly sharp.' Wines are carefully served and
interesting (from £2·60 for French Shiraz or
Marsanne): the '70 château-bottled clarets (from
Ch. Giscours at £6·30) may be a little hard as yet

but the '67 Hermitage or Côte Rôtie from £7·80 should certainly help with food of this kind. Music and decor are also personal: the former is described as '1920–30s soft dance music'.

App: L. & C.T., O.J.P., Thomas Ward

FINDON West Sussex   Map 3

Darlings Bistro
The Square
off A24
4 m N of Worthing
Findon 3817

Closed Sun; Mon; Sat L;
Dec 25 & 26; Jan 1
Must book
Meals 12–1.45, 7.30–10.45

Tdh L £3·95 (meal £6·05)
Alc £5·70 (meal £8·60)

Children's helpings L
(under 10)
Seats 18
Access, Barclay

Brian Lavers' converted teashop opposite the Gun pub is a modest enterprise, in both scale and experience, beside Findon's other new place. But he has begun as though he believes that small means beautiful, or at least fresh. The unsalted butter and hot brown bread that open meals are an early promise; so is 'delicious pork satay (85p) with a lively dip tasting of coriander and peanuts'. Stuffed mushrooms (85p) and onion soup are also creditable beginnings, and lamb with Cumberland sauce (£2·65) argued a good butcher but a rather heavy-handed sauce-maker. 'Pigeon with cherries was excellent, but the venison was not tender enough to roast.' Scallops royale (£3·65) tasted 'fishy and lovely'; vegetables are lightly if naively cooked. Sweets (Black Forest gateau, prune and cognac ice-cream, and so on) and wines (from £2·35 for Caldorino Italian ordinaire) are less out of the way. Recorded music. No dogs. More reports, please.

Findon Manor
Findon 2269

Closed L (exc Sun);
D Sun & Mon (exc res)
Must book
Meals 12.30–1.30 (Sun),
from 7

Tdh Sun L £4·50 (meal
£8·05)
Alc £5·40 (meal £9·10)

Cover 50p
Seats 35 (parties 18)
♿ rest
Car park
No dogs
5 rooms (4 with bath,
1 with shower)
B&B from £9·50

Adrian and Mary Bannister are gluttons for punishment, say people who have watched them doing up and running this 500-year-old house a matter of months after leaving their inconvenient (but admired) restaurant in Brighton. It is too early to be sure about the hotel side (additional rooms are planned in 1979), where they aim at 'peace and quiet and country-house informality', but in the elegant 'dusty-green and brilliant white' dining-room inspectors and others have already reported characteristic dishes: a moist and gamey venison pâté with orange slices (95p), 'very marine' bisque de crabe in an antique tureen designed for the purpose, fresh grilled sardines, avocado with grapefruit and cream cheese (for a nice change) and carefully cooked main dishes – veau au romarin (£3·50), carré d'agneau, guinea-fowl with gin and juniper ('a rather bitter-tasting sauce, though'), and poached salmon. Grey mullet grilled with fennel and Pernod, with butter sauce, is £3·25, good vegetables are included, and game is a speciality in season. Peaches in brandy, pot au chocolat, or raspberry sorbet may be expected as sweets. The house wines are closely related to Muscadet (£3) and Rhône red (£2·85), and there are fine white burgundies or '71 hocks at fine prices. No music; no pipes; and either the Bannisters or their resident Airedales variously discourage other tableside smokers, 'plastic money', young children, and visiting hounds. More reports, please.

Chequers Inn
off B482
7 m NW of Marlow
Turville Heath 335

Closed Mon; Sun D;
Dec 26; Jan 1
Must book
Meals 12.45–2, 7.30–10

Tdh L £3·95 (meal £7·05)
Alc £6·30 (meal £9·60)

VAT inc
Service 10%
Cover 30p
Children's helpings
(Sun L under 12)
⌷ rest (2 steps)
Car park
No dogs in public rooms
Barclaycard

The Browns' 'simple country pub' (their description) stands opposite the 13th-century church in a charming village. There are a few suggestions that their not-so-simple à la carte prices reflect too closely what the surrounding country will bear, and a test meal confirmed reports that although the kitchen will pass inspection (because you walk through it to eat) the loos may not. Whether at table or at the bar, it is best to take robust food rather than would-be continental. 'Rack of lamb was most generous' (for many people, helpings are far too generous) 'and cooked to perfection.' Veal, duck, and ratatouille are also praised. Grouse and hare pie is a speciality. Profiteroles were 'fresh and delicious' when tried, a banana and meringue concoction was 'swimming in rum', and another inspector hails 'one of the best fruit salads I've lately seen'. Wine prices verge on the disgraceful (£3·60 for Lutomer Riesling reported in 1978), but it is a pleasure as well as a duty to take the Brakspear bitter from the wood. No music.

App: Mrs J. E. Diwell, Michael Lyster, Mary Moore, J. & M.B., P.M., J.G., and others

White Hart
off A507
2½ m SE of Ampthill
Silsoe 60403

Closed Sun; public hols
(exc Apr 13)
Must book
Meals 12–2, 7.30–10

Tdh £3·25 (meal £5·65)
Alc £5·85 (meal £8·50)

VAT inc
Cover 25p
Seats 50 (parties 16)
Car park
No dogs in d/r
No rooms

For 'a village on the edge of nowhere' (writes a correspondent from Welwyn Garden City) Somerset Moore's fish dinners, *pétanque*, travelling sign exhibitions, and traditional potato races must be a better draw than the parish church, fine though it is. Most customers continue to admire both the enterprise and the accomplishment of Mr Moore and the long-haired girls who surround him in the kitchen, like some latter-day saint. But one or two shrewd accounts suggest that the results cannot yet be called a divine gift to Beds. 'The reception and service were polite, but of the kind that sums up your bank balance on the way. Fish pâté en croûte was fresh and intriguing, with good mayonnaise. Smoked trout mousse hovered on the borderline between the delicate and the bland. Fish pie (£2·50), though irritatingly described, had crisp pastry and a good mélange of fish.' 'Monk-fish Newburg (one of the various ways with this fish, £3·20) was delicious, but swimming on the plate in copious sauce that cooled quickly. The cheeses were interesting, but mostly well over the hill. Bread and other accompaniments were excellent.' Less guarded praise is to hand for the assortment of shellfish (£1·65), turbot with fennel, venison sausages, strawberry syllabub, Amaretti in burgundy and cream, and other things. The brief,

lighter set menus are sensibly composed. To drink,
there is Charles Wells bitter of two gravities, or
Sauvignon de Touraine at £2·75, and a dozen
well-chosen bottles at £3·80 (£2 the half): guess for
yourselves which cost Mr Moore most or least.

*App: Colin & Jane Read, Dr Aldwyn Cooper,
J.R.M., Ronald & Maureen Hinde, and others*

FOLKESTONE Kent   Map 3

**Emilio's Restaurant
Portofino**
124a Sandgate Road
Folkestone 55762 *and*
55866

Closed Mon; Apr 15;
Dec 25 & 26
Must book
Meals 12–2.15, 6–10.30

Tdh L £2·50 (meal £4·75)

Alc £4·55 (meal £7·55)

Cover 30p alc
Children's helpings
(under 12)
Seats 55
♿ rest; w.c.
Air-conditioning
No dogs
Access, Am Ex, Barclay,
Diners

Eric Randall's cooking for Emilio Bevilacqua has
been the salvation of the seaside for longer than
Jacob served for Rachel, and it is a rare reproach
that comes from a July visitor, whose lunch was
slipshod by comparison with a previous dinner, and
brought dry roast duck, long-soaked potatoes and
jaded prawns with spaghetti. However, 'salsify au
gratin (90p) with slivers of tomato and bubbling
cheese made a delicious change from the ever-reliable
pasta.' Many main dishes are cited: sweetbreads alla
Sassi (£2·50) 'a real delight', chicken sorpresa,
'heavenly scaloppine alla cacciatore with scrunchy
sauté potatoes and admirably cooked cauliflower',
and other house nominations such as gamberetti in
conchiglia (£1·70) and fegato alla veneziana. 'I very
much like their trifle-like pudding called spumone,
soaked in Marsala.' Zabaglione and lemon sorbet are
also worth noting. The absence of music and the
readiness of the staff to discuss the food shows
further respect for customers, 'with Emilio walking
the deck as usual'. Pedrotti carafes are £2·50 and
even the better Italian wines were under £4 in 1978.

*App: Brian Congreve, C.E.G., P. Y. Dudgeon,
A.R.C., and others*

FOWEY Cornwall   Map 1

Cordon Bleu
3 Esplanade
Fowey 2359

Rolf Keilbart has not written this year, but
reporters of crab au gratin, 'enormous soles either
grilled or Colbert' (£4) and 'just-crunchy courgettes
in a tasty tomato and cheese sauce' suggest that he
at least read the strictures compelled by last year's
test meal. Snails, poached turbot, and 'veal with
buttered cauliflower and a delicious sauce' have
pleased others. The quality of meat and fish make
up for dullish first and last courses, and wines
(from £2·40). But this place has now spent over 14
years in the *Guide*: please see that what it does well
(or not) is adequately reported this fifteenth time.

Closed L; Sun; mid-Dec
to Mar
Must book
D only, 7–10.30

Tdh from £3·50
(meal from £5·45)
Alc £5·30 (meal £7·75)

VAT inc
Seats 38 (parties 30)
No dogs

Coach House
off B2102
2 m SE of Uckfield
Framfield 636

'Old world style' restaurant, with swimming-pool. The Granthams are welcoming and attentive hosts, and members appreciate the bargain set lunches with a reasonable choice in each course. The 'gourmet menu' is richer fare for longer purses: avocado Rothschild (with crab, cream cheese mousse, mayonnaise and caviare, £1·25), veal Cordon Bleu (£3·25) or boned duck breast with ham and mushroom stuffing, served with apple sauce (£3·75). Carefully cooked vegetables and a 'fabulous choice of sweets'. Roussillon wines, £1·60 for 50 cl. Classical music on record. A few outside tables. No children under five at dinner. Pipe and cigar smokers are asked to take coffee in the bar.

Closed Mon; Sun D; 1st week May; last 2 weeks Oct; Dec 25 & 26
Must book
Meals 12.15–1.45, 7–9.30

Tdh L £2·50 (meal £3·80),
Sun L £2·75 (meal £4·15)
Alc £6·70 (meal £8·65)

VAT inc

Service 10%
Seats 32 (parties 12)
♛ rest (1 step)
Car park
No dogs

FRAMFIELD see also pub section

Teignworthy Hotel
3 m SW of Chagford
Chagford 3355

Closed L (exc Sun & bar)
Must book
Meals 12.45–2 (Sun & bar), 7.30–9

Tdh Sun L £4·50 (meal £5·80), D £7·50 (meal £8·80)

VAT inc
Seats 20
♛ rest (1 step)
7 rooms (6 with bath, 1 with shower)
B&B £10–£11·50
D, B&B £16–£17·50

It is very early days yet for this hotel conversion of a granite-and-slate house, built half a century ago at the top of a south-facing combe by the craftsmen who moved on from Castle Drogo. But John and Gillian Newell's spell at Chittlehamholt (q.v.) lends credence to accounts of a friendly reception and careful family cooking of tomato soup, fish pâtés, roast stuffed lamb or roast pork with prunes, poached brill with mushroom sauce, boeuf Stroganoff, kidneys with green peppers, and other dishes. Apple pie, blackberry sorbet, or 'a type of brown bread ice-cream' round dinner off satisfactorily, and breakfast is 'a meal to savour'. Chantovent ordinaires (the red from the Aude district) are £1·70 for 50 cl, and 'we hope to have Blackawton bitter soon.' No music. No children under 14. Smoking at table is discouraged. There are bar snacks at lunch-time on weekdays. Car park. No dogs. More reports, please.

Unless otherwise stated, a restaurant is open all week and all year and is licensed.

Do not risk using an out-of-date Guide. A new edition will be published early in 1980.

FRILFORD Oxfordshire   Map 2

Noah's Ark
on A415
4 m W of Abingdon
Frilford Heath 391470

A comfortable place in the 'stockbroker and scampi belt', with Roman remains, lawns for your helicopter, and whirring prices. But regulars appreciate the consistency of service and dishes like mussels Capri ('in a strong tomato and garlic sauce', £1·50), scampi flambé à la crème (£5) and the veal in various ways. Try, too, quails in a sweet-sour sauce (£3) and crêpes Suzette (£3 for two). 'Old partridge should be casseroled, not roast.' The set lunch offers a reasonable choice. Italian house wine, £2·95 for 75 cl; Frascati Fontana Candida '76, £4·75. Taped music. Dancing on the last Friday of the month.

Closed Mon; Sun D;
Apr 13; Dec 26
Must book
Meals 12.30–2.30, 7–11

Tdh L £3·50 (meal £6·25),
D £4·50 (meal £7·40)

Alc (min £3·50)
£7·32 (meal £10·55)

VAT inc
Service 12½%
Cover 20p

Seats 60
⅃ rest (3 steps)
Car park
No dogs
Am Ex, Diners

FROME Somerset   Map 2

Mendip Lodge
Bath Road
1 m N of Frome
Frome 3223

Comfortable motel in three acres with a view. The à la carte dinner (with a simpler set menu, £6) offers a 'Taste of England', or Levantine masquerade, with yoghourt, mint and avocado in Somerset summer cocktail (£1·10), and apricot, yoghourt and cinnamon sauce with Beckington chicken. Veal Cordon Bleu, chicken Urchfont, crisply roast duck and sweets are praised – but not during a deplorable fortnight or so in early summer. Coffee is poor. Good service, unless Charles Worz's eye is elsewhere. Bar snacks at lunch except on Sunday. French house wine £3 for 50 cl. Usher's pale ale on hand-pump. No pipes and cigars at table. Children under eight should finish eating by 8 p.m.

Meals 12.30–2, 7–9.45

Tdh Sun L £4·50 (meal
£7·95), D £6 (meal £7·95)
Alc (min £3·50) £6·10
(meal £8·05)

VAT & service inc
Children's helpings
(under 12)
Seats 60 (parties 50)
⅃ rest (3 steps)
Car park
No dogs in public rooms

Access, Am Ex, Barclay,
Diners, Euro
40 rooms (all with bath)
B&B £9·50–£10·50
D, B&B £13–£14·50
Fire cert

FROME see also pub section

For the explanation of ⅃ denoting accessibility for the disabled,
see 'How to use the Guide', p. 4.

Combe House

off A30
2 m SW of Honiton
Honiton 2756

Closed L Mon–Sat (exc
bar); Sun D (exc res);
Jan & Feb
Must book
Meals 12.30–2 (bar
Mon–Sat), 1 (Sun);
7.30–9.30

Tdh Sun L £4·50 (meal
£7·95)
Alc £6·75 (meal £10·70)

Service 12½%
Children's helpings
(Sun L, under 6)
Seats 60 (parties 40)
 rest; w.c. (2 steps)
Car park
No dogs in d/r
Am Ex, Barclay, Diners
13 rooms (7 with bath,
4 with shower)
B&B £11–£15
Fire cert

In spite of the private grief that overshadowed the
Boswells' year, most guests have taken their usual
pleasure in their meals and stays at this demandingly
handsome Elizabethan house and park. The rooms
are better furnished, equipped and kept than they
used to be, and on a good night it is possible to
think yourself into an Upstairs role after 'crudités
with mayonnaise, creamily melting crêpe de fruits
de mer, duckling Grand Marnier (£4·20, including
'young vegetables') and brandied chocolate mousse,
ending with plenty of coffee and cream before the
enormous fireplace in the panelled hall'. Others
remember equally well the gazpacho, fresh crab
tart, fish pâté and scallops, suprême de volaille aux
écrevisses, tournedos madère, and lamb cutlets with
peperonata; while Mrs Boswell's even grander
specialities include fresh lobsters with coral, Pernod
and cream (£8), stuffed Dover sole Mère Récamier,
and chateaubriand (£10 for two). Some of these
dishes seem to demand a salad rather than cooked
vegetables. Sweets usually taste well, even if
'raspberry mille-feuille was delivered – albeit
apologetically – collapsed in a pudding-bowl.'
Roasting beef and compiling a menu for Sunday set
lunch is a different kind of challenge, not always
triumphantly surmounted. Sunday evening is a
buffet meal. A visit for afternoon tea was –
perhaps predictably – a disappointment. The
Corney & Barrow wines are well chosen (from
£2·90) and it is the kind of place where you might
risk one of the two '64 clarets, c.b., at under £7.
Beaujolais Villages '76 (Marc Dudet) is £4·80. But
'rather loud' service and VAT add 20% to all these
prices and some people find this disconcerting.
Children under ten may stay, and eat high tea (not
dinner). No music.

*App: David Gladwell, S. G. Langford, V. F. Ireland,
R. O. Marshall, Pete & Sue Chesterman, and others*

No 3 Dining Rooms

Magdalene Street
Glastonbury 32129

Closed L (exc Sun);
Mon; Sun D; Dec 25
Must book
Meals 12.30–1.30 (Sun),
7.30–9.30

In the last year or two George Atkinson and
Charles Foden's handsome Georgian house has
provided a sobering lesson in restaurant
accountancy. They opened too cheap for the
extraordinary quality in which they believed,
doubled their price overnight, then stabilised, but
have been slow to recover the custom they lost.
However, it was no restaurant tyro who claimed his
terrine of chicken, chateaubriand with garlic butter,
carrots au gratin and courgettes with almonds, and
home-made ices as the best dinner the *Guide* had
led him to. Others who began with turbot aïoli and

Tdh from £7·50
(meal £11·55)

Seats 24 (parties 12)
⏦ rest (2 steps)
Car park
No dogs

coquille de saumon gratinée, followed by veal with lemon and fresh rosemary and ris de veau en brioche, questioned nothing in the dedication of Mr Atkinson's cooking, though wondered precisely how he thickened his sauces. Minor virtues include the bread and the black olives; major specialities include the green soup (fresh vegetables with local green peppers), lobster thermidor, and Scottish roe venison in port wine with juniper. The chocolate truffle, a jealously guarded recipe, is a 'cocoa-dusted brick that is utter bliss in its light, smooth butteriness', and other sweets – liqueur bavarois, fresh fruit zucotta, and the ices with first-rate tuiles – run it close. The Cheddar is liable to be better than the Stilton. The brandy sorbet is perhaps too sweet to be served between courses in the old manner. The owners are their own servants and sommeliers: they make good Kirs but after that their advice is less dependable, though their buying is good, with a choice in 1978 of local English, Spanish Rioja, and Gigondas '72 or Rubesco Torgiano '73 under £4, and Ch. Le Pape '70, a red Graves, £5·50. No music. No children under 16. No pipes. There are plenty of flowers, and a terrace overlooks the Abbey park. Formal dress is preferred.

App: Drs Willem A. & Helene W. Koppejan, Roger Williams, P. C. Currall, Susan Pike, and others

---

GLOUCESTER Gloucestershire   Map 2

Don Pasquale
19 Worcester Street
Gloucester 25636

Gloucester's single sentry these last ten years looks after its guests well enough, but at a test meal seemed in need of competition, Italian or otherwise. That is, chicken liver pâté, fettuccine, sole Colosseo and the lemony herb butters or dressings are liked, but devilled sardines and chicken saltimbocca proved mediocre, and crème brûlée was neither crème nor brûlée. Philip Schettini's specialities include rack of lamb à la carte, and on the set meal, chicken parcel. Be careful how you order (or accept) vegetables. Wines are routine (from £2·95 a litre). Stella Artois on tap, and various bottled beers. Avoid the 'inner sanctum' of the long thin restaurant if it is hot, but 'strong tobacco' is banished to the bar – where lasagne and other snacks can be had during opening times. 'Light' recorded music.

Closed Sun; 2 weeks July; public hols
Must book D
Meals 12–1.45, 7–9.45

Tdh £5 (meal £7·75)
Alc (min £2) £4·80
(meal £7·55)

Service 10%

Seats 24 (parties 16)
⏦ rest
No dogs
Access, Am Ex, Barclay, Diners

GLOUCESTER see also wine bar section

Gosforth Hall
off A595
on Wasdale Road
Gosforth 322

'A useful stop if business or science takes you to Seascale' is one verdict on this 17th-century manor-house in its own grounds. Others find it more relaxing than that might imply, and enjoy the simple set dinners: perhaps cucumber and celery soup, consommé italienne ('beefy, with noodles'), or pâté; roast chicken, baked brill or pork chop, with garden vegetables; and coffee cake or pineapple Melba. Sauces and coffee could be improved. Friendly and unobtrusive service. About forty wines, with Hirondelle at 40p the glass. Good bar snacks (soups, open sandwiches) with pressurised and bottled beers. Recorded classical music.

Clos d L (exc bar);
mid ec to end Jan
Mus. book
Meals 12.30–1.30 (bar),
7–8

Tdh from £5 (meal
£7·10)

VAT inc
Children's helpings
(under 10)
Seats 30
&. rest
Car park

No dogs in public rooms
6 rooms
B&B £6·85–£7·25
Full board £71·75–£80
Fire cert

Michael's Nook
Grasmere 496

Must book
Meals 12.30 for 1,
7.30 for 8 (Sat in season:
7 for 7.15, 9 for 9.15)

Tdh L £5·25 (meal £8),
D from £7·95 (meal
£11·20)

Service 10%
Seats 30
&. rest; w.c.
Car park
No dogs in public rooms
10 rooms (6 with bath,
2 with shower)
D, B&B £18–£27·50

Mr Gifford's effetely furnished Edwardian mansion and garden lie at the foot of Wordsworth's Greenhead Ghyll (turn off the A591 at the Swan, north of the village). It has had its vicissitudes, but if Nigel Marriage, the latest of a long line of chefs, lasts as well as his name promises, all should again be well, for the creature comforts, service and table settings are up to the best Lake District standards. At best, this is also true of the cooking, and sweetbreads, either as a first or main course, leek soup, and 'an aggressively home-made steak and kidney pudding' have various admirers. On the five-course dinner menus, duck and orange soup, roast best end of local lamb with rosemary and garlic, tenderloin of pork en croûte with sage, onion and mushroom, and gateau McMahon are among the chef's favourites. Fools and syllabubs are also well made, and people like the Costa Rican coffee. Wines, too, though not always served promptly, form a substantial collection, with Touraine Cabernet or Sauvignon £3·20, French-bottled Aloxe-Corton '71 (Charles Vienot) £6·50, and Ch. Cos d'Estournel '70, c.b., £7·25. But beware the fading '62 clarets also listed. No music. No children under 12. To earn Mr Gifford's smiles, wear jacket and tie, and refrain from smoking in the dining-room. More reports, please.

Meal times refer to first and last orders.

White Moss House

Rydal Water
on A591
1 m S of Grasmere
Grasmere 295

Closed L; Wed; Nov 1 to
mid-Mar
Must book
D only, 7 for 7.30

Tdh £7·50 (meal £9·50)

VAT inc
Seats 18
♿ rest (1 step)
Car park
No dogs
7 rooms (4 with bath)
D, B&B £16·50–£20·50
Fire cert

Criticism, both given and received, is the life-blood of this book, so it is hard to know how to treat a small hotel whose guests have learnt to 'value it above all others', and whose quality of food 'occasionally drops as low as good'. Ordinary lapses are few: one member regrets the 'hideous' new sign, but finds the quiet disquieting: an interesting disagreement between eye and ear. But it is evident that the Butterworths decided long ago to perfect, rather than expand, what they offer in their handsomely (and thoughtfully) furnished stone house and its even more peaceful annexe up the hill. Enthusiasm for cooking, and affection for the countryside, save it from pretension. Anyone who needs to know what the English Tourist Board's Taste of England campaign was meant to foster should be taken through one of Jean Butterworth's dinners: cream of mushroom soup 'just what it says'; hot avocado with garlic shrimps and a little cheese (English eclectic rather than English traditional, the individual flavours carefully preserved); chicken breasts with celery and parsley stuffing and sorrel sauce (slightly obscured by leeks in cream sauce and cabbage with caraway among the vegetables); and a difficult choice between home-made yoghourt with honey ('heavenly, beyond earthly praise') and a light, creamy, sweet but sharp, apricot brandy flan. 'This was rounded off with home-made oatmeal biscuits, a slice of Lancashire cheese, and potted Stilton.' Smoked mackerel hot-pots and guinea-fowl with cider on a bed of Cox's apples are other innovations; Sussex steak and Sussex pond pudding, Westmorland raisin and nut pie, and apple Grasmere are perennial favourites. In a meal that lacks choice till the sweet stage it matters that the main course should not fail, and it hardly ever seems to. 'The coffee, though abundant, was not a strong brew.' Breakfasts and packed lunches match the rest. The wines are well chosen and worth discussing with Mr Butterworth. He does not press them, for the Chanson or Latour burgundies cannot help being dear, though in 1978 there were also six good Loires under £4. Half-bottles encourage experiment, and a sweet white is offered by the glass. Recorded classical music. No smoking at table. No children under 15 unless by arrangement. Jacket and tie 'preferred'.

App: R. A. Hamilton, N. V. Crookdake, T. E. Crompton, D. E. Saunders, D. E. Westoby, and others

---

Entries for places with distinctions carry symbols (pestle, tureen, bottle, glass). Credits are fully written entries, with approvers' names below the text. Passes are telegraphic entries (useful in the area) with details under the text. Provisional entries are in italics (see 'How to use the Guide', p. 4).

The Starr

Market Place
Great Dunmow 3824

Closed L (exc Sun); Mon;
Sun D; Apr 13; Dec 25,
26 & 31
Must book
Meals 12.30–1.30 (Sun),
7.30–9

Tdh Sun L £3·50 (meal
£5·60), D (exc Sat) £5·50
(meal £7·95), Sat D £6·50
(meal £9·15)

Children's helpings
(Sun L)
Seats 30 (parties 10)

Last year's provisional entry seems to have sent to the Jameson family the kind of people who appreciate their spacious, blessedly un-restaurant-like Elizabethan house and its personally assembled pictures and decorative pieces. Mother and daughter serve, son (a professional chef) cooks, and father keeps the books; it is an economical system and this shows in the prices. The food is unforced English: a home-made tomato soup or pâté, perhaps, steak and kidney pie or roast duck with apple sauce or chicken casserole, a fruit sorbet served between other courses, and 'rich and melting walnut pudding with a light sauce' or Victorian prune jelly 'served without cream so that the flavour comes through'. At Sunday lunch there is no choice of main course. The Stilton might sometimes be moister and the celery crisper. The wine list, by Dolamore's Cambridge branch, and its ungrasping prices, betray an enthusiast. There are several French bottles under £3, and Crozes-Hermitage Blanc and Ch. Langoa-Barton '73, c.b., could be had for under £10 the pair. Chassagne-Montrachet must be a family taste, for it appears in three different guises. Wine drinkers also benefit from the old wine-coolers ('can't stand those chrome buckets,' says Mrs Jameson robustly) and the curb on smoking at table. No young children except at Sunday lunch. Classical records. Wear a tie.

App: Mrs A. Page, Q.D., Geoffrey Carr, M.F., C.P.D., A. B. Goad, P.W.B., and others

---

GREAT DUNMOW see also pub section

Hundred House

on A443
11 m NW of Worcester
Great Witley 215 *and* 565

Closed D Sun & Mon;
Dec 25
Must book L & weekends
Meals 12–2, 8–9

Tdh buffet L £2·75
(meal £4·25), D £6·95
(meal £10·05)

Everyone seems to like what the Tansleys offer at this simply furnished restaurant, in spite of the marked difference in expense and style between midday and evening. The problems are those of success: uncontrolled smoking at night, and at lunch, gluttony that may bring tears to the eyes of St Michael and All Angels in the baroque parish church. ('Spinsters carrying plates heaped with food can be seen putting a couple of apples or pieces of cheese into their handbags on the way out,' reports one ungallant male.) Soups, salads, terrine and coffee are all good, though there is an occasional grumble about tasteless ham. A superior version of the cold table appears as an option at dinner, along with fresh sardines, sole, salmon and other fish very deftly cooked, sweetbreads en brochette, roast duck

VAT & service inc L
Service 10% D
Children's helpings L
Seats 75 (parties 22)
&. rest (2 steps)
Car park
No dogs
Access, Am Ex, Barclay

with orange sauce, 'superb lamb's kidneys', good
vegetables 'too lavishly helped', and similarly
generous sweets: at least a pause is allowed before
embarcation on the orange soufflé, rhubarb
cheesecake, strawberry mille-feuille and 'excellent
cheeses'. Wines are fairly priced, with Ch. Marquis
de Mons '73, c.b., £3·60 and dry white Ch.
Carbonnieux £3·85 in 1978. No music.

*App: Frank Carrigan, Michael Copp, T.G., Dr &
Mrs T. S. Worthy, P.B.W., and others*

GREAT YELDHAM Essex   Map 3

White Hart
Poole Street
on A604
7 m NW of Halstead
Great Yeldham 250

Must book D & weekends
Meals 12.30–2, 7.30–10

Alc £6·60 (meal £9·25)

VAT inc
Children's helpings
Seats 60 (parties 30)
&. rest (2 steps)
Car park
No dogs
Access, Am Ex, Barclay,
Euro
No rooms

Brian Jones manages and Cliff Jones cooks at this
500-year-old Gough hotel with its own garden,
stream and antique dungeon. The house is well kept,
if amateurishly served, and a member's criticism of
the deep-frying was well taken. But even so, on a
later occasion, another member's aubergine fritters
were still oily. The best features of meals tend to be
the generously helped main courses: roast lamb or
pork on the trolley, or 'well-stuffed and crisply
roasted' ballotine of duck. Soup or crab-stuffed
tomatoes or galantine may be tried, but expect little
of fish soufflé; take the 'less rococo' sweets. The
Lay & Wheeler wines are fairly priced (from £2·85,
with other house wines under £3): note under £5
Muscat d'Alsace '76 and Château de Juliénas '76
(domaine-bottled). Hot and cold dishes can be had
in the bar during all opening times. 'Avoid the cask
sherry.' The Garden Room is open to parents with
young children. No music.

*App: H. Glover, Mr & Mrs A. Mitchell, D. M.
Gaythwaite, and others*

GRESSINGHAM Lancashire   Map 8

The Haven
Hornby 21274

Closed L; Sun; Mon; Fri
Must book
D only, 8 p.m.

Tdh about £5

VAT inc
Seats 25
Car park (6)
Unlicensed

Mrs Hogg reads but does not respect the *Guide*.
This is no reason not to respect either her views or
her cooking, which is 'simple but excellent, with a
choice only for hors d'oeuvre and dessert'. You need
to arrange a dinner at her charming cottage well in
advance. People have begun with, for instance,
artichoke soup, or 'a rich and robustly flavoured
borshch', or 'a meltingly light cheese and onion
quiche'. Next, there may arrive a little ramekin of
fresh sole in a well-made sauce, and she has a happy
knack of cooking duck with a crisp skin, neatly
detached from the bones, and a 'not too violent'
sage stuffing. Vegetables – parsnips in pine kernels,
perhaps, or celeriac, or broccoli – 'taste as vegetables
should.' Duke of Cumberland tart comes with a
'smooth and eggy custard', meringues and
profiteroles are popular, and there is a note of 'fresh

211

passion-fruit with home-made ice-cream'. Not the least pleasure of the place is that you may, indeed must, take your own wine. No music. Details approximate.

App: P.J.F., F.H.S., J.K.L., and others

GRIMSTHORPE Lincolnshire Map 6

Black Horse Inn
on A151
4 m NW of Bourne
Edenham 247 *and* 253

Mrs Fisher bats for England – or at least for this minor county – in the taste trials, and scored all round for one visitor on Stilton pâté (90p), cottage broth, fish pie (£3·10), Abbot John beef (with the brandy and Bénédictine of Old England, £3·75), and hot raspberry jam omelette (80p). Omelette Arnold Bennett, chicken livers Osbert Sitwell, and poachers' game pot (£4·20) are also suggested, but guests for their part mention 'unsubtle' sauces and 'sweaty' Stilton. Good grapefruit and bacon and egg for breakfast, but coffee weak. Wines (no vintages) from £2·70. No music. No jeans. No under-fives in the dining-room. Ties preferred.

Closed Sun; Dec 25	Service 10%	Car park
Must book	Children's helpings	No dogs in d/r
Meals 12–1.30, 7–9.30	Seats 50 (parties 12)	5 rooms
	🔧 rest; w.c.	B&B from £9
Alc £5·25 (meal £8·85)		

GRIZEDALE Cumbria Map 7

Ormandy Hotel
Hawkshead
off B5286
6 m S of Ambleside
Hawkshead 532

Closed Tue; Jan
Must book
Meals 12–2, 7–8.30

Alc £5·55 (meal £8·50)

VAT inc
Children's helpings
Seats 36
🔧 rest
Car park
No dogs
5 rooms (all with shower)
B&B £7–£9
Fire cert

Down in the forest, something is being stirred by the hand of Yves Champeau, late of the Normandie in Birtle, who is working himself more gently as chef to this sylvan hotel (rooms called Hazel and Birch ought to beguile flagellant couples). The McInalleys, who run it, keep close ties with the Forestry Commission and the theatre in the forest, and perhaps the former provide the venison steaks for M Champeau's famous chevreuil Coupigny. (The materials for canard sauvage, caille rôtie, and homard chaud must have to be sought elsewhere.) A summer test meal yielded excellent examples of more everyday staples of a French table: 'very creamy but not overwhelming vegetable soup', 'a fresh herb butter for snails', grilled meats with pan juices, and true vanilla in the flavour of ice-creams and meringues. Vegetables reported include 'well-buttered French beans, and courgette-based ratatouille, with flavoury boiled potatoes'. The cellar and bar are modestly stocked, to put it mildly, and a litre of ordinaire cost £3·80 in 1978. No music. More reports, please, since not all autumn experiences have been happy.

1979 prices are as estimated by restaurateurs in the autumn of 1978.

GUILDFORD Surrey   Map 3

Cranks
35 Castle Street
Guildford 68258

The mixture as before: pine tables, plenty of customers, everything vegetarian and wholefood, prices high – but high quality materials too. Soups, 'savoury and filling' vegetable stew, flans, baked potatoes, salads, various breads and cakes in the self-service juice bar attached to the shop. The coffee is rather better than the wines – or try Aspall Hall cider. No music. No smoking between 12 and 2.

Closed Sun; public hols
(exc May Day)
Open 10–5

Alc meal £3·05

VAT & service inc

Seats 20
♿ rest (1 step)
No dogs

GUILDFORD see also pub and wine bar sections

GUIST Norfolk   Map 6

Tollbridge Restaurant
on B1110
10 m SW of Holt
Foulsham 359

Closed Mon; Sun D;
1st week Oct; Dec 25 &
26; last 2 weeks Jan
Must book
Meals 12.30–1.45,
7.30–9.30

Tdh L £2·75 (meal £4·95),
Sun L £3·20 (meal £5·45)
Alc £4·65 (meal £7·20)

Children's helpings
Seats 30
♿ rest (1 step)

Central Norfolk is a large and emptyish space from this book's partial point of view, but the delight numerous members express in nominating this handsomely converted toll cottage on the upper reaches of the Wensum river suggests that William Stark's imaginative menus and the relaxed atmosphere would find the couple friends anywhere. Huge joints of beef with fresh vegetables for Sunday lunch, preceded by local cockles and oysters, caught one couple's attention and they returned for more another day. But in the evening people have been just as happy with pike and parsley fritters (65p), salmon mousse, hot crab in season with prawns and Pernod (£2·75 – and the price includes 'excellent' vegetables), pigeon with chestnuts and port, and other dishes. 'The puddings – and Brie or Stilton – seldom disappoint.' Croix St Pierre ordinaire is £2·30, and Ch. Gloria '66, c.b., a very reasonable £8; Clos Vougeot '70, £5. No music. No dogs. Car park. More reports, please.

GULWORTHY Devon   Map 1

Horn of Plenty

off A390
3 m W of Tavistock
Gunnislake 832528

Closed Thur; Fri L;
Dec 25
Must book D & Sun L
Meals 12.15–2, 7.15–9

'Sights remain unlowered,' writes Patrick Stevenson after a dozen fraught years in this remote family house overlooking the Tamar valley. There are some visitors who would reply, 'I do not ask to see – The distant scene: one step enough for me': for instance, slightly more dependability about the often excellent vegetables, puddings, and coffee; a slightly less offhand attitude to current English taste in pre-prandial drinks. But it is not for predictable experiences that professional cooks and critics wear out their tyre treads on the westward run. Rather, they know Sonia Stevenson as an inspirational cook who can do things with food that others

213

Tdh D (inc wine) £10·75
(meal £14·10)
Alc £7·90 (meal £12·35)

Cover 55p
Children's helpings L
(under 10)
Seats 60
♿ rest (3 steps); w.c.
Car park
No dogs

cannot. The combinations that result – of dish with
dish, or food with wine – often reflect her husband's
robustly idiosyncratic tastes and views; never mind
that, for there are reprobates resting on Abraham's
bosom who have done worse with their lives than
supervise the evolution of those aristocratic salmon
quenelles, or the humble but ever-crisp potato
pancakes, or trenette col pesto, or marinated
venison with pine-kernel sauce (venison pie keeps its
appeal too) or lambs' sweetbreads en brioche: these
'look unnervingly like profiteroles' but 'the brioche
was divine, and the taste of those sweetbreads in
their very rich sauce will never fade.' There are two
comparably devotional accounts of the Languedoc
regional dinner (perhaps Oc is the language the
family's wolfhound understands). It included fruits
de mer en brochette à l'aillade toulousaine, canard
poêlé with olives, peppers and aubergines, good
cheeses from Patrick Rance, and 'a hot marinated
orange in a lovely spicy sugar syrup'. The waitresses
are well trained and natural, 'though sometimes they
may seem brusque as they greet your car enquiring if
you have a reservation.' Wines eddy weekly all the
way from Yugoslav Prokupac or Australian Shiraz
at under £3 to irreplaceable Richebourg at over £40.
David Wolfe helps Mr Stevenson with the list, and
mistakes are owned up to: of a still champagne,
'fell off, began to taste of iodine'. No music. No
under-tens at dinner, but proper fish and chips for
them at lunchtime.

*App: D. M. Gaythwaite, Pete & Sue Chesterman,
M. E. Cohen, C. Ford, T.J.G.S., Julia & James
Warner, and many others*

HADLEIGH Suffolk   Map 3

Taviton's
103 High Street
Hadleigh 2820

Closed from 22nd to end
of every month (exc Dec);
Dec 25 D; Dec 26
Must book
Meals 12–1.30, 7.30–9.30

Tdh L £4·50 (meal £6·75),
D £5·50 (meal £7·95)

Service 10%
Seats 22
♿ rest (1 step)
Access, Am Ex, Barclay
3 rooms (1 with bath)
B&B £7·50

*Gerald and Patricia Lomax's Georgian townhouse has
been an actor-manager's cliffhanger this year, and the
latest intelligence, though not precisely from the
owners' lips, is that the wine bar has been sold within
the family and that quality rather than quantity will be
the object in the adjoining restaurant, with set meals,
three-course at lunch, four-course at dinner. The italic
type therefore implies guarded hope whereas last year's
Roman type expressed some despondency. Even the
snack lunches, now discontinued, have included
excellent soups, quiches, salads, treacle pudding and
suchlike; and as well as what one member unkindly
calls 'headachy wines' there is, for instance, Ch.
Tronquoy-Lalande '62 at £9. No music. No children
under eight. No dogs. Note the sabbatical week's
closure every month, and the provision of rooms. More
reports, please.*

HALESWORTH Suffolk   Map 6

Bassett's

London Road
Halesworth 3154

Closed L; Sun; Dec 25,
26 & 27; Jan 1
Must book
D only, 7.30–10

Tdh £5·75 (meal £7·65)

VAT inc
Seats 40 (parties 16)
⅃ rest (2 steps)
Car park (6)
No dogs

In the award of a 'pestle' to a single-handed chef-patron, character counts as much as cooking; otherwise, the next year's file reads like a bed of nettles. Stewart Bassett, no doubt because he is 'more gruff than gush', has survived the test, along with the 'show-me' visitors and the reneging table-bookers that offset – in his own words – 'proud regulars and some very interesting and knowledgeable new people'. Clearly, he has not pleased everyone: choice is very narrow (a menu displayed outside would help here); helpings are refined by East Anglian standards; quirks, or errors, or long waits are not uncommon. But through all the evidence of a very busy year gleams a certain integrity. It has been a good year for fish, he says, and his baked brill with persillade, or mackerel with mint and gooseberry, or herring with olives and garlic are admirable beginnings. Nor does he always make things easy for himself: aduki bean salad can be prepared in advance but what of 'poached egg on chicken liver mousse in a vol-au-vent with hollandaise sauce'? New dishes arrive frequently – perhaps too often for safety, but an inspector approves the herbed loin of lamb in puff pastry and fillet of pork with apricots and rosemary; others delight in baked crabs, game ('this is the only place I dare eat pigeon'), and 'splendid chicken breast stuffed with veal forcemeat, in an onion and mushroom sauce which did not pall.' A fellow restaurateur dined well off chicken terrine, veal stuffed with chicken and spinach and garnished with nasturtium, and 'a slab of blue Cheshire', and risked sounding 'like one of those dreadful food writers in a woman's magazine' to tell us so. Crème brûlée, chocolate brandy cake and home-made ices are generally excellent but 'would Herr Sacher have recognised the Sachertorte?' The house Corbières or Loire white cost only £2·45 in 1978 but it is for claret that you come here: gruff '66s (Ch. Gruaud-Larose, c.b., £9·95); more gushing '73s (Ch. Grand Ormeau, c.b., £3·35), and legendary '61s and '45s from £9·30 to £88·90 precisely. No music. No cigars before 9 p.m.

App: D. R. Reid, Mrs J. Ellis, Derek Drummie, K. S. Vaus, Sarah Hamp, Peter Coulson, and others

---

'Must book' is the restaurant's information, not ours. The context of the entry usually indicates how much or how little it matters, but a preliminary telephone call averts frustrated journeys. Always telephone if a booking has to be cancelled: a small place may suffer severely if this is not done, and customers are also the losers in the end.

Halland Motel and Old Forge Restaurant
on A22
3 m SE of Uckfield
Halland 456

A sprawling, begonia-begirt motel which the Barltrops run in friendly and efficient fashion. Staff and many customers are long-stay regulars. The menu is basically grills and good fresh fish, with a few made-up dishes. Sauces and pâtés may lack character, but there is praise for crab soup, 'a large steak' (£3·50), steak and kidney pie, sweetbreads in wine and cream, poached halibut hollandaise (£2·75), and hot fruit pie. Some fine wines (Ch. Chasse-Spleen '67, c.b., £6·60); wine by the glass, 50p. No music. 'Pipes and large cigars (10 cent?) in the lounge area only.' Bar snacks and Whitbread Tankard at lunch-time (except Sunday). No children under five. Men should wear a jacket at night.

Closed Dec 25 & 26	VAT inc	Am Ex, Diners
Must book	Service 10%	12 rooms (all with bath)
Meals 12.15–2, 6.15–8.45	Seats 70	B&B from £9
	♿ rest; w.c.	Fire cert
Alc (min L £3, D £4)	Car park	
£6·05 (meal £8·90)	No dogs in public rooms	

Chef's Kitchen
on B3311
St Ives 6218

Closed L; Sun; Dec 24, 25 & 26
Must book
D only, 7–10

Alc £4·55 (meal £7·55)

Seats 34
♿ rest (3 steps)
Car park
No dogs

'They asked all the right questions about the food and wine and obeyed all the answers' is an uncommon compliment to a restaurant, but Frank Tetley is a professional chef – and he also expects his own advice to be listened to, which is only fair: besides, you may get a better meal, and perhaps a 5% reduction, if you discuss a menu in advance. The furniture is pine, the light dim, the food 'well above *Guide* average for Cornwall'. A subsequent test meal suggested that this assertion about the duckling bigarade 'with imaginatively prepared vegetables' was also true of the John Dory with parsley, shallots and mushrooms (£3), and the accompanying potatoes (correctly sauté). Soup was less impressive, but 'crab fritters were crisp enough to be heard 10 feet away', and gravadlax or escabèche of mackerel are other good first courses. Salad was nicely oily. Even one of the sweets could be given marks for originality at least: tinned lychees dusted with cinnamon on a base of Cornish 'white cake', made with fruit, peel and spices. Wines begin at £3·15 a litre and while there is nothing of note, at least much is still under £3 a standard bottle. Recorded music.

App: R. C. Peattie, K.M.B., Henry Potts, and others

If you think you are suffering from food-poisoning after eating in a restaurant, report this immediately to the local Public Health Authority (and write to us).

HALSTEAD Essex   Map 3

Luigi's
1 High Street
Halstead 2184

An ordinary corner house 'with a pleasantly warm and pink interior'. Luigi Russo produces tasty Italianate food, 'efficiently if brusquely served'. Many dishes are standard, but the minestrone is rich in vegetables (30p), the beef hongroise (£2·60) comes with a well-flavoured sauce, and the pollo della casa (£1·60) is original. Vegetables are ordinary and sweets may disappoint. Italian house wine, £1·60 for 50 cl. Recorded Italian music.

Closed L (exc Sun); Mon;
Dec 25
Must book
Meals 12.30–2 (Sun),
7–10·30 (9 Sun, 11 Fri
& Sat)

Tdh Sun L £2·25 (meal
£3·90)
Alc (min £1·50) £4·20
(meal £6·80)

Children's helpings
(under 12)
Seats 40
 ⅃ rest
No dogs

HAMPOLE South Yorkshire   Map 5

Hampole Priory
off A638
1 m W of A1(M)
Doncaster 723740

The Priory continues to be voted 'a very recommendable restaurant for the area' and retains its endearingly amateur service in quiet and comfortable surroundings. Despite soaring prices in the past year, members speak warmly of seafood pancakes and onion tart; veal Savoy, chicken hongroise, sole bonne femme, all with plain but carefully cooked vegetables; ginger syllabub and Aunt Flo's fruit pie. House wine £2·60 for 70 cl. Recorded classical music. No dogs.

Closed L; Sun; Mon
Must book
D only, 7–9.30

Alc £6·40 (meal £8·10)

VAT & service inc
Children's helpings

Seats 24
 ⅃ rest; w.c. (m)
Car park
Access, Euro

HARROGATE North Yorkshire   Map 5

Apollo
34 Oxford Street
Harrogate 504475

The Ivy Cafe Ltd appears to be the Vassiliou family, and it is worth planning ahead before a visit, since most of their Greek-Cypriot dishes require advance notice. Failing that, you can settle for the omelettes, grills and made-up dishes on the main menu, or take souvlakia or sheftalia from the Cypriot one. Sheftalia (£2·45) were 'bursting with flavour but delicate in texture' when tried, and the salad, kataif and coffee rounded out the meal pleasantly. Courteous but leisurely service. Spanish house wine £2·40; Othello £2·95. No dogs.

Closed Sun; Mon (exc by
arrangement); Dec 25 D;
Dec 26
Must book

Meals 12–2.30, 5.30–10.30
(11.30 Fri, 12 Sat)

Alc £4·90 (meal £7·50)

Children's helpings
Seats 70
Air-conditioning
Access, Barclay, Diners

217

**Au Charbon de Bois
Studley Hotel**
Swan Road
Harrogate 60425

A comfortable small hotel, related to the Cardinal in Wetherby, with a Breton manager and delightful staff ('no trouble and no tempers'). The set lunch is sensibly simple (celery soup, chicken espagnole or beef stew and dumplings, sweets or cheese). At night the charcoal grill produces tasty steaks and kebabs ('Judi, the boss's favourite dish, is marinated chicken served with aubergines and a kebab sauce, £3·35') and the kitchen attempts famous French dishes: casserolette de filets de sole Lasserre (£3·70), escalope de veau Brillat-Savarin. Soups and vegetables sound better than they did last year. Stowells wine list, with Les Celliers carafes at £2·70 for 72 cl. Recorded music.

Must book	VAT inc	Access, Barclay, Diners
Meals 12.30–2, 7.30–10.30	Seats 55	25 rooms (13 with bath,
	♿ rest	1 with shower)
Tdh £2·50 (meal £4·65)	Car park	B&B from £10·25
Alc £5·95 (meal £8·45)	No dogs in public rooms	Fire cert

Number Six

♟

6 Ripon Road
Harrogate 502908

Closed L; Mon;
3 weeks July/Aug;
Dec 25 & 26; Jan 1
Must book
D only, 7.30–10

Tdh £6·95 (meal £9·75)

VAT inc
Seats 60 (parties 26)
♿ rest
Car park
No dogs

For its 'number six' appearance in these pages, Mr di Silvestro's restaurant has a new chef, but no hiccough has been perceived in what has always been a very smooth production. The dim light and pink effects are not universal taste, but the good manners of the staff are: 'There was no pressure to leave'; 'I was alone, but treated like a duenna.' The crudités on the tables have been much fresher this year, and the Melba toast is praised too. First courses – poached quenelles of sole and salmon, another pink-and-white effect, or hot creamed shrimps with paprika – are better than the soups in the table d'hôte meals, but these revive with main dishes such as quails en cocotte – 'two lovely little browned birds, glistening in apple and madeira cream sauce, with juicy croûtes underneath, and lightly cooked green beans and cauliflower.' 'Moist chicken Kiev was carefully punctured by the waiter to avert a spurt', and carré d'agneau (served for two) was 'the first quality, accurately cooked'. Black Forest gateau has pleased even inspectors who have 'grown weary of these concoctions', and lemon soufflé was light too. 'Coffee was kept hot too long.' The cellar is imposing, and if the long list of sparkling wines and sweetish hocks tells a tale about this house's trade, few restaurants in Britain have better German and Alsace lists, the '71 vintage being particularly well represented. Nor are the French whites and reds inferior, unless perhaps in half-bottle, with one or two '45, '53 and '61 clarets still, a choice between '57 and '67 vintages of Ch. Rauzan-Gassies under £10, and sweet white Ch. Filhot '69, c.b., at £7·25. The burgundies and

Rhônes need a knowing eye as to shippers, but the evidence is given, and if they learn to be firm with smokers, and decant fine wines instead of uselessly cradling them, this year's 'glass' might be next year's 'bottle'.

App: C. R. Handley, Dr & Mrs T. S. Worthy, J. & K.L., R.B.C., and others

---

Oliver Restaurant
24 Kings Road
Harrogate 68600

Closed L; Sun; public hols
Must book
D only, 7.30–10.15

Tdh from £5·25 (meal £9·15)

VAT inc
Seats 80 (parties 40)
♿ rest
Air-conditioning
No dogs

There is a certain family resemblance in the tastes – visual and gustatory – to which the two serious Harrogate restaurants appeal, and though Peter Jones (who cooks, with three assistants) may not match his rival for professionalism of service, the Wedgwood-set tables and the cooking keep him well in the race. 'Everything tasted as if it had been just prepared for us,' says one visitor after a set meal that included onion soup and beef Wellington; another was not surprised to see that grilled trout with Bercy butter was a speciality after meeting a well-grown example as a first course before a crisply roasted half-duckling with fresh pineapple and 'a delicious orange liqueur juice'. Vegetables are well cooked too: 'tiny new potatoes in skins, and well-buttered green beans.' Celery and basil soup, roast lamb with Yorkshire sauce, chicken with langoustine, and quail Marcel Provence are other dishes to look out for, they say, and for sweet, coupe Cardinal or crème brûlée; an apricot and almond trifle turned out 'rather wet and innocuous'. The Manor Wine Company list (from £3 for Anjou rosé) is long and interesting, with Viña Vial Paternina £3·70, Masseria Viglione '68 £4·50, Muscat Les Amandiers '75 (Dopff & Irion) £5·70, and Ch. Giscours '73, c.b., £7·15. Burgundies are also quite good. Recorded music.

App: J. & A. Hartley, S.S., C.P.H., and others

HARTLEY WINTNEY Hampshire   Map 2

Tullio Restaurant
High Street
Hartley Wintney 2960

Tullio Maraviglia's wife copes fairly well with a long menu at his informal restaurant and wine bar. The home-made pasta always pleases (and can be had in the wine bar during opening hours), veal and steak dishes are good, but vegetables are more perfunctory. Fresh fruit, cream and brandy sweets are better than 'soggy Suzettes'. Italian wines (Brunello di Montalcino '69, £6·50); house wine £1·20 for 36 cl, 35p the glass. Recorded music might include 'jazzed-up Beethoven'. No dogs.

Closed L; Mon; Apr 13 & 15; first 2 weeks Aug; Dec 25 & 26	Must book D only, 7–11	Cover 20p Seats 40 ♿ rest Am Ex card
	Alc £6·35 (meal £9·85)	

The Mitre
56 High Street,
Old Town
Hastings 427000

Closed L (exc Sun); Mon;
Sun D; 1st 2 weeks Oct &
Feb; Apr 13; Dec 24–26
Must book
Meals 12.30–1.45, 7–10

Tdh Sun L £4 (meal
£6·40)
Alc £5·10 (meal £7·75)

VAT inc
Service 12½%
Children's helpings Sun L
(under 8)
Seats 26

To an Oxford man, the Mitre is a memorable
restaurant name, or used to be, and in Hastings,
where distinctive cookery has been a rare commodity
since the Conquest or thereabouts, the Anglo-French
Gibbons family's brown-furnished restaurant in the
old town fills a felt want. Just too late for proper
investigation last time, a local couple thought Rodney
Gibbons's soups, turbot à la crème and steak au
poivre (£3·60) 'and general niceness' an answer to
prayer. This year, a test meal yielded 'exquisite
terrine de volaille (95p), the slices of breast layered
between a herby *farce*'. Summer-seasonal filets de St
Pierre ma façon (£3·40) were 'just as good, gently
poached in white wine, and served with a sauce of
diced mushrooms, parsley and cream.' Mushrooms à
la grecque, seafood pancake, 'very fresh' lemon sole
meunière, kidneys in sherry sauce, salads, meringues,
sauté potatoes and bread are praised by others, and
Mr Gibbons is also proud of his mousse au kirsch
(95p). Cheeses may be a little jaded. Expect slow
service if pressure builds up. Wines, from £2·80,
include Ch. Meyney '73 at £5·40 and Crozes-
Hermitage Les Meysonniers '73 at £4·45.
Recorded music.

*App: Mr & Mrs T. Rowland-Entwhistle, M.S.,
Peter & Sheilah Ling, J. & M.B.*

George Hotel
Hatherleigh 454

The Giles family run their thatched 15th-century
coaching-inn 'ably assisted by fifteen lovely local
ladies'. Set meals are priced according to main
course: mussel chowder or crêpe surprise; loin of
pork with orange and wine sauce (£4·50); lamb
biriani, turkey vol-au-vents, or steak moutarde;
treacle tart and clotted cream, raspberry meringue,
or devils on horseback. Vegetables are carefully
cooked. French house wine, £1·80 for 50 cl. Usher's
best bitter from the cask and snacks in the bar (till
2 p.m. and 10 p.m.). No music.

Closed Sun D (winter exc
res); Dec 25 D
Must book
Meals 12.15–1.45, 7–9.30

Tdh L from £3 (meal
£5·55), D from £4 (meal
£6·75)

Seats 42 (parties 50)
♿ rest (1 step)

Car park
No dogs in public rooms
Diners card
14 rooms (5 with bath,
1 with shower)
B&B £7

Inspections are carried out anonymously. Persons who pretend to be able
to secure, arrange or prevent an entry in the Guide are impostors and
their names or descriptions should be reported to us.

HEALD GREEN Greater Manchester   Map 5

La Bonne Auberge
061-437 5701

Closed Sun; Mon D;
public hols (exc
Chr Day L)
Must book L & Sat D
Meals 12–1.45, 6.30–9.30

Tdh L £2 (meal £4·20)
Alc £4·80 (meal £7·55)

Service 10%
Children's helpings
Seats 36 (parties 40)
No dogs
Am Ex, Diners

For 15 years now (a dozen of them in the *Guide*)
Roger and Cecilia Boutinot's stock-pot has been
bubbling in Stockport, and both food and service
probably remain as good as the clientele – 'more
guzzle than gourmet', in one description – allows
them to be. This does not excuse an inspector's
dinner of 'tedious' asparagus soup, 'ill-cooked'
duckling and 'bodiless' Châteauneuf-du-Pape (of all
wines) but adds lustre to the salade niçoise,
coquilles St Jacques (£1·30), crêpe aux fruits de mer
(£2·50), steaks (médaillons de boeuf au madère,
£2·80), pork escalope, and poulet aux amandes that
may appear on dinner menus in these rather spartan
surroundings. Salads may be better than vegetables,
apart from 'pommes frites enough to satisfy the
appetites of student sons'. Set lunches remain
excellent value, sweets and all ('an enterprising
lemon sorbet once appeared as a first course').
Crêpes normande (£2·40 for two) are another sweet
speciality. Granvillons ordinaires are £2·50 (£1·75
for 50 cl) and Ch. Giscours '62 or '70, c.b., is £11
or £9. The recorded music is, alas, inextinguishable,
even at the request of a solitary party dining
upstairs. But 'we do not stock tobacco'.

*App: M. L. Goddard, M.S., A. M. Reid,
M. S. Hicks, and others*

HECKFIELD Hampshire   Map 2

Andwells
on A33
8 m S of Reading
Heckfield 202

'The Ritz *in rure*' – or Claridge's, rather – is a fair
description of this brocaded restaurant, and for 20
years here and elsewhere members have kept the
owners in the style to which they are accustomed.
The virtue, in a needy district, is that Mrs Stratton
can and does cook. Lower prices and faster turnover
might evoke more zestful tastes, and indeed a
'shorter, changing' menu is promised for the spring.
As things are, filets de sole Walewska (£3·95 in 1977,
£5·50 in 1978, who knows about 1979?), noisettes
d'agneau 'la patronne', escalope de veau au
marsala and suprême de poulet au Champagne are
properly conceived. Besides, hazelnut meringue
(£2·25) was 'fresh and crumbly and super', and the
cellar is excellent in all the main French regions if
you resign yourself to £10 and on up. No music.

Closed Sun D (winter)
Must book D & weekends
Meals 12.15–2, 7.15–10

Alc £11·25 (meal £16·65)

VAT inc
Service 12½%
Cover 65p
Children's helpings
Seats 40 (parties 15)

🔥 rest; w.c.
Air-conditioning
Car park
No dogs
Access, Am Ex, Barclay,
Diners, Euro

Riverside

off B3293
Manaccan 443

Closed L (exc Sun);
D Sun & Mon (exc res);
2 weeks Chr
Must book
Meals 12.45–2.15,
7.30–9.30

Tdh from £8·50 (meal
£10·10)

VAT & service inc
Seats 40
Car park (res only)
No dogs
3 rooms (all with bath)
B&B from £8

George Perry-Smith and Heather Crosbie's customers this year have included one couple who came 400 miles and another who came 14,000 miles for the experience: no doubt the Martians will be here one day, but if they fail to enquire about low tide they too risk a long wait or a drive round from the wrong side of the estuary, and Tantalus himself was not more cruelly punished. The owners of this meridional house, as of old, have the knack of seeming carefree even if they are not, whether to restaurant or overnight guests, and 'an artist in our party stopped short at the display of lemons, lettuce, and scarlet lobsters in the porch.' You nibble the irresistible black olives, then sit down, perhaps to 'incandescent cheesy globes called petites fondues', or aillade toulousaine, or fish soup, or 'consommé with a glass of Malaga and provocatively flavoured "rissoles" in tissue-thin pastry'. At times, the white fish so long admired here has been over-poached and its sauce too assertive, but sea bass or Dart salmon with sorrel sauce or fennel salad are among the other choices. Spicy lamb with garlic, peppers and courgettes, carré de porc provençale and goose à la poitevine (one of the many specialities this house shares with the sister place at Dartmouth, *q.v.*) arrive with the usual gratin dauphinoise potatoes. Helpings are restrained. Steaks can be unreliable and there are those who claim to have made or tasted better St Emilion au chocolat, *lèse-majesté* though they know it to be: perhaps this is an excuse to try lemon soufflé, walnut treacle tart, rhubarb fool or 'wonderful raspberry ice-cream'. Another member, slightly disappointed in his dinner, was 'surprised by joy' at breakfast: 'fresh grapefruit, home-baked croissants and brown rolls, good butter, the best marmalade I have had in years, ample good coffee, and to cap it all, a huge plate of fresh strawberries.' The wine list betokens a long-established house that knows the value of what it sells, from Laymont & Shaw of Falmouth's sound Riojas under £4 to splendid Averys burgundies under £10 and putative masterpieces at around £25: Echézeaux '55 of the Domaine de la Romanée-Conti; Ch. Latour '53, and so on. Note also the eaux-de-vie and single malts. Service is competent, smoking at table sometimes a nuisance. No music.

App: by too many members to list

HELFORD see also pub section

HEMEL HEMPSTEAD Hertfordshire   Map 3

Lautrec
95 High Street
Hemel Hempstead 55146

Closed L; Sun; 1st 2
weeks Jan; public hols
Must book
D only, 7.30–11

Alc £5·10 (meal £7·95)

Service 10% (parties
over 6)
Cover 20p
Children's helpings
Seats 40
No dogs
Access, Barclay, Diners

There have been one or two disappointments here
with tepid or under-seasoned dishes, but the
friendly service, the carnations on the house
and the itemised bills suggest a desire to please, and
Pierre Briançon's cooking is good at its best. 'We
began with delicately flavoured poireaux vinaigrette
and fish soup. Veal kidneys had been well cooked to
allow the blood to seep into the herby sauce.'
Menus change every six weeks, and often look
distinctly long for the place's resources. M Briançon
himself suggests pojarsky de saumon (£2·95),
noisette de chevreuil grand veneur (£3·50) and filet
Brillat-Savarin, but people who have settled for
steaks with various butters also sound content.
Begin, perhaps, with mackerel or smelts and finish
with 'choux pastry swans sailing in chocolate sauce'.
French-bottled ordinaires are £2·50 and it may be
worth paying another 25p for Côtes du Roussillon
red or Corbières white; Ch. Rauzan-Gassies '72,
c.b., at £7·50 is more debatable. Recorded music.

App: Ann Spencer, Peter Liechti, D. Brabants, S.S.

White Hart
High Street
Hemel Hempstead 42458

Closed D; Sun; public hols
Must book
L only, 12.30–2.15

Alc £5·50 (meal £8·65)

Service 10%
Seats 30
Car park
Am Ex, Diners

*Relaxation and generosity sound the keynotes of the
L-shaped restaurant in Stanley Vasey's 17th-century
pub (mind your head). Mrs Vasey runs the kitchen,
supplying the bar with home-made pies of rabbit, or
prawn and plaice, or steak and kidney, and the
dining-room with excellent and capably cooked
materials (though mallard in red wine and Parson
Woodforde's rabbit and onion dish were both rather dry
when tested). An August visitor was offered all to
himself a 'football-sized' Ogen melon and a fresh,
dressed crab that 'could have played a terrifying
second lead in Jaws'; it was served with a spare plate
for débris. Soups 'with good fresh croûtons',
'well-garlicked and moist pâté', fresh plaice stuffed
with prawns (£3·50) and roast duck with apple sauce
are other possibilities, and 'there was grated orange
rind in the creamed potato with game, and kiwi fruit
in the fruit salad' at a test meal. 'There only seems to
be one copy of the wine list' (from £3 for Nicolas).
'Mature women' serve helpfully. More reports, please.*

HENLEY-IN-ARDEN Warwickshire   Map 2

Filbert Cottage
64 High Street
Henley-in-Arden 2700

Closed Sun; Sat; public
hols (exc Dec 24)
Must book

Quimper and Coventry do not sound like the ideal
town-twinning, but Jean-Yves Guerrot from the one
and his wife from the other, with competent French
girls serving, have made a fetching restaurant out of
this Tudor nook in Arden. Many people admire
M Guerrot's sabayon de St Jacques sur lit d'épinards
(£2·60) and his subtly varied sauces for trout.

Meals 12.30–1.45,
7.30–9.30

Tdh L £3·75 (meal £6·10)
Alc £6·95 (meal £9·85)

VAT inc
Children's helpings
Seats 25
Air-conditioning
No dogs in public rooms

'Crêpes are also exquisite.' These opinions were
borne out by an exacting inspector's gratin de fruits
de mer in a 'buttery, boozy and classic' armoricaine
sauce on the à la carte menu, which changes every
eight weeks or so. Soups and frogs' legs have been
praised too, and main courses that have pleased
various people include duck bigarade, carré d'agneau
rôti à la provençale (£7·70 for two), steak
grand'mère, and poached salmon béarnaise.
Chicken à l'estragon at a test set lunch maintained
the same standard but vegetables 'are presumably
better at night'. (They are, according to others.)
Sweets are less ambitious, but expect îles flottantes,
tarte aux pommes, or cheesecake. Coffee is 'strong,
freshly ground, and hot'. Wines, from various
sources, begin with Litre Vin carafes at £1·85, Loire
Gamay at £3·05 or Muscadet at £3·40, and are
surprisingly strong on claret, divided into
communes: Ch. Cissac '70 from Haut Médoc, £5·90;
Ch. Pavie '62 from St Emilion, £11·70. French
recorded music. The Saturday evening closure, and
'a scallop shell drawn freehand with a knife in the
butter' are both in their way signs of caring.
Remember how small a place it is.

*App: Katharine Goodwin, Carol Hilton & Chris
Beetles, A.H., J. W. Dunn, T.M.F., P. & S.C., and
others*

HERSTMONCEUX East Sussex   Map 3

The Sundial
Herstmonceux 2217

Closed Mon; Sun D; last
2 weeks Aug; Dec 25 &
26; Jan
Must book
Meals 12.30–2.30,
7.30–10.30

Tdh L £3·95 (meal £7·25)
Alc £7·80 (meal £11·80)

Children's helpings
Seats 45 (parties 20)
⟨&⟩ rest; w.c.
Car park
No dogs
Barclay, Diners

Even last year, after a benevolent entry, Giuseppe
Bertoli was touchily conscious that his lavishly
restored cottage might be full of spies waiting to
report him for some misdemeanour. There are indeed
one or two people who criticise a certain
peremptoriness, or particular miscarriages ('very
undercooked pastry for lamb' . . . 'rather similar
sauces for both duck and kidneys' . . . 'far too sweet
chocolate mousse'). But most meals described,
including a test one, have been successful: 'a good
lunch of champignons farcis, sole meunière and
soufflé glacé'; 'impressive paupiettes of turbot'
(£4·75). Those deep-fried mushrooms with their
contrasts of texture are an alluring though substantial
first course, and oeufs pochés florentine (£1·45) do
indeed come in the plural. Bouillabaisse à la rouille
(£1·75) is a speciality. One of the best main dishes
tried was the breast of duckling with peach sauce
(£4·25), 'crisp and succulent as a good Chinese duck,
though foolishly garnished, like almost everything,
with a tired lettuce leaf'. Vegetables, though perhaps
too numerous for the hardworking staff to control,
include good ratatouille and courgette fritters.
'Rum baba could have done with a teaspoon of
rum at the table' – a gesture that would be the

more welcome because of the fierce prices charged for admittedly superior claret and burgundy (Ch. Talbot '67, £11·75). If you wish to improve on house Merlot or Sauvignon at £3·50 look first at the Rhône and Loire sections. Laurette Bertoli receives and serves pleasantly, but the place attracts people who like being smoked by their fat cigars. Recorded music.

App: A. G. Thompson, H.R., D. & M.S., W. McKinlay, and others

---

HERTFORD Hertfordshire   Map 3

Maison Carton
6 Parliament Square
Hertford 52193

David and Anne Ricketts's former shop for tea and haberdashery may be overreaching itself. The menus, still changed every few weeks, propose elaborate, mostly classical dishes which would tax a grand hotel, and so there are some growls about sauces 'adequate' rather than inspired, tournedos en croûte overcooked, crème brûlée 'inauthentic'. But soups, garlic bread and vegetables win praise, as do the profiteroles, hazelnut meringue with strawberries and the Stilton. Les Frères ordinaire is £2·15. 'David's bin-ends' offer a few bargains. Recorded classical music. 'Pipes unwelcome early in the session.'

Closed Sun; Mon; Sat L;
Aug 1–21; Dec 26; Jan 1
Must book
Meals 12.30–2.30,
7.30–9.30 (10.30 Fri &
Sat)

Tdh L £2 (meal £3·65)
Alc (min £2) £4·70 (meal
£7·25)
Service 10%

Seats 40
rest (1 step); w.c.
No dogs
Barclaycard

HERTFORD see also wine bar section

HIGH EASTER Essex   Map 3

Punch Bowl
off A414
6 m NW of Chelmsford
Good Easter 222 *and* 264

Closed L (exc Sun); Mon;
Sun D; Dec 25 & 26
Must book
Meals 12.30–2.30 (Sun),
7.30–10.30

Tdh Sun L £3·75 (meal
£6·65)

Alc £6·30 (meal £10·05)

Cover 30p D

One dinner early in January tasted distinctly hungover, but since then, whether or not members have had a high old time on punch when they got to Brian and Liz Clark's expensively refurbished inn, they have clearly enjoyed themselves at table. There are signs too that Mr Clark heeds criticism: 'There are fewer service delays, and apparently less sugar in sweets.' The set Sunday lunch, perhaps with fish pâté, roast beef and fresh vegetables, and cinnamon or peach flan, seems a good buy. At dinner, 'casserolettes of crab and Roquefort quiche (£1·25) were outstanding first courses, followed by almost equally good carré d'agneau à la diable (£3·15) and beef in pastry.' Clams, scallops, quail and guinea-fowl are also popular, and light eaters appreciate the choice offered between one or two quail (£2·35 or £4·50). Syllabub, or oranges in

Children's helpings
(under 12)
Seats 52
♿ rest (1 step)
Car park
No dogs
Access, Am Ex, Barclay,
Diners, Euro

Grand Marnier, appeal to those daunted by pastry
or meringue. Castel Frères ordinaire is £3·10 a
litre, but there may be better value in the house
burgundy at £3·60 a bottle, or Poitou at £3·70.
Ch. Citran '73, c.b., is £5·75. Recorded music.

*App: P. S. Luckin, R. E. Gardner, Jean Taylor,
C. J. Carroll, M. L. Goddard, J.M.R., and others*

HILLESLEY Avon   Map 2

Portcullis
3 m SE of Wotton-under-
Edge
Wotton-under-Edge 2313

Closed Mon; Sun D;
Sat L; Dec 25 & 26
Must book
Meals 12.15–1.30, 8–9.30

Alc (min £3·50) £5·85
(meal £8·80)

VAT inc
Service 10%
Seats 40
♿ rest
Car park
No dogs

Pub and beer – but not lunchtime snacks – have
vanished together now that the Jakemans have
bought the premises they tenanted, and made a few
alterations (with more on the way). Log fires take
the chill from the large bar and the welcome is
warm too. Beware of the 'massive' first courses
unless you are very hungry, but soups or mussels in
mayonnaise are liked, and mushrooms in light garlic
sauce or chicken-stuffed pancakes are among Terry
Jakeman's recommendations. After that, best end of
lamb, rare contrefilet of beef in red wine sauce
(£3·25) or escalope of veal Evita suggest themselves.
'No room for a pudding' is a common cry, and there
are only two or three (brandy eclairs, 75p). Chianti
Classico at £3·50 a bottle sounds a better choice
than Monte Campo at £3·75 a litre, and Ch. Talbot
'73 is £7. No music. 'A rare beef sandwich (55p) for
lunch in the bar could not have been better.' Take
the Hawkesbury turn off the A46 to find the village.

App: R. Thersby, J. M. Bone, R. J. Bond, P.M.R.

HINDHEAD Surrey   Map 3

La Masia d'Avinyo
15 London Road
Hindhead 5171

Closed L (exc Sun);
Dec 25 D
Must book
Meals 12–2.30 (Sun),
6.30–12

Tdh Sun L £3·20 (meal
£5·90)
Alc £5·95 (meal £9·20)

Seats 42
♿ rest (1 step); w.c.
Car park
No dogs
Access, Am Ex, Barclay,
Diners, Euro

'Basically a good place for Sunday eating in darkest
Surrey' is a guarded compliment indeed from a
visitor who wondered how much Mr Dunster's
Spanish chef had had to do with the prawns in
garlic mayonnaise, and at what stage wine had been
added to the copious sauce for steak with pâté.
However, barbecued prawns, grilled sardines, and
veal in white wine sauce were better at that same
meal, and the paella (£7 for two), zarzuela (£4·95) or
Spanish mixed grills of either fish or meat (£4·25)
sound worth ordering. An inspector also praises
gazpacho and veal Masia. Some vegetables may be
frozen and confected sweets mediocre, so salad and
fruit may be better, as well as more Spanish, options.
Still, lemon torte was 'light and sharp'. Red, white
or rosé ordinaires are £1·50 for 50 cl, and there are
some better Torres wines under £5, though we have
not seen a recent list. Spanish music tapes are
played and there is a live guitarist sometimes.

App: A. C. Sayer, P. N. Wilson, D.B., and others

HINTLESHAM Suffolk   Map 3

Hintlesham Hall

on A1071
5 m W of Ipswich
Hintlesham 268 *and* 227

Closed Dec 26 D; Jan 1
Must book D
Meals 12.30–2.30,
7.30–10.30

Tdh L from £8 (meal
£11·25), D from £9·20
(meal £12·70)

Service 12½%
Children's helpings
Seats 100 (parties 110)
& rest (1 step)
Car park
No dogs
Am Ex card

Frank Harris, in a characteristic image, claimed that literary London was spread out before him 'like a willing woman'. Robert Carrier's boasts would be in better taste, but with this grandee one has the same sense that American tourists are queuing up to be fed, ducks to be stuffed, and grand houses to be restored by a man who doubles the roles of patron and *patron*. Much is left at his imposingly furnished country mansion to his manager Paul Lewis and his chefs Nigel Rolfe and Stig Henricksen, which is fair enough, except that the innovations everyone expects from this style sometimes tend to bolt, lettuce fashion. Blandness or – oddly – over-reduction leading to saltiness are among the faults noticed from time to time in the set meals, which are less elaborate (or rather, more *nouvelle*) than they used to be. Perhaps you should state at the outset where your tastes lie and await advice. Among inspectors' meals, the best things have been the bouillabaisse fish salad (a mixture of fishes lightly poached and served vinaigrette), fillets of trout in a lettuce packet, terrine de rouget, soups and quiches composed of green vegetables from the walled garden, and among main courses the lamb chops with herb butter, chicken with soy sauce or guinea-fowl with lemon, and trout again, this time in filo pastry. Others would add the duck sausages, rillettes d'anguilles and other beginnings, but comparatively few main dishes: gourmandise of veal has critics, and control sometimes falters – 'too much fat on the smoked pork loin and too few lentils with it.' Sweets usually recapture any lost inspiration: 'superb' mince pies with brandy cream, or a tulip of fresh pineapple and ice-cream in crisp pastry; Bavarian nut pudding; or 'les trois sorbets' (kiwi fruit, raspberry and mango), 'exquisite to eye and palate'. Savoury canapés at the beginning and petits fours at the end are also stylish. The wines, from £2·50 in 1978 for a choice of four house ones, are meagre in Germany and Alsace but strong in Rhône, Loire, Bordeaux and Burgundy. Nor is £5·75 bad at this level for Ch. d'Angludet '73, c.b., or £32 for Ch. Mouton-Rothschild '62, or £6·75 for 'surprisingly good' Ch. Talbot '68, c.b., as a change from the numerous '66 and '70 clarets, still on the hard side. Ch. Doisy-Védrines '61, c.b., at £7 is a sweet snip. 'A woman who is choosing wine for a man throws the service utterly.'

App: by too many members to list

See p. 120 for the restaurant-goer's legal rights, and p. 118 for information on hygiene in restaurants.

227

Low Hall
Calverley Lane
off A6120
Horsforth 588221

Low Hall – a well-modernised Elizabethan building
and garden – is not quite liberty hall when people
seek to criticise the Monkmans' service and food
(cooked by their co-director, Roger Doughty). It
sounds as though the year's fervent admirers and
scolders (in two-to-one proportion) would be equally
surprised by each other. Happily a test meal veered
towards praise after a good crab soup and
spinach-stuffed turbot; you may also start with
Yorkshire pudding and continue with the trolley
roast ('but the beef was nowhere pink'). Fruit and
sorbet may be better than lemon pancakes to finish.
Waiters may be 'chatterboxes or butter-fingers'.
Many wines are dear for what they are, but '76
Beaujolais or Ch. Gloria '69 at about £5 seem fair in
an executives' place. Recorded music.

Closed Sun; Sat L;
Aug 27–Sept 3; most
public hols
Must book
Meals 12.30–2, 7.30–10

Tdh D £7·75 (meal £9·60)
Alc L (min £2·85) £5·05
(meal £6·90)

VAT & service inc

Children's helpings
(prior notice)
Seats 70 (parties 112)
♿ rest
Car park
No dogs
Access, Barclay

French Partridge

on B526
6 m SE of Northampton
M1 exit 15
Northampton 870033

Closed L; Sun; Mon;
mid-July to early Aug;
10 days Chr
Must book
D only, 7.30–9.30

Tdh from £6·50

(meal £7·60)

VAT & service inc
Seats 50
♿ rest
Car park
No dogs

Fourteen years have passed since David and Mary
Partridge – he the chef, she described as 'barmaid,
B Sc Econ' – first took their roadside inn into
this book. They are now substantial citizens whose
services to the county have not been confined to
browsing and sluicing the gentry. Still, 'for consistent
excellence this restaurant never fails' is a comment
that could have been made at any time. True, the
excellence is of a now unfashionable kind. There are
people who find – especially after a long wait in the
uninspiring bar – individual dishes uneventful,
sweets undistinguished, and the feminine service
well-meaning rather than professional. But in each
of the past three years, test meals eaten by different
people have shown the same result: 'first-class raw
materials, economically and skilfully treated,
presented with flair but without flamboyance, to
make – with the fine cellar that the owners have
presciently accumulated – a singularly harmonious
evening out.' There are always four courses, in the
old manner, and though the soups and terrines, or
pâté en brioche, or mushrooms à la grecque, or
stylishly assembled plate of hors d'oeuvre that may
begin the meal are creditable, it is usually the
second course that excels: 'A wedge from a hot tarte
de tomates suggests that someone has a loving hand
for quiche-making, and quenelles de lotte (monk- or

angler-fish) were served with the kind of buttery white wine sauce you usually have to go to the Loire for.' Equally light pastry may encase meat in one of the main dishes ('though the lamb would have been better boned and trimmed first'), and pepper steak, or 'very handsome' lambs' tongues in tomato sauce with spinach cream, or bitoks ('some would say superior beefburgers') with sauce smitane are mentioned this year. Nor was there anything amateurish about a superbly confected apricot and coffee bombe served to an inspector, or 'lovely oeufs à la neige, with a proper vanilla custard and the cloud of egg white seeded with toasted almonds'. Wines from Provence and Tarn under £3 have joined the Ch. Chasse-Spleen '69 or '70 at £4·90, Hattenheimer Heiligenberg Riesling '75 at £4·60, Morey-St-Denis '71 (Clerget et Fils) at £6·70, and half-bottles of Ch. Suduiraut '70 at £2·50 on the list: on the whole here it is worth paying more for more. No music. They do their best to segregate smokers, but it is an uphill task ('worst luck,' they say).

App: L. Ratcliffe, R. C. Godber, J. & P.S., O.J.P., Colin & Jane Read

---

HOVINGHAM North Yorkshire   Map 8

Worsley Arms Hotel
on B1257 between
Malton and Helmsley
Hovingham 234

Closed Dec 25
Must book
Meals 12.30–1.45, 7–9

Tdh L £3·25 (meal £4·90),
D £5·50 (meal £7·15)

VAT & service inc
Children's helpings
Seats 60 (parties 12)
 ⅙ rest (2 steps)
Car park
No dogs in d/r
Access, Barclay
14 rooms (all with bath)
B&B £8–£10
Fire cert

The village is charming, 'perfumed with the scent of minor royalty', as an inspector puts it, and guests at Mr Rowe's comfortable and traditionally served hotel (though it is 'more G-plan than Georgian') relish their sniffs. Last year's entry, and a report or two since, suggested that they would be better employed scolding the vinegary hors d'oeuvre, pedestrian 'blancmange-like' pâté, gelatinous sweets, and senescent Stilton. But if you remember what old-fashioned British hotels used to do competently, take the set menu with soup followed by generous and tender meat dishes, confine yourself among supplementary items to the more straightforward grills, butter your own vegetables at table, and take a careful look at the sweets trolley to see what wobbles and what sits ('there were some good oranges in kirsch'), it is possible to feel a little less republican about it all. The house claret, too, was sound at £3·65 in 1978. Either side of it, Litre Vin ordinaire was £1·50 for 50 cl; Ch. Fourcas-Hosten '66, c.b., at £8·90. No music. Lunchtime bar snacks are substantial, like the Theakston's beers that go with them.

App: E. Eisenhandler, A. Kerr, P. C. H. Newbold, R. Sykes, D. R. Saunders, C. D. Mathews, and others

Thompson's
17 High Street
Hungerford 2056

A new team has taken over the 'eating-house' near the railway bridge ('prepare for alarming rumblings from time to time'). Some rumbles, too, about Terry Thorpe's uncertain seasoning ('bland' oeufs à la crème, 'mouth-puckeringly salt' côte de veau aux anchois, £3·95, in the same test meal), and erratic helpings. But terrine de canard à l'orange and lamb cutlets in a brandy, cream and walnut sauce (£3·75) on the often-changed menu tasted well, as did the vegetables. Service and the look of the kitchen have inspired less confidence. Snacks are available at the bar with wine by the glass (60p) or 50 cl carafe (£1·95). Interesting Alsace wines (Muscat, Richard Ancel Cordon Mauve, '74, £3·90). Recorded music.

Closed Sun; Dec 26	Tdh L £2·25 (meal £3·20)	Children's helpings
Must book D	Alc £6·40 (meal £9·10)	(under 14)
Meals 12–2, 7.30–10.30		Seats 36
(11 Fri & Sat)	VAT inc	⅁ rest (1 step)
	Service 10% D	No dogs
		Am Ex, Diners

Old Bridge Hotel
1 High Street
Huntingdon 52681

Closed Dec 24 D; Dec 25
Must book
Meals 12.30–2.30,
7.30–10.30

Alc £5·50 (meal £8·40);
buffet L from £2·25

Service inc
Cover 30p
Children's helpings
Seats 50 (parties 25)
⅁ rest (4 steps)
Car park
No dogs in d/r
Access, Am Ex, Barclay,
Diners
25 rooms (13 with bath)
B&B £8·75
Fire cert

Numerous reports this year give a chiaroscuro impression of this Poste Hotels' creeper-clad, well-equipped, and 'dressily but amiably served' headquarters. Stays would be a pleasure but for 'Le Mans-like' traffic. The food is within their control – or nearly. James Bate has replaced the more experienced Graham Harbisher as chef and though the group has an established formula by now for its dining-room and (generally excellent) all-day bar meals, there are some new ideas and new lapses. Exacting critics have enjoyed the cheese croquettes, lasagne, and mushrooms in batter as first courses, then (as usual) the baked ham and pink roast beef on the trolley, and even 'less pink' lamb cutlets with Cumberland sauce, or more ambitious chicken stuffed with crab and adorned with a crab claw – 'though the sauce was parsley, rather than white wine.' There is also a trolley laden with smoked fish. But duck, whether tough or grossly sweet, crab-filled but mediocre 'Bridge bun', variable vegetables ('salad bowls are now better'), and sweets whose content often seems a mystery to the staff, suggest there is plenty left to learn. 'I liked blackberry mousse but cheesecake was bitty because they had used cottage cheese rather than curd.' 'Coffee was terrible but there were *nine* beans in a Sambuca.' Breakfasts are good. The Poste Hotel group's wines (from £3·35) are often crassly served, but sensibly chosen, listed alongside the menu, and given a flat-rate mark-up that leaves Ch. Batailley '73 and

Gewürztraminer '76 under £5, and Aloxe-Corton Les Boutières '71 (Doudet Naudin) or Würzburger Innere Leiste Riesling Kabinett under £6. There are several ports by the glass too. Wines – and pots of pâté – may be bought to take away. Pressurised beers. No music.

App: John Scott, John C. Baker, Colin R. Hawke, N. C. Dee, T. D. Ellison, F. Westcott, D.W., and many others

---

HURST GREEN Lancashire   Map 5

Shireburn Arms
on B6243
5 m NW of Whalley
Stonyhurst 208

'A small, comfortable hotel in beautiful country', built on the solera system since the 16th century. It could be warmer in winter (the food too, some say). That apart, people approve a rather runny lasagne, filets de limande en sabots (a 'nugget' of sole in potato nests with a good cheese sauce on top, £1·80), baby chicken casseroled with tomatoes and white wine (£2·80), interesting fresh vegetables ('never straight'), with a fluffy baked apple to finish. The chef proprietor is Italian, but the eclectic menu also takes in chachouka, curry, and gammon Mendip Hills. The long wine list is equally catholic, with a page of Australians, others from Greece, Spain and England (and Ch. Margaux '55 at £35). The Italian section yields various Valpolicella Amarones, from £3·75 to £6·70. No music.

Closed L (exc public hols)
Must book D
Meals 12.30–2 (public hols), 7–8.30

Alc £5·25 (meal £7·40)

Service inc
Seats 45 (parties 10)
Car park

No dogs in public rooms
Barclaycard
11 rooms (6 with bath)
B&B from £7–£10
Fire cert

HUSBANDS BOSWORTH Leicestershire   Map 5

Fernie Lodge
on A50
6 m SW of Market Harborough
Market Harborough 880551

Closed Sun; Mon; Sat L; last 2 weeks July; Dec 25 & 26; Jan 1
Must book
Meals 12–1.30, 7–9.30

Tdh L from £2·50 (meal £4·40), D from £5·50 (meal £7·60)

If hotel and catering schools taught systems worth learning, there would be a tableful of students every lunch-time at Richard and Ishbel Speight's mid-Victorian mansion, trying to work out how to produce an attractive three-course meal with choice for £2·50 or so when no one else in the East Midlands can. True, the turnover is brisk, for plenty of M1 travellers are capable of reading the *Guide*. True again, not everything every day is worthy of the owners ('it was a mistake to order the creamed prawns'). But the good dishes people report on at either lunch or dinner include Fernie Lodge smokies, mushrooms in herb and garlic butter, smoked salmon and crab pâté, crunchy vegetables with mayonnaise dips, 'crisp roast Norfolk duckling with fresh apples as part of the accompanying salad', lamb's sweetbreads cooked with cream and mushrooms garnished with bacon, pork with cream,

VAT inc
Children's helpings L
Seats 96 (parties 25)
🔲 rest (1 step)
Car park
No dogs

chives, cider and apples ('rather sweet though'), 'generously served bilberry and apple pie', Eton mess, 'delicious profiteroles', and mincemeat, almond and brandy tart. Green salads are not always green, the bar chimney is apt to smoke, and the coffee is merely passable. Wine prices are kept low: many bottles are under £3, including a house red burgundy; Ch. Laborde '67, c.b., is £3·70. The pressurised bitter is Marston's Pedigree. A pianist plays light classical airs at night.

App: Martin Cowlyn, Trudy Reid, R. A. Jones, K. W. Wilkinson, R. J. Haerdi, S.T., and others

HYTHE Kent   Map 3

Gambrinos
74 High Street
Hythe 60571

Real – but erratic, and eccentrically served – cooking is done by Mr Gonçalves in this 'rococo Victorian' house, say inspectors and others who have enjoyed their coquilles St Jacques Mornay (£1·50), ris de veau au calvados, entrecôte poivre vert (£3·15), and crème amandine (when freshly made). But flavours seem more vigorous à la carte: at a test set dinner, brandade and agneau à l'ail were anaemic, while for porc au vin blanc (£2·75) 'the garlic came in lumps.' The house white (£2) seems better than the red. They are planning morning coffees now. Please continue to report.

Closed Sun; Apr 13;
Dec 26
Must book weekends
Meals 12.30–1.45, 7–9.30

Tdh L £2·50 (meal £4·55),
D £4·75 (meal £7·20)
Alc £5·45 (meal £8·25)

Cover 20p alc
Seats 40
🔲 rest; w.c.
Car park
Access, Diners

IDDESLEIGH Devon   Map 1

Duke of York
on B3217
3¼ m NE of Hatherleigh
Hatherleigh 253

Closed Dec 25
Must book
Meals 12–2 (bar), 8–10

Tdh £5 (meal £6·65)

Service inc
Children's helpings
(under 10)
Seats 24
🔲 rest (1 step)
No dogs in d/r
10 rooms (3 with bath,
3 with shower)

'This is a place that I would keep to myself and a few close friends were it not for the fact that the *Guide* had first led me to it,' writes one correspondent. Several people still judge Tony Ball by his graceful predecessor Peggie Rafferty and find his snappish humour unrestful, but others are well content, and Elizabeth Ball's food pleases almost everyone. There is little choice, but her repertoire varies enough for a short stay, and at least two puddings are normally attempted by diners. 'The smattering of mint-flavoured rice with the fine roast lamb, the Norwegian cream and the breakfasts' impressed one visitor; liver pâté, parsley pie, beef olives, chocolate brandy cake, and lemon meringue pie are other possibilities. 'Diabolical mashed potato' is an extreme but not an unsupported criticism. In a thatched house of such unforced charm (with communal tables), Inch's cider or Trophy bitter from the cask seem natural drinks but there are also

B&B £5
D, B&B £9

fifty wines, from £1·85 for French Sauvignon or
Chardonnay. No smoking till the coffee stage.
Rooms are simple, except perhaps in the new
extension which locals call 'the Iddesleigh Hilton'.
Families with children may find the inn
inconvenient. A substantial buffet lunch, laid out in
the dining-room, with items from 60p to £2, may be
eaten where you wish.

*App: A. R. P. Reid, R. McIsaac, E. H. Plaut,
John Phillips, W. P. G. Feiner, and others*

ILKLEY West Yorkshire   Map 5

Box Tree
Church Street (A65)
Ilkley 608484

Closed L; Sun; Mon;
Dec 25 & 26; Jan 1
Must book
D only, from 7.30

Tdh £10·50 (meal
£15·45)

Seats 50 (parties 25)
 [&] rest
No dogs
Access, Am Ex, Barclay,
Diners

From this nest of ornately furnished rooms,
Malcolm Reid, Colin Long and their director-chef
Michael Lawson have this year supplied a wine list
and other details, for which due thanks. It is a pity
that the year's reports are not themselves more
cordial in tone, for the winding-up of the Kildwick
Hall branch ought by the summer of 1978 to have
produced more *élan* and a tighter control here. Both
excellent and indifferent meals have been reported
by members. But the owners have a high opinion of
what they offer (it is more than shared by the 'high
priestess' who introduces dishes in the restaurant).
They are best judged by people who are used to
eating in the best places and – an important
provision in the West Riding – noticing what they
eat. Parts of most of the four-course meals are well
achieved. They begin well with a hot almondy roll
and butter, and the kitchen's instinct for interfering
with food does not preclude, for instance, 'lovely,
crunchy mange-tout peas', 'a well-dressed salade
verte' and more robust salade grande femme.
Balmoral grouse pie is a speciality. 'Splendid and
unctuous sauces' for cuisse de volaille vallée d'Auge
and noisettes d'agneau Edouard VII are also
reported, though sometimes the effect is spoilt by
over-reduction and consequent excess salt. But 'the
noisettes themselves were overcooked, the pâté
disagreeable, and the potatoes, some distant cousin
of pommes lyonnaise, poor.' Even the mousseline of
sole on which the house's reputation rests (with
Frenchmen) would not excite remark in Lamastre
or Tours. Sweets and pâtisserie are more reliable:
marquise au chocolat et au Cognac, or tartelette de
fraises, or meringue Alicia Markova, are examples.
'Coffee was good, thanks (we are told) to the
Wa-Chagga tribe on the slopes of Kilimanjaro': a
pity delegates cannot be invited to Ilkley. The
Yorkshire Fine Wines list is vigorously marked up,
with little to drink under £4. French-bottled Fleurie
'76 (Robert Sarrau) is £6·90. It makes a formidable
collection, and, to be fair, at the upper levels it
might be hard to replace the '69 Romanée-Conti or

'49 Ch. Rausan-Ségla, c.b., at much under the £30 or so here charged. However, a member reasonably objected to an attempt to remove not only him but his bottle to the lounge to make room for a second sitting. No music.

App: R. David Hall, D. M. Gaythwaite, P.M.A., O.J.P.

ILKLEY West Yorkshire   Map 5

Sabera
9 Wells Road
Ilkley 607104

Charmingly incongruous Alpine kitsch and well-groomed, courteous Indian staff make this a novel experience. The menu is helpfully descriptive, and includes a star-rating for degrees of heat. Standards of cooking are variable, and though some members have liked the shami and sikh kebabs (65p) and mulligatawny soup (45p) at the start, and then chicken biriani with whole almonds and an omelette (£1·80) or chicken curry (£1·55), others have been disappointed by prawn dhansak and meat korma. Chapatis and parathas, too, have their ups and downs. There is a plain set lunch on weekdays. A few wines; lager and Worthington E, 22p the half-pint. Recorded music. No dogs. More reports, please.

Closed Dec 25
Meals 12–2.30, 6–12

Tdh L (Mon–Fri) £1·40
Alc meal £4·65

Seats 44
♿ rest; w.c.

IPSWICH Suffolk   Map 3

Rosie's Place
200 St Helen's Street
Ipswich 55236

Closed L; from 23rd to
end of every month;
2 weeks summer
Must book
D only, 7–10.45

Tdh Sat £6·50
(meal £8·40)
Alc (min £3) £5·15
(meal £7·20)

VAT inc
Seats 32
♿ rest
Car park (4)
No dogs

Three weeks shalt thou labour and the fourth week shalt thou rest, say Rosemarie Farrell and Buddy Woolsey, scripture revisionists who submit this year opening times that 'may seem weird but make life tolerable for us and at least ensure that there's one place in Suffolk open on a Sunday (unless it falls on the 23rd or after).' Otherwise, the dim light, plant jungle, nervous service, and informal English cooking (the Italian light lunches have been abandoned) remain roughly as before. One member 'heard the chef (presumably Buddy) say that the sauce on the overcooked salmon "seems to have boiled away a bit"', but the *Guide*'s own critics were lucky with a generous helping of well-flavoured, coarse liver and ham pâté baked in cider (70p) and 'brownish and unexpected egg and walnut pâté (65p)'. The lamb hot-pots may taste less exotic than names like china cholla or panjotheram suggest, but are sound enough, and vegetables are buttered. Pork with black cherries was 'meltingly tender meat in rich gravy', with well-cooked parsnips and cabbage. Grimsby fish or Kentish chicken pies (£3·80) are worth trying, and 'some are surprised that nut-stuffed cabbage rolls with mushroom curry are tasty even though vegetarian,' the owners say. Treacle tart has vanished from the menu now, but Cumberland Rum Nicky now rivals chocolate Marie. Coffee is nondescript. Wines are enterprising and modestly priced, from Spanish at £2·25; Crozes-Hermitage Rochefine '73, £3·19; Hattenheimer Engelmannsberg Spätlese '71, £4·92. Recorded music. Smoking is discouraged. 'We don't believe in a service charge.'

App: V. & F. Irish, J. & M.B., O.J.P., and others

ISLE OF WIGHT   Map 2

Peacock Vane

🍷

Bonchurch
Ventnor 852019

Closed Jan 5–Feb 20
Must book
Meals 1–1.30, 8 & 9

Tdh L £5 (meal £7·25),
D £7 (meal £9·40)

Seats 40
🚹 rest (1 step); w.c.
Car park
No dogs in d/r
Access, Am Ex, Barclay,
Diners
10 rooms (7 with bath)
B&B from £8

'A dangerous place to go when the owner remembers from prep school days how you beat him for not rowing hard enough.' Perhaps it is no surprise that the world of *Eric, or, Little by Little* has lasted longer on the Isle than anywhere else, even though a younger generation of Wolfendens are now in charge of this long-loved hotel. Perhaps, too, it should be made diplomatically clear that school history is not repeating itself, for it is a subsequent *fin de saison* inspector, not the scourge of juvenile galley-slaves, who convicts the kitchen of not rowing hard enough, at least for a 'tureen' hotel. Main courses were not as authoritative as they should have been, given the narrow choice, and the cheeses were not well kept. (Neither were the swimming-pool or the cottage annexe, incidentally.) Some have also deduced, from the soup and fish courses and the breakfasts, that delicate appetites are catered for here. But others praise the generosity of, for instance, the Sunday evening buffets with 'salmon, crab, guinea-fowl, duck, and other meats, with an infinite variety of salads'; and happily the home-made bread and soups, the sea bass stuffed with fennel, stuffed quail, carré d'agneau, beef Wellington and other dishes with island-grown vegetables, the mousses of lemon or chocolate, and the orange tart and other things, make it clear that when the family is not absent or overstretched quality remains high. The same is true of the wines. Burgundy prices, though they will be up this year, were generous last year with Chanson Réserve at £2·40, Beaujolais Villages '76 (Paul Sapin) at £3·80, and Clos de la Roche '70 (Chanson again) £6·50. Remember, with the sweet wines, that Mr Wolfenden will decant a half-bottle at 60 per cent of the full price. Sometimes classical records are played.

App: Angela Bailey, Alan Stevens, Ivor Hall, S.E., G. Berown, and others

---

ISLE OF WIGHT see also pub section

King's Head
Cheddington 668388 *and*
668264

Closed Dec 25 D
Must book D & weekends
Meals 12.30–1.45,
7.30–9.30

Tdh £5·25 (meal £7·75)
Alc £7·15 (meal £10·80)

VAT inc
Service 12½%
Cover 40p alc
Seats 65 (parties 100)
♿ rest (1 step)
Air-conditioning
Car park
No dogs
Access, Am Ex, Barclay,
Diners, Euro
No rooms

There is more joy in heaven over a Trust Houses
Forte pub with a manager who makes food his
priority than there is over places that start out with
more advantages, and even members who admired a
long-vanished regime are warmly in favour of
Georges de Maison and his welcoming staff. The à la
carte menu is at first sight typical Home Counties
posh, but there are unexpected variants: stuffed
cabbage with sour cream, scrambled egg with
smoked salmon in a tartlet, coulibiac of salmon, and
braised oxtail. Curried prawns, grilled sardines with
mustard sauce (£1·50), and pollastrella al mattone
(poussin in a brick, which sometimes appears, like
the oxtail, on the 'agreeable rather than
outstanding' set menus) and collops of veal with
prawns and lobster sauce (£3·95) are all praised.
There is 'a grand sweets trolley, including many
additions to the usual display'. The all-too-usual
display of THF wines (from £3·25) with Ch. Ségur
'73 at £5·75 may be expected, with pressurised beers.
No music. Men should wear a tie at night.

*App: Bel & Kevin Horlock, Robert Ellis, Marion B.
Dewar, F. Joan Heyman*

JEVINGTON East Sussex   Map 3

Hungry Monk
on B2105
4 m NW of Eastbourne
Polegate 2178

Closed L (exc Sun);
Dec 24 & 25; Jan 1
Must book
Meals 12.15–2 (Sun),
7.15–10

Tdh Sun L £5 (meal
£7·95), D £5·75 (meal
£8·85)

Seats 30
Car park
No dogs in d/r

Nigel and Sue Mackenzie, with their chef Ian
Dowding, have had a decade now to put down
taproots from these cottage rooms to the water-table
of monied Sussex, and bookings and reports alike
confirm their success. True, the 'dinner in a private
house' feeling to which they aspire sits awkwardly
with the way guests are 'whisked from A to B to
make room for the next big spenders', and unsmiling
faces, cold plates, opened wine bottles and small
coffee cups have been regretted on occasion by
otherwise contented customers. The actual cooking,
though, has benefited from stability (even Kent
Austin, the alternate chef, is in his eighth year here
now), and from the 'hot home-made rolls' to the
smoked eel pâté, prawn and cheese terrine, rack of
lamb Shrewsbury, roast beef, 'celery and carrots
done to perfection', ices, and hot chocolate cake with
chocolate sauce, content is pretty general. Caramany
red or Taichac white wines are £2·90, and there are
eight other house wines under £5, including '76
Muscadet (£3·80) and Juliénas (£4·75). There are a
few finer bottles too, from good sources, and old
brandy or madeira by the glass, but the
complimentary port they offer is definitely not in
that category. No cigars. No children under five.

App: A. M. Reid, S.P., J.C., J.M., and others

KENILWORTH Warwickshire   Map 5

Restaurant Bosquet

97a Warwick Road
Kenilworth 52463

Closed L; Sun; Mon;
2 weeks Easter; 3 weeks
Aug; 1 week Chr
Must book
D only, 7–10

Alc £6·45 (meal £9·15)

VAT inc
Seats 24
♿ rest (2 steps)
No dogs

David Groves' restaurant raises in an acute form the question of whether a good chef needs the right audience to stay at the top, for only a minority of visitors to this over-patterned south Midlands room give signs of knowing what – apart from the price, and the wait while a dish is prepared – differentiates this kitchen from others in the same county. Yet the Groves family (who wait at table very efficiently) consider their customers, whether or not they order one of those sublime *petites entrées* – soufflé de merlan (£1·10), perhaps, golden on top, creamy inside, with a surprise ballast of tomato sauce at the bottom of the dish; or courgettes with generous prawns and a lemony hollandaise. Moules farcies and other seafood dishes are praised too, and prawns naturally appear (standing in for the écrevisses Napoleon's chef is supposed to have found on the battlefield) in an 'exceedingly fresh-tasting' veal Marengo (£2·85). Pintade aux raisins (with Malmsey as well as grapes), beef with walnuts and mustard, and venison in season, are other main course possibilities. Filet de boeuf Edouard VII had too much curry, in one visitor's view, and vegetables, though well cooked, tend to arrive in slightly too elaborate guises, given that sauces generally are rich. End, if not with the crêpe aux fraises praised last time, with soufflé omelette parisienne (£1·25) or nectarine with raspberry and kirsch. Under £4 there is Muscadet or Côtes du Ventoux to drink, or even cheaper Chenin and Gamay, and over £5 there is Gewürztraminer '76, or Santenay La Maladière '73 (domaine-bottled) at £6·80. No music.

App: S.F., J. Homan, H.A., and others

Romano's
97 Warwick Road
Kenilworth 57473

A small, family-run Italian place next-door to Le Bosquet (*q.v.*) though moving a few doors away (to 60 Weobley Road) in the autumn. Romano's wife and mother-in-law produce 'exceptionally rich and tasty' stuffed aubergine (95p) and cannelloni (75p), veal Cordon Bleu (£2·35), scampi pizzaiola (in a red wine sauce, £2·95), 'crisp and fresh vegetables', bistecca con olive nere (£2·60), and zabaglione. 'Romano serves genially, and unleashes an evil Gorgonzola.' A wide range of Italian wines (including ten Sardinian), with litre carafes at £3·30. Taped music.

Closed Sun; July 30–
Aug 26
Must book D & weekends
Meals 12.30–2, 7.30–
10.30

Tdh L £2 (meal £4)
Alc (min £2·85) £5·30
(meal £7·55)

Service inc

Seats 34
♿ rest (3 steps)
Car park
No dogs

KERSEY Suffolk   Map 3

Quill's
The Street
off B1070
1½ m NW of Hadleigh
Hadleigh 7161

Closed L; Sun; Mon;
Dec 25 & 26
Must book
D only, 7.30–9

Tdh £6 (meal £7·25)

VAT & service inc
Children's helpings
(under 10)
Seats 28
No dogs

In this pretty wool village 'the street descends from both sides to a duck-dotted ford in the middle', and the Coopers' weaver's cottage has been converted to make a diminutive restaurant with timbers, an open fire, and spiral stair to a bar upstairs. Mrs Cooper's hard work, large helpings, and interesting ideas for her quarterly menus are the most obvious virtues, and inspectors have enjoyed their crab or spinach and lemon soups, hot smokies, marinated kippers, lamb Stroganoff, veal with sultanas and almonds, and, above all, potato pie. 'Monochrome' hors d'oeuvre need more flair in presentation, duck curry more flavour and better-cooked rice, and the rich puddings flat plates. They are 'presented in turn by a waitress because there is no room to wheel a trolley and by the time you've seen them all you've forgotten the first.' 'Banoffly' pie, chocolate roulade and meringues were good and even light when tried. Cafetière coffee is fresh too. Argentine ordinaires are a sound choice at £2·50, as are other bin-ends on the short, mutable wine list. No music. No cigars or pipes. More reports, please.

KINGS LANGLEY Hertfordshire   Map 3

Old Cottage
18 The High Street
Kings Langley 63823

Closed Sun; Mon;
Dec 25 & 26; Jan 1
Must book
Meals 12.30–2, 7.30–9.30
(10.30 Fri & Sat)

Alc L £2·25 (meal £4·60),
D £5·50 (meal £8·85)

Seats 65 (parties 35)
♿ rest (3 steps); w.c.
Access, Am Ex, Barclay,
Euro

Nominations for Annie Maudsley and Ron Titley's restaurant and catering service have been guarded, for trial suggests that the experience of the staff could be written on a very small corner of the menu's vast white spaces. But Mr Titley himself has cooked in private service for five years, and visitors report well of his gazpacho (85p), spicy potted meat (£1), slivers of pork with ginger and peppers (£2·50), chicken chaud-froid, gently treated vegetables, strawberry sorbet and prune mousse. The à la carte menu is sensibly short, and they offer to cook anything else within reason to prior order: filet en croûte and soufflé Grand Marnier (£1·25) are popular elections. House red and white wines, provenance unstated, are £2·90 (55p the glass) and the few better bottles are fully priced. No music. Children's helpings. No dogs. They also do morning coffee, teas, and lunches. More reports, please.

KINTBURY Berkshire   Map 2

Dundas Arms
♟
off A4
5½ m W of Newbury
Kintbury 263

Apart from the dining-room atmosphere which even smokers object to ('I was offered a cigar when others had not even finished eating') the two-generation Dalzell-Pipers' house between Kennet and Avon has most of the qualities members seem to look for in a weekend hotel within striking distance of London: comfortable rooms, the quack of ducks, mostly excellent cooking, and a serious wine collection. A clanking radiator, absence of a

Closed L (exc bar); Sun;
Mon; Dec 25 & 26;
Jan 1; Ascot week
Must book
D only, 7.30–9.15

Tdh from £6·80 (meal
£10·25)

VAT inc
Service 10%
Seats 40
♿ rest (3 steps); w.c.
Car park
No dogs
Access, Barclay, Diners
6 rooms (all with bath)
B&B £12·50–£18
Fire cert

residents' lounge, inappropriate potatoes for
delicate dishes, and other minor errors, weigh for
little against people's pleasure in 'outstanding'
watercress soup, crab andaluz, walnut and mushroom
pâté, 'light quenelles of pike with a good fishy
taste', deep-fried smoked salmon pancakes (if you
can imagine), crisp honey-roast duckling with mint
and lemon ('the best for a long time'), stuffed
chicken breasts, roast poussin with prawn sauce,
steak and oyster pudding, young grouse, guinea-fowl
with ginger and orange, and other good things cooked
by David and Jane Dalzell-Piper and their assistant
Marina Scarpitta. 'Offal' is a proud boast too. Good
puddings may include torte Malakoff, syllabubs and
chocolate brandy cake, though 'we found apricot
mille-feuille over-sweet.' The wines (from £3·80 a
litre for Valgardello) rest most firmly on white
burgundy (Averys Puligny Aligoté '71, £4·50) and
formidable clarets, including nearly three dozen '70s
and '71s. (Ch. La Lagune, almost the only one to
appear in both vintages, is £6·90 and £8 respectively.)
Ch. Léoville-Barton, c.b., survives from the '62
vintage at £9. There are inviting half-bottles too.
No music. No 'screamers or under-sevens'; and at
least no pipes. Beware of both Ascot week, when
they close, and Newbury race meetings, when they
do not. Bar lunches, with Morland and Arkell 3B on
hand-pumps, offer good bread, cheese, and pâté.

App: by too many members to list

KIRKBY STEPHEN Cumbria   Map 8

King's Arms
Kirkby Stephen 71378

'Mrs Hibbert's dachshund still reigns supreme . . .',
and long may Mrs Hibbert reign over us too, say
holiday-makers (non-residents may dislike the
unpriced set menu and 'all in by eight' atmosphere).
Guests like the game soup, egg mayonnaise, beef
with Marsala and mushrooms, baked ham with
Cumberland sauce, and roast beef, as well as the
'splendid assortment of sweets on the trolley'. They
are less happy about the vegetables and some
'glutinous' sauces. Pleasant and competent service.
Stowells wines on a limited list. No music.

Must book	VAT inc	Car park
Meals 12–1.30, 6.30–8	Children's helpings	No dogs in d/r
	(under 10)	11 rooms
Tdh L £2·85 (meal £4·80),	Seats 45	B&B £10·55
D £5·55 (meal £7·55)	♿ rest (1 step)	

We rewrite every entry each year, and depend on fresh, detailed reports
to confirm the old, as well as to include the new. The further from
London you are, the more important this is.

KNOWLE West Midlands   Map 5

Florentine
15 Kenilworth Road
Knowle 6449

A snug little restaurant in a converted shop near Solihull, with a long, mainly Italian menu on which the simplest dishes are often best. Flavours may be too low-key for the sophisticated, but others have enjoyed the chef-made pastas (65p), veal zucchini (with a Marsala and tomato sauce, £3·45), scampi in cream, cassata, and the coffee. Considerate service. Unambitious wine list, with several Italians, from about £2·80. 'Soft' recorded music.

Closed Sun; Mon L;
public hol Mons &
following Tues L;
Dec 25 & 26; Jan 1
Must book D & weekends
Meals 12.30–2.30,
7.30–10.30

Tdh L from £2·25
(meal £4·25)
Alc £4·40 (meal £6·50)

Service inc

Children's helpings
Seats 40
♻ rest
No dogs
Access, Am Ex, Barclay,
Diners

KNUTSFORD Cheshire   Map 5

La Belle Epoque
60 King Street
Knutsford 3060

Closed L; Sun; public
hols
Must book
D only, 7.30–10

Alc £6·90 (meal £10·45)

Service 10%
Seats 70 (parties 100)
♻ rest (2 steps)
No dogs
Access, Am Ex, Barclay,
Diners, Euro
5 rooms (3 with bath,
1 with shower)
B&B from £8·70
Fire cert

There are still one or two suggestions that Keith and Nerys Mooney's restaurant is neither as good nor as French as the proprietors and some of the guests think it is. But Richard Harding Watt's eclectic style of architecture and art nouveau interiors – not to mention, if you stay, the comfort of the rooms – disarm misgivings about, for instance, excessive creaminess. People remember their leek and potato soup, crêpe aux fruits de mer, foie de volaille au madère (£1·25), stuffed quail with orange butter, and paupiettes de veau au concombre 'reminiscent of French Canada' (£4·25). Less ambitious steaks with jacket potato, buttered parsnips and other well-presented vegetables are also capably done. A good choice of flans, dacquoises, chocolate roulade and other delectables round off the meal, and they do their own baking. House burgundy is £2·75. We have not been shown the current wine list but one member says that it is more impressive and better value in whites than in reds. There is 'rather repetitive' recorded music. Children under 13 are discouraged.

*App: D. Waller, Lt-Col. M. E. Bransby-Williams,
Anne Bird, Dr & Mrs R. J. Wheler, and others*

David's Place
10 Princess Street
Knutsford 3356

Closed Sun; Mon L;
Apr 16; Aug 16 & 27;
2 weeks Aug/Sept;
Dec 25 D; Dec 26; Jan 1

'Southerners may need to be reminded to leave the M6 at the Manchester Airport exit,' but northerners seem well aware that the Stirling family's 'Hat and Feather' tradition that has kept them eating in Knutsford for years past is well continued in the younger generation's rather close-packed olive-and-green restaurant (once a cake shop). The set lunches (especially on Sundays) and the à la carte dinners

Must book
Meals 12.30–2.30,
7.15–10.15

Tdh L £3·85 (meal £6·65)

Alc £6·60 (meal £9·95)

Children's helpings
Seats 50 (parties 40)
 rest
No dogs
Access, Am Ex, Barclay,
Diners

both have their admirers. 'The former, though without choice till the sweets, yielded mushroom and madeira soup that I would not have missed, then ample rare roast beef with real Yorkshire pudding and good vegetables including hot beetroot.' For an evening inspector, the turbot in cream and tomato sauce (£3·45) and tenderloin of pork (£3·50), both with well-balanced sauces, were the best things, along with their vegetables, 'crisp and light' chips, sauté parsnips, and lightly cooked broccoli. But the meal began well, too, with terrine (£1·15), and melon with prawns in curry mayonnaise; and orange mousse, spiced plum flan, hazelnut roulade, and other sweets generally appeal, though some find them too rich or sweet and take refuge in the fine blue Cheshire kept. Colin Williams in the kitchen is also proud of his Jamaican fillet fingers with rum and bananas (£4·50) and chicken breasts with juniper berries and brandied apricots. French or Argentine ordinaires are £2·75, and there is little claret to drink under £4. Recorded music 'sometimes'. Confine pipes to the bar.

App: P. A. J. Andrew, M.L.R., M.M., S. & A.G., and others

LACOCK Wiltshire   Map 2

At the Sign of the Angel
3 m SW of Chippenham
M4 exit 17
Lacock 230 *and* 470

Closed Sun D; Sat L;
L public hols; Dec 22–
Jan 1
Must book
Meals 1–1.30, 7.30–8

Tdh L £5·50 (meal £7·90),
D £6·50 (meal £9)

Service inc
Seats 36 (parties 12)
No dogs in public rooms
6 rooms
B&B £8·50–£12
Fire cert

The Levises' medieval inn – 'it feels like living in a large cupboard' – in a village protected by the National Trust can be confidently recommended to foreign visitors who do not mind being conscious of plumbing noises. The price you pay reflects the small numbers that can be housed, but is justified by the genuineness of the food. That includes the home-made yoghourt, fresh orange juice and other good things at breakfast. Lunches and dinners offer no choice of main course, unless it be an omelette or steak, and depend on a sound English roast of pork, beef or stuffed duckling, perhaps with cabbage 'cooked not a moment too long'. Fine soups or 'less inspired fish mousse or potted crab' appear beforehand, and afterwards there will be home-made profiteroles, or meringue, or ice-cream; treacle lick may be altogether too sweet. Stilton would be fine if customers did not insist on spooning it, and the Cheddar is good too. The seventy wines include the owners' own Tarn red at £2·80. They do not say so this year, but doubtless there is still a good port kept decanted. No music. 'Preferably' no smoking at table. No children under ten for dinner or under eight overnight. Note that there is no food at all on Sunday evenings, and no pub licence.

App: M. S. Hicks, B.A. Marder, A.A.D., Christopher Bradshaw, M. E. Cohen, and others

LAUNCESTON Cornwall Map 1

Dockie's Bistro
20 Westgate Street
Launceston 3873

Casual, cheerful bistro with brisk service and loud
music, offering à la carte lunches and set meals at
night. Crab and prawn coquille, deep-fried mussel
pancake and Caribbean pepper-pot are among
successes, but some dishes have been called dull or
dismal. The 'steak dinner' (£2·99) might suit some.
Wines 'from the local cash and carry' – £2·99 the
litre for Bonatelo (40p the glass). Restricted opening
January to Easter.

Closed Sun; April 13; Dec 25 D; Dec 26; Jan 1; L most public hols Must book weekends & Aug Meals 12–2.15, 7–10	Tdh D £5 (meal £7·05) Alc L £2·45 (meal £4·55) VAT inc	Children's helpings Seats 40 (parties 12) 🔄 rest (1 step) No dogs

LAVENHAM Suffolk Map 3

Timbers
High Street
Lavenham 247218

The Clarkes offer à la carte lunches and set dinners
of 'firsts, fillers and finishers' at their 15th-century
restaurant in the centre of this show-piece village.
Even gluttons have quailed at the helpings.
Batter-fried mushrooms, moussaka, steak with
mustard and honey, and the vegetables are
mentioned in reports this time. Sweets may look
better than they taste. Lay & Wheeler wines; litres
of Choix du Roy are £3·25, 45p the glass. Bar snacks
(not Saturday), with Greene King beer. Recorded
classical music. No dogs.

Closed Tue; Mon D; Dec 26; Jan 1 Must book D Meals 12.30–2.15, 7.15–9.30	Tdh D £5·25 (meal £7·65) Alc L £3·40 (meal £5·60) VAT inc	Children's helpings (under 11) Seats 40 🔄 rest (2 steps) Access card

LAVENHAM see also pub section

LEAMINGTON SPA see **BISHOP'S TACHBROOK**

LEEDS West Yorkshire Map 5

Jumbo Chinese Restaurant
120 Vicar Lane
Leeds 458324 *and* 458547

Meals noon–11.45

'Only the uniformly high quality of all dishes tested
on three visits have persuaded us to return and
suffer the smoke, noise and uncaring service about
which many fierce complaints are only too audible,'
and this London comment is echoed by northern
ones, from both sides of the Pennines. Perhaps it is
the effect of having eight men named as chefs, as

Alc meal £3·55

Seats 132
Air-conditioning
No dogs
No cheques

though it were a boat-race. Anyway, the dishes to note are the fried rice, the mixed meat and vegetable soup, on which other places use up yesterday's left-overs, bean curd soup, Peking sour and chilli soup (75p), satay beef or pork, chicken or king prawns with broccoli, 'very accurately cooked beef with seasonal vegetables', chicken breast or brown mushroom with prawn meat stuffing (for virtuoso chopstick-wielders), and Hong Kong style roast duck. Peking capital spare ribs and Canton fillet steak (£1·30) are other recommendations of Lin Dai Lai's. The menu is à la carte but they will do special meals to prior order. There are wines of no moment from £2·20; drink tea or beer. Recorded music (in Chinese for the waiters).

App: W. B. O'Neill, N.J., Jill & Raymond Barnett, and others

Shabab
2 Eastgate
Leeds 468988

'My restaurant is very different . . .' and members agree – reporting bells on the chairs and joss sticks in the loo – for dishes here show signs of individual spicing. Among those admired are alloo or chicken tikka, shami kebab, chicken tandoori and the unusually wide choice of Indian sweets. The menu makes good reading, and the decorative staff are efficient and courteous. Bottled beers. Recorded Indian music; occasional dancing. No dogs.

Closed Sun L
Must book D & weekends
Meals 11.30–2.30, 6–11.45

Tdh L £1·75 (meal £4·35)

Service 10%
Seats 70 (parties 80)

Air-conditioning
Access, Am Ex, Barclay,
Diners, Euro

Ya Koge
166 Lower Briggate
Leeds 468664

Since last year's tentative entry, Mr Chak has introduced forks and spoons to the restaurant and European furniture in the *tatami* room. Little sign, though, of westernisation in the cooking, though veterans who praise it wish, nevertheless, that the cloths were cleaner and the cat less friendly. For £4 at a set dinner, try double fresh chowder, harlequin hors d'oeuvre, Peking duck, beef steak on sizzling plate, lemon chicken, Chinese leaves, rice and a pudding. Excellent tea. Licensed. Oriental music.

Closed Dec 25
Must book D & weekends
Meals 12–1.30, 5.15–11.30

Tdh L 95p, D from £3·50
Alc meal £5·05

Service 10%

Seats 85 (parties 16)
♿ rest
No dogs
Access, Am Ex, Barclay

The Guide accepts no advertising. Nor does it allow restaurateurs to use its name on brochures, menus, or in any form of advertisement. If you see any instances of this, please report them to us.

For the explanation of ♿ denoting accessibility for the disabled see 'How to use the Guide', p. 4.

LEICESTER Leicestershire   Map 5

Acropolis
270 Loughborough Road
(A6)
Leicester 63106

The Menicou family's five years of toil in this
Hellenic restaurant will bear fruit in 1979 with a
face-lift for the outside and vast expansion within.
But the authentic flavours in the Greek-Cypriot
dishes offered left admirers blind to their
surroundings in 1978. No 'improvements', please, to
the trahana soup, stuffed courgettes, Acropolis
special, afelia and moussaka. The English coffee is
another matter. Othello seems dear at £2·50 the
half-litre; other Greek-Cypriot wines begin at
around £3·25. Recorded Greek music.

Closed Sun; Sat L;
July 1–14
Must book
Meals 12–2.15, 6.30–10.15

Tdh L from £3 (meal £5),
D £4·50 (meal £6·60)
Alc £4·10 (meal £6·15)

Children's helpings
(under 12)
Seats 45 (parties 35)
  rest (1 step)
No dogs

LEWDOWN Devon   Map 1

Lew Trenchard Manor
off A30
9 m SW of Okehampton
Lewdown 256

Sabine Baring-Gould once lived in this handsome
old manor house, and outside there are '14 acres of
tranquillity', inside, oak panelling, ornate ceilings
and log fires. There are generous bar snacks (soup,
40p; 'wild fowler's snack' – cold duck, salad and
rolls, £2·90) with a hot dish or two at lunch-time,
and pressurised beers. We have not seen the set
dinner menu, but the *carte* (changed twice a year)
offers chef-made soup, dabs meunière (85p as a
starter, £2·60 as a main course), pork fillet with apple
stuffing (£3·60, including vegetables), nut cutlets for
vegetarians (£2·15), and various sweets with clotted
cream. Wines from Colliers of Plymouth; Carafino at
£3·25 the litre. 'Discreet and welcoming staff.' No
music, not even 'Onward, Christian soldiers'.

Must book D
Meals 12.30–2 (bar), 7–9

Tdh D £5 (meal £7·25)
Alc (bar L) £3, D £5·45
(meal £7·75)

VAT inc
Service 10%
Children's helpings
Seats 150 (parties 76)
  rest

Car park
No dogs in d/r
Access, Am Ex, Barclay,
Diners, Euro
12 rooms
B&B from £7·50
Full board from £80

Numbers are given for private parties only if they can be accommodated
in a room separate from the main dining-room; when there are several such
rooms, the capacity of the largest is given. Some restaurants will take
party bookings at times when they are normally closed.

LEWES East Sussex   Map 3

La Cucina
13 Station Street
Lewes 6707

Closed Sun; Dec 24, 25,
26 & 31; Jan 1
Must book D
Meals 12–2.15, 6.30–11

Alc £4·25 (meal £6·60)

Service 10%
(parties over 6)
Seats 48 (parties 22)
Access, Barclay

The Cuthbertsons and the Lincolns seem to have
established themselves firmly in this little place
near the station since last year's tentative entry.
Cannelloni or minestrone, or the house's suggestion
of mussels in crispy bacon (95p) may begin a meal,
and breast of chicken with ham and cider, trout
with almonds, veal in various sauces, specialities of
the day such as feuilletage of salmon with prawns,
and half-ducklings with greengages in vinegar
(£2·75) sound interesting. 'Vegetables are also
recommended.' Drawbacks include 'close-packed
tables, and mediocre profiteroles and coffee'. The
house Barbera is £2·10. Recorded music. No dogs.

App: S. Jellis, B. Hurl, M. Rose, Gordon McEwan

Nitchevo
199 High Street
Lewes 2343

Harry Meissner's Russian cooking in this cosily
ethnic but far from cheap cellar is real enough,
though oddly bland sometimes, and the service is
good when it is Madame's. However, £4·55 for outka
(duck with blackcurrants) and similar prices for veal
in a caviare sauce, or marinated charcoal-grilled
pork and beef in cream sauces, may restrict turnover
(though main dish prices include vegetables). The
best things at a test meal were the minor ones least
likely to have known a freezer: borshch, herrings in
sour cream, 'moist' kasha, and sweet and sour white
cabbage. Decent house burgundy £2·95; rare vodkas.
No pipes. Russian music tapes.

Closed L; Wed; Apr 13 &
15; Dec 24 & 25; Jan 1
Must book
D only, from 7 p.m.

Alc £6·55 (meal £10·35)

Cover 30p

Seats 30
No dogs
Access, Barclay, Euro

Pelham Arms
Sussex Kitchen
High Street
Lewes 6149

This 17th-century pub-restaurant has bounced back
again in members' affections, and is often crowded.
But once you are seated, the 'efficient and charming'
staff give you a chance to enjoy the simple set
lunch or, à la carte, smoked mackerel, crab cocktail
(75p), Pelham pie, the batter-fried 'Sussex fish
dish' (£2·15), pot o'chocolate or raspberries and
cream. The vegetables are carefully cooked and the
tartare and mayonnaise chef-made. French or
Italian house wine, £2·60 the bottle. Good bar
snacks with hand-drawn Harvey's ale. No music.

Closed Sun; Mon; 2 weeks
Aug/Sept; public hols
Must book
Meals 12.15–1.30, 7–9.30

Tdh L £2·30 (meal £4·25)

Alc (min £2) £3·50
(meal £5·70)

VAT inc
Service 10%
(parties over 5)
Cover 15p alc

Seats 38
 ♿ rest (1 step)
Air-conditioning
Car park
No dogs in d/r
No rooms

Trumps
19–20 Station Street
Lewes 3906

Closed L; Sun; Mon;
3 weeks March; last
2 weeks Sept; Dec 25 &
26; Jan 1
Must book
D only, 7–10

Alc (min £3·95) £6·30
(meal £9)

VAT inc
Service 10%
Seats 28
♿ rest (2 steps)
No dogs

Bryan Chaffer and Christopher Goff (who cooks) call this their 'fourth and final' restaurant: if so, customers (some of whom have faithfully patronised them all) hope that the final appearance will be indefinitely extended. A certain preciousness, perhaps, often goes with extravagantly rich food, and so it is here, and visitors late on a Saturday evening found choice restricted. But normally there is no quarrel with the variety, nor with the cooking of, for instance, mushrooms in a bacon, garlic, and vermouth cream sauce (£1·20), chicken Christopher (the breast filled with their own terrine) and 'Christopher's brief-case' (fillet steak in puff pastry, £4·50). The duck, when tried, tasted 'far better than the restaurant norm', and vegetables were good. It is nutritional suicide to continue with home-made vanilla ice-cream with honey and rum, or other similar sweets, and if you fancy one of these, or a genuine peach Melba, then gazpacho (85p) or crudités with herb mayonnaise (90p) might be the wisest first course. Achat ordinaires are £2·85 and prices rise fairly fast thereafter: even the house claret and white burgundy are £4 or so, and Gewürztraminer '73 is £6·20. Recorded music.

App: K. B. Harrison, P.D., Henry Fawcett

Bolton Arms
Wensleydale 23327

Must book D & weekends
Meals 12–2 (bar exc Fri &
Sun), 7.30–8.30

Tdh Sun L £3·50 (meal
£5·75), Fri L £1·30
(meal £3·60)
Alc £4·55 (meal £7·40)

Seats 90 (parties 14)
Car park

This typical, plain-looking, Dales pub hides an upstairs dining-room 'long, like the Mauretania's', and surprisingly good food and drink, according to members and an inspector who liked Mr and Mrs Stevens's carefully cooked guinea-fowl in port and cream sauce, 'excellent duckling and venison', 'thick slices of locally killed beef for Sunday lunch, with good Yorkshire pudding and horseradish sauce too', and 'rich but light sweets': charlotte russe in the Beeton manner, profiteroles coated with dark chocolate, and walnut and cherry meringue. Even so 'plain cooking is more essential than things you tart up,' Mr Stevens says, and at the right time of year they will make a game pie to advance order. Weekday lunches are bar meals except on Fridays (market day), when there is a set version at a modest £1·30. French ordinaires are £2·75 a litre. Recorded music. More reports, please.

LICHFIELD Staffordshire   Map 5

Thrales
40 Tamworth Street
Lichfield 55091

An abandoned abattoir and butcher's shop, with 15th-century cottages, went to make this relative of the Casserole in Stone. (Their chef went too.) Lunchtime buffet offers salads, pâtés, taramosalata, savoury pancake (£1·35, including a glass of wine and coffee) and sweets. Dinner is a set menu, mainly casseroles: moussaka, caneton normande, pintade aux marrons (75p extra), jugged hare. Vegetables may be a weak point, sweets rather better (chocolate praline, lemon cheesecake). Helpful service. Various house wines, £3·50 the litre. No music.

Closed Sun; Sat L; last week Apr; last 2 weeks Aug; last week Dec
Must book D

Meals 12–2.30, 7.30–11

Tdh D £5·90 (meal £7·85)
Alc L £2·65 (meal £2·90)

VAT inc
Seats 64 (parties 30)
♿ rest (2 steps); w.c.
No dogs

LITTLE LANGDALE Cumbria   Map 7

Three Shires Inn
off A593
5 m W of Ambleside
Langdale 215

Closed L; late Nov to Mar 1
Must book
D only, 7–8.30

Tdh from £7 (meal £8)

VAT & service inc
Children's helpings
Seats 24
♿ rest
Car park
No dogs
7 rooms
B&B £8·50
D, B&B £13·50
Fire cert

The Poole family's zest for running this stone-built inn at the foot of Wrynose did not – understandably – long survive the retirement of the senior generation, but customers have been unusually buoyant about the regime that has taken their place. There are, it is true, a few who feel that their dinners were unmemorable, at best, and even one who thinks – unkindest cut – that Mr Price would be happier in front of the fire with a volume of Sartre than running a hotel. But other evidence suggests that the owners – condemned in this remote if trafficked place to do much of the work themselves – are learning fast. 'The gentleness and fair prices remain, and the cooking gets better and better. Tonight we had seafood Mornay, spiced mallard with fresh vegetables, damson cobbler with plenty of cream, and cheeses including superb fresh Cheshire.' Trout with mushrooms and Pernod, turbot provençale, roast lamb, pigeon, and 'marvellous cheesecake' are also mentioned. Chanson ordinaires are £4·65 a 'magnum' or 60p a glass; Touraine Gamay or Sauvignon under £3, and Savigny-les-Beaune '73 (Louis Latour) £5·90 on the Youdell list. There are lunchtime bar snacks with pressurised beers. No music. No smoking. No children under five. Dress 'tidily'. More reports, please.

The Guide News Supplement will be sent out as usual, in June, to everyone who buys the book directly from Consumers' Association and to all bookshop purchasers who return the card interleaved with their copy. Let us know of any changes that affect entries in the book, or of any new places you think should be looked at.

Everyman Bistro
Hope Street
051-708 0338

Closed Sun; Mon D; Sat L
No bookings
Meals 12–2, 6–11.30

Alc £2·70 (meal £3·85)

VAT inc
Seats 130 (parties 50)
No dogs

A co-operative quintet run this cheerful restaurant and cafe-bar, new to the Guide, opposite the Roman Catholic cathedral and underneath the theatre. The menu changes daily, with the food displayed on a long self-service counter. Hot dishes are microwaved to order, 'but at least they are intended for that treatment.' Expect soups, pâtés, dips (hummus or guacamole), quiches and pies ('always fresh and not doughy'), hot meaty and vegetarian dishes, salads and 'generous' sweets, whether fresh fruit salad in yoghourt or a home-made cake with cream. The cheeses rival the wines and include a good range of English and others. House wine is £1·90 (40p a glass); sangria is £2·30 a litre; other wines are over-described but not over-priced; Higson's bitter and mild are on hand-pump. No music. Smoky atmosphere, though 'we do not sell tobacco or matches.' More reports, please.

Lau's
358 Prescot Road
051-228 1103 *and* 6447

There is a Chinese tea called Buddha's ear: Buddha's armpit would be an apt description of the approach to this flavoury Pekinese place 'up a flight of stairs opposite the abattoir'. Mr Lau and his son exude an appropriately plump and saintly calm, furnishing banquets at modest prices. Note the cold hors d'oeuvre, grilled beef Peking-style, king prawn special (£1·80), chicken and cashew nuts, sweet-and-sour fish à la squirrel. Less praise for the sometimes oversweet spare ribs and 'almost chickenless' chicken and agar-agar. 'Pancake rolls hot, crispy duck lukewarm' reversed expectation. Pleasant service ('like a Jewish mother, our waiter muttered "enjoy", every time a new dish appeared'). Various wines; Chinese tea. No music.

Closed L; Sun; Dec 24,
25, 26 & 31
Must book
D only, 6–11

Tdh from £4·20
Alc meal about £4

Seats 180
No dogs

Oriel
Oriel Chambers,
Water Street
051-236 4664

Closed Sun; Sat L; most
public hols
Must book
Meals 12–2.15, 7–10.15

Tdh L £4·50 (meal £8·15),
D £6·90 (meal £10·55)
Alc (min L £4·50, D £7)
£10·80 (meal £14·45)

The mauve-to-geranium decor and the discreet entrance to this basement restaurant in an office block near Pierhead may seem to promise an exclusive bordello, an impression reinforced for one Christmas-time diner who found at his right ear, among other electrically driven furry toys, 'a macaw on its perch, gently rotating'. However, if one eats as well as this in bordellos, they should certainly be on the National Health. The chef has changed, and the service seems more excitable than it was, but there are few places in the north where both set and à la carte meals reach as high a standard as they do under Andrea Coticelli's management for R. I. Roberts's Groveland Inns (see also Beeston, Wild Boar). One member who dropped in for a set lunch

248

VAT & service inc
Cover 45p
Seats 100 (parties 40)
Air-conditioning
Access, Am Ex, Barclay,
Diners, Euro

after queueing at the passport office nearby had
'extraordinarily good pâté, wiener Schnitzel and
strawberry flan'; another, at a set dinner, had a
seafood pancake that wanted only more heat,
followed by ill-trimmed but tender noisettes
d'agneau au Brouilly 'in a rich, dark wine sauce
with mushrooms, little onions, and a heart-shaped
croûton'. There is then free access to the rich trolley
sweets (choux pastry ones seem the best). A la carte,
crab soup was well-balanced, in spite of being
brandied and ignited at the table, turbot (£4·95)
could be had with various well-differentiated sauces,
and tender boeuf Stroganoff was served with good
saffron rice. Sea-bass with fennel and Pernod is a
speciality (£5·10). 'Vegetables at a test meal were a
good antidote to the richness of the rest.' Normandy
butter and radishes on ice appear at the start or
with the fine Cheshire cheeses, and good petits fours
are served with the fragrant coffee. The cheapest
(VAT and service included) house wine is Lalignant
& Chameroy burgundy at £5·10, or, for the fish,
Pinot Blanc de Blancs (Hugel) at £5·80: one can
hardly counsel better bottles at these prices, but
Beaujolais Villages '76 (Drouhin) is £8 or so, and
Chx. Talbot or Margaux '71, £15 or so. 'Faint'
recorded music. Wear a jacket and tie. Remember
that the set meal may disappear round holiday
periods.

App: E. Parry, T.S., J.R.

**Peking and Shanghai
(Peter Gee)**
54 Berry Street
051-709 2555

Closed Apr 16 & 17;
May 7 & 28; Aug 27;
Dec 26–28
Must book D
Meals 12–2.15, 6–11.45

Tdh D £3
Alc (meal £3·50)

VAT inc
Service 10%
Seats 80 (parties 50)
No dogs

Though just down the hill from the Philharmonic
Hall, this restaurant in shabby-garish taste is the
gateway to Chinatown, where two errant visitors
describe a walk past 'the click of mah-jong pieces
and the spectacle of axe-wielding Chinese chefs
dismembering a carcase in a basement'. The walk
proved a good appetiser for one of Bui-Yuen Lock
and Yuet-Ming Yau's set meals. Menu B at £3
offers cold hors d'oeuvre and crispy duck as well as
hot-and-sour soup (which owes plenty to the lethal
chilli sauce on the tables), shredded beef with bean
shoots, and filled dumplings called siu mai.
Regulars, though, often eat from the *carte*, noting
gratefully that prices have not risen much lately, if
at all. Fried seaweed 'if the oil has been lately
changed', barbecued or spiced spare ribs, prawns in
chilli and tomato (£2·50), chicken with almonds,
toffee apples and, for lovers of that shy taste, the
sweet red bean pancake, are all worth trying.
Service is mostly good, and tea willingly refilled.
There are wines. Recorded Chinese music.
Customers seem to prefer the ground floor.

App: W. J. & R. Webster, H.D., F.S., and others

Old Farmhouse Hotel
on A436
1 m W of Stow
Stow-on-the-Wold 30232

The Gladstones' civilly served hotel is useful to know but its charms do not erase memories of an 'incompletely thawed' dinner early in 1978. Since then, others advise that the simpler cold and hot dishes and home-made bread served buffet-style in bar or garden at lunch are the best reason for a visit. At sit-down meals too the straightforward dishes may be better than the composed ones. Vegetables and, among sweets, the syrup tart are liked. Nicolas ordinaires are £2·76, and thereafter Gewürztraminer '71 or '75 at £4·25 are perhaps the best of a humdrum bunch. No music. No smoking at table.

Closed Sun D & Mon L (exc res); Dec 24 to mid-Jan
Must book D & Sun L
Meals 12.15–2, 7.30–9

Tdh L £4 (meal £5·25), D £6 (meal £7·25)

VAT & service inc
Children's helpings
Seats 25

Car park
No dogs
Access, Euro
5 rooms (1 with bath, 1 with shower)
B&B from £8·80
Fire cert

Penny Anthony
5 Church Street
Ludlow 3282

Closed Sun & Thur (Sun D & Thur L June–Oct); 1st 2 weeks May & Dec; Dec 26
Must book weekends
Meals 11–2, 7–10
(6.30–2 Festival)

Alc L £2·25 (meal £3·45), D (min summer £2·50) £4·55 (meal £6·70)

VAT inc
Children's helpings
Seats 30

It cannot be coincidence that Ludlow has a Penny Anthony while Shrewsbury has a Penny Farthing, but in this case the name really is the owner's. Apart from the ominous Shakespearean Festival dish titles – 'The taming of the stew' for sauté of lamb with aubergines; 'Half a Shylock' for 8 ozs of rump steak – both the decor and the cooking are free from affectation, and Mrs Anthony designs her menu so that anyone can obtain freshly cooked food, whether just a plateful with a glass of wine or a full dinner. The trained chef, Colin Hingston, is a local man who was first known to the place as a customer. Inspectors and others have admired his mushroom soup, pâté (75p), seafood pancake with a cheese and fennel sauce (£1·75 as a main course), lasagne, steak au poivre, and cream caramel. A test meal found the garlic bread heavy and not garlicky enough, and the salad (otherwise excellent) innocent of dressing. French ordinaires are £1·50 for 50 cl and there is normally a 'wine of the month', with two dozen others from £2·55. Service is well supervised. Recorded music. Physical expansion is under way, and 'since the owners do not themselves cook and Housman tells us that Shropshire lads and lasses are sometimes fickle', more reports, please.

LUDLOW see also pub section

LUSTLEIGH Devon   Map 1

Moorwood Cottage
on A382
2 m S of
Moretonhampstead
Lustleigh 341

Closed L; Sun; Dec 25
Must book
D only, 7–9.30

Alc £5·65 (meal £7·35)

Service inc
Seats 24 (parties 20)
 ⬥ rest (1 step)
Car park
No dogs

'With Michael Harris in the kitchen, "the unabridged Claudia Harris" (her own description) out front, and Tamburlaine in the lavatory, this comfortable place has a lot going for it,' writes one member. Doubts are voiced from time to time about individual dishes: 'Very good soles were rather drowned by too much shrimp-type sauce.' But the sorrel-flavoured soup, 'crisp and melting' seafood bonnes bouches, pork with cheese and peaches, seasonal offerings such as venison, salmon, and fennel, and sweet confections (chocolate and brandy mousse with the local cream, or a mixture of black cherries, raspberries and pineapple called after the Harrises' daughter) are all popular. Wines, from various sources, include Ch. Canon-la-Gaffelière '70 (£5·75) and sound Muscadet or moselle; Primanova ordinaires at £1·65. No music. No children under ten or so. Men are asked to button their shirts, and 'we would rather people did not smoke since it is smelly and anti-social.'

App: David Gladwell, John F. Pescott-Day, A. Crowther, B. W. Adams

LUTON Bedfordshire   Map 3

Acropolis Kebab House
33 West Side Centre
Luton 36724

An unexpected touch of Greece in a modern shopping centre. Beams and alcoves, slow but generally genial service, and occasional live bouzouki music wing you much-needed miles from Luton. Order accordingly: meze (twelve different dishes, £3·95), taramosalata, loukanika (spicy sausages, 85p), moussaka (£1·85), kleftiko (£2·20), afelia and various honey-soaked sweets. Salad and rice or potatoes are included. If you must eat English, steaks seem expensive when vegetables are extra, and the fruit salad may be mostly apple. Greek and Cypriot wines, from £2·95 the bottle.

Closed L; Sun; public hols
D only, 6–12

Alc £3·55 (meal £6·35)

Children's helpings
Seats 60
 ⬥ rest
Air-conditioning

Car park
No dogs
Access card

LYME REGIS Dorset   Map 2

Toni
14–15 Monmouth Street
Lyme Regis 2079

Peter Taylor and his Austrian wife run a cheerfully informal seasonal restaurant with an eclectic, Italianate menu. Members praise gamberetti pil-pil (prawns in garlic and wine sauce, £1·20), spaghetti alla carbonara, filetto alla norcese (steak in a truffle sauce, £4), scaloppine al Marsala (£2·80 –

251

prices include vegetables), and glazed oranges in
Cointreau. A confusing wine list hides some good
buys (Ch. la Croix-Millorit '71, £5·80); house wines
(French and Italian) £2·50 for 70 cl. Recorded
music; sometimes 'spur of the moment' dancing.

Closed L; Sun;	Alc £5·20 (meal £7·45)	Seats 28
Oct–Easter		No dogs
Must book	VAT inc	Access, Barclay, Diners
D only, 7–10.30	Children's helpings	

LYMINGTON Hampshire   Map 2

Limpets
9 Gosport Street
Lymington 75595

Closed L (exc Sun in
winter); Mon; Sun D
(Nov–Easter); Dec 25 &
26
Must book
Meals 12–2 (Sun in
winter), 6.30–10.30

Tdh Sun L from £3·50
(meal £6)
Alc £5·90 (meal £8·50)

VAT inc
Seats 40
♿ rest (2 steps)
No dogs

Hundreds, even thousands, of members must have
eaten and drunk well over the years in this and its
sister seaside restaurant in Christchurch (q.v.), not
to mention the inland branch in Winchester, so the
shortfall of reports comparing performances is a
disappointment. The notable wine cellar and the
stripped pine booths are the chief common features.
Here, Douglas Craig varies his menus adequately
according to supplies, but mistakes in cooking or
service have been too common for comfort this
year: even at a test meal arranged after a grumble
on these lines, a vegetable order was forgotten and
a frying medium was beginning to 'turn'. However,
both the soups – onion, tomato, cressonnière – and
emphatic-tasting crabe au gratin (£1·15) make good
first courses, baked sea trout with shallot butter
(£3·40) is the chef's favourite among fish dishes, and
sauté de porc with celery and walnuts (£3·20) also
speaks of a taste for 'forward' flavours. Boeuf
Stroganoff, when tried, overdid the emphasis.
Vegetables are carefully cooked, and sweets – but
here, 'assembled' might be a more accurate term –
suit the style. The girls who serve will probably not
be able to advise you between, say, Ch. Cantemerle
and Ch. Léoville-Lascases, both '67 and £7·50, or
between the four '72 red burgundies at £10·50, but
the house Gros Plant is a good buy at £2·95, and
generously served by the glass too. No music. No
young children after 8 p.m. No pipes at table.

App: M. E. Shepherd, C.P.D., Thomas Potts

LYTHAM ST ANNE'S Lancashire   Map 5

Lidun Cottage
5 Church Road
Lytham 736936

Closed Mon; Tue L;
Dec 25
Must book
Meals 12–2, 7.30–9.30

*For a place in Lytham – or Lidun, as Domesday called
it – where people can eat without winning a Premium
Bond first, this little bow-windowed place run by recent
university and catering college graduates has much to
be said for it, say Guide-followers of varying vintages.
In spite of the small capacity and price, Paul Caddy
does not double-book tables, and visitors have had time
to enjoy the fresh wholemeal bread, 'cream of onion soup
made with good stock', 'fresh and runny' pepper and*

Tdh Sun L from £3·50
(meal £5)
Alc L £2·45 (meal £4·55),
D £4·20 (meal £6·35)

VAT & service inc
Seats 28
 ⅃ rest
Barclaycard

tomato omelette (55p), stuffed mushrooms, 'delicious chicken with mint done somewhat in the Kiev style' (£2·70), and tender lambs' kidneys. The menu changes monthly, but apple pie and Lancashire cheese are surely constant. Wines include '76 Beaujolais at £3·30 and Muscadet at £2·75. Recorded music. Smaller helpings for children under ten. No dogs. More reports, please.

MAIDENHEAD Berkshire   Map 3

Chef Peking
74 King Street
Maidenhead 32591 *and*
32851

Closed Dec 25 & 26
Must book weekends
Meals 12–2.30, 6–11.30

Alc meal £3·80

Seats 80
No dogs
Access, Am Ex, Barclay,
Diners

Whatever may be the case in Peking itself, free-market competition between King Street and Queen Street has done wonders for Pekinese eating in Maidenhead, and since they keep pinching each other's chefs, and the situation is doubtless fluid, not to say hot and sour, comparative reports will be welcome. Members are anyway divided this year, but a return visitor to Mr Yi and Mr Ching here reports on different occasions 'generous' crispy seaweed with almonds, and sesame prawn toasts with 'not too much toast'. Fish in lemon and egg was 'very delicate – eat it on its own', chicken with almonds and crispy deep-fried beef tasty but on the sweet side, prawns with green peppers 'big, juicy and tender', and stewed seasonal vegetables 'succulent and flavoursome on both occasions'. End with toffee apples or fresh fruit salad. Sometimes they produce Cantonese crab in black bean sauce 'to perfection', and as well as Peking duck to order at £8·50 they have ideas of their own: 'fried three with spring onion offers pork, beef and prawns cleverly combined.' Service is 'anxious to please'. Wines from £3·25 (stiff for a Chinese place). No music.

Maidenhead Chinese Restaurant
45–47 Queen Street
Maidenhead 24545

Closed Dec 25 & 26
Must book D
Meals 12–2.30, 6–11.30

Tdh from £3·80
Alc meal £4·65

Service 12½%
Seats 80
 ⅃ rest (1 step); w.c.
Air-conditioning
Am Ex, Diners

There is nothing wrong with Mr Keung's restaurant that a touch of competition (now supplied, see above) cannot cure, for Mr Ng the noodle-knitter is still in the kitchen, and members remain more than content with his typically Pekinese set or à la carte meals, including crispy seaweed, sesame prawn toasts, chicken in yellow-bean paste, prawns or shredded beef in chilli sauce, lamb with leeks, shredded pork with Szechuan pickles and, of course, 'crunchily delicious' deep-fried duck with pancakes. 'Seasonal vegetables in oyster sauce were also very good and not flabby.' However, the hot-and-sour soup, the service, and quantity for the money, have lately shown signs of unwelcome westernisation, so please assess critically. There are wines, and recorded music. No dogs.

App: Jane Diwell, V. & P. Tseng, Mr & Mrs F. Williams

253

Michel et Valérie
Bridge Avenue
Maidenhead 22450

The Hédouins' restaurant français ('very Maidenhead, very popular') pleases locals with filet au poivre, côte de veau and garlicky snails. Inspectors liked the hors d'oeuvre (£1·60), crêpe de volaille, the duck (£3·05) – but not its jam-like sauce – and the spinach, but at these prices deplored signs of penny-pinching and patchiness elsewhere: 'The Stilton might have been painted by Francis Bacon, and coffee was weak.' Competent service. French regional wines (£4) and others, in pretentious goblets. Recorded music sometimes. No dogs. A couple of tables on the terrace.

Closed Sun; last 3 weeks Aug; public hols Must book D Meals 12–2.15, 7–10.15	Alc (min £3) £6·35 (meal £10·30) Service 10%	Cover 25p Seats 53 Access, Am Ex, Barclay, Diners

La Riva
2 Raymead Road
Maidenhead 33522

An elegant and relaxing setting, overlooking floodlit Maidenhead Bridge. Franco Trapani takes his corners rather close, some think, for cheeses and avocados may be past their best and 'coffee is not as good as it used to be.' But for substantial main courses of carefully cooked veal or liver (at about £2·30 each), you could go further and fare worse. Vegetables may assort oddly with the rich sauces (cauliflower béchamel and ratatouille were a recent pair). Chocolate eclairs and oranges in liqueur are popular sweets. Frascati costs £3·20. Recorded music. No dogs. More reports, please.

Closed Sun Must book Meals 12.30–2.30, 7.30–10.30	Alc (min £3·50) £5·65 (meal £8·75) VAT inc Service 10% Cover 35p	Seats 40 ⅙ rest (3 steps) Car park Access, Am Ex, Barclay, Diners, Euro

Cottage in the Wood
Holywell Road
off A449
2 m S of Malvern Wells
Malvern 3487

Must book
Meals 12.30–2, 7 & 8.30

Tdh L £5·50 (meal £6·50),
D (res only) £6·25
(meal £7·25)
Alc £7·10 (meal £9·25)

A minor catering mystery of the 1970s is why Michael Ross's modernised, but not spacious, dower house on a wooded scarp still wavers. (It slipped out of the *Guide* altogether while he was also occupied at Corse Lawn, now in other hands.) Keith Maby cooks, and inventive dishes have been served, both on the set meals and à la carte: leek and potato soup, avocado with walnuts and curry mayonnaise, fresh brill 'perfectly matched to its sauce of tomato, mushrooms and red peppers', mousse of pike with dill and sour cream, breast of chicken with liver stuffing and a touch of Pernod, almond bombe, and others. But unluckier visitors – sometimes the same ones – report besides not only actual failures such as 'overcooked roast lamb cut

VAT & service inc
Cover 50p Sat D
Children's helpings
Seats 30
 ♿ rest
Air-conditioning
Car park
No dogs
Access, Am Ex, Barclay,
Diners
20 rooms (17 with bath)
B&B from £14
Fire cert

too long in advance', 'disappointing mallard', and 'heavy' puddings, but also an insipidity that may be ascribed to Mr Ross's 'Taste of England' enthusiasms: 'Carrot soup evoked baby food, fish pie had delicious pastry and a smooth sauce that wanted only salt and lemon juice, guinea-fowl with madeira sauce tasted like chicken in English gravy, and the salad dressing was sweet. At least the cheeses were excellent.' Garlic bread is also an exception to the blandness rule. Two evening sittings bear hard on the service, which may remind you that the Malverns are noted for girls' boarding schools. The wines are seriously chosen and often good value, from Loire or Chenin Gamay at £3·30 to Ch. Canon-la-Gaffelière '67 or a couple of '71 Erbachers at £9 or so. Local English wines are also stocked, and 'we have just planted 80 vines,' Mr Ross threatens. There are bar or terrace snacks with Litre Vin wines by the glass or pressurised beers. No music. As a hotel, the place is very comfortable, with praise for the bedroom breakfasts.

App: S. E. & M. S. A. Fishburn, V. H. Vanstone, C. J. Richardson, Geoffrey Stone, Frank Cummins

---

Croque-en-Bouche
221 Wells Road
on A449
2 m S of Malvern
Malvern 65612

Closed L (exc Sun); Mon;
Tue; Sun D; Dec 26;
Jan 1
Must book
Meals 1–2 (Sun),
7.45–9.15

Tdh Sun L £4·10 (meal
£6·85), D £6·80 (meal
£10)

Children's helpings
Seats 22 (parties 12)
♿ rest
Air-conditioning
Car park
No dogs
Access, Am Ex, Barclay,
Diners, Euro

Most people from the Lavender Hill district of London might find it hard to settle in the twinset and knickerbocker ambience of the Malverns, but Robin and Marion Jones's hunch that they were badly needed here has been endorsed by local residents, who have fallen eagerly on this converted house opposite a filling station. The owners find it difficult to obtain good fish and even good vegetables (what is the Vale of Evesham coming to?), but in fact there are warm accounts of their 'very marseillaise' fish soup, hors d'oeuvre, and salmon mayonnaise; and lotte à l'américaine appeared on a recent Sunday lunch menu. The five-course dinner begins with soup and ends with a platter of cheeses ('many seldom seen in the Midlands, including four goat ones'), and a choice of puddings. In between there are usually four choices of both entree and main course. Mrs Jones's own favourites include her crêpe filled with langoustines, avocado and mushrooms, and her guinea-fowl 'truffée' à l'estragon (the new home by the Severn valley includes a herb garden). For a sweet, try pear sorbet or chocolate almond cake. Sometimes there are choiceless set regional dinners with wines included. As at their London restaurant, the wine list emphasises the Loire, and the run of Vouvrays begins with a '47 moelleux at £14·80. The house Azay-le-Rideau whites are about £4, Saumur or Côtes du Forez red just under. Half-bottles, brandies, and eaux-de-vie are not forgotten; poire de Touraine is 80p a glass. Cigarettes are not sold. No music. More reports, please.

MAMHEAD Devon   Map 1

Old Stable
off B3381
3 m NW of Dawlish
Mamhead 276

Turn south at the top of Telegraph Hill to find this stable conversion (with self-catering flats) on the Ashcombe road. In both bar and restaurant ('every table has its own stall') the Hatchers' food is simple and local 'and long may it stay that way.' Demand may have compelled some advance roasting for Sunday lunch, but hearty soups, good vegetables, vegetarian dishes, and junket, summer pudding and others with Devonshire cream give pleasure, and there is rough cider from the wood.

Closed D Mon & Sun
(Oct–Easter); Dec 27,
28 & 29
Must book
Meals 12–2, 6.30–9.30

Tdh Sun L from £3·50
(meal £5·85)
Alc £5 (meal £7·50)

VAT inc

Children's helpings
Seats 50
Car park
No dogs in d/r

MANCHESTER   Map 5

**(1) Hotel Armenia
Shish Kebab House**
125 Palatine Road,
Didsbury
061-434 1122

Closed Sun; Sat L;
Apr 13 & 16; Dec 25 &
26; Jan 1
Must book weekends
Meals 12–2.30, 7.30–10.45

Alc £4·10 (meal £7·25)

Service 10%
Children's helpings
Seats 70 & 50 (parties 50)
Air-conditioning
Car park
No dogs
23 rooms (5 with bath,
18 with shower)
B&B from £13·75

By the volatile standards of Armenians, George Mardirossian and his still-obtrusive cigar have become comparative fixtures in south Manchester. The same cannot quite be said for his prices, at which one local businessman of substance expected less dilatory service and better cooked Tale of Three Cities kebabs. But the soups and first courses, including hummus, falafel, tabbouleh, and lahma-bi-ajeen ('a very crisp thin pancake with a spicy meat filling, eaten with the fingers', 50p) are all good. So are most of the family kitchen's ways with aubergines, stuffed with rice and walnuts, or fried and served on a bed of yoghourt, or interspersed with lamb chunks in Kars kebab (£2·35). Angel-hair pilaf is as good as ever, and the well-known letzvarz varyag (£6·30 for two to prior order) is roast chicken that needs and gets no adornment but its crisp skin, pan juices, and a stuffing made from pine nuts and its own liver. Aryan, a yoghourt concoction somewhere between a drink and a pudding, may suit if you feel unequal to very sweet kataif or to tavuk geoski (95p) whose ingredients are worth enquiry. Hungarian Riesling is £2·95; Lebanese red £3·80. Middle-Eastern recorded music. Feel free to speak Arabic and Hebrew, Greek and Turkish in the restaurant, but not concurrently, perhaps. The hotel offers civilised comfort to those who tire of concrete palaces.

App: A. T. Roberts, S. C. Coverley, O.J.P.

'Meal' indicates the cost of a meal for one, including food, coffee, half the cheapest bottle of wine, cover, service, and VAT (see 'How to use the Guide', p. 4).

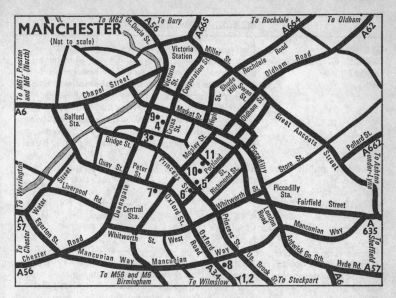

MANCHESTER
(Not to scale)

(2) Casa España
100 Wilmslow Road,
Rusholme
061-224 6826

Closed Sun; public hols
Must book weekends
Meals 12–2.30, 6.30–10.45

Tdh L £1·75 (meal £3·75)

Alc £4·65 (meal £7·20)

Service 10%
Children's helpings
Seats 48
No dogs

Galdeano and Puro's long-loved Spanish basement
has 'kept itself up to the mark', says one
informant, 'even after 14 years in the same hands'
(12 of them in the *Guide*). Unbooked diners are
turned away nightly. Perhaps the lunch menu
should vary more, and flavours are less emphatic
than they would be in Spain. But meatballs are
freshly made, tortillas tasty, mejillones (mussels) a
la marinera spicy enough, and zarzuela (mixed fish
with olives in tomato sauce, £2·65) an ample and
varied plateful. Juan Lopez in the kitchen also
recommends his pato Cazadora (duck cooked with
vegetables, £2·50) and, naturally, paella (for at least
two). A hyped-up version of flan (cream caramel) or
fresh pineapple with anisette may or may not appeal
as sweets, and it would be nice to see dulce de
membrillo too. Sangria is £2·75 a jug for a hot day,
but the Rioja estate bottlings are not to be ignored
(Paternina Viña Vial red £3·20 in 1978). Look at the
special offers too: 'We had a rich but dry white
Montecillo at £2·95.' 'Fuzzy-sounding' Spanish
music on tape – 'they might at least clean the head.'

*App: S. C. Coverley, Ronald Schwarz, Brid & Tony
Weeks, H.R., and others*

Towns shown in black on our maps contain at least one recommended
restaurant or pub (see map key). The dot denotes the location of the
town or village, not the restaurant. Where necessary, we give
directions to the restaurant in the entry. If you can, help us to
improve them.

(3) Cesare
14 South King Street
061-832 7669

Cheerful, smart, white-walled ristorante off Deansgate. Pasta, scampi and veal dishes have given pleasure; vegetables are well cooked and trolley sweets above average, but standards as a whole are variable and prices on the high side. House Valpolicella or Soave is £2·70 for 72 cl, 50p the glass; other Italian wines are around £4 the bottle. Recorded Italian music. Reports, please, on their new pizza place, the Venezia in Mount Street.

Closed Sun; public hols (exc Dec 25)
Must book weekends
Meals 12–2.30, 6–11.30 (12 Sat)

Tdh L from £2·20 (meal £4·55)
Alc £6·15 (meal £9·30)

VAT inc
Children's helpings (under 12)

Seats 100 (parties 30)
 rest (1 step)
No dogs
Access, Am Ex, Barclay, Diners, Euro

(4) Danish Food Centre
Royal Exchange Buildings,
Cross Street
061-832 9924

Unchanging and popular formula: self-service restaurant (the Danmark Inn) open 9 a.m.–11.15 p.m. for open sandwiches (40p–£1·25) and pastries; in the Copenhagen Room, a choice between the short *carte* of simple dishes (smoked pork loin with potatoes, £2·95) or the help-yourself cold table, with waitress-served soup. 'The best choice of seafood in the north-west' is one verdict, depressing if true. Meats and cheeses are more limited now. The Theatre Platter (served 6–7.30 and 10.30–11.15) provides a small selection of cold dishes (including gravadlax) for £2·75. Drink akvavit, lager or Charbonnier at £1·75 for 50 cl. Music is sometimes live. No dogs.

Closed Sun; public hols
Must book (Copenhagen Room)
Meals 12–2.15, 6–11.15 (Copenhagen)

Tdh cold table L £4·75 (meal £6), D £5·75 (meal £7)
Alc (Copenhagen) £6·65 (meal £7·90)

VAT & service inc
Children's helpings
Seats 200 (parties 80)
Air-conditioning
Access, Am Ex, Barclay

(5) Kai's
16 Nicholas Street
061-236 2041

Open noon–2 a.m.

Tdh L 95p, D from £3
Alc meal £3·70

VAT inc
Service 10%
Seats 90
Air-conditioning
No dogs
Am Ex, Diners

'An authentic Cantonese restaurant of the old down-market kind,' says an inspector who has found the faintly anglicised set lunch unreliable, but evening crumbed-and-fried prawn cutlets (£2·40 with various dips), spare ribs with plum sauce, 'fatty but delicious' brisket chow mein, wun-tun soup with greens, and duck with crispy pork, fit for the numerous Chinese customers. The menu and Kai Lee's culinary experience are both long, so note his specialities: steamed fish (from £3), crispy chicken Cantonese-style (£5 for a whole one), and casserole dishes, including tripe, fish lips, ducks' webs, chicken blood, and other delectables that sound more intimidating than they are. Wines from £3. Recorded music. More reports, please.

(6) Kwok Man
34 Princess Street
061-228 2620 *and*
236 9298

Closed Jan 1
Must book
Meals noon–4.45 a.m.

Tdh L £1·15
Alc meal £4·45

VAT inc
Service 10%
Seats 200 (parties 40)
Air-conditioning
Am Ex, Diners

Everything that sanitary engineers and other contractors can do has been done to help the migrated Kwok Man live down some aspects of its past: now all that Tony Lai and his manager Albert Tung need do is cook, and control the waiters. Early trials of the set lunches and, at dinner, such dishes as crab claws stuffed with prawn meat and Hong Kong roast duck (hot or cold) have been satisfactory, dim-sum snacks (till 2 a.m.), spring roll, prawn and fresh fruit salad, and other appetisers are suggested, and steamed fish Hong Kong style is another speciality. Pedrotti carafes are £3·50; tea 'does not seem to arrive automatically'. Recorded music. No dogs. It is no doubt a sign of the times that they supply Cantonese buffets in the small hours to two Manchester casinos. More reports, please, on all these developments.

**(7) Midland Hotel
French Restaurant**

Peter Street
061-236 3333

Closed Sun; Sat L; Aug;
Dec 31; public hols
Meals 12.30–2.30, 7–11

Alc £9·05 (meal £11·75)

VAT & service inc
Seats 70
Air-conditioning
No dogs in public rooms
Access, Am Ex, Barclay,
Diners, Euro
304 rooms (244 with
bath, 2 with shower)
B&B £17·50
Fire cert

A regular customer who understands food often receives a very different impression of a restaurant from the one a casual visitor forms, especially in a grand and traditional place like this, whose senior staff have 'stood' for years, ministering benignly to Manchester celebrations both polite and vulgar. On the whole, though, the day-to-day variations noted this year by one individual, in a rough proportion of four successes to one failure, correspond closely enough with both the virtues and flaws of a test meal and other people's isolated experiences. Gilbert Lefèvre is a skilled French chef; head waiter and wine waiter are communicative and worth hearing; the service is decorous, even ritualistic. But since you are paying a vast sum anyway, choose dishes that M Lefèvre is unlikely to depute: soupe du Var (£1·55), for instance, possibly crêpes morvandelle au jambon (£2·50) and oeufs en cocotte Mirabeau, then grouse in season (pink by request) or caneton bigarade (if you can catch it as it leaves the kitchen at the start of a sitting) or médaillon de veau berlinoise (£5·35) – 'a great success, excellent veal, pink in the middle, an admirable madeira sauce, and a lightly cooked chicken liver perched on a buttery half-apple.' Salad may be better than vegetables, though it often comes with a vinegary dressing. Lapses of taste or judgement occur ('turbotin spoilt by thin white wine sauce and peppery lobster sauce') and are multiplied at the sweet stage ('they have an incomprehensible affection for cheap jam and other substitutes'). Again, it is best to order a soufflé, which gets an expert hand. The wines, likewise, are expertly handled in the BTH cellars, and prices are modest here by current grand hotel standards: note the '76 Beaujolais and '73 clarets at about £5, or the Rhônes and '71 hocks and Ch. Fombrauge '70 at £1 or so more. And if you feel giddy after drinking or merely sniffing the 30-year-old BTH cognac, blame the new carpet, which affects teetotallers the same way. Wear a tie. Expect a pianist. 'Infants under the age of 12' stay at home.

App: A.V., J.R. & G.A.B., F. J. Noble, O.J.P., and others

MANCHESTER   Map 5

---

(8) **On the Eighth Day**
111 Oxford Road,
All Saints
061-273 4878

A vegetarian co-operative 'run by enthusiasts with missionary zeal'. 'If you object to squashing up on benches with strangers, don't go.' They aim to provide soup, a hot main dish and a sweet, as well as salads, wholemeal bread, fruit juices and various teas. Always a Vegan dish; half-portions for the young and the elderly on request. Hearty soup stocks and very fresh ingredients convert carnivores, at least temporarily. Recorded music, 'rock to classics'. No smoking. Unlicensed.

Closed D; Sun; public hols; 1 week Chr	Alc meal about £1·45	Children's helpings
		Seats 32
L only, 12–3.30	VAT & service inc	♿ rest (1 step)
		Unlicensed

---

(9) **Royal Exchange Restaurant**
The Royal Exchange
St Anne's Square
061-833 9682

Closed Sun; Sat L;
Aug 27 D; Dec 25
Must book
Meals 12–2, 6–11

Alc L £3·05 (meal £4·90),
D £5·95 (meal £8·35)

VAT inc
Service 10%
Children's helpings
Seats 69
Air-conditioning
Access, Barclay

It is hard for a theatre restaurant to excel, because customers are apt to insist on seeing the play. So it is all go before and after, and doldrums in between. But do not miss the total *mise en scène* of this theatre suspended in King Cotton's marble halls. In the kitchen, Roy Pegram seems to have settled down for a long run. Lunches have been simplified but also delegated: 'go at night' is the message from admirers of sensibly composed hors d'oeuvre (80p), 'particularly good' warm onion and cream tart, crab mousse with Escoffier sauce (walnuts, that is), and main dishes ranging from tagine (Moroccan lamb stew) to Lancashire hot-pot (£2·30). The critics' circle is divided about chicken Tremalki, as one would expect of a sauce combining garlic and sweet red plums, but jugged hare or blanquette de veau with Royal Exchange potatoes may also appear, and there is raspberry vacherin if you are daunted by Russian paskha (cheesecake with crystallised fruits). Early in 1978, there were a few grumbles of niggardly meat helpings. The Ch. Lescadre '70 one member admires seems to be exhausted now, and the Gilbey list is printed without vintages, so better not stray far from the house Gaillac or Muscadet at £2·50. The recorded music is a mild irritant.

App: J. D. Mitchell, Michael Hicks, J. R. Norman, A. P. B. Harston, and others

(10) Woo Sang
19–21 George Street
061-236 3697

Closed Dec 25 & 26
Must book
Open noon–11.30

Tdh L £1·10
Alc meal £4·20

VAT inc
Seats 160 (parties 80)
Air-conditioning
No dogs
Access, Am Ex, Barclay,
Diners, Euro

Although Manchester's bourgeoisie long since penetrated beyond the lacquered ducks and plastic fruit at the top of the stairs here to where they are fed so well for so little, they do not seem to have diluted the tastes or edged out the Cantonese family parties. Yik Yen Tsim and Kwai Wah Chan cook. At lunch or early in the evening, try their dim-sum (steamed snacks), notably the siu mai dumplings (kon jin based on prawn meat, bat col on pork, with a black beret of a Chinese mushroom). After that, experienced visitors with pronounced tastes and robust stomachs commend the baked spare ribs with salted pepper ('pig, butcher, and chef are all to be congratulated'), roasted pork with rice (£1·40), stewed beef brisket with vegetables and rice (£1·40 – 'superb if you like fat'), fresh fried squid with seasonal vegetables, baked king prawn with chilli and salt (£2·30), and soups, both Peking sour and duck with pickled vegetable. Oysters and crabs are other temptations. Fried sliced beef with chilli and black bean sauce (£1·50) was 'exemplary, cooked just beyond the point of redness'; Hong Kong roast duck (£2·80 for a half, best ordered by a party of more than two so that other dishes can also be contemplated) was 'the best Chinese duck dish I remember, redolent of star anise, soy and probably honey.' (Heaven knows what would be said about the special-order 'duck with skin peeled, £18'). Gluttons have also enjoyed the Chinese pastries afterwards. The service is courteous and efficient, even on the rare occasions when a dish has to be returned, and the air-conditioning can even cope with 'a party of cigar-smoking executives who gave living expression to Hume's *Critique of Natural Religion.*' Recorded music.

App: Yvonne Williams, J.F.N., Michael Mowbray Silver, John McClenahan, and others

---

(11) Yang Sing
17 George Street
061-236 2200

Must book
Meals noon–11.45 p.m.

Tdh £1
Alc meal £3·55

VAT inc
Service 10%
Seats 70

The old slogan about Avis and Hertz may already be applying to the Cantonese neighbours in George Street, and this is the one that has to try harder. Consumers reap the benefit in the two places: it would be literally possible to eat a Chinese dish every night of the year and never the same one twice. The staff here are helpful – 'they asked me at what stage in the meal I wanted the dim-sum to arrive and got it right.' Inspectors who have tried both places find them mostly comparable, and have so far been pleased by 'a Caen-like variety' of ox tripe with noodles in soup (£1), 'intriguing, meat-loaf-like' steamed pork pie with dried squid (£1·40), mixed spiced roasted meat with rice, roast duck congee, brisket chow mein, and the dim-sum, including crab meat-balls, stuffed Chinese mushrooms, beef-balls, and fried wun-tun – 'the prawns had a clear fishy flavour.' A diner who

261

Air-conditioning
No dogs
Am Ex, Barclay

ordered crispy belly pork with rice was warned that it was very fatty – 'as in the Monty Python sketch about the runny Camembert: "It's runnier than you'd like, sir." ' The sweetmeats too are worth trying: sesame bun, peanut shortbread, and melon cake. Wines from £2·90. Moderate tea. Recorded music. More reports, please.

MANCHESTER see also pub and wine bar sections

MANCHESTER see also **HEALD GREEN**

MARLBOROUGH Wiltshire   Map 2

Pharoah and Clarke's
4 The Parade
Marlborough 52139

Closed Sun D; D Apr 13;
D Dec 25; Dec 26
Must book L & weekends
Meals 12.30–2 (bookings
only), 7.30–10.30

Tdh L £3 (meal £5·20),
D £5·40 (meal £6·10)

VAT inc D
Service 10%
Seats 77 (parties 50)
⑤ rest (1 step); w.c.
Access, Barclay

Marlborough is a popular eating-place, and from a side street, Trevor Pharoah (who cooks) and Roger Clarke, both experienced young caterers, have to compete through quality rather than flamboyance. They seem to be succeeding, but the results are still uneven: even a good-value test lunch that included 'outstanding' baked eggs florentine and spicy pork with aubergines fell back a little when it came to the sweets, and others have variously reported 'wholesome but unspectacular Vienna steak,' 'delicious bread', and 'overcooked and tasteless sole catalane'. Try the specialities (zrazy Nelson, marinated lamb steak and, in season, fresh scallops gratinée). They make their own ice-creams, and recommend black-bottom pie or butterscotch gateau too; a black fruit fool also pleased an inspector. Tricolor ordinaires are £1·85 for 50 cl, alarming cocktails are popular, and there are a few other wines. Recorded music. Smaller helpings for under-tens. No dogs. More reports, please.

MARSTON TRUSSELL Northamptonshire   Map 5

Sun Inn
off A427
3 m SW of Market
Harborough
Market Harborough
65531

The Farmers and their 'family of families', who live on the spot and run this modernised inn, keep their rooms 'immaculately' and try to be all things to all men, from local businessmen to overnight families. But the long à la carte menu has yielded tasteless steaks and mediocre sauces or sweets as well as substantial helpings of shellfish, meat, syllabub, and so on. Try also roast quail, or sauté of chicken archduke (£2·55). Breakfasts are good. The wine list, from £2·75 for French ordinaire, lacks vintages. No music.

Closed Dec 25 & 26
Must book D & weekends
Meals 12.45–1.45, 7–9.30

Tdh Sun L £2·95 (meal
£4·35)
Alc £5·60 (meal £7·25)

VAT & service inc
Children's helpings
(under 8)
Seats 40 (parties 12)
⑤ rest (1 step); w.c.
Car park

No dogs
Am Ex, Diners
10 rooms (all with bath)
B&B £8
Fire cert

262

MATLOCK BATH Derbyshire   Map 5

Hodgkinsons
150 South Parade
Matlock 2113

'A Victorian parlour tinged with bistro' sits oddly in this lead mines extension (which you may now explore in 'caving gear' borrowed from the owners). Tables are small and seats hard, but the food atones, it seems: onion soup, prawns or mushrooms in garlic, roast sucking pig (£3·95) served with herb jelly in an apple, beef and mussel pie, tarragon chicken (£3·65, including vegetables). Fresh fruit or treacle pudding sound the best of the sweets. Italian house wine is £3·40 the litre; Marston's Pedigree ale from the cask. Recorded classical music.

Closed L (exc Sun); Mon; Dec 25 & 26; Jan 1
Must book
Meals 12.30–2 (Sun), 7–10

Alc £5·80 (meal £8·60)

VAT inc
Children's helpings
Seats 34 (parties 20)

♿ rest
No dogs
Access, Am Ex, Barclay, Diners

MELBOURN Cambridgeshire   Map 3

Pink Geranium
on A10
11 m S of Cambridge
Royston 60215

Ellen Shepperson's 15th year in this 'pretty', 'cosy', or even 'twee' cottage finds her 'still battling on', and experience tells: 'It is one of the few places I would care to order prawn cocktail, and roast duck' (with orange curaçao sauce £2·95). Salmon mousse in season, soles plain or fancy, and often-interesting vegetables are also in her chef David Rogers' repertoire. Cheeses are well kept; sweets seasonal. Wines start at £2·50 and include some finer clarets.

Closed L; Sun; Mon; last 2 weeks Aug; public hols
Must book

D only, 7–9.30

Alc £5·45 (meal £8·25)

Seats 32 (parties 18)
Car park
No dogs

MENTMORE Buckinghamshire   Map 3

Stag Inn
off B488
4 m S of Leighton
Cheddington 668423

Heaven knows what the goings on at the Towers – antique-dealers out, meditators in – will do for the Stag, a Victorian pub once part of the estate. But at a test meal, everything looked spruce enough, and though quiche was 'doped with dried herbs', boeuf Stroganoff a country version, and chocolate cake on the dry side, tournedos Rossini (£4·60) was unexpectedly good, and cheesecake capably made. Quite good wines (£3·95 for Gigondas), but vintages are missing. Long à la carte menu; bar snacks too.

Closed Mon; Dec 25 D
Must book
Meals 12.30–2.15, 7.30–10

Tdh L £2·50 (meal £5·20)

Alc £5·70 (meal £9)

Service 10%
Children's helpings
Seats 45 (parties 30)

♿ rest
Car park
No dogs in d/r
Access, Am Ex, Barclay, Diners, Euro

Mr Bistro
East Quay
Mevagissey 2432

People like this plain, harbourside place (once a pilchard store) for its natural air, reasonable lunch prices, and the zest of the owners (an old Cornish family). Fish lovers approve the local squid, mackerel, sole and crab. Cornish or 'old English' dishes appear often in the evenings. Children's lunch menu. Locally supplied wines. Litres of Bacchante £3, 45p the glass. Friendly service. No music.

Closed Nov–Feb (exc weekends); Jan 1
Must book D
Meals 12–2, 7–10

Alc L £2·20 (meal £4·35), D £5·15 (meal £7·65)

VAT inc

Children's helpings
Seats 30
♿ rest (1 step)
No dogs
Access, Am Ex, Barclay

Millers House
Market Place
Leyburn 2630

Must book D
Meals 12–1.30,
HT 3.30–5.30, 7–10

Tdh L £2·10 (meal £3·55),
D (7 p.m.) £4·40
(meal £5·85)
Alc (from 8.15 p.m.)
£5·60 (meal £7·05)

VAT & service inc
Children's helpings
Seats 24
♿ rest (1 step); w.c.
Car park
No dogs
Access, Am Ex, Barclay,
Diners
7 rooms (3 with bath)
B&B £6·50–£8·25
Fire cert

If you want to fish, walk the moors or listen for the sound of thoroughbreds clip-clopping through a Dick Francis novel, this Georgian house is a place worth knowing. The cooking, though, is not yet as reliable or consistent as you might expect from Michael Rawcliffe's catering college background, and it may be wise to settle for the straightforward English set meal at 7 rather than the French à la carte menu that begins at 8.15. Besides, the setting seems a little stark to some, and though in distant times young ladies were 'finished' in this house, suavity is at a premium: 'Hosts and staff should heed their own fire safety notice – "Shouting and running tend to create panic."' All the same, there are sufficient good reports of the bar lunches (Monday to Saturday), roast joints, fruit pies and crumbles to justify an entry, and the French or gourmet evenings (less frequent in winter) attract more cautious support for oeufs sur le plat forestière, escalope de veau, and individual chocolate and rum gateau. Other puddings are often fruit-based, such as the 'pears in amber sauce' one visitor loves. But at the price charged, warm sherry, cold plates, 'deep-freeze' Wensleydale, and other misjudged details should not occur. Spanish Santa Marta ordinaires from a firm in Pateley Bridge are £2·90. Ch. Meyney is £6·50, but since no vintage is listed, it could be either a bargain or not. Pressurised beers. No music. No children under eight after eight. No cigars at table.

App: Arthur Guest, M.C., H. K. Heseltine, James Knight, R. Sykes, Philip Britton

See p. 440 for the pub section, and p. 505 for the wine bars.

MIDDLE WALLOP Hampshire   Map 2

Fifehead Manor
on A343
7 m SW of Andover
Wallop 565

Closed Sun D; Dec 26;
Jan 1
Must book D & weekends
Meals 12–2, 7.30–9.30

Alc £5·50 (meal £8·10)

VAT inc
Children's helpings
Seats 36 (parties 15)
⟨⟩ rest (1 step)
Car park
No dogs in public rooms
Access, Am Ex, Barclay,
Diners, Euro
12 rooms (7 with bath,
5 with shower)
B&B £10
D, B&B £14
Fire cert

A peaceful country hotel run by women too tactful to criticise each other vigorously may lack a certain edge to its performance, and there are occasional notes of a dull pâté, under-trimmed sweetbreads, or desultory service. But Mrs Leigh Taylor has a genuine desire to please ('We were given a table in her private drawing-room because the restaurant was prepared for a reception') and her cooking of baked mushrooms in a nutmeggy onion cream sauce (£1·10), trout Père Louis (£3·30), veal scaloppine, and stuffed breast of chicken confirms last year's tentative entry. Besides, steaks are tender, vegetables carefully done, and the coffee meringue or butterscotch fudge that follows 'quite an experience'. The hotel is comfortable, and 'well-chosen antiques' adorn the dining-room: perhaps the 'tacky art-work' another member reports was only temporary. The choice and service of wine still leaves something to be desired, and vintages have not been notified. Monte Campo ordinaires are £2·60 a litre (£1·30 for 50 cl) and Ch. de Pez, c.b., £5·80, if you wish to hope for the best. There are various pressurised beers, and bar lunches include soup, smoked mackerel, salads and coffee. No music.

App: Stanley John, A. N. Black, Joseph Gazdak, Timothy Frost, J.P., and others

MIDDLEWICH Cheshire   Map 5

Franco's
51 Wheelock Street
Middlewich 3204

You need a copper lining for this friendly little Italian place, whether you arrive by road or canal, since prices are high and flavours can be 'overpowering'. Those who can take it report pleasure in spaghetti bolognese, bistecca pepata (£4·40, vegetables included), veal alla Franco (stuffed with cheese and ham and served in a good demi-glace with mushrooms, £3·60), garlicky (sometimes stringy) beans and 'as good a zabaglione as we've had', luckily, as the sweets are very limited. Mainly Italian wines (Chianti Brolio, £4·50); no house wines. Light recorded music.

Closed L; Sun; Mon;
Dec 25
Must book
D only, 7–9.45

Alc £6·40 (meal £8·85)

VAT inc
Service 10%

Cover 5p
Children's helpings
Seats 40
⟨⟩ rest (1 step)
No dogs

Bed and breakfast prices have been quoted to us by hoteliers; where possible, we have given minimum off-season and maximum in-season prices for one person sharing a double room.

Milton Ernest Hall
on A6
4 m N of Bedford
Oakley 4111

Closed Mon; Sun D;
10 days Aug; Dec 25 &
26; L Dec 31; 1st 2
weeks Jan
Must book
Meals 12.30–1.30, 8–9.30
(Sat 10)

Alc (min D £5) £6·40
(meal £9·75)

Service 10%
Seats 50 (parties 30)
&. rest (1 step)
Car park
No dogs in public rooms
Access card
6 rooms (5 with bath)
B&B £15
Fire cert

It was important to be earnest in the days when William Butterfield, fresh from his triumphs in the chapels of Rugby and Keble, designed his first and last country house between the upper Ouse and the Grand Union Canal. But the Harmar-Browns, a faintly gothic couple from the advertising world, have survived here and kept their chef (Robert Andrews) for seven years, so this year's inspector felt apologetic for minding the hall's heroic scale and 'clanging silences'. As a hotel, the house is comfortable and humane, if casually managed and served. In the dining-room, most first courses are cold (apart from soup), and prawns with garlic mayonnaise had too much rice. Roast duck with apple sauce was depressing when tested. But terrines and pâtés, or tomato and onion salad, make useful openers, oxtail (£2·95) was 'rich and delicious', and charcoal-grilled guinea-fowl or roast poussin with brandy and tarragon are other good main course choices. Baked prawns with mushrooms and garlic butter (£3·65) are a speciality. The vegetables are fresh, and show that butter is plentifully used in this kitchen, but 'they are served in a solemn pavane that tends to cool them.' Chocolate and almond cake, Norwegian cream, and lemony syllabub or mousse with toasted almonds are praised, as is the coffee. Mr Harmar-Brown buys wine carefully (from £2·75 here for Loire or Côtes du Rhône) and his advice is worth heeding. Recorded classical music. No children under five in the dining-room.

App: Christopher Rae, D.G.B., Helen Macintosh, and others

Parson's Nose
Church Lane
Mobberley 2651

Closed L; Sun; Mon;
Apr 13; Dec 25 & 26;
Jan 1
Must book
D only, 7–10

Alc £5·75 (meal £8·45)

VAT inc
Children's helpings
Seats 30
&. rest (1 step)
Access, Am Ex, Barclay,
Diners, Euro

Messrs Holland-Smith and Southerton, and their chef Gotfried Ribbeck, are making a good thing of this cosy two-year-old restaurant opposite the church, though the affability of the service and the closeness of the quarters may mean that only smokers can enjoy their meals. That is a pity, for soup had a good stock, pâté was coarse and chunky, lemon sole whether plain grilled, or with shrimp sauce, tasted fresh, and vegetables, though underseasoned, were carefully cooked, when tested. Other good dishes include mushrooms à la grecque, and 'wine-drenched pork fillets in a buttery, garlicky sauce' (£4 including vegetables). 'Chocolate mousse (80p) had a distinctly orange flavour', but strawberry vacherin was a little disappointing. Coffee is copious but weak. The wine list (from £3·20 for French ordinaire) is under revision. Recorded music. Car park. No dogs. More reports, please, and book well ahead for weekends.

MONTACUTE Somerset   Map 2

Milk House
17 The Borough
4 m W of Yeovil
Martock 3823

Closed L (exc Suns before
public hol Mons); Sun;
Mon (exc D public hols);
2 weeks Mar; 2 weeks
autumn; Dec 25 & 26;
Jan 1
Must book
D only, 7–9.30

Alc £5·45 (meal £7·15)

VAT & service inc
Children's helpings
Seats 50 (parties 25)
⑆ rest
No dogs

For want of sufficient reports by closing-time in
1978, members nearly 'lost' Charles Donovan's
well-set and personally run 15th-century stone
house in Montacute's Ham stone quadrangle, so be
warned. However, there is no doubt of the owner's
cooking – 'even on a crowded Saturday night our
hors d'oeuvre, chicken pâté, breasts of chicken
marinated in herbs and grilled, and home-made
ice-cream were excellently prepared and served.'
Another visitor says, 'I had occasion to take a party
of ten there, including four children from five up,
and dreaded it. But they were welcomed, splendidly
fed, and much impressed.' Other dishes that
succeeded at a test meal were good spinach
gnocchi, scampi provençale 'not quite garlicky
enough for Provence or me, but enclosed in a
delicious croustade', and turbot and scallops 'very
courteous to each other'. Filet de porc en croûte,
boned duck Grand Marnier (£3·15), 'large and
sharp' grapefruit sorbet, and 'singularly toothsome'
chocolate and hazelnut torte (95p) are also reported.
'There are no hidden extras apart from vegetables'
(70p), for VAT and service are included, and the
waiting is often done by acquaintances of the
owner's who make up for their inexperience by
friendliness. The wines are numerous, well chosen,
and well signalled: it would be a pity to drink the
Notre Dame carafes at £2·70 when Yugoslav
Traminer is £2·85, and plenty of other good-value
choices £1 or so more. Ch. Fombrauge '71, c.b., at
£6·40 is also a good buy, Mr Donovan thinks. No
music.

*App: Leo & Betty Clynes, Ian J. Philip, F.I.,
and others*

MORETON-IN-MARSH Gloucestershire   Map 2

Lamb's
High Street
Moreton-in-Marsh 50251

Closed Mon; Sun D;
Tue L
Meals 12–2, 7–9.30

Tdh Sun L £5
Alc £7·10 (meal £9·90)

VAT inc
Service 10%
Seats 55 (parties 20)
⑆ rest
No dogs in d/r

*Plenty of restaurants come in like lions and go out
like – well, let's hope Ian MacKenzie's first
independent venture (he was at the Dormy House,
Broadway, before) will reverse the procedure. The
setting behind the plate-glass, with vast comfortable
spaces into which several London restaurants could be
fitted, is tastefully muted. The cooking, by Paul
Barnard, happily does not follow suit, and people who
have started their lunches with large garlic prawns or
plump sardines 'served very hot in a cast-iron
frying-pan', or even tomato soup and 'very yellow'
haddock mousse, sound pleased. Black pudding and
bacon (£1·10) or salmon fish-cakes on Sunday are
among lunchtime possibilities reported. At night the
kitchen favourites include petits pots de champignons
(£1·25), baked avocado with hard-boiled egg and*

267

Access, Am Ex, Barclay,
Diners

hollandaise, allumettes of pork (£3·80) and medallions of beef with a mushroom cream sauce. Bourride, chicken Célestine, and game pie have proved equally successful, vegetables are carefully treated, and the service treats customers carefully too, if a little impersonally. There are about 50 wines (from £2·80 for Baronette), including good Spanish reds under £5, and halves of sweet Ch. Coutet '73 at £3·20; £7·80 for Muscat de Beaumes de Venise will surprise those who know how little it costs at source. No music. More reports, please.

MORPETH Northumberland   Map 8

Gourmet
59 Bridge Street
Morpeth 56200

Flamboyant decor and menu camouflage rather low-key flavours in this carefully served restaurant. Crêpe de poisson russe (95p) was dull and bland, poussin aux pêches and médaillon de veau tricolore (£2·95) 'very creamy' when tried. But 'someone is making a genuine effort', and others fared better with crab cocktail, chicken Kiev (£2·55), steak, and good vegetables. Sweets are on the heavy side. 'The hot and cold bar food is good, varied and modestly priced', with pressurised beers. Italian carafe wine, £3 the litre. No dogs. Recorded music.

Closed Sun; Mon; Apr 13;
Dec 25 & 26; Jan 1; 1st
3 weeks Feb
Meals 12–2.30, 7–11.30

Tdh L from £1·75 (meal £5·10)
Alc (min L £1·75, D £2·50) £6·15 (meal £9·45)
Alc (Bistro) meal £3·20

Children's helpings (under 10)
Seats 50
Car park
Access, Am Ex, Barclay, Diners, Euro

MOULTON North Yorkshire   Map 8

Black Bull
🍷
off A1
1½ m SE of Scotch
Corner
Barton 289

Closed Sun; Dec 24–31;
Apr 13 L
Must book D (exc fish bar)
Meals 12–2, 7–10.30

Tdh D (main rest)
from £7 (meal £10·45)
Alc (Hazel) £8·30 (meal £11·15); (fish bar) £7·25
(meal £10·05)

'I like this creeper-clad place because it is still at heart the local boozer,' says a normally fastidious inspector, and indeed, says another, the service 'seems sincere even when it is slapdash'. The girls have plenty to do anyway, since George Pagendam offers three different ways of eating: the fish bar with blue-and-white tiled tables, the regular dining-room, and in the evening Hazel, which now sounds as though it must be a rabbit bar but is, in fact, a handsome, converted London–Brighton Pullman car, vintage 1932. A casual lunch of 'vinegary' smoked mackerel pâté and 'dryish, uninteresting' casserole of pigeon barely reached 'useful in the area' level, but the fish that comes fresh from Whitby makes a very different impression, by inspectors' accounts of grilled mullet and pan-fried plaice with delicious buttery vegetables. In Hazel, a visitor's avocado with fresh crab and 'huge and succulent' grilled Dover sole were also reassuring. Dublin Bay prawns gratinée (£2·50), turbot en croûte sauce mousseline (£4) and calf's

VAT inc
Seats 22, 20 & 28
(parties 20 & 10)
🔥 main rest & fish bar
Car park
No dogs

liver in wine sauce are also among Charles
Somerville's specialities, and they have a *vivier* for
lobsters. If you want a sweet, consider brandy-snaps
or crème caramel. A large collection of wines is
sensibly chosen and priced (from only £3 for
Marqués de Murrieta '73). The house Muscadet '76
at £4, the Georges Duboeuf Beaujolais '76 at £4·50,
and '71 Wachenheimers fairly represent the whites;
clarets include Ch. Malescot-St-Exupéry '73 at
£5·25, Ch. Grand-Puy-Lacoste '66 at £6·50, and Ch.
Cos d'Estournel '61 at £15, with several serious
half-bottles under £3. A vintage port is kept
decanted. No music.

App: G.P., H. L. Horne, J.R., S.S., and others

NANTWICH Cheshire   Map 5

Churche's Mansion
150 Hospital Street
Nantwich 65933

Closed Sun D; Dec 24 D;
Dec 25 & 26; Jan 1
Must book
Meals 12–2, 7–8.30

Tdh L from £3 (meal
£4·50), D from £6 (meal
£7·75)

VAT & service inc
Cover (weekends) L £1,
D 50p
Seats 60 (parties 12)
🔥 rest (1 step)
Car park
No dogs

Richard and Margery Churche's town house was
built by Thomas Clease under the first Elizabeth
and restored to its original glory by the Myott
family under the second. As one visitor remarks,
this authenticity enables them to dispense with
'fake beams, bulk-buy horse brasses, and costumed
serving-wenches' and the food that usually goes
with these things. Instead, there has been for 23
years an honest attempt to serve imaginative
English food at a modest price. Knighthoods have
been conferred for less, under both Elizabeths, and
though a few meals may miscarry, vegetables may
be 'rather soft' and some dishes (usually main
courses) may be ill-advised in view of their resources,
most members and inspectors are well content with
their visits. One couple who landed from a narrow
boat for cream cheese and cucumber mousse,
pigeon casserole, and junket with stewed plums
made the canal locks deliver them back another day
for dinner, an over-ambitious meal with prawns in
garlic mayonnaise, slightly bitter braised grouse,
and grapes in Cointreau custard, but notable still
for the home-made rolls and wheaten biscuits.
Numerous other dishes praised include mussel
brose, herring and sour cream casserole (more like
herring and potato pie), scallop au gratin, roast
guinea-fowl or mallard, sweetbreads in madeira,
steak and kidney pie with 'black, tasty
mushrooms', 'superb' jugged hare, Malakoff pudding,
and walnut fudge flan that might be better served
in smaller nibbles with coffee. The English cheeses
may not look much when they are presented, partly
because (as Mr Myott says) 'it would be a kindness
to cheese if customers learnt how to cut it', but
they are formidably good. Drinks measures are
generous, wine prices about average (though wines
are robustly listed by price groups rather than
regions). But as well as St Maroc at £2 for 50 cl

269

and Averys Santenay Gravières '72 or Ch. Meyney '67, c.b., at £7·75, Mr Myott now keeps several dessert wines, and Hyde's Anvil ale in cask. No music. No pipes, but too much smoking of other kinds.

App: by too many members to list

NAYLAND Suffolk   Map 3

The Bear
Bear Street
Nayland 262204

Closed L (exc Sun);
Sun D; Apr 15–21; Aug
19–Sept 4; Dec 23–30
Must book
Meals 12.30–1.30 (Sun),
7.30–9

Tdh Sun L £5·50 (meal
£8·10)
Alc £4·90 (meal £7·80)

Children's helpings
Seats 50 (parties 20)
♿ rest (2 steps); w.c.
Car park
No dogs in public rooms
Am Ex card
7 rooms (all with bath)
B&B £8–£12

The founders of Colchester's Bistro Nine (*q.v.*) have not wanted for custom since the word got round that they had set up in this inviting old house, with panelling and hessian lining the dining-room walls. Alas, there have clearly been some evenings on which they have taken more customers than either the kitchen or the service could cope with adequately, and sometimes the creaminess of everything takes them beyond customers' powers of coping too. It is possible to admire the moules marinière, the seafood mélange in a 'very thin and buttery pastry case of delicate texture', the home-made pasta, the chicken leg boned and stuffed with pâté, the brown bread ice-cream and the crème brûlée (70p), but it is inadvisable to attempt more than one at a sitting. Mackerel fillets in oatmeal (75p) started a test meal well, and the properly kept cheeses finished it nicely – but it did take a long time to serve. Wines are well chosen, especially the '73 red Graves that is their current house wine, and other clarets are also accessibly priced. Pressurised Abbot ale. No music.

App: Mrs R. L. Harding, L.S.H., J.M.B.,
V. R. Sladden, P.H.S., B. M. Newman, and others

NEWBURY Berkshire   Map 2

Curry Garden
73b Northbrook Street
Newbury 46935 *and*
40162

A popular new tandoori house, candlelit in the evening, with Mr Khan cooking the tandoori dishes and Mr Ali the curries, 'all the way from sweet and creamy to very, very hot'. Service is pleasant, prices modest – and booking essential in the evenings. Try onion bhajia (30p), chicken or mutton tikka (75p and 80p as starters, double as main courses) with nan (30p), chicken and prawn special (£1·50), chicken korma (£1·10), prawn vindaloo (£1·20) with okra, aubergine or mixed vegetable curry (60p). Tandoori mixed grill is £2·80, and there is a set dinner at £3·50 per person. Various wines; lager. Recorded music. Take-away too.

Closed Dec 25
Meals 12–3, 6–11.30
Must book D

Tdh L £1·50, D £3·50
Alc meal £3·65

Seats 56

No dogs
Access, Am Ex, Barclay, Euro

La Riviera
26 The Broadway
Newbury 47499

A cheerful family-run restaurant with an international menu, from which regulars prefer the Greek dishes. But as well as taramosalata (75p), there is praise for scampi, whether fried or provençale, and 'delicious' zabaglione (£1·60 for two). The chef recommends his moussaka and chicken Kiev. French and Italian house wines, £2·75 the bottle (45p the glass). No music. Dress smartly. No dogs.

Closed Wed; 2 weeks Apr; most public hols	Meals 12–2.30, 6.45–10.30	Seats 40
		🔥 rest (1 step)
Must book D	Alc £5·05 (meal £7·95)	Barclay, Diners

Sapient Pig
29 Oxford Street
Newbury 44867

Closed Sun; Mon; Sat L;
Apr 13; 1st 2 weeks Aug;
Dec 25 & 26; Jan 1
Must book D
Meals 12–2, 7.30–10

Tdh D £5·95 (meal £9·40)
Alc L £4·30 (meal £7·45)

Children's helpings
(under 12)
Seats 44
🔥 rest
No dogs
Access, Barclay

Most bistros in this plain but honest style lean towards jokiness: one visitor finds this one 'earnest', even though Lynda Franklin and Jenny Page in the kitchen now have a male manager to leaven what used to be a single-sex menage. Earnestness should not have allowed the meagre coquille St Jacques and lamb chops, or ill-chosen fresh fruit, that are mentioned, but most people are well content with the varied short menu and the cooking of soups, prawn and leek quiche, beef casserole, turbot Marguéry, brochette d'agneau, and 'spring vegetables admirably timed and presented'. Rognons de veau Robert is a favourite dish. Sweets are less often reported, but they make their own cheesecake and the chocolate gateau is praised. Mâcon is £3·50 a litre. Recorded music.

App: Richard Cawston, P. W. May, Andrew Dakin, D. R. Whitbread, S. J. & E. Monkcom

---

NEWCASTLE UPON TYNE Tyne & Wear   Map 8

Black Gate Restaurant
The Side
Newcastle upon Tyne
26661

Closed Sun; Mon D;
Sat L; Apr 16; Dec 25 &
26; Jan 1
Must book
Meals 12–2.15, 7–10

Tdh L £2
Alc £7 (meal £10)

VAT inc
Children's helpings L
(under 10)
Seats 75
🔥 rest; w.c.
Air-conditioning
Access, Barclay, Diners

Newcastle members, and the southerners they advise about where to eat in their modestly endowed city, have been quick to find this Edwardian room in an old shipping-office by the Cathedral, for the Lant family and Stephen Falconer (who cooks) 'give every sign of enjoying their job'. Lunch menus are short and simple, the evening carte perhaps too ambitious, with six hot hors d'oeuvre as well as soups (venison broth, or Northumbrian yellow split pea soup with ham hock) and cold escabèche, a house speciality of marinated pike, cod and halibut (£1·25). Among main dishes, pâté-stuffed chicken with vermouth sauce (£4·75 with vegetables) and entrecôte Café de Paris are praised, and duck with honey and walnuts and cuisse de lièvre rôtie au poivre vert (£4·50) are house suggestions. 'Plates are too small for the food put on them.' They make their own ice-creams, they say, and sherry trifle and strawberry cheesecake have given pleasure. Valgardello ordinaires are £3·30 a litre, and a list is being built up slowly. Recorded music. No dogs. More reports, please.

271

Moti Mahal
1 Forth Place
off Clayton Street West
Newcastle upon Tyne
20301 *and* 29148

Closed Dec 25
Must book D
Meals 12–2.30, 5.30–11.30

Alc meal £4·35

Service 10%
Children's helpings
(under 12)
Seats 60 (parties 25)
⚹ rest (1 step)
No dogs
Access, Am Ex, Barclay,
Diners, Euro

Apart from one *grande dame* of the theatre who was depressingly received and fed at lunch, members and inspectors find this a refreshingly lively place, from the khaki walls, dried flowers and jungly mural that make a change from normal Indian restaurant decor, to the Punjabi dishes on a menu that promises (rather unwisely) a full range of the sub-continent's cooking. Prices allow the young to eat here, and they do. There is praise for the seekh kebabs (75p) and chicken tikkas (95p) that make useful openers, 'conspicuously good' lamb pasanda in a mild, creamy sauce (£1·65), chicken or mutton masala (£2·30), fresh-tasting brinjal bhajia (65p), well-cooked pilau rice, and 'crisp-soft nan with sultanas and almonds'. To special order, whole stuffed chickens and ducks are offered at £8–£9·50, and a vegetarian trayful costs £2·50. There are wines from £2·75, but Drybrough heavy or lager is more popular. Even the coffee is drinkable. Recorded music.

App: David & Jane Copeland, David West, J.C., C.P.D., and others

---

NEWENT Gloucestershire **Map 2**

Bistro One
1 Culver Street
8½ m NW of Gloucester
Newent 820896

Closed L; Sun; Mon
(exc May 7 D); Dec 25 &
26; Jan 1
Must book
D only, 7.30–9.30

Alc (min £3) £7·15
(meal £9·85)

VAT inc
Children's helpings
(under 12)
Seats 18 (parties 18)
No dogs

The Soutters 'put everything they have' into their lovingly planned cottage restaurant, with Laura Ashley tablecloths, 'real oil-lamps instead of candles', and a wood stove. The food is also more than competent. The short blackboard menu changes frequently 'and avoids hackneyed dishes': people speak of smoked chicken or quail, ham and mushrooms Mornay (£1·35), or giant prawns with garlic mayonnaise for first courses. Afterwards, roast blackcock was 'a little tough but worth the hard work', and a massive veal chop Normandy at a test meal had 'a delicate wine and calvados sauce' (£4·75). Steak béarnaise, or grilled prawns with an anchovy dip and garlic rice are other main courses. Vegetables are included, and are carefully cooked ('roasted, slightly caramelised parsnips') and there is good garlic bread, but puddings are unambitious and coffee is poor. Mrs Soutter serves charmingly. French Notre Dame ordinaire is £3·50 the litre (45p the glass); Portuguese Dão and English Three Choirs '76 are both £3·95. 'Occasional' recorded music.

App: Mary Bailey, R.B.J., R.T.H., P. Martin, D.J.B.

Meal times refer to first and last orders.

NEWTON POPPLEFORD Devon Map 2

Bridge End House
on A3052
Colaton Raleigh 68411

Closed Sat L; Sun D
(Oct 1–Apr 1); Dec 25 &
26
Must book
Meals 12–1.45, 7–10

Tdh L from £1·30 (meal
£3·90), D £2·85 (meal
£4·85)
Alc £4·55 (meal £7·10)

VAT inc
Children's helpings
Seats 41
♿ rest; w.c.
Car park
No dogs in d/r
3 rooms
B&B £4
D, B&B £60 p.w.

The awkward main road site commends dinners to cautious drivers and overnight stays to sound sleepers, but warmth of service and the value given spread the invitation to this well-altered house much more widely. In the summer of 1978 four people lunched with a glass of wine for under £3 a head, including home-made soup or hors d'oeuvre, interesting vegetables with the pork chop or steak and kidney pie, and blackberry pie or apricot and almond tart at the end. Similar accounts of generously priced club dinners have been received, and on an ordinary evening 'creamed potatoes with almonds, and a beautiful cauliflower with a herby sauce, almost broke my concentration on Barry Cox's rack of lamb marinated in white wine and oregano.' Duck roast in cider, fresh broad beans in cream sauce, peppers and onions, and dauphinoise potatoes are also praised. Salmon en croûte (£3) is a speciality. On the other hand, a party in May was depressed by 'hard and cold' smoked trout pâté, 'amateurish' main course sauces and 'over-sweet' syllabub. Ice-cream and brandy-snaps may both be home made. Spanish and Italian ordinaires are £3·15 a litre; Coeur des Lanciers red and white is better value at £3·20 a bottle; Ch. Fombrauge '70, c.b., is £5·50. No music.

App: R.S., P. J. Lovett, D. I. Baddeley, Mr & Mrs C. E. Newbegin, Ron L. Graham, and others

NORTHALLERTON North Yorkshire Map 8

Romanby Court
High Street
Northallerton 4918

Closed Sun; Mon; Sat L;
Aug 12–Sept 3; Chr;
L Apr 13 & Jan 1
Must book D
Meals 12–1.30, 7.15–10.15

Tdh L £2·50 (meal £4·50),
D from £5·35 (meal £8·45)

VAT inc
Seats 30 (parties 14)
♿ rest (1 step)
No dogs

The Collu family from Clapton, E., are a metropolitan gift to North Yorkshire, in one inspector's opinion, and their lasagne was 'marginally better than at the Gritti in Venice'. Pheasant, too, is good, though probably easier in Yorkshire than in the Veneto. Less exotic minestrone, pork fillet with vegetables, veal alla crema, and mille-feuille among the sweets are also praised. Lunch remains good value most days, though one inspector disliked overcooked vegetables, 'limp and bland' calf's liver in a batter overcoat, and 'creamy cake innocent of spirit'. The young Italian waiters are brisk. Carafe wines vary with what can be bought; house claret is £3·20, and other wines are at least interesting: Ch. Lynch-Bages '73, c.b., £6·90; Clos de Tart '70, domaine-bottled, £8·80. However, 'Frascati was not chilled at all on a very warm evening.' Recorded music.

App: W. A. Rinaldi-Butcher, M. Clarke, A.T., C. B. & L. W. Rutter, D.C.M., and others

St Matthews Hotel
Cellar Restaurant
23 St Matthews Parade,
Kettering Road
Northampton 713821

'Never mind the decor, enjoy the food,' says one admirer of the Colleys' small hotel restaurant. There is a log fire in the new bar, a pleasant atmosphere and careful presentation. Try cream smokies (90p), moules provençale, gratin de langoustines (£3), half a roast pheasant with walnut stuffing (£3·40), or roast beef or lamb. (Main dish prices include a salad or vegetables.) Monte Campo house wine, £3 a litre. 'Light jazz' on tape. No dogs.

Closed Sun; Mon; L Sat;
Dec 25 & 31; Jan 1
Must book D
Meals 12.15–2, 7–10

Tdh L £2 (meal £3·85)
Alc £4·80 (meal £7·90)

VAT inc L
Service 10%

Children's helpings
Seats 40
9 rooms
B&B £4·50
Fire cert

Old Woolhouse

The Square
Northleach 366

Closed L; Sun; Dec 25
Must book
D only, from 8.15

Tdh £7 (meal £9)

VAT & service inc
Seats 14
[⚬] rest (1 step)

Cooking is Jacques Astic's vocation, and he studies day-to-day variations in the taste and texture of his raw materials as other restaurateurs study men and women. In other words, until you have gained his confidence by booking (very difficult), turning up (reneging is unthinkable) and appearing *sympathique*, you are at best a necessary evil, and the guide that sent you to him is much better not mentioned. Remember, if piqued, all the offences that attend much 'French' eating-out in prosperous parts of England and try to understand what a sensitive Lyonnais craftsman must feel who has to earn a living for his growing family in the same milieu. Not that M Astic and his English wife (who makes the desserts) are entirely beyond criticism. The balance of meals is not always wise, and their dependence on special deliveries of Lyonnais cheeses is inconsiderate (no-one pretends it is easy to obtain good French cheeses here, but it is possible). Kitchen noises and remarks are audible. All this said, few places offer dishes such as this cottage's hot chicken liver mousse, or crab tartlet, or spinach-stuffed trout ('they nearly had a turn when I asked for salt'); followed perhaps by poulet au vinaigre, or 'exquisite' ris de veau à la crème, or veal cutlet in armagnac sauce, or kidneys in port or cassis. The dauphinois potatoes remain more to the house's taste than to that of members, and salad dressing is vinegary 'though by this stage you need the astringent effect,' says one fellow cook. 'Chocolate gateau looked and tasted marvellous, but I would have preferred crème pâtissière to cream as a bed for marzipan-stuffed prunes in the tarte.' We have not seen the wine list this year but even with a bottle of Pouilly Fuissé or Montagny, another of Bonnes-Mares '71 and brandies with the coffee, the price of a meal for four people was little over £10 a head in 1978, and seemed good value to everyone who paid it. No music. Details are approximate.

App: Pete & Sue Chesterman, G.L.M., P.M.S., D.S., F.R.B.A., H. B. Walton, and others

---

NORTHLEACH see also pub section

NORTHREPPS Norfolk   Map 6

Church Barn
off A149
3 m SE of Cromer
Overstrand 588

Inconsistency and inattention to detail have marred what would otherwise be a sound English restaurant – 'indeed, a major find' – in these flint farm buildings. Dressed crab, kidney soup, potted pigeon, roast lamb (not pink) or sirloin, gammon in red wine, pheasant and garden vegetables have many admirers, and 'chocolate cabbages and blackberry meringue flan were just two of the interesting sweets.' But vinegary hors d'oeuvre, tough birds, bland sauces and chalky Stilton are described too, though the Foxalls cope surprisingly well with large parties. Adnams' and Greene King beers in cask; French ordinaires from £2·95. Friendly service. Pipes discouraged. Recorded music.

Closed L (exc Sun);
Sun D; Mon (exc public
hols & Aug); Dec 25 & 26;
Jan 15–Mar 15
Must book (summer)
Meals 12.15–2 (Sun),
7.15–11

Tdh Sun L £3·50
(meal £6·60), D from
£4·65 (meal £8·90)

Cover 25p
Children's helpings
(exc Sat)

Seats 45 (parties 35)
♿ rest (2 steps)
Car park
No dogs
Access, Barclay

NORWICH Norfolk   Map 6

Bistro Beano
72 Prince of Wales Road
Norwich 614195

'Vaguely 1920s bistro' on a corner site which has housed both pub and pizza parlour in its time. The cast-iron furniture is 'not as uncomfortable as you might fear'. Ambitious menu with chef's daily specials on a blackboard. Praise for fresh sardines in garlic butter (65p), chicken provençale (£1·95), kidneys Turbigo, rump steak (£2·75), 'outstanding' vegetables, and a light orange gateau. Pâté and cassoulet were below French standard when tried. Friendly service. Lunches – a new venture – offer soups, pancakes, omelettes (£1·30) with salad. House wine £2·20 the unspecified carafe; Marqués de Riscal '73 (red) £3·95. Recorded music. No dogs.

Closed Sun; Apr 16;
Aug 27; Dec 25 & 26
Must book D & weekends
Meals 11–3, 7–11.30

Alc £4·85 (meal £6·74)

VAT inc
Service 10%

Children's helpings
(under 5)
Seats 36
♿ rest

Marco's

17 Pottergate
Norwich 24044

Closed Sun; Mon;
Apr 13; Dec 25 & 26;
Jan 1
Must book
Meals 12.30–2, 7.30–10

Tdh L £3·50 (meal £6·30)
Alc £6·60 (meal £10)

Seats 40
⚹ rest
No dogs
Access, Am Ex, Barclay,
Diners

Restaurant-goers lead interesting lives: 'We had to pursue the young women (ours was Guianese) into the kitchen to attract their attention,' writes one of them about Marco Vessalio's long-admired Italian place. But the service is good, really, like Marco's cooking, and if the room were better lit, gesticulating customers might be noticed more quickly. The 'real' menu is not as long as it looks, but does not need to be, given the standard reached here by the crespelle and lasagne ('very hot, with real tomato and a light sauce'). Fishy dishes to note include scampi in Spumante, burrida alla genovese, and cozze alla marinara; main dishes praised included 'very good' boned, grilled chicken with lemon and butter, and osso buco. Saltimbocca is worth trying. Minestrone, 'overcooked and over-buttered' green beans, and uninteresting sweets are criticised. Wine prices for this year have not been notified, and the Italian whites are mediocre, but if you want something better than ordinary reds try the Gattinara. Recorded music. 'Unplanned closures sometimes, so be sure to telephone.'

App: M. F. Cullis, H.W., L.W., and others

Parson Woodforde

1 Old Post Office Yard,
19/21 Bedford Street
Norwich 24280

Closed Sun D; Apr 15 &
16; Dec 25 & 26; Jan 1
Must book D
Meals 12–2.30, 7–11

Alc £6·10 (meal £9·45)

Seats 50
Car park
No dogs
Access, Am Ex, Barclay,
Diners, Euro

Norfolk's clerical trencherman and diarist is nobly remembered in this medieval hall (the beams are exposed to the roof trusses), and there is a seafood bar in the crypt below. Paddy Heyland, who cooks, and his partners insist that theirs is an eating-house, not a restaurant, and their favourite dishes include anchovy whets (90p) as a first course and Woodforde's favourite pie 'The Charter', whose composition has long puzzled cooks but here contains chicken, leeks and cream (£3·25). Skate in black butter is offered too, wild duck is praised, and 'two of us had huge slices of fore-rib of beef admirably cooked, with good vegetables.' There are few reports as yet of the sweets and English cheeses, but the coffee is decent. They stock one or two English wines and real ale (Greene King) too, but the Englishman's traditional affection for claret is given full rein. 'Let others drink up the tiring '62s while there are still enjoyable '73s from £4·75.' Recorded music. More reports, please.

Tatler's

21 Tombland
Norwich 21822

Closed Dec 25 & 26;
Jan 1
Must book D
Meals 12–2.30, 6–11.30
(Sun 7–11)

One inspector found the group of young people who run this Edwardian house near the Cathedral amusing rather than presumptuous, 'though they presume too much with the type and volume of the unavoidable music.' Cooking and service, members also agree, exhibit both the virtues and the faults of amateurism, with 'entirely successful' buttered samphire, and 'not at all bad' rabbit casserole, jugged hare, and stuffed pigeon, and robust pies of similar materials. 'A good

Tdh L Sun £3 (meal £5·10)
Alc £3·75 (meal £5·95)

VAT inc
Children's helpings
(under 10)
Seats 70 (parties 25)
[&] rest (3 steps)

*meal is possible if one catches a dish early in a
session, before it has been around too long.'
Vegetarians like the cheese and vegetable pie, the baked
potatoes, and the mushrooms in an earthenware dish.
Sweets are less mentioned. The menu changes often,
and so does the wine list, but apart from basic Cuvée
Jean Perruchot at £2·50, 'soi-disant Beaune', there are
surprisingly extensive clarets: Ch. du Tertre '71,
£5·35. No dogs. More reports, please.*

NORWICH see also wine bar section

NOTTINGHAM Nottinghamshire Map 5

Ben Bowers
128 Derby Road
Nottingham 47488 *and*
43288

Good humour and cheerful service are to be found
in this crowded restaurant and wine bar, called
after a 19th-century coachman, 'on an unfashionable
corner of an unfashionable town'. The menu is
wildly international, so that you could find yourself
following gambas con ajo (90p) with Highland steak
(cooked in Glayva and cream, £4·25) and green figs
in ouzo. One Monday a month is gourmet night,
perhaps a Spanish meal and flamenco, or an
English one with Morris dancers. Self-service buffet
lunches (95p) in the wine bar and Betty's Buffet
Bar. Various house wines, from £3·12 the litre.
Live music most nights. No dogs.

Closed Sun; Sat L;
Dec 25 & 26; L public
hol Mons; Jan 1
Must book
Meals 12–2, 7–11

Alc £4·90 (meal £7·15)

VAT inc
Children's helpings
(under 10)

Seats 48
[&] rest
Air-conditioning
Access, Am Ex, Barclay,
Diners, Euro

La Grenouille
32 Lenton Boulevard
Nottingham 411088

Closed Sun; Sat L;
Dec 23–Jan 1; public hols
Must book D
Meals 12.30–1.30,
7.30–9.30

Tdh £3·50 (meal £5·90)
Alc £5 (meal £7·55)

VAT inc
Children's helpings
(under 8)
Seats 24
No dogs

As the *Nottingham Evening Post* judiciously
remarked when last year's entry appeared, 'Few
local restaurants have been listed twice in recent
years', so Alain Duval and Yves Bouanchaud are
already one up on a few competitors. True, two
lunchers on separate occasions wonder whether the
actual cooking would pass *routier* muster in France,
let alone at £3·50 for the set meal. But it is not the
owners' fault that there is so little competition, and
diners have reported well of most things (except the
vegetables) on the prudently short menu. Jambon à
la crème (£1) and cuisses de grenouille (£2·10) as
entrees, and escalope de veau normande (£3·50) and
chateaubriand maître d'hôtel are the best dishes, it
is claimed, but soup, omelette champignons, cheese,
and bananes flambées are also praised. Chaumière
ordinaires are £2 for 50 cl, and there are a few
others, including Tarn red at £3·10. Recorded music.

*App: John Inman, D.W.D., C. P. Scott-Malden,
Leslie Henry*

277

NOTTINGHAM Nottinghamshire   Map 5

Laguna Tandoori
43 Mount Street
Nottingham 49110 *and*
411632

Mr Baij Verma brings a touch of class (from his stint with the Indian High Commission?) to his smart tandoori house near the Playhouse: informed service, sandalwood-scented towels, and some delicate spicing in the cooking. People like the tandoori mix (tastes of several tandoori dishes, £2·60), chicken shashlik (£1·50), muttar paneer, raita, and gulab jamun. The chef recommends Begum Behar (£1·40) and lamb moghlai (£1·40). But kulfi is seldom on, the adding-up favours now you, now them, and sometimes dishes lack sparkle – even the chapatis and nan may seem leaden. Drink lager; French house wine is £2 the carafe. The cocktails include Pussyfoot – another diplomatic borrowing, presumably. Recorded Indian music.

Must book D
Meals 12.30–2.45,
6.30–11.45

Alc meal £4·35

Service 10%
Seats 80

♿ rest
No dogs
Access, Am Ex, Barclay, Diners, Euro

ORFORD Suffolk   Map 3

Butley-Orford Oysterage
Market Hill
on B1084
12 m E of Woodbridge
Orford 277

Closed Dec 25 & 26;
D Jan & Feb
Must book
Meals 12–2.30, 6–8.30

Alc £2 (meal £3·75)

VAT inc
Seats 46 (parties 20)
♿ rest; w.c.

'If you stick to raw or near-raw food you can eat like a king in a cafe.' That means simple decor, marble-topped tables and oysters (natives at £2·80 the dozen or Butleys at £2), or their home-smoked fish: 'generous and superb' salmon (£1·45 or £2·40), cod's roe 'of excellent quality', 'moist and not aggressively smoky' eel with thick, hot toast (90p), mackerel or pollan ('a fish of the salmon family', 70p). Risk the stewed eels, oyster soup, angels on horseback, and pork and clam stew, but avoid the eel and salmon mould ('bouncy and grey') and hot salmon with oyster sauce. The coffee is good. The house wine is local Finn Valley (what else?) '76 at £2·80 and a decent Muscadet is £2·50. Mrs Pinney is a firm lady, but service is pleasant enough. No music. The indispensable take-away shop is round the corner.

App: V. & F. Irish, Pat & Jeremy Temple, John C. Baker, N. A. Punt, D.W., and others

---

Wine prices shown are for a 'standard' bottle of the wine concerned, unless another measure is stated.

Unless otherwise stated, a restaurant is open all week and all year and is licensed.

OTTERY ST MARY Devon   Map 2

The Lodge
Silver Street
Ottery St Mary 2356

Closed Mon; Sun D;
3 weeks Jan–Feb; Apr 13;
1 week Nov; Dec 25 & 26
Must book
Meals 12.30–1.30,
7.30–9.30

Alc £5·20 (meal £7·20)

VAT inc
Seats 20 (parties 20)
No dogs

Not only the church, but the butchers, the bakers and, for aught we know, the candlestick-makers are out of the ordinary in Ottery, and so is the Freeman-Cowen family's restaurant, according to visitors who have followed up last year's provisional entry. Rather than succumbing to increased pressure, the kitchen has grown in confidence. Duckling may be variably cooked, and Italians have a better knack with aubergines in batter, but the almond-stuffed mushroom Cockaigne (£1), spicy tomato soup, locally farmed trout, seafood casserole 'with a sauce that enhanced rather than smothered the flavour of the fish', sole meunière, and guinea-fowl with cider and apples do the house credit, and vegetables are deftly cooked too. Jugged hare and Elizabethan pork (£3·20) are other dishes to look out for, and lunch is curry on the first Sunday of the month. In Ottery it is still safe to offer négresse en chemise, whatever may be the case in Brixton, and there is further sociological interest in the fact that a confection of biscuit crumbs, chocolate, and rum-flavoured soufflé only began to sell when they called it Admiral's Tart (70p). The David Baillie Vintners Fino sherry and cognac are appreciated, and under £4 there is a fair choice between, say, Chianti Classico and Alsace Muscat. There is good value in the Spanish section too. No music. 'Well-paced' family service. Children, pipes, and men *en déshabillé* 'at discretion'.

App: R. J. S. Marsh, C. A. Stubbings, D.J.S., A. Carrington, and others

OUNDLE Northamptonshire   Map 6

Tyrrells
6–8 New Street
Oundle 2347

Closed Mon; Sun D;
Dec 25 & 26; Jan 1
Must book D & weekends
Meals 12–2, 7–10.30

Alc £5·25 (meal £8·30)

VAT inc
Service 10% (Sat D)
Cover 25p
Children's helpings
Seats 42
Access, Barclay

Hilary Tyrrell has chosen a needy locality for her small, informal restaurant, and people have been glad to find it this year. Richard Pool and Frances Taylor cook, and one man even calls their kebabs – either lamb with yoghourt sauce or Portuguese pork marinated in sherry and paprika (£2·75) – 'the best since Turkey 20 years ago.' People also mention beef bourguignonne, stuffed quails in red wine (£3·30), fresh sardines or mussel brochettes among first courses; halibut with crab and mushroom; and chocolate orange cheesecake among 'sweeties' (ugh). There is a 3-course weekday 'business lunch' for £2·95. Mâcon and upper Mosel ordinaires are £3·80 a litre, and there are a few others, with some character but no vintages stated. A glass of white port as aperitif or digestif costs 40p. Recorded music. Children must be well-behaved. No dogs. More reports, please.

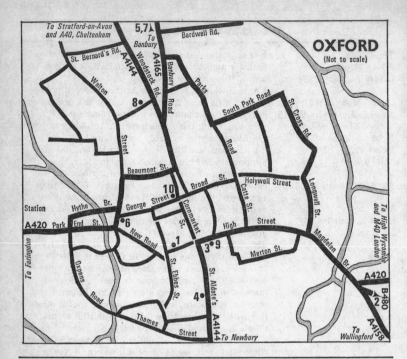

OXFORD Oxfordshire   Map 2

(1) La Cantina
34 Queen Street
Oxford 47760

Closed Mon; Dec 26 &
31; Jan 1
Must book
Meals 12–2.30, 6–11.30

Alc £4·75 (meal £7·95)

VAT inc
Service 10%
Cover 25p
Children's helpings
(under 8)
Seats 56
No dogs
Access, Am Ex, Barclay,
Diners

In 1977 La Cantina reverted to its former manager,
Reno Pizi, and, says one member, 'the people of
Oxford know what they are doing in trooping
back.' A test meal confirmed this opinion. Queen
Street was pedestrianised while Reno dwelt in
Nottingham, and perhaps this has improved the
passing trade. An inspector, dropping names with
uncharacteristic abandon, compares the fettuccine
(£1·30) with Alfredo's in Rome 'where I once heard
Stewart Granger calling for chopsticks to eat it
with'; rigatoni were almost as good. 'Rather
stringy' abbacchio alla marchigiana (£2·15) was
generously helped and admirably sauced, as were
the involtini; fresh buttered spinach and 'clean,
crisp' courgettes appeared as vegetables.
Minestrone, trout with almonds and grapes, frogs'
legs, and stuffed squid (Reno's mother's recipe) are
also praised, and what sounds like spumone makes a
good sweet. Merlot or Tokai ordinaires are £2·80
and there is an adequate choice of better bottles
under £4. Service of both food and wine is much
better than average. The room is apt to be stuffy,
and there is 'languid' Italian music.

*App: V. S., G. Cotton, Michael Copp, P.O'R.S.,
Dr D. H. Clark*

280

(2) La Capannina
247 Cowley Road
Oxford 48200

Modest, very popular, shanty-like cafe at the wrong end of the Cowley Road, enthusiastically run by a family from Capri. Skip the conventional dishes and keep to pasta, osso buco or saltimbocca, and zabaglione. Italian house wine is £2·10 for 75 cl, 40p the glass. No music.

Closed Apr 15 & 16;	Meals 12–2, 6–11	Children's helpings
Dec 25 & 26		Seats 60
Must book D & weekends	Alc £3·80 (meal £6·10)	No dogs

---

(3) Casse Croûte
130a High Street
Oxford 41320

This down-market relative of the Sorbonne (*q.v.*) off the High, is 'about as spartan as could be', with shared tables, diminutive chairs and bare light-bulbs. 'A casual and tardy waiter is expected to cope single-handed.' But the blackboard menu may offer civet de lièvre (£1·50) and paupiettes de veau à la crème (£1·90) as well as more run-of-the-mill soupe au pistou (short on pistou when tried), a *baveuse* omelette and a crème brûlée so freshly made it was warm on top, chilled below. The coffee, when tried, would have been nasty at half the price (35p). Carafino wines, £2 for 50 cl. No music.

Closed D; Sun; 2 weeks	Alc £2·65 (meal £4·40)	Seats 18 (parties 30)
Aug; public hols		No dogs
L only, 12–2.15	VAT inc	

---

(4) Restaurant Elizabeth

84 St Aldates
Oxford 42230

Closed L (exc Sun); Mon;
3 weeks Aug; public hols
Must book
Meals 12.30–2.30 (Sun),
6.30–11 (7–10.30 Sun)

Alc (min £5·10) £6·70
(meal £10·25)

Service inc
Cover 70p
Seats 55
No dogs
Access, Barclay, Euro

Diners in Antonio Lopez's bijou but lately extended upstairs restaurant sometimes feel that they have been staring across at the friable masonry of Christ Church long enough for the scaffolding irons to enter their souls. At least, the delays reported, and failures with particular dishes (boeuf Stroganoff for instance), suggest that it is not all joy pasturing with 'the tourist-and-knowledge industry at the leading edge of post-industrial capitalism', as one overheated inspector expresses it. Colleagues of his, who cannily chose lunch-time instead, did very much better. True, the cover charge was the same. The carelessly printed, seldom varied menu, especially the stereotyped potatoes and sweets, also bore to tears some of those who have to spend years instead of hours in Oxford. But the mellow golden ttoro (fish soup with aïoli, £1·60), the quenelles de saumon sauce Nantua, the taramosalata (also £1·60) and the mussels baked (but not overbaked) in butter are hard to beat as fishy first courses. Then 'carré d'agneau was ordered rare and came rare, a rarity in Britain', 'poulet au porto (£3·75) was boned, succulent and wine-dark in an only slightly sweet sauce', and entrecôte au poivre vert was tender and *bleu* with an equally refined – but not, as some have called it, bland – béarnaise-like sauce. Mange-tout peas are well cooked; and if you do not feel equal to another crème brûlée there are always champagne sorbet or chestnuts in kirsch. Sometimes, too, the mustachioed Spanish waiters make up for the *longueurs* by zeal beyond the call of duty 'like making more of the excellent coffee at 1.15 a.m. for a party who came in at 8.30'. The wines, though unavailable bottles are sometimes said to be 'in Antonio's cellar in north Oxford', begin with Haut Poitou '76 at £3·90, and Marqués de Riscal '73 at £4·25, and rise to splendid heights: ten '61 clarets, and even Ch. Boyd-Cantenac '67 at £7·85 (c.b.), showing nicely. Corton-Charlemagne '73 (Tollot-Beaut) is £14·50, and Ch. Filhot '59, £18·05 (a pity there are no halves of these dessert wines). Try the Manzanilla too. No music.

App: M. H. Gough, Mrs H. A. Swan, B.B., Andrew Tindell, J.O.H., F.I., R.W.D. Orders, and others

---

OXFORD Oxfordshire   Map 2

---

(5) **Lotus House**
197 Banbury Road
Oxford 54239

'A Chinese eating-place with something extra' – several things, in fact: 'authentic' decor, 'pleasant' Chinese music, and an interesting menu, on which the 'sizzling dishes' are most popular – fresh squid with black-bean sauce (£1·95), sliced duck with ginger and spring onion (£2·25) and beef with black pepper sauce. Others worth trying might be grilled scallops with garlic and butter sauce (£2·75), wafer-wrapped prawns, deep-fried shredded beef, bean curd family-style and the tea called 'tit koon yum'. The set meals are unambitious. Service is 'quick and good'. House wine £3 the carafe.

Must book D & weekends
Meals 12–2.30, 6–11.45

Tdh L £1·20, D £3

Alc meal £4·70

VAT inc
Service 10%
Seats 70 (parties 40)

☺ rest
Car park (3)
No dogs
Am Ex, Barclay, Diners

---

(6) **Opium Den**
79 George Street
Oxford 48680

Closed Dec 25 & 26
Must book D & weekends
Meals 12–2.30, 6–11.45

Tdh L £1
Alc meal £4·50

VAT inc
Service 10%
Seats 130 (parties 80)
☺ rest

Some have their doubts about Shu-Man Tse's much-frequented and agreeably designed central Oxford restaurant, but most people are content for it to appear here for the 'sizzling dishes' (for instance, beef in black pepper sauce, £2·05, oysters with spring onions and ginger, £1·85), salted king prawn in garlic dressing (£1·70 for two as a first course), and baked vegetable in coconut sauce with chicken or pork (£1·65); deep-fried squid in wine and garlic, or steamed duck in plum sauce, are specialities. An Englishman exiled to the American west coast even attempted sea-snails in black bean sauce with green peppers without regretting it, while mentioning that the bowls were cold, and pork with pickled cabbage soup too sweet. 'I don't

Air-conditioning
No dogs
Access, Am Ex, Barclay,
Diners, Euro

recommend Chinese fondue,' says someone else. Tea
may be too strong. Wines from £3 a litre. Chinese
recorded music.

*App: Angela Bailey, Esther Kaposi, M.M.,
T. M. S. Tosswill, and others*

---

(7) Les Quat' Saisons
272 Banbury Road
Oxford 53540

Closed Sun; Mon L;
public hols; last three
weeks July; Dec 24–Jan 6
Must book D
Meals 12.15–2, 7–10

Tdh L £3·10 (meal £5·30)

Alc (min £2·50) £6
(meal £8·75)

Children's helpings
(under 10)
Seats 48
[&] rest; w.c.
Air-conditioning
No dogs
Barclaycard

No posse of Ph D assessors could have been more
rigorous in their scrutiny than the people who went
to Raymond and Jenny Blanc's Summertown
restaurant after last year's first *Guide* entry. On the
whole the candidate has emerged with honours,
both for the food and for the owners' evident desire
to please, though critical customers have sometimes
been disappointed in some particular. Service is the
main problem: 'Though the ratio of waiters to
customers was perfectly adequate by French
standards, the former were overwhelmed and the
latter gritted their teeth for a long wait.' (It is just
as well that the summer of 1978 was a cool one.)
Under similar pressure, individual dishes may also
falter, but there is little better cooking for many
miles. One inspector even ate chez Blanc three
times in one week and 'so light was the food I
actually lost 2 lbs in this memorable period.' The
cassolette de fruits de mer (£1·25) and the soufflé de
sole aux deux sauces (£4·75) were perhaps the high
points, but other equally good judges mention the
hot turbot pâté au beurre blanc (£1·50); poached
eggs with chicken livers (80p); mousse of duck
liver, veal, and beef with a port sauce; and two fine
chicken dishes, one with morels in a sauce made
with vin jaune and marc de Jura, the other stuffed
with mousseline and (not much) foie gras. 'With an
excellent côte de boeuf I had a vol-au-vent filled
with a puree of Jerusalem artichokes; just imagine
how long that must have taken,' writes a professional
cook. In season, various fungi are imported from the
Franche-Comté for tournedos aux saveurs des
sous-bois (£4·60). Vegetables and cheeses are not
neglected, and in a check-clothed place the sweets –
such as the mousse glacée au praline (90p) and
crème brûlée au salpicon de poires – might well
astonish a visiting Frenchman used to little more
than crème caramel. The wines, from Edward
Sheldon, are admirably chosen, with ordinaire £1·80
for 50 cl, house burgundy £2·75 a bottle, and at £5
or so, a choice between Louis Latour's Mâcon-
Lugny '77, Georges Duboeuf's Chiroubles '76, and
Ch. Fombrauge '73, c.b., with many other fairly
priced clarets and burgundies. Expect too much
smoke. No music. Note the price for a well-varied
set lunch.

App: by too many members to list

(8) Quincey's
10 Little Clarendon Street
Oxford 50662

'A posh bistro on a Gallic nostalgia trip.' The main assets are 'fetching and efficient waitresses' and large main dish helpings. The menu is 'fairly free of banalities' and might offer crudités with aïoli and skordalia (£1), prawn profiteroles, smokies, Greek roast lamb with lemon and herbs (£2·30), rabbit à la moutarde (£2·10) or steak au poivre (£3·20). Prices include rice and vegetables, neither of them impeccably cooked. Chocolate mousse in a small pot 'is rich and good' (60p). Arc de Triomphe house wine, £2·50 the bottle. Recorded music. 'Our canine visitors sit outside on the steps.' Some would send smokers to join them.

Closed Sun; Mon;
Dec 25 & 26
Must book D & weekends
Meals 12–2, 7.30–10.30
(11 Fri & Sat)

Alc (min L £1·25, D £2)
£4·25 (meal £6·70)

VAT inc

Cover L 25p, D 30p
Seats 50
♿ rest
No dogs

(9) La Sorbonne
130a High Street
Oxford 41320

Closed Sun; 2 weeks Aug;
public hols
Must book
Meals 12–2.30, 7–10.30

Alc £7·15 (meal £9·50)

VAT inc
Seats 60 (parties 30)
Air-conditioning
No dogs
Am Ex, Diners

The timbers here are older than any college's, and ventilation standards are fairly medieval too. Reception and service – unless you are one of André Chavagnon's boon companions – range all the way from the abrupt to the unforgivable, though there is a certain charm in a waiter's reply, when told the chateaubriand was excellent: 'I know.' However, an inspector who took the brunt of all these faults could not withhold admiration from M Chavagnon's robust soupe de poissons marseillaise (£1·60), and delicately cooked and decorated médaillons de veau orangina (£3·10 – and good veal too) with crisp, pikelet-like potato pancakes and crunchy haricots verts. Others, also in spite of themselves in some cases, report equally good omelettes, veau à la crème, and seasonal chevreuil grand veneur or râble de lièvre sauce poivrade (quenelle de brochet lyonnaise, and suprême de volaille à l'estragon, £2·80, are also worth trying). 'Whitebait and pommes frites were negligently cooked, alas.' Sweets are not ambitious, but they are proud of their sorbets now, especially the calvados one, and a soufflé may also be attempted. Coffee is only fair. You pay £2 for 50 cl of Carafino, and wine prices for full bottles are to match: Morey St Denis '72 (Bouchard Père et Fils), £6·70; Bereich Schloss Böckelheim '77, £4·60. But dons come here to eat, not drink.

App: Helen Macintosh, Roger Baresel, O.J.P., C.J., and others

---

1979 prices are as estimated by restaurateurs in the autumn of 1978.

(10) **Sweeney Todds Pizza Parlour**
6–12 George Street
Oxford 723421 *and* 45024

'Echoing wooden cavern' a few yards from the Broad, where you steer round the loudspeakers and the arch menu prose to arrive at 'wholly admirable' pizzas (Sicilian or Neapolitan, 85p–£2·10). Soups and pies are worth a miss; and better to keep to beer (or cocktails, around 80p). Service is youthful and cheerful. Music is live sometimes. Other branches in Bath and Canterbury (reports welcome).

Closed Dec 25 & 26; Jan 1
Meals noon–midnight

Alc (min 90p) £2·90 (meal £4·90)

Service 10% (parties of 8 or more)
Seats 160
Access, Barclay, Euro

OXFORD see also wine bar section

PAINSWICK Gloucestershire   Map 2

Country Elephant
New Street
Painswick 813564

Closed L (exc Sun); Mon; Sun D; 3 weeks Oct/Nov; public hols (exc Apr 13)
Must book
Meals 12.30–2 (Sun), 7.15–10.30

Tdh Sun L £2·95 (meal £5·70)
Alc £5·35 (meal £8·45)

Service 10%
Children's helpings (Sun L)
Seats 36
&. rest (1 step)
No dogs
Am Ex, Barclay, Diners

The pink in the file for this Cotswold stone house mostly belongs to the Medforths' menus and billhead rather than to the *Guide*'s 'disapprove' forms. But there are one or two of those too for mediocre soup and chicken Kiev, along with praise for tasty grilled sardines, mushrooms with garlic and herbs in cheese sauce, prawn and cheese quiche, 'liberal' rack of lamb with herb and onion sauce (£7·55 for two, including vegetables), and pies of steak, pigeon and mushroom, or duck with sage and apple, or game. Stuffed fillet of plaice with prawns, onions and bacon also has an admirer. Vegetables may lack inspiration. Not everyone gets as far as the 'excellent' chocolate roulade, but lemon meringue pie at Sunday lunch pleased another visitor. The Lionel Bruck house burgundy, red or white (£2·95) is popular, and there are some Californian wines to be noted on the way to Ch. de Pez '67 at £6·10 and the other clarets. No music.

App: Lt Col. D. A. R. Clark, Mrs G. B. Thersby, P.B.W., L.M.L.

PAINTER'S FORSTAL Kent   Map 3

Read's
2 m SE of Faversham (M2 exit 6)
Faversham 5344

Closed Sun
Must book
Meals 12–2, 7–11

Various people over the past 18 months have nominated David and Rona Pitchford's brown-and-oatmeal restaurant in a modern single-storey building that might be mistaken for a library or clinic, but reminded an inspector of 'something in northern France' (an impression confirmed by authentic boeuf flamande). 'Outstanding' dishes have included avocado balls with fresh shrimps and prawns in a light and delicate mayonnaise, fish soup, and 'three lamb

285

Alc £6·70 (meal £9·30)

VAT inc
Children's helpings
Seats 40
🔆 rest (1 step)
Car park
No dogs
Barclay, Diners

cutlets Reform (£2·80), perfectly cooked with a very thin coating and a piquant sauce'. Flétan Toscana, and blanquette de veau à l'ancienne may be pleasing alternatives. Pommes lyonnaise and the garden vegetables (£1), including cauliflower with a correct hollandaise and mange-tout peas, keep up the standard. The menu is arranged to allow for seasonal or short-notice dishes, and also 'sudden subtractions if something runs out unexpectedly'. 'A light minty pudding' (unnamed) and others from the trolley have given pleasure, and beignets soufflés au Parmesan (90p) are a savoury alternative. Pasquier-Desvignes ordinaire is £2·85. Alsace Sylvaner is £4, Louis Latour's Beaune or Meursault over £6, and half-bottles of Sauternes £2·10. Recorded music. More reports, please.

PARKHAM Devon   Map 1

Foxdown Manor
off A39
5 m SW of Bideford
Horns Cross 325

Closed L; Jan; Feb
Must book
D only, 8 p.m.

Tdh £5 (meal £7·35)

Service 10%
Seats 36
🔆 rest
Car park
7 rooms (3 with bath, 3 with shower)
D, B&B £60–£80 p.w.
Fire cert

Belinda Luxmoore and Bruce Ross have transformed this handsome Victorian manor house into a comfortable hotel, with family cottages in the converted stables (one is suitable for a disabled person). Their ten acres provide a heated swimming-pool and a sandpit, plenty of room for games, as well as vegetables and free-range chickens and ducks. Cottagers may cater for themselves, but most adults join the hotel guests for the set six-course dinner (Belinda is Atholl-Crescent trained and has run restaurants in New York and Wales; Bruce has a financier's eating experience): asparagus or crab soups, fruits de mer en cocotte, tournedos Rossini, roast chicken or pork, peaches Grand Marnier or lemon soufflé, with generous cheeses and baskets of fruit to finish. The wine list is under revision; Choix du Roy is £2·50 the litre. Attentive service. Guests remark on the lack of noise, though a pianist plays in the drawing-room after dinner and discos may arise in the games room 'well away from the house'. No dogs, except in the cottages. More reports, please.

PENZANCE Cornwall   Map 1

Bistro One
46 New Street
Penzance 4408

Closed L; Sun; Apr 13;
Dec 25 & 26; Jan 1
Must book
D only, 7–10

Alc £5·40 (meal £8·95)

Service 10%
Cover 20p

Inevitably, after last year when everyone ate onion soup in this Victorian setting, no-one seems to have done so this time. But Roger Harris must have long tired of the topic. This year people have enjoyed his mushrooms arménienne and avocado with crab at the outset of meals that are more carefully cooked than the bistro format suggests. 'We were warmly welcomed on a cold and wet evening and were very content with John Dory Mornay and gateau with plenty of cream and kirsch.' Scampi Bréval and beef Stroganoff are called 'competent, rather than subtle or inspired', but duckling in a port sauce and chicken in a sherry one pleased another member, and sauté

Seats 30
No dogs
Am Ex, Barclay

potatoes are crisp. Syllabub and poached oranges
are also praised. Pasquier-Desvignes ordinaires are
£3·50 a litre, and Ch. Beau Rivage '73, c.b., £4·45.
Recorded music. No children under five.

App: R. C. Peattie, B.K.S., P.J.W.

PHOENIX GREEN Hampshire   Map 2

The Stilton Dish
on A30
8 m E of Basingstoke
Hartley Wintney 2107

Knick-knackery, comfortable chairs and a warm
welcome get the Schweimlers' cosy little restaurant
off to a good start with guests. The long menu
alarms, but reports describe 'excellent moules
marinière', crisp whitebait, a hearty game soup
(50p) served with tiny home-made brown rolls,
grilled langoustines with rice and salad 'impossible
to fault', and escalope de veau Mozart – the
harmonic infilling was uncharacteristically thin but
the tender meat was carefully crumbed and fried
(£2·95). Sweets are attractive: lemon meringue pie
with lemon curd filling and thick meringue, walnut
pie. Over 30 wines. Recorded music.

Closed L (exc Sat, and
by arrangement); Sun;
Apr 16; Dec 25 & 26
Meals 12.30–1.30 (Sat),
7–9.30
Must book

Alc £5·85 (meal £9·45)

VAT inc
Cover 25p
Children's helpings

Seats 35 (parties 10)
  rest (2 steps)
Car park
No dogs
Access, Am Ex, Barclay

PLUSH Dorset   Map 2

Brace of Pheasants
off B3143
2 m N of Piddletrenthide
Piddletrenthide 357

The evocative 16th-century thatched pub still
draws weekenders, but resources seem stretched at
times, and Mrs Chandler's hot sardines with lemon
and watercress, local mushrooms, and 'excellent'
boeuf en croûte do not quite erase other people's
memories of April chills, hit or miss bar lunches, sad
cheeses, and 'collapsed, icky-tasting' coffee mousse at
a test meal. Alouette ordinaires are £2·35; Chianti
Classico '74 is £3·95; Gibbs Special is in cask. No
children under 12. Smoking is rife, whichever room
you eat in.

Closed L (exc bar); Sun;
Mon (exc May–Sept);
Dec 25 & 26
Must book
Meals 11.45–1.45 (bar),
7.45–9

Alc £5·95 (meal £8·25)

VAT inc
Seats 35 (parties 20)

Car park
No dogs
3 rooms
B&B £7·50

Since each restaurant has a separate file in the Guide office, please use a separate
form or sheet of paper for each report. Additional forms may be obtained free
(no stamp required) from The Good Food Guide, Freepost,
14 Buckingham Street, London WC2N 6BR.

Warehouse
The Quay
Poole 77238

Closed Sun; Sat L;
Dec 23–Jan 2; L Apr
13 & 16; L May 28;
L Aug 27
Must book
Meals 12–2, 7–10
(11 Fri & Sat)

Alc £6·55 (meal £9)

VAT inc
Service 10%
Seats 75 (parties 35)
Access, Am Ex, Barclay,
Diners

Rachel Greig has got a new chef again, this time a young Frenchman, and though the service stuttered for a while, the food seems to have improved markedly. Grandfather clocks and the wheel of the old grain hoist decorate the place. Marc Bertrand's favourite dishes sound ambitious for the context, and we would welcome more accounts of his coquilles St Jacques en brochette (£2·25), pâté de canard à l'orange en croûte, ballotine de volaille Curnonsky ('stuffed with a rich forcemeat and creamily sauced', £3·50), and gratin de langoustine thermidor (£5). There is even a Lyonnais-style salad with a hot vinaigrette, the lot then flamed in brandy at the table, to remind you of Dorset's little oil well, perhaps. However, humbler salad of avocado and crab, fresh tomato soup in a help-yourself tureen, steaks, fish in all forms, and 'the good fresh vegetables and fruits of early summer' are all praised (but shellfish provençale would be more authentic without the cream). The 'creamy extravagances' on the sweets trolley are more appealing. Rhône red and Loire white ordinaires are £2·50 and the good Averys claret and burgundy is in most cases ludicrously marked up. No dogs. Recorded music.

Pool Court

4 m E of Otley
Arthington 842288

Closed L; Sun; Mon;
2 weeks Dec/Jan;
2 weeks July/Aug
Must book
D only, 6.30–10

Tdh from £6·45
(meal £11·60)

Seats 65 (parties 24)
⑤ rest (1 step, Regency)
Air-conditioning
(Regency)
Car park
No dogs
Barclay, Diners

The Gill family's slap-up place in the Dales is one of the few in Britain that have gone from strength to strength over the years in spite of a relatively uncritical local clientele and, last year, further extensions. Staff relations are cherished, and it shows, says one member who 'parted *happily* with £300 for a golden wedding party for 18' and another who recalls the service 'unobtrusive, timed to the second, and above all serious: Mr Gill reminds me more of a family solicitor than of an estate agent (last year's phrase).' Roger Grime cooks, as before, with 'an exact balance of richness and size of helping, so that you emerge replete but not overfaced.' The same judgement appears in the dishes themselves: 'terrine de volaille with a delicate port and mint sauce, spiced salmon with hints of dill and fennel', 'a perfect balance, again, between taste and smoothness in the mousseline of sole'. Fish is usually good, with no apologetic leftovers in the crêpes de fruits de mer. Rich main courses – 'melting' venison with Margaret Costa's Cumberland sauce, canard rôti à la façon du chef, 'crisply roasted and alluringly presented' – come with well-cooked vegetables ('chips of beetroot in a translucent honey and tarragon sauce'), and it is a pity there is no description to hand of Mr Grime's *cuisine minceur* borrowings: carrot gateau with chervil and a fresh artichoke sauce, and volaille 'truffée' au persil (actually the cheapest centre-piece of that day's set menu). Puddings run a similar gamut from Amaretti Schokoladentorte and spun-sugar confections to the 'continental fruit platter with fresh mango and a counterpoint of raspberries and strawberries'. Coffee and petits fours are now served in a separate lounge. Criticisms are very few: too much smoke sometimes, too much sugar in the bread rolls, 'first courses limited (on that night's menu) for someone who does not eat cheese'. The wine list, and Mr Gill's advice about it, both have several admirers. 'The cheapest white was a bargain'; 'we were warned off a starred wine because it had deteriorated, and Muscat les Amandiers '73 was superb' ('75 is now £7·55). Clarets and burgundies are exemplary: not many half-bottles but, irresistibly, a full run of Ch. Cissac for every sound year since 1962, between £6·30 and £15·65. No music.

App: R. J. Stansbridge, R.K., J. B. Wilkin, Shirley Wise, John Wilkes, A. J. Murison, and others

---

PORLOCK WEIR Somerset   Map 1

Ship Inn
on B3225
1½ m NW of Porlock
Porlock 862753

Must book D & Sun L
Meals 12.30–1.45,
7.30–8.45

Tdh L from £3 (meal
£5·15), D from £5 (meal
£7·50)

Seats 24 (parties 24)
 rest (2 steps)
Car park
No dogs in public rooms
6 rooms (all with bath)
B&B £7–£10

Many sons of family catering businesses think of the life as a meal ticket till doomsday. Pandy Sechiari gives every sign of enjoying both work and customers, and visitors seem to respond, in spite of the alterations and extensions that are making a little more space and comfort in a seaside inn that was already old when it was first altered in 1651. Mr Sechiari and his chef are proud of their taramosalata, steak and kidney pie, and crab thermidor. The value given is fair, and menus enterprising, with boudin aux pommes a favourite first course, and sound pâté auvergnate and cream of onion soup, then 'real mayonnaise with lobster salad at a meal price (£5) that some would charge for the one dish', tongue with madeira sauce, and conventionally rich puddings, or perhaps hot mince tart. Bass and Courage bitters are on hand pumps, and there are lunchtime snacks in bar or courtyard. Primanova Italian ordinaires are £2·70 a litre or 60p for a large glass. The David Baillie Vintners wines rise to Ch. Cantemerle '67, c.b., at £6, and include half-bottles of sweet Cérons at £1·80 or glasses of late-bottled Taylor port at 65p. No music. No pipes at table. 'No shorts', and Mr Sechiari evidently feels young enough at 26 to discourage children.

App: R. D. & S. A. Mackay, Rita Masseron, Robert McFarland, Drs B. & A. Henderson-Sellers, and others

---

'VAT inc' means that an inn's policy is to incorporate VAT in its food prices.

That Mott
Cliff Road
Helston 62460

'*A southerly gale at spring tide could bring the sea up over this mott*', and the young, inexperienced proprietors also worry about a spring tide of exacting members. But they have already pleased people with their marinated mushrooms, crab (by special request), fresh-grilled megrim with good vegetables and salad, and amateurish but agreeable sweets. 'Pouilly Fumé '76 (£2·60 the half) was correctly served but they put a bottle of Côtes du Rhône on the Calor gas heater to warm up.' Recorded music. Details are approximate; ask about closures. More reports, please.

Must book

Tdh D £4·75 (meal £6·80)   VAT inc
Seats 28

Slipway Hotel
Port Isaac 264

Quiet, small hotel with pleasant, galleried dining-room. No lunches. The set meals are stressed, usually with a choice of meat or fish for main course (local turbot, skate, John Dory, sea trout). Lobsters and steaks are reserved for the *carte*. Soups and bread are home-made. Carafe is La Vie de France (£2·30 for 75 cl, 45p the glass); about 35 other St Austell Brewery wines. No music. Emphatically no dogs. Parking for residents only.

Closed L; mid-Oct to Easter
Must book
D only, 7.45–9.30

Tdh £5 (meal £7·20)
Alc meal about £8·65

VAT inc
Seats 40

Children's helpings (under 12)
11 rooms (2 with shower)
D, B&B £13–£16
Fire cert

Gerrans Bay Hotel
Gerrans
Portscatho 338

People still enjoy their stays, Hilda Addison's cooking, 'and Mr Key's dry wit', at this quiet hotel on the upper road. 'They are particularly good with sole (in a white wine sauce).' Roast topside of beef with horseradish sauce is another favourite, and 'though residents have no choice of main course, an alternative is offered if you ask.' Start with shrimp flan, perhaps; end with treacle tart or apple pie with cream. Argentine Estancia wines are £2·80 a litre. Recorded music. No resident under-tens. Car park.

Closed L (exc Sun);
Apr 15 D; Oct 16
Must book
Meals 12.30–1.30 (Sun),
7–8

Tdh Sun L £3·30 (meal £5·40), D £4·95 (meal £7·20)

Service inc
Children's helpings (under 7 Sun)

Seats 50
♿ rest (1 step)
No dogs in public rooms
Access, Am Ex, Barclay
15 rooms (12 with bath)
B&B from £8·25
Fire cert

POTTERS BAR Hertfordshire   Map 3

Potters Lodge
Barnet Road
Potters Bar 59976

The Nichols and Nicola brothers cater to traditional and ethnic tastes in the Barnet Road with prawn cocktail and steak Diane ('may cause delay of up to half an hour') or sousoukakia (spiced meat balls) and stifado. Note the cover charge, and 15p surcharge for cream. Hatch Mansfield wine list, with Greek and Cypriot bottles among the cheapest. French carafe £2·40. 'International' recorded music. 'No jeans, please.'

Closed Sun; Dec 25 & 26;
L Jan 1
Must book D & weekends
Meals 12–2.45, 6–11.45

Alc £3·55 (meal £5·90)

VAT inc
Service 10%
Cover 30p
Children's helpings
(under 11)

Seats 60
rest; w.c.
Car park
No dogs
Access, Am Ex, Barclay,
Diners

POUNDISFORD Somerset   Map 2

Well House

3½ m S of Taunton
Blagdon Hill 566

Closed L (exc Sun); Sun D
Must book
Meals 12.30–1.30 (Sun only), 7–9

Tdh Sun L £4·25
(meal £6·80), D £5·25
(meal £8·30)

Children's helpings
(Sun L)
Seats 40
rest (1 step)
Car park
No dogs

It is always gratifying when a restaurant that earns its first pestle lives up to the expectations of members, and especially so when a total change of team in the kitchen still leaves a critical visitor saying: 'Clearly deserves it. Delicious tomato and herb soup, excellent lamb and vegetables and equally excellent puddings.' True, the new chef-manager, Graham Cornish, comes from the Horn of Plenty in Gulworthy (q.v.) via Hatch Beauchamp (see the 1978 Guide). Less clear, even to himself, is the future extent of Laurie Boston's own involvement, now that he is giving his own health some of the care he has lavished on his partner Ralph Vivian Neal's historic house, which a team of energetic young people have built up to its present repute. The prix fixe meals offer no more than four choices in each course, and less than that for Sunday lunch, but have seemed excellent value to people who have encountered Dutch beetroot salad, haddock mousse, chicken liver pâté, 'ecstatically received' poached chicken with peppers and cardamom, sweetbreads Catalan, 'more pommes dauphinoise than even addicts could finish', 'impeccable' grapefruit sorbet, rhubarb and ginger compote, and Russian paskha (cream cheese, cream, and chopped glacé fruits). English Sunday joints and cheeses are also beyond reproach. Various good merchants help Mr Boston with the wines, and on the list make their own nominations of bargains that have helped to keep sound basic drinking here below £4. (Note too wines from Gaillac and Cahors that were unfashionable when their cause was first espoused.) At higher levels, some prices and niggardly vintage information may be criticised, but

291

it is worth looking first at the Beaujolais and burgundies, from Chiroubles '76 at £5·60 to 'blockbusting' Bonnes-Mares '70 (Averys) at £18. There are also nice hocks, halves of sweet Cérons, and a red or white wine by the glass if you want it. No smoking. No music. While the 'pestle' pends to allow the new regime to settle, please report in detail.

App: C. R. Doherty, John Halliday, T. D. Hemming, H.P., T. McK. Shortt, and others

---

POYNINGS West Sussex Map 3

Au Petit Normand
2 The Street
off A281
6 m NW of Brighton
Poynings 346

Closed L (exc Sun); Mon;
Feb
Must book
Meals 12–2 (Sun), 7–9.30
(10 Sat)

Tdh L (Sun) £3 & £4
(meal from £5·50)
Alc £5·75 (meal £8·80)

VAT inc
Cover L 15p, D 40p
Children's helpings
Seats 22
Access, Am Ex, Barclay

Everyone seems to wish Christian and Wendy Debu well in their tiny home-made restaurant (they are both graduates from Brighton's Le Français in Yves Bottasso's time). The à la carte and set lunch menus are at least short enough for tastes to be genuine, and people have reported good ficelle normande, onion soup, tripes à la mode de Caen, filet St Pierre dieppoise, and other dishes from the French littoral. 'I had salmon mousse followed by delicious canard aux poires' (£2·70). 'Tender and tasty gigot was accompanied by mange-tout peas.' But inspectors' goodwill was strained by a long smoky wait for good mousse de truite au poivre vert (£1·50), and optimistically sauced escalope cauchoise and médaillons de boeuf périgourdine, ending with 'rather soft' tarte normande and 'dire' coffee. Vin du patron is £2·95, or try the Norman cider at £1·85. (If this can be sold successfully, why don't more places find the elusive but good and relatively cheap English equivalents produced here and there?) No dogs. More reports, please.

PRIOR'S HARDWICK Warwickshire Map 2

Butcher's Arms
5 m SE of Southam
Byfield 60504

Closed Sun D
Must book D
Meals 12.30–2.30,
7.30–11.30

Tdh L from £2·70
(Sun £3·25) meal £5·30
Alc £5·10 (meal £8·15)

Service 10%
Seats 90 (parties 38)
♿ rest (3 steps)
Car park
No dogs

Like some butchers, Lino Pires' 600-year-old inn is high on temperament, and moods seem to change as rapidly as his countrymen change governments. Critical visitors, as well as the local industrial or farming families who throng the place at Sunday lunch, have found Mr Pires charming and generous, but another who dined in one of the not infrequent go-slow periods had his head bitten off when he grumbled. The food, though, sounds consistent, apart from a poor May Day lunch. One visitor 'had never had a better Christmas turkey'; another recommends nearly everything on the menu from gazpacho and grilled sardines as first courses to the grills and roasts and more expensive langoustines a la plancha (£4·95). A test Sunday lunch proved a bargain, for the terrine of venison was well flavoured if slightly dry, steak and kidney pie good with crunchy cabbage from their own gardens, and

292

an expertly made crème caramel with 'more lovely yellow cream' to pour over it. Wines, from £2·85, are surprising, whether you are a party taking a double magnum of Ch. La Lagune '73, c.b., at £30 (not a bad price), or a couple trying one of the Portuguese estate-bottlings, Garrafeira Particular Caves Alianca '63 at £4·95. A half-bottle of Rebello Valente '63 port is £4. No music. There are weekday lunchtime bar snacks with pressurised beers.

App: F. E. Ford, Michael Copp, M.J.M., and others

PULBOROUGH West Sussex   Map 3

Stane Street Hollow
Codmore Hill
on A29
Pulborough 2819

Closed Sun; Mon; Sat L;
last 2 weeks Apr; 3 weeks
Nov; Dec 25 & 26
Must book
Meals 12.30–1.15,
7.15–9.15

Tdh L £2·05 (meal £4·50)

Alc £4·20 (meal £7·05)

VAT inc
Children's helpings
Seats 36 (parties 20)
♿ rest
Car park
No dogs

Everyone likes the Kaisers and the efficiency – 'Swiss but charming' – with which they run their cottage-style restaurant, hen-run, and vegetable garden. At tests of both the set lunches and the more leisurely dinners, inspectors felt more confident than is common in this district of the sincerity with which materials are chosen and cooked. Lunch may be veal Marengo or 'rather textureless' goulash followed by a fruit fool. Julienne of tripe in a minestra pointed to courage; eggs en cocotte and apple fritters argued technical competence too, 'if you did not mind crunchy onion in the first.' Crêpe à l'aiglefin (75p) is another first course speciality. Among main dishes, duck with gooseberry sauce was 'one of the best restaurant ducks I can remember for flavour and crispness' and another visitor's caneton Chambertin was equally good, with delicious courgettes, spinach puree and new potatoes, though 'the Chambertin might have been applied with a spray.' Other good dishes include sweetbreads, noisettes d'agneau René (£3·85 with vegetables), and suprême de volaille fribourgeoise. The taste of sour-cream cheesecake and fresh raspberry puree is as irresistible as the name in Quark Kuchen mit Himbeeren (85p), and vacherin with coffee parfait or choux bun with bananas are also praised. Coffee is likewise good value. The ordinaires are Nicolas at £1·80 for 50 cl. Among other wines, Sancerre '76 and Barolo '73 under £4, and fine hocks and moselles around £5, cast a certain light on other people's prices. Recorded music in the bar only.

App: J. R. Tyrie, John Sherlock, Blanche Holmes, J. & R.C., M.E., A.J.V.B., and others

---

Entries for places with distinctions carry symbols (pestle, tureen, bottle, glass). Credits are fully written entries, with approvers' names below the text. Passes are telegraphic entries (useful in the area) with details under the text. Provisional entries are in italics (see 'How to use the Guide', p. 4).

The Bell at Ramsbury
5 m NW of Hungerford
Ramsbury 230

Closed Mon; Sun D;
Apr 13; last 2 weeks
Aug; Dec 25 & 26;
Jan 1; first 2 weeks Feb
Must book D & Sun L
Meals 12.15–1.45,
7.15–9.45

Tdh L (exc Sun) £4·75
(meal £7·35), D & Sun L
£5·50 (meal £8·15)
Alc £8·50 (meal £11·45)

VAT inc
Service 10%
Children's helpings
Seats 60 (parties 40)
⑤ rest (1 step)
Air-conditioning
Car park
Am Ex, Diners

Brian O'Malley takes his own enthusiasms seriously, and though in his youth he bade fair to be 'everything by starts and nothing long', he has kept this bow-fronted inn in the *Guide* for a dozen years now. Log fires in the bar make a warm welcome, and though the food is robust rather than delicate, regular visitors seem happy to make allowances. Trout, mackerel pâté and pork loin, all smoked, make good beginnings on the set menu (nowadays called 'the Ordinary'), and salmon, devilled kidneys, and escalope of pork with mushrooms and cream are praised among main dishes. So is the steak and venison pie, though sometimes it is very obviously more steer than stag. Proprietorial favourites include salmon and turbot bisque (£1·25) and Dublin Bay prawns with dill-weed sauce (£2). Cold sweets are generally alcoholic and vigorously priced à la carte if they do not happen to figure on the Ordinary. Service may need more guidance. The bar snacks are substantial variants of what is offered in the main restaurant; Wadworth and IPA beers are on hand-pump. The wines come from Berry Bros, and are fairly priced though not always fairly treated, according to a member whose '66 Corton should have been decanted, not cradled. Ordinary claret is £3·10, Sauvignon or Sancerre (n.v.) a little more, and there are good '71 clarets in the £6–£8 range. No music. No pipes or cigars in the restaurant. No children under ten at night.

App: A. T. Langton, P. G. Urben, T. M. Wilson, E.S., C.N., A. C. Tozer, and others

Mallet's
58 Queen Street
Thanet 52854

Closed Sun; Mon; most
public hols
Must book D & weekends
Meals 12.30–2, 7.30–10.30

Alc L £3·75 (meal £6),
D £5·10 (meal £7·60)

VAT inc
Cover 30p
Children's helpings
Seats 35
⑤ rest
Access, Barclay

The frontage is 'typical Ramsgate', which is a compliment, and the food is not typical Ramsgate, which is also a compliment, for Simon Mallet used to be Michael Waterfield's partner at Wye (q.v.) and in this little place which he has opened with his wife 'everything seems home-made, even the bread and the fudge, and is varied, original, and over-generous.' Spinach and orange soup (55p), squid cocktail, 'delicate fennel fritters with a gentle tomato and garlic sauce', bream with sorrel, sea bass in pastry with dill cream, and pork cutlets with apricots are contained in that and other early descriptions. A few true trenchermen have soldiered as far as walnut and treacle tart, 'thick, heavy, nutty and soft' hazelnut ice-cream, or lychees with cream cheese. Coffee is good. The short wine list naturally includes Waterfield's Marriage Hill (£3·85). House wines (Costières du Gard red) are £2·40 the bottle. Recorded music. More reports, please.

REDLYNCH Wiltshire   Map 2

Langley Wood
off B3080
6 m SE of Salisbury
Earldoms 348

Enquire for directions through the wood when you book an evening's table at the Pearces' isolated suburban-style house. No raptures this year, but people like the tomato and orange soup, gougère or quiche, followed by veal with black cherries or filet de porc en croûte, with 'moderate' vegetables (spinach and courgettes sound the best). Expect about a dozen choices in each course. 'Champagne Charlie was full of well-blended orange, lemon and wine flavours', but 'the heat hadn't reached the middle of the apple tart.' Hallgarten Bordeaux is £2·60, and the choice beyond is fair. Pressurised beer. No music now. No children under eight. Wear a tie for preference.

Closed L; Sun;
Dec 25 & 26; Jan 1
Must book
D only, 7.30–9.30

Alc £6·65 (meal £9·25)

VAT inc
Children's helpings

Seats 40
♿ rest (1 step); w.c. (m)
Car park
No dogs

REDRUTH Cornwall   Map 1

Basset Count House
Carnkie
between B3297 & A30
1 m SW of Redruth
Redruth 215181

Closed Sun; Sat L;
Apr 13; Dec 26; Jan 1
Must book D & weekends
Meals 12–2, 7–10

Alc £6·35 (meal £8·80)

VAT inc
Children's helpings L
Seats 95
Car park
Diners card

Yet another change has put the Pages into this lush Italianate restaurant in the old tin-mine count house. A test meal included duck and bacon terrine with a crisp salad, scallops Mornay, veal in a white wine sauce with fresh tomatoes and peppers, and pork cooked in cider with orange peel strips. Vegetables, moreover, were above the Cornish norm, particularly courgettes in batter, French beans, and sauté potatoes. The cheeses are perfunctory and the bread mass-market, but most people no doubt prefer the fresh fruit salad or the strawberry meringue, possibly even with extra Cornish cream at 30p for kamikaze diners. The Hicks wines (from £2·60) are adequate: Ch. Rausan-Ségla '70, £6·70. The previous owners left behind them a very well-stocked bar, and it sounds as though there were a few tins of this and that in the kitchen cupboard too, perhaps by now used up. A guitarist sometimes plays on Saturday evenings. No dogs. More reports, please.

REETH North Yorkshire   Map 8

Burgoyne Hotel
9 m W of Richmond
Reeth 292

Closed L (exc Sun);
Nov 1–Apr 13
Must book

Textiles and music are married in the Cordingleys, and they have both been married to this stone-built house for ten years, with three bedrooms still to decorate because they really prefer talking to people. And cooking, of course, though they find the diet fads of contemporary customers as puzzling as 'the rise in the number of feather allergies'. Neither the decor nor the cuisine are *haute*, but inspectors and others enjoy soup, rice-stuffed peppers, steak

Meals 1–1.45 (Sun),
7.30–8.15

Tdh Sun L £2·40 (meal
£4·20), D £4·45 (meal
£6·65)

Service 10%
Children's helpings
Seats 35
⟨♿⟩ rest
No dogs in d/r
9 rooms
B&B £6·35
Fire cert

and kidney pie, beef in beer, duckling, steaks and –
welcome revival – boiled mutton with caper sauce,
on the short, easily priced set menus. Brûlées, hot
gingerbread and cream, and Dacquoise are Mrs
Cordingley's favourite sweets, though one couple
calls kissel 'the one memorable feature' in this
section; another likes the lemon summer gateau.
The large breakfasts are liked. Spanish red and
Hungarian white wines are £1·35 for 50 cl and the
Cameron list is undistinguished; but consider the
Rioja '71 at £3, or Mouton Cadet '75 at £4·75, with
the farmhouse Wensleydale, or fall back on the
pressurised bitter. Small car park.

App: Prof & Mrs Ian Oswald, L. M. Luscombe,
A.V., D. G. Barlow, R.C.R.

RIPON North Yorkshire   Map 8

Hornblower
Duck Hill
Ripon 4841

'A surprisingly elegant little place to find in a rather
down-at-heel town' is a back-handed local compliment,
but he adds, 'everything is as cool and quiet as the
patronne.' Service can be slow, though. Mrs
Weston's husband cooks the sort of food they
themselves like, on a set and seldom changed menu,
with a dish of the day for slight variety. Inspectors
found flavours bland on the whole, but there is
praise for aubergine gratinée, cheese poppets,
chicken Delmonico, veal viscayenne, profiteroles and
chocolate mousse. Vegetables are good. Rhône wines
remain good value; house claret, French-bottled, is
£3·25. No music. Children must eat early.

Closed L; Sun; Mon;
Dec 25 & 26; Jan 1
Must book
D only, 7.30–9.30

Tdh from £5·50
(meal £7·85)

VAT inc

Children's helpings
(under 10)
Seats 22
No dogs

RIPPONDEN West Yorkshire   Map 5

Over the Bridge
on A58
6 m SW of Halifax
Ripponden 3722

This tranquil, flower-bedecked restaurant lies 'over
the bridge' from the related Bridge Inn (which is
open for buffet lunches, £2). It serves set dinners,
mainly to contented regulars, who appreciate the
careful cooking and service of tomato and orange
soup, baked stuffed clams, sole Véronique, sauté
kidneys, game (at a small supplement), rum tart or
summer pudding. No wine details this time, but 'the
port is properly decanted.' No music. No children
under ten.

Closed L; Sun; Apr 16;
Aug 27; Dec 25 & 26;
Jan 1
Must book
D only, 7.30–9.30

Tdh £6·75 (meal £8·80)

Seats 45
⟨♿⟩ rest (1 step)

Car park
No dogs
Cheques by arrangement
Am Ex card

ROMILEY Greater Manchester Map 5

Waterside Restaurant
166 Stockport Road
3 m E of Stockport
between A560 & A626
061-430 4302

Closed Mon; Sun D;
Sat L; Apr 13; Dec 25 &
26; Jan 1
Must book
Meals 12–1.45, 7–9.30

Tdh L £3 (meal £4·85)

Alc £5·70 (meal £7·75)

Service inc
Seats 36
 ⟦&⟧ rest
Car park
No dogs
Access card

One visitor found the Smalls' restaurant rather cold and dispirited at the nadir of the year, but a veteran inspector who made the trip out from Manchester for lunch as the weather got warmer complained only of the number of Stockport Roads he seemed to traverse before finding this medieval cottage by the canal. An excellent fish soup, Oxford sausages, and a blackcurrant and apple tart 'with very short pastry and lots of cream' sent him home markedly heavier but not much poorer. Dinner is dearer but there is general praise for 'a real home-made cock-a-leekie', 'delicious champignons frits', 'pâté made to an old family recipe', and for main course perhaps turbot Christine, salmon trout, tournedos farci fougère (£3·25) or 'an almost excessive helping of game pie'. Tipsy hedgehog is another family favourite. The Gilbey wines (from £2·50 a litre for Valpolicella or Soave) are adequate if you control their service a little: ask the vintages before paying upwards of £5 for Ch. Léoville-Barton or Ch. Pichon-Longueville that may not be ready to drink, and retire perhaps to Gewürztraminer or Barolo. Pressurised beers. Recorded classical music.

App: Cherry Ann Knott, J. F. M. West, G.B., M.M., Michael Hicks, and others

ROWSLEY Derbyshire Map 5

Peacock Hotel
3 m S of Bakewell
Darley Dale 3518

A comfortable and well-run Allied Breweries' house and garden by the Derwent, at the gates of Haddon Hall (fish for brown trout and grayling here, rainbow trout on the Wye). The set meals – 3-course at lunch, 4-course at dinner – offer rather limited choice (with heavy surcharges for prawn or crab cocktails and smoked fish): lasagne, cold cucumber soup, sweetbreads in tomato sauce, steak and kidney pie, salmon hollandaise (£1 extra), 'creamy' black cherry ice-cream or waffles with maple syrup. Complaints are courteously and sensibly received. Nicolas house wine, £4·10 the litre, £2·80 the bottle. Cold bar snacks, except on Sundays and public holidays, with Burton ale from the cask. No music.

Must book weekends
Meals 12.30–1.30, 7–9
(8 Sun)

Tdh L from £3·65 (meal £5·35), D £6·35 (meal £7·30)

VAT & service inc
Children's helpings
(under 12)
Seats 50 (parties 30)
Car park
No dogs in public rooms

Access, Am Ex, Barclay,
Diners, Euro
20 rooms (11 with bath,
4 with shower)
B&B £8–£10·50
Fire cert

Andalucia
10 Henry Street
Rugby 76404

Closed Dec 25 D
Must book
Meals 12–2.30, 7 (Sat &
Sun 6.30)–11 (Sun 10)

Tdh L £2·75 (meal £5·65)
Alc £5·70 (meal £9·40)

Cover 20p D
Children's helpings
(under 10)
Seats 120 (parties 50)
⎣ rest
No dogs
Access, Am Ex, Barclay,
Diners

The Izquierdos and their chef Carlos Garcia (whose thoughts, duly translated into 'Chef's English', figure largely on the à la carte menu) have reigned as cock restaurant in Rugby for 12 years, and some inspectors think them overdue for toppling, after over-trumpeted shellfish Mornay and Carlos' Temptation (a Dover sole dish) at brassbound prices (£3·50 and £4·50) that grate somewhat in these modest, bar-less surroundings. Sweets are best ignored. But, if you keep your head and take the place at commonsense evaluation rather than at its own, the paella (three versions, from £2·75), zarzuela, kidneys al Jerez, and other Spanish classics are normally admirable, and the set lunch is ungrasping: 'The new menu features monk-fish grenobloise which is extremely good.' They bottle their own Rioja in Spain, keep good Fino, and a range of red and white Spanish wines that are commoner than they used to be, but a surprise here still: Viña Tondonia '69 white, £5·25, and '61 red, £6·50 (both Lopez de Heredia bottlings). A guitarist plays most nights. More reports, please.

The Monastery
6 High Street
Rye 3272

Far-from-ascetic restaurant-with-rooms in the town centre. Floodlit ruins, a peppermint-and-white decor, and classical tapes set off food which has sometimes let people down this time. No complaints about guinea-fowl, pepper steak, trout with celery and almonds, and the Romney roast lamb. But first-course ingredients, 'variable' vegetables, and ice-cream-based sweets may not live up to the rest. 'Pleasant, welcoming service' at times. Varied clientele. House wine is St Pierre, £1·95 for 50 cl, 55p the glass (6 oz). Note that lunches are served in summer only. No children under seven.

Closed Tue; Wed L;
L Oct–May (exc Sun);
Mon–Wed (Nov–Easter)
Must book
Meals 12.30–2
(June–Sept), 7–9.30

Tdh L £3 (meal £5·70)
Alc £5·60 (meal £8·55)

VAT inc
Service 10%
Cover 20p D

Seats 46
⎣ rest
No dogs
7 rooms (6 with shower)
B&B £8–£9·50
Fire cert

RYE see also pub section

Numbers are given for private parties only if they can be accommodated in a room separate from the main dining-room; when there are several such rooms, the capacity of the largest is given. Some restaurants will take party bookings at times when they are normally closed.

ST ALBANS Hertfordshire Map 3

Aspelia
17 Heritage Close
St Albans 66067

A lively place in a shopping precinct, attentively served by the Charalambous family. The cooking is Greek-Cypriot, though seasoned travellers long for more vigour with olive oil and garlic. You eat either in the basement wine bar or upstairs in the main restaurant (or outside in summer): taramosalata (by itself or with avocado), calamares, afelia (pork with wine and coriander, £2·75), moussaka (£2·05) or, perhaps, meze, a taste of most of the menu for £4·75. Pitta, salad and coffee are authentic, and the house wine is drinkable (£2·55 for 70 cl). 'Classical Greek' music on record, and candles, of course. No children under five.

Closed Sun; Apr 16;
Dec 25, 26 & 31; Jan 1
Must book D
Meals 12–3, 6.30–11

Alc £4·75 (meal £7·55)

VAT inc
Cover 50p
Seats 82
♿ rest
Air-conditioning

Car park
No dogs
Access, Am Ex, Barclay,
Diners, Euro

ST DOMINICK Cornwall Map 1

Cotehele House
off A390 *or* A388
2 m E of St Dominick
St Dominick 50434

You pay the National Trust entrance fee to eat at this medieval barn whether you view the 15th-century manor or not, but people seem to regard this 'cover charge' as more than reasonable for 'superb' cream of onion soup; fresh local mackerel; homely savoury pies; plump chicken and home-cooked ham for the cold buffet; a strawberry cream sponge 'about a foot high'. Cornish cream teas, too. Licensed. Countryman cider from Milton Abbot. No air-conditioning but 'plenty of fresh air' and no smoking. No music.

Closed D; Nov–Mar
Open 11–5.30
(L 12–2.30)

Alc £2·55 (meal £4·45)

VAT inc
Children's helpings
Seats 80

♿ rest (1 step); w.c.
Car park
No dogs

ST IVES Cambridgeshire Map 6

Slepe Hall
Rugeley's Restaurant
Ramsey Road
St Ives (Cambs) 63122
and 62824

Closed Dec 25 & 26
Must book
Meals 12–2.15, 7–9.45

'Strong men have blanched and shot their wives, rather than send them to St Ives', is a line the Editor found himself murmuring after being buttonholed about his shortcomings by Mrs Scott, who shares the cooking here with James Edwards. But never mind, she and her husband have turned the Revd John Rugeley's 19th-century school for young ladies into a pretty pink-and-brown restaurant with a 'very well-run' hotel attached, according to the experienced inspectors who followed up one or two nominations in 1978. One of

Tdh (D res only) £4·35
(meal £7·15)
Alc (exc Sun L) £6·45
(meal £9·65)

Children's helpings
Seats 60 (parties 28)
♿ rest (1 step)
Car park
No dogs in d/r
Access, Am Ex, Barclay,
Diners, Euro
15 rooms (9 with bath)
B&B £11–£12·85
Fire cert

the set menus may include 'a sound version of Bell Inn smokies', a fluffy, buttery mushroom flan, good roast beef and Yorkshire pudding with 'unassisted' gravy on the trolley, and chocolate truffle 'stunningly hedgehogged' with flakes. They also offer as favourite dishes a spinach and cheese pancake (for vegetarians and others, £1·40), grilled lemon sole with herb butter (£4·25 à la carte), and venison in various ways (though it is unlikely to be high, and may well be under-seasoned). Vegetables leave room for improvement. The buffet lunch is praised, and there are evening bar snacks too. The service, though inexperienced in wine, responds well. Wines, from £2·70 for Bouchard Aîné et Fils red or white burgundy, mostly hover above £5, but at least below £8 for château-bottled Chx. Beychevelle and Batailley. Various beers. Dress smartly. Recorded music.

ST JUST IN PENWITH Cornwall   Map 1

Count House
off B3306
1 m N of St Just
St Just 788588

Closed L (exc Sun); Mon
(exc public hols D); Tue;
Sun D
Must book
Meals 12.30–1.45,
7.30–10

Tdh Sun L £2·95 (meal £4·95)
Alc £5·30 (meal £7·85)

VAT inc
Children's helpings
Seats 30
Car park
No dogs
Access, Am Ex, Barclay,
Diners, Euro

From St Just on the B3306, take the second left past the Queen's Arms to find Ian and Ann Long's 'sociable and delightful' restaurant contrived out of the old Botallack mine buildings, with memorable views of sunsets and the Scillies. 'Every time, I leave looking forward to my next visit,' says one lucky man of Kent exiled to Cornwall, for Mrs Long varies her short menus cleverly. Prawn with cream cheese and onion, chowder (80p) or Stilton and onion soup (75p), salmon mousse flavoured with orange (£1·10), chicken and veal loaf, ballotine of duck (£3·10), and roast leg of lamb stuffed with minted crab and a mild curry sauce are among the dishes she or her guests nominate, and the value given at Sunday lunch is 'amazing': 'green pea and mint soup, abundantly filled steak and kidney pie with olives, admirable cauliflower, courgettes, carrots, and rich butter-baked potatoes, and outstanding puddings, with chocolate mint (again) cheesecake, raspberry oatmeal gateau, and the very apotheosis of lemon meringue'. With prior warning it seems that they will do anything from 'crawfish to a birthday cake', and they may suggest you write home about it. The wine list is being rewritten, but for the time being Argentine Estancia is £2·95 a litre, and on the short, unvintaged wine list, English Lamberhurst Priory is £3·85 and Mouton Cadet £4·65. No music.

App: Mike Bristow, P. F. Marnham, N.F., and others

ST JUST IN PENWITH see also pub section

ST MARTIN IN MENEAGE Cornwall   Map 1

Boskenna

off B3293
5 m SE of Helston
Manaccan 230

Closed L; Dec 24, 25 & 26
Must book
D only (res), 7.30–8

Tdh £4

VAT inc
Service 10%
Seats 8
[access] rest (1 step); w.c.
Car park
No dogs
Unlicensed
4 rooms (1 with bath)
B&B from £6·50

One member returned from 'four heavenly days being waited on by Mr and Mrs Munro' so overcome by the hospitality that he sat down to 'tell everyone about this place that the *Guide* led us to', even before he had unpacked his suitcases. Almost equally good examples have been set by others anxious to repay the natural welcome, rich but fine cooking, and unusual value they have found at this civilised house. Remember, first of all, that residents only are fed, with no choice till the sweet stage, and that you must bring your own liquor. Guests may feel almost too at home: 'One man asked to have four bottles of wine opened for his dinner'; 'My friend and I ate crème caramel and treacle tart for breakfast the last day because we had no room the night before.' The best dishes seem to include the devilled local crabs, consommé with cream and caviare, lasagne, and mushrooms provençale; then 'thick slices of Cornish lamb with mint jelly'; 'roast pork with crackling and an original aubergine garnish'; 'the *beau idéal* of roast duck'; roast beef and steak and kidney pie; garden vegetables and pommes dauphinoise; finally raspberry bliss, pear crème brûlée, and kinky pie. Breakfasts to match make midday hikes compulsory. No music. No children under 14. No pipes or cigars. No open necks (male) at dinner; and apart from a few minor culinary points, no breath of rebuke in reports.

App: S. Damaluji, Ron Graham, F. Power, O.K., G. R. & J. F. Pritchett, R. Gromb, and others

ST MAWES Cornwall   Map 1

Green Lantern
Marine Parade
St Mawes 502

Closed L (exc Sun);
Mid-Dec to mid-Feb
Must book
Meals 12.30–2.30 (Sun),
7–9.30

Tdh Sun L £3 (meal £5·10), D £6 (meal £8·65)

Service 10%
Seats 52
Am Ex, Barclay, Diners
11 rooms (5 with bath)
B&B from £7·50
D, B&B from £12·50
Fire cert

The Browns are no country bumpkins when it is a matter of managing and cooking for a simple family-served hotel 'where all residents are given their own front door keys.' But pressures were heavy in 1978 and 'significant blemishes' or 'monotonous vegetables over a week' or 'hors d'oeuvre put together too long in advance' have betrayed them at busy times. Still, the deep-fried mushrooms with garlic mayonnaise, whitebait, coquilles St Jacques, sole fillets in a wine and shrimp sauce, and 'plain roast duck with crisp, rich skin and apple sauce on the side', suggest that when timing is of the essence, Mrs Brown can still be depended upon. There is no need to spend more than about £3·50 on good wine, and Rocamar is £2 a pint. No children under ten. No dogs. Recorded music. Pressurised beers.

App: W.G., L.P.C., B.M.

Rising Sun
St Mawes 233

Closed Dec 24, 25 & 26
Must book D
Meals 1–1.45, 7.30–8.45

Alc (min £4) £6 (meal
£8·85)

Service 10%
Seats 50
[&] rest (2 steps)
Air-conditioning
Car park
No dogs in d/r
20 rooms (14 with bath,
2 with shower)
Prices on application
Fire cert

Mrs Campbell Marshall's gem-like hotel by the
sea-front, with its flowers and china cabinets and
'breakfasts ideal for après-beachcombing', changes
little, as one would expect after forty years. At the
price, members are less impressed by Jeffry West's
à la carte menu than they were by the old table
d'hôte, which they voted good value year after
year, and a Sunday luncher in May found the food
'over-complicated' and the waiting slack. Still,
other reports and an inspection later left much to
praise: fried mushrooms stuffed with pâté (£1·35),
avocado and grapefruit salad, trout and almond
mousse (95p), roast pheasant or grouse with
appropriate trimmings, sauté of venison steaks with
'nicely tart' fresh pineapple, and fish of course:
notably sole with braised fennel, or salmon peel
baked with asparagus. Sweets are mostly ice-cream-
based. Wines, though limited, are decently priced,
with Gewürztraminer '75 (Hugel) just over £4, and
Ch. Beychevelle '73, c.b., £6·40. Yugoslav Riesling
is £2·33. No music. No children under ten as
residents.

App: Mrs J. Harries, Richard Bond, M.B.K.

**Rivermede Country
House Hotel**
on A586
9 m NW of Preston
St Michaels 267 *and* 653

'Four clear rounds and good marks for dressage,'
quips an irreverent spectator of the Fieldings'
feminine, horse-struck country-house hotel in the
Fylde, worlds away from Blackpool lights (but near
enough for top Tory and BBC signatures in the
visitors' book to be good for a giggle). The four-
course set dinners continue to please, with cream of
lovage and sorrel soup, green summer pâté, lettuce
and shrimp roulade, roast quail, steak au poivre
vert, lemon ice-box and raspberry Pavlova. Club
dinners, cookery courses and a popular Friday night
cold buffet are among the sidelines. Sidi Larbi or
Yugoslav Riesling is £3·75 the litre, 45p the glass.
Recorded classical music. 'Chintzy' service.
Children are asked to behave well, smokers to
desist, and mint-eaters 'not to feed Ben and
Rumble'.

Closed L; Tue;
Dec 25–Jan 31
Must book
D only, 7–9

Tdh from £6·95 (meal
£9·70)

VAT inc
Children's helpings
Seats 50
[&] rest
Car park

No dogs in d/r
Access, Am Ex
4 rooms (1 with bath)
B&B £9·50–£11

SALISBURY Wiltshire   Map 2

Crane's

🦢 🍷

90-92 Crane Street
Salisbury 3471

Closed Sun; Mon; Apr 13;
last 2 weeks June;
3 weeks Dec/Jan
Must book
Meals 12.30–2 (Sat 1.30),
6.30–10.30

Tdh L £6 (meal £8·10)
Alc £8·30 (meal £10·40)

VAT & service inc
Cover 50p (for meal
under £3)
Children's helpings
Seats 36 (parties 18)
♿ rest
No dogs

Nothing is harder in England than to believe that a restaurant can stay good without changing much. Moreover, Tim and Sue Cumming even started good: seven years ago they had a 'pestle' in their first year, which more wary counsels now forbid. The seriousness this implies is a first and last impression of the staff and of the converted and soberly if elegantly furnished shop near the Close. Compared with last year, mistakes have been fewer – indeed, very rare – but helpings, especially of sweet things, seem to be creeping towards West Country *grosseur*, 'and I wish they wouldn't slap cream on top of the delicate ice-creams.' If there is a dish this year that sums up the couple's achievement it is perhaps the timbale of coquilles St Jacques with crab sauce: 'the lightest of scallop timbales, with the red part done as a stripe in the middle and a most flavoursome, not over-thick brown crab sauce that just coated each delicate forkful. It was too good even to dip bread into and I finished it off with a spoon.' But similar language has been used about the crespolini with chicken, spinach and cream cheese, the taramosalata that 'starts watering my mouth as soon as I write the word down', the tomato soup with fresh basil, and the crab tart pastry 'so buttery compared with everyone else's loathly quiches'. If you begin with aillade toulousaine you will hardly want more than a sweet afterwards, though one doughty pair proceeded to the old Perry-Smith favourite, salmon in puff pastry, stuffed with ginger and currants (possibly the most English, in all its resonances, of great dishes invented since the war). Pheasant with braised red cabbage, poulet canaille, stuffed escalope de veau with madeira sauce, and sorrel omelette ('lovely flavour – not a supreme omelette but about twice as good as any British eater expects') are among other main courses. 'Cumulus clouds' of crémets d'Angers with raspberries, redcurrants and blackcurrants, or the fruity ices, may be the best sweets. Coffee is no longer variable. The set lunch, with two alternatives in each course, looks worth taking. The wine list is thoughtfully composed, though the prices of the Yapp Loires and Rhônes creep ever nearer the clarets and burgundies: note Ch. Meyney '64 at £7·50 as a dignified survivor of an accident-prone vintage. No music. Please smoke in the lounge only.

App: Julia & James Warner, A. Kerr, W. J. Legg, W. S. Blanchard, Jean Vella, and many others

---

Do not risk using an out-of-date Guide. A new edition will be published early in 1980.

Haunch of Venison
Minster Street
Salisbury 22024

Comfortable, well-tended first-floor restaurant in a 14th-century building, offering set lunches (soup; fish, game or roast; cheese or sweet), an appealing cold table, and at night a reliable *carte*. Marinated mushrooms, veal with paprika, beef with madeira, and the vegetables have been liked. Rolls are better now, but pastry needs a lighter touch. 'Tasty and ample helpings of haunch of venison (£3·90) lived up to expectations.' House wine is Bon Esprit, £3·90 the litre, 50p the glass. Other wines from Saccone & Speed. Bar lunches on weekdays. No music.

Closed Sun; Mon; 2 weeks July; 2 weeks Feb; Dec 25 & 26 Must book weekends	Meals 12–2, 7–10 Tdh L £3 (meal £5·80) Alc (min £3) £6·65 (meal £9·80)	VAT inc Seats 37 (parties 25) No dogs in d/r Access, Am Ex, Diners

Le Provençal
14 Ox Row
Market Place
Salisbury 28923

Closed L; Sun (Nov–May); 5 days Chr
Must book
D only, 6–10.30

Alc (min £3) £6·50 (meal £9)

VAT inc
Service 10%
Seats 34 (parties 20)
Air-conditioning (lower rest)
No dogs
Access, Am Ex, Barclay, Diners

Winning manners have done wonders over the years for Edward and Geraldine Moss's 'wholesome bourgeois' (his description) restaurant on two floors overlooking Salisbury's main square. In 1978 these qualities even survived a test meal's heavy-handed cooking (of lamb with herbs and apricots) and absent-minded service (with boudin blanc and too many wines 'off' when enquired for). For other members and inspectors fared much better with Mr Moss's enterprising dips and crudités at the start of a meal, 'paper-thin pancake with savoury stuffing', sweetbreads in black butter ('almost too rich and filling, but you are courteously warned'), mussels, braised kidneys, the lamb dish already described (though the bone was surprisingly large for a tranche de gigot), and red cabbage 'done to a crunch'. Caneton poêlé aux pruneaux (£3·60) is a speciality. The brown bread, salads, and bouchée vallée d'Auge were among the test meal's more notable successes, and good home-made ices or crème brûlée (95p) are also reported. Cheeses are disappointing. Wines begin modestly with Gamay or Sauvignon at £2·50, and the Gros Plant, Menetou-Salon or Chinon under £4, Gigondas '74 under £5, and especially sweet Coteaux du Layon under £3 are worth tasting. No music. No children under six in the confined but cleverly exploited space.

App: F.I., R. J. Stansbridge, E.R., H.S.E., Elizabeth Salter, M.J., and others

Prices of meals underlined are those which we consider represent unusual value for money. They are not necessarily the cheapest places in the Guide.

SCARBOROUGH North Yorkshire   Map 8

Lanterna Ristorante
33 Queen Street
Scarborough 63616

Closed Sun; Mon; Easter;
Chr; New Year
Must book D
Meals 12–1.30, 7–9.30

Alc £5·90 (meal £9·95)

Seats 36
& rest
No dogs
Barclaycard

There is a strong temptation to overeat in Gianluigi
Arecco's bay-windowed restaurant, not just because
it has no serious competition in the district
but because it is in many ways a model of how an
Italian chef-proprietor's restaurant far from London
should be run, and seldom is. True, marketing is
sometimes a struggle, and the printed menu is
conservative (take note of any manuscript
additions). But the quality Mr Arecco learnt about
in famous London kitchens lasts all the way from
his spaghetti carbonara (£1 as a first course) through
his pollo principessa (£3·50) to his special pudding,
described by one visitor as 'sponge soaked in
Strega, topped with fresh fruit and whipped cream,
and, teetering on the tip, choux buns containing
sliced strawberries'. The backbone of the menu is
steaks and escalopes in various ways, sole and
lobster (either hot or 'with home-made mayonnaise'),
but fritto misto or polpette in herbs and tomato will
also be classic in their homelier way, and the
vegetables included in main dish prices are not
scamped – 'new potatoes in their skins, mange-tout
peas, and creamed cabbage, all left on the table for
us to help ourselves.' Bread and brandy-snaps are
both made on the premises. Janet Arecco supervises
the girls who serve, and it was a six-year-old, made
welcome here, who remarked of her fruit salad:
'Everything that always has skin and pips hasn't
here.' The coffee is praised this year. The Barbera
red imported from the proprietor's own region is all
you need for meat dishes, though for fish one or two
better chosen and described whites would help.

App: Peter & Avril Rimmer, H.K.P., D.C.M.,
Joan Todd, U. M. Goodger, A. Cavill

SCOLE Norfolk   Map 6

Crossways Restaurant
at junction of A140 &
A143
Scole 638

Old Mr Josef's widow is carrying on (and sharing the
cooking) with the younger generation in this
friendly, Tudor-built restaurant. Members still enjoy
tava à la grecque, chicken paprika (£2·50) and beef
goulash (£2·30), served with vegetables and both
rice and sauté potatoes. Other courses are less
memorable and 'it is a pity the excellent coffee is
sold by the cup' (30p). Spanish house wines, £3·30
the litre. Greene King IPA on tap, and bar snacks
every day except Sunday (sandwiches only,
evenings). Recorded music. Children's helpings.

Closed Dec 25 D; Dec 26
Must book
Meals 12–1.45, 7–10

Alc £4·45 (meal £7·25)

Service 10%
Seats 53 (parties 28)

& rest (2 steps)
No dogs in d/r
Access, Am Ex, Barclay,
Diners

305

Masthead
5 High Street
Seaford 896135

After six years in the book, Mr Sillett's spryly-run place on the way to the sea is in danger of being forgotten, and, indeed, the only things remembered after a set lunch were mixed grill, cheesecake and thoughtful service. But the new chef Peter Sharrard's favourite dishes à la carte in the evening are worth trying: pork tenderloin in Marsala and mushroom sauce (£3·15, including vegetables or salad), beef Stroganoff (£3·20), sweetbreads in white wine sauce (£2·95). Decoration of food is more effervescent than judicious. Puddings are mostly routine. Cuvée St Pierre house burgundy is £3 in both colours; Ch. Chasse-Spleen '67 a promising choice at £5·90. Recorded music. More reports, please. (See also Eastbourne: Porthole.)

Must book
Meals 12–2, 7–10

Tdh L from £2·40
(meal £3·25)

Alc £5·30 (meal £7·80)

VAT inc
Seats 28

▣ rest
No dogs
Access, Barclay, Diners

Yew Tree
8 m SW of Keswick
Borrowdale 634

The Martins appear to be carrying on in the Hunters' tradition at this cottagey hikers' refuge at the foot of Honister pass. Pleasant informality, speedy service, and helpings geared to mountain appetites: ham and vegetable broth (40p), fresh orange juice, bacon and egg, Cumberland sausage with salad and mushrooms (£1·65), steak, omelettes or salads, apple pie and cream (50p) or ices. Various wines, with Italian carafes at £2·20 for 75 cl; Tetley's pressurised bitter. No music. (Note the 10% surcharge at weekends.)

Closed Mon; Sat L;
Nov–Mar
Must book D
Open noon–8 (6–9.30
Sat)

Alc £2·80 (meal £3·80)

VAT inc

Children's helpings
Seats 45
▣ rest
Access card

Inspections are carried out anonymously. Persons who pretend to be able to secure, arrange or prevent an entry in the Guide are impostors and their names or descriptions should be reported to us.

We rewrite every entry each year, and depend on fresh, detailed reports to confirm the old, as well as to include the new. The further from London you are, the more important this is.

The Guide accepts no advertising. Nor does it allow restaurateurs to use its name on brochures, menus, or in any form of advertisement. If you see any instances of this, please report them to us.

SEAVINGTON ST MARY Somerset   Map 2

The Pheasant
off A303, at Seavington
St Michael
South Petherton 40502

Thatched farmhouse, tucked away off the A303, mentioned here for nine years as a travellers' refuge. Smart rooms now, and varied food. Bar meals of soup, pâté, cold fish and meat with self-service salads ('less varied than of yore') and pickles, curries and spaghetti. A la carte dinners may include home-made duck-liver pâté, salade niçoise, pork in cider with apples, daube de boeuf. Wines from various sources, mostly in the £3–£6 range. No carafe. Worthington E. A few tables outside. Not a suitable place for very young children, they say.

Closed Sun D (exc res);
last 2 weeks Feb & Sept;
Dec 25 & 26
Must book D
Meals 12–2, 7–10

Alc L (buttery) £1·85
(meal £2·60), D (rest)
£4·35 (meal £6·75)

VAT inc
Seats 50 (parties 20)

♿ rest
Car park
No dogs
11 rooms (8 with bath)
B&B £6·50–£7·50
Fire cert

SELMESTON East Sussex   Map 3

Corins
Church Farm
off A27
7 m SE of Lewes
Ripe 343

The Corin family's 17th-century farmhouse in peaceful countryside is an endearingly amateurish concern – 'it seems churlish to criticise.' Service is agreeable, but the set meals are sometimes over-ambitious, and praise for lamb en brioche, the vegetables, meringue Chantilly and the coffee is balanced by tales of disappointing duck, oily mushrooms provençale and variable seasonings. 'They have the right ideas and standards', but have not yet fully achieved them. French house wine, £2·90 for 74 cl. No music.

Closed L (exc Sun); Mon;
Dec 25 & 26; Jan 1
Must book
Meals 1 (Sun), 7.30–11

Tdh Sun L £3·25 (meal
£5·15), D £5·25 (meal
£7·35)

VAT inc

Service 10%
Seats 24
♿ rest; w.c.
Car park
Access, Barclay

SHEPTON MALLET Somerset   Map 2

Blostin's
29 Waterloo Road
Shepton Mallet 3648

Closed L; Sun; Dec 25 &
26; Jan 1
Must book
D only, 7–10

Alc £4·95 (meal £7·95)

'Chaotic service' spoilt one August inspector's meal at Bill Austin's converted cottages at the north end of the town. Perhaps his new manager was too busy mixing the terrifying cocktails in which she specialises, for other impressions have been much more favourable, and the cooking (now shared with Adrian Derrick, late of the Miners' Arms in Priddy) is called 'delicately and discretely flavoured, in spite of helpings robust enough for my husband's appetite'. Avocado and sorrel soup, scallops and bacon, garlic bread, and above all salmon baked in

Children's helpings
(under 10)
Seats 28
No dogs

pastry with lemon, crab-meat and a variety of
herbs, and served with cucumber yoghourt, are all
popular. Try, too, mushrooms with aïoli (85p) and
chicken breast stuffed with Stilton (£2·65). Steak
and loin of lamb have also been found 'meltingly
tender', and calabrese 'gorgeous'. Walnut ice-cream,
'tart and creamy syllabub with a little flower
perched on it', crème brûlée and chocolate mousse
are mentioned among sweets, and chocolate
turinois is a speciality. The Austins have their own
farm now. Wine bar lunches have been discontinued.
Moroccan red or Bordeaux white wines were £2·75
in 1978, and Ch. Latour '67, c.b., a comparatively
reasonable £13·50, though it would be better left a
while. Six wines may be had by the glass. Recorded
music.

App: M.E.J., Mrs D. J. Ferrett, and others

SHEPTON MALLET Somerset   Map 2

Bowlish House
Wells Road
just off A371
Shepton Mallet 2022

Closed L (exc by
arrangement); Dec 25 &
26
Must book
D only, 7.30–10.30

Alc £6·75 (meal £10·45)

Service 12½%
Children's helpings
Seats 24 (parties 30)
Car park
No dogs in d/r
5 rooms (1 with bath)
B&B £7

*Ten entries have been written for four different regimes
at this solid 18th-century merchant's house over the
past ten years. The latest incumbents are Brian and
Pat Jordan with Martin Schwaller as chef, whose
father used to keep the Old Manor House at
Knaresborough. Mr Jordan's experience lies elsewhere,
but when he learns to leaven conversation with
observation he will make a good maître. Mr
Schwaller's problem is that he invents too much and
tastes too little. Vide his poulet de tonnerre which, for
£4·95 including vegetables, offered at a test meal rather
dry chicken in a too thin sauce which needs only three
of its ingredients (cream, Meaux mustard, and
walnuts) but also laboured under tarragon, chervil,
mushrooms, and malt-vinegary onions. Other things –
even parts of a game terrine – have on occasion
tasted too bland. But enough is said in praise of the
bread, the chicken breasts in pastry, tournedos
Médicis, and the vegetables, not to mention the owners'
desire for betterment, to justify tentative inclusion.
Local suppliers of raw materials are listed on the
menu. There is a wide choice of interesting wines at
fair prices, and some fine clarets, dessert wines and
ports are kept decanted so that you may drink a
glassful instead, or as well, if you wish. No pipes or
cigars at table. No music. They only put up people
who dine. More reports, please.*

See p. 440 for the pub section, and p. 505 for the wine bars.

PLEASE keep sending in reports as soon as possible after each meal.
Closing date for the 1980 Guide is September 30, 1979, but reports are even
more useful earlier in the year, especially for the remoter areas and new places.

SHIPSTON ON STOUR Warwickshire   Map 2

White Bear Hotel
High Street
Shipston on Stour 61558

Closed Sun; D Mon & Tue
(exc res); Sat L;
Dec 25 & 26; Jan; public
hols
Must book L & weekends
Meals 12–1.45, 7.30–9.30

Alc £4·70 (meal £6·90)

VAT inc
Service 10%
Seats 24
Car park
No dogs in d/r
6 rooms
B&B £5
Fire cert

*A thoroughly modern impresario toting a group of
Polish musicians round the country found that Hugh
and Suzanne Roberts's new regime in this modestly
priced pub 'made up for Huddersfield'. Last-minute
nominations from others too stir hopes that Mrs
Roberts has begun as she means to go on, with fresh
home-cooking and a flexible weekly menu that
nevertheless offers unexpected red pepper and tomato
soup or 'rose et noir' (pork fillet in white wine with
prunes and redcurrant jelly), as well as more
predictable but competently done chicken liver pâté and
steak and kidney pie. Vegetables are good, and among
the sweets 'a creamy cheesecake on a buttery biscuit
base' and not over-sweet Mont Blanc suggest
themselves; pastry for blackberry and apple pie 'could
have done with more lightness and sweetness'. The
pottery is a local craftman's. Service is tentative as
yet, wines (from £2·40 for Rocamar) unpromising.
There are lunchtime bar snacks with Bass and
M&B XI on hand-pump. No music. More reports,
please.*

SHREWSBURY Salop   Map 5

Penny Farthing
23 Abbey Foregate
Shrewsbury 56119

Closed Sun; Mon; Apr 13;
Dec 26
Must book
Meals 12.15–1.45, 7–9.45

Tdh L from £3·65 (meal
£6·90)
Alc (min main dish) £5·65
(meal £8·90)

Service 10%
Seats 32 (parties 10)
♿ rest (1 step)
Air-conditioning
Car park (5)
No dogs
Diners card

Chris and Audrey Greenhow are still cooks as well
as owners for this Victorian-style restaurant near the
Abbey, gleaming with copper and mahogany. They
take trouble to please (one member reports a
booking honoured over a bank holiday when it
might have been cancelled) and inspectors' carrot
and orange soup, and sea trout or salmon, have
shown welcome freshness and authenticity. They
buy good meat, too, according to people who have
tried their veal provençale, Scotch beef, and rack of
lamb with rosemary and Marsala (£3·95 with
vegetables included). Scallops au gratin (£1·65) and
peppers toulonnaise are among specialities. Breast
of chicken in cream and calvados, leaf spinach,
apple and plum tart, and home-made rum ice are
other dishes praised. The coffee is Cafetière, and the
Tanners of Shrewsbury wine list better than most
provincial ones. Pressurised beers. No music. Dress
tidily. Smaller helpings for children under nine.
Smoke in the bar only.

App: A. B. Ward, M.M., J.K.L., J.R., E.S.

'Must book' is the restaurant's information, not ours. The context of the
entry usually indicates how much or how little it matters, but a preliminary
telephone call averts frustrated journeys. Always telephone if a booking has
to be cancelled: a small place may suffer severely if this is not done, and
customers are also the losers in the end.

Oats
Chapel Hill
Skipton 3604

Peppe Montuori's staff remain civil and cheerful in this 'chrome and smoked-glass place' whose hard seats and close-packed tables detract little from people's enjoyment of, say, mushrooms with tartare sauce, cannelloni, lamb with tarragon, strawberry vacherin or oatmeal and whisky syllabub. Valgardello is £3·20 the litre. A few tables outside. Recorded music.

Closed Sun; Mon;
Dec 25 & 26; Jan 1
Must book D
Meals 12.15–1.30, 7.30–9

Tdh D £7·75 (meal
£10·45)
Alc L £3·30 (meal £5·55)

VAT inc

Seats 62 (parties 24)
  rest
Car park
No dogs
Access, Barclay

Oaklands

8 Palmer Street
South Petherton 40272

Closed (rest) L (exc Sun);
Mon; Sun D; 2 weeks
spring & autumn;
Dec 25 & 26;
Closed (Pump Room)
Dec 25

Meals (rest) 12.30–1.45
(Sun), 7–9.30; (Pump
Room) 12–2.30, 7–9.30

Tdh Sun L £3·45 (meal
£5·25), D £5·60 (meal
£7·60)
Alc (Pump Room) £2·50
(meal £4·40)

VAT inc
Service 10%
Children's helpings
Seats 42 (parties 14)
  rest; w.c.
Car park
No dogs
Am Ex, Diners
3 rooms (1 with bath)
B&B £6–£7

Accounts of the Chapmans' early-Victorian family house off the A303 grow warmer year by year, reflecting the proprietor's own view that what they offer is 'the same but better'. The rooms supply 'pretty well everything, including well-chosen books', the furniture is in good taste, the service relaxed, and the food scrupulously prepared by Hilary Chapman and several assistants. Dinners are table d'hôte, with three main dishes and more choice before and after; if the abandon of genius is missing, the coquilles St Jacques mayonnaise, porc Casimir, boeuf Edouard VII and – the owners' own preference – sole Mont Bry, or pintadeau pays du chêne, are all consistently good. Perhaps they should offer their 'creamily moist' Stilton before the sweets, for many people come to a halt after grazing among the apricot Pavlova, well-sherried trifle, chocolate and Grand Marnier mousse, and fresh fruit sorbet. The wines, drawn from various sources, are a noteworthy and catholic collection. Rhine and Mosel stand out, with two beerenauslese Mettenheimers '71 under £7 and two Mosel '75 Eisweins that are dear enough to be left alone till the '80s. But the red burgundies from Averys, and the Châteauneuf-du-Pape (both red and white) from Yapp, are good, and the clarets (rising from humble Ch. Guionne '73 at £3·60 to Ch. Latour '66 at £20·70) are just as imposing in half-bottles as in full ones. Classical records are played. Smoking is not restricted (though not complained about either). The separate Pump Room has a more limited menu and wine list, but makes a useful driving stop. Breakfasts are good, and guided explorations of the district can be arranged.

App: D.G. & A. M. Pert, C. P. Hill, Stanley John, Group Capt. F. Westcott, and others

SOUTHPORT Merseyside Map 5

Le Coq Hardi
1 Royal Terrace,
West Street
Southport 38855

Closed L; Sat; Sun; Aug;
public hols (exc Apr 13)
Must book
D only, 7–9.30

Alc £4·85 (meal £7·70)

Seats 24
No dogs

Simon and Margaret Parmegiani have the hardihood to close on Saturdays now, usually a sign of seriousness in a restaurant, and the understated decor here conveys the same message. Mr Parmegiani is proudest of his main courses, but 'sea trout quenelles made an exquisite first course' (95p), cuisses de grenouille are generously helped, and 'squid with prawns, mushrooms and wine sauce was particularly enjoyed.' Breaded and deep-fried prawns with a curry sauce, and humble potage, are other possibilities. Woodcock and wild duck turn up on menus in their seasons, and duck generally is a speciality, perhaps with honey and almonds. Try also veau en croûte, noisette d'agneau with onion, mint and chicken livers (£3·20) or pork fillet with cream and mushrooms (£3·20). Fennel may appear among the well-cooked fresh vegetables (included in the dish prices). Most people seem to find fruit or cheese enough afterwards, though a light lemon flummery has been reported. The wines, from £2·80 for Gamay or Chenin, are not numerous, though sometimes a good bin-end appears, and £5 is not bad for Ch. Rauzan-Gassies '73. Recorded music.

App: F.R., A. Lockley, T.E.C., and others

Squires
78 King Street
Southport 30046

Closed L; Sun; 2 weeks
June; 2 weeks Chr
Must book
D only, 7–10.30

Alc £4·95 (meal £7·90)

Service 10%
Seats 40 (parties 30)
♿ rest (1 step)
Air-conditioning
No dogs
Access, Am Ex, Barclay,
Diners

Enrique and Susan Darias have come a long way since they started the Bistroquet in this town and had to cope with the kind of customer who demanded paella without the fish. Their move to this pinkly gentrified, Frenchified, and cramped setting has not been an unmixed blessing. French cooking is very different from Spanish, needing a lighter hand and more accurate seasoning to control its richness. Since last year's provisional entry many people report fine dishes, notably tartelette de fruits de mer ('good crisp pastry full of fresh and tasty shellfish', £1), carré d'agneau aux aromates (£6·80 for two), sweetbreads Marsala, médaillons de boeuf à l'armagnac, and 'memorable' ratatouille, spinach, and 'transformed' spring cabbage. Paella and zarzuela can still be ordered at a day's notice, and almond ice-cream is praised. But some things have been bland, over-rich, or served at the wrong pace. The wine list is not yet to hand this year, but Spanish red and white Riojas may be a better buy under £4 than anything else. Classical guitar music is played on record.

App: Mr & Mrs P. Holland, W. J. & R. Webster, Dr N. E. Hand, David & Helen Hughes, and others

Dutch Barn
53 Ferry Road
Southwold 723172

Closed Mon; Sun D
Must book
Meals 12.30–2, 7.30–9.30

Alc £6·40 (meal £9·05)

VAT inc
Seats 35
♿ rest (1 step)
Car park
No dogs
Am Ex card

There is an 'earnest good breeding' about the Wiltons' well-spaced timber-frame restaurant – 'almost a beach hut' – by the shingle, and its personally assembled bric-à-brac. The atmosphere pleases many who would be quick to take against pretentiousness, and the cooking – though the owners' absence quickly shows – appeals to visitors from Bougival to Brightlingsea. The local smoked mackerel, mushrooms either in soup or à la grecque, and 'a perfect avocado heaped with delicious juicy crab and flanked with crunchy cabbage instead of wet lettuce' (£1·95) are all praised, 'though more than a mere sliver of lemon would have been welcome.' Plaice in breadcrumbs (£2·45) was 'perfectly crisp, juicy and hot, with home-made tartare sauce'; pigeon à la Stroganoff 'could hardly have been improved upon', and escalope de veau à la crème passed a Frenchman's yardstick. Pork fillet in pastry with cider and cream sauce is not quite right yet. Vegetables are fresh and well cooked, and sauté potatoes crisp; tomato sauce with custard marrow 'seemed too aggressive both for the vegetable and the dish it accompanied'. 'Pithless' oranges in caramel will be enough for many afterwards, though chocolate goodie is smooth and dense, and trifle creamy. When he was engaged elsewhere, 'Nicholas Wilton kept an unobtrusive eye from a distance', and he is careful about wine too, offering a house dry sherry, Domaine de la Borie red wine at £3·10 in 1978, and Ch. Guionne '73 at £4, Savigny Dominode '72 (Chanson) at £7, and other interesting if rather dear bottles. The coffee at 50p is at least Cafetière. No music.

App: Philip Britton, V. R. Sladden, L. & J. H., L.S.H., L.W., and others

---

SOUTHWOLD see also pub section

STEEPLE ASTON Oxfordshire Map 2

Red Lion
South Street
Steeple Aston 40225

Closed L (exc bar
Mon–Sat); Sun; Mon;
public hols (exc Apr 13)
Must book
Meals 12–2 (bar),
7.30–9.30

From this warm and hospitable inn Colin Mead reports 'fewer *Guide*-clutchers and more academics or buyers of good wine', which sounds contradictory, except that these scholarly topers have mostly been too torpid to report. But although regular admirers of Margaret Mead's dinners report a miscalculated dish of veal with anchovy sauce, they also say that pâté, taramosalata, and celery with almond soup as first courses, and pepper steak, pork in calvados, and conger eel with pine kernels and a tomato and raisin sauce, are as good as ever. 'Sweets have, if anything,

Tdh from £6·10 (meal £7·25)

VAT inc
Children's helpings
Seats 20
Car park
No dogs
Access, Barclay

been more adventurous, with baked pears in marzipan, and unusual golden raspberries in July.' Lunch is a bar meal (Monday to Saturday). Les Frères ordinaires are £2 for 50 cl. The clarets and other names on the wine list are well-known and therefore dear, and there are no half-bottles, but Christopher's Côtes du Rhône (£3·40) and Uerziger Schwarzlay '75 (£4·10) help the middle ranges. Wadworth's 6X on hand pump. No music. No children under 14 in the bar, of course, but tolerance of all but barefoot guests. 'Smokers are asked in writing to be considerate.'

App: C.M.C., D. & P.M., and others

STOKE GOLDINGTON Buckinghamshire   Map 3

Forest Retreat
Eakley Lanes
Stoke Goldington 305

Closed Mon; Sat L;
Sun D; Dec 25 & 26
Must book weekends
Meals 12–1.45, 7.30–9

Alc £5·50 (meal £8·60)

Seats 24
♿ rest (2 steps)
Car park
No dogs

The Forest (Salcey) is a view rather than a sylvan embrace, and the roadside aspect of the Randall sisters' restaurant is humdrum enough for members to have overlooked them for four years – perhaps a record, if 1978 reports of simple dishes, well cooked from good materials, are borne out. Lucilla cooks; Alicia serves. A full à la carte lunch brought home-made pâté, an individual chicken casserole tasty with peppers, fresh calabrese from the market, and an unusual peach cheesecake, with a choice of several cheeses, and ample coffee with home-made mints. Apart from, say, scallops Mornay, most other dishes are straightforward steaks, soles, and trout. Wines, from £2·80, are conventional. Recorded music. More reports, please.

STOKEINTEIGNHEAD Devon   Map 1

Harvest Barn
Stoke Road
Shaldon 3670

Closed Tue; last 2 weeks
Oct; Dec 26; Jan 1
Must book weekends
Meals 12–3, 7.30–10

Tdh Sun L £3·50, D £7
(meal £9·90)

VAT inc
Service 10%
Seats 40 (parties 20)
♿ rest
Air-conditioning
Access, Barclay

Michael Weston formerly ran a hotel in Torquay and his chef Mr B. M. Davies is said to have fed Lord Mountbatten: at any rate, they seem to have drawn in their train to this converted old farmhouse a number of colleagues who need a change from the Torbay rat-race. The menus change fortnightly and service is professional, with superior fish pâté, avocado with rum sorbet, sole with orange, mussels bourguignonne (£2 extra on the set meal), stuffed shoulder of lamb with plum sauce, and broiled steak on creamed parsnips among the choices notified. 'Vegetables are very original', sweets perhaps less so, but competent enough, and the coffee is Cafetière. There is a cold buffet at lunch-time, except on Sunday when a roast appears. Primanova or Coeur des Lanciers ordinaires are £4, and Beaujolais or Fleurie worth trying if they still have the '76s (at about £6 though). Pressurised beers. Recorded music. No dogs. More reports, please.

See p. 440 for the pub section, and p. 505 for the wine bars.

313

STOKESLEY North Yorkshire   Map 8

Golden Lion
27 High Street
Stokesley 710265

Last year's account of erratic cooking and marginal
accommodation provoked no contention – just
agreement that, even with little change, the
Hutchinsons offer the best there is in the district
and deserve mention for effort. So expect clean but
spartan rooms, and nothing special in the dining-
room, although soups are reasonable and beef
Stroganoff or bourguignonne adequate. Bar snacks;
various beers. French house wine £3·20 the litre.
Recorded music, 'but at least the bedroom set had
Radio Three.' Wear a tie.

Closed Sun D (exc res);
Dec 25 D
Must book D & weekends
Meals 12–2.30, 7.30–9.30

Alc £4·80 (meal £8·10)

Cover 15p
Children's helpings
(under 12)
Seats 75 (parties 30)
🔥 rest (2 steps)

Car park
No dogs
15 rooms (12 with bath)
B&B from £7

STORRINGTON West Sussex   Map 3

Manleys
Manleys Hill
on A283
Storrington 2331

Closed Mon; Sun L;
Dec 26; D Dec 25 &
Jan 1; 1st 3 weeks Jan
Must book D & weekends
Meals 12.30–1.45,
7.30–9.30

Tdh Sun L £5·20 (meal
£8·45)
Alc £8·20 (meal £12·05)

VAT inc
Service 12½%
Cover 25p alc
Children's helpings
Seats 40 (parties 10)
🔥 rest (3 steps)
Car park
No dogs
Access card

'Gosh, posh nosh,' says one of the Guide's *Daisy
Ashfords who happened on Karl Löderer's second
night at this revamped Queen Anne house and garden
on the Steyning road. Subsequent inspection confirmed
that Mr Löderer, whose Scottish wife fronts the house
with competent male assistance, is carrying on as
though he had never left Gravetye Manor (q.v.) and
must be cooking himself into an early grave to cope
with such a rich and complex menu. The prices, too,
are first rather than second division, but with a few
exceptions everything tried did him credit. 'Crêpe
pêcheur (£1·80) might not be much but for its crisp
coating and very hot filling, and avocado filled with a
light smoked salmon mousse showed signs of too-early
assembly. But filets mignons Rubens (£4·20), which
came with three sauces looking like a child's drawing
of a traffic light, was ingeniously done, with crisp
straw potatoes.' 'Turbot in lobster sauce (£4·90) was
fresh and correct but needed some of the piquancy that
was present – in excess form – in Zuri G'schnätzlets
with rösti.' Other specialities to note include sole Café
de Paris (£5·80), and steak de chevreuil. The cold
puddings are a Daisy Ashford dream, especially the
meringue aux framboises with kirsch, which had
raspberries lurking somewhere in the plasterwork
(£1·10), and crêpe fraisalia (£1·30). The wine list is
'woefully inadequate' by Gravetye standards, but there
are some good Germans, or Muscat d'Alsace '75
(Loeb) at £5 or so, to make up for the double-figure
clarets. No music. 'Ties requested for dinner.' More
reports, please.*

314

STOW-ON-THE-WOLD Gloucestershire   Map 2

Rafters
Park Street
Stow-on-the-Wold 30200

Closed L (exc Sat & Sun);
Sun D; Dec 24, 25 & 26;
Jan 1
Must book
Meals 12.15–2 (Sat &
Sun), 7–10

Tdh L £2·35 (meal £4·85),
D £2·95 (meal £5·50)
Alc £4·15 (meal £6·80)

VAT inc
Children's helpings
(under 8)
Seats 50
⬕ rest (2 steps)
No dogs
Access, Am Ex, Barclay

As the name implies, mind your head in the cramped
bar upstairs. Expect, too, a few blemishes – or worse –
in cooking and service. But reports improved
during the year, and with David Price back in the
kitchen, determined to cook from a simplified menu
out of a conviction that restaurant meals have
become too complicated and expensive, it is fair to
give them the benefit of any doubt going. The
trouble with '*faites simple*' is that both materials
and their treatment have to be that much better if
they are not to seem ordinary. Pepper steak has had
its critics, and 'a waiter's description of the
bavarois – "coffee cream with gelatine" – was all too
accurate.' But good judges have enjoyed their à la
carte and weekday set meals much more positively
too: crudités with anchovy mayonnaise, 'delicate'
carrot soup, eggs, prawns, courgettes and cheese in
various combinations (though the taste of the prawns
tends to get lost), 'succulent' pork casserole with
cider and apple, 'rich and meaty beef casserole with
bacon and mushrooms', 'excellent trout with fresh
and crisply cooked vegetables', and so on. Meringues
'even tempted a curate in the middle of a sponsored
slim'. Wines, too, have been slimmed to keep meal
prices within bounds, but we await details. French
ordinaires are £3·40 a litre. No music; and a
pleasingly relaxed attitude to clothes, children, and
other problems.

*App: Philip Britton, Joan Chenhalls, Leon Kaufman,
Catherine Kroon, J. & J.W., and others*

STRATFORD-UPON-AVON Warwickshire   Map 2

Ashburton House
27 Evesham Place
Stratford-on-Avon 2444

Closed L; Sun; Dec 24,
25, 26 & 31; Jan 1
Must book
D only, by arrangement

Tdh £4·50 (meal £5·90) &
£7 (meal £8·40)

VAT & service inc
Seats 12
Car park (2)
No dogs
5 rooms
B&B £6·30
Fire cert

Second years are usually more difficult than first,
and some have found the *Guide*'s discovery of virtue
in a modest guest-house next door to the Elfin
Nursery School ('fortunately not in academic
session') distinctly unnerving. An inspector
overheard one half of a couple who had just
entered enquire 'Should we leave?', followed by the
gratifying reply, 'The book hasn't let us down yet.'
Most – not all – of Mrs Fraser's meals justify this
confidence. She is better at soups, bread, sauces,
puddings and ice-creams (sorbets less so) – indeed,
anything requiring little more than close attention
to a sound recipe – than she is at roasting meat and
timing vegetables. (Steaks are tender, though.) The
supply of indifferent, imperfectly understood wines
(from £2·80) has increased both work and tension.
But the ideas that the Frasers brought with them
out of Africa – groundnut and green pepper soups
('the colour passed straight through me'), eggah,
and Fez carrots, with raisins to bring out the

315

natural sweetness – are all praised. So are mushrooms with sweet-sour sauce, trout with prunes, chocolate brandy cake and 'a wonderful buttery-gingery topping to apple crisp'. Breakfasts are copious, rooms scrupulous. The cheaper three-course table d'hôte meal allows you time to get to the theatre, but 'Mr Fraser drove us there when he thought we would be late.' No smoking at table. No music. No children under 12. There are no meals on Sundays, even for residents.

App: J. S. M. Whitaker, E. C. Kirby, Colin & Jane Read, M.R., H.L., Mr & Mrs R. Bentley, and others

---

STRATFORD-UPON-AVON Warwickshire   Map 2

Marianne
3 Greenhill Street
Stratford-on-Avon 3563

Closed Sun; Dec 24;
public hols
Must book D
Meals 12.30–2, 7–11.30

Tdh L £3 (meal £4·70)
Alc D £5·05 (meal £8·20)

VAT & service inc L
Service 10% D
Cover 15p D
Seats 50 (parties 25)
⑤ rest (1 step)
No dogs
Am Ex, Diners

In 'a district full of showy vulgarity in pubs and restaurants' the no-nonsense austerity of Pierre Denervaux's decor – and even sometimes service – hits some people like a cold shower, and at lunch-time the set meals have at times fallen well below the standard expected, even at the price. Evening visitors have sounded very much happier, but as we went to press, Bernard Lignier moved to the Old House at Wickham, so it is uncertain how his successor will treat his inventions such as snails with peppers and walnuts (£1·40) or 'rather strong and weird, but nice' gâteau de foie de volaille au caramel d'estragon, and a 'winter salad' dressed in walnut oil. Tourte aux oignons, gigot de poulet in a garlicky sauce, and 'moist, generous' faisan aux raisins are also praised. A test meal yielded not only good rognons gasconne but really saignant lamb, alas at the price of undercooking the pastry that surrounded it. (Other faults included poor Brie, and stewed milk with stewed coffee.) Glace aux pruneaux (70p) or imported fruit sorbets sound dependable sweets, and oranges en ruban au Cointreau were charming in conception and execution. The Languedoc ordinaires are £2·70, and French-bottled house wines include Touraine Gamay (£3·30) and Côtes du Rhône Villages (£4·60). More reports, please.

STRATFORD-UPON-AVON see also pub section

STURMINSTER NEWTON Dorset   Map 2

Plumber Manor
off A357 (on road to
Hazelbury Bryan)
2 m SW of Sturminster
Newton
Sturminster Newton
72507

For some years Richard and Brian Prideaux-Brune (who cooks) have been at or near the top of the Dorset country house market, and since the family has lived here since Bad King Charles's time they would expect no less. Americans and Frenchmen alike love the family portraits, 'gorgeous rooms', rich and studied food, and the brothers' willingness to walk that 'difficult path between service and

Closed L; Mon;
Sun (Nov–Mar exc res);
2 weeks Nov; Jan 1; Feb
Must book
D only, 7.30–9.30

Tdh £6·50 (meal £8·85)

VAT inc
Seats 56 (parties 40)
♿ rest
Car park
No dogs
6 rooms (all with bath)
B&B £9–£10
Fire cert

friendliness'. Oddly, it is a Californian who complains of muted garlic even in dishes that advertise it, and a Briton who resents (in a house that values wine, too) a high risk of sweet sauces with main courses. Much is finely achieved, though: fresh clams from Poole; an individual coulibiac stuffed with rice, salmon and smoked mackerel, with sauce Choron on the side; 'dreamy' chicken indienne; best end of lamb 'rare, but with highly edible fat'; salads (Brian prefers walnut to olive oil apparently: too bad if you differ); and 'lethally rich' sweets. Never mind the richness, for you can skip the Atholl brose and the profiteroles if your character is strong enough, and take fresh fruit or peach in wine or ripe Stilton. But a coffee gateau tasting of salted butter and meringue tasting of baking-tin suggest a need for tighter control. The wines are Averys, whose deliveries stutter sometimes, but whose house labels hide good champagne at £7 or '73 red burgundy at £5. The Comte de Monceau '73 white (£6) is also very fragrant. Wear a jacket and tie. No music. No children under 12. Note that there are no meals even for residents on Mondays.

App: Lynn Hay, J. K. L. Scott, J. W. McClenahan, J. Ridley Thompson, A.H.A., C.P.D., and others

---

SUTTON BINGHAM Somerset   Map 2

Sutton Bingham Manor
off A37
3 m SW of Yeovil
West Coker 2110

Closed Mon; Sun D;
Dec 25 D; Dec 26
Must book
Meals 12–2, 7.30–10

Alc £4·05 (meal £6·35)

VAT inc
Service 10%
Children's helpings
(under 10)
Seats 40 (parties 25)
♿ rest (1 step)

Ted Stiles' migration from the Plucknett to this old family manor and garden beside Sutton Bingham reservoir is a promising addition to the (thin) choice round Yeovil, people feel. 'Prices are sensible and the snack meals (during opening hours) useful,' says one inspector. In the dining-room, there is praise for Eric Vercruyssen's pâté, whitebait, soups, saltimbocca, chicken Kiev or Cordon Bleu, and other dishes: try, he suggests, his seafood provençale, pork chops with apples, celery and cheese, or Burgundian beef. The Eldridge Pope wines (from £2·80 for French ordinaires) appear to offer Corton Les Maréchaudes '71 (Doudet Naudin) at £3·75: go now while stocks last, perhaps, and pick up the dry version of Ch. Filhot Sauternes too (£3·05). Pressurised beers. Recorded music. Dogs are not allowed in the dining-room. Car park. More reports, please.

SWAVESEY Cambridgeshire   Map 3

Hotel de la Poste
20 Market Street
Swavesey 30241

As for many years past, André Arama's ill-kempt villa in the Fens can be safely suggested only to people whose quest for expert cooking enables them to ignore a want of social or decorative graces. His wife cooks, and his son waits, under André's

Closed Mon; Sun D;
Apr 15; Aug 12–Sept 4;
Dec 25 & 26
Must book
Meals 12.15–2.15,
6.30–10.15

Alc £7·80 (meal £12)

Service 12½%
Seats 20
&. rest
Car park
No dogs
Am Ex, Barclay, Diners

basilisk eye. The repertoire seldom changes, or needs to, when the quenelles de brochet are so feathery, the langoustines grillées with a 'spectacular' sauce so succulent, and the duck (served either au cassis or au poivre vert, £4) so eminently capable of standing up even to the *patron*'s claims for it: a crisp skin all over, no subcutaneous fat, but tender and moist. The blackcurrant sauce is perhaps more original, but the creamy pepper one is refined, and apparently also flourless. With two days' notice and four or more diners, beef or lamb en croûte, or bouillabaisse, can be prepared. Salads are good. Parfait au caramel is well achieved, profiteroles not, and if there is time or unanimity, crêpes Suzette or a soufflé Grand Marnier might be a better idea. Muscadet Château de la Moinerie '76 is £3·90 and prices have been better held lately: Crozes-Hermitage Rochefine '73, £4·20; Niedermenniger Sonnenberg Spätlese '71, £5·20. A request for a half-bottle of sweet white yielded Ch. Doisy-Daëne '70 at £3·25.

App: Christopher Forman, P.S.A.W., and others

SWAY Hampshire   Map 2

Pine Trees
Mead End Road
(NW of station)
off B3055
4 m NW of Lymington
Sway 2288

Closed L; Dec 24, 25 &
26
Must book
D only, 7.45–9

Tdh £6·50 (meal £7·65)

VAT & service inc
Children's helpings
Seats 18 (parties 8)
&. rest (1 step)
Car park
No dogs
Am Ex, Barclay
7 rooms (1 with bath,
4 with shower)
B&B £6·50–£9
Fire cert

Most visitors to this slightly shabby but mostly peaceful New Forest hotel know not to expect any excitement, unless it be a goldcrest outside the bedroom window or the faint feeling that Willie Maugham in his carpet slippers is about to appear from behind a sideboard. The Davids themselves have learnt much in their first three years without losing the individuality implied by a choiceless dinner, or a bathroom that needs a spanner to turn the tap. Criticisms of the kitchen are few: some would like a larger breakfast, or at least proper marmalade as well as the admirable croissants, and one visitor reports 'too many creamy or pureed things, with nothing crisp or fresh (even in July) to offset the richness of a five-course meal'. But these are small matters beside the virtues: very light first-course soufflés of cheese or salmon, 'perfectly cooked trout not smothered with almonds', delicate sole with lemony hollandaise, escalope de veau ma façon, good salads (avocado and tomato, Danish cucumber), well-judged roasts ('beef red in the middle moving through various shades to light brown'), 'the best cauliflower cheese I can remember', 'carrots a dream', and for sweet not only orange soufflé or well-balanced Atholl brose, but on occasion peach Melba made with fresh fruit, home-made ice-cream and real raspberry sauce, which is enough to get an English hotelier lynched by his more cynical colleagues. Better carafe wines might be found, even at £2·30 for 70 cl, and while '72 burgundies are all very well, '72 clarets should not be over-represented on a modest list. But prices are kept down below £5 in almost all cases. No music. No children under 12. There are no lunches now, 'but one June picnic included soup, salmon trout, cold veal, and home-made mince pies.'

App: John & Laura Parker, J. R. Michaelis, R. D. Boyer, Louisa & George Ogilvie, Ivor Hall, and many others

TALKIN Cumbria Map 8

Tarn End Hotel
off B6413
2 m S of Brampton
Brampton 2340

Closed Oct; Dec 25
Must book
Meals 12.30–1.45, 7.30–9

Tdh L from £3·50 (meal £5·90), D from £4·50 (meal £7·65)
Alc £6 (meal £9·20)

Service 10%
Seats 40
Car park
No dogs
6 rooms
D, B&B £11

The *accueil* at the Hoefkens family's 'horrendously decorated' hotel (which owns its own tarn) remains, in various descriptions, 'courteous', 'condescending', and 'chilly', but after five years here and many more elsewhere, no sudden conversion can be expected. Happily, accounts of Martin Hoefkens' cooking are warmer. Set menus are 'so good there was no need to go further', with a wide (perhaps too wide) choice of enterprising dishes: cockle chowder, oeuf périgourdine, beignets de crabe, 'delectable' salmon en brioche, quenelles of fresh haddock, sweetbreads en croustade, breast of chicken with apple and calvados, and many more. 'Pike in a light, crisp pastry case, stuffed with lemon and fennel, was superb.' 'It is a few years since I last tasted confit d'oie and it was as good as I remembered it, with a little garlic in the accompanying sauté potatoes.' Profiteroles, mille-feuille with various fruits, fresh nectarine shortcake and other sweets end a meal no less impressively. 'Since I was only halfway through my wine I was offered a fine Stilton before my sweet.' Breakfasts bring 'melting croissants and tasty eggs'. Spanish or Italian ordinaires are £1·75 for a pint, and other wines, fully priced and skimpily described, include Chorey le Beaune '73, estate-bottled, (£6·20, and £3·30 for a half) which 'went admirably with the confit'. 'A request for the loan of an iron was curtly refused.' No music, children under eight, or pipes. Wear a tie at dinner.

App: C. Williams, Mrs J. A. Sankey, Dr Ian Sims, W. J. Hallett, Mrs M. W. Kerr, and others

TEIGNMOUTH Devon Map 1

Churchill's
Den Road
Teignmouth 4311

Closed Mon; Sun D (Oct–May); Sat L;
3 weeks Oct/Nov;
Dec 25 D; Dec 26; Jan 1

Business is often brisker in the evenings during the season but a lunchtime visitor on a 'cold, foggy, July day' was 'very sad' to see a chain restaurant in this bourgeois resort full, while food from a different world was being served at reasonable cost in Stafford and Martin's discreetly set upstairs room. The terrine (90p) was 'rich and coarse', kidneys Turbigo (£3) and poussin in wine and mushroom

319

Must book
Meals 12.30–2, 7.30–10

Tdh L £2·95 (meal £5·05)

Alc £5·05 (meal £8)

Seats 36
No dogs
Access, Barclay

sauce (£3·15) were alike dexterously cooked, and courgettes provençale 'perfect'. Other lunchers report onion soup 'still hot when I finished it', good plaice and sole, 'and creamy Stilton, refreshing orange salad, or profiteroles'. At night, service may be very slow, and the bar at the end of the room is not large. But Mr Stafford's omelette Arnold Bennett (85p), watercress soup, cuisses de grenouille fines herbes (£1·95), and râble de lièvre grand veneur (£8·50 for two) are among dishes worth trying. Main course prices include four fresh vegetables. Les Frères red or Primanova white ordinaires are £2·60; the rest of the David Baillie Vintners wine list is not yet to hand. Recorded music.

App: T. M. S. Tosswill, M.E.D., A. Jones

THETFORD Norfolk   Map 6

Anchor Hotel
Bridge Street
Thetford 3329

Formerly a coaching inn, now a brewery Relais Routier, the Anchor feels a good place to ride out a storm in. Members usually take the set lunch, which offers a fair choice of carefully cooked food (some of it kept warm over-long, though) : egg mimosa, grilled fresh sardines, Cromer crab (30p extra); pork chop, plaice or sole, shoulder of lamb, with fresh vegetables; creamy sweets and good coffee. 'Tiny, home-made rolls were a delight.' There is a very ambitious carte and a daily cold carvery in the bar; more reports on both, please. Various house wines at 95p for 25 cl; pressurised beers. Recorded music.

Must book
Meals 12.30–2, 7–9

Tdh L from £2·95
(meal £5), D £3·75 (meal
£5·90)
Alc (min L £2·95,
D £3·50) £7·10 (meal
£9·55)

VAT inc
Service 10%
Children's helpings
(under 10)
Seats 60 (parties 120)
 rest

Car park
No dogs in d/r
Access, Barclay, Grand
Met
22 rooms (20 with bath)
B&B from £11·50
Fire cert

THORNBURY Avon   Map 2

Thornbury Castle

Thornbury 412647

Closed L (exc Sun); Mon;
Sun D; Dec 25 & 26;
Jan 1
Must book
Meals 12.30–2 (Sun),
7.30–9.30

The cliché says it is tough at the top. It is actually rather easy at the top, provided you are, say, a world-famous conductor or restaurateur rather than a heavyweight boxer or a revolutionary, because most people go by your reputation rather than by your performances. Kenneth Bell, who has practised the high art of cookery for a dozen years now in this Henrician castle, surrounded by its own vines, is a shy man who fell out with the *Guide*'s fallible assessments some time ago, but is self-aware enough to confess in print that his life is spent serving too rich food to too rich people. The style is seductive.

Tdh £8·50 (meal £12·45)
Alc £7·05 (meal £10·70)

Service 12½%
Cover 50p (weekend)
Seats 60 (parties 40)
♿ rest
Car park
No dogs
Access, Am Ex, Barclay

Even an inspector who found his palate and spirit cloyed after devilled crab, 'subtly spiced with cinnamon and mustard', and 'first-rate but overpowering' paupiette de veau with madeira sauce and gratin dauphinoise potatoes, came back after a *Luftpause* for fresh raspberry syllabub. Other experienced visitors lately report triumphant and better-judged set meals that included avgolemono and other good soups, fillets of John Dory with hollandaise on a puree of green peas, beignets de soufflé au fromage, 'unexpectedly tender pigeon in a delicate red wine and celery sauce', and 'rough and moist marzipan latticed with pastry and caramelised'. There is now once again a full *carte* that should, even with the weekend cover charge, work out more cheaply for three courses than the slimmed-down set menu does for five. But alas, in the summer of 1978, with Mr Bell away and no alternative *carte* offered, a strong test party ate not excessively but just indifferently, with nothing in eight different savoury dishes really worthy of remark except for a superbly crisp roast duck with a sauce tasting nicely of dried apricots. Even the cheeses were all three of them badly over the hill. An earlier report of 'a tepid main course and rather weatherbeaten salad' and a later one of curdling sauces and pappy textures lent conviction to this finding. The wines are accessibly priced, not just the house Traminer at £2·10 for 50 cl but 'green and gooseberryish' Poitou or Loire wines at £4, Ch. Fombrauge '71 at £6·40, or halves of Ch. Nenin '59 at £4, noble burgundies, and a sensible clutch of Spanish. Service is cool but competent in these high dining-rooms, segregating smokers from the rest as best it may. No music.

App: Adrian Gammon, Mary Elizabeth Devine, J.R., Mr & Mrs F. D. Hillson, C.P.D., and others

---

TIVERTON Devon   Map 1

The Lowman
45 Gold Street
Tiverton 57311

Closed Thur; Wed D;
2 weeks Apr/May;
2 weeks Aug; Dec 25 D;
Dec 26; Jan 1
Must book D
Meals 12.30–2, 7–10

Alc L £3·50 (meal £5·15),
D £4·25 (meal £6),
L (quick service) £1·65
(meal £3·15)

As the name implies, the little restaurant is at the foot of Tiverton's main street (use the nearby car parks) and 'how nice it is to run a familiar wine cellar to ground once again,' says a customer of the Harveys' former place near Ross-on-Wye. They are thoughtfully aiming here for 'a middle market of people paying their own bills' and an inspector in 1978 was pleased to find at lunch-time some properly cooked dishes under £1: fried mussels with sauce tartare, egg and mushroom pancakes, and so on. At night or Sunday lunch, pepper soup, cold curried prawns, and mushrooms in garlic butter are also praised as first courses, followed by chicken Limpopo (£2·35), 'excellent' fillet of beef in madeira sauce, and a few others. The fruit pies might be better hot, or at least warm, and the 'Sailor's Lament'

VAT inc
Children's helpings
Seats 30
No dogs in public rooms

needed more rum, a soldier lamented. The wines and their prices are most unusual, with Chilean Cabernet at £2 (or £1·45 for 50 cl) and various other ordinaires to choose from; then Jura or Cassis or Lamberhurst Priory whites at £4 or so; and superior claret and burgundy: Ch. La Conseillante, c.b., '64, £7·90; domaine-bottled Bonnes-Mares (Drouhin-Laroze) '70, £9·30; and French-bottled Clos de la Roche '21 (a Barolet wine), £25. Rhônes, Loires, and halves of sweet white are also to be noted. No music. More reports, please, including ones on the 'quick-service' lunch.

TONBRIDGE Kent   Map 3

A la Bonne Franquette
20 Barden Road
Tonbridge 358457

Closed Sun; L Wed &
Sat; L Apr 13; Apr 15 &
16; May 28; Aug 27;
Dec 25 & 26; L Dec 31;
Jan 1
Must book
Meals 12.30–2, 8–9.30

Tdh L £2·35 (meal £2·60)
Alc £4·90 (meal £7·75)

VAT inc
Cover 25p D
Seats 28
♿ rest (1 step)
No dogs

The station car park approach and slightly austere interior have long ceased to deter lovers of Michel Maillard's uncompromisingly French cooking. Forgivable lapses occur, such as a thin, tough steak replaced by another no better, a niggardly helping of pommes dauphine, or failure to tell a guest that mushrooms figure twice in the meal he has ordered. The set lunch is almost always excellent value, perhaps with pâté de campagne, gigot, profiteroles, coffee and a glass of wine. But evening prices are also modest for the quality of the mushroom tartlet (70p), gnocchi or fish soup among first courses; then ris de veau beurre noir, perhaps, or individual cassoulets, or lapin provençale, or canard aux olives (£2·90). Some vegetables are annotated, no doubt prudently, with the single word 'garlic'. Salads are good too – 'Density or similar lettuce in a nice oily dressing.' If you order an ice, ask if it is M Maillard's or someone else's. Cheeses may vary with deliveries but are usually French and good. Bread is also praised. Coffee is not infallible. Smoking 'should be controlled in the interests of both customers and chef'. Among the wines in bottle, French-bottled Rully Varot white and Côtes du Rhône red, both about £4, suit this kind of food. No music.

App: Catherine Kroon, Rosemary Cunningham, A. J. A. Leys, Nicholas Roberts, Nancy B. Eddy, and others

TORQUAY Devon   Map 1

Fanny's Dining Room
53–55 Abbey Road
Torquay 28605

Closed L; Sun; Dec 26
Must book
D only, from 7.30

Most reports on Gully and Summers' ornately Victorian terraced house (knock for entry) begin with 'the food is good but . . .' A restaurant that notifies the next year's prices to the Guide in October and is charging 30% to 40% more for some of the same dishes six months later cannot expect to keep its friends easily, and neither the service nor the sense of detail lays claim to the league to which the owners and

Alc (min £5) £7·15 (meal £10·80)

Service 10%
Seats 36 (parties 12)
No dogs in d/r

their chef (this year unnamed) may aspire. However, the chilled cucumber soup (£1·25), fruits de mer diable, petites limandes, chateaubriand bordelaise, and especially the roast duck, boned, rolled and stuffed au poivre vert (£9·50 for two) are good, and vegetables well cooked, even if suprême de poularde and filet de boeuf O'porto were undistinguished. 'Cherry brandy ice-cream was triumphant.' French ordinaires are £1·50 for 50 cl. Only booked customers are accepted. The neighbouring Mousetrap wine bar invites nibbles from all comers, midday and evening: tell us about either place, or both.

John Dory
7 Lisburne Square
Torquay 25217

Closed L; Sun; Mon;
2 weeks Nov; 2 weeks
Jan/Feb; Dec 25 & 26
Must book
D only, 7–9.30

Alc (min £2·10) £5·40
(meal £8·25)

Seats 30
Car park
No dogs

'Look for a Rolls-Royce garage,' said a policeman directing a visitor up the hill from central Torquay to the little square housing Luggie and Woodman's soigné restaurant and matching antique shop. Table settings and the satirical prints on the walls make an impression confirmed by dexterous service and fish-cookery. Ronald Luggie also likes to cook game, but summer visitors gravitate to his John Dory grilled with fennel or grilled salmon hollandaise, 'both exquisitely fresh and not overcooked'. Lobster-lovers may prefer the beast buttered rather than in a thermidor version (£3·95) with more sauce than lobster, but the sauce itself, along with crab bisque and other basics, is capably made. Note also skate with black butter, and fish pie at £2·95. Vegetables, too, are accurately cooked and not piled on the plate. Sweets vary somewhat: at a test meal crème caramel was 'watery and disappointing'. But fresh pineapple mille-feuille and fresh orange mousse were very light. The carafe white is rather sweet for drinking through a meal, but there are better Alsace wines from £3·95, or Muscadet '76 at £3·85, and Warre '60 port at £14 (or '63 at 90p the glass). Recorded music.

App: G. J. Carwithen, C.P.D., Tony & Jenny Gould, W.A.M.S.

Toorak Hotel
Chestnut Avenue
Torquay 27135

'Near to perfection for family holidays,' writes one *père de famille* of the Edmonds' comfortable hotel which they, with faithful retainers, have run for forty years. Set meals offer a fair choice – at lunch, spaghetti bolognese, perhaps, then sole with tartare sauce, and an apple and raspberry compote; dinner may offer vichyssoise, a fish dish, roast duck and lemon soufflé. Recorded music. No wine details. Wear a jacket and tie.

Closed Dec 24, 25, 26 & 31; Jan 1
Must book
Meals 1–2, 7–8.15

Tdh L £3·25 (meal £4·80),
D £5 (meal £6·70)
Alc meal about £10

Service inc

Seats 200 (parties 30)
Car park
No dogs in public rooms
89 rooms (49 with bath)
Prices on application

Elbow Room
6 North Street
Totnes 863480

A 300-year-old converted cider press with log fire, candles and elbow room to enjoy the Sellicks' crab chowder, soft roes on toast, turbot Marguéry (£5), escalope de veau Argenteuil (with mushrooms and asparagus in a cream sauce, £4·25), roast duck (with sage and onion or mushrooms and burgundy, £4), or pui gu caise (Rumanian chicken with apricots and wine). Prices include fresh vegetables. House wine (provenance unspecified) £2·80 the bottle, 50p the glass. 'Romantic' recorded music. Mr Sellick wears a dinner jacket and the menu displayed tells you in several languages not to wear jeans. No under-sixes.

Closed L; Sun; Mon; Apr 13; Dec 25 & 26 Must book	D only, 7.30–10 Alc £6·85 (meal £10·25)	Seats 32 No dogs Am Ex, Barclay, Euro

ffoulkes
30 High Street
Totnes 863853

Closed L; Sun; 2 weeks
Feb & Nov; Dec 25 & 26
Must book
Meals 7–10.30 (11 Sat)

Alc £5·50 (meal £8·30)

Service 10%
Children's helpings
Seats 36
♿ rest
No dogs
Access, Am Ex, Barclay,
Diners

A tentative switch of enthusiasms in this civilised town proposes the Darroll-Broughs' emphatically Elizabethan restaurant, towards the top of the steep main street. The owners should relax a little, for dishes, descriptions and service are too busy. But very fresh scallops (£2·45) 'marinated in cider and fried in lager batter' with a lemony mousseline sauce survived the treatment well, and may also be divided between two as a first course. The salmon, whether fresh or locally smoked, is also good, and speciality meat dishes include filet dijonnaise (£3·30) and chateaubriand with a brown oyster sauce (is there a Chinese influence in Totnes?). At a test meal, the sauce for paupiette vallée d'Auge showed signs of 'breaking', and plainer vegetables, or more fruity and fewer creamy textures in the sweets, would have been welcome. Good Cheddar is kept, and the wines – chiefly from Averys and David Baillie Vintners – are startling in the context: among '70 château-bottled clarets under £10, for instance, Chx. Batailley, Beychevelle, Canon-la-Gaffelière, Gloria, Pédesclaux, and Rausan-Ségla. The ordinaires are Baronière red and white at £2·70, and Rhônes and Loires under £5 also repay attention. One wonders, perhaps unworthily, how all these bottles are binned. No music. More reports, please.

Kea House
Tregony 642

Closed L; Sun; Dec 25;
Jan 1
Must book
D only, 7.30–10

Alc £4·30 (meal £7)

Paul and Teresa Folkes, in this pine-and-wicker ex-pub that has proved to be more than a nine days' wonder, are still concentrating on 'the fish, the whole fish', without plunging on to 'nothing but the fish'. 'As the sea bass are sold by weight, a 1½ lb fish made a most satisfying main course for two – and a cheap one at £4·50 – and scallops en brochette were a model of sweet succulence.' Others have taken equal pleasure in the deep-fried crab-meat

Children's helpings
Seats 32
⟐ rest
No dogs
Access card

balls, baked bream with herbs, or gurnard, or John Dory in orange sauce, that are their reward for travelling so far from Billingsgate. 'Stuffed squid needs a more pronounced flavour.' Turbot sauce ma femme, with lime, is another innovation. Local regulars who can take fish or leave it are apt to begin with the crab pot ('fresh crab from Portscatho and a slightly curried flavour to the creamy sauce') or spinach pancake, and diverge to Glamorgan sausages (70p) and 'moist and pink pigeon in cabbage with cranberries and sweetcorn between bird and leaf'. Sweet-lovers expect sorbets and chocolate pots and consider themselves lucky if they are offered rhubarb fool or raspberry and almond tart as well. Service may be slow or unprofessional and the *patron* can seem rebarbative at first brush, though others find both the Folkes 'friendly and informative'. The Spanish wines from Laymont and Shaw of Falmouth continue to please both taste and pocket. Well-tempered Masía Bach and Extrísimo Bach are modestly marked up, which makes for well-tempered customers, and there is sound drinking even under £3. No music.

App: Neil Fairlamb, Mrs M. A. Grant,
C. P. Lowell, J. B. & S. Barnes, P.J., and others

TRING Hertfordshire   Map 3

Trattoria Pinocchio
56 High Street
Tring 4210

Closed Dec 25 & 26
Must book D & weekends
Meals 12–3, 6–11

Tdh L £3 (meal £5·45)
Alc £4·15 (meal £6·80)

Cover 25p
Seats 42
⟐ rest (2 steps)
No dogs
Access, Am Ex, Barclay,
Diners, Euro

The Tudor origins of Dominici and Tramontin's building by the car park are well concealed by Italianate tiles, alcoves and drapes, but the robust, personal cooking has caught a few people's attention lately. An inspector who pecks at his food wisely took along juniors who eat like pigeons to make the most of the kidneys in 'an enticingly flavoured red wine sauce' (a first course) and the generous poultry dishes: half a guinea-fowl tenderly roasted, offered with lemon or sour cream sauces, and half a crisp duck in lemon and wine sauce (£3·10). Chicken stuffed with pâté and ham is also praised (£2·05). Vegetables are competent rather than inspired (a 40p charge is made for them on Friday and Saturday evenings). Brandy-snaps and blackcurrant cheesecake, if bought in, come from a good source. Wines, from £2·20 for French or Spanish ordinaires, are routine. More reports, please.

Most places will accept cheques only when they are accompanied by a cheque card or adequate identification. Information about which credit cards are accepted is correct when printed, but occasionally restaurants add to or subtract from the list without notice.

For the explanation of ⟐ denoting accessibility for the disabled, see 'How to use the Guide', p. 4.

Hoover Chinese Restaurant
Calverley Road
Tunbridge Wells 33723

Fills a vacuum, you might say, for genuine Pekinese food is not so common in rural Kent, and an inspector's first experience of prawn toasts with sesame seeds (80p extra on the banquet), paper-wrapped prawn, pork satay with a chilli and aniseed sauce, spare ribs, and batter-fried 'butter-cups' filled with mixed vegetables was eminently satisfactory. So were beef with pepper and black bean, pot-roast chicken, hot-and-sour soup, and other things, though on a second visit the demands of denim'd Tunbridge youth for less complex chinoiserie had dimmed standards somewhat. Wish it well and report please. No details.

Alc meal £3·50

Mount Edgcumbe Hotel
The Common
Tunbridge Wells 20197

Closed Sun; Mon; Dec 26
Must book
Meals 12–2, 7.30–12

Alc £7·95 (meal £10·95)

VAT inc
Service 10%
Seats 24 (parties 10)
Air-conditioning
Car park
No dogs
10 rooms (3 with shower)
B&B £7·50–£8·50
Fire cert

Parry of the Arctic once lived in this house and 'perhaps in his memory the central heating was blasting away on a muggy evening.' The Higgins family have been sweeping away the tasteless accretions of the years to make a 'slickly run' hotel, and a brown-and-cream dining-room (with running water from the hothouse plants and 'romantic music' as aural distractions) that displays the cooking of Ian Higgins, a Karl Löderer pupil. The style is comparably rich, and needs a more delicate hand, but at a test meal crab pancakes with Mornay sauce and a hint of fennel (£2·25), and lavishly helped beef Stroganoff with plenty of paprika (£3·75), were alike admirably cooked. 'A pity that the lamb steak – rare, with a good madeira sauce – was overwhelmed by spikes of fresh rosemary.' Steak au poivre of 'Texas rather than Kentish' size is also praised, but the plates are too small for vegetables as well. Fish dishes are also well worth considering. Not everyone reaches the sweets, but hot apricot omelette suggested to one visitor that this may be a shame. Wines, a modest collection, begin at £3: Crozes-Hermitage Les Meysonniers '73, £4·30. Dress conventionally. No pipes or cigars. More reports, please.

Royal Wells Inn
Mount Ephraim
Tunbridge Wells 23414

Meals 12.30–2, 7.30–9.30

Tdh L £3·45 (meal £5·65),
D (res only) £3·25
(meal £5·45)
Alc £5·30 (meal £8)

VAT inc
Seats 48 (parties 40)

The white-painted hotel on Mount Ephraim gives you a faint feeling that you are dining with the Romanoffs, or at least the Forsytes fallen into indigence. But this architectural first impression is belied by the Sloan family, owner-chefs who claim only to believe in real food as in real ale (here Shepherd Neame and Courage on hand-pumps). There are times, certainly, when a beleaguered brother parks a sole in the oven too long, and some customers also report a sense of having been parked unattended in the dining-room. But on the whole the set meals seem 'cared for and delicious', with affectionate accounts of fresh tomato soup, brill,

Car park
No dogs in d/r
Access, Barclay, Diners
16 rooms (15 with bath,
1 with shower)
B&B £7·15–£8·15
Fire cert

chicken paprika with savoury rice, salmon trout
meunière, 'côte de veau Marengo almost like a
young joint', and half-forgotten syrup pudding, or
bread-and-butter pudding, 'creamy and succulent
inside, crispy outside'. Bar meals are good value too,
with a main dish from the dining-room set menu if
you like, and a visitor who notified in the same
breath a mild complaint and a substantial mistake
on the bill in his own favour had his money
cheerfully waved away. Wines, from Cuvée St Pierre
at £2·80, include Ch. Meyney '73 at £5·40. No music.

*App: Vida Bingham, N. A. Singers, L. Ratcliffe,
Kenneth Young, H. K. Heseltine, and others*

TUNBRIDGE WELLS see also pub section

ULLSWATER Cumbria   Map 7

**Sharrow Bay Country
House Hotel**

2 m S of Pooley Bridge
M6 exit 40
Pooley Bridge 301 *and*
483

Closed Dec to mid-Feb
Must book
Meals 1–1.30, 7.45–8.30

Tdh L from £7 (meal
£9·15), D from £8·50
(meal £10·20)

Service inc
Seats 60
♧ rest (1 step)
Car park
No dogs
28 rooms (19 with bath,
1 with shower)
D, B&B £22–£29

Very few restaurants or hotels of any distinction are
now older (in the same hands) than the *Guide* itself:
Francis Coulson and Brian Sack's stone-built
'Shangri-la' on the Howtown side of the lake is one
of them. It might take Muriel Spark or William
Trevor to do justice to the clientele of the one and
the readership of the other over the past 30 years,
but subtract the superabundant trimmings from
both hotel and book, and you are left here with the
spectacle of self-motivated craftsmen offering to
the cosseted guests of the late 70s what must have
seemed, in the late 40s, like the starving man's
dream of plenty. 'Does anyone take lunch here as
well as dinner?' 'We made one packed lunch last
two people two days.' 'There was the sorry sight of
too many full vegetable dishes being taken back by
the staff.' Those very commentators list the luscious
food that they did in fact enjoy: smoked trout pâté,
smoked salmon quiche, 'an exceedingly rich chicken
liver parfait bouchée, said to have been a favourite
of the late Queen of the Belgians', sole or fresh
scallops Mornay, salmon cutlets with dill sauce,
poussin vallée d'Auge served from the pan, lamb in
pastry with watercress *farce*, roast game; and
'superb sweets', with strawberry cheesecake, peach
and pear clafoutis, and lime chiffon pie among them.
(The kitchen would add their chocolate and rum
cream pie, and one wonders, somehow, what the
lads eat on their days off.) However, the last
Guide's phrase about 'flaws of taste and technique'
is upheld this year by a famously articulate visitor
who 'cannot abide beautiful plump fish, fresh as one
hardly ever gets it nowadays, made into a poultice
by cheese dissolving into thick white sauce. Texture
is of importance in cookery, and this and other
otherwise admirable dishes had the texture of an

327

Irish bog. I hate to grumble, for I felt the owners were working on some strange religious principle.' As a hotel, Sharrow is luxurious both in the house and the lakeside extension, but, from the point of view of a guest seeking an aperitif or a cup of coffee, it is hardly efficient. A former serious admirer finds the wine service casual, but wines themselves are admirable and their prices relatively modest, from £2·90 in 1978, with famous '71 auslese hocks under £10, and Romanée-Conti '69 burgundies £35 or so. No music. One of the dining-rooms is non-smoking. No under-13s. Dress conventionally.

App: by too many members to list

UNDERBARROW Cumbria   Map 7

Greenriggs Country House
3 m W of Kendal
M6 exit 36 or 37
Crosthwaite 387

Closed L; Sun;
Mon–Thur (Nov–Mar)
Must book
D only, 8 p.m.

Tdh £6 (meal £8·10)

VAT inc
Seats 40 (parties 14)
♿ rest (2 steps)
Car park
No dogs in public rooms
12 rooms (6 with bath,
1 with shower)
B&B £8·50–£10·50
D, B&B £12–£14

A good few people, many of them new to our files, are warm in praise of Frank and Christine Jackson's peaceful 18th-century house in the Lyth valley. Gratifying though this is, one half-wonders whether in catering colleges (where Mr Jackson used to teach) there are by now courses in guide management as well as in mere cooking. Not that there is all that much wrong with the four-course dinners (with modest choice) that the courteous owner provides at comparatively low cost, and people who have reason to know have been very happy with 'chicken livers with marjoram to begin with, and admirably cooked local lamb with an apricot and herb stuffing', or 'subtle and interesting watercress and lemon soup followed by thick, moist roast pork with apple and almonds'. Even a severe critic says that 'Stilton and onion tart really tasted of Stilton' before going on to regret mediocre fish and main courses, frozen raspberries and bought ice-cream in a June coupe, liquid tinned tomatoes on the plate at breakfast, and inappropriately small fluted glasses for the sensibly chosen wines (Ch. Meyney '70, c.b., £5·80; halves of Ch. Climens '70, c.b., £2·80). Basic Spanish is £2·20. No music. No children under ten.

App: Tim Harper, Shirley Mackenzie, T. P. Walter, Gerald France, Harry Robinson, G. Coop, and others

---

Tullythwaite House
4 m W of Kendal
M6 exit 36 or 37
Crosthwaite 397

Closed L (exc Sun); Mon;
Fri; Sun D; mid-Dec to
mid-Mar
Must book
Meals 12.30 (Sun),
HT 4–5, 7

Perhaps it is insultingly age-ist to express surprise, as one or two members do, that Mrs Johnson in her Lakeland farmhouse should be cooking some of the district's best food in her eighties. (After all, when cooks are tired of cooking they are tired of life.) Anyway, Mrs Johnson's daughter-in-law shares responsibility for locally traditional potted char, 'very delicate fresh salmon mousse', superb soups of cauliflower and cheese or Stilton and onion, 'tender and crisp' roast duckling or Lakeland lamb with apple and walnut stuffing, and imposing sweets: 'A

Tdh Sun L from £7,
D from £7·50

VAT inc
Seats 20 (parties 8)
[&] rest
Car park
No dogs
Unlicensed

whole raspberry Pavlova and freshly made
profiteroles were brought and left on each table.'
Damson soufflé or peach crème brûlée might arrive
on other days. Stilton in its pierced dish is then
brought from what one connoisseur describes as 'a
most unusual Gillow walnut sideboard with serpentine
front'. The service of both food and wine (take your
own bottle) is unaffected and skilful. Remember
that there is no choice to speak of, and that early
booking is essential. No music.

App: R. T. Davies, M.J.D., V. B. Cole, and others

WALTON-ON-THAMES Surrey   Map 3

Angelo's
70 Terrace Road
Walton-on-Thames 41964

Angelo Minerva and his staff tread an amiable
lobster quadrille among their customers; most
admire the performance but a few scurry for cover.
As well as the favourite lobsters, try the sensible set
lunches (soup or ravioli; fritto misto, pollo paesana,
or veal; pancakes or fruit salad; coffee and petits
fours, £3·50) and traditional Italian dishes. The
lobster soup is usually delicious, the prawn cocktail
generous on prawns, veal Cordon Bleu 'superb', the
monkey gland steak 'nothing out of the ordinary'.
'The waiter does not understand when you say
"enough".' (Try 'basta'.) Italian house wines, £3·20
for 95 cl. 'Flamingo or classical music', live at
weekends. Wear a jacket and tie in the evening.

Closed Sun; public hol
Mons; Dec 25 & 26;
Jan 1
Must book
Meals 12.30–2, 7–11

Tdh L £3·50 (meal £6·10)
Alc £6 (meal £9·80)

Cover 35p alc

Children's helpings
Seats 40 (parties 20)
No dogs
Am Ex, Barclay, Diners

WANSFORD Cambridgeshire   Map 6

Haycock Inn
8 m W of Peterborough
Stamford 782223

Queen Victoria once stayed at this 17th-century inn
(a Poste Hotel since 1971). Today's travellers find
it a useful pull-in from the A1, and though not all
are amused by the sporadic lapses, most consider the
all-day bar food reasonable ('good cold salmon') and
the roasts, guinea-fowl and jugged hare in the
dining-room admirable. Lilliano Chianti Classico is
£4 the litre; for details of the wine list, see under
Huntingdon. Tollemache & Cobbold and Bass on
hand pump. Bar meals also served in the garden.
Jeans frowned on in the restaurant. No music.

Closed Dec 25
Must book
Meals 12.30–2, 7–10.30

Alc £5·25 (meal £7·85)
Service inc

Children's helpings
(under 10)
Seats 36 (parties 70)
Car park
No dogs in d/r

Access, Am Ex, Barclay,
Diners
25 rooms (6 with bath,
1 with shower)
B&B from £9·25
Fire cert

329

Oliver's
West Street
Wareham 6164

The owners are called Twist, so the bistro's name and large helpings were inevitable. Soup, haddock mousse, entrecôte bordelaise (£3·25) and pigeon aux cerises (£2·70) have pleased people. A test meal yielded 'delicate' kidneys and courgettes but also signs of strain: a pre-cooked taste to pork, crème brûlée still hot on top 'like Chinese toffee apples' and 'terrible' lemon meringue pie. Carafe Italian is £2·85. Wines, and service, show more enthusiasm than knowledge. Pop records. More reports, please.

Closed L; Mon; Dec 25 & 26
Must book weekends
D only, 7–10.30

Alc £5·15 (meal £7·50)

VAT inc
Service 10% (parties of 6 or more)

Seats 30
♿ rest
No dogs
Barclaycard

Flower Drum
16 Market Street
Watford 26711

Closed Dec 24, 25 & 26
Must book weekends
Meals 12–2.30, 7–11

Alc meal £3·80

Service 10%
Seats 55
♿ rest (1 step)
No dogs
Access, Am Ex, Barclay, Diners

London inspectors have for years been exposing the roofs of their mouths in Chinese restaurants in the hope of peppery Szechuan flavours, mostly in vain. But Richard Yuen in the kitchen and his English manager Linda Penny are offering both Pekinese and Szechuan 'feasts' in this well-set place ('apricot linen, cane-seated tubular chairs, and discreet dragons on the walls'). On the Szechuan side, prawn fingers, seaweed, and chicken pancake were delicate when tried, but spring rolls in rice paper with chilli sauce, and, to a lesser extent, the juicy prawns, 'had a kick like a mule'. On the Peking side, when tried, the mixed hors d'oeuvre were 'accompanied by halved spicy hot sausages', and kungpo prawns in batter with sesame seeds and black-bean sauce were generous and lightly cooked. They have evidently been successful in persuading their Watford customers to drink the Bouchard Aîné et Fils wines (from £2·70) with Chinese food, but the tea is good too. Recorded music. More reports, please.

Bed and breakfast prices have been quoted to us by hoteliers; where possible, we have given minimum off-season and maximum in-season prices for one person sharing a double room.

'Meal' indicates the cost of a meal for one, including food, coffee, half the cheapest bottle of wine, cover, service, and VAT (see 'How to use the Guide', p. 4).

Since each restaurant has a separate file in the Guide office, please use a separate form or sheet of paper for each report. Additional forms may be obtained free (no stamp required) from The Good Food Guide, Freepost, 14 Buckingham Street, London WC2N 6BR.

WELL Hampshire   Map 2

Chequers
off A32
3 m SE of Odiham
M3 exit 5
Long Sutton 605

The Chequers, an old coaching inn, licensed since 1704, has a '*sens interdit*' sign outside – to let you know the owners are French, presumably. In the bistroish restaurant that has been grafted on, the sensibly short menu might offer mushrooms à la grecque (£1·05), moules farcies, frogs' legs provençale (£2·25); then grilled daurade with herbs (£2·75), pork fillet niçoise 'with a real tomato sauce' (£2·95), or venison, either with sauce poivrade or in a pie. Vegetables are properly cooked but swamped in butter. Sweets are 'fair', though a rum baba 'like a little sultana pudding' sounds intriguing. Some interesting French wines; house wine £2·85 for 70 cl. Bar snacks (lunch only, Tue-Sun): onion soup, quiches, steak and kidney pie (95p), with Badger best bitter on hand pump. No music.

Closed Sun; Mon; Dec 25 & 26	Alc £5·65 (meal £8)	Seats 50 (parties 12)
Must book D & weekends	Service inc	🛇 rest
Meals 12–1.30, 7.30–9		Car park
		No dogs in d/r

WELLS Somerset   Map 2

Rugantino
Ancient Gate
House Hotel,
Sadler Street
Wells 72029

Wells has run dry of good restaurants lately, and last year's tentative suggestion of the Rossis' place at the edge of Cathedral Green has provoked, along with praise of Italian seafood cocktail, veal rustica (£2·70), and steaks pizzaiola or boscaiola (£3·50), vigorous complaints of mediocre veau à la crème, poorly cooked vegetables, and 'trifle (70p) that a children's party would have turned up its nose at'. (Try crêpes Suzette, perhaps, but they are £3·20 for two.) 'Vino sfuso' (Valpolicella or Soave) is £2·80 a litre and there is little else.

Closed D Dec 25 & 26	VAT inc	🛇 rest (2 steps)
Must book D	Service 10%	No dogs in d/r
Meals 12–3, 7–10	Cover 15p	Access, Barclay, Euro
(10.30 Fri & Sat)	Children's helpings (under 8)	9 rooms
Tdh L £2·60 (meal £4·75)	Seats 35	B&B £8
Alc (min £2·50) £4·65 (meal £7·15)		Fire cert

Please report to us on atmosphere, decor and – if you stayed – standard of accommodation, as well as on food, drink and prices (send bill if possible).

Prices of meals underlined are those which we consider represent unusual value for money. They are not necessarily the cheapest places in the Guide.

WESTERHAM Kent   Map 3

Alison Burt's
1 Market Square
Westerham 62245

Alison Burt is actually only one half of this brown-and-pink little place with a short monthly menu, smocked waitresses, and mildly uncomfortable ladderback chairs, for her sister Kate Sutherland shares the management and the cooking. The Kentish dearth has filled it with customers for taramosalata, jugged hare, tongue with caper sauce and so on, but none of these dishes was very good of their kind when tested. Pâté, pork tonnato, 'buttery potatoes in their skins', and almondy cheesecake were better, though, and chocolate and chestnut roulade is called 'crisp, creamy and delicious', so please report further. Wines from £2·50; Ch. Ricaud '71, £3·20. Recorded music.

Closed L; Sun; Mon;
1 week summer & winter;
Dec 25
Must book

D only, 7.30–9.30
(10 weekends)

Tdh £5·25 (meal £7·15)

VAT inc
Seats 40
No dogs
Access, Barclay

WESTERHAM see also wine bar section

WEST RUNTON Norfolk   Map 6

Mirabelle
Station Road
West Runton 396

Closed Mon; first 3 weeks
Nov; Dec 25;
Sun D (Nov–May)
Must book
Meals 12.30–2, 7–9

Tdh L £2·60 (meal £4·90),
D £4·40 (meal £7)
Alc £6·60 (meal £9·65)

Children's helpings
Seats 48
□ rest; w.c.
Car park
No dogs
Am Ex card

It is no coincidence that Weybourne (*q.v.*) nearby and West Runton should both boast competent Swiss restaurants, and in five years Manfred Hollwöger has not strayed far from the formula that has kept his former employers in the *Guide* for twenty-five. His set meals behind the net curtains in this suburban setting are substantial and usually good value. One dinner began with a whole 'ripe but not sloppy' Ogen melon; another with a puree of avocado with cream cheese and tomato-flavoured mayonnaise; a third with minestrone from a large tureen left at the side of the table. Duckling with home-made apple sauce was generous, steak and venison steaks similarly liberal; vegetables competent; cream meringues 'enormous and light in the best continental tradition'; Sachertorte workmanlike, crème caramel stiff. À la carte, though salmon hollandaise was disappointing, kidneys on toast (90p) made a splendid first course. Lobster thermidor (£4·85 à la carte, but sometimes lobster appears as an extra on the table d'hôte too) and sauté of beef are among Manfred's own favourites. Gironde or Roussillon ordinaires are £2·60, and on a moderate list Ch. Chasse-Spleen '69 is £5·50 and Brauneberger Kurfürstlay Spätlese '75, estate-bottled, is £6·50. But service, though willing, is sometimes restlessly supervised. No music.

App: B. M. Newman, Paul L. Joslin, E.R., Iain Alexander, and others

WEST STOUGHTON Somerset   Map 2

Eethuys
Cypress House
off A38
4 m S of Axbridge
Wedmore 712527

Closed L; Sun; Mon;
2 weeks Chr
Must book
D only, 7–9.30

Tdh £6·50 (meal £9·10)

VAT inc
Seats 18
[&] rest
Car park
No dogs

*It is back to base (not far from her old place at Cross)
for Karen Roozen and her friend Erie Ten-Oever,
after a spell managing the Priory at Rushlake Green
(in the 1978 edition). Evidence is naturally sparse as
yet, but Mrs Roozen's cooking is a known quantity,
and her remote farmhouse is worth signposting,
especially after early reports of her 'sizzling hot' pea
and mint soup with croûtons, 'amply filled devilled
prawn pancakes', and steaks of lamb 'with a
deliciously light, thin, vermouth and lemon sauce'.
The vegetables are characteristically well cooked,
especially the gratin dauphinoise potatoes, and apple
sorbet with apple brandy 'rounded off an excellent
meal, modestly priced for what it was'. Another early
visitor picks out vanilla soufflé with crème de cassis.
Look out, too, for gougères with snails and a delectable
parsley and garlic sauce, hare in red wine,
'free-range duck with various sauces', and cabinet
pudding. Rouge du Gard or Frascati wines are £2·50;
Beaujolais Villages, a.c., '76, £4·50; Ch. Ausone '66
'magnificent at £8·50'. Pipes and cigars are confined to
the bar. No music. More reports, please.*

WETHERAL Cumbria   Map 7

Fantails
on B6263
5 m SE of Carlisle
M6 exit 42 or 43
Wetheral 60239

Small, family-run restaurant opposite the village
green, included here – after five years out of the
book and a change of ownership – for its shortish
carte. Try the Fergusons' prawns in aïoli, whitebait,
salmon, or Welsh pork (with cheese and brown ale).
Reasonable vegetables and puddings. Affable
service. House wine is Pinot Noir, £2·50 the bottle.
Other wines from Youdell of Kendal. Bass and
Tennent's beer (pressurised). No music.

Closed L Nov–Apr;
Jan 1; Feb
Must book D
Meals 12–2, 6–9.30

Alc £5·45 (meal £7·60)

VAT inc
Children's helpings

Seats 50 (parties 30)
Car park
No dogs
Access, Am Ex, Diners,
Euro

WEYBOURNE Norfolk   Map 6

**Gasché's Swiss
Restaurant**
on A149
3 m W of Sheringham
Weybourne 220

Closed Mon; Sun D;
Dec 25
Must book
Meals 12.30–2, 7–9

'When is Gasché's not full?' a regular customer
reasonably enquires after the restaurant's 33 years
in the same hands. There are faults, of course, some
of them surely curable: tepid vegetables sometimes
because of overloaded silver service, off-putting wine
prices, and a dining-room tinged with kitchen
odours. But these last were not too apparent at this
year's test meal, in spite of deep-fried aubergines
and sole Colbert (both competent) on the menu.
Other creditable dishes in that meal included the

333

Tdh L £2·95 (meal £4·80),
D £4·80 (meal £6·80)
Alc £8·05 (meal £10·40)

VAT inc
Children's helpings
Seats 70 (parties 35)
[symbol] rest; w.c. (m)
Car park

cream of vegetable soup, dressed crab (rather too cold) and sweetbreads à la crème. 'Heaps of rustling whitebait', chicken suprême in a flavoury sauce, steaks, 'tender and crisp' duckling (usually), and 'the way they remember you and your reservation' are also remarked. A la carte, the fish risotto at £7·70 for two should be memorable. Café liégeois or a fresh peach may be the best of the unexciting sweets. In view of the set meal prices, wines that start at £2·20 for 50 cl of French ordinaire and march quickly past Swiss bottles at £6·60 to mostly indifferent claret vintages in double figures are excusable, but a pity. At least some of the vintages are declared now, so try Ch. Meyney '61 at £14 if you are in funds, and Gewürztraminer or Chianti (n.v.) around £5 if you are not. No music.

App: Paul L. Joslin, R. Whitehead, N.M.B., N. & L.R., and others

---

WEYBOURNE see also pub section

WEYBRIDGE Surrey   Map 3

Casa Romana
2 Temple Hall,
Monument Hill
Weybridge 43470

Closed Mon; Sat L;
public hols (exc Apr 13 &
L Apr 15)
Must book
Meals 12.15–2.15, 7–10.45
(Sun 7–10)

Tdh L £2·85 (meal £5·75)
Alc (min main course)
£7·15 (meal £10·45)

VAT inc
Cover 50p
Seats 70
[symbol] rest (3 steps); w.c.
Car park
No dogs

Eight years have brought prosperity to Corrado di Michele and Roberto Ballerini, and they have lately opened a take-away outlet, La Cucina Italiana, in Oatlands on the outskirts of the town. All this has not diminished people's pleasure in their meals at the original restaurant, which is 'got up in not too off-putting mock-classical style'. But it has loosened control somewhat, especially in the dress and deportment of the waiters, and they were unwise to mistake a fish trader and fellow Italian for a guest who would not know the difference between a fresh Dover sole and 'an over-grilled, tasteless slip'. Still, 'you would go a long way to find better king prawns or duck in Marsala', and 'how right the last entry was about the delicious chicken breast in pastry with Mozzarella, ham and herbs.' 'For mussels in white wine and tomato, they removed the shells at half-time and brought a fresh plate for discards.' A dish of veal with lobster made an enterprising combination.' The trolleys of fishy hors d'oeuvre at the beginning and sweets at the end lift people's hearts – 'fruit salad was really fresh and brandy-snaps delicious.' The set lunch is normally good value. Drink Italian house wines under £3, and there are other lesser-known Italian bottles too. Recorded music 'only adds to the hubbub'.

App: V. & F. Irish, B.S.A., Mrs S. Blissett, M.F.R. A.M., G. Webster-Gardiner, and others

Dulcinea
73 Queen's Road
Weybridge 42895

Closed Sun L; Apr 13;
Dec 25 D
Must book weekends
Meals 12–2.30, 6–11

Tdh L £2·50 (meal £4·75)
Alc £6·50 (meal £10·20)

VAT inc tdh
Cover 30p alc
Children's helpings
Seats 40
No dogs
Access, Barclay

Even now, more people visit Longinos Benavides'
neat little Spanish restaurant than ever think of
recounting their meals to the *Guide*, but one couple
who ate there 'frequently and well' in 1978 have
been through most of the menu from calamares en
su tinta (£1·60) and tortilla de patatas to rape en
cazuela (monk-fish in casserole, £3·50, not just
another exploit of Don Juan's) and devilled squab en
crapaudine (£2·80). 'The paella (£4) is about the
best we have had in Britain, or Spain either, for that
matter.' Inspection confirms the Spanishness of both
the cooking and the waiting – 'one boy looks as
though he'd stepped straight out of a Murillo
painting.' Fish soup was incandescent in
temperature and equally lively in flavour, with well-
fried croûtons, and courgettes were also deftly fried,
in a light, thin batter. The house veal dish was less
memorable. Specialities, which should probably be
ordered in advance, include spiced crab-meat crêpes,
striped bass in flaming fennel, suckling pig with three
sauces, and the sweet (not otherwise explained)
called natillas de la casa (£1·60). Nougat is 'friable,
and exquisite too'. Rioja red or white wines are
£2·90 and there are better ones as well (Spanish not
French), but the full list has not been supplied this
year. 'The pictures are better than the music.'

*App: Brian, Arlette & Bob Singleton, C.P.D.,
O.J.P., and others*

Valencia
47 Church Street
Weybridge 47443

Jesus Freire's Spanish place in the Quadrant now
boasts a bright new stucco façade, and the inside
has been renovated too; but Saturday nights can
still be 'crowded and airless'. No complaints,
though, of the à la carte dinners: calamares, paella,
gazpacho, zarzuela, a few sweets. Reasonable-
sounding set lunch. Service is committed. Fair list
of Spanish bottles at £3–£4; house Rioja is £2·60, or
50p by the glass. Spanish records.

Closed Sun; Mon L;
Apr 13; Dec 25 D;
Dec 26; Jan 1
Must book D & weekends
Meals 12–2.15, 7–11

Tdh L £2·50 (meal £4·50)
Alc (min D £2·50) £5·40
(meal £7·95)

VAT inc
Cover 25p alc

Children's helpings
(under 10)
Seats 40
🔾 rest; w.c.
No dogs
Access, Am Ex, Barclay,
Euro

WEYMOUTH Dorset   Map 2

Sea Cow Bistro
7 Custom House Quay
Weymouth 3524

It may be easier to find the Jonzens' popular
restaurant by yacht or harbourside train than by
car, but the 'nicely dated air' of the townscape is
irresistible, and the low white building worth
finding. In holiday season it can be overrun and the
kitchen overwhelmed, but a test meal earlier in the

Closed Sun; Aug 15;
3 weeks Oct; Nov 5;
Dec 24–26; Jan 1
Must book D
Meals 12.15–2, 7.30–10.30

Alc £4 (meal £6·20);
(smorgasbord) L £1·80,
D £3

VAT inc
Children's helpings
Seats 54 (parties 36)
  rest (2 steps); w.c.
Air-conditioning
No dogs
Access, Barclay, Diners,
Euro

year was a distinct success, including a russet crab soup, cheeks of skate in a lightly curried cream sauce (75p), baked bass (slightly overcooked) coated with hardboiled egg and parsley (£2·80), and good jacket potatoes, even in May. Others endorse this opinion, and there are good meat dishes too: aubergine with bacon, mushrooms and cream as a first course, Swedish spiced pork with red cabbage, and perhaps quails flared in calvados (£2·80). There are smorgasbord lunches upstairs (also dinners from June to September and on winter Saturdays) and these are good value, says an inspector strayed from an ill-fed course in a nearby college. A vegetarian, too, was given 'an impromptu but delicious dish' at dinner. Mrs Jonzen and her helpers' favourite sweet is their fresh blueberries in kirsch with home-made shortbread, and the fruit tarts are competent; trifle, chocolate mousse and cheeses were poor relations in comparison. Carafino ordinaires are £3·20 a litre and there are pressurised beers; '76 Muscadet was £3 in 1978. They make 'nice big cold Kirs'. No music.

App: Julian Corbluth, G. W. Disbrey, P. & J.S., Henry Potts, and others

WHITSTABLE Kent   Map 3

Giovanni's
49–55 Canterbury Road
Whitstable 273034

Closed Mon; Dec 26;
Jan 1
Must book D
Meals 12–2.30, 6.30–10.45

Tdh L £2·95 (meal £5·15)
Alc (min £2·50) £5·90
(meal £8·85)

VAT inc
Service 10%
Cover 35p
Children's helpings
Seats 60
  rest (3 steps)
Access, Barclay, Diners,
Euro

'A bypassed and rather unhappy little port', Postgate called Whitstable in this restaurant's first (1969) entry, but if there is joy in Whitstable, even without oysters, Giovanni Ferrari has contributed his share, and been rewarded by the extensions to bar and kitchen that are now under way (and whose results should be reported, please). The cold table is always adorned with freshly landed fish, and a party whose lunch included 'a huge plate of hors d'oeuvre,' and 'lasagne of main course quantity', followed by freshly cooked, hot lemon sole on the bone and veal Parmentier with celery and aubergines, emerged astonished by the value given. A la carte specialities include veal cutlet (£2·75) and aubergines with seafood (£1·35). Others praise the home-smoked trout, mussels in white wine, pigeon casserole, 'splendid chicken cooked with figs and Marsala (£2·40)', various not over distinguished but rich sweets, and 'topical' (as opposed to tropical) fruit. 'Good grappa and macaroons too.' The house Italian wines are £2·65 but we have not seen the full list lately. Air-conditioning. Car park. No dogs. Recorded music.

App: Kenneth Young, Stephen Ward, A.R.F.C.

See p. 120 for the restaurant-goer's legal rights, and p. 118 for information on hygiene in restaurants.

WILLITON Somerset   Map 2

White House Hotel
on A39
1½ m SE of Watchet
Williton 32306

Closed L; Oct to mid-May
Must book
D only, 7.30–8.30

Tdh £5·25 (meal £7·35)

VAT inc
Seats 30
⟐ rest (1 step)
Car park
No dogs in d/r
14 rooms (7 with bath)
B&B £8·50–£9·50
D, B&B £12–£13
Fire cert

Williton is now once more a steam railway terminus. Perhaps jazz (Dick Smith's former occupation) is on its way in again too, but in recent years he and his family have made an appealing hotel of their shuttered white house, and people have lately started to write about the food which three of the Smiths cook together (a barefoot fourth serves). Borshch and pork with lentils seemed a winter rather than a summer evening's programme, but were well cooked, and at a test meal smoked mackerel mousse had 'a very delicate flavour and consistency'. Other soups – red bean, and chicken and leek – are also praised, and main courses do not disappoint, to judge from 'a marvellous dish with turkey breasts and bacon, accompanied by garlicky potatoes', and fennel-flavoured cod provençale. Stilton-baked eggs sound good. The Smiths like their own strawberry crème brûlée and Viennese chocolate cream, but nut roll, loganberry trifle and 'pale brown meringue with delicious gooseberry puree' are noted too. Bread is good, and breakfasts are adequate: 'I asked for the impossible – a soft-boiled egg – and got it.' There is also warm praise of lunch ordered in advance for a large party. Wines begin with Yapp's Gamay de l'Ardèche or Muscadet at £2·40 for 50 cl; thereafter note the Vacqueyras and three Gigondas under £6. No music. More reports, please.

WILMINGTON Devon   Map 2

Home Farm Hotel
on A35
3 m E of Honiton
Wilmington 278

Closed Sun D; Jan 1–
Feb 15
Must book D
Meals 12.30–1.45,
7.30–9.30

Tdh L £3·75 (meal £5·65),
D £6 (meal £7·90)
Alc £7·35 (meal £9·25)

VAT & service inc
Children's helpings
(under 12)
Seats 36
⟐ rest (3 steps)
No dogs in d/r
12 rooms (5 with bath)
B&B £10–£12
D, B&B £90–£100 p.w.
Fire cert

At the second attempt, so to speak, the Crastons' converted 16th-century dairy farm seems to have secured its foothold on the *Guide* slopes – and not at the nursery level either, to judge by contented and informed accounts of Susan Rowatt's hardworking but cheerful kitchen, working on its vegetable soups, chicken liver pâté, cold sweets and apple pie before turning to the more topical business of cannelloni with creamed haddock, coq au vin, spiced rabbit casserole, or sweetbreads in cream and white wine. They have not quite mastered the art of roasting pigeon without dryness (who has?) and lamb cutlets have occasionally shown the same fault. But vegetables are carefully cooked on the whole, and orange chocolate cheesecake, lemon meringue pie, or chocolate brandy crunch do credit to the sweet-makers. Lunches are lighter, and much cheaper. Service is affable, and rooms comfortable. There are half a dozen modest French house wines under £4, and though the supplier is sound, there is no overpowering temptation to go beyond them. No music.

App: P. M. Arnold, D. J. Hawkins, E. S. Bedell, Norma Gordon, R. J. S. Marsh, S.P.B., and others

Splinters
9 Great Minster Street
Winchester 64004

Across the green from the Cathedral's west door is a Victorian-style splinter from the original Christchurch and Lymington timbers (both q.v.). Cooking here falls short of the well-chosen and extensive wine list (see under Christchurch) and mousses may 'bounce'. But bream and other fish, fried potatoes, and other daily dishes have admirers. No children under six. Reports, please, of the daily dishes in the new lunchtime Brasserie downstairs: 'anglicised curry but real soup, Brie and coffee' is one early description. 'No music in the restaurant, but Land of Hope and Glory downstairs.'

Closed L (exc bar); Sun;
Dec 24, 25 & 26; Feb
Must book D

Meals 11–2.30 (bar),
6.30–10.30

Alc £6·10 (meal £8·70)

VAT inc
Seats 42
No dogs

Miller Howe

Rayrigg Road
on A592
Windermere 2536

Closed L; Jan–Mar
Must book
D only, 8.30 (Sat 7.30 &
9.30)

Tdh £9 (meal £12·10)

VAT inc
Service 12½%
Seats 70
🔲 rest
Air-conditioning
Car park
No dogs in public rooms
Am Ex, Diners
13 rooms (11 with bath)
D, B&B £20–£32
Fire cert

Unlikely as it may seem, there is something of Wodehouse's Uncle Fred in dapper Mr Tovey, whose culinary life is a perpetual upbeat to some mischievous new tune, and whose articles of belief include feeding residents Buck's Fizz before breakfast. Somehow, between tours of America and courses of instruction for cooks and guide inspectors (not ours) he invents new creature comforts for this Firbankian house with its sublime view of lake and Pikes. He is a good pedagogue, too, for Robert Lyons, Tom Peter, and Phillip Hornby in the kitchen need less direction than they once did. The style, at this level, inevitably divides opinion. Some of the year's letters read like Webern criticising Richard Strauss, for Mr Tovey will seldom use three notes in a gustatory chord where seven will do, and there are times when a miscalculated effect makes one look in vain for a robust helping of plain meat, or wish for a pause in the *buffo* pace of the blazered service (which outside the dining-room naturally considers residents before casuals). 'I see little point in having *both* mayonnaise *and* Pernod cream with the salmon.' But the vast majority of reports are best summed up by the (Welsh) inspector for whom this is 'the only British restaurant whose meals are both technically superb and light and uncloying in their effect.' The technique indeed dazzles: most people who could devise a *jeu d'esprit* such as sole cream with a core of watercress and orange, baked to a shiny brown and served with hollandaise, would make more fuss about it than Mr Tovey, whose favourites listed to the *Guide* this year are merely 'triple pâté terrine, loin of pork with ginger, lime, and yoghourt, and walnut fudge tart'. Others admire no less the consommé, almost all pastry dishes ('superb chestnut and brandy quiche'), the sense of taste, colour, and texture contrast ('gamey duck terrine with cream cheese and water chestnuts'), and the élan, 'as of a finely tuned sports car', with which seventy close-packed diners can be served all at once (admittedly with no choice, except of sweet), and given unambiguously delicious meals such as 'deep-fried crumbed duck's liver with hot Cumberland sauce, pea and carrot soup, smoked trout mousse with salad, roast sirloin with blackcurrant and beetroot jelly and the famous seven vegetables, and whisky coffee meringue gateau.' Take a long walk midday if you stay, for breakfasts, teas and packed lunches for residents are also hard to resist. Coffee is variable. Wines are distinguished and normally well served by Wolfgang and his wolverines. There is little under £4 and some will feel that the cheapest, plainest bottles (Sauvignon, Cabernet, Pineau, or Gamay de Touraine, all £4·15) are the best solutions to so many complex, un-French flavours. However, the run of Beaune Clos des Fèves (from £6·75), or Louis Latour '71 burgundy bottlings from £11·45, will tempt those who can afford them. No smoking in the dining-room. No children under 12. Recorded 'nice' music – too nice, perhaps.

App: by too many members to list

WIVENHOE Essex Map 3

The Casserole
30 The Avenue
Wivenhoe 2221

A converted Victorian house, homely and comfortable. Good ideas – some of them Creole, though that partner has gone – on Halcyon Palmer's short menus. Praise for cauliflower Mornay, spiced prawns New Orleans, moules bordelaise, lapin aux deux moutardes, pork in cider with chestnuts, and Caribbean curried pork (served in a half-pineapple). Doubts about an apricot sauce with cauliflower tart, shortage of calvados in veal normande, and over-sweet puddings. Vegetables are nicely *al dente*. Friendly and unobtrusive service. French house wine, £3·20 the litre. 'Intermittent' recorded music.

Closed L; Sun; Mon; Apr 13; last 2 weeks Aug; Dec 25 & 26; Jan 1 Must book D only, 7.15–9.30	Tdh (Tue–Thur) from £3·50 (meal £6·80), (Fri & Sat) £5·50 (meal £7·90) VAT inc	Children's helpings (under 10) Seats 28 ♿ rest (1 step) Car park No dogs Diners card

---

For the explanation of ♿ denoting accessibility for the disabled see 'How to use the Guide', p. 4.

Tandoor
46 Queen Street
Wolverhampton 20747

'Marvellous, spicy food'; 'warm reception'; 'handy for the theatre'. People still consider this dimly lit, personally run restaurant an ornament to the Black Country. Praise for keema nan (stuffed with minced lamb), chicken Begum Behar (£1·70) or Jal Frazy. They also recommend lamb moghlai, and tandoori chicken masala (£1·95), and seem to make their own kulfi or gulab jamun as a sweet. Fresh fruit too would be welcome, and you may wait long for the bill. Various beers; Hirondelle £3·25. Indian records.

Closed Sun L; Dec 25;
L public hols
Must book weekends
Meals 12–2.30, 6.30–12.15

Tdh L £2, D £3
Alc (min D £3)
meal £3·90

Seats 90 (parties 40)

♿ rest (1 step)
Air-conditioning
No dogs
Access, Am Ex, Barclay, Diners

Luis
19 High Street
Woodstock 811017

Closed Mon L; Apr 16;
May 28; Aug 27; Dec 26;
Jan 1
Must book D & weekends
Meals 12.15–2.30, 7–11

Tdh D from £3·15 (meal
£6·65)
Alc L £4·05 (meal £6·25),
D £6·75 (meal £9·25)

VAT inc
Service 10%
Cover 25p
Children's helpings
(under 5)
Seats 32
♿ rest
No dogs
Am Ex, Barclay, Diners

The Castro family come from the northern Pyrenees, which accounts for such specialities as shellfish soup (£1), turbot à la basque (£3·80) and lobster tails au Ricard (£3·60). But it is not just for fish that members – provided they are not copious wine-drinkers – praise this restaurant, which was new to the *Guide* last year. Onion soup is sometimes good, sometimes greasy or 'anaemic', and carbonnade of beef likewise varies in tenderness and juiciness. But a brace of pheasants has been successfully attempted, chicken Cordon Bleu is a favourite dish, tournedos Opéra and veal cutlets are praised, and vegetables, even when included as they are in the set dinner price, are carefully cooked. The Castros seem by now to have got the hang of sherry trifle and crème brûlée too. Spanish or Italian carafe wines are £2 for 50 cl, which is too much, and the rest of the Bouchard Aîné list is in proportion. No smoking unless by common consent – but even so one diner's eyes were smarting. Recorded classical music.

App: C. D. Legg, T. A. Stevenson, Mrs Charles Raff, J.M., R.A.R.H., G. Caldwell

---

WOODSTOCK see also pub section

If you think you are suffering from food-poisoning after eating in a restaurant, report this immediately to the local Public Health Authority (and write to us).

See p. 120 for the restaurant-goer's legal rights, and p. 118 for information on hygiene in restaurants.

WOOLVERTON Somerset Map 2

Woolverton House Hotel

on A36
8 m S of Bath
Beckington 415

Closed L (exc Dec 25);
Sun; 2 weeks Nov;
Dec 24 & 26; Dec 25 D;
2 weeks Jan
Must book
D only, 7–9.30

Tdh from £6·75 (meal
£8·55)

VAT & service inc
Seats 40
rest (1 step)
Car park
No dogs
Access, Am Ex, Diners
8 rooms (all with bath)
B&B from £10
Fire cert

The Dove at Corton was a regretted deletion from
the 1978 *Guide*, but the Conways have been quick to
resurface, in spite of taking on here not just a
Victorian house but a hotel conversion too.
'Wouldn't mind a rainy day there' is one fairly
particular lady's comment, and she is even more
benevolent to the food, which is still cooked by Mrs
Conway and Beverley Sullivan together. The menu
has changed a little, with a new set of customers
not yet demanding their old favourites, and there is
warm praise for 'the smoked mackerel mouthfuls on
toast that came before dinner when we asked for a
glass of moselle', for 'light and fresh-tasting ham
and watercress mousse' and vegetable hors d'oeuvre,
and for stuffed pork fillet, wild duck with cherries,
ballotine of duck with apricot sauce, and jambalaya
– 'every item in the exciting mixture kept its own
taste.' Steaks, vegetables and salads are well done
too, and among current specialities note roast rack
of lamb with orange and lemon sauce, and cushion
of sole. The puddings for once taste as good as they
look, and most people try at least two: chocolate
praline, perhaps, or choux pastry with cream and
raspberries, or strawberry mille-feuille, or 'a
confection of meringue, good cream and sugared
redcurrants worthy of Rumpelmayer's'. 'Coffee
steaming away at a distance throughout our meal' is
less worthy. Mr Conway moved many of his clarets
from the Dove, and he is glad he did when he looks
at the replacement costs. That leaves Ch. Gloria '67,
c.b., at £6·55 and Ch. Rauzan-Gassies '61 at £9·15.
There are not many halves. Touraine Sauvignon is
£3·35, halves of Averys Barsac for the puddings
from £2·35, and French ordinaires £2·90. No music.
No children under seven in either restaurant or
hotel. 'Great care is taken over pipe and cigar
smokers.'

*App: Major J. K. C. Scott, George Harris,
Janet Tomalin, E.L.F., C.H.C., and others*

WOOTTON BASSETT Wiltshire Map 2

Loaves and Fishes
The Old Lime Kiln
on A420
M4 exit 16
Wootton Bassett 3597

Closed Mon; Sun D;
Sat L; July 6–16;
Dec 25 & 26; Jan 1
Must book

'Some people have never even heard of Wootton
Bassett,' writes Nikki Kedge from this Elizabethan
house and walled garden once occupied by the
town's Inspector of Nuisances. However, company
presidents from New Jersey and middle-aged
tearaways bound for Wroughton motor-cycle track
unite with others to praise her 'earth-goddess'
colleague Angela Rawson's cooking at this small,
gentle, but in the best sense professional restaurant
– 'it stood up very well to a visit after 17 days'
eating round France.' With so few tables, prices

Meals 12.30–1.30,
7.30–8.45

Tdh L £4 (meal £6·20),
D £6 (meal £8·40)
Alc £5·85 (meal £8·25)

VAT inc
Children's helpings
Seats 20
Car park
No dogs in d/r
Access card

cannot be low, and choice is minimal. The set meals seem to be an innovation (and please report) but visitors may begin à la carte with consommé cream, avocado mousse, and devilled crab or mushrooms ('hot from the grill, garnished with a twist of lemon and a spike of rosemary', 60p). Pork in mushroom and lemon, or brandied lamb (one visitor was dubious about the cut but not about the sauce), and grilled chicken with herb butter, moist meat and 'very crisp and brown skin' may cost up to £4·60, including such vegetables as 'a delicious casserole of sliced parsnips and tomatoes in a cheese sauce, plain boiled sprouts, and very creamy potato.' The sweets stage may bring pear meringue, mille-feuille, home-made ices, or 'very sozzled oranges', and though Stilton is best not spooned, at least the antique spoon itself was irreproachable. 'Coffee should be better at 45p.' La Bonne Franquette (Argentine) ordinaires are £2·40; as well as well-chosen white wines and magnums of Ch. Canon-la-Gaffelière '70 (£15) they offer various ports and madeira by the glass. Recorded music. You may eat in the walled garden in summer. No children under eight at dinner. You may smoke in the bar but not the dining-room.

App: Alan Cathcart, Peter Little, J. R. Michaelis, T.G.K., Roger J. Isted, and others

---

WORCESTER Hereford & Worcester   Map 2

King Charles II
29 New Street
Worcester 22449

Light-footed Charles bolted through the back door of this half-timbered house, now a stylish restaurant well cared for by the Pedrini family. Set lunches remain fair value, and à la carte dinner prices are reasonable too. The vichyssoise, 'genuine' lasagne, soused sardines, saddle of lamb, roast veal and zabaglione are all mentioned with relish this time. Half-litres of Valpolicella are £1·30. No music. No under-eights at dinner. Dress 'decently'.

Closed Sun; Apr 16;
May 28; last 3 weeks
July; Aug 27; Dec 25 D;
Dec 26; Jan 1
Must book

Meals 12.30–1.45,
7.30–9.30

Tdh L £3 (meal £5·70)
Alc (min L £3, D £5)
£6·30 (meal £9·60)

Seats 35
No dogs
Access, Am Ex, Barclay

WORTHING West Sussex   Map 3

The Paragon
9–10 Brunswick Road
Worthing 33367

Soft lighting, polished furniture and good table settings deserve, one visitor thinks, a slightly more cordial welcome from Mr Fornasari to strangers as well as to Worthing's senior citizens who throng the place. But others are happy enough, and the cooking (by Graham Edwards and Andrew

Closed Sun; Tue; 1st
3 weeks June; Dec 24 &
31; public hols
Must book
Meals 12–2, 7–10

Tdh from £4 (meal £6·50)

Alc (min £4) £6·90
(meal £9·70)

VAT inc
Service 10%
Seats 36 (parties 12)
♿ rest
No dogs
Am Ex, Barclay

McGlennon) seems well adjusted to the milieu –
perhaps too well, to judge by rather anaemic soups
at a test meal. Happily sole Véronique (£4·20) was
much better, plump and fresh with a good sauce
and peeled white grapes, and buttery leaf spinach.
Veal is good too, whether 'sizzling' veal Cordon
Bleu with the right kinds of cheese and ham, or
escalope Sandeman with mushrooms, red peppers
and sherry (£4·50), or in other ways. Entrecôte or
rump steaks in other elaborate treatments (£5) are
also specialities. Set lunches remain good value, and
may be more imaginative than à la carte meals,
with lasagne or fried herring roes as possible
preludes to pot-roasted leg of lamb with caper sauce,
or omelette lyonnaise. Among sweets tried, either at
midday or in the evening, crème brûlée was a
comparative failure – 'like eating sugar mice', but
crêpe à l'orange (with ice-cream inside and hot
orange curaçao sauce on top) was much better.
Wines begin at £3 for Valpolicella or Soave and
there are others: Ch. Larrivet-Haut-Brion '67, c.b.,
£8 in 1978. Recorded music.

*App: A. G. Coleman-Cross, A. J. V. Baker, R.A.,
A.P.*

WRAFTON Devon   Map 1

Poyers Farm
off A361
4 m NW of Barnstaple
Braunton 812149

*Even under new ownership, this comfortable
16th-century restaurant seems to have kept up its
standards of cooking, though the pacing of meals has
stuttered on occasion. The set lunch offers a reasonable
choice and à la carte there are various steak and
scampi creations. Duck (at 24 hours' notice) comes in
three styles (£3·95); trout in a cream sauce with
almonds, mussels and chives is £3·75. Main dish prices
include vegetables or salad. Bread-and-butter pudding
sometimes. About 50 wines, with Valpolicella at £2·60
the bottle. 'Intimate' recorded music: 'inappropriate'
is another description. More reports, please*

Closed Mon; Sat L;
Sun D; Dec 25 & 26
Must book D
Meals 12.30–2, 7.30–9.30
(10 Sat)

Tdh L £2·85 (meal £4·35),
Sun L £3·20 (meal £5·60)
Alc £5·65 (meal £8·55)

VAT & service inc
(weekday tdh L)

Service 10% alc
Seats 42 (parties 32)
♿ rest; w.c.
Car park
No dogs
Am Ex card

WRELTON North Yorkshire   Map 8

Huntsman
on A170
2 m NW of Pickering
Pickering 72530

*David and Annette Bell's stone-faced restaurant in
hunting and golfing country appeared in the last
Guide's pub section, but members who have tried not
only their soup, and fish fresh from Hull, in the bar
at lunch-time, but also fish pâté, roast beef and
Yorkshire, and blackberry and apple pie in the*

Closed Mon; Sun D;
Dec 25
Must book
Meals 12–2, 7–9.30

Tdh L from £2·50 (meal
£5·15), D from £4·50
(meal £7·20)
Alc (bar) meal £2·65

VAT inc
Seats 50 (parties 16)
Car park
3 rooms
B&B £4·50–£5·50
Fire cert

*restaurant, think they are worth a higher rating. An
inspector is inclined to agree, for shellfish barquette
(95p extra on the set meal) and médaillons de porc
with ham and almonds, 'and a sort of Yorkshire
ratatouille of cabbage, carrot and celery with
cinnamon' showed both skill and imagination. Other
dishes praised include truite bretonne, noisettes
d'agneau à l'estragon, 'juicy' chicken à la maréchale,
hazelnut meringue, walnut pie, and the fresh grapefruit
and bacon and egg at breakfast. Coffee is sound too,
and the feminine service welcoming. The Yorkshire
Fine Wine Co list is short and conventional with
Côtes du Rhône £3·40 and Muscadet '76, £3·70.
Recorded music. Children's helpings. Air-conditioning.
No dogs in public rooms. More reports, please.*

WYE Kent Map 3

Wife of Bath

♟

4 Upper Bridge Street
Wye 812540

Closed Sun; Mon; Apr 13;
1 week Chr
Must book
Meals 12–2, 7–10

Alc £5·30 (meal £8·10)

VAT inc
Cover 35p
Children's helpings
Seats 50 (parties 18)
🪑 rest
Car park

'I must not be too critical of this establishment,'
begins one newcomer who goes on to recognise that
while many restaurants find it easy to avoid this
one's bad points – the erratic menu-building, the
shabbiness noticed by inspectors and others in the
furnishing and housekeeping – few places match the
good points that have kept Michael Waterfield and
his partner-chef Robert Johnson at the top of the
Guide tree for the past six unbroken years. At a
test meal, the main courses – the fatal flaw of most
kitchens – had a touch of class: turbot with prawns
in a buttery, winey sauce of good French pedigree
(£4 with fir apple potatoes, 'an endearing conceit
that did not suit the dish', and crisp lettuce); and
wild duck, 'lean and tasty, with a delightful sauce of
tart oranges, redcurrants, and red wine'. Others
report with equal enthusiasm on home-made
saucisson sec, fritters of fennel and pepper, or 'light,
crisp, and flavoury' beignets de fromage, 'stylish and
satisfying tunny-fish and pork terrine', 'gorgeous'
saumon en croûte, 'admirably spiced skewered lamb,
cooked just right', crab sauce with brill, gooseberry
pickle with lamb, and many other inventions.
Salted duck (£3·75, including VAT and vegetables)
and chicken mode ancienne are other kitchen
favourites, and meals end with the usual home-made
ices and sorbets, or peaches with fresh raspberry
puree, perhaps. But alas, not everything has lately
had this quality of attention. Dishes are apt to
vanish early (serious, on so limited a daily menu),
soup may arrive tepid or a sauce turn out 'inedibly
salt', and when tried, both vacherin aux pommes
and coffee profiteroles were unworthy. The house
wines (from £2·80 or so for Chianti or Soave, with
Côtes du Ventoux or the house's own local Marriage
Hill white £1 more) are various, if humble; other
bottles are also apt to be listed absent when

roll-called. Sancerre '77 or Ch. Citran '69 are over
£6 now. Tio Guillermo sherry, and, in summer,
glasses of sweet white Quarts de Chaume, are
welcome. No music.

App: M. F. & I. D. Walsh, Neil Fairlamb,
Nova Whyte, M.A.S., H.D.R., Adeline Hartcup,
and many others

WYE see also pub section

YORK North Yorkshire   Map 5

Ristorante Bari
15 The Shambles
York 33807

Peppino's rose from its ashes last spring with a new
name, new interior and a brand new pizza oven
which is earning its keep with well-filled, generous
platefuls (95p–£1·30; the chef's special one is topped
with a fried egg, not to everyone's taste). The pasta
for lasagne is home-made, and scaloppe Sophia
Loren is 'worth propositioning'. Avoid soup, and do
not expect the puddings to be inventive. Bonatello
is £2·60 the litre, 45p the glass. Italian records.

Closed Dec 25 & 26	VAT inc	Seats 80
Meals 11.30–2.30, 6–11	Service 10% (parties)	♿ rest (1 step)
	Children's helpings	No dogs
Alc £2·65 (meal £4·70)		Access, Barclay

Lew's Place
King's Staith
York 28167

'Large helpings, large help, small comfort', runs one
report on the lunchtime bar snacks at this
ill-arranged fast-food cafe down by the Ouse. 'Long
queues (no booking) eat off scruffy cloths at
close-packed tables' is another view of the same
scene at night. But enough stalwarts sway the
balance, vouching for the lamb kebab, steak and
kidney pie, stuffed pork fillet, Barnsley chops,
lemon sole, chips with everything and the salads.
Some call cheesecake and apple crumble 'lovely',
some do not. Litre Vin is £2·95, and there is draught
Bass, and Worthington White Shield. Loud music.

Closed Sun; Sat L;	Meals 12–2, 7–10 (6 Sat)	Children's helpings
Dec 25 & 26		Seats 45
No bookings	Alc £3·95 (meal £6·75)	No dogs

YORK see also pub section

WALES

Bronheulog Hotel
off A499
6 m SW of Pwllheli
Abersoch 2177

Closed L; Sun; Mon (exc
summer); Nov–Feb
Must book
D only, 7–9

Alc £6·25 (meal £8·40)

VAT & service inc
Seats 45
Car park
No dogs
6 rooms
B&B £7–£7·50
Fire cert

Even a land-lubber not afraid to express his dislike
of yachtsmen – as restaurant customers, anyway –
enjoyed his meal in the Zaniers' comfortable little
Lleyn peninsula hotel (designed by the late and
lamented Clough Williams-Ellis). Considerate service
was part of this, but personal and scrupulous Italian
cooking mattered too, and it was 'difficult to think
how the cannelloni (£1·25) could be improved'.
Smoked mackerel, though, could have been juicier,
an inspector thinks. Escalope of veal sorpresa in 'a
rather heavy batter', and rare steak Dijon, were also
competently done, and the former came with 'three
admirable vegetables: cabbage braised in cream,
runner beans finished in butter, and crisp, freshly
roast potatoes.' Crab and lobster thermidor (£5·20),
roast guinea-fowl in calvados sauce (£3·50) and veal
with lemon and parsley are house specialities.
Sweets are less interesting – 'the cherry pie filling
was not as good as the pastry' – but crème caramel
and brandy-snaps restored confidence. Drink
Verdicchio at £3·50 or Barolo at £4, perhaps, since
the French wines are of no moment and little is
known of the red ordinaire at £3·40 a litre in 1978.
No music. No children under twelve.

*App: Thomas Ward, P.O'R.S., Henry Potts,
and others*

Porth Tocyn Hotel
9½ m SW of Pwllheli
Abersoch 2966

Closed Nov; Dec;
mid-week (Jan–Easter)
Must book
Meals 1–1.25, 7.30–9.30

Tdh L £4·75 (meal £7·45),
D £6·85 (£5·50 winter)
(meal £9·90)

Children's helpings
(under 14)
Seats 50
♿ rest
Car park
Access, Am Ex
18 rooms (15 with bath)
B&B £12·50
D, B&B from £17·75

It is a well-found hotel that survives an entry like
last year's (which James Bond would have
recognised as a 'Brooklyn-stomping, sixty-percenter').
Naturally, regulars came to the defence of Mrs
Fletcher-Brewer and her comfortable, dramatically
sited house above Cardigan Bay, but cooler critics
also feel that while perfection or even high
imagination still eludes the kitchen, much has been
improved. The atmosphere is more relaxed than it
was in the old days, and all authoritarian regimes
know that a loosened curb brings their most perilous
moments. Anyway, a test meal that included a
small helping of 'very light and tasty' smoked
salmon quiche, mushroom and parsley soup, steak
en croûte with a piquant sauce, 'crunchy' carrots and
cabbage, and liquorous Jamaican rum pie carried
off the honours for North Wales, in the eater's
opinion. Another, less enthusiastic account in
August of cloying sauces for coupe indienne and
veal Bénédictine mentions with pleasure the
'massive bowl of fresh fruit from which there was
unrestricted choice'. The kitchen's own view is that

the best dishes include lamb terrine, smoked chicken with raisin slaw, soups of chicken and chestnut or parsnip and apricot, baked stuffed trout, barbecued lamb, roast veal with peach and walnuts, and various desserts including avocado ice-cream and chocolate brandy cake. The dining-room is dimly lit, wine (and water) service is sometimes stretched, and 'a gaggle of waiters and waitresses seem to congregate by the Welsh dresser.' The wines, from £3·10, are moderate; perhaps only an impatient Frenchman would broach Ch. Meyney '76, c.b., at £5·40 so precipitately, but £6·30 is not bad for Ch. Lynch-Bages '73, c.b. No music. In spite of the heated outdoor swimming-pool, it is 'not really a hotel for children'. Dress conventionally. No dogs.

App: J. L. Cameron, John Idris Jones,
K. Charters, Brian Rowley, J.R., and others

ABERYSTWYTH Dyfed   Map 4

Y Dewin
6 Portland Road
Aberystwyth 617738

Another modest, very Welsh place ('Y Dewin' means 'the magician'), of the type more noticeable this year, but Dilys Myrddin does her own cooking, and inspectors and others report well of her creamy onion soup, quiche or pizza, 'admirably assembled salads of everything in season', apple tart and syllabub. The dysgl y dydd (dish of the day) varies: 'a wonderful Guinness hot-pot', but 'mediocre' sweet-and-sour chicken (£1·15). Try also liver and bacon casserole. French carafe wine £1·60 for 50 cl; better drinks would be welcome. 'Celtic' recorded music. More reports, please.

Closed Sun; Wed L
(Sept–May);
Dec 25 & 26
Meals 12–3 (12–2
Sept–May), 5–10

Alc (min 70p) £1·90
(meal £3·20)

Children's helpings

Seats 28
 🔲 rest
No dogs

BEAUMARIS Anglesey (Gwynedd)   Map 4

Hobson's Choice
13 Castle Street
Beaumaris 810323

Closed Sun; Mon L;
Dec 25 & 26
Must book D (summer &
weekends)
Meals 12–2.30, 7–10.30

Alc L £2·20 (meal £4·35),
D £6 (meal £8·80)

VAT inc

The 1978 Bank Holiday joker who put 'Anglesey full up' notices on the Welsh side of the Menai straits may only have been disappointed of a table at Patricia Talbot's modest but – for this region – desirable restaurant in a 16th-century building. On a chillier holiday evening a member found a cheerful fire and helpful service of good pâté and vegetable soup, followed by freshly cooked scallops Mornay (£3·30) and pork fillet. Pork kebab with rice (£3·80), roast stuffed guinea-fowl, and Ian Mirrlees' special lobster at £7·50 are prides of the kitchen, and others praise 'generous slabs of roast lamb, and good salads at an awkward season for green things'. Mayonnaise is bought in, but they make their own

Service 10%
Cover 15p D
Children's helpings
Seats 66 (parties 40)
♿ rest (1 step)
No dogs
Access card

fruit fools, mousses, meringues and other puddings.
Litre Vin ordinaires are £3 for 80 cl, and the
owner's interest in wine is reflected in, for instance,
Ch. Gruaud-Larose '73, c.b., £6·50, and
Morey-St-Denis '71 (Moillard) at £5·75. 'The young
guitarist kindly adapted his repertoire for our
eight-year-old.' 'They sell cigarettes, unfortunately.'
There are weekday bar snacks, though an inspector
found that buffet and service alike wilted near the
end of the season.

*App: E. Smith, Kenneth F. Macrae, B. A. Maguire,
Dr C. Knapper, W. T. Winterbottom, R. V. Myott*

BROAD HAVEN Dyfed   Map 4

Druidstone Hotel
2 m N of Broad Haven
on coast road
Broad Haven 221

Closed Sun D (exc res);
Nov; Dec 24, 25 & 26
(exc res); Jan 1 (exc res)
Must book D & Sun L
Meals 12–2, 7.30–9.30

Tdh Sun L £4·25 (meal
£6·65), D from £5·25
(meal £7·85)

Children's helpings
Seats 36 (parties 12,
winter)
♿ rest; w.c.
Car park
No dogs in d/r
8 rooms
B&B £7
D, B&B £70 p.w.
Fire cert

Nothing divides members like the Bells' housekeeping
at this idyllically sited house. Most of them are
happy to gaze steadfastly at the wild flowers and
the sunsets, ignoring the peeling paint, but one
couple who visited in the spring (but before
spring-cleaning) suggest eating the dinners and
retiring to a tent. Well, better a dish of herbs where
love is, and the Editor is personally ill-placed to
complain about 'Burmese cats among the breakfast
cereals'. Jane Bell, for that matter, is particularly
good with herbs, and everyone from pernickety
pensioners to benighted BBC teams likes at any
rate most of the food. For want of a Pekinese
restaurant in Pembs. they make their own sesame
prawn toasts, if not to Soho standard; soups are
excellent; so is tarte à l'oignon. Steak of sewin
baked with lemon, orange and spices is an admired
traditional speciality. Rolled ribs of beef, lamb
Edward VII, Egyptian chicken and the Sunday
buffet are also praised. Sweets occasionally miscarry
– 'a delicious lemon soufflé but the sourest, most
crystalline water-ice (damson) I have ever tried to
eat.' But even severe critics praise the bread rolls
and the expertly cooked breakfasts, including
properly scrambled eggs. On Sundays, lunch is a
traditional roast and dinner a residents' buffet.
There are weekday bar lunches (with tables outside)
and Worthington in cask; also Weston's cider and
perry. Ordinaires vary, but in 1978 Hungarian
bottles were still under £3, and good '75 hock or
moselle under £5. No music.

*App: D. G. Randall, P.R.M., John Timpson,
N.R.H., M.M.G.J., David Head, and others*

Within parts of these old county boundaries, alcohol is not served on Sunday,
except to hotel residents: Anglesey, Cardigan, Carmarthen, Merioneth.

Meal times refer to first and last orders.

BULL BAY Anglesey (Gwynedd) Map 4

Pot Luck
Amlwch
Amlwch 830885

Ann Peters, an agriculture graduate who runs a one-woman-show at her plain, whitewashed cottage, is 'at the mercy of a mixed clientele', according to one (discerning) admirer, but her Stilton soup, steak and kidney pie, pheasant with apples and celery, and lemon mousse or mille-feuille are liked. Note the seasonal closures and that the name means what it says, and be sure to book. Wine list unresolved for 1979. Recorded music; piano in the bar. More reports, please.

Closed L; Sun; Oct–Mar;
Sun, Mon & Tue (Apr,
May, June & Sept)
Must book

D only, 7.30–9

Alc (min £3·50) £3·80
(meal £5·70)

Seats 18
No dogs

CARDIFF South Glamorgan Map 4

Gibson's
8 Romilly Crescent,
Canton
Cardiff 41264

Closed Sun; Mon; 2 weeks
summer; public hols;
Tues after public hol
Mons
Must book D
Meals 12.30–2, 7.30–10

Tdh D (Tue, Wed, Thur)
£5·75 (meal £8·60)
Alc £6·60 (meal £9·95)

VAT inc
Service 10%
Cover 40p alc
Children's helpings
Seats 34
No dogs
Am Ex, Barclay, Diners

Take your map and compass, a member advises, to find Irene Canning's place, whose uninviting exterior hides 'a set for a 1940s situation comedy about a P & O cruise'. The service is careful-to-slow, and the cooking personal enough to justify the price. The mid-week regional set menus are probably the best choice, says an inspector whose Languedoc night included respectable pâté, daube, fish soup and civet de lièvre. Another visitor enjoyed on a similar occasion the hors d'oeuvre, 'tasty terrine of chicken', langoustines with mayonnaise, and 'pink and succulent gigot boulangère with thinly sliced potatoes in a well-flavoured stock'. On the whole, a test à la carte meal endorsed these findings, for oeufs durs soubise (95p), green salad, and mocha and walnut ice-cream (85p) could hardly have been improved. But crab pâté and fillet of beef grand veneur (£4·40) were both under-seasoned and boring. Good soft white mints come round with admirable coffee, and cheeses are not neglected. The wines and their descriptions are rather disappointing for this genre of restaurant, though under £5 Crozes-Hermitage les Meysonniers '73 is worth trying. Saumur '76 white is £4. No music. 'Far from being discouraged, as is claimed, smoking is promoted by the sale of cigars and cigarettes, and by books of matches, published by Egon Ronay.'

App: J. S. Waters, Denys Gueroult, F.I., J.R., B.W., and others

Harvesters
5 Pontcanna Street
off Cathedral Road
Cardiff 32616

Most harvesters these days – at least the grosser *légumes* of agribusiness – tend to confuse quantity with quality, and the same is true of this cheerful, close-packed place which might be in Chelsea, but for the sound of Giampero Fama speaking Welsh.

Closed L; Sun; Mon;
3 weeks Aug; Dec 25 &
26
Must book
D only, 7–11

Alc (min £2) £5·55
(meal £8·75)

Service 10%
Children's helpings
Seats 38
 rest
Air-conditioning
Am Ex card

'Helpings still make people gasp: one steak, kidney and mushroom pie (£2·50) could easily be enough for two or more.' It was a very good pie, at a test meal, and brains in black butter (£2·50) were even better: 'a rare treat in Wales'. Grilled king prawns with mayonnaise (£2·25), crab soup, and rare roast rib of beef with Yorkshire pudding (£3·25) are other specialities. Blackcurrant fool is praised. But kipper pâté with a crust on it, bread-and-butter pudding with too much bread, and mediocre coffee and ice-creams are also reported. House burgundy is £2·95, and there is little incentive to go further. Pressurised Carlsberg. No music. Pipes are discouraged. No dogs.

App: M.J.R., O.J.P., Henry Potts, R.J.

CARDIFF South Glamorgan   Map 4

Field's
(formerly Prashadam)
99 Wyeverne Road,
Cathays
Cardiff 23554

A relaxed vegetarian wholefood restaurant (with new name, though everything else as before), so dedicated to fresh ingredients that even tomato puree is banned. The menu, changed frequently, might include spinach lasagne; celery, mushroom and cheese crumble in an individual casserole (£1·50); aubergine with cheese and herbs; aduki onion pie with miso sauce; chili *sin* carne (meatless and sinless); banana fritters. Unlicensed; various teas, fruit juices and grain coffee. Recorded music. One room for non-smokers.

Closed Sun; Mon; 1 week
Easter; Aug; 1 week Chr
Meals 12–2, 6–11

Alc meal £4

Service 12½%
Children's helpings

Seats 44 (parties 27)
 rest; w.c.
No dogs
Unlicensed

Riverside
44 Tudor Street,
Riverside
Cardiff 372163

Must book
Open noon–midnight

Tdh from £3·20
Alc meal £5·35

VAT inc
Service 10%
Seats 140
Air-conditioning
No dogs
Access, Am Ex, Barclay,
Diners, Euro

It is not every Chinese restaurant that is opened for business by the Speaker of the House of Commons, but members and inspectors trying Yin Kiu Chan's Cantonese cooking (and the well-stocked supermarket next door) are impressed and perhaps surprised by George Thomas's taste, and recall 'hazy memories of childhood feasts in Tiger Bay during the 30s'. The set meals are best bypassed in favour of Mandarin braised king prawns (not exactly braised, rather deep-fried, £2·90), steamed sea bass ('a great dish by any standard'), duck with ginger and pineapple, fried sliced beef Cantonese-style (£2·70), and crispy chicken with a 'brown-glazed, salty, crisp skin, cut into pieces manageable with chopsticks'. Among the dim-sum snacks (served from 12 till 8), prawn har-kowloo, pork dumplings and prawns in rice paper were 'carefully prepared and delicious'. Tea and service are good. There are no sweets to speak of, but several wines, including Chinese Shansi dry white at £3·80. Recorded Chinese music. More reports, please.

CASTLE MORRIS Dyfed   Map 4

Y Gwesty Bach
5 m SW of Fishguard
Letterston 337

Closed L; Sun; Mon–Wed
(winter); mid-Oct to
mid-Nov; Dec 24, 25 &
26; Feb
Must book
D only, 7.30–9.30

Tdh £6·50 (meal £8·25)

VAT & service inc
10% service (wine)
Children's helpings
(under 10)
Seats 30
&. rest (1 step)
Car park
No dogs

Whiz Collis's domestic difficulties in 1978 do not seem to have affected the quality of meals eaten in this tastefully adapted village post-office; indeed, perhaps she is the kind that flies to cookery books for solace in emergency, for her menus (with three or four choices in each course) may include Greek meatballs with egg and lemon sauce, coulibiac of salmon, tandoori chicken, porc aux pruneaux de Tours, and the ever-popular colonial goose (which is actually a leg of lamb marinated and stuffed with apricots, and 'the best piece of lamb I have seen on a restaurant plate for many a day.') First courses may have a similar Levantine flavour, with aubergine and tahini pâté or baba ganoue one possibility, and stuffed courgette flowers another. More conventional mushrooms and shrimps flambé, generous fillet steaks, and 'capital duck with orange' are also praised. Puddings 'are on the hefty side, with pastry and cream in all directions', and 'a slice off a gigantic hazelnut meringue' is reported. Cranberry and banana pie, chocolate charlotte Malakoff, and 'a proper baked Jewish cheesecake' are also wiz, says Whiz. 'They were kindness itself when one of us felt unwell (no fault of theirs) during the meal.' Rieumon French ordinaires are from Hérault, £3·40 a litre; red Gaillac is £2·48; and Ch. Chasse-Spleen '66 a very decent £5·45 (but note that wines carry a 10% service charge). No music; and the rule about dress is 'please wear some'.

App: H. D. Farmer, D.R.J., and others

COLWYN BAY Clwyd   Map 4

Holland Arms
on B5113
6 m S of Colwyn Bay
Tynygroes 308

'A plain, whitewashed building, about 1,000 feet up, in an almost empty expanse of hills' south of Colwyn Bay. A homely atmosphere and friendly service enhance the enjoyment of the summertime cold buffet, with routine meats but imaginative salads and 'lovely sweets', and of the dinners served four nights a week all the year round. The menu sounds ambitious 'with flaming this and flaming that', but early reports of seafood provençale (£3·90), brown sugar meringues with apricots or chocolate sauce and 'excellent' coffee are encouraging. Carafe wines £2·60 for 75 cl. 'Soft' recorded music.

Closed L Sept 17–May
25; Mon (exc May 28 &
Aug 27); D Sun & Tue;
Dec 26
Must book

Meals 12.15–2.15,
7.30–9.30

Tdh L £3 (meal £5·05)
Alc £5·85 (meal £8·90)

Children's helpings
Seats 50 (parties 20)
&. rest
Car park
No dogs

Moelwyn Restaurant
29 Mona Terrace
Cricieth 2500

Cheerful little seaside restaurant, popular with holiday-makers. Special children's menu (from 60p; £1·25 Sunday lunch) and weekday cold buffet (also from 60p). Local fish and shellfish are well cooked, and the Booths also recommend their Welsh lamb cutlets. Vegetables are more variable. Friendly service. Italian and French wines, £1·60 for 50 cl. Recorded music.

Closed Mon & Sun D
(exc July–Sept);
Nov–Easter
Must book D
Meals 12.15–2, 7–9.15

Tdh L £1·95 (meal £3·30),
D £2·95 (meal £4·40)
Alc £4·10 (meal £5·65)

VAT inc

Children's helpings
Seats 40
♿ rest (1 step)
No dogs

Gliffaes Country House Hotel
off A40
2½ m W of Crickhowell
Brecon 730371

'The air of a Saki-like country-house party survives,' reports a visitor to this hotel and shrubbery on the banks of the Usk. For many, the generous cold buffet at lunch and on Sunday evening is the highlight: cold meats, pâté, imaginative and exotic salads, with hearty soups first and hot or cold sweets after. The set meals won more praise this year with carefully cooked roasts and casseroles. Wines from Christopher's (Savigny-les-Beaune '72, £4·37), or help yourself and sign for house wine at 40p the glass (£3 the litre). The Brabners prefer you to change for dinner and not to smoke in the dining-room.

Closed Dec 31–Feb 28
Must book
Meals 1–2, 7.45–9

Tdh L £3·50 (meal £4·75),
D £5 (meal £6·25)

VAT & service inc
Seats 46 (parties 20)
♿ rest (2 steps); w.c.

Car park
No dogs
21 rooms (10 with bath)
B&B £7·70–£11·50
Full board £12·10–£18·60
p.d.

Inspections are carried out anonymously. Persons who pretend to be able to secure, arrange or prevent an entry in the Guide are impostors and their names or descriptions should be reported to us.

We rewrite every entry each year, and depend on fresh, detailed reports to confirm the old, as well as to include the new. The further from London you are, the more important this is.

Wine prices shown are for a 'standard' bottle of the wine concerned, unless another measure is stated.

Unless otherwise stated, a restaurant is open all week and all year and is licensed.

Nantyffin Cider Mill
Talgarth Road
at junction of
A40 & A479
Crickhowell 810775

A man who can coin the word 'pubstraunt' is capable of any excess, but Tony Ambrose has good in him: he has kept the Bulmer's cider on tap in this old house (as well as Marston's and John Smith's bitters on pump). His wife and daughter's vegetable soups, quiches, fisherman's or steak and kidney pies, pâté, poached Usk salmon hollandaise sometimes, and apfelstrudel or fresh fruit, take the place 'well ahead of its pub competitors'. The Ambroses also suggest their trout pickled in cider (£1·15) and pigeon in cream and brandy (£3·60), but these, like some of the other dishes, may appear in the dining-room only. Expect crowds and noise in summer, and in winter 'an enormous log fire, and on the chair beside it, clusters of comatose cats'.

Closed (rest) L & Sun;
Dec 25
Must book weekends
Meals 11.30–2.30
(Sun 12–1.40), 6.30–10.30
(Sun 7–9)

Alc (bar) £3·55, (rest)
£4·90 (meal £7·25)

VAT inc

Seats 30
rest (3 steps)
Car park
No dogs in d/r

CROSS INN Dyfed   Map 4

Rhos-yr-Hafod Inn
at junction of B4337 &
B4577
Nebo 644

Free house, with substantial bar snacks (not Sunday) and fixed-price dinners in the converted stables (rickety chairs need an overhaul). Not much heard this year, but there is a sensibly short menu with reassuring soups, crisp salady starters, choice of half-a-dozen imaginative main dishes (a floury sauce has disappointed) and creamy sweets. Various wines: Ch. Haut-Marbuzet '72, c.b., £6·34; Nicolas £2·90 the litre. Hancock HB on hand pump. Tables outside for bar lunchers. Children may eat in the bar until 9.30 p.m. No music.

Closed L; Sun; Mon;
Dec 25 & 26
Must book
D only, 7–9

Tdh from £5·50 (meal
£7·85)

VAT inc
Children's helpings

Seats 24
rest (2 steps)
Car park
No rooms

Entries for places with distinctions carry symbols (pestle, tureen, bottle, glass). Credits are fully written entries, with approvers' names below the text. Passes are telegraphic entries (useful in the area) with details under the text. Provisional entries are in italics (see 'How to use the Guide', p. 4).

The Guide accepts no advertising. Nor does it allow restaurateurs to use its name on brochures, menus, or in any form of advertisement. If you see any instances of this, please report them to us.

Within parts of these old county boundaries, alcohol is not served on Sunday, except to hotel residents: Anglesey, Cardigan, Carmarthen, Merioneth.

Maesllwch Arms
Glasbury 226

'A pleasant, old-fashioned sort of place' under new ownership, plain but comfortable for a stay. The owner-chef cooks elaborately for both set dinners and à la carte menus: smoked mackerel mousse, rolled prawn soufflé (90p), duck with a tart peach sauce (£4), chicken in Pernod and cream (£2·70), crème de menthe parfait. The various vegetables (80p à la carte) are freshly cooked and enterprising. Home-baked bread and rolls. Some unusual wines from good sources on a poorly annotated list; wine by the glass 60p. John Smith's Yorkshire bitter on electric pump, and lunchtime snacks in the bar. No music. More reports, please, as the Williamsons settle down and invite the builders in.

Closed L (exc bar snacks)
D only, 7–9.30

Tdh £4·25 (meal £7·35)
Alc £6·55 (meal £10·10)

Service 10%

Children's helpings
(under 10)
Seats 38
♿ rest (3 steps)
Car park

No dogs in d/r
Access, Am Ex, Barclay, Diners
12 rooms (3 with bath)
B&B £6–£7·50

Cwmllechwedd Fawr
off A483
on road to Knighton
Llandrindod Wells 83267

Must book
Meals by arrangement

Tdh D £5

VAT & service inc
Children's helpings
Seats 10
Car park
6 rooms
D, B&B £12

The Guide was deliberating whether to break normal practice and allow Geraldine Barnes a year's grace to develop her defiantly Welsh repertoire in peace (at her own request), but four pages in a catering magazine then suggested that she is no stranger to either tourism or publicity, and an inspector had previously confirmed that she is a genuine, historically conscious cook, who expresses her view of Anglo-Saxons by writing her menu in Welsh and French. She makes her own bread, and sometimes butter and cheese too. A meal is like eating with friends in a farmhouse kitchen, sometimes with songs and harp music afterwards: expect cockle cakes, perhaps, 'terrine with a good jelly' or laver bread, followed by trout 'in a delicious astringent sauce', 'very tender' mutton, ham in cider, vegetables either from the farm or Newtown market, then apple pie or elderberry jelly, or violet pudding (an 18th-century recipe 'soothing for irritable husbands'). The house French ordinaire is £2·50, or you can take your own, and there is herb tea. The family serve. You must book your meal at least 24 hours in advance. Treat them all gently – after all, Mrs Barnes's husband gave her a butcher's cleaver for Mother's Day. More reports, please.

Do not risk using an out-of-date Guide. A new edition
will be published early in 1980.

LLANDEWI SKIRRID Gwent Map 4

Walnut Tree Inn

on B4521
3 m NE of Abergavenny
Abergavenny 2797

Closed Sun; Dec 25 & 26
Must book D (d/r)
Meals 12.30–2.30,
7.30–10.30

Alc £6·95 (meal £10·95)

Cover 40p D
Seats 45 (d/r)
♿ rest; w.c. (m)
Air-conditioning
Car park
No dogs

You get all sorts at the Taruschios' whitewashed pub at the foot of a brackeny hill, which is roughly where the rainbow ends and the dual carriageways peter out. This year's crop include 'a brash young man overheard explaining to some Germans that syllabub was a British dish at least 1500 years old', and a family who were mistaken for French because (a) they were speaking Welsh and (b) they were teaching themselves marine biology on the way through the plat de fruits de mer with 'shrimps, mussels, langoustines, whelks, clams, prawns, Pacific prawns, écrevisses, winkles and a crab'. And a solitary Londoner took the *Times* crossword for company: 'The first clue down was "Ye gods, the food's so good" (answer, "ambrosial").' Franco Taruschio's own Italian origin is chiefly relevant when you come to the ice-cream and espresso stage (and most British Italians have forgotten how to make both). A test meal this year included taramosalata (£1·49), veal Bénédictine (£3·79) and strawberry granita (98p – are these chain-store prices a joke?) which would not have been approached, let alone surpassed, if the eater had gone round London and eaten these dishes in the three separate restaurants that might be expected to do them best. Sadly, chicken Rossini at the same meal was a travesty, and it is perhaps inevitable that at cramped tables in a perpetually thronged bar (the restaurant is open only at night, and is usually booked months ahead) a dish 'gets away' every now and then. If game is listed – partridge or grouse or rabbit in red wine or, for that matter, kid with coriander and Marsala – consider it seriously. Remember that helpings are robust (lasagne is not an appetiser). The Viennese torten are as revelatory as the ices. The house Verdicchio white or Montepulciano red at £2·89 a litre are quite adequate for the smoky surroundings, though an inspector who found Ch. Haut-Bages-Monpelou '61, c.b., at £9·95, was not disappointed. No music.

App: Michael & Naomi Hull, Catherine Kroon, J.R., J. & M.B., G. Short, J.T., T.C. Davison, and others

LLANGADOG Dyfed Map 4

Plas Glansevin
off A4069
1½ m E of Llangadog
Llangadog 238

Closed L (exc Sun in winter); Dec 24, 25 & 31
Must book

There is a 'restful silence' round William and Gwenda Rees's porticoed mansion off the Llandovery road (except presumably when there is a 'crescendo of Welsh or charabanc voices' at the *hwyrnos*, or singing suppers, in the Tudor wing). At least, that is what the brochure says, amid much else, for the Reeses know they have something worth selling in their 'taste of Wales' cooking, and in the affable if

355

Meals 12.30–1.30 (Sun in winter), 7.30

Tdh Sun L £3·50 (meal £6·40), D £5·45 (meal £7·35)

VAT & service inc
Children's helpings
Seats 20 (parties 60)
 rest
Car park
No dogs
Access, Am Ex, Barclay, Diners
7 rooms (3 with bath)
B&B £8·75
D, B&B £13·75

sometimes subdued atmosphere. It is a mistake to miss tea, which may produce teisennau ar y maen (apple turnovers with brown-sugar and cream) as well as wholemeal and currant loaves. But it is also a mistake to miss soup at dinner ('a beetroot one was exquisite'). Choice is modest, but as main dishes there may be loin of pork with orange sauce and ginger, or leg of lamb with marrow. Vegetables have included 'outstanding onions cooked in wine vinegar, honey and lemon juice', and 'sliced courgettes with onions and tomatoes looked well too.' Blackberry fool, lemon cream, or pancakes in orange may appear as sweets. 'Pears in red wine, and chocolate pots were more ordinary.' Coffee seems to be cheaper than last year, but still weak sometimes. Mr Rees specialises in Loire wines, found on the spot or ordered from Yapp, from £2·95 for Gros Plant to £5·30 for red St Nicolas de Bourgeuil '75 and £5·75 for sweet Château de Suronde '61 from Quarts de Chaume. Felinfoel and Double Dragon bitters are in cask. Recorded harp music. High teas for the young.

App: Ian Oswald, J.H., W. M. D. & P. E. Berry, J.R.T., R.E.

LLANGYNIDR Powys   Map 4

Red Lion
on B4558
10 m NW of Abergavenny
Bwlch 730223

Pretty creeper-clad, stone-built, 15th-century inn beside the church in the peaceful upper village. Competent cooking of fresh local lamb, 'impeccable' steak and kidney pie (£2·95) and smoked poussin. But vegetables and sweets falter. Excellent coffee. Toujours £3·50 the litre. Bass from the cask. Enthusiastic local service. Wear a tie in the restaurant, or eat in the (crowded) bar (same menu, lower prices). No music.

Closed L (exc Sun); Sun D; Dec 24, 25 & 26; Must book
Meals 12–1.30 (Sun), 6.30–10

Alc £4·75 (meal £6·35)

VAT inc
Seats 60 (parties 30)
 rest; w.c. (m)

Air-conditioning
Car park
No dogs
7 rooms
B&B £6·50

LLANRWST Gwynedd   Map 4

Meadowsweet Hotel
Station Road
Llanrwst 640732

Closed L (exc Apr 15 & 16 & Dec 25); Dec 26; Jan 1; Sun–Wed (Oct–Easter)
Must book
D only, 6–9.30

Stephen Bull has followed the well-trodden road from Wales to London (see Lichfield's) and John Evans (who is English, and a repentant banker) has taken his place, with results that deserve tentative auditing. The Victorian terrace house is a comfortable place to stay and the dining-room will look graceful enough with a few more customers. There are about half a dozen choices in each course of the à la carte menu. Try roulades au fromage (£1) or coquilles St Jacques à la parisienne (£1·35) to start with, perhaps, though spare ribs, pears in tarragon cream, and miniature

Alc £6·15 (meal £8·65)

VAT inc
Service 10%
Seats 36
 🔼 rest (1 step)
Access, Am Ex, Barclay
4 rooms
B&B £6–£7
D, B&B £11–£12
(min 4 nights)

pizzas are also liked. Sauté de veau Marengo (£3·30) tasted pleasantly astringent to an inspector jaded by too many syrupy sauces, and another speciality, guinea-fowl in cider and calvados, also has admirers. Lamb is preferred to beef. End with 'a light coffee and ginger mousse' or 'a remarkably fine Stilton'. Breakfasts are praised: 'This was only the second place I found in Wales to serve kidneys; gargantuan black pudding and smoked haddock too.' Tanner of Shrewsbury's Moroccan red or Italian white wines are £2·50; Ch. Cos Labory '70, £6·95. Recorded music. Children's helpings. No dogs in the dining-room. More reports, please.

LLANTWIT MAJOR South Glamorgan   Map 4

Colhugh Villa
Flanders Road
on B4270
16 m W of Cardiff
Llantwit Major 2022

'Shabby-looking' late-Victorian house perched above a narrow road. Inside, though, all is Palm Court elegance, with a grand piano in the conservatory, red plush in the bar, and candles and lace cloths in the dining-room. The cooking falls just short of this splendour, with authentic crab soup or mayonnaise, crevettes au beurre (£1·60) and fruit salad, but too much tomato in boeuf bourguignonne and vegetables not as they should be. Coffee is weak. Signor Villa organizes his local girls with gusto, but sometimes they cannot match it. Modestly priced wines; house wine is Valpolicella at £3·30 the litre. Recorded music.

Closed L (exc Sun); Mon;
Sun D; Dec 25 & 26;
Jan 1
Must book
Meals 12–1.45 (Sun),
7–9.30

Tdh Sun L £3·20 (meal £6·15)
Alc £6·50 (meal £10)

Children's helpings Sun L
Seats 60
Car park
No dogs
Access, Am Ex, Barclay

LLANWDDYN Powys   Map 4

Lake Vyrnwy Hotel
on B4393
10 m W of Llanfyllin
Llanwddyn 244

Closed mid-Jan to Mar 1
Must book
Meals 1, 8 (7.30
Nov–Easter)

Tdh weekday buffet L
£3·50 (meal £4·50), Sun
L £3·75 (meal £4·75), D £4
(meal £5)

'One of the very few British hotels I know that seems to operate for the comfort of its clients rather than the convenience of its staff' is one verdict on this remote, sedate house at the east end of Liverpool's water supply. An equally extreme counterblast, 'would go down well in Caithness provided they have Rennies up there', is happily not borne out by an inspector's Sunday lunch visit for 'unthickened potage Crécy with a sweet carroty tang, served with fresh home-baked rolls; steak and kidney pie with meat just short of tenderness; adequate vegetables with particularly good red cabbage; and delicious bread-and-butter pudding or hot rhubarb tart.' 'Only someone with a robust taste for robustas could cope with the mocha soufflés.' Mrs Moir is proud of her smoked trout and game dishes, and others praise the roasts, home-made pork

357

VAT & service inc
Children's helpings
(under 10)
Seats 55
🔥 rest; w.c.
Car park
No dogs
30 rooms (9 with bath,
2 with shower)
B&B £7–£13
Full board £11–£18 p.d.
Fire cert

pie, damson chutney and rice pudding, noting only that 'the second-floor bedrooms are unashamedly spartan', loos sparse, and that the coffee is still served to its detriment from vacuum flasks in the lounge. Choix du Roy ordinaires are £1·45 for 50 cl and Tanner of Shrewsbury's claret is £2·50. There are some good '70 château-bottled clarets in the £5–£7 range. Breakfasts – kippers and marmalade included – are ample but variable. The Tavern pub for snacks is attached to the hotel; Worthington E in cask. Children under three must eat in the nursery. Wear a tie at dinner. There is plenty of shooting and fishing, and bicycles may be hired.

App: E.D., S.J.W., Michael Mowbray Silver, J.R., I. J. Campbell, J.S.M., and others

---

LLANWRTYD WELLS Powys   Map 4

Llwynderw Hotel
Abergwesyn
5 m NW of Llanwrtyd
Wells
off Tregaron Road
Llanwrtyd Wells 238

Closed L (exc by
arrangement); Dec 24,
25, 26 & 31; Jan 1
Must book
D only, 7.45–8.30

Tdh from £7 (meal £9·50)

VAT & service inc
Seats 25 (parties 15)
Car park
No dogs in d/r
12 rooms (10 with bath)
D, B&B £20–£30
Fire cert

Either Michael Yates has been mellowed by wind and rain on this wild mountain road, or last year's entry must have reconciled people by advance warning of the eccentric 'hair tax' for dogs, or 'soap tax' if you leave yours at home, and other supplements. The bill remains high, but good judges report 'poetically balanced', virtually choiceless meals, served by cheerful youngsters (another improvement). A delicate egg mousse, ratatouille soup 'smoothly blended but not with flour', very pink and tender roast beef with sauce béarnaise and caraway cabbage, and pears in white wine, made one of these meals; kipper quiche, 'an exceptional spinach soup with red wine in it', mildly gamey local grouse, and lemon meringue pie made another; cheese soufflé and roast lamb or duck have figured in yet others. The cellar is good, but 1979 prices are unknown, and at £25 or so per head for dinner, bed and breakfast, the hotel is unlikely to attract – as one member says it should – 'retired archdeacons' (unless they are all Grantleys). Picnic lunches can be taken. No children under ten. No pipes.

App: A. C. Tozer, L. C. J. Wilcox, L. W. Ashton, R.N., and others

---

LLANYCHAER BRIDGE Dyfed   Map 4

Penlan Oleu
off B4313
4½ m SE of Fishguard
Puncheston 314

Closed L; Jan; Feb
Must book
D only, 8

It is a far cry from the Peacock in Liverpool Road, Islington (where Ann Carr first caught members' attention) and the shores of Turkey (where she has spent some of the intervening years) to this whitewashed farmhouse – pronounced Penlan Olé – up in the Preseli hills above Fishguard. She and her painter husband Martin MacKeown are here tending an extended family of children, cows, sheep, hens and geese – and a few diners or overnight stayers as well.

Tdh £7 (meal £9·35)

VAT inc
Seats 12 (parties 6)
Car park
No dogs
Access, Am Ex, Barclay
4 rooms (2 with bath,
2 with shower)
D, B&B £14·50

Take the 'Pu' sign off the B4313 (the Nats have removed the 'ncheston') and expect a dinner (with no choice until the sweet stage) of fastidious cooking that begins with home-baked brown bread and unsalted butter with 'creamy onion soup with chives', followed by 'dreamy cheese mousse with walnuts', or spinach and egg tartlets, or parsleyed ham with tartare sauce; a main course of brown trout stuffed with lemon and sorrel, or North African chicken tagine with 'properly cooked rice', or noisettes of Welsh lamb with apricot sauce, or stuffed chicken fillets with tarragon. Stilton is served before you are invited to indulge in hazelnut cream or walnut torte, or Caledonian ice-cream with whisky. The coffee is good, sherry greets your arrival, and hot-water bottles and early morning tea are not forgotten, nor books for wet days and maps for fine ones. The few wines from Berry Bros are well chosen and mostly about £3·50, though there is also Clos de Tart '66 (Robert James) at £7·90. No under-12s. No smoking at table. No music. More reports, please.

LLOWES Powys Map 4

Radnor Arms
on A438
3 m W of Hay-on-Wye
Glasbury 460

Closed Sun; Dec 25
Must book weekends
Meals 12–2.30, 7–10

Alc £4·35 (meal £7·10)

Children's helpings
Seats 25
  rest
Car park
No dogs

Academics have been out in force judging their own kind in this tactfully restored and enlarged stone-flagged pub, which has a terrace overlooking the Black Mountains. Some have had the impression that Julian Whitmarsh (who cooks) and his wife Juliet (who minds the house with a touch of asperity) took on more than they bargained for, at least while the builders were in, and the careful casualness of the lunches and the bar seating coupled with the enterprising dinner menus may leave a confused impression. But a test meal, even at the height of the alterations, was creditable, notably the pigeon and walnut pâté (£1·05) which most people like, and guinea-fowl normande (£3·85 including vegetables). Walnuts amount almost to an obsession, for they also turn up with boned shoulder of mutton (£2·95) and (in pickled form) with beef in Guinness. The trouble with scholars is that they travel, and are accordingly critical of the lasagne and moussaka they meet here. But a specially ordered lunch (amusingly enough, 'to celebrate the completion of a research project on Welsh rural development') was a success, and so was a dinner that included chicken lemon terrine and roast duck with green figs. Praline ice-cream and frangipane tart are praised. Wines, from £2·75 a bottle or £3·50 a litre, are an injudicious bottle tombola of Averys and Stowells ordinaires, but Felinfoel Double Dragon bitter is hand-pumped. No music. Children under 14 must be out by 9 p.m. 'Even the *patronne* smokes.'

App: William Woods, D. G. Foot, Maurice Broady, Philip Knight, John Scott, J. & M.B., and others

Pantry Restaurant
Market Street
Newport 820420

Closed L (Sept–May);
Sun; Mon; Dec 25 & 26;
Jan 1
Must book D
Meals 12.15–2 (summer),
7.15–9.30

Alc L £3 (meal £4·35),
D £6·20 (meal £8·10)

VAT inc
Service 10%
Children's helpings
Seats 45
Car park
No dogs

Apart from 'dispiriting, overcooked and dear' specialities over one public holiday, people continue to admire this now time-worn restaurant in an old-fashioned estuary town. Robin Evans, the owner-chef, and his assistant Hennie Jenkins offer as their favourite dishes mushrooms arménienne (£1·20), shellfish pie (£4·80), and filet en croûte bordelaise (£10 for two – main dish prices include vegetables). But others have equally enjoyed their melon balls with curried prawns, salmon and fennel in pastry with cream sauce, hazelnut meringue gateau, and cherries Lorette. Lunch (June to August), which used to be served across the road at the Barley Mow, offers a different menu but is served in the restaurant and has its own inspiration, according to admirers of the 'moist and rich' pâté, duck salad, and seasonal fruit tarts. Children have been considerately treated by the Evans family. The wine list betrays a lack of interest; André Simon ordinaires are £1·50 for 50 cl. Pressurised beers. No music.

App: Marjorie & David Harris, D.R.J., Thomas Ward

George III Hotel
2 m SW of Dolgellau
Dolgellau 422525

'Taste the treats of Penmaenpool,' urged Gerard Manley Hopkins in skittish mood, and the George is one of them, for as pub and ship's chandler's it has overlooked the Mawddach estuary for 300 years or so. Polished furniture and genially slow service make the local fish, roasts and grills, home-made soups and sweets taste better. Vegetables are 'out of the rut'. Some interesting wines; Choix du Roy by the glass, 40p. Snacks in the Welsh dresser bar (good steak and kidney pie); and in summer sandwiches and pizzas in the Cellar bar. Pressurised beers. Some outside tables. No music. 'Families with children like the old railway with signal nearby.'

Closed Sun D; Dec 25
Must book D & Sun L
Meals 12.45–2, 7.30–9

Alc (min £3·50) £5·75
(meal £8·60)

Service 10%
Children's helpings
(under 12)
Seats 36
🔓 rest
Car park

No dogs in d/r
Access, Am Ex, Barclay,
Diners, Euro
12 rooms (7 with bath)
B&B £8·50–£14·50
Fire cert

Numbers are given for private parties only if they can be accommodated in a room separate from the main dining-room; when there are several such rooms, the capacity of the largest is given. Some restaurants will take party bookings at times when they are normally closed.

RHYDYMAIN Gwynedd   Map 4

Rossi's Ristorante
on A494
8 m NE of Dolgellau
Rhydymain 667 *and* 227

Must book
Meals 12–1.45, 7–9

Alc £5·85 (meal £9)

Service 10%
Seats 35
⟨&⟩ rest; w.c.
Car park
No dogs
Access, Am Ex, Barclay,
Diners
8 rooms
B&B from £8
Fire cert

RR is a symbol which Roberto Rossi has gratefully appropriated, and on the whole members do not grudge it to this quietly furnished old inn. Susannah Rossi's cooking is a successful marriage of Italian and Welsh, with oatmeal porridge and cream for overnight guests, and dinner first courses of antipasto misto, tortellini in brodo, or tagliatelle alla crema (lasagne may be had as a main course too). 'The local vegetables in minestrone reminded me more of our native Welsh *lobsgows* (the origin of Liverpool's scouse) but we would not have had Parmesan on it where I was brought up.' Game is a speciality, and there is praise for pheasant with walnuts as well as for fillet steak in a mustard and cream sauce, and veal in a tomato and garlic one. Vegetable cooking is plain. Sweets are 'heavy with cream' and chilled zabaglione may be a better choice. Coffee is strong. The set lunch now seems to have been discontinued. Mr Rossi, though normally affable, even to children, can be maladroit: there are rules about dress, but one booked customer's young son was turned away without being told what they were, and the *Guide* is no wiser from the owner's reply to its routine question on this point. House wines are Valpolicella or Soave at £2·75. Recorded music.

*App: A. W. John, J. C. Tyrie, J.R.,
Mr & Mrs R. N. Temple, Allan & Anne Heason*

ROBESTON WATHEN Dyfed   Map 4

Robeston House
Narberth
on A40
8 m E of Haverfordwest
Narberth 860392

Closed L (exc by
arrangement); Sun D
(exc res); Dec 24–26;
Jan 1
Must book
Meals L by arrangement,
7.30–9.30

Tdh L £4·50 (meal £6·80),
D £5·50 (meal £7·90)

VAT inc
Service 10%
Children's helpings,
by arrangement
Seats 56

Last year's provisional entry, the Barretts say, brought them many visitors. The old vicarage is warmer and better furnished now than it ever was, perhaps (and they plan to have more rooms soon). Sea and river fishing are among nearby recreations, and local catches or bags frequently appear on menus, which expand as the week proceeds. First courses praised include melon balls with prawns in a mild curry sauce, but spare ribs may not reach Chinese standard. Look out for game in season, and sea bass Dugléré. 'My only criticism in three otherwise faultless meals was an overcooked loin of lamb containing more stuffing than meat. Vegetables are cooked *al dente*, and dauphinoise potatoes and salads are brought round.' 'Fresh season's salmon with a shrimp sauce (£1 extra) was enormous and superb', and roast duck 'had a crisp and delicious skin'. Brandied peach surprise was 'not another name for peach Melba as we had feared'. Hazelnut crunch with raspberry sauce 'reminded us of Debussy's description of Grieg's music'. The coffee (with lovely fudge) tasted of freshly ground beans.

361

♿ rest (1 step); w.c.
Car park
No dogs
Access card
5 rooms (3 with bath)
B&B £8·50

'Service is cordial enough but 'there are rather too many notices telling you what not to do.' The Barretts aim to make their wine list one of the largest in Wales. One hopes that by that time burgundy shippers will be named, and other small errors put right, but there are interesting choices from Argentine red at £2·65 and sweet white Hungarian at £6 to good hocks and clarets: Ch. Fonbadet '70, £4·95. The house Bordeaux at £2·75 is also liked. No music. Smoking at table is frowned upon, sometimes in vain. Children are expected to behave and, if they stay, to be over 14. Adults should dress neatly.

App: Jeremy Temple, Roberta Collins, Henry Joseph, Leonard Jones, D. S. N. Brierley, and others

---

ST DAVID'S Dyfed   Map 4

St Non's Hotel
St David's 239

Must book D
Meals 12–2, HT 5–6, 7–9
(9.30 summer)

Tdh buffet L £2 (meal
£3·90)

Alc £5·20 (meal £7·40)

VAT inc
Children's helpings
(under 6)
Seats 75
♿ rest; w.c.
Car park
No dogs in public rooms
Access, Am Ex, Barclay,
Diners
24 rooms (22 with bath)
B&B £9
Fire cert

Sandy Falconer still manages and Simon Periam still cooks for the Stirling family's modernised hotel near the cathedral. It shows no sign of reaching the heights, at least until the sweet stage, but everyone seems to have enjoyed their stay. The set meals offer little choice, but whether table d'hôte or à la carte it is worth noting guests' and the kitchen's favourites: soups (especially celery and Stilton), kidneys in sherry, seafood hors d'oeuvre when the boat has come in, and Gianni's flambé dishes, notably veal vallée d'Auge. 'You need to be in good training for the lunchtime buffet' ('sausages stuffed with pickle were succulent, but quiche was at once too salty and too cheesy'). Dobostorte and lemon soufflé are also praised. Argentine Franchette carafes are £2·80 a litre and Ch. Fonbadet '70, c.b., was £5·45 (£2·80 a half) in 1978. No music. 'No crying babies', but 'my two children were allowed two buffets for the price of one though they must have eaten quite as much as the very refined old dear at the next table.' The bar and patio for casual lunchers, 'full of rather superior sailors', are being extended.

App: Denis Tate, Philip Knight, John Willmington, B. G. L., Graham Woodville, John Morton, and others

---

Warpool Court Hotel
St David's 300

Closed Jan 1–28
Meals 1–2, 7–9.30

Tdh L £3·80 (meal £4·80),
D £5·70 (meal £6·70)
Alc £7·35 (meal £9·60)

Members (at least the ones who ate dinner rather than the set lunches) responded well to last year's request for more reports on the Lloyd brothers' spreading house, lined with armorial tiles, overlooking St Brides Bay. The Lloyds say they enjoy striving to improve what they offer, and there is evidently something left to work on (for instance, breakfasts, cheeses, and staff training). But the set menu cooking rises to most occasions. Hors d'oeuvre remain 'outstanding'. 'Creamy shrimp salad with

VAT inc
Service 10% alc
Children's helpings tdh
Seats 100
♿ rest; w.c.
Car park
No dogs in public rooms
Access, Am Ex
25 rooms (16 with bath,
9 with shower)
B&B from £10·50
Full board from £16 p.d.
(3 days min)
Fire cert

lemon slices' and pommes Suzette (in spite of the
description 'a twice-baked potato') are also admired.
Main course sauces may be floury (or capery) on
occasion, but the local fish is good, and 'we had a
very tasty blanquette, and duck with a crispy skin
and juicy flesh.' Lamb Dewi Sant (with duxelles and
mint in a pastry crust) is a speciality. Strawberry
soufflé, mille-feuille, and chocolate mousse with
orange are among sweets praised. The wine list,
called 'unbalanced' and sent to us unpriced, does
indeed lack half-bottles. One night when a rugby
club was expected 'the pourer filled five glasses and
then said "you can't get six glasses out of this
bottle so you'll have to have another" – just as well
it wasn't the '59 Latour, at £19·77.' Under £4, there
are various Bergeracs and other wines from
Bordeaux Direct. Lunchtime bar snacks. No music.

App: Dr & Mrs A. W. Pendlington, Joseph Gazdak,
E. J. Grossman, and others

SOLVA Dyfed   Map 4

Old Pharmacy
5 Main Street
on A487
3 m E of St David's
Solva 232

*So many members have found good medicine in the
Willsons' quiet, small-scale and unpretentious
dining-room that it will be a shame if they give up –
but it will be wise to telephone before a visit in 1979.
Sometimes the menu contracts to very little, but
expanded versions have offered good crab soup and
pâté, 'lovely salmon either poached with hollandaise or
with home-made cole-slaw as salad', steak and kidney
pie, Swiss apple tart, and other sweets. Bread and
scones may be on the heavy side. Wines from £3·15.
'Baroque' music.*

Closed Mon; D Sun–Wed;
Oct–Easter
Must book D
Open 10.30–5.30; meals
1–2.30, 8–9.30 (Thur–Sat)

Tdh D £5·25 (meal £7·80)
Alc L £3·15 (meal £5·50)

VAT inc

Children's helpings
Seats 25
♿ rest; w.c.
No dogs

SWANSEA West Glamorgan   Map 4

Drangway
66 Wind Street
Swansea 461397 *and*
51603

Closed Sun; Mon;
July 29–Aug 14;
Dec 21–Jan 1
Must book
Meals 12.30–2.15,
7.30–10.15

*Italic type is no derogation of Colin Pressdee's
upstairs-and-downstairs restaurant in one of Swansea's
drangways, or passages. But after David Brooks left a
year ago, he himself took charge of the kitchen with two
assistants, looked for new or seasonal dishes to put
beside such old favourites as bass au beurre blanc,
stuffed mushrooms and carpet-bag steak, and paid
more attention to sauces and sweets. The effect of all
these changes (including a complete refit of kitchen
and restaurant) is not clear, though most visitors have
enjoyed their meals. The best dishes now, Mr Pressdee
thinks, are hot artichaut avec mousse de crabe and cold*

363

Tdh L £3·25 (meal £5·40),
and from £5·25 (meal
£8·40), D (mid-week)
£5·45 (inc wine)
Alc £8·20 (meal £10·35)

VAT & service inc
Seats 28 (parties 26)
&. rest
Air-conditioning
Access, Am Ex, Barclay,
Diners, Euro

*terrine de saumon au poivre vert (both £2·25), and
filet de boeuf 'en chevreuil' (£11·50 for two). But if
these prices seem high, the mid-week four-course set
dinner is called good value. (The basic lunch has three
courses and less choice, though dearer options exist at
midday too.) For sweet try a fresh fruit tart, or crème
brûlée. The wines, from £3·80 a litre for French
ordinaire, are suitably chosen, with Gros Plant '76
(£3·75) for the shellfish, Berry Bros house claret or
Côte de Nuits-Villages '72 (£5·25), and Ch.
Léoville-Lascases '62 (£8·95) among good clarets.
Sometimes there is live music. Children's helpings.
No dogs. More reports, please.*

THREE COCKS Powys   Map 4

Three Cocks Hotel
on A438 at Aberllynfi
4 m SW of Hay-on-Wye
Glasbury 215

Must book weekends
Meals 12.15–1.50,
6.45–9.50

Tdh L £4·45 (meal £6·70)
Alc £6·60 (meal £9·30)

VAT inc
Service 10%
Seats 45 (parties 24)
Car park
No dogs in d/r
Access, Barclay, Diners
7 rooms
B&B £6·50
Fire cert

*It is always gratifying when a long-admired place
keeps an entry of any kind in its own right after a
change of hands, but it is particularly hard to be sure
about the Barber and May families' regime at this
creeper-clad roadside inn (ask for a room at the back
if you stay). This is because the Hines' young chef
stayed on for several months but now seems to have
gone, and a test meal taken later was by no means
faultless. The best things were the noisettes of venison
in madeira sauce ('tender meat with a touch of
sweetness in the cream sauce, and a garnish of thin
and crisp croûtons', £3·55) and a cold chocolate
pancake filled with mint cream from the sweets trolley.
On another occasion, 'roast quail with roebuck sauce
(£3·55) was successful, though the vegetables were
dreary.' Hot shrimps en croustade (£1·35) also
remain on the speciality list, along with honey-roasted
duckling with pineapple, (£3·95, vegetables not
included). Late in the year excellent grouse and
guinea-fowl were reported. But cheeses and minor
service details suggest that the sociable partners have
plenty to improve backstage; the coffee is also poor.
French ordinaires are £2·70 and on the Averys and
Stowells list Aloxe-Corton '71 is £6·70, Ch. le Pape
'70, £4·20, and half-bottles of Sauternes or Barsac
£2·15. There are bar lunches with pressurised beers.
'Breakfasts are magnificent and include kidneys and
mushrooms.' No music. No toddlers. Dress
conventionally. More reports, please.*

Most places will accept cheques only when they are accompanied by a
cheque card or adequate identification. Information about which credit cards
are accepted is correct when printed, but occasionally restaurants add to or
subtract from the list without notice.

Since each restaurant has a separate file in the Guide office, please use a separate
form or sheet of paper for each report. Additional forms may be obtained free
(no stamp required) from The Good Food Guide, Freepost,
14 Buckingham Street, London WC2N 6BR.

WHITEBROOK Gwent   Map 4

Crown Inn
2½ m off A466
at Bigsweir Bridge
5 m N of Tintern
Trelleck 254 *and* 504

During 1978, numerous members supplied vivid and mostly admiring accounts of their meals at the Crown, and we are extremely grateful to them. But as we went to press, it became apparent that Neville and Sonia Blech were on the point of negotiating a sale. If you are contemplating a visit, enquire first; and please report developments.

Towns shown in black on our maps contain at least one recommended restaurant or pub (see map key). The dot denotes the location of the town or village, not the restaurant. Where necessary, we give directions to the restaurant in the entry. If you can, help us to improve them.

The Guide News Supplement will be sent out as usual, in June, to everyone who buys the book directly from Consumers' Association and to all bookshop purchasers who return the card interleaved with their copy. Let us know of any changes that affect entries in the book, or of any new places you think should be looked at.

Since all restaurants have a separate file in the Guide office, please use a separate form or sheet of paper for each report. Additional forms may be obtained free (no stamp required) from The Good Food Guide, Freepost, 14 Buckingham Street, London WC2N 6BR.

PLEASE keep sending in reports, as soon as possible after each meal. Closing date for the 1980 Guide is September 30, 1979, but reports are even more useful earlier in the year, especially for the remoter areas and new places.

Within parts of these old county boundaries, alcohol is not served on Sunday, except to hotel residents: Anglesey, Cardigan, Carmarthen, Merioneth.

'VAT inc' means that an inn's policy is to incorporate VAT in its food prices.

Meal times refer to first and last orders.

Wolfscastle Country Hotel
off A40
7 m N of Haverfordwest
Treffgarne 225

Meals 12.30–2, 7–9
(9.30 summer)

Alc L (bar) £2·60,
D £4·80 (meal £7·50)

Children's helpings
Seats 50
♿ rest (2 steps)
Car park
No dogs in d/r
Access, Barclay
8 rooms (2 with bath)
B&B £5·50–£9·50
D, B&B £9·50–£14·50

It sounds as though Andrew Stirling, whose second local hotel enterprise this is, has some hard choices to make between the interests of summer residents and those of local parties. At any rate, the sounds of revelry by night ('not to mention crows in the morning') have marred the stays of some, who also report that for want of lounge space, bedrooms should be better furnished for sitting. Otherwise, the young staff do what they can, and Rosanna Lloyd remains in the kitchen. Her materials are local and good, especially the sewin and garden vegetables, and her preferred dishes, such as spinach and mushroom roulade (£1), cold curried apple soup (85p), Lisanne's chicken with mussels (£3·40), and aillade de veau (£3·70), are worth looking out for on the short à la carte menus. For sweet try hazelnut meringue. A teatime visitor tells of 'chunks of excellent Dundee cake' too, but a Sunday night one reports a tedious meal. The ordinaire is Patriarche at £2·50, and there is a short wine list (Ch. Fonbadet '70 was £4·95 in 1978). Recorded music. No children under four in the restaurant. Lunchtime bar snacks (home-made cheeseburgers, soups, paté, pizza); pressurised beer.

App: R. C. Lang, Rosemary Marsh, R. J. McGrath, N.R.H., Jill Briggs and others

WOLF'S CASTLE see also pub section

SCOTLAND

ABERDEEN (Aberdeenshire) Grampian   Map 9

Le Dodo
15 Crown Street
Aberdeen 26916

Closed L Sun & Sat;
Dec 25
Must book weekends
Meals 12–2.30, 7–11

Tdh L £2·55 (meal £4·65)
Alc £5·75 (meal £9·05)

Service 10%
Seats 60
⟨⟩ rest (1 step)
Car park
No dogs
Access, Am Ex, Barclay,
Diners

Several people hope that the Dodo will not quickly become extinct, for the setting, the menu and the staff of this French restaurant – owned by food-loving Scottish accountants – exhibit a spiritedness that deserves exacting customers. (One man even caught himself talking to a table neighbour about the food – 'always a good sign.') Pleasures described include salmon in sorrel sauce, délice de sole Nantua 'with a shrimp sauce far removed from the usual amorphous mush', and sauté of kidneys in madeira with 'artichokes in cream sauce and cabbage in a nicely glazed stock'. Specialities of David West and his assistants include courgettes farcies (£1·50), langoustines provençale (£4·95) and médaillons de venaison aux cerises. The set lunch also looks well worth a try. Errors reported include far too bland 'piquant' sauces with crab claws; and, says someone, the use of 'poivre vert' to mean peppers not peppercorns is misleading. The carafe wines are Bonatello; house Bordeaux is £2·75, and Franconian Volkacher Kirchberg '76 at £7·60 or Ch. d'Issan '70 at £7·95 are a further steep step up. Recorded music. More reports, please.

ACHILTIBUIE Ross & Cromarty (Highland)   Map 9

Summer Isles Hotel

16 m off A835
NW of Ullapool
Achiltibuie 282

Closed L (exc
Smokehouse); **early**
Oct–Easter
Must book
Meals (Smokehouse)
10–6, 7.30–9 (D mid-July
to mid-Sept only);
(rest) D only, 7 for 7.30

Tdh (rest) D £6·50 (meal
£9·35)
Alc £3·45 (meal £5·95)

Service 10%
Seats 30
Car park

Stabilisation seems to be the year's theme in this hotel that has attempted and achieved so much in the nine years it has spent in the *Guide*. True, cheese production may depend on the unstable sex life of the Irvines' goats, but further expansion of the house has been forsworn – 'Roberta refuses to cook for more people' – and guests can imagine few improvements on 'the simplification of life to walking, fishing, eating, talking, and sleeping profoundly'. 'We stayed two weeks and had not one poor meal. Our favourites were scallops in various ways, very subtle Armenian lamb with cumin, and stuffed peppers.' Another visitor has 'nothing but praise for the Levant-inspired chilled soups and taramosalata, the lamb, sucking-pig, and venison, roast, casseroled, and even made into moussaka. Enquire if there's fish for breakfast, and you may be offered trout meunière.' 'Mogul roasted kid with spicy yoghourt sauce tasted marvellous.' 'Where else in the Highlands would you be offered home-grown courgettes?' Salads and sweets are both good – 'we liked crème de menthe bavarois and banana galette.' Perhaps there should be alternative cheeses

367

No dogs in public rooms
17 rooms (7 with bath)
B&B £8·50–£15
Full board £110–£175
Fire cert

at dinner. Verdicts on the price and quantity of the packed lunches depend on energy and appetite: some take one between two, some do not, but 'giant prawns on Quinag and smoked salmon on Suilven enhance the charm of these mountains.' Casual callers, 'from student hikers to caravanning professors and their families', may eat in the separate Smokehouse restaurant (and the smokehouse itself is now producing smoked mutton hams and saucisson sec as well as more usual salmon and mackerel). Wines are well chosen and fairly priced. If the main course dictates a red wine, Robert Irvine now offers a glass of an appropriate white with the earlier course ('it feels like an offer you can't refuse'). A serious toper has first-rate clarets at his disposal, many still in half-bottle, with sweet Ch. Suduiraut '70, c.b., £5·70 or £2·95, for pudding, and if he chooses, a decanter of Warre or Delaforce '60 port to last him (or her) through a stay. No smoking, either. No music. No children under eight in the hotel.

App: B.R., R. & J. Hardwick, Peter John Dyer, F.P., P. & J. I. Findlater, and others

---

ALYTH Perthshire (Tayside)   Map 9

Lands of Loyal Hotel
Loyal Road
Alyth 2481

Loyal, yes, but after eight years some members wonder if the Billinghursts' cooking, helpings and staff are what they once were. Happily, an equal number report from different times of year a warm welcome and good bread, Loyal cheese soup, eggs en cocotte, 'delicious haddock mousse', seafood pancakes, chicken Marengo, kidneys Turbigo, pork escalope, and fried sweetbreads in the four-course dinners. Syllabub and trifle are possible sweets; cheeses are a good alternative if in condition. There are 66 wines, from £2·40 for Spanish Cumbrero '75. Pressurised beers. Bar lunches. No music.

Closed Dec 24–Jan 2
Must book
Meals 12.30–2, 7–8.30

Tdh L £3·50 (meal £6·05),
D £5·50 (meal £8·40)

Service 10%
Children's helpings
Seats 40 (parties 12)
Car park
No dogs in public rooms

Am Ex, Diners
14 rooms (6 with bath,
1 with shower)
B&B £7·50–£8·50
Fire cert

ARDENTINNY Argyll (Strathclyde)   Map 9

Ardentinny Hotel
Loch Long
on A880
Ardentinny 209

Closed Nov; Dec 25 & 26

On the western shore of Loch Long, with a view of the Cobbler 25 miles away, John and Sylvia Harris have revived an old pub in Harry Lauder land to the point where it is nominated for decent accommodation and enthusiastic cooking at an ungrasping price. 'Snack lunches, inside or outside, are admirable,' says a

Must book
Meals 12–2 (Sun 12.30),
HT 5–6, 7–8.30 (Sun
7.30)

Tdh D £4·50 (meal £6·50)
Alc (bar meal) £3·20

VAT inc
Seats 36 (parties 20)
Access, Am Ex
8 rooms (4 with bath)
B&B £6·75–£9·50
D, B&B £57·50–£78 p.w.
Fire cert

*regular visitor, and the smoked trout salad, fish pie
with salmon and prawns (£1·50) and strawberry
Pavlova (60p) served midday may turn up on the set
dinner menus too. When tried, steak and mushroom
pie, lemon pancakes and Caledonian cream – 'a sort of
marmalade syllabub' – were good of their kind; more
ambitious trout Père Louis left room for improvement,
as does the coffee. Australian reds at just under £4 are
perhaps the best if not the cheapest wine choices.
Recorded music. Wear a jacket and tie. Early evening
meals for residents with children, and a 'buttery' for
non-resident families, too; children under ten may have
smaller helpings. No dogs in the dining-room. More
reports, please.*

ARDUAINE Argyll (Strathclyde)   Map 9

Loch Melfort Hotel
on A816
Kimelford 233

Closed end Oct to Easter
Must book D & Sun L
Meals 12.30–2 (bar exc
Sun), 7.15–8.30

Tdh Sun L from £5
(meal £7·40), D from £6
(meal £8·60)

Seats 50
Car park
No dogs in public rooms
Access, Am Ex
28 rooms (23 with bath)
B&B from £11·50

Not for the first time, some people think that Colin
Tindal's glorified motel belongs in a good view guide
rather than a good food guide, and an early summer
visitor's account of dry pork, sugar-dredged ham,
tasteless herrings in mustard, 'primitive' wine
service and watery coffee carries conviction, for Mr
Tindal seemed to resent last year's much milder
criticisms. In September, a mediocre bar lunch did
not encourage a member to stay for dinner.
However, nearly everyone has something good and
some have nothing but good to say about the place:
comfort, 'staff who called us by name', ample
breakfasts (apart from the foil-packeted butter
ration), 'tasty green pepper soup', 'an impressive
help-yourself selection of fresh salmon, dressed crab
and giant prawns, followed by roast beef pink by
request', and sweets such as chocolate pear crisp
and blackcurrant cheesecake. 'Perhaps avocado filled
with tinned grapefruit segments should appear, if at
all, in this section.' Lamborghini white wine at £2·90
and Chianti Classico '72 Castell' in Villa at £3·25
may be the best choices. Recorded music. No
children under eight at dinner. Smoking is not
encouraged. Sunday lunch is a hot and cold buffet.

*App: B. M. Newman, Mr & Mrs K. Garside,
Enid G. Adam, Mr & Mrs Alan Cleave*

Scottish public holidays do not all coincide with English ones.

For the explanation of 🔄 denoting accessibility for the disabled,
see 'How to use the Guide', p. 4.

Entries for places with distinctions carry symbols (pestle, tureen, bottle, glass).
Credits are fully written entries, with approvers' names below the text. Passes
are telegraphic entries (useful in the area) with details under the text.
Provisional entries are in italics (see 'How to use the Guide', p. 4).

Gleneagles Hotel
1 m W of Auchterarder
off A9/A823
Auchterarder 2231

As a man-made monument, Gleneagles is in the
Ozymandias class, serving American stalkers and
Japanese golfers rather than native Brits, 'so don't
forget your sporran when you come to pay the bills',
as the house pop song has it. Service is mostly
amiable and swift (during August, they draft in
reinforcements from further south); set meals are
variable (all the way from good mushroom soup and
roast to 'Byron potatoes' that tasted recycled).
M Cottet's 'handsomely prepared hors d'oeuvre with
no bottled beetroot', veal Vaucanson (£7·65), 'unusual
sliced aubergines and courgettes in a very garlicky
sauce', and intensely flavoured Kümmel sorbet may
reach a much higher level, and the wines are
excellent: note Mâcon-Prissé '75 (Duboeuf) £4·95;
good Rhônes now, and Ch. Cos d'Estournel '64,
£10·50. 'Jacket required.' Bar lunches. Car park.

Closed Nov to mid-Apr	Alc (min L £4·50, D £5·50)	No dogs in public rooms
Must book	£15·15 (meal £17·55)	Access, Am Ex, Barclay,
Meals 12.45–2, 7.30–9.15		Diners, Euro
	VAT & service inc	210 rooms (207 with bath,
Tdh L from £6·75 (meal	Seats 275 (parties 476)	3 with shower)
£8·45), D from £8 (meal	🔲 rest; w.c.	B&B on application
£9·70)	Air-conditioning	Fire cert

Bumbles
9 New Shopping
Development
Aviemore 810392

Closed 3rd week May;
5 weeks Nov/Dec; Dec 24
Must book D
Meals 12–2.45, 6.30–9.30

Alc L £2·75 (meal £4·85),
D £5·35 (meal £7·85)

VAT inc
Children's helpings
(under 12, before 8 p.m.)
Seats 42
No dogs

The address sounds like something from Calcutta or
the Comintern, but Fraser and Bridget Clyde have
risen very capably above this handicap in a
two-season town where real food is an unfashionable
concern. They think themselves that their Below
Bumbles Diner is also below *Guide* notice, and it
sounds as though they are right. Afternoon 'hot
chocolate and scones', alas, proved uneconomic. But
they themselves cook the dinners, and simple lunches
upstairs, which give pleasure without pretension,
whether their guests come in après-ski finery or
knickerbocker glory. One visitor was luckier with
main courses than first ones (an unusual way
round) and praises chicken in sherry and rabbit in
mustard sauces, with 'generous vegetables decently
cooked'. But try also crab soup or garlic mushroom
tartlets with béarnaise (£1); then trout Père Louis
or Barbizon (£3), kebab en croûte, or fillet steak
(£3·90–£4·60) 'since our butcher has excellent fillet
at a reasonable price'. Sweets ('an appetising Pernod
syllabub') and service are also praised. Ordinaire is
£2·90 a litre; and good Riojas, '75 hocks, and
Bonnezeaux '70 express the owners' own taste at
£5 or so.

App: Irene Hepburn, Ian T. Wilson, J. M. Broom

High Range Hotel
on A9
Aviemore 810636

Closed L (exc Sun in summer); Nov; 1st week Dec
Must book weekends
Meals (Sun in summer) 12.30–2, 7–10 (9 in winter)

Tdh Sun L £3 (meal £5), D £3·50 (meal £5·60)
Alc £5·75 (meal £8·85)

Children's helpings (under 11)
Seats 50
⟨⟩ rest (1 step); w.c.
Car park
No dogs in public rooms
Access, Am Ex, Barclay, Diners
22 rooms (9 with bath, 13 with shower)
B&B £5·50–£9
D, B&B £8·10–£12·50

Last year's provisional entry sounded somewhat sceptical, but Mr and Mrs Vastano, by all accounts, have taken a firm grip on this hotel with chalet rooms in wooded ground by the main road, overlooking the Forest of Rothiemurchus and the peaks and runs of the Cairngorms. The bar and lounge still need a decorator's brush, but the rooms are warm, and the set meals have improved greatly under Peter Morris in the kitchen: 'soups and lamb navarin were excellent;' 'each night, all three courses showed unstinted effort and style, especially the vegetables, such as potatoes sauté with bacon and carrot, whole baby turnips in batter, and salsify.' 'Waldorf salad, cauliflower and tomato soup, poached trout, braised beef Huntingdon, and pork chop normande all succeeded, and though the trifle was a trifle heavy, we liked the chocolate and rum gateau, and grapefruit cheesecake.' 'Haggis and neeps appeared on the set lunch.' A la carte, Mr Morris suggests his champignon Dordogne (85p), fresh lobster soup (£1) and gigot d'agneau (£9 for two). Valpolicella or Soave are £1·70 for 50 cl; Beaujolais Villages '76, £3·95. Recorded music. Plans for 1979 include a dinner-dance on Fridays; après-ski entertainment on Wednesday evenings until May; and Italian bar snacks in the summer.

App: Peter John Dyer, Mr & Mrs R. G. Bateman, and others

BALLATER Aberdeenshire (Grampian)   Map 9

Tullich Lodge

on A93
1½ m E of Ballater
Ballater 406

Closed Jan–Mar
Must book
Meals 1, 7.30–9

Tdh L £4·50 (meal £5·50), D from £5 (meal £6)

VAT & service inc
Seats 34
⟨⟩ rest (2 steps)
No dogs in public rooms
Am Ex, Diners
10 rooms (8 with bath, 2 with shower)
B&B from £12·50
Full board from £130
Fire cert

'Impeccable and idiosyncratic' is one description of Neil Bannister and Hector MacDonald's lovingly furnished sub-baronial house. Users of the *Guide* will naturally see no contradiction in that coupling of adjectives. Users of the hotel are not so sure: from time to time, people have been given to understand that their own or their dog's faces do not precisely fit. However, cynophobia may be forgiven a man who wears a pullover woven from the superfluous hair of his own sheepdog, and the vast majority 'like everything about this place: the friendly and welcoming owners, the careful but unobtrusive attention to detail, and above all the food.' 'The set meal – grouse soup, baked chicken with herbs and cream cheese, and gooseberry pie – could easily have been dull, but wasn't: it was as well cooked as one could possibly want, and a crisp green salad was admirably dressed. As a diabetic, I could not have the pie, and was given a good choice of fresh fruit and a farmhouse Cheshire instead.' Other meals notified include iced beetroot consommé with sour cream and chives ('a gorgeous colour and texture'), roast lamb and parsnips with 'delicious spinach', and Deeside blue cheese; or venison soup, sea trout with

371

gratin dauphinoise potatoes, and unadorned white
currants still on their stems: the owners are not
afraid of their own idiosyncrasies in compiling their
virtually choiceless (and far from gross) menus.
Sunday evening meals may fall off somewhat.
Service is minimal, and breakfast 'a do-it-yourself
meal', but it is usually efficient, and tiresome waits
in the bar to be called to dinner may be solaced by
'a plateful of fresh-gathered radishes from the
garden and a saucer of salt'. No cigars or pipes, they
say, but people are allowed to smoke cigarettes
through meals to the annoyance of others. The
wines, from £2, are well judged and reasonable, with
Mâcon-Prissé '76 (Duboeuf) £3·40 and Ch. Haut
Beychevelle Gloria '70, £3·85 in 1978. There are
numerous single malt whiskies. Books and a grand
piano are other signs of civilisation. No babies;
young children are given a kitchen high tea. No
music in the dining-room. Wear a tie.

App: David de Saxe, R. L. White, S.E.,
Elisabeth Aylmer-Kelly, D.T., and others

BEATTOCK Dumfriesshire (Dumfries & Galloway)
Map 7

Old Brig Inn

2 m SW of Moffat
Beattock 401

Closed Jan & Feb
Must book D
Meals 12.15–1.30, 7–8.30

Tdh L £3 (meal £4·85),
D £4·75 (meal £7·35)

Service 10%
Seats 36
♿ rest (1 step)
Car park
No dogs
Diners card
8 rooms (1 with shower)
B&B £7–£9
Fire cert

Last year's first 'glass' distinction sent more
members than before to the Worthys' solid Telford
posting-house off the main road. Lunches, by several
accounts, including a test meal, barely rise above a
'useful in the wilderness' category, and a few people
find the owner disconcerting: 'I felt like damping
him down with a soda syphon.' But on the whole
dinners well sustain the praise given for mushrooms
in garlic butter, ratatouille ('they skin the aubergines
but not the tomatoes, which is surely the wrong way
round'), spiced lamb with apricots ('more spice and
apricot flavour needed'), pork fillet with orange
cream sauce, beef in red wine, and pink lamb chops.
Poussin dijonnaise is a speciality and vegetables are
better cooked in the evening. The bramble or
blackcurrant puddings sound the best. 'Greying
Scotswomen' serve. Mr Worthy buys wine shrewdly
and sells it fairly, from little over £2, with Ch.
Pichon-Longueville-Baron '67, £5·25; magnums of Ch.
Branaire-Ducru '61, c.b., at £20, and eight vintage
ports ('60 and '63) under £8, one of them kept
decanted for sale by the glass. No music.

App: Jenifer & Geoffrey Rowntree, R. L., B.W.,
M. Russell-Carter, R. J. Haerdi, and others

PLEASE keep sending in reports, as soon as possible after each meal.
Closing date for the 1980 Guide is September 30, 1979, but reports are even
more useful earlier in the year, especially for the remoter areas and new places.

CLEISH Kinross-shire (Tayside) Map 9

Nivingston House
off B9097
2 m SW of Kinross
Cleish Hills 216

Closed L (exc bar, and
Sun buffet) Mon; Oct;
Jan 2–16
Must book
Meals 12.30–1.45 (bar),
7.30–9

Tdh Sun buffet L £3·50
(meal £5·75) and D £5
(meal £6·35); Mon–Sat D
£8·50 (meal £11·70)
Alc £8·05 (meal £11·75)

Service 10%
Children's helpings
(under 12)
Seats 54 (parties 16)
🔲 rest; w.c.
Car park
No dogs in public rooms
Am Ex, Barclay
7 rooms
B&B £10·50
Fire cert

Take exit 5 from the M90 and follow first Crook of Devon, then Cleish, signs to find the Scott-Smiths' small, personally run hotel. The chef, William Kerr, has worked there several years, and though there are sometimes signs of over-ambition or over-use of cream and salt, the effect is generous and good, especially when – as has sometimes happened – there are only a few diners to tackle the imposing Sunday night buffet. (Overnight guests are not taken on Sundays without due notice, for the hotel is closed on Mondays.) From weekday set dinners, most soups, hot avocado with prawns and cheese sauce, chicken livers, pike mayonnaise, asparagus mousse, roast loin of lamb with artichokes, 'a brace of quail with orange, fresh pineapple and mushroom', and 'excellently underdone beef Wellington and matching vegetables' are all praised. 'Cul de veau bourgeoise' may be worth a try, but chicken suprême Camembert was 'on the dry side'. Stilton – if they would but cut it, not spoon it – may be a wiser choice than the sweets, but 'black cherry flan did not suffer from softened pastry this time.' The wines, from £2·70 in 1978, are eccentrically chosen; Ch. Calon-Ségur '70, c.b., £8. There are bar lunches, and pressurised beers. No music. Wear a tie at dinner.

App: A. H. M. Adam, Elisabeth Aylmer-Kelly, M. E. Lipkin, P. & J. I. Findlater, and others

CORSOCK Kirkcudbrightshire (Dumfries & Galloway) Map 7

Glaisters Lodge
Corsock 245

Closed L; mid-Nov to
mid-Feb
Must book
D only, 7.30 for 8

Tdh £4 (meal £5·50)

Service inc
Seats 12 (parties 6)
Car park
No dogs in public rooms
6 rooms (1 with bath)
B&B £6·50–£11·50
Fire cert

'Discotheque types and the gin-and-It brigade would find the silence shattering', for the company in the Urr valley is mostly birds and black Galloway cattle. After three years in the business the Edwardses have gathered a clientele that recognises 'a haven for honest, well-cooked food' and does not mind 'a warm house but a claustrophobic atmosphere'. There is limited choice at dinner, and hungry walkers would find quantities delicate, but 'soups were subtly flavoured, especially cock-a-leekie, game broth, and potage Parmentier. Another delicious first course was a quenelle of pike with prawn sauce. Good main ones included pigeon casserole, steak and mushroom pie, pork escalope and roast beef.' Not all sweets succeed, but there is praise for chocolate brandy cake, apfelstrudel, and 'home-made ice laden with strawberries'. Mrs Edwards also nominates her sweet pancakes and Dundee tart. Cheeses are more than adequate. Mr Edwards makes an admirable breakfast cook and wine waiter, but there are normally no lunches (though they will provide picnics). Wine prices (from £2·20 for carafe burgundy) are kept down, and so are the bar ones. 'Semi-formal dress is usual at dinner.' No music. No children under 12. The self-catering cottages are comfortable, but cotters count as non-residents, for whom there is little room in the hotel dining-room.

App: Mr & Mrs K. Garside, J. B. Collins, D. J. Perry, and others

---

CRINAN Argyll (Strathclyde)   Map 9

Crinan Hotel
off B841
7 m NW of Lochgilphead
Crinan 235 *and* 242

Closed Dec 24, 25 & 26
Must book D
Meals 12.30–2, 7–9

Tdh L £2·25 (meal £4·35),
D £4·95 (meal £7·50)

Seats 50 (parties 20)
♿ rest
Car park
No dogs in d/r
Access, Am Ex, Diners
19 rooms (all with bath)
B&B £6–£9
Fire cert

'This is potentially such a good place that some seemingly minor improvements to the beds, the heating system, and other matters would make it irresistible,' says one (representative) guest of Nicholas and Frances Ryan's modern hotel. A serious fire late in 1978 makes a telephone call essential if you are contemplating a visit this summer. As for the cooking, if the sublime fish and shellfish were subtracted from Bella MacLeod's repertoire there might be some blaze-ups too, for 'standards' such as Mornay sauce, mayonnaise, and trifle are at best indifferent, and salads wince with malt vinegar. However, the sunset view across the Sound of Jura to the islands 'excuses any confusion or delays in the dining-room', and all the loving critics hail the clams and giant prawns that may appear on the table within an hour of landing. Loch Sween mussels, lobster, and poached (but not baked) salmon are also praised. Steaks are good too. Stilton or fresh fruit may be the wisest endings. Coffee is poor, but real orange juice and Loch Fyne kippers for breakfast help to make a fish-lover's holiday. Beers are pressurised, and the wine list standard, 'though Mr Ryan produced from his personal stock a superb '73 Meursault at £6·95.' There are teas for resident under-fives. No music. More reports please, on account of the uncertainties.

CUPAR Fife   Map 9

Timothy's
⚲

43 Bonnygate
Cupar 2830

Closed Sun; 3 weeks from
mid-June; Dec 25 & 26;
Jan 1
Must book
Meals 12–2, 7–10

Alc (min £3 after 9.30
p.m.) £4·10 (meal £6·55)

'Big, boyish and breathless' Athole Laing presides over this homely place, a slightly soberer twin of the Perth Timothy's (*q.v.*). In a cold spring, an inspector found a welcoming fire to set off the bar and dark furniture downstairs, and the Scandinavian-style food, cooked by Mrs Laing and others, was conscientious. The home-made soup and roll is an obvious beginning to the main-course open sandwiches. When tried, smoked marinated mackerel (82p) seemed better value than crab-meat with mushrooms (£1·10), and 'seafood medley (£2·85) needed a little help from the freezer to make it up during the winter.' But crab and prawn koenig (£1·20) and pâtés of chicken liver or kipper (75p) are

374

VAT inc
Cover 15p D
Seats 32 (parties 10)
⟨&⟩ rest (1 step)
No dogs

kitchen suggestions, and the roast sirloin of beef or clove-tinged ham are well cooked and sensibly served. 'The day's sweet, Danish fruit tart (37p), had good crisp pastry, raisins, and an almost toffee-like filling.' Coffee was good too. The wine glass distinction is earned here not by anything out of the way but by wines, carefully chosen by Mr Laing, that surpass expectation in such a place, with Barolo '73 or Marqués de Riscal '71 under £4, St Johanner Königsgarten Auslese '71, £4·80, and Ch. Magnan-Gaffelière '70, £6·60. The Spanish Santa Fé ordinaire is £3 for 75 cl.

App: W. Frankland, Henry Potts, Christine Duncan, and others

DALBEATTIE Kirkcudbrightshire (Dumfries & Galloway)   Map 7

Granary
Barend,
Sandyhills
off A710
7 m SE of Dalbeattie
Southwick 663

Tiny bar-cum-restaurant in a converted barn, amid new Swedish-style holiday chalets. Fixed-price dinners with little choice, but more imaginative and better cooked than people expect hereabouts. Pork noisettes with prunes, moussaka, and mincemeat tart pleased one party. The weekend cold buffet lunch is adequate but not very lavish, and pastry can be 'a bit hard'. Good filter coffee. A few wines: Spanish red is £2·40 the bottle, 50p the glass. Bar snacks. No music.

Closed L (exc buffet Sat & Sun); Mon; Sun D (exc July & Aug); Jan–Easter; Dec 25
Must book D (Sat & Sun)

Meals 12.30–2 (Sat & Sun), 7.30–9

Tdh £4 (meal £6·45)
Alc buffet L £1·75 (meal £3)

Children's helpings
Seats 40
⟨&⟩ rest (1 step)
Car park
No dogs

DIRLETON East Lothian (Lothian)   Map 9

Open Arms
off A198
2½ m SW of North Berwick
Dirleton 241

'Civilised surroundings, many interesting dishes at each stage of the menu, but I do wish they would ginger up the waitresses', is a fair resumé of people's views on Arthur Neil's traditional little hotel. 'Dismal' pork with cream cheese and whisky, reported in October, but warm praise for mussel and onion stew, mutton broth, smoked trout (usually), 'excellent venison', cranachan (creamy oatmeal with brambles and whisky) on the varied set menus. Children's menu at lunch-time. Some eighty wines on a list we have not seen this time. No music.

Must book weekends
Meals 12.30–2.30, 7–10

Tdh L £3 (meal £5),
D £7·25 (meal £9·70)

VAT inc
Service 10%
Children's helpings
Seats 65 (parties 30)
⟨&⟩ rest

No dogs in d/r
Am Ex, Barclay, Diners
7 rooms (all with bath)
B&B £7
Fire cert

Gunga-Din
99c–101 Perth Road
Dundee 65672

Jacob Chacko has renovated his popular Indian restaurant – perhaps there is even a punkah by now. The menu is still divided into 'Colonial' and 'Traditional British' (prawn cocktail, steak and trifle, of course – how could you ask?). The Indian dishes range wide: tamarind soup, stuffed nan, iddly with sambar, parsindah (strips of meat cooked with couscous and yoghourt, £1·65), South Indian pork vindaloo, tandoori meals and vegetarian thalis ('six items, nicely balanced between moist and dry, spicy and mild', £1·85). Helpful service. Drink lager, or water à la Gunga, of course.

Closed Sun L; Dec 25 D;
Dec 26; Jan 1
Must book D
Meals 12–2.15, 6–11.30

Alc meal £3·40

VAT & service inc
Children's helpings
(under 10)

Seats 46
🚻 rest
No dogs
Diners card

Cringletie House

on A703
2½ m N of Peebles
Eddleston 233

Closed early Nov to
mid-Mar
Must book
Meals 1–1.45, 7.30–8.30

Tdh L £3·50 (meal £5·85),
D £6 (meal £8·60)

VAT inc
Children's helpings
Seats 65 (parties 26)
Car park
No dogs in public rooms
16 rooms (7 with bath,
1 with shower)
B&B £8·50–£11
Fire cert

The 'teeming garden' and well-worn baronial house in rolling country by the Eddleston water invite a stay. So too do the reception and the cooking, if you have caught Mr Maguire on the right foot and his wife in the right recipe. 'No criticism,' says one inspector after sole aurore, soup, roast beef and chocolate brandy pudding for a set meal, and others have contributed equally warm accounts of Mrs Maguire's wholewheat rolls, cheese aigrettes, ham mousse, and coffee nut rings, lemon crumble or cheesecake. Look out for her own preferred main courses: roast leg of lamb with courgette stuffing, oven-baked chicken Parmesan, and braised gammon. Good Brie or Stilton are often served. But main courses are sometimes a disappointment – 'deep-frying did nothing for a pork escalope' – and the inevitable gaps in the phased supply of garden vegetables and soft fruit are not always filled from other sources. The wines, as expected from the family connection with Uphall (q.v.), are admirably chosen and fairly priced. The inspector who drank it predicted correctly that Ch. Rauzan-Gassies '64 would not last long at £6·50, but Ch. St Christoly '70 is £5, and two '76 Beaujolais and Brouilly bins (Robert Sarrau) are just being opened at about £5. Spanish Lagunilla Gran Reserva '71 (a Rioja) is £4·75. Lutomer Riesling is still under £3. Afternoon teas are 'a bargain at 90p'. No music; and every encouragement not to smoke, since the dining-room is not too well ventilated.

App: John Dixon, N. V. Crookdake, W.F., A.F., Gerald H. France, J. E. F. Rawlins, and others

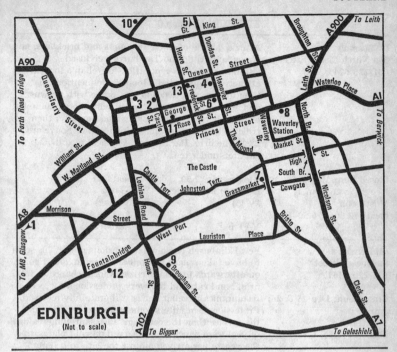

EDINBURGH Map 9

(1) Anatolian
13 Dalry Road
031-346 0204

Closed L; Sun
Must book
D only, 6.30–11.30

Alc £4·75 (meal £8·10)

Service 10% (parties)
Cover 20p
Seats 32
No dogs
Am Ex, Barclay, Diners

Restaurants are often the best ambassadors that some countries can afford to maintain in foreign parts, but avowedly propagandist ones are rare. There is nothing political about the unfortunately sited but tastefully laid out restaurant that Coskun and Engin Karadeniz, two Turkish architects, have opened, but handicrafts, music and slides in the bar convey something of Anatolia to guests even before they have reached the deep-fried börek pastries (80p), brains, or tripe soup ('a restorative for intemperance') on occasion, and aubergine, green peppers or courgettes fried with yoghourt and garlic. The kebab section is purist enough to eschew pork but it is worth considering two house specialities: sole in wine sauce (£3), and baked aubergine nests with lamb (£6 for two). 'Flavours are distinctive, unlike anything that I make in my own kitchen or can find in other ethnic places,' says a member who tried the 'mezeler' (mixed hors d'oeuvre for several people, from 65p an item). Better still, there is as yet no multiple Levantine baker in Edinburgh, so the baklava, sekerpare, tulumba and other sweets (including a sumptuous caramel-creamy rice pudding) taste as they should. So does the pitta bread. Turkish coffee is good, and not over-sweet. Efes Turkish red wine is £3·10, and there are a few others. No under-fives. More reports, please.

(2) Cosmo's
58a North Castle Street
031-226 6743

After a decade of *Guide* bouquets and brickbats, and a new layout, Cosmo Tamburro's civilised ristorante holds its reputation for reliable food, attractively presented. Honourable mention this time for lasagne, avocado in a puree with prawns and other seafood to start with; saltimbocca and most of the other veal dishes or seafood pancake; then trifle or testina di negro. Valpolicella or Soave are £3·10 the litre. Bar lunches. Classical records. No children under ten.

Closed Sun; May 7 & 28; Dec 25 & 26; Jan 1
Must book
Meals 12.30–2, 6.30–10

Alc (min L £2·50, D £3·50) £6·65 (meal £9·45)

VAT inc

Seats 60
 rest
No dogs
Access, Am Ex, Barclay, Euro

---

(3) Denzler's
80 Queen Street
031-226 5467

Closed Sun; Dec 25 & 26; Jan 1
Must book
Meals 12–1.55, 6.30–9.50

Alc L £3·55 (meal £5·70), D £5·40 (meal £7·75)

VAT inc
Service 10%
Children's helpings
Seats 120
 rest (1 step)
No dogs

Few Edinburgh ceremonial occasions in the '70s seem to have taken place without someone involved going on afterwards to Sämi Denzler's for a chance to talk, drink, and eat, and this very professional Swiss restaurant and cellar bar is still gratefully received. Professionalism falters sometimes – more often in the service than the cooking: 'Pheasant and escalope of veal were delicious but served on cold plates, and the vegetables arrived almost too late to be eaten with the meat. White wine arrived after our first courses. But all credit to the waiter who refused to serve smoked eel because it was not so good that night.' Air-dried cold meats from Bündnerland are always popular (£1·40), and croûte aux champignons on one of the regularly changed menus was impeccably cooked, an inspector reports. So was the crisply roast pork with apple sauce that followed, lavishly helped. Salade niçoise, steak mexicaine, and venison with noodles or pommes berrichonne are also praised. For sweet try Apfelstrudel perhaps, or banane à la Gruyère (60p – and no cheese involved). The strength of the Swiss franc puts the unfamiliar Swiss wines – such as l'Arbalète Dézaley white or Nüssbaumer Beerli red – into the same £5 range as red Chassagne-Montrachet '74 (Chauvot Labaume) or Ch. de Pez '70; but Rioja can be had for £2·80, and the list as a whole is substantial and well chosen. No music.

App: T.R.A., Geoffrey Carr, Mrs P. E. Moore, and others

---

(4) Henderson's Salad Table
94 Hanover Street
031-225 3400

It is sometimes surprising how little notice restaurants take of each other. For instance, if either Cranks in southern England or every Scottish hotel that serves a lunchtime buffet in the summer sent a deputation to Henderson's to see how

Closed Sun; Dec 25, 26 &
31; Jan 1
Open 8 a.m.–10.45 p.m.
Meals 11.30–2.45,
4.30–10.30

Alc £1·85 (meal £3·35)

VAT & service inc
Cover 10p D
Seats 200
Air-conditioning
Am Ex, Diners

vegetarian dishes and salads should be prepared and presented (not to mention priced), how happy we would all be. Service, table-clearing, control of disorderly customers, and so forth, is not impeccable here, though, and you must expect to queue, the value being what it is. 'For £1·25 in 1978 I had a large helping of broad bean and tomato hot-pot with crisp cheese topping, and a slice of a featherlight wholemeal sponge gateau, with plenty of whipped cream and dribbles of dark chocolate, and coffee.' Another man who ate here five times in three days during August did not feel he had exhausted the menu – and also discovered that the 'superb' vegetable curry (70p) was different every day. Other items to look out for (and it would be nice if they named and priced them in the display) include lasagne, nut roast (80p), courgette and mushroom soufflé ('oddly called flan'), cherry tart (30p) and the 'soured Jersey cream with fresh and dried fruit and stem ginger' (45p): 'Not many expensive restaurants would find such cream and such fruit for a pudding at twice the cost.' You may drink dandelion or ginseng tea – or fair coffee – if you like, but wines (from £1·50 for 50 cl of French ordinaire) are sensible, with Yugoslav Traminer or Cabernet £2·40, '76 St Véran or Beaujolais £3·70, and Ch. Puyblanquet '73, £4·20. Recorded or live guitar music. There is a separate wine bar with a shorter menu. 'Smoking is allowed in three-quarters of the restaurant' – even the London Underground reverses that proportion, but it is a start.

App: by too many members to list

---

(5) **Loon Fung**
2 Warriston Place
031-556 1781

Closed L; Dec 25;
Chinese New Year
Must book
Meals 2 p.m.–1.30 a.m.

Alc meal £3·80

VAT inc
Seats 45 (parties 55)
No dogs
Unlicensed

Mr Tam (o' the Shanta dynasty?) is a good name for a Cantonese chef in these parts, and, as a local doctor points out, 'since it is one of the few places anywhere where two adults and three healthy children can eat well for under £2 a head, it is unwise to go along on spec unless you are prepared to queue in Warriston Place's Siberian east wind.' You get what you pay for, perhaps, and 'there is little identifiable protein in many of the meat dishes.' But among much else, people like the dim-sum (the sweet items such as lotus paste buns are useful as puddings), fishball and watercress soup, spicy spare ribs, baked crab and black bean sauce, lemon chicken, ginger beef, Cantonese steamed duck with Chinese mushrooms, scallops Loon Fung; and the pretty Chinese waitresses. The place is mercifully unlicensed, and the Garrads' (late of Wester Howgate) wine shop is not too far away.

App: Yvonne Williams, D. G. Bradley,
D. H. J. Goodall, Ian Ragg, Kenneth F. Macrae,
and others

(6) Madogs
38a George Street
031-225 3408

In his crowded basement Howie Wright stuns some people with 'loud and raucous' music, offends others with his 'Poor Boy' sandwich (Kosher salami with Genoan smoked ham) and might repel still others with formula food and an unchanging menu. But many remain well pleased by lunchtime offerings of lightly poached eggs Benedict, crisp salads and well-filled sandwiches (around £1·20, with trimmings). At night, crab claws, tenderloin of beef and a gooey chocolate cake impressed one critic. Cheapest wine is Mateus Rosé, £2·80. Various American beers. Iced water and hot bread arrive when you do.

Closed Sun; Dec 25; Jan 1	Alc L £1·60 (meal	VAT inc
Must book	£2·20), D £5·70 (meal	Seats 90 (parties 15)
Meals 12–3, 6–11.30	£8·25)	Air-conditioning
		Barclaycard

(7) Ristorante Milano
7 Victoria Street
031-226 5260

Guiseppe Ferrari's bright but unobtrusive ristorante near the Castle does not always live up to his aim of 'high standards in all departments', for critics find the cooking here 'ordinary'. But there remain admirers for mussels in tomato and garlic, fresh tomato soup, saltimbocca, pollo bolognese, halibut and game dishes. Good trolley sweets too. Barbera and Frascati are still £2·60 for 75 cl, 50p the glass. No music. No dogs.

Closed Sun; Dec 25; Jan 1	Alc £6·05 (meal £8·75)	Cover 30p
Must book D		Seats 65
Meals 12–2.30, 6.30–10.45	VAT inc	Am Ex, Barclay, Diners

**(8) North British Hotel
Cleikum Restaurant**
Princes Street
031-556 2414

'An uninviting basement entrance' leads to 'substantial furniture, plenty of room, and horse-boxes for privacy'. If you survive the hoots-mon dish names (BTH with its sporran in its cheek), try the simpler dishes, which surpass such flights of fancy as chicken Cleikum Club (with saffron rice, cider sauce and vegetables, £2·90). Potted hough (80p), broth, kipper pâté, mince and tatties (£1·95), haggis, and the occasional omelette and steak win praise. Other steaks at other times, the vegetables, the cheese and the coffee have been less satisfactory. Service is friendly, even mostly efficient. The wines (from £2·95) are a mere sampler from the fine BTH list (available on request). Bar lunches. No music.

Closed Dec 25 & 26	VAT & service inc	Access, Am Ex, Barclay,
Must book weekends	Seats 180 (parties 400)	Diners, Euro
Meals 12–2.30, 6–10.30	♿ rest (lift)	195 rooms (168 with
	Air-conditioning	bath, 13 with shower)
Alc (min £2·25) £4·35	Car park	B&B from £15·30
(meal £6·15)	No dogs in public rooms	

(9) Shamiana
14 Brougham Street
031-229 5578

Closed L; Sun
D only, 6–12

Alc meal £6·35

Service 10%
Seats 42
No dogs
Access, Am Ex, Barclay,
Diners

'They'd never get away with the prices – or, for that matter, some of the cooking – in Westbourne Grove,' says a Londoner who knows her dopiazas, and Edinburgh folk do well to be as critical of Mr Jogee's coolly decorated, well-set pair of rooms, for at a test meal, lamb korma (said to contain saffron, £1·85) tasted of little, and aubergine masala of stale oil. However, enough else on this and other inspectors' visits justifies a tentative entry: try the chicken tikka (£1·80), and 'puffy fresh nan, like a deflating ball from Murrayfield' (there are two chefs, one for the tandoor, one for the curry); then lamb pasanda (£1·80), or Jaipur chicken with fresh bhindi (£1·25), or 'crunchy and addictive' spiced chick peas. Basmati rice is well-cooked. Dhal and raita 'seem rather soupy'. Some like the Indian sweets, some do not; but at least there are sometimes fresh mangoes, and the coffee is drinkable. Among the wines (from £2·95) try Gewürztraminer (£4·50) with the mild curries, but halves of a sweet white for the end of a meal might be a better idea for Mr Jogee to consider. Indian music. More reports, please.

---

(10) Snobs
1 Dean Bank Lane,
Stockbridge
031-332 0003

Mr Bevilacqua and Mr Bottiani have set up their small, vigorously coloured restaurant out of the way of passing trade, unless you happen to be buying antiques in St Stephen Street, and they have confided little information to the Guide for that matter. But an inspector confirms assertions during 1978 that their food is 'well cooked, fresh and hot', with good pollo alla crema or agrodolce (£2·25) and scampi in lemon and wine sauce, preceded by minestrone or lasagne, or perhaps courgettes parmigiana (£1·20). The chocolate gateau and the coffee also surpassed normal trattoria standards. Torrenova red or Colle Albani white wines are £3·10 for 75 cl. Recorded music. More reports, please.

Closed Sun L; Dec 25,
26 & 31; Jan 1
Must book D
Meals 12.30–2.30, 6.30–11

Alc (min £2·50)
£4·65 (meal £7·25)

VAT inc

Seats 26
♿ rest
No dogs
Access, Am Ex

---

(11) Town & Country
72 Rose Street
North Lane (between
Frederick St & Castle St)
031-225 3106

Closed Sun (exc Festival);
Sat L (exc bar); Jan 1
Must book
Meals 12–2.30, 7–11
(bar 12–3, 6–11)

It must have been galling to take a pensioners' free train trip 200 miles to Edinburgh only to find Ann Smith's restaurant serving a bar lunch because it was Saturday. But it shows what people will do for a good meal, and on the whole, the snug little place provides this, both in bar and dining-room. Indeed, another senior citizen finds helpings too large. The menu is Scottish, 'most of the customers seem to know each other', and Robert Muir cooks. Scots like their soup salty, remember, but kipper pâté and not-too-Scottish beef curry have been praised at a set meal. A la carte, this year there are better accounts of potage savoyarde, whole avocado with

Tdh L £2·80 (meal £4·50),
D (bar) £3·75 (meal £5·60)
Alc £7·65 (meal £8·45)

VAT inc
Cover 25p alc
Children's helpings
Seats 30
🔄 rest (2 steps); w.c.
No dogs in d/r
Access, Am Ex, Barclay,
Diners, Euro

good vinaigrette, marinated smoked haddock, egg mousse, 'very gamey venison casserole', and excellent veal in wine and cream sauce, with fennel and parsnips for vegetables. Sweets, cheeses, and coffee may tail off somewhat, but competent mousses of apricot, or chocolate and orange are reported. Wines begin with litres of Carafino at £2·70 or André Simon claret at £4·30, and they keep interesting bottled beers as well as, for instance, Santenay les Gravières '71 (bottled by Bouchard Père et Fils) at £5·85, and Eltviller Taubenberg Spätlese '71 at £4·85. No music.

App: D. N. Whyte, Alasdair Adam, J. H. Duffus, G. S. Carr, E.L.F., C. P. Lowell, I.N., and others

EDINBURGH Map 9

(12) **Vito Restaurant**
109 Fountainbridge
031-229 2747

Closed L; Sun; Dec 25 & 26; Jan 1
Must book
D only, 6–11.30

Alc £5·80 (meal £8·20)

VAT inc
Seats 45
No dogs
Access, Am Ex, Barclay

'The entrance stairs are off-putting, but inside the atmosphere is relaxed, with Italian families, an elderly man dining his secretary very closely, and a choice group from the Usher Hall to raise the cultural tone.' Festival time, obviously, and the very next night another visitor had to wait till the ice-cream and coffee stage to obtain food as sprightly as the first man's Parma ham and melon, scaloppine Montiff, 'tender and generous' veal al limone (£2·40), and hot, well-cooked vegetables. Lorenzo Crolla's lasagne (£1·30), saltimbocca fantasia (£2·80) and speciality pollo Kiev or scampi Lorenzo are also worth ordering, and indeed the cassata or affocata di Amaretto sweets are 'delicious'. Valpolicella or Frascati are £2·80, house Chianti £3·30. No music. (See also the Crolla family's other place, below.)

App: P. J. Witchell, I.O., Thomas Ward

(13) **Vito Spaghetti House and Restaurant**
55a Frederick Street
031-225 5052

Closed Sun; Dec 25, 26 & 31; Jan 1
Must book D
Meals 12–2, 6–11.30

Alc £6·15 (meal £8·75)

VAT inc
Seats 65
No dogs
Am Ex, Barclay

The year's reports suggest that Vito Crolla's Mediterranean sunspot in the grey New Town, with Frank Fusco in the kitchen, outshines most places of the kind elsewhere. 'From the first warm welcome onwards everything was so good that we went back for lunch the next day. Lasagne and grilled crawfish were alike delectable.' Other visitors recall a 'genuine-tasting' zuppa pavese, pollo all'italiana with a surprising sweet-sour sauce and orange slices, and equally surprising (because chilli-hot) braciola bruciadito, deep-fried rolls of veal, ham and hard-boiled egg, served with 'decadent' fried onions. 'Very garlicky and buttery fagiolini' are also noted, and house specialities include scampi Bréval, scaloppine deliziose, and spaghetti carbonara. Profiteroles are good, and one critical visitor put testina di negro – 'a light and boozy sponge with a good chocolate sauce and cream' – high up on her list of restaurant sweets. The coffee is liked.

Some have found the service rather hasty. Italian ordinaires are £2·90, house Chianti £3·40. You drink out of the pottery goblets – pity. Recorded music.

App: J. R. Harries, John Dixon, E.L.F., H.W., E.K., and others

---

EDINBURGH see also pub section

ERISKA Argyll (Strathclyde) Map 9

Isle of Eriska Hotel
12 m N of Oban
Ledaig 205

Closed Nov–Mar
Must book D
Meals 1–1.30, 7.30–8.30

Tdh L £4 (meal £5·90),
D £9 (meal £11·30)

Service inc
Seats 50
Car park
No dogs in public rooms
Am Ex card
28 rooms (all with bath)
Full board £160–£190
Fire cert

You get a high class of worshipper at the Buchanan-Smiths' peaceful and comfortable house, reached by a Bailey bridge from the mainland, and the collection is a silver one, as befits a noble padre whose wife remains 'the Hon' even behind her kitchen apron. But loyal, friendly, and efficient service suggest that there is more to the owners than a £9 dinner price (for five courses, albeit with little choice till the sweets stage). One American thought his stay 'no step down in any respect from the Connaught in London' which he had just left, with 'a cuckoo on the island to match the nightingale that no longer sings in Berkeley Square'. The best dishes, the kitchen thinks, are haddock Montrose, Loch Linnhe langoustines, and pibroch of chicken; others would add Sally Collier's 'desserts and baked goods'. But 'fruit cocktail looked and tasted as though it had been made up well in advance.' Clarets are reverentially treated with Ch. Cos d'Estournel '64, c.b., £10·75, and ordinary Bordeaux £3·35. No music. No children, except as residents prepared to eat high tea. Wear a suit.

App: Charles S. Drew Jr, I. Samuels, R.G.H., and others

FALKIRK Stirlingshire (Central) Map 9

Hatherley Hotel
Arnothill Lane
Falkirk 25328

'Plain food, attractively served, but the service was frosty.' Well, the accommodation and the plumbing at this listed building have been improved, the Gausters tell us, so perhaps the waitresses squeeze a few smiles now. The smorgasbord – about 30 from 55p–£1·20 – are still popular, with a soup (the only hot dish on the menu) to start with and an excellent Austrian cheesecake afterwards. The seafood salad (£3·95) is good, too. Wines from T. H. Robertson; Italian half-litre carafes £1·70, 45p the glass.

Closed Sun; Wed L;
part of July; Dec 25 &
26; Jan 1
Must book D
Meals 12–1.45, 7–9.30

Alc £3·75 (meal £5·50)

VAT inc
Seats 32 (parties 15)

♻ rest (3 steps)
Car park
No dogs in public rooms
5 rooms (3 with shower)
B&B £8

Redgauntlet
36 Market Street
Galashiels 2098

Closed L; Tue; Dec 25 &
26; Jan 1; public hol
Mons
Must book
D only, 6–10.15

Alc £5·20 (meal £7·35)

VAT inc
Seats 32
[&] rest

*Benito Cardinale and Carlo Campari (the chef) have
customers for their restaurant (not far from Scott's
Abbotsford) who seem to conspire to keep the* Guide *in
ignorance of its survival. Fortunately, itinerant
inspectors report as well as ever of its 'not especially
Italian' menu and cooking. Probably most people eat
steaks and peach Melba, and pasta is apt to be cooked
to toothless texture, but the cannelloni alla ricotta, and
the fresh tomato sauce for fettuccine, the rich brown
sauce for osso buco, a juicy escalope milanaise
(£2·50), 'excellent creamy spinach with a hint of
garlic', and well-made choux à la crème save these
indefatigable partners for another year. Barbera or
Frascati are £1·50 for 50 cl. Recorded music. No
pipes at table. Children's helpings. No dogs. More
reports, please.*

Tweeddale Arms
4 m SE of Haddington
Gifford 240

'A very pleasant little pub', slightly in need of
refurbishment, but a convenient country retreat for
Edinburgh Festival-goers. Service may be snooty
(in brass-buttoned blazer) or slow (at table) but it is
willing. Sensibly limited set meals might offer egg
in cocotte, pâté, or good smoked mackerel;
'pleasingly hot' lentil soup; 'superb' pork escalope
Holstein, trout with almonds or chicken paprika;
Atholl brose, chocolate bombe or 'uninteresting'
cheeses. 'A generous supply of self-service coffee.'
'I could have made better porridge myself.' Nicolas
house wine, £3·20 the litre. No music. Bar lunches
daily, with pressurised Belhaven ale.

Must book
Meals 12.30–2, 7.30–9.45

Tdh Sun L £3·50 (meal
£6), D from £5·95 (meal
£8·70)
Alc £3·60 (meal £6·10)

VAT inc
Service 10%
Children's helpings
(under 12)
Seats 85 (parties 200)

[&] rest (1 step)
No dogs in public rooms
Am Ex, Barclay, Diners
8 rooms (2 with bath,
2 with shower)
B&B £8·50–£13·50
Full board £85–£115

La Bavarde
9 New Kirk Road,
Bearsden
041-942 2202

Closed Sun; Mon; last
3 weeks July; Dec 24;
1st week Jan
Must book
Meals 12–1.30, 6.30–9.30

Space is at a premium in Armenio Trevisan's
Bearsden restaurant – but first things first: he goes
to market early, and his chef Peter Bannister knows
how to cook. There is the odd disappointment, but
regular and irregular visitors praise both the
'bustling' set lunches and more leisurely dinners. A
test lunch, indeed, proved satisfactory value,
especially if you began with salade Orloff (shredded
cabbage with ham in mayonnaise) and then took
tripe Trevigana (an enterprising notion for a

Tdh L from £2 (meal
£4·10)
Alc £5·80 (meal £8·40)

VAT inc
Children's helpings
Seats 50
🔾 rest (2 steps)
No dogs
Access, Am Ex, Diners,
Euro

Glasgow lunch-time). Dinner with coulibiac (90p), tongue salsa verde, and 'the tenderest venison I recall in a rich honey and whisky sauce under a lid of herby pastry' also proved satisfying. Puddings are comparatively simple, but a plum tart at lunch confirmed praise of the pastry-maker, and plums maltaise or date and almond cream are other suggestions. Roast hare with chocolate and nut sauce is a speciality (£3·20). Wines, from £3, are mediocre. No music.

App: L. Ratcliffe, J. & K.L., G.F., and others

Beacons Hotel
La Bonne Auberge
7a Park Terrace
041-332 9438

Neither the prices nor the *mise en scène* are those of the Malmaison (*q.v.*) but the cooking and waiting are French enough in a more casual genre, with regional set meals sometimes. When tried, onion soup was robust, and fish soup, though fairly reticent as to fish, fortified by good rouille; suprême de volaille, too copiously sauced, tasted of apples and cider; gibelotte de lapin (£3·10) was an honest casserole; and Waldorf salad was fresh. Venison and steak au poivre are specialities. The gratin dauphinoise potatoes ('more milky than creamy, and not hot enough') and the sweets could be bettered, but try their mousse au chocolat or poire au vin rouge, they say. Coffee (35p) includes petits fours. Reynier ordinaires are £2·60. French music, live or not.

Closed Sun; Sat L;
L Apr 16; May 28;
Aug 27; Jan 1
Must book
Meals 12.30–2.15, 7–10.45

Tdh L £4·50 (meal £7·45)
Alc £5·65 (meal £8·85)

Service 12½%

Seats 80 (parties 80)
No dogs
Access, Am Ex, Barclay,
Diners

Central Hotel
Malmaison Restaurant

▮

Gordon Street
041-221 9680

Closed Sun; Sat L;
Apr 16; Dec 25 & 26;
Jan 1
Must book
Meals 12.30–2.30, 7–10.15

Tdh L £6·50 (meal £8)
Alc £10·85 (meal £13·35)

VAT & service inc
Seats 70 (parties to 600)
No dogs in public rooms

It is a pleasure to welcome back to full-entry status this jewel in British Transport Hotels' rather gap-toothed crown, for fingers had to be crossed after Jean Labat left the kitchen here. Mr Moretti and his Scottish chef Stewart Cameron have pleased almost all the members who have reported (and please keep up the flow of information so that fair assessment can be made next year, too). The set lunch 'with good meat and particularly well-cooked broccoli' is short of choice for the price, but dinner has brought on occasion truffled fillets of sole in lobster sauce in a short pastry case which 'looked like a large pork pie and far transcended even normally good restaurant cooking.' Fish soup, hors d'oeuvre (often travestied in other BTH hotels), petite marmite and 'superior prawn cocktail' are worthwhile first courses, and for suprême de volaille Douro 'the sauce was excellent and the chicken done to a turn.' 'L'aile de caneton Auguste Escoffier was worthy of the name it bore.' Other diners' memories

385

Access, Am Ex, Barclay,
Diners, Euro
211 rooms (150 with
bath, 20 with shower)
Prices on application

include 'a neighbouring Canadian buying me a liqueur because he so enjoyed watching me eat the delicious French beans from a side dish with my fingers' and a sommelier who 'brought a fresh wine of his own recommendation when I said casually that I thought I had made a wrong choice'. (True, another member's claret arrived too warm and 'improved as it cooled'.) Profiteroles, rum babas and spun sugar confections 'finish off a quite wicked indulgence exquisitely'. The maître talks well and remembers names, and the pianist plays soothingly. BTH sell their wines to the public through the 'Malmaison Wine Club' now and the restaurant prices here are not out of proportion to the retail ones: after sensibly chosen ordinaires at £2·05 for 50 cl note the French or Spanish regional wines under £4 (Rioja Ardanza '70, £3·95), Montagny Les Coères '76 (£5·50), Ch. Laville-Haut-Brion '73, c.b. (£8), Fleurie and Chiroubles '76 (both Georges Duboeuf) at £5·50, and (though nearly exhausted) '61 clarets at inclusive prices that Londoners would hardly credit. Wear a jacket and tie.

App: Russell Thersby, Prof Ian Oswald, W.H., Mrs J. Stephenson, P. R. Jeffreys-Powell, and others

GLASGOW   Map 9

Charlie Parker's
21 Royal Exchange
Square
041-248 3040

Stylish hamburger joint, all black velvet and palm trees, 'a night-club atmosphere at 2 p.m.' Prices less clip-joint than this implies – ¼ lb burgers with good-quality trimmings, £1·65; filled pancakes around £1·80; pasta, steak, fish, chicken too. Daily dish at lunch-time around £1·40. House wine is Velletri, £1·60 the half-litre, 45p the 5 oz glass. Mechanised cocktail-shaker in the bar. Nippy service by Charlie's Angels. Recorded music ('hard to hear above the clatter').

Closed Sun; Dec 25 & 26;
Jan 1
No bookings
Meals 12–2.30, 6.30–11.30

Alc L £3 (meal £4·85),
D £4·20 (meal £7·20)

Seats 55

  rest (3 steps)
No dogs
Access, Am Ex, Barclay,
Diners

Ubiquitous Chip
12 Ashton Lane
041-334 5007

Closed Sun; Dec 31 D;
Jan 1
Must book
Meals 12–2.30, 5.30–11

Alc L £4·55 (meal £6·85),
D £6·10 (meal £8·70)

The covered, umbrella'd, heated courtyard that leads to Clydesdale and Brydon's long, Scandinavian-style dining-room is not what Glasgow expects, least of all in the Byres Road district. Sometimes the (mainly Scottish) cooking has not lived up to members' expectations either, but the revolution in Scottish licensing laws distracted Mr Clydesdale's attention to the bar side in 1978, and a test meal in the autumn, though not faultless, left the impression of a soundly based and sincere place whose problems should not be beyond solution. One frequent visitor reports much better meals (naturally

Children's helpings (under 12)
Seats 130 (parties 50)
♻ rest
No dogs

with less choice) for parties in the upstairs room. Downstairs, lemon sole on the bone and other dishes that had to be cooked to order proved much better than lamb and venison. Soups at the beginning and Caledonian ice-cream at the end are also good, and lunches at least sound interesting, for pike in orange mayonnaise, excellent smoked salmon, halibut au poivre, and goulash with caraway dumplings occasionally appear then. Meringue with walnuts (65p) proved an agreeable sweet at an inspector's meal. The bitter is Belhaven 70/- on hand pump, and Hérault red or Yugoslav white are only £2·75 a litre, even if as late-comers to the market they have to price their many good clarets firmly. But there is other good drinking under £4. No music. 'A small no-smoking area.'

App: Mrs J. M. Tracy, John Duffus, J. & K.L., and others

GLEN CLOVA Angus (Tayside) Map 9

Rottal Lodge
off B955
6 m N of Dykehead
Clova 224

The Earl of Airlie's comfortable 19th-century shooting lodge in the midst of fine grouse moors appeals to neighbours and globe-trotting sportsmen alike. Fauna *du pays* adorn the view and the plate, along with other local produce. From the short set menu people praise cheese and pear salad, Stilton pâté, roast grouse, filet de boeuf en croûte, cider-baked gammon, noisettes of lamb, with mostly fresh vegetables, a healthy Stilton and 'imaginative' sweets. No house wines, but others are reasonably priced (Ch. Pontet-Canet '70, £5·45). Inexpert service. No music. Wear a tie.

Closed Apr 13, 15 & 16; Dec 24, 25, 26 & 31; Jan 1
Must book
Meals 1–1.45, 7.30–8.30

Tdh L £4 (meal £5·90), D £6·50 (meal £8·85)

Children's helpings (under 10)
Seats 26
♻ rest

Car park
No dogs in d/r
12 rooms (all with bath)
B&B £10–£14
Full board £18·50–£22 p.d.
Fire cert

GULLANE East Lothian (Lothian) Map 9

La Potinière

Gullane 843214

Closed D (exc Sat); L Wed & Sat; Oct; Dec 25 & 26; Jan 1
Must book

Hilary Brown can cook. David Brown understands wine. That is at once the most and the least that can be said about this unassuming cottage restaurant whose busy lunchtime scene 'could be taken to France without changing anything except the customers'. It is not the 'best' restaurant in the book, whatever that may mean, but it may be the one most completely faithful to the principles which its owners and the *Guide* share. The price is part of that, and southerners or foreigners can sometimes be seen doing slow double-takes as they examine their

387

Meals 12.45 for 1, 7.30
for 8 (Sat)

Tdh L £3 (meal £4·45),
Sat D £5 (meal £6·60)

Service inc
Seats 34 (parties by
arrangement)
&. rest
Car park (3)
No dogs

bills. But it is not the main part. At twice the cost,
the 'delicate and fresh-tasting' soups – St Germain,
for example – the pale-green, creamy-centred
courgette soufflés, and the juicily browned farmyard
chicken with a sauce based on pan-juices,
mushrooms and Pernod, would all be noticed, even –
or especially – by the most jaded food critic. Poulet
au vinaigre is another fine chicken dish. Menus are
set, with minimal choice, ending with well-kept Brie,
Mr Moffat the local baker's crusty loaves, and a
sweet, 'unctuous' chocolate velours perhaps, or
peaches poached in white wine with strawberry
cream. As Mr Brown says, it is a satisfying
occupation to create a complete product from the
raw materials each day, and see it through to
consumption. The wines are kept longer, and
'Volnay Caillerets '71 at £5·25, discreetly decanted,
rounded off my study of Scotland's bargain
burgundies,' writes one 1978 visitor. Clarets are
fairly priced too, with Ch. Mouton-Rothschild '67
under £10 and Ch. Malartic-Lagravière under £5, and
you could start with Muscat les Amandiers '75
(Dopff & Irion) at £4·20 (£2·20 the half). For
economical or Lenten moods, Carafino is £2·25 for
75 cl. No music. No smoking until the coffee stage.

App: Dr G. H. France, E:M.D., Henry Fawcett

HARRIS Western Isles   Map 9

Scarista House
Scarista
on A859
15 m SW of Tarbert
Scarista 238

A Georgian manse with 'views of white beaches'
sympathetically converted by a young couple. Mrs
Johnson uses local and home-grown produce for her
set dinners; choice is limited, but give your
preferences when you book. Moules, mouclade, roast
venison, moussaka, lobster thermidor and a variety
of fruity puddings have admirers. The home-made
bread and oatcakes go down well, too. Unlicensed
(for Presbyterian reasons, apparently). No corkage
charge. No music. No children under 12.

Closed L; Dec 24, 25,
26 & 31; Jan 1
Must book
D only, by arrangement

Tdh £6·50

VAT & service inc
Seats 12
&. rest
Car park (6)
No dogs in public rooms

Unlicensed
4 rooms (2 with bath)
B&B £8–£11
Full board £15·50–£18·50
p.d.

INVERNESS Inverness-shire (Highland)   Map 9

Dunain Park

on A82
2½ m SW of Inverness
Inverness 30512

'Everything for the comfort of life may be had in
the Highlands at least nine months in the year,'
wrote Colonel Thomas Thornton 200 years ago, but
the Bulgers, in quoting him, add 'Does anyone
realise the complications involved in getting any
sort of food on the table up here?' They do pretty

Closed Nov–Mar
Must book
Meals 12.30–1.30 (res),
7.30–9

Tdh D £8 (meal £9·35)

VAT & service inc
Seats 20 (parties 6)
🔂 rest
Car park
No dogs in d/r
6 rooms (4 with bath)
B&B from £11·30
Fire cert

well at that though, with their own sheep, pigs and
vegetables where practicable, and most people think
that last year's tureen for this old house in six acres
by Loch Ness was well earned. True, two or three
visitors in early spring found the food consistently
over-seasoned or under-inspired, with 'amateurish'
service in bar and dining-room. But the tone of
reports picked up markedly as the year progressed,
and both new visitors and returners speak warmly
of the Bulgers' unforced hospitality and their
imaginative four-course dinners. Mrs Bulger thinks
her best version may be avocado and melon salad,
lentil soup, roast veal with orange sauce, and burnt
almond cream; but others have been equally happy
with, say, salmon mousse, apple and cabbage soup
('a masterpiece'), venison ('the sauce marginally
over-thickened'), and 'light yet rich' chestnut and
chocolate cream. The bread rolls – and 'Stornoway
black pudding for breakfast' – are mentioned too.
Wines, from £2·90 for a litre of Carafino, are adequate
if a bit unbalanced: Ch. Lalène '67, c.b., £5·50.
Lunches are for residents only, and light, but
'packed lunches (£2·50 in 1978) were worth every
penny.' 'Preferably no children and no tatty clothes
at dinner'; 'no pipes or cigars at table, and no
cigarettes either until everyone else has left
the room.'

*App: A. Tomlinson, H. D. O'Reilly, Phebe Cambata,
Mrs P. J. Marshall, Bel & Kevin Horlock, and others*

ISLE ORNSAY Skye, Inverness-shire (Highland)
Map 9

Kinloch Lodge Hotel
off A851
6 m S of Broadford
Isle Ornsay 214

Closed L (exc bar);
Nov–Feb
Must book
Meals 12–2.30 (bar),
8–8.15

Tdh £5·50 (meal £8·10)

Children's helpings
(under 10)
Seats 30
🔂 rest; w.c.
Car park
No dogs in public rooms
12 rooms (6 with bath)
B&B £8·30–£9·80
Fire cert

'The most varied collection of individuals I have
ever encountered in a hotel (the guests, I mean)' is
one description of the house parties at Lord and
Lady Macdonald's white shooting-lodge on the Sleat
peninsula, a good striding-off point for the least
accessible parts of the Black Cuillin. The Macdonalds
are individual too, in the style of today's Scottish
aristocracy, using a training in accountancy and a
flair for cooking to fight off capital transfer tax.
The lodge looks as shabby as the laird's
hacking-jacket, and reception is casual, but people
accept it happily and 'ceaseless rain somehow
added to the beauty of the surroundings.' The food
is erratically excellent. One guest who has nothing
to learn about the problems and opportunities of
small hotel kitchens reports a crab soup 'full of meat,
and delicious', 'a rather sad onion flan with very dry
pastry', 'tender and tasty lamb chops in port sauce',
well-stuffed but again rather dry chicken, a light and
well-flavoured apricot mousse, and 'unmemorable'
chocolate brandy cake. 'Breakfasts were more
imaginative than dinner, especially the

help-yourself bowls of fruit salads and home-made
muesli.' Others mostly echo this: 'On the one hand
superb salmon in butter sauce with browned
mousseline potatoes and chicory; on the other a
"délice" de sole that was anything but.' The cooks
(Lady Macdonald is assisted by Mrs MacLure and
Mr Macpherson) also like making smoked salmon
cream tart, braised beef provençale, Polish almond
cake with plum and port compote, and chocolate
vacherin. A fine Stilton is usually kept. The service,
whether from Coruisk or Qantas, does its best, and
though the Justerini & Brooks wine list is short it is
fairly priced if you can get it well served: Ch.
Meyney '67 at £6·70 only 80p up on last year;
French-bottled Echézeaux '70, £7·40; dry Frascati
£2·70. There are bar lunches. Smoking and young
children are both discouraged. No music.

App: B. M. Newman, Peter John Dyer,
B. Webb Ware, N. V. Crookdake, and others

KILMARTIN Argyll (Strathclyde)   Map 9

The Cairn
on A816
8 m NW of
Lochgilphead
Kilmartin 254

There is nothing amateur or crafty about this
converted granary above a craft shop. It is a
comfortable place, the dinner-jacketed owner knows
his wines, service is friendly, and good use is made
of local produce. The menu may yield smoked
mackerel or salmon, soused herring, Cairn pâté, fresh
scallops, entrecôte garnie (£2), braised venison in red
wine, or various cold roast joints and salad (from
£1·60). Baked potato and salad are included in the
main-course price. Sweets are less reliable. French
house wine £2·95 the litre. Recorded music. Snacks
(soup, filled rolls, steak) and pressurised beers from
10.30–5.30. No children under ten at dinner.

Closed Sun D; 1st 2 weeks Nov; Dec 24 D; Dec 25; Jan 1; Feb Must book D Meals 12.30–2.30, 7.30–9.30	Alc L £3·05 (meal £5·15), D (min £4·50) £4·25 (meal £6·45) VAT inc	Children's helpings L (under 10) Seats 60 Car park No dogs Am Ex, Barclay

---

'Must book' is the restaurant's information, not ours. The context of the
entry usually indicates how much or how little it matters, but a preliminary
telephone call averts frustrated journeys. Always telephone if a booking has
to be cancelled: a small place may suffer severely if this is not done, and
customers are also the losers in the end.

We rewrite every entry each year, and depend on fresh, detailed reports
to confirm the old, as well as to include the new. The further from
London you are, the more important this is.

Scottish public holidays do not all coincide with English ones.

KINGSKETTLE Fife   Map 9

Annfield House
between A92 & A916
6 m SW of Cupar
Ladybank 245 *and* 608

You may need the 'sublime' view from the bedroom window to distract you from the decoration within, and the culinary mishaps described by various hands over the year preclude the full entry that others still advocate. But if Mrs Kelly will taste everything before it leaves the kitchen and throw away bottled products that nobody sensible buys, people's praise of her whitebait, duckling with apricot sauce, lemon and walnut meringue and other sweets may be less qualified. Given the high price of à la carte items, more choice of main course on the set meal might be wise. Carafino is £2·50; Chianti Classico '74, £3·90. No music. No under-fives for dinner.

Closed Sun D; Mon (Nov–Mar); 1st 2 weeks Nov	Tdh L £2·50 (meal £4·35), D £4·50 (meal £6·55)	Seats 50 (parties 70) Car park
Must book weekends Meals 12.30–1.45 (Sun 1),	Alc £5·60 (meal £7·85)	No dogs in d/r Access card
HT 4.45–5.45 (Sun 4.30–6.30), 7.30–9	VAT inc Service 10% Children's helpings (under 10)	9 rooms (6 with bath, 1 with shower) B&B £8–£10 Fire cert

KIRKCUDBRIGHT Kirkcudbrightshire
(Dumfries & Galloway)   Map 7

Coffee Pot
5 Castle Street
Kirkcudbright 30569

This 'neat, spartan little cafe' has changed little in six years, but now it boasts a licence. Reasonable lunchtime prices still invite families here for home-made soups (French onion is always good), then omelettes, burgers, fish and chips or the daily hot dish. Ice-cream-based puddings. Dinners are dearer, with coq au vin, roast venison or chicken Kiev approved this time. Coffee fair. Italian ordinaire 80p for 25 cl, 40p the glass. 'Repetitive' tapes. No dogs.

Closed Sun; Oct–Apr Must book D Meals 12–1.45, 6.45–8.30	Alc L £1·70 (meal £3·25), D £3·40 (meal £5·25) VAT inc	Service 10% Children's helpings Seats 24 ♿ rest

Ingle Restaurant
St Mary's Street
Kirkcudbright 30606

The railway station here is now partially converted into a cheerful Italian restaurant with a serenading guitarist and dancing at weekends. The set dinner (no lunches) seems fair value – pea soup, veal with cream and mushrooms, well-cooked vegetables and chocolate meringue cake or trifle. Large *carte* too. Italian ordinaire is £3·60 the litre.

Closed L; Mon Must book D only, 7–11	Tdh £4·50 (meal £7·50) Alc £5·30 (meal £8·65) Service 10%	Seats 60 (parties 40) ♿ rest (1 step) No dogs Am Ex, Diners

391

Carraig Mhor
Lamlash 453

'Perhaps I am going soft after a typical Scottish fortnight of chicken, soggy chips and tinned peas,' says an East Anglian, 'but I really enjoyed the vegetable soup, haddock Mornay, roast duckling with orange sauce, and banana split that they gave me for dinner here.' Another visitor to Tom Langmuir's house in the middle of the village reports queues, even on Arran for his omelettes (65p–90p), vol-au-vents, and seafood pancakes at lunch-time (à la carte) or dinner (table d'hôte). Service is 'a trifle stern but efficient'. Spanish Viña Zaco '69 at £2·35 is probably the best-value wine. Recorded music. More reports, please.

Closed Sun; Mon (exc Dec 31); Jan 1	Tdh D £5·50 (meal £7·60)	Children's helpings
Must book D	Alc L about £2·30	(under 5)
Meals 12.15–1.45, 7–9		Seats 26
	VAT inc	🔾 rest (1 step)

Champany
on A904
3 m NE of Linlithgow
M9 exit 3
Philipstoun 532

A handsome, farmhouse pub with a smart restaurant attached, handy for Edinburgh Festival refugees and other subsidised patrons. Service is smooth and considerate, though overfond of the lamp ('my rare steak became medium before my eyes'). Praise for game soup (95p), porterhouse (£14·50 for two), double loin of pork, and brandy-snaps. Pâté may be disappointing, veal tasteless, or vegetables inappropriate. Various wines; house French, 50p the glass. No music. Parties well catered for in the gallery. Bar snacks (toasted sandwiches, etc) and pressurised beers in the Country Life bar. Wear a jacket and tie 'except in hot summers'.

Closed Sun; Dec 25 D; Jan 1, 2 & 3	Tdh L £4 (meal £6·40)	Seats 45 (parties 20)
Must book	Alc (min £5) £9·40	🔾 rest (2 steps)
Meals 12.30–2.15, 7–10	(meal £11·70)	Car park
		No dogs
	VAT & service inc alc Service 10% tdh	

'Meal' indicates the cost of a meal for one, including food, coffee, half the cheapest bottle of wine, cover, service, and VAT (see 'How to use the Guide', p. 4).

Bed and breakfast prices have been quoted to us by hoteliers; where possible, we have given minimum off-season and maximum in-season prices for one person sharing a double room.

Please report to us on atmosphere, decor and – if you stayed – standard of accommodation, as well as on food, drink and prices (send bill if possible).

LOCHGAIR Argyll (Strathclyde) Map 9

Lochgair Hotel
on A83
15 m SW of Inveraray
Lochgair 233

The welcome and the rooms at the MacLeans'
country house are warm, though the residents'
lounge may be 'rather drear' by contrast. Breakfasts
are excellent, with porridge and kippers, but the set
dinners have been 'patchy': very good haddock or
salmon kedgeree but ordinary soups; good-quality
roast beef and baked salmon, but dull shepherd's pie
and vegetables. The Gigha cheese with oatcakes
pleases everyone. Bar lunches with pressurised beers.
Wines from Justerini & Brooks; Italian house wine
85p for 25 cl. No music. 'Discretionary' children's
helpings.

Must book D	VAT inc	Am Ex, Diners
Meals 12.30–2, 7–8.30	Seats 100 (parties 50)	20 rooms (9 with bath)
	♿ rest (1 step)	B&B £9·90–£12
Tdh D £5 (meal £7·30)	Car park	D, B&B £13–£16
Alc bar L £1·80 (meal £3·35)	No dogs in public rooms	

LOCHMADDY North Uist, Inverness-shire (Highland)
Map 9

Lochmaddy Hotel
Lochmaddy 331

Choice on North Uist is limited, but George
Maclellan's local venison, lamb and shellfish await
consumers at modest prices in this hotel 100 yards
from the car ferry, and 'a memory of the leek broth
and the perfect sea trout outweighs the near-raw
apple fritters and plastic cheeses on the night I was
there.' Breakfasts and weekly lunchtime bar snacks
are substantial. Ordinaires are Hirondelle, and malt
whiskies almost outnumber the wines. Pressurised
beers. No music.

Closed Dec 25 & 26; Jan 1	VAT inc	Car park
Must book D	Service 10%	No dogs in d/r
Meals 12.30–1.45, 7–9	Children's helpings (under 12)	18 rooms (1 with bath)
		B&B from £8·50
Tdh L £2·50 (meal £4·10), D £5 (meal £6·85)	Seats 56 (parties 25)	Full board from £90
	♿ rest (1 step)	Fire cert

Towns shown in black on our maps contain at least one recommended
restaurant or pub (see map key). The dot denotes the location of the
town or village, not the restaurant. Where necessary, we give
directions to the restaurant in the entry. If you can, help us to
improve them.

If you think you are suffering from food-poisoning after eating in a restaurant,
report this immediately to the local Public Health Authority (and write to us).

See p. 120 for the restaurant-goer's legal rights, and p. 118
for information on hygiene in restaurants.

Maryculter House
South Deeside Road
on A943
7 m SW of Aberdeen
Aberdeen 732124

Peaceful Deeside house offering bar lunches (Maggie's green soup, £1; salmon salad, £1·50) in the Knight's Hall and a short *prix fixe* lunch in the restaurant (taramosalata, lamb casserole, wild apricot fool). The evening *carte* borders on the expensive and the exotic (eight different countries' cooking on one occasion); one party were charmed by their rabbit and lemon or tomato and crab soups, guacamole, roast quail with grapes ('wonderfully moist and tender'), and brown bread ice-cream. Shortish wine list from Smith of Perth; Anjou Rosé £2·40. The proprietress fears the service may be slow, but no-one has remarked on it. No music.

Closed Sun; Jan 1	Tdh L £3 (meal £5·55)	Children's helpings
Must book	Alc £6·80 (meal £10·05)	Seats 80 (parties 50)
Meals 12.30–2, 7–9.30		🔥 rest; w.c.
		Car park

Woodlea Hotel
on A702
1½ m W of Moniaive
Moniaive 209

Last year's reports of Robin McIver's do-it-himself hotel ('I am the cook and the crazy-paving layer and the mate of the "Nancy Bell" ') earned it a toehold in the book, for there is little competition in the district. This year's accounts are warmer, and several people not easily pleased report satisfactory soups, smoked trout, poached sole, duck with orange, and pigeon in rowan sauce, even if some dishes may be cooked during the winter and frozen, and vegetables are mediocre. Strawberry flan is perhaps the best sweet. Afternoon tea with fresh scones and cakes is much better value than the early morning version. Ordinaires began at around £2 in 1978, and there are other goodish wines. No music.

Closed Nov; Dec 25 D	Alc £5·80 (meal £7·85)	Car park
Must book D		No dogs in public rooms
Meals 12.30–2, 7.30–8.30	VAT inc	13 rooms
Tdh L (res) about £3	Children's helpings	B&B from about £6·50
(meal £4·45), D (res)	(under 10)	Fire cert
about £4·50 (meal £6·10)	Seats 40	

Clifton Hotel
🍵

Viewfield Street
Nairn 53119

'Gordon Macintyre may be an actor-manager by temperament, but the bit parts are well taken here, too,' writes one admirer of this hotel, which is firmly rooted in the culture of the locality. There are times when you may wish the owner had an eye or a moment to spare for a lick of paint here and there (though the attics are being done) or for a taste of

Closed L (exc bar);
mid-Nov to Mar 1
Must book D
Meals 12–1.30 (bar),
7–9.30

Tdh £6·80 (meal £9·40)

VAT inc
Children's helpings
Seats 60 (parties 25)
 rest (3 steps)
Car park
No dogs in d/r
19 rooms (11 with bath)
B&B £8·80–£12·10
Fire cert

the rather soft vegetables that may emerge from the kitchen. But the total effect is generous, especially the cold table that is an opening option at dinner ('it included salmon mousse and a vast array of other good things'). Mushroom and other soups, roast lamb, saddle of venison with 'excellent rowanberry jelly', blanquette of veal, and liver parisienne are also praised, and as you would expect here, the fish – crawfish, or salmon with beurre blanc – is normally excellent. Terrine de tête de porc aux pistaches, and gigot boulangère, are among favourite dishes of the kitchen. The choice of sweets and cheeses is more restricted, but breakfasts include home-made muesli and marmalade 'and if you are lucky a fried fish'. There are 110 bins in the cellar and even though prices are reasonable, with quite a few bottles under £5 in 1978, there is no pressure to buy. Aloxe-Corton '70 (Berry Bros) at £6·25 and Ch. Gloria '67, c.b., at £8 indicate what awaits people who can. There are no half-bottles. Bar lunches 'with excellent soups' or packed lunches ('one of them included strawberries and cream') are also served, and smoking is allowed only in the small restaurant. Dress 'reasonably smartly'. Sometimes there is classical music from Mrs Macintyre's piano.

App: Anthony Kerr, A. A. Tait, David Harcus, Dr & Mrs Paul Wraight, and others

---

OVERSCAIG Sutherland (Highland) Map 9

Overscaig Hotel
17 m NW of Lairg
on A838
Merkland 203

Closed Dec 24, 25 & 26
Must book D
Meals 12.30–2, 7.30–10.30

Tdh L £3 (meal £4·80),
D £6 (meal £7·35)
Alc bar L about £2·10

VAT inc
Service inc D
Children's helpings L
Seats 36 (parties 16)
 rest (1 step)
Car park
No dogs in public rooms
Am Ex card
15 rooms (5 with bath)
B&B £8–£10
Fire cert

Like the Highland wild-cats, Sheila Hamilton-Hesse prefers to retire before the advance of civilisation. Still, winter blizzards and a long food supply chain help to explain why this white outpost on the brown moor is the *Guide*'s northernmost point. Perhaps it was unfair in the past to 'hit her on her puds', as one of the catering magazines oddly put it last year. Anyway, everyone has liked the place this time once they have beaten its systems: in other words, don't lock your room and lose the key, or jovial Jimmy Hamilton-Hesse will have to break the door down because he hasn't got a key either; don't be late for dinner because 'the fennel au gratin that was a dream at 8 was a burnt offering at 9', but don't be too early either because the main course is not served till it's done. Service is another hazard – 'three Italian waiters arrived one evening and left at breakfast' (where for?). But never mind, for there are many single malts in the bar, and in the dining-room the chance of 'superb' crab soup, 'sea trout freshly caught by a guest', salmon whether in salad or vol-au-vent, monk-fish in brandy and cream, Kinlochbervie plaice on the bone, chicken envelopes with haggis stuffing ('a sauce would have helped it, though'), and first-rate pork, beef and mutton. Stags abound nearby, but venison is not always well cooked. The seafood platter (£3·50) and game pie (£3 including vegetables) are also suggested. Sweets are improved, to judge by the strawberry gateau and the cheesecake. The system for ordering packed lunches works admirably. Italian, French or Spanish ordinaire is £1·80 for 50 cl but the red or white Beaujolais at £4, house claret at £3·20, Ch. Lestage '61 at £8, and sweet white Ch. Doisy-Védrines '67 at £6 (spread it over two or three evenings) are tempting. Terrace lunches overlooking Loch Shin; high teas for residents' children. No music. Non-smokers may be separate but not equal.

App: D. R. Ellis, B. Webb Ware, Jenifer & Geoffrey Rowntree, R.B.J., and others

PEAT INN Fife Map 9

Peat Inn
on B940
6 m SE of Cupar
Peat Inn 206

The Wilsons' 18th-century inn, which gave its name to the village, offers bar lunches – soup (28p), omelette, quiches, salads, sandwiches. At night in the little dining-room people have enjoyed smokie and cream cheese pâté, stuffed mushrooms, guinea-fowl and salmon. Home-made ices or fresh fruit Pavlova are popular sweets – and half-bottles of dessert wines are listed alongside them on the menu. The wines are ungraspingly priced; several bottles under £3 on a sound list. No music. No pipes.

Closed L (exc bar); Mon;
Dec 25 & 26; Jan 1
Must book
Meals 12.30–1.45 (bar),
7.30–9.30

Alc bar L £2·05 (meal
£3·80), D £5·30 (meal £8)

VAT inc (bar L)
Service 10%

Children's helpings
(under 10)
Seats 46
♿ rest; w.c.
Car park
No dogs

PERTH Perthshire (Tayside) Map 9

Timothy's
♟
24 St John Street
Perth 26641

Closed Sun; Mon;
Dec 24 & 25; Jan 1
Must book
Meals 12–2.15, 7–10

Alc (min £3·25 after
9.30 p.m.) £4·15
(meal £6·45)

VAT inc

Domestic emergency robbed Major Norman of his cook in 1978 but his wife and Sandi Lamb have kept this long-popular, cheerfully jumbled, smørrebrød restaurant in members' favour, and little changes, not even the puns. Egg mayonnaise with anchovies, Andrea's hamful (£1·10) with a jacket potato (22p), beef and chicken salads, and about forty other variants including a well-stocked board of cheeses are honest of their kind, and on winter weekday evenings they do by request fondue bourguignonne with sauces and salads. There are a few suitable pastry or liqueur ice-cream sweets. Iced akvavit is 47p, Tuborg lager and Bass special beer are 44p a pint, and the wines are mostly excellent, from the house burgundy at £2·80 (ordinaires are £1·60 a pint) to Ch. Grand-Puy-

Service 10%
Cover 25p D
Children's helpings
Seats 56
♿ rest
No dogs

Lacoste '67 at £8. Stocks tend to vary with
purchases at Christies or elsewhere. Recorded
music. Go early in a session if you dislike tobacco
smoke (and note the minimum charge after
9.30 p.m.). No children under five.

*App: Betty Lawson Barnes, P. & J. I. Findlater,
Colin R. Murray, C. J. Richardson, and others*

PORT APPIN Argyll (Strathclyde)   Map 9

Airds Hotel
2 m off A828
Appin 236

*This old ferry inn overlooking Loch Linnhe is under
new ownership with a new chef, but 'the staff, style
(and regimental pace) remain unchanged.' Good soups,
pâtés, whitebait; roast pork, fresh salmon, haunch of
venison with apple and beef forcemeat and a wine
sauce; Highland bonnets (choux pastry with
strawberry jam), Drambuie flummery. Vegetables are
variable, and fish may gasp for breath in thick crumbs.
Breakfast kippers and packed lunches are popular. No
wine details; pressurised beers. Home-made rolls in the
bar. No smoking. No music, though Mr Allen is
taking bagpipe lessons to keep up with his predecessor.
More reports, please.*

Closed mid-Nov to
mid-Mar
Must book D
Meals 12.30–1.30, 7–8.30

Tdh L £2·50 (meal £4·10),
D £5·50 (meal £7·40)

VAT inc
Children's helpings
(under 10)
Seats 46
Car park

No dogs
14 rooms (5 with bath)
B&B £8·50–£10·50
D, B&B £93–£107 p.w.
Full board £108–£122
Fire cert

PORTPATRICK Wigtownshire
(Dumfries & Galloway)   Map 7

Knockinaam Lodge
off A77
2 m S of Portpatrick
Portpatrick 471

Closed mid-Nov to
mid-Mar
Must book
Meals 12.30–1.15, 7–9

Tdh D £5·75
Alc £6·10 (meal £9·05)

Children's helpings
Seats 35
♿ rest; w.c.
10 rooms (7 with bath,
1 with shower)
B&B £13–£14
Fire cert

Raymond Baudon is still in the kitchen at the Vere
Nicolls' tranquil hotel in a rocky cove, facing
south-west across Port of Spittal Bay, and long may
he remain, say people who have enjoyed his sensibly
composed set dinners with about three choices in
each course. His watercress soup may be slightly
grainy, or his oeufs en cocotte not always perfectly
timed, but tastes are true and ideas good, from
lobster soup with avocado to suprême de volaille à
la Mancha ('sizzling with butter and a saffron cream
sauce', £2·90 à la carte). One party, going the
whole Scot, ordered Galloway collop, filet mignon
Robbie Burns (with haggis and whisky sauce, £3·10)
and Caledonian cream (cottage cheese, marmalade
and brandy), yet lived to tell the tale. Pork
Devonshire ('kept juicy, with an apple to offset it'),
crisp pommes berrichonne, and sweet
Pernod-flavoured pancakes are also praised. So is
the 'quiet and helpful service'. The wines (from
£2·50) are not very interesting, though there is

adequate claret and burgundy at £6 or so. There are bar lunches, with scallops and lobster often 'in the basket', and pressurised Bass. No children at dinner after 8 p.m. There may be two dinner sittings at busy weekends. No music. No dogs.

App: J. A. C. Marples, O.J.P., J.K.L.

ST ANDREWS Fife   Map 9

Pepita's
11 Crails Lane
between South Street
and Market Street
St Andrews 4084

By day this cramped cottage serves students and tourists with salads, cakes, pastries and good coffee. At night it sports red check tablecloths, candles and 'a cosy informal air', but dinner prices are not low and reports are very mixed: good pâté, asparagus quiche, fresh Tay salmon, langoustines and 'Hebridean beef' (in a sauce of pine kernels, whisky and yoghourt); but poor spinach soup, 'dry and over-kept' paupiette de sole and 'stringy' veal Marengo. Fair list of sweets. French ordinaire is £2·70 for 73 cl. Live music on Tuesday evenings (classical guitar). Service 'patient even of guests who sing'. Children's menu.

Closed Sun; Mon D;
June 11–23; Dec 24–
Jan 9
Must book D
Open 10–5.30, 7–10

Alc L £2·05 (meal £2·90),
D £6·35 (meal £8·65)

Service inc

Children's helpings
(under 12)
Seats 60 (parties 20)
[&] rest
No dogs

SEIL Argyll (Strathclyde)   Map 9

Dunmor House
15 m SW of Oban
½ m E of Easdale Village
Balvicar 203

Closed L (exc bar);
Oct 16–Apr 30
Must book D
Meals 12.45–1.45 (bar),
8–9

Tdh £6 (meal £8·50)

Service inc
Seats 34
[&] rest (2 steps)
Car park
No dogs in d/r
12 rooms (4 with bath,
6 with shower)
B&B from £9
D, B&B from £14·50
Fire cert

Lt Commander Gibson and his Alsatians run 'a very well-ordered ship' at this hotel with attached farm, reached from the mainland by one of Telford's bridges, and endowed with a matchless view. 'It is quiet, except for sheep's evensong. Fortunately no dawn chorus of the same,' writes one guest; and another found the place improved after four years' absence, though 'I thought I was politically apathetic until I met the Commander' (a very audible host). Jackie Morris now does most of the cooking. 'I was impressed by a professionally cooked and gracefully served bar lunch of nettle soup, cheese and ham quiche, and crisp salad.' Out of his three days' stay another visitor picks out the egg mousse and cheeses as 'very good', poached sea trout, black mushroom soup, prawn mayonnaise and mussels as 'excellent', and cold chicken breasts in cream sauce with a hint of curry and wine as 'superior'. Roast duck Hymettus with good vegetables left on the table for second helpings, and sweetbreads in puff pastry, are also liked. Look out for the roasts, and venison and mushroom pie. 'Gorgeous' sweets approved include orange and chocolate mousse, brandy-snaps, and apricot and

brandy tart. Wines, from £2·70 for Valpolicella or
Soave, are few, but Mâcon-Lugny Les Genevrières
'76 (Louis Latour) was £4·60 in 1978, and Ch.
Léoville-Lascases '69, c.b., £5·80. No under-eights
at dinner. No music. Wear a tie in the evening.

*App: Peter John Dyer, T.P., Margot Graham,
M. N. Rodger, and others*

SELKIRK Selkirkshire (Borders) Map 8

Philipburn House Hotel

♥

on A707
¾ m W of Selkirk
Selkirk 20747 *and* 21690

Must book
Meals 12.30–1.30, 7.30–9

Tdh L £3·75 (meal £5),
D from £7 (meal £8·25)
Alc L £3·95 (meal £5·50)

VAT & service inc
Children's helpings
Seats 75 (parties 25)
⏃ rest; w.c.
Car park
No dogs
16 rooms (10 with bath)
B&B £8–£10
D, B&B £13–£15
Full board £15–£17 p.d.
Fire cert

Jim and Anne Hill have modified their policy at
this 18th-century house ('which a glut of stripped
pine in bar and dining-room does not entirely suit')
to allow residents demi-pension terms as well as full
board. This reduces the patter and clatter of
children and leaves more determined eaters to
concentrate on their two meals a day. Otherwise,
children's needs are paramount here (except for 'no
under-14s at dinner', and a prudent notice
discouraging ball-games), and an inspector reflected
that the view from the dining-room window of the
fairy-lit young round the heated swimming-pool,
willing a waitress to fall in while she tried to rescue
stray frogs, would have delighted the more epicene
Roman emperors. Set menus are sensibly balanced
and varied. The kitchen has something to learn
about cooking rice, and stufatino di manzo at a test
meal looked 'chewy and glutinous'. But terrine with
Cumberland sauce and brown toast, homely duck
soup, pork fillet with green peppers, orange and
rosemary, and 'sticky ginger cake with Emmenthal
cheese, green apple slices, and cream' made an
entertaining meal. Other visitors praise the lasagne,
poached salmon, duck bigarade, and chicken in
ginger, while Mr Hill is proud of his fish soup,
pigeon breasts in vermouth, and boned stuffed
poussin. Pressurised beers and Rondinella or
Trebbiano carafes pale beside an enthusiast's wine
list with good Loires and Riojas under £4, '76
Beaujolais under £5, and enviable claret and
burgundy in well-chosen years and price ranges: Ch.
Haut-Brion '62, £12; half-bottles of Clos Vougeot
'70 (Remoissenet) at £5; and (if not as a partner for
the sticky ginger cake) Ch. d'Yquem '58 at £7·20.
No smoking at table. Recorded music sometimes,
and dancing on Saturdays.

*App: W. Frankland, William Thomas, A.L.,
A. T. Sedgefield*

Wine prices shown are for a 'standard' bottle of the wine concerned, unless
another measure is stated.

1979 prices are as estimated by restaurateurs in the autumn of 1978.

Skeabost House Hotel
6 m NW of Portree
Skeabost Bridge 202

'Cook simpler things more carefully,' suggests a
rueful visitor who loved the setting but found little
to praise in three people's Sunday evening set meals.
'Quite extraordinary value,' writes another, whose
family of five dined here twice on 'chunky soups,
delicately varied fish dishes, perfectly cooked
vegetables and at least one delicious pudding each
time'. Others concur, so perhaps Mrs McNab puts
her feet up on Sunday nights. Wines are 'adequate';
no carafe on the Justerini & Brooks list. Service is
agreeable, but they may forget to tell you that
coffee is served in the lounge. Bar lunches. Wear a
tie in the restaurant. No music.

Closed Dec 24, 25, 26 &
31; Jan 1
Must book D
Meals 1–1.30, 7–8

Tdh L £2·50 (meal £4·40),
D £4·50 (meal £6·80)

Seats 70
♿ rest
Car park

No dogs in public rooms
21 rooms (10 with bath)
B&B £9·60
Full board £100 p.w.
Fire cert

Western Isles Hotel
Tobermory 2012

Imposing, turreted building which dominates the
harbour but proves 'infuriatingly inaccessible'.
'Old-fashioned' is the general opinion of the meals
(and the rooms), but basic materials, especially the
fish and shellfish, are impeccable, and few fault the
soups, the breakfast kippers, beef roasted or braised,
seafood cocktail (with crayfish and whole scallops),
and the light pastry and cakes. A pity that bread is
poor and vegetables tend to be watery. Wines from
Thomson of Perth; French ordinaire £2·35 for 50 cl.
Service by nippy youngsters. Lunch in the bar only
(from 80p); pressurised beers. No music.

Closed L (exc bar)
Must book D
Meals 12.30–2 (bar),
7–8.45

Tdh D £5·50 (meal £6·65)

VAT & service inc
Children's helpings
(under 10)
Seats 70
Car park
No dogs in public rooms

Access, Am Ex, Barclay,
Euro
43 rooms (11 with bath)
B&B £9–£12·50
D, B&B from £78 p.w.

Scottish public holidays do not all coincide with English ones.

Prices of meals underlined are those which we consider represent
unusual value for money. They are not necessarily the
cheapest places in the Guide.

Do not risk using an out-of-date Guide. A new edition
will be published early in 1980.

ULLAPOOL Ross & Cromarty (Highland) Map 9

The Ceilidh Place
West Argyle Street
Ullapool 2103

Two houses and a boat shed, joined together round a courtyard by the actor Robert Urquhart, make 'a fine place for casual summer eating'. The coffee shop buffet, open all day, can be 'disorganised' with 'plain eatable, rather than mouthwatering' food. Salads, though, are more varied than anyone expects in these parts, and lentil soup, quiche, haggis and chips and even the lurid ice-creams have pleased some. We need more reports of the set or à la carte dinners for residents and others, with fresh fish a feature. The back-garden theatre may be a distraction this year. House wine £3·10. Classical records.

Closed Dec 31; Jan 1
Open (buffet) 8 a.m.–11 p.m.; meals (buffet 12–2, 5–8.30; (rest) D only, 7–9.30

Tdh (rest) £4·90 (meal £7·50)

Alc (buffet) £3·15 (meal £6), (rest) £5·80 (meal £9·75)

VAT inc
Children's helpings (under 12)
Seats 40 (d/r), 100 (buffet)

 rest
Car park
No dogs in public rooms
Diners card
26 rooms (6 with bath)
B&B £6–£10·25
Full board from £9·45 p.d.
Fire cert

UPHALL West Lothian (Lothian) Map 9

Houstoun House
🍷

off A8/M8
1¼ m W of Broxburn
(turn N at only traffic lights on A8 between Edinburgh & Glasgow)
Broxburn 853831

Closed Dec 25, 26 & 27
Must book
Meals 12.30–2, 7.30–9

Tdh L £3·75 (meal £5·50), D £7 (meal £8·75)

VAT & service inc
Children's helpings
Seats 75 (parties 40)
Car park
No dogs in d/r
29 rooms (26 with bath, 3 with shower)
B&B £12–£13
Fire cert

It is ten years since Keith Knight moved from Comrie to this enlarged and enlarging 16th-century laird's house set back from the main road, and in 1979 there may again be a new departure, a restaurant in an old mill down the road, run in harness with Houstoun. How far planning of the new place excuses lapses here in 1978 is hard to tell. As before, the set meals, with minimal choice, are imaginative in content and quite modest in price: they would be good value but for curious lapses into 'cafe cooking' (gammon creole at a test lunch), and the technique which sometimes 'perfects dishes at 7.30 for service at 9'. But at the same test meal, mussel and onion stew, and bramble and apple tart, were unusually nice of their kind, and others report, amid much else, good nettle kail or kümmel soup, flan à l'écossaise (or chausson de crabe à l'oseille), truffle omelette for an (unannounced) vegetarian, coq au vin, roast widgeon with wild rice, gratin de framboises, spritzkuchen ('but they are better hot'), and Stilton. It is essential, though insufficient, to order your wine from one of Britain's best and best-priced lists at an early stage, perhaps over a malt whisky ('try Ardbeg or Bruichladdich for a change') in the crowded bar. Bear in mind that even if they have got the bottle of wine you want (and it is wise to have others in mental reserve) they are not very likely to serve it either well, or in time. All

the same, there are those who have extracted, for
instance, Ch. Gloria '67 at £6, Savigny-les-Beaune
les Lavières '71 (Bouchard Père et Fils) at £5·20,
Bonnes-Mares '69 at £11, and halves of Ch. Bastor-
Lamontagne '70 (a Sauternes, £2·60), or of
Wachenheimer Goldbächel Riesling Auslese '71 at
£7·30, among other treasures. Bottles began at
£2·80 in 1978. No pipes. No music. You sleep under
duvets. If you are agile enough for the stairs, the
old house is more atmospheric, and the breakfasts
are excellent.

*App: B. A. & M. G. Furse, T.S., Russell Thersby,
Kenneth & Mary Macrae, A.F., J. M. Ragg, and
many others.*

WEEM Perthshire (Tayside)   Map 9

Ailean Chraggan Hotel
on B846
1 m NW of Aberfeldy
Aberfeldy 346

A small family-run hotel, with comfortable
bedrooms (and tea-making facilities). Prices are
perhaps too high and helpings over-generous on the
set dinners (priced according to main course):
herring in oatmeal, green pea soup, carbonnade de
boeuf, banana fritters, and coffee (£5·90 in 1978).
Good Tay salmon. Popular bar meals (main dishes
from £1·30, including vegetables) and pressurised
beers. Some interesting wines (wine by the glass 45p)
and a dazzling list of malt whiskies that would
betray a Russian (or English) spy if you asked him
to read it aloud. No music.

Closed Jan 1	Tdh L from £2·70 (meal	Seats 50
Must book D; Sun L	£5·40), D from £4·50	♿ rest (2 steps)
Meals 12.30–1.30,	(meal £7·85)	Car park
HT 5–6, 7.30–8.30		No dogs in public rooms
	VAT inc	4 rooms
	Children's helpings	B&B from £8·50
	(under 8)	Fire cert

WESTER HOWGATE Midlothian (Lothian)   Map 9

Old Howgate Inn
on A6094
2 m SE of Penicuik
Penicuik 74244

Little has changed at this inn 11 miles south of
Edinburgh since the Di Rollos' purchase late in
1977 provoked wide-spread fears of a change in style,
and a hiccough in its *Guide* appearances. Some say
the Laura Ashley wallpaper and curtains overdress
the place, and at one time the bread, the spinach
soup and the mayonnaise seemed variable, but at
least the food and wine are served by familiar
hands. One regular speaks for many: 'It is still a
charming, unspoilt inn, with a warm welcome in the
bar, though rather offhand dining-room service at
times, excellently kept real ales (Belhaven and
McEwans on hand pump), a wide range of cold
Danish-style snacks (a generous plateful is £1·25),
admirable home-made soups and puddings, good

Closed Sun; Dec 25; Jan 1
Must book
Meals 12–2, 6.30–10

Alc £3·80 (meal £6·60)

VAT inc
Cover 20p (d/r)
Seats 50
♿ rest; w.c.

Air-conditioning
Car park
No dogs

coffee, pleasant surroundings, decent wines and lots of malt whiskies.' The smørrebrød, quite a novelty when the inn first appeared here in 1957, now cost between 35p and £1·55, soup 45p, cheeses or fresh fruit from 30p. There are a few more substantial dishes: cold meats and salad (£1·95), fondue bourguignonne or lobster. Coffee served from copper pots with whipped cream (50p) is strong and good. Drink it at table or in the garden in summer, or 'sitting in an Orkney chair by the open fire in winter'. There is akvavit, cider, draught stout and lager as well as the ales. Exploration of the fuller wine-list is well worth it, but prices of some of the best on their 1977 list have nearly doubled. The St Saturnin Vin d'une Nuit from the previous owners' own vines in Hérault is recommended at £2·95, and there are other house wines for £2·75 (or £1·50 a half, 60p a glass).

App: Elspeth Johnston, P. G. Spencer, E.M.A., Ian Oswald, T.S., J. M. Ragg, and others

CHANNEL ISLANDS

GUERNSEY

La Frégate
Les Cotils
Guernsey 24624

Closed Dec 25 D
Must book
Meals 12.30–1.30, 7–9.30

Tdh L £3·50 (meal £5·45),
D £4·50 (meal £6·55)
Alc £6·35 (meal £8·60)

Service 10%
Seats 44 (parties 14)
Car park
No dogs
Access, Am Ex, Barclay,
Diners
13 rooms (all with bath)
B&B from £11
Fire cert

Konrad Holleis is still in the kitchen at this well-favoured 18th-century mansion high above harbour and town, but a change of manager put the issue in doubt until seasonal visitors reported yet again that they had felt 'cosseted as we had not been for many, many years, from croissants and coffee in the bedroom for breakfast to considerate bar and dining-room service, and uniformly first-class cooking in the evening.' Naturally, whether table d'hôte or à la carte, fish and shellfish play an important role on menus, especially scallops and plaice on the former, and Dover soles and lobster on the latter. Chinese and Indian beef or poultry dishes also appear. But 'we also remember with pleasure the iced cucumber and walnut soup, most tender chateaubriand with a mass of varied vegetables (elsewhere in the Channel Islands inferior versions of the same dish arrived at the same price), sorbet au Grand Marnier, excellent profiteroles, and of course the sublime peach à la Frégate.' Rhône or Anjou ordinaires are £2·30, and clarets still accessible, with Ch. Gloria '67 or Ch. Lynch-Bages '60, both c.b., £6 in 1978. No music. No children under eight in the restaurant or under 14 in the hotel (for the cliff is steep). Wear a jacket and tie for dinner. More reports, please.

JERSEY

Moorings Hotel
Jersey Central 53633

Closed Dec 25 & 26;
Dec 24 D
Must book D
Meals 12.45–2.30,
7.30–10.30

Mr Fitzpatrick's hotel, in the centre of the quay just below Mont Orgueil castle, has not appeared here for some years, and there is still little externally to distinguish it from its neighbours. But inside, visitors report this year, there is a chef who cooks and a maître who rules the dining-room 'with a rod of iron', to excellent effect. At least, two separate people report the best lobster soup and avocado with crab they recall in the Channel Islands, along with deftly prepared eggs

Tdh L £3·85 (meal £5·35),
D £4·40 (meal £5·90)
Alc £6·50 (meal £8)

Service inc
Children's helpings
(under 8)
Seats 64 (parties 30)
[&] rest; w.c.
12 rooms (7 with bath)
B&B £9·25–£13
Fire cert

*florentine ('85p, and they could not have made much
of a profit on that'), coquilles St Jacques (£1·90),
langoustines mayonnaise, and poached turbot
hollandaise (£3·50). Vegetables and salads are good
too, and conger soup (70p) is worth noting, but more
conventional pâté, sole bonne femme and cheesecake
'somehow failed to inspire us'. Mary Ann bitter is in
cask, and wines (from £2·40 a litre for Italian)
include interesting '71 Germans and '64 or '66 Ch. de
Lescours (a St Emilion) at £6 or so. A pianist plays.
No children in the bar, and no children's high teas.
No dogs in public rooms. More reports, please.*

ST AUBIN   Map 1

Portofino
Jersey Central 42100

Closed Wed; Dec 25
Must book
Meals 12–2.30, 7–10.30

Tdh L £2·25 (meal £3·85)
Alc £5·45 (meal £7·35)

Service 10%
Children's helpings
Seats 67 (parties 35)
[&] rest
No dogs

*Brian Skelley runs this newly nominated upstairs
restaurant with an Italian partner (Renzo Acronzio)
and chef. It quickly began to do well, because it has a
comfortable and enthusiastic air – perhaps too
enthusiastic over displaying food that would be better
prepared when about to be eaten. At test and other
meals, well-dressed avocado Portofino, 'delicately
coloured and authentically flavoured lobster soup', fresh
grilled sardines 'almost like young herrings' (£2·80),
paillard of veal, veal kidneys 'cooked to the right
chewy moistness, in a light herb and white wine sauce',
and duck à l'orange (£3·75) with a crisp skin, and
juice rather than a thickened sauce on the side, are all
praised. Cacciuco livornese (£4·30) and fegato alla
veneziana (£2·80) are other suggestions from Pasquale
Fuschetto. Bardolino or Soave are £2·10 a litre.
Recorded music. More reports, please, especially on
the set lunch.*

ST BRELADE   Map 1

La Place Hotel
Cartwheel Restaurant
Route du Coin,
La Haule
Jersey Central 44261

Hans Hiller is still cooking at this Delrich hotel
near the airport, though a change of manager was
pending as we went to press. The style is
international, and some of the pretensions tiresome –
it is a London businessman who complains of not
being able to wear less formal clothes in the
evening because the restaurant demands a tie. But
the food is competent, not just the elaborate à la
carte dishes but the set meals with generous hors
d'oeuvre, good soups, 'whole crab with salad', and
'excellent roast beef and Yorkshire pudding on
Sunday'. They have not bothered to send a wine
list, but there are about 100 listed. Live music.

Meals 12.45–1.45,
7.30–9.30

Tdh L £4 (meal £6·05),
D £4·50 (meal £6·60)
Alc £7·35 (meal £9·85)

Seats 90 (parties 100)
Car park
No dogs in public rooms
Access, Am Ex, Barclay,
Diners, Euro

37 rooms (all with bath)
B&B from £15·50
Full board from £22 p.d.
Fire cert

La Capannina
67 Halkett Place
Jersey Central 34602

Closed Sun; most public
hols
Must book
Meals 12–2, 7–10

Alc £5·35 (meal £7·70)

Service 10%
Seats 65 (parties 18)
Air-conditioning
No dogs
Am Ex, Barclay, Diners

There is a distinctly clubby atmosphere in Valentino
Rossi's comfortable light and dark blue rooms – in
spite of the colours, it cannot be the Oxford and
Cambridge club; more like the Junior Tax Avoiders,
or the Pot and Belly – for there has long been
first-rate Italian cooking here. Faults noticed include
blander flavours than real Italians like, and a
tiresome choice between a draught if the door is
open and stifling tobacco if it is not. Mr Rossi keeps
the loyalty of his staff, and a test meal was expertly
served, quite apart from the skilled cooking of
praires farcies with a sweet (in this instance, very
garlicky) butter mixture (£1·50), and sweetbreads
with cream and mushrooms (£3·30) and good fresh
spinach. The mixed fish salad – unpriced on the
menu, but sometimes now they put prices of the
day's specialities in the window – cost £2·50 when
tried. It seemed good value for praires, mussels on
the half shell, a little oyster, shelled prawns in a
tomato dressing, scallops, a cold sardine, and an
adolescent crayfish. Steaks are copiously sauced;
sauté potatoes are competent. The usual Italian
wines can be had for about £2·80, with house
Chianti £2·60 and Mâcon-Lugny '73 (Louis Latour)
£3·80. Recorded music.

App: H.W., S.L., K.G.J.

ST HELIER see also wine bar section

Greenhill Country Hotel
Coin Varin
Jersey Central 81042

A useful little hotel near the airport; comfortable
accommodation, on the whole, though recent
'improvements' are not soundproofed. Stone, pine
and a swimming-pool make a more pleasant
background than the recorded music – 'even at
breakfast it tinkled away.' Unambitious set meals
(soup or melon or Parma ham; bouchée à la reine;
a joint – beef better than 'tough' lamb – fish,
omelette or steak, and a 'predictable' sweets
trolley); lengthy *carte* with 'ten variations on
everything and leaping flames'. House wines £2·10
for 50 cl, too much for almost duty-free Jersey.

Closed Dec 24, 25, 26 &
31; Jan 1
Must book D
Meals 12.30–2, 7.30–9.45

Tdh L £3·70 (meal £5·25),
D £5 (meal £6·65)

Alc £5·55 (meal £7·70)

Service 10%
Seats 60
🔲 rest
Car park

No dogs
Am Ex, Barclay
18 rooms (11 with bath,
7 with shower)
B&B £10–£17
D, B&B £14·50–£21

SARK

Aval du Creux
Harbour Hill
Sark 36

Closed Oct–Apr 13
Must book
Meals 12–1.30, 7.30–8.30

Tdh £3 (meal £4·80),
D £4 (meal £5·90)
Alc (min £3·50) £4·80
(meal £6·75)

Service 10%
Children's helpings
(under 10)
Seats 50 (parties 25)
⟨ rest (3 steps); w.c.
No dogs
10 rooms (all with
shower)
D, B&B £13

After four seasons, Peter Hauser has markedly
improved the physical comfort of his house, and his
own high ability as a chef, coupled perhaps with his
Austrian origin, is gathering round him an
international clientele. Their conversation may be
limited from an English visitor's point of view, but
they need only their own language to admire
irreproachable frogs' legs (£2). The goulash soup
and consommés are also praised, and fish platters
'combined in a lobster shell all kinds of white and
shellfish with a delicious sauce'. The Sark lobsters
themselves are naturally popular, and other
speciality dishes include poulet sauté Voronoff
(£2·50), escalope de veau Mirza (£3), and
chateaubriand. Quiche Lorraine is not to be despised
either, and 'Mr Hauser has not forgotten how to
make Apfelstrudel and other Austrian desserts.'
French vin de table white and red is £1·10 for 50 cl,
and on a fairly modest list white Hermitage is £2·60
and Gigondas '70, £3·50. No pipes or cigars at table.
Recorded Austrian music. Dress neatly.

*App: V. Delgua, A. K. Ashford, J. H. Myring,
Ian Culley, and others*

Dixcart Hotel
Sark 15

Closed mid-Oct to
mid-Apr
Must book
Meals 12.30, 7.30

Tdh L £3·25 (meal £4·40),
D £4·25 (meal £5·50)
Alc £5·50 (meal £6·75)

Service 10%
Seats 65 (parties 14)
⟨ rest
No dogs in d/r
18 rooms (7 with bath,
2 with shower)
Full board £13·50–£16·75
p.d.

After a 21-year regime in which the physical
comforts of this atmospheric hotel have got
gradually less Swinburnian ('no bathroom or
lavatory has more than five beds competing for it,'
writes Peggy Ravenshaw enigmatically), radical
changes are not to be expected, and at least there
has been no further change of chef. One student of
the Sark hotels puts Gary Owston well up in the
field, but another visitor, not content with reproving
his eye for colour and 'his attempt to use up the
EEC's butter mountain at a single meal' suggests
that his marshmallow-based 'surprise' be banned
from the island. However, gazpacho, crab claws
with almonds (£4·30), limande meunière, gelinottes
rôties à l'anglaise, rump steak Café de Paris, and
soufflé omelette are all liked, and cheeses are good.
Every other Sunday there is a choice of two curries,
and medallions of veal Verlaine (with Pernod and
pineapple, £3·50) and leg of lamb with herbs en
croûte are other specialities. There is an element of
cronydom, unsurprising after Queen Peggy's long
reign, and one couple report a very mediocre meal
and unhappy overnight stay. Breakfasts are well
cooked, though. Guests tend to be catholic in their
drinking, and need to be told what may be good on

the wine list and what is not. St Joseph '70 at £2·90 or Sancerre '76 at £2·65 seem wise choices. Ordinaires are £1·40; pressurised beers or Strongbow cider with bar snacks. No music. Children are not encouraged; ties at dinner are.

App: R.A., W. N. Greenwood, T.R., E. G. Liddell, and others

SARK Map 1

Hotel Petit Champ

Sark 46

Closed Oct–Easter
Must book
Meals 12–1, 6.30–8

Tdh L from £2·50 (meal £3·75), D from £4 (meal £5·40)

Service 10%
Children's helpings
Seats 50 (parties 20)
No dogs
Access, Barclay, Diners
17 rooms (7 with bath, 4 with shower)
Full board £13–£16·50 p.d.

You now need to book for next year not on the day you leave but on the day you arrive, writes one member, and casual dinners in season are impossible without a week or so's notice, too. This does not mean that Terry and Janie Scott's well-loved hotel can be left to coast along without reports: for one thing, the concerned, but unobtrusive service (though it should scrutinise cutlery more carefully) is a model even to places that cannot manage a horse and carriage to meet guests at the harbour, or a gardener-fisherman to provide reliable weather forecasts. Brian Rolls remains in the kitchen. Soups are always good. Bar chaud à la maison, assiette de fruits de mer, okra vinaigrette, mousse au jambon en cocotte, and vol-au-vent indienne ('stuffed with a curry-flavoured goat's milk cheese') are among the best first courses, and then there may be filet de boeuf en croûte with sauce madère and pommes brioche, caneton rôti en canapé or rheinische sauerbraten with choux flamande and spätzli, or local veal. 'Another memorable meal included iced strawberry soup and delicious skate with a true hollandaise, not a vinegary custard.' French cheeses vary with deliveries; Stilton, though, is reliable. Sweets are refreshing rather than elaborate, in spite of the tempting Sark cream: mousse au citron, pêche au cognac, with apple pie for any surviving corners. Packed lunches are good, and it will never be possible to criticise the coffee again, since Mr Scott lent his machine and blend to the Seigneurie to help with a royal visit, and the Palace mentioned it approvingly in the bread-and-butter letter. Mainland visitors – and some French ones – may well be startled to find Loire and Côtes du Rhône wines at a mere £1·60 a litre, not to mention Ch. Cos d'Estournel '70, c.b., at £5·50, Aloxe-Corton Valozières '71, £4·20, half-bottles of dessert Ch. Coutet '69, £1·80, and (with due notice) Fonseca Guimaraens '62 port at £5. Decanting is done without fuss and smoking firmly discouraged. 'Some guests retire to the bar to smoke between courses.' No music. Wear a jacket and tie at dinner. Children can be accepted only if they stay up for the meal.

App: C. R. Handley, A. Grove, S.P., and others

ISLE OF MAN

BALLASALLA Map 7

Coach House
Silverburn Bridge
Castletown 2343

Closed Sun; 2 weeks
Oct/Nov; Dec 25
Must book D
Meals 12.30–2.15, 7–10.30

Alc £7·55 (meal £10·65);
(Saddle Room) £3 (meal
£5)

Seats 60 (Rest) & 30
(Saddle Room)
♿ rest (2 steps)
Am Ex, Barclay

The comings and goings of chefs during the year, and a couple of dismal meals at different dates (dinner in the main restaurant, and lunchtime steak and kidney pie in the cheaper Saddle Room) make it hard to be sure about this sparkling white, low-rise building owned by Terry Croft of a local seafood firm. Yet others have been luckier, even with the same steak and kidney pie (as well as 'delicious walnut and apple salad') and fortunately a late-season test lunch showed signs of quality, notably an enterprising salade japonaise as a first course, the rare fillet steak, and the sherry cream sauce for tender suprême de volaille Sandeman (£4·10). Even so, monotonous lobster soup (95p) and over-sweet Pavlova suggest that the current chef (whose specialities include coquilles St Jacques en brochette, £4·20, and truit Belin) still has problems calling for his attention. Car park. No dogs. More reports, please.

DOUGLAS Map 7

Crows Nest
Sea Terminal
Douglas 5009

'Panoramic views of harbour and promenade' from the third floor of the modern 'lemon squeezer' sea terminal. Italian-run, but lacking atmosphere and warmth (even literally on occasion). The long menu offers fish (including local queenies), pasta, roasts and grills. The seafood platter (£1·60) is 'very English' (in other words, vinegary), spanako soupa (60p) is a tangy spinach and yoghourt soup, whitebait are crisp, marinated lamb kebab (£2·80 with vegetables) tasty and tender. Vegetables, sweets and coffee were less successful when tried. Various wines (Chianti Melini, £3). Recorded music.

Closed Sun (Oct–May)
Must book
Meals 12–2, 7–9.45

Tdh L from £2·45
(meal £4·35)

Alc (min L £2·50, D £3)
£4·35 (meal £6·45)

VAT inc
Service 10%

Seats 90
Car park
No dogs
Access, Diners

Inspections are carried out anonymously. Persons who pretend to be able to secure, arrange or prevent an entry in the Guide are impostors and their names or descriptions should be reported to us.

We rewrite every entry each year, and depend on fresh, detailed reports to confirm the old, as well as to include the new. The further from London you are, the more important this is.

Villiers Hotel
Clarendon Grill
Loch Promenade
Douglas 21889

These natural stone cellars make a pleasant hideaway. Standard grill menu, with commercial overtones, but careful choice may be rewarded: try 'our second chef's pâté', perhaps, rather than some of the other seven on offer; avoid the soup; have the vast mixed grill (£3) or queenies sautéed in garlic butter (£2·25); keep to the fruit salad for sweet, 'all fresh, apart from the cherry'. 'Young adults under 11' may have chef-made fish fingers with chips and peas (40p). With luck, elderly toddlers' goujons of local fish on the set lunch will be equally virtuous. Interesting and reasonably priced wines; house Loire, £2·50. Efficient and friendly service. Recorded music.

Must book	Service 10%	Access, Am Ex, Barclay,
Meals 12.30–2, 7–10.30	Children's helpings	Diners, Euro
	(under 11)	130 rooms (43 with bath,
Tdh L £2·25 (meal £4·15)	Seats 90 (parties 30)	49 with shower)
Alc £4·20 (meal £6·85)	Air-conditioning	B&B £8–£13·50
	No dogs in public rooms	

Grosvenor
4½ m NW of Ramsey
Kirk Andreas 576

A lunchtime queue may form at Bernie Hamer's pub-restaurant, for 'an enormous helping of black pudding with English mustard', 'seafood shell with plenty of variety', 'delicious kidneys and bacon with well-cooked cabbage among the vegetables', 'hot roast lamb', 'home-made eclairs with natural rather than inflated cream'. The cold buffet, the service and the coffee are also praised. Tell us how they do at dinner when you may begin with queenies in garlic butter and go on to roast duckling. Conventional wines from £3 or so. No music.

Closed Tue; Sun D;	Alc L £3·40 (meal £5·75),	Seats 45
D 3 days Easter;	D (min £2·50) £5·25	♿ rest; w.c.
1st 3 weeks Oct; Dec 25	(meal £7·95)	Car park
Must book D & Sun L		No dogs
Meals 12–2, 7.30–9	Service 10%	

'Must book' is the restaurant's information, not ours. The context of the entry usually indicates how much or how little it matters, but a preliminary telephone call averts frustrated journeys. Always telephone if a booking has to be cancelled: a small place may suffer severely if this is not done, and customers are also the losers in the end.

Numbers are given for private parties only if they can be accommodated in a room separate from the main dining-room; when there are several such rooms, the capacity of the largest is given. Some restaurants will take party bookings at times when they are normally closed.

PORT ST MARY   Map 7

The Barn
Harbour Road
Port St Mary 832064

Gastone and Sue Quaglio now have quite a
following for their candlelit barn with bare tables
and pews. Roast joints – beef, lamb, ham – are out
on display; poached salmon and the wide choice of
hors d'oeuvre (as main course if you like) are
popular too, and the accompanying vegetables are
plain but virtuous. Coffee and walnut gateau is
light, cheese 'a little tired' sometimes, coffee
acceptable. Unlicensed, but no corkage. No jeans,
please. Orchestral records. You go through the
'spotless kitchen' to the loo.

Closed Mon; Sun D	Tdh D £5·50	Seats 40
Must book	Alc L (min £1·75) meal	Air-conditioning
Meals 12.30–1.30, 7.30–9	£3·45	No dogs
		Unlicensed
	VAT inc	

RAMSEY   Map 7

Harbour Bistro
5 East Street
Ramsey 4182

*Informal little place in a converted shop, with white
walls, black beams, 'the occasional fishing net' and
tiled tables. Reasonably priced menu, and some
imaginative cooking: kipper mousse, seafood
mayonnaise (chef-made), chicken blunderbust (£1·95,
no details . . .), casseroles served with sweetcorn and
onion fritters. Good-humoured service. French house
wines, £1·80 for 75 cl. Recorded music, 'trad, pop and
country'. More reports, please.*

Closed L; Sun; Dec 24 & 25	Alc £3·70 (meal £5·35)	Seats 40
Must book	VAT inc	♿ rest (1 step); w.c.
D only, 6–11		No dogs

IRELAND

PREFACE

In matters of food, and especially the service of cooked food outside
the home, few European countries are static. They are going from
somewhere to somewhere else, and in their own gloomiest moments
food critics are sure that it is mostly downhill all the way. But if
there is any country that has a genuine opportunity to make a
marked improvement in the meals it offers to its foreign visitors,
that country is Ireland. It possesses the essentials, which cannot be
developed without a century or so's notice in any nation that lacks
them: first-rate in-shore fish, meat, and dairy products in
abundance; and men and women who do not (like so many of the
English) become self-conscious or aggressive when they find
themselves 'in service'. What is missing in Ireland is the network
of secondary systems that are taken for granted in, say, France,
which has made a comfortable living out of tourists ever since the
Napoleonic Wars. If only, for instance, Ireland had an effective
fish-marketing structure capable of getting bass, scallops, mullet
and mackerel from sea to table inside 24 hours on every day in the
year that they can be caught; if only there were automatic
provision for the in-service training of chefs and waiters, at the
hands of people whose own standards are as high as the best of the
restaurateurs and hoteliers named in the ensuing pages. . .

There are not many years left. For the Irish problem, as
perceived by the *Good Food Guide*'s touring inspectors, is not
precisely the one identified in a vivid and intelligent report on the
attitudes of tourists to eating (and drinking) in Ireland, published
last year by the Irish Tourist Board (*Thought for Food*, free from
Bord Fàilte, Baggot Street Bridge, Dublin 2). Understandably, the
authors of the report, and many of the tourists they interviewed,
look upon Ireland as an underdeveloped country in matters of the
table, where meat and vegetables are cooked to destruction,
hygiene is unreliable, and a proper cup of coffee is unobtainable.
Shortcomings of this kind may even be noticed by a visitor who
confines his eating to the places mentioned in this book, and will
certainly be apparent in any more random sample of Irish
restaurants, hotels, and pubs. But a selective visitor will encounter
some remarkably fine food too, and besides, there is hope for a

412

country whose tourist authority (unlike Britain's) is anxious to identify and discuss in public what needs to be mended, rather than peddling optimistic taradiddles about what visitors can expect.

However, the danger less often recognised is that improvement itself will be arrested or misdirected, as soon as the profits arrive, by people who never properly understood the reasons for it. If 'thick brown gravies' simply yield place to 'refined' French sauces from a commercial sauce refinery, if deep-freezes are installed so that a dry salmon steak can be offered every day of the year to a tourist who demands one, if brown bread with smoked salmon is ousted by sliced, and Irish potatoes boiled in their skins give way to Smash piped round plastic scallop shells, Ireland's last state will be worse than her first. And initially, hardly anyone will notice, because half the incoming tourists from North America and Germany will be so dazzled by the view and the Georgian silver that they will not notice the fake orange juice for breakfast and the packet soups at dinner, while the ones from France and Britain will stay in hotels once and do their own catering the next time. Ireland's own people, meanwhile, will gradually forget their own food heritage, except when the Myrtle Allens and Declan Ryans of the land appear on television, as quaint figures from the past, to remind them.

So if you like Ireland and the riches it has to offer in food, drink, and entertainment – and no *Good Food Guide* inspector has ever, as far as I know, regretted a tour of this maddening but disarming country – please remember that by the simple act of filling in the report forms at the back of this book, you can help to encourage the best, and repress the worst. But don't expect eating in Ireland to be cheap. Quantity for quantity and quality for quality, our own rule-of-thumb calculations suggest that meals out in 1978 cost at least ten per cent more than they did in the British Isles. You may think that this gives you every reason to be exacting.

REPUBLIC OF IRELAND

Armstrong's Barn
Wicklow 5194

Closed L; Sun; Mon;
public hols
Must book
D only, 7.30–10

Tdh from £9 (meal £12·50)

Seats 45 (parties 14)
♿ rest (1 step)
Car park
No dogs
Am Ex, Barclay

Members were understandably put off visiting and reporting on this much admired restaurant on the Glendalough road because our 1978 news supplement reported that Peter Robinson (who built it up) had sold out. This was true, but Paul Tullio, the new owner, has been able to keep Humphrey Weightman as chef, along with several of the staff. The Gillray prints have given way to Mrs Tullio's pictures in the bar, and the wines are not quite what they were, but the cooking seems to have the same verve, to judge from crab puff, and field mushrooms with garlic butter, followed by turkey breasts with smoked ham and fresh sage, and roast spring lamb (£9·75 – the price of the main course on the short menu dictates the cost of the whole). Other seasonal dishes include roast lamb's kidneys with garlic and coriander, and sweetbreads in black butter: Mr Weightman is fond of offal. If you do not fancy crème brûlée he may offer elderflower and gooseberry fool, for 'wild food', from nettles to rowans, represents both men's enthusiasms. Italian Cabernet or Soave are £2·50 a litre, and there are in fact good clarets still, divided into communes on the list: Ch. Branaire-Ducru '69, £6·10, the '66 and '67 vintages of Ch. Calon-Ségur at £12 or so. No music. No pipes. More reports, please.

Fishery
Doohulla
2½ m SE of Ballyconneely
on L102
9 m SE of Clifden
Ballyconneely 31

Closed Oct–May
Must book D
Meals 12.30–2.30,
7.30–9.30

Alc £6·10 (meal £8·40)

Service 10%
Cover 20p
Seats 40

Nick Tinne of Snaffle's in Dublin (q.v.) exercises a 'benevolent supervision' over Edward O'Brien's informal restaurant between Ballyconneely and Roundstone, and '50 miles from Galway but near my favourite golf course'. It is bright, clean, and not over-decorated, and devoted to fish, naturally: fish soup with rouille (£1·25), baked crab (£2·50), and lobster 'still twitchy under the grill' (as it may well be at £8). Garlic soup (£1) and crab 'with a really exceptional crisp salad' also pleased an inspector, and according to Mr Tinne himself, 'I doubt if there are many places outside the Iberian peninsula where you can get angulas (baby eels) from the restaurant's own river.' Local girls serve. Drink Valpolicella or Soave at £2·15; other wines have not been notified. Classical records. Children's helpings. No dogs. More reports, please.

In the Republic of Ireland some restaurants are licensed to sell wines only (not spirits or beer).

BALLYDEHOB Co Cork   Map 10

Audley House Hotel
Ballydehob 74 *and* 51

Meals 1–2, 7.30–10.30

Tdh L £4·10 (meal £5·20),
D £7·25 (meal £8·35)

Service inc
Children's helpings
Seats 35
🛗 rest
Car park
10 rooms (all with bath)
B&B £7·50

Ballydehob may be surprised at its own rise to gastronomic prominence, but John Konig and Elisabeth Konig-van Essen have begun well in their modern but appealingly designed and furnished hotel on a headland by an old copper mine. Mr Konig's substantial but not over-elaborate set menus are priced on the taxman's deductive principle: a meal price is named and you claim back for what you have not consumed – soup, dessert, coffee or whatever. However, a critical visitor who began with excellent smoked salmon 'from the smoke-house of a small Bulgarian in the neighbourhood' filed a complete return for what followed: a red-peppery bouillabaisse, 'admirably moist' grilled turbot with green pepper sauce, and dame blanche. Steak Florentino – 'really blue if you ask for it' – is £3·80 (including vegetables) à la carte, and sometimes there is an Indonesian rijsttaffel – 'very popular,' Mr Konig says – at £9·50 a head, and two days' notice, including 16 dishes ranging from sajur lodeh to pisang goreng. La Tourelle red or la Gravette white ordinaires are £2·25, and Gewürztraminer (which might suit the rijsttaffel) £4·75. Recorded music. Slow service – but they like to cosset residents with breakfast in bed, and even offer to polish their shoes. More reports, please.

Basil Bush
Main Street
Ballydehob 10

Closed Sun; Dec 24, 25, 26 & 31; Jan 1
Must book
Meals 12.30–2, 7–10

Alc £5·50 (meal £8·05)

Service 10%
Children's helpings
(under 12)
Seats 20
No dogs

It was good to hear that the Basil Bush had not burnt or withered when the owners fell silent last time, but that they were moving round the corner to this elegantly converted, blackstone-flagged cottage. For the daily bake of sour-dough bread and drip of mayonnaise show that Shirley Foster and Alfie Lyons care, and do not attempt more than they can perform: 'We had egg mayonnaise and marinated mackerel, followed by sole Basil Bush, stuffed with breadcrumbs and herbs (£4 including vegetables), superbly finished chicken and tarragon, plum and brandy ice-cream, and as good a blackberry mousse as I remember.' Others have been equally impressed by the chicken pâté, locally grown globe artichokes béarnaise, chicken cacciatora, rainbow trout, grilled salmon hollandaise, 'the superb flavour of marrow or chard', the freshness of the salads, and various ices. Even the coffee is good enough for someone to name the bean. 'The service was exceptionally slow' even by Irish standards, but perhaps not by those of Ballydehob, and anyway they really do cook to order. Sensibly chosen wines begin at £3 for French Blanc de Blancs, and the music suits too. Note that the telephone number belongs to the pub next door.

App: Graham & Gail Nunn, Vyvian Gundry, G. H. Hafter, M.G., and others

415

BEARNA PIER Co Galway   Map 10

Ty Ar Mor
Sea Point
3 m W of Galway
Bearna 65031

Hervé Mahé's 'house on the edge of the sea' has had a new chef since June and 'the beautiful lacy crêpes gave way to stodgy Irish pancakes.' Even the fish was patchy for a month or two: fish soup seemed dependable, and scallops bretonne 'excellent', but salmon was dry when grilled, and poached hake or turbot unexciting. Main dishes begin at £3·20, and there is a summer seasonal set lunch. Service 'had a fatal air of self-satisfaction, culminating in cold coffee served with milk, and replaced with a bad grace.' French ordinaire is £2 for 50 cl. More reports, please.

Closed L (exc July–Sept); Sun; Feb	Tdh L (summer) £3 (meal £4·90)	Service 10% Seats 50
Must book	Alc £6·15 (meal £8·35)	♿ rest (2 steps)
Meals 12–2 (July–Sept), 7–11		Car park No dogs

BETTYSTOWN Co Meath   Map 10

Coastguard Restaurant
6 m S of Drogheda
on coast road
Drogheda 27115

The Robsons' little stone house on the strand offers 'homely, elegant comfort, but don't be in a hurry.' Fish appears frequently on the short, often-changing à la carte dinner menus: sea trout, lobster, turbot, Boyne salmon, brill. People have liked vegetable soup or the light, crab-filled crêpe as a first course; then lamb with rosemary ('pink and juicy'); and a sharp damson sorbet. But late in the year pâté was poor, mallard tough, and boeuf Stroganoff tasteless. French house wines (£2·20); some unusual bottles too. No music. No dogs. Dress 'respectably', and try not to smoke in the restaurant. Car park.

Closed L; Sun; Mon; last week Jan to mid-Feb; Dec 25 & 26	D only, 7.30–10	Service 10% Seats 40
Must book	Alc £7·85 (meal £10·15)	♿ rest (1 step) Am Ex, Barclay, Euro

CAHIRCIVEEN Co Kerry   Map 10

Murray's Seafood Restaurant
on N70
1 m S of Cahirciveen
Cahirciveen 246

Converted schoolhouse facing Valentia Island where you eat fish and shellfish 'from the waters in view of the restaurant'. The 'seafood platter' at £3·50 is the star turn – 'all that it should be.' Mussels, scallops, sole, lobster, too. Nicolas Vieux Ceps or Orvieto Antinori is a reasonable £2·60 the litre, 45p the glass. Sandwiches at lunch-time. Irish music.

Closed Sun; Nov–Easter	Service 10%	♿ rest
Meals 12.30–2.30, 6.30–9.30	Children's helpings (under 13)	Car park No dogs
	Seats 34	
Alc £4·15 (meal £6·35)		

CARAGH LAKE Co Kerry   Map 10

Caragh Lodge
3½ m SW of Killorglin
Caragh Lake 15

Guest house (meals for residents only) run 'with Teutonic efficiency', set in nine acres overlooking the lake. Not surprisingly, the fish dishes are 'outstanding' – grilled sole and poached bass especially. Soups, too, are 'uniformly delicious', vegetables fresh and carefully prepared ('kohlrabi with pickled beef was a revelation'). Fish and chicken salads are less praiseworthy. No choice of sweets but all sound fresh and tempting. Excellent breakfast (on terrace). No children under ten. No dogs. Dress 'decently'. No music.

Closed Sept 21–Easter
D only (res only), from
7.30

Service 10%
Seats 18
Car park

8 rooms (7 with bath,
1 with shower)
B&B £8·50

Tdh £5·50 (meal £7·45)

CARRIGBYRNE Co Wexford   Map 10

Cedar Lodge
on N25
14 m W of Wexford
New Ross 24386 *and*
24436

For people who know and hate motels, Thomas and Ailish Martin's 'spanking new' single-storey building in gentle country on the Waterford road from Rosslare is a surprise, because she has good taste and cooks carefully. Scallops in vermouth (£3·95), and salmon mayonnaise in season (£3·25), are her set pieces, but there is praise too for 'succulent' lamb chops, 'refined' trout with almonds, and 'juicy smoked salmon sandwiches for a snack' (though the coffee was instant). Rochelle ordinaires are £2·40 for 50 cl. Recorded music. No young children after 7.30. More reports, please.

Closed L (exc summer);
Dec 25
Meals 12–2.30, 6–9.30

Alc £5·40 (meal £7·65)

Service 10%
Children's helpings

Seats 36 (parties 84)
Car park
No dogs
6 rooms (with shower)
B&B £7

Tdh L £4 (meal £5·85)

CASHEL Co Tipperary   Map 10

Chez Hans
Rockside
Cashel (Tipperary) 61177

Closed L; Sun; Apr 13;
Nov; Dec 24 & 25
Must book
D only, 6–10

Tdh £7·50 (meal £10·45)

Service 10%

Hans-Peter Matthia is a talented and experienced chef who seems to be able to feed seventy as easily as he can feed seven. But his staff have not always stood the pace since the expansion of his converted Wesleyan-Gothic chapel, and summer visitors found the service 'brusque, brisk, or disingenuous', and even the cooking erratic. Happily both in spring and autumn much higher standards are reported, with excellent crab and mushroom soup, goose-liver pâté 'on top of Hans's omnium-gatherum salads', followed by cassoulet of fresh Atlantic langoustines, or loin of lamb, or chicken

Seats 70
⑤ rest (1 step); w.c.
Car park
No dogs

with lemon and almonds. 'Beware of over-eating, for quantities are large and sweets too are good' (blackberry or blackcurrant mousse, and Black Forest gateau, for example). You will pay about £4 for Muscadet or St Emilion, but they have been dashing about too fast to send a wine list this year. Recorded music.

App: Henry Potts, J.C. & L.K.A., J.G.R., and others

CLOON Co Wicklow   Map 10

Enniscree Lodge
4 m from Enniskerry
Dublin 863542

Variously described as a 'pre-war bungalow' with 'Tudor decor', and 'just like a Swiss chalet', with staggering views over Glencree. Conventional first courses; then fondues of massive dimensions – Gaelic cheese (as a starter too), chunks of beef or lamb (to cook à la bourguignonne) or prawns with a dip. Sorbets or fruity sweets. Set Sunday lunch includes a buffet. French house wine £3 for 70 cl, 50p the glass, and a dearish but varied list (nothing Swiss). Cocktails on the patio. 'Infants welcome.' Dress neatly.

Closed L (exc Sun); Mon; Sun D; Apr 13; last 2 weeks Oct; 1 week Chr Must book
Meals 1–2, 8–9.45

Tdh Sun L £3·75 (meal £5·90)
Alc £8·05 (meal £11·10)

Service 12½%
Children's helpings L (under 10)

Seats 55 (parties 35)
⑤ rest (2 steps)
Air-conditioning
Car park
No dogs

CORK Co Cork   Map 10

Arbutus Lodge

St Luke's Cross
Montenotte
Cork 501237

Closed Sun L (exc bar); Sun D (exc res); Dec 24, 25 & 26
Must book
Meals 1–2, 7–9.30

Tdh L £7·35 (meal £9·25), D £9·60 (meal £11·50)
Alc £8·80 (meal £12·55)

Service 12½%
Seats 75 (parties 30)
⑤ rest
Air-conditioning
Car park

'Declan Ryan is the greatest. Delicious bread. Take the fish. Aaaaaaaahhh.' For an inspector's report, that ought to get the volunteer drummed out of the regiment for dereliction of duty to detail, but the ones that go on for pages convey substantially the same message about this much refurbished Georgian house overlooking (from a height) the industrial Lee river. Mr Ryan has had his ups and downs, and the list of names in his kitchen reads like an Irish Uncle Tom Cobbleigh, but his own talent and training ability are not in doubt. It is hard to think of three better first courses than his crudités (fennel and purple broccoli among them) with a 'dragon's breath' of garlic mayonnaise, saumon cru with coarsely ground coriander (£2·50) or cassolette of fresh prawns, 'very fresh and sweet, with plenty of wine, butter and cream'. His kitchen pulverisers will cope with everything from mushrooms for soup and pigeons for terrine, to almonds for chocolate St Emilion (not all at once), and after the soup you may consider escalope of salmon with sorrel sauce, crab-stuffed plaice ('a blander taste than I had

No dogs
Am Ex, Barclay, Diners
20 rooms (16 with bath,
4 with shower)
B&B £13·25–£16·25

hoped'), râble de lièvre rôti sauce moutarde (£5) or the côte de boeuf à la moelle sauce Beaujolais (£9·70) for two – good meat, hung in the hotel's cold-room, and given a correctly brown and winey sauce to offset its red rareness. Vegetables are extra, but also worth it, if the crisply fried aubergines, creamy spinach, and garlicky, barely-curdled gratin dauphinoise potatoes at a test meal were anything to go by. After all this, anyone still in the running for rhubarb fool, the St Emilion, or oeufs à la neige 'like caramelised eiderdowns', not forgetting the good cheeses (unusual in Ireland), rich petits fours and the Cafetière coffee, is an eating man to be envied. The service is described by a severe judge as 'the nicest egalitarian mix of the professional and the friendly I've met in a long while.' The set lunches are a sensibly curtailed version of the *carte*, and packed lunches are also good. The cellar is one of Ireland's last claret repositories, and that includes Chx. Cheval Blanc '24, Latour '45, and Pape-Clément '61 at appropriate prices as well as Ch. Malescot-St-Exupéry '67 at £9·95 (nearly 50% up on last year, though). At £5 or so, desirable '75 German wines are joining the list. No pipes, and please do your best to suppress all smoking here. Bar snacks. No music.

App: Terence A. Clegg, Margaret-Anne Mackay, P.S., Thomas Ward, A.V., and others

---

CORK see also pub section

COURTMACSHERRY Co Cork   Map 10

Courtmacsherry Hotel
12 m S of Bandon
Bandon 46198

Severe critics who readily applaud Terry Adams' 'unparalleled social mix' and 'touches of finesse' at this handsome house in a dramatic setting have been saddened to find good fish ruined by ill-conceived sauces, and too many short-cuts, especially with puddings. Lasagne, the salmon and the trout seem reliable. Valpolicella is £1·40 for 50 cl, 45p the glass. Bar snacks (not Sunday). Music 'on request' only. More reports, please.

Closed L (exc Sun);
Oct–Mar 16
Must book
Meals 12.45–2.15 (Sun),
7.30–9.15

Tdh Sun L £4 (meal
£5·35), D £6 (meal £7·35)
Service inc
Seats 70 (parties 30)

rest; w.c.
Car park
No dogs in public rooms
17 rooms (6 with bath)
B&B £6·50–£9

Irish public holidays do not all coincide with English ones.

The Guide accepts no advertising. Nor does it allow restaurateurs to use its name on brochures, menus, or in any form of advertisement. If you see any instances of this, please report them to us.

CROOKHAVEN Co Cork   Map 10

Journey's End
12 m SW of Schull
Skibbereen 35183

Closed L; Mon;
winter; May 7
Must book
D only, 7.30–9.30

Alc £7·55 (meal £10·25)

Service 10%
Children's helpings
Seats 22
♿ rest

It is certainly hard to re-start a journey after an extended evening at Ina Manahan's house on the outskirts of this little fishing village (include Skibbereen in the mailing address), and she adds, on writing her annual letter 'through a glass darkly': 'Tis a great part of the world for installing and maintaining hangovers.' In other words, she enjoyed most of the guests the last *Guide* sent her, and guests who remember where they have been – and notice her excellent cooking – reciprocate. The menu does not depart very far from scallops or pâté, steak or duckling, gateau or cheese. But 'the French people present seemed as pleased as we were with the very fresh scallops in garlic butter with wine sauce, the fillet steak béarnaise, and the duckling bigarade. Vegetables were also well cooked.' The gateau and coffee may decline somewhat from the standard of earlier courses, but everything is home-made, including the soda bread, of course. Cépage d'Or house wine is £3, Muscadet £4, St Emilion £4·50. Children are 'best over seven', and 'oilskins to mink' still describes people's dress. You may choose your own records over your first drink, and by the time you reach your last, Mrs Manahan may be singing to a guitar by the turf fire.

App: Henry Fawcett, O.J.P., G.M., and others

CURRAGH Co Kildare   Map 10

Jockey Hall
2 m E of Kildare
Naas 41416 *and* 41401

Closed L; Sun; Apr 13;
Dec 25
Must book
D only, 7–10

Tdh from £5 (meal £6·35)
Alc £8·95 (meal £10·65)

Service inc
Children's helpings
Seats 65 (parties L 90,
D 50)
♿ rest
Car park
No dogs
Access, Am Ex, Barclay

'Consistently delicious' is one visitor's verdict on Paul McCluskey's food at this long, low restaurant near the racecourse. With Willie Ryan also in the kitchen, and vegetable and sweets specialists too, the team can obviously cope with a menu that is in any case not over-long. Whether they have eaten table d'hôte or à la carte, people seem equally content with their watercress soup, mussels either poulette or marinière (£1·95), deep-fried crêpe Gruyère, mayonnaise verte with smoked salmon, spring lamb Irish stew, roasts and charcoal-grilled steaks, and other dishes (specialities include escalope de veau cauchoise and petits filets au poivre vert, £5·75). Noticeable vegetables include spinach à la crème and carrots with bacon (95p). 'Home-made ice-creams are always super', and apple tart was well cooked too, an inspector says. Chocolate and orange mousse (95p) is one of the kitchen's favourites. Service is capable and friendly. There is nothing much to drink under £4, apart from house Chianti at £2·75, but there are a few sensibly chosen red and white burgundies at about twice that. No music.

App: D. Nagle, A.K. & L.C.J., Henry Potts

DINGLE Co Kerry   Map 10

Doyle's Seafood Bar
John Street
Dingle 144

Closed Sun; Apr 13;
Nov–Feb
No bookings
Meals 12.30–2.15, 6–9

Alc (min main course)
£4·85 (meal £7·15)

Service 10%
Seats 23
🔾 rest (1 step)
No dogs
Am Ex, Barclay

'There should be a *Guide* medal struck for those who do but one thing and do it superbly', and Stella Doyle, in charge of the kitchen of this natural stone-and-wood cafe in 'Europe's most westerly port' would qualify. True, John Doyle, who runs the place with deceptively casual charm, may have grander ambitions, and takes her to Windermere (*q.v.*) for John Tovey's cookery courses. These would be unlikely to improve on the oysters in garlic butter or the 'wriggling blue lobsters from the *vivier*' or the 'heaped plates of prawns and mussels' that Frenchmen and Americans chomp at between their inconsiderate cigars. But though there are good accounts of trout with mushroom sauce, and of the chicken and scallop pie speciality (£3·50), quenelles in lobster sauce at a test meal badly needed professional help (the excellent bread they bake twice a day here makes a heavy panada). Soups and salads are good; chocolate choux is 'given away at 60p', and rhubarb tart is good too if you don't mind your rhubarb sour. Valpolicella or Soave are £3 a litre, and '76 Muscadet on a well-chosen list 'goes like snuff at a wake', according to Mr Doyle, which must make him, to borrow an expression from another seaboard, as happy as a clam at high tide. No music.

App: Nigel Thomas, Jenny Rathbone, Henry Potts, Martin Cowlyn and Trudy Reid

DUBLIN   Map 10

(1) Le Coq Hardi
29 Pembroke Road,
Ballsbridge
Dublin 689070

Closed Sun; Sat L; public
hols; 2 weeks Jan
Must book
Meals 12.30–2.30,
7.30–11

Tdh L £4·25 (meal £6·60)
Alc £10 (meal £13·50)

Service 12½%
Seats 40
🔾 rest (3 steps); w.c.
Air-conditioning
Car park
No dogs
Am Ex, Barclay

Last year's request for more reports on John Howard's dear but devoutly run restaurant in the basement of the Lansdowne Hotel has been handsomely met from near and distant addresses: thanks to all concerned. It would certainly have been a shame to miss accounts of the fish that Mr Howard and his co-chef Brendan O'Neill prepare: 'very lobstery lobster bisque, and a whole dinner plate full of Dublin Bay prawns in a light and tasty Mornay sauce – it broke my heart to leave some.' If you do not fancy the *patron*'s own sole dish at £7·50, 'lobster in garlic butter and plain sole on the bone are as good as anywhere in Ireland.' Coq Hardi smokies (£1·60), expert chicken Kiev (£4·20), 'memorable' jugged hare and game pies or casseroles are also mentioned. Vegetables (from 85p) are usually good, from mange-tout peas to red cabbage. Sweets are comparatively disappointing, though one visitor who asked for 'some simple berries' after much rich food was given redcurrants and sugar. 'Service is good even down to the infamous Irish coffee made at the table', but the

421

lighting is rather unfriendly. Arc de Triomphe ordinaires are £3·20, and clarets and burgundies rise rapidly to double figures, but try Ch. Belgrave '73 at £9·50. Louis Latour's '73 Chambolle-Musigny is £10·60. No music. Wear a suit.

App: S. F. Stanton, Janet Morgan, P. Kirby, L.S., Mary Ann Gralka, Dr D. Waldron-Lynch, and others

DUBLIN   Map 10

(2) **Kilkenny Kitchen**
Kilkenny Shop
Nassau Street
Dublin 777066

Light and spacious balcony above the Kilkenny Shop, overlooking Trinity. Irish produce wherever possible (in the shop too), pine tables, bright green chair seats, creamy delft. Self-service morning coffee, lunches and teas; tea is 'real', coffee mediocre; cakes are 'country' solid rather than creamy; salads are fresh and imaginative. Limited range of hot dishes (soups, quiches, stews). House wine by the glass at lunch. No music. Leave time to enjoy the Avoca bedspreads and other crafts products in the ground-floor shop.

Closed D; Sun; public hols (exc May 7 & 28; Aug 27) Open 9–5.30 (L 12–2.30)	Alc (min 75p) meal about £2·45 Service inc	Seats 80 Air-conditioning No dogs

VAT is, by law, included in Irish restaurant and hotel prices.

(3) **Royal Hibernian Hotel Rôtisserie**
48 Dawson Street
Dublin 772991

The warm brown grill-room of this traffic-noisy Georgian hotel is a favourite with Dubliners and transatlantic visitors. Avuncular or trainee service helps the clublike atmosphere. Simplest things are best: good smoked salmon (£2·50) or crab, with a steak or rib of beef to follow – 'thick, bloody and tough, but worth the chew.' The accompanying salad and baked potato are not successes. Apple pie or prune ice make appealing sweets, and the coffee is good. Water comes with ice. Typically, the wine list is a shadow of its former self since THF took over, but not greedily priced. French house wine is £2·75 the bottle. No music.

Closed Sun; public hols	Service 12½%	Access, Am Ex, Barclay,
Must book	Children's helpings	Diners, Euro, THF
Open noon–10.45 p.m.	Seats 70	109 rooms (all with bath)
	No dogs in public rooms	Room only, £9·50–£17
Alc £6·35 (meal £9·05)		Breakfast from £1·50

---

(4) **Snaffles**
47 Lower Leeson Street
Dublin 760790 *and*
762227

Closed Sun; Mon D;
Sat L; public hols
Must book
Meals 12.30–2.30, 7–11

Alc £7·45 (meal £10·40)

Service 12½%
Cover 25p
Seats 40 (parties 10)
Am Ex, Barclay, Diners

Nick Tinne's Georgian basement, with (they say) the owner cooking as well as Jack Williams, and flavoury masculine service under John Nolan, has been honoured here for eight editions, and only an editorial accident last time made us accuse them of not making their own bread. There are still some who hold, with one inspector after a fine rack of lamb, that 'Snaffles has survived Stanley Kubrick.' Let's not be unkind to film directors, but the un-Irish tinfoil round the baked potatoes tells you, even if you are blind or deaf, that Irishmen and Englishmen are usually in a minority here, and a more formal test meal, eaten by a long-time admirer, suggested strongly that some of the heart of the place has flown away to Mr Tinne's new project in Connemara (*q.v.* under Ballyconneely). Seafood bisque, turbot en croûte hollandaise, grape pud and (especially) the service were all 'shadows of what they once were'; neither is this an isolated judgement. As always in Ireland, control and morale seem to be the problem, rather than lack of talent, for the same turbot can be exquisite on occasion, Snaffles mousse as a first course retains its appeal, and critical people write of 'superbly tender, just high enough quail, stuffed with grapes, all in a *jus* atop a piece of lightly fried bread' or 'splendid spinach and puree of carrot and parsnips', or lambs' kidneys with mustard sauce (£2·50); and calves' brains in black butter (£2·95) are still worth ordering. Plums in red wine are not 'very persuasive', and Stilton ought to be better kept, says a member who found it 'gamey, scooped, and port-fed'. Neither the atmosphere nor the wine prices encourage fine drinking: 'silly prices for good names in poor years' is a caricature, perhaps, but you need care to find, say, promising '73 clarets

423

under £6, and strength of mind to resist 'lovely' Taylor '63 port at £2 a glass. No music.

App: Terence Clegg, H. W. Gardner, G.W., D.W., Antony Verney, Vernice Darnley, and others

---

DUBLIN   Map 10

(5) Tandoori Rooms Golden Orient
27 Lower Leeson Street
Dublin 762286

Closed L; Sun; public hols
Must book
D only, 7–12.30

Tdh £8·50 (meal £11·70)
Alc (min £5) £10·05 (meal £13·45)

Service 12½%
Cover 15p
Children's helpings (under 10)
Seats 60 (parties 30)
Air-conditioning
No dogs
Am Ex, Diners

Mike Butt (whose 'lifeline is giving people some joy') is in a class of his own as chef and barker alike, and *Guide* forms have floated down like leaves in Vallombrosa this year. Genuinely critical accounts of meals served in his 'caverne d'Ali Baba' (by one Belgian description) are rarer, no doubt because the culinary dialect is unfamiliar: Kenyan-Asian spicing applied to mostly first-rate Irish fish, poultry and game. For instance, one meal began with seafood honey-sour, which was monk-fish deep-fried in a piquant batter with a fair sweet-sour sauce crowned with a julienne of carrot. Lemon chicken, Peshawari roast lamb, the ever-popular beef rickshawboy, turbot seychelloise, sole Lahori and other marinated dishes, and highly personal treatments of game, all invite a visit. But Indian classics do not, says an autumn visitor who found shami kebab, cabbage dolma, and tandoori chicken 'antiseptically spiceless', and pilau rice 'short-grain, overcooked, and turmeric-saturated'. Moreover, you must expect a stiff bill if you also drink wine: Gewürztraminer (Dopff) £5·50; sweetish Vouvray £3·65. Recorded music. Dress up to the owner's ambitions.

App: Mary Ann Gralka, H.C., Jean & Yvette Pigeon, Mr & Mrs Leo F. Cone, and others

---

DUBLIN see also wine bar section

DUNDERRY Co Meath   Map 10

Dunderry Lodge
5 m SW of Navan
on L23
Navan 31671

Closed L; Sun; Mon
Must book
D only, 7.30–11

Tdh £4 (meal £5·75)
Alc £5·85 (meal £8·05)

Service 10%
Seats 36
🔲 rest (1 step)
Am Ex card

This 'converted barn and cow-house in the lush countryside of County Meath' shelters Nicholas and Catherine Healy (who cooks), migrants from Jaws and Slane Castle in the same district. Little information is yet to hand except for praise of their prawns wrapped in slices of ham with mayonnaise, cucumber and apple, ratatouille, garlic bread, and noisettes of lamb in fresh apricot sauce (a seasonal dish at £3·75 including well-cooked fresh vegetables). But venison pie, roast widgeon with fresh plums and madeira sauce, veal cauchoise, prawns à la crème, and salmon hollandaise are also to be noted, and they make their own ices. Wines for 1979 (from £2·50 for French ordinaires) are uncertain, but may include promising Riojas and Barossa Valley Australians as well as the usual French ones. No dogs. More reports, please.

DUN LAOGHAIRE Co Dublin   Map 10

Digby's
62 Upper George's Street
Dublin 802204

Closed L; Apr 13;
Dec 24–26
Must book
D only, 7–11.30 (Sun
10.30)

Alc £6·30 (meal £8·95)

Service 12½%
Seats 32
♾ rest
No dogs
Access, Am Ex, Barclay,
Diners

This small, informal restaurant was formed by amoebic fission when Trudi's moved elsewhere and Paul Cathcart, the chef, stayed put to work with a new partner and Georgina Foley to help in the kitchen. Last year's visitors report that they are trying hard and, moreover, trying the right things with a menu that changes with the season and the market, and offers a daily vegetarian dish too. The best things at a test meal were the mussel and squid first courses, the agreeably high venison, pheasant, and wild duck with red wine and orange (sensible, too, to offer a whole bird for £4·75, a half for £3·65), and the chocolate orange mousse, made with good chocolate and liqueur. Rack of lamb, rabbit casserole, pork fillet in white wine with cream and apricots, and spinach, are also praised, but keftedes tend to be dry, and couscous 'null, apart from the hot sauce'. 'Surely their gratin dauphinoise potatoes had been boiled first?' Specialities include stuffed pirogi and peperonata (£1·25), and fillets of plaice stuffed with fresh crab (£3·60). Wines, from £3 a litre for Bardolino or Soave, in 1978 offered Alsace Sylvaner and other French bottles well under £3. Vacqueyras '76 (£3·30) will be good with more bottle age. Recorded music. More reports, please.

Trudi's
107 Lower George's Street
Dublin 805318

Closed L; Sun; most
public hols
Must book
D only, 7.30–11

Alc £6·30 (meal £8·90)

Seats 56
♾ rest
No dogs
Am Ex, Barclay

There are three partners: Trudy Kiernan (who cooks), and David Kiernan and Johnny Robinson, who manage. They have plenty of space in this house ('we like the tables for two upstairs that overlook the main dining-room'), and both cooks and waiters work hard. 'A delicious onion and leek soup followed by nicely dressed crab' is one memory, crab with garlic mayonnaise and fillets of pork with a well-made mushroom and white wine sauce, another. Courgettes in cheese sauce, potted crab (£1·25), braised lambs' tongues with mustard sauce (90p), pigeon breasts with black cherries, 'moist and well-timed breast of chicken en croûte', and potatoes baked with onions, cheese and cream are also praised (though the last dish tasted warmed-up on Trudy's night off). It may not be worth leaving room for the puddings. Specify the brand if you want sherry, a member advises after an unworthy tulipful, and expect little of the wines. Torre Franc French ordinaires are £3·70 a litre. Recorded jazz. No children under ten.

App: Richard Foster, A.K. & L.C.J., C.H., James C. Doherty, and others

Irish public holidays do not all coincide with English ones.

See p. 440 for the pub section, and p. 505 for wine bars.

Towers Hotel
Glenbeigh 12

Closed mid-Oct to
mid-Nov; Apr 13;
Dec 24 & 25
Must book
Meals 12.30–2.30, 7.30–9

Alc £6·85 (meal £9·80)

Service 15%
Children's helpings
(under 5)
Seats 128 (parties 60)
 rest
Air-conditioning
Car park
No dogs in public rooms
Access, Am Ex, Barclay,
Diners, Euro
21 rooms (4 with bath)
B&B £9·50

Not so much dreaming towers (for they don't seem
to sleep much at Ernie Evans's convivial hotel),
more bats in the belfry. Perhaps that's why Paul
Bocuse liked it, as do Britons, Americans and others
in love with the kind of Irishness you find on the
Ring of Kerry. The public rooms, pictures and all,
are better decorated than the bedrooms; and in the
dining-room the fish is better than anything else,
which may mean trawling in your pocket for Mr
Evans's filets de sole aux crevettes (£6·75 including
vegetables), turbot aux fruits de mer, baked scallops,
and crab Mornay, and grilled buttered lobster
(£9·90). But 'humbler plaice is also excellent.' The
seafood curry is worth considering too (£4·75) and
there are the usual steaks, though the pig's head
and cabbage invitingly depicted on the menu does
not seem to be on offer. Sweets are 'better skipped'.
Wines, mostly bought direct from France, are dear:
St Véran '75 (Ferraud) £5·25. However, they include
good '76 Beaujolais and even (at £22·50) Vouvray
Tranquille '47. Wear a tie. The pianist is not
universally popular, but is in character.

*App: James F. P. Fischer, R.W., Thomas Ward,
and others*

Marlfield House
on Courtown Road
1 m SE of Gorey
Courtown Harbour 21124

Closed L (exc bar); Sun;
Mon; Dec 25 & 26
Must book D
Meals 1–2.30 (bar),
7.30–8.30

Tdh D from £7 (meal
£8·35)
Alc L (bar) £3·30 (meal
£4·90)

Service inc
Seats 60 (parties 30)
 rest; w.c.
Car park
No dogs
11 rooms (all with bath)
B&B £12–£14

Mary Bowe from Esker Lodge at Curracloe (see the
1978 *Guide*) has opened this 'heavenly' Regency
dower house in 35 wooded acres (part of the
Courtown estate). Good taste is apparent in both the
furnishing of the house and the composition of the
menus, and if she can resist booking more evening
customers than even her competent staff can cope
with, the potential is high. Numerous nominations
describe everything from 'a feast of Slaney salmon',
'outstanding' scallops in cream and brandy sauce,
brill provençale, and beef ribs with parsnip puree, to
whiskey cake and home-made praline ice-cream. A
touring inspector enjoyed the Irish eavesdrops that
emerged from the cigar smoke ('my great-grandfather
got married at 65 and had eight children in ten
years') and ate extremely well: 'a useful reminder
that Ireland is not *all* boarding-house cookery.'
Mushrooms fried in batter with garlic sauce (90p)
were deliciously crisp and light, and the aïoli
compelling; different meats in a salad were admirably
cooked and presented, and vacherin with mocha and
almonds was also good. Coffee itself was less so. La
Tourelle or La Gravette ordinaires are £3, Aloxe-
Corton '73 (Louis Latour) £10·60, and Ch. Grand
Pontet '70, c.b., a reasonable £10. Lunches, 'varied
and solid enough for anyone', are eaten in the

drawing-room bar, beside the rosewood grand piano
on which Lawrence of Arabia is reputed to have
played. No music of this or any other kind with
dinner. Smoking, young children, and tieless men
at night are gently discouraged.

*App: John M. Farrell, H. N. Piper, M.A., A.H.,
Ann Kierans, and others*

HOWTH Co Dublin   Map 10

Belmont Restaurant
10 Harbour Road
Dublin 323334

Overlooking Howth harbour and the encouraging
bustle of fishing-boats landing their catches, the
Kollmers' little restaurant lives up to expectations
with careful cooking on an interesting set menu:
fresh asparagus soup, ragoût fin gratinée (chicken
in mushroom and cream sauce), roast pork with
'admirable' crackling, apple sauce and stuffing,
Wicklow trout in court bouillon and melted butter,
sauerbraten with hand-made spätzli, monk-fish,
calf's liver Berliner-style (with apple rings and
onions), apple tart, fresh fruit or ice-cream.
'Presentation is a delight.' Wine licence: Italian
house wines, £3·10 the bottle. Recorded music.

Closed L (exc Sat & Sun);	Tdh L from £2·85	Seats 49
D Sun & Mon; Oct;	(meal £5·35), D £6	🔲 rest (1 step)
public hols	(meal £7·20)	Car park
Must book		No dogs
Meals 12.30–2.15,	Children's helpings	Am Ex, Barclay
6.30–10.30	(min £1·30)	

King Sitric
East Pier,
Harbour Road
Dublin 325235 *and*
326729

Closed L; Sun; 10 days
Chr; public hols
Must book
D only, 6.30–11.15

Alc £7·95 (meal £10·90)

Cover 25p
Seats 72 (parties 24)
🔲 rest (1 step)
No dogs
Access, Am Ex, Barclay,
Diners

*'A delightful place with some very good cooking of fish
purchased off the boats in the harbour the same
morning,' says one inspector about Aidan McManus's
'clubby' restaurant on Howth Head, and that was what
earned Mr McManus and his co-chef John
Houraghan a pestle last time. But, alas, that
inspector was lucky. It is not yet so good a restaurant
that the owner can afford to leave the kitchen, let alone
the house, for long. A test meal, incompetently served
from start to finish, at least began with a light fish
soup (95p) tasting of shellfish, good stock and butter.
John Dory and monk-fish also tasted fresh. But
details went downhill all the way: a strong taste of
dried thyme and past-it Stilton in the mousse (£1·20),
'overwhelming dry mustard' in a gummy sauce for
monk-fish thermidor (£4·20), the frying oil fading fast,
and mediocre meringue, ice-cream and chocolate sauce
combined in the house sweet. Cafetière coffee is
excellent. Both the pros and cons are reflected in other
accounts, with the further touch that 'they book more
people than they can cope with.' Bergerac ordinaires
are £2·80, and though we have not seen the current
list, clarets, vintage ports and sweet white wines are
admirable. Recorded music. More reports, please.*

427

Fitzpatrick Castle Hotel
Victorian Dining Room
on T44
Dublin 851533

A comfortable Victorian castle (with sauna and heated pool) overlooking Dublin Bay. Mixed pickles in the past year, but 'dilute' vichyssoise, over-cooked vegetables and unripe strawberries are more than balanced by 'half a perfect Ogen melon filled with fat, fresh prawns, with real mayonnaise served separately'; tender steak Rossini 'cooked exactly as asked'; roast turkey 'with a succulent stuffing'; apple pie with 'real' apple chunks and crisp, thin pastry. A formal buffet for a conference was 'immense and beautiful'. Service may be rather rushed. Wines from £2·75. Snacks in the grill bar.

Must book	Service 12½%	No dogs
Meals 12–2.15, 6.30–10.30	Children's helpings (under 12)	Access, Am Ex, Barclay, Diners, Euro
Tdh L £4·50 (meal £7),	Seats 100 (parties 300)	50 rooms (all with bath)
D £6·75 (meal £9·50)	Air-conditioning	B&B about £11
Alc £9·15 (meal £12·20)	Car park	

The Vintage
Main Street
off N71
17 m S of Cork
Cork 72502

Closed L; Tue;
Wed (Oct–May);
Dec 25 & 26; Jan & Feb
D only, 7–10.30

Alc £6·40 (meal £9·05)

Service 10%
Seats 40
♿ rest (1 step)
No dogs

Beams, plastic vines, and a stone wall adorn the Galvins' restaurant, which one visitor calls the market-leader (in price as in quality) in a town where eating-out seems to be the main pastime. Several reports since last year's provisional entry confirm this, though not without scepticism: 'My cotriade (fish stew) tasted of pure bay-leaf'; 'soufflé aux fruits de mer was hardly a soufflé, more a casserole crowded with cockles.' However, good meals are also reported, and hors d'oeuvre, rabbit terrine, scallops with bacon, a better cotriade 'with salmon, monk-fish, scallops, clams and prawns', 'mild and tender beef curry' and poularde champenoise (£2·85 in 1978), are all praised. Courgettes in white sauce and aubergines in tomato indicate effort with vegetables, though they do not always suit the dishes served. 'Sauté potatoes were poor.' Crème riche aux abricots (and walnuts too) may be the best sweet. Beware of off-year clarets, but the house burgundy at £3 is fair. Recorded music. Details are approximate.

App: D. J. Hogan, R.S., C.H., A.K. & L.C.J., Mark & Heather Williamson, and others

KINSALE see also wine bar section

For the explanation of ♿ denoting accessibility for the disabled, see 'How to use the Guide', p. 4.

KNOCKFERRY Co Galway   Map 10

Knockferry Lodge
Roscahill
off T71
6½ m N of Moycullen
Galway 80122

'Good home-cooking presented without fuss in a pleasant dining-room overlooking Lough Corrib.' Visitors appreciate Des Moran's dedication, and the quality of the soups, the 'mustardy mayonnaise' for smoked pike or mackerel, chicken Maryland, roast lamb with whinberry jelly, and boeuf bourguignonne. Cheese tends to be dull, and the ice-cream is 'still at the experimental stage', though guests confirm that texture, not flavour, is the problem. House wine is Italian, £2 the litre, 40p the glass. The taped music palls. One twelve-seater table for outdoor eating. There are grumbles about 'rooms and house-keeping – straight out of Edna O'Brien'.

Closed Oct 27–Apr 12
Must book
Meals 12.15–1.30, 7–8
(9.30 Sat)

Tdh L £2·20 (meal £3·50),
D from £4·75 (meal £8·10)

Children's helpings
(under 10)

Seats 39 (parties 50)
Car park
No dogs (exc bar)
10 rooms (2 with bath)
B&B from £5

LETTERFRACK Co Galway   Map 10

Rosleague Manor
8½ m NE of Clifden
Moyard 7

Closed L (exc bar);
mid-Oct to Easter
Must book D
Meals 12.30–2.30 (bar),
8–9.30

Tdh D £6 (meal £7·80)
Alc (bar) L £2·70

Service 10%
Seats 65 (parties 10)
♿ rest; w.c.
Car park
16 rooms (14 with bath)
B&B £7–£8·50
D, B&B £12–£13

The Foyle family run this Connemara hotel with charm and consideration. The house was built in 1830, and its gardens run down to the water's edge. It is closed in winter, and there are no set lunches, but substantial snacks can be taken in bar or lounge. At night, Patrick Foyle and Nigel Rush in the kitchens make overtures towards haute cuisine, but their forte lies in their magnificent salmon and sea trout (freshly caught), with alternatives of deep-fried shrimps or 'beautifully tender beef in a delicious sharp red wine sauce'. First courses (except for soups), vegetables and some of the sweets have been found disappointing, and at breakfast the 'fruit juice' (of a type all too often met in Eire) and the toast should be avoided. To go with the fish there are acceptable white burgundies and Alsace wines on the otherwise humdrum list; house red or white is £2·20 a half-litre or 55p a glass. Guinness and Smithwick's in the bar. No music. No dogs. Children under 12 may eat in the restaurant only with prior notice. Though the bedrooms are comfortable and spacious, two couples in 1978 complained of sheets too small for the double beds.

App: A. J. Wardrop, J.M., S. McGovern, N.D.P., and others

PLEASE keep sending in reports, as soon as possible after each meal. Closing date for the 1980 Guide is September 30, 1979, but reports are even more useful earlier in the year, especially for the remoter areas and new places.

MALAHIDE Co Dublin Map 10

Johnny's
9 James Terrace
Dublin 450314 *and* 452206

Closed L; Sun; Mon;
1 week Easter; mid-Sept
to mid-Oct; 1 week Chr;
public hols
Must book
D only, 7.30–11

Alc £7·60 (meal £10·80)

Seats 65
Access, Am Ex, Barclay,
Diners

Johnny Oppermann, the chef-patron of this hospitable
cellar with a blazing fire and a view of the kitchen –
'a great place for a jolly evening's eating and drinking'
– was rapped rather sharply last time so it is a relief
to find diners praising not only the chicken Kiev
(£5), noisettes d'agneau grand'mère (£5·70) and
tournedos au poivre vert that are specialities, but also
salmon pâté, medallions of pork, ratatouille, croquette
potatoes, and 'a mouth-watering chocolate layer-cake
which for once tasted even better than it looked.' There
are not many single-figure clarets among the wines
(from £3·80 for Beaujolais '76) but Louis Latour's
Savigny-les-Beaune and Aloxe-Corton, '72 or '73,
were under £10 in 1978. Recorded music. Air-
conditioning. No dogs. Wear a jacket and tie, and
report, please.

MALLOW Co Cork Map 10

Longueville House

4 m W of Mallow
on Killarney Road
Mallow 27156

Closed L (exc res); Sun
& Mon (exc res);
mid-Oct to mid-Apr
Must book
D only, 7–8.30

Tdh from £7·50 (meal
£10·05)

Service 10%
Seats 50
⟨⟩ rest (3 steps)
Car park
No dogs
20 rooms (18 with bath,
2 with shower)
B&B from £8·50
D, B&B from £89·50
p.w.

This serene and (for Ireland) unusually well-kept
mansion, overlooking its own park and the
Blackwater valley beyond, is one of the few that
have steadily improved over the years through its
owners' refusal to rest on their laurels or profits.
Mrs O'Callaghan goes to John Tovey at Windermere
(*q.v.*) for cookery courses and her husband to
Germany or France for wine ones; both are determined
'to cook everything fresh from our farm, garden,
vineyard and river'. Their reward is people with
memories hailing 'the country-house cooking of
before 1939 – even the consommé', and younger
visitors reporting that 'we were called by name
throughout and pressed to eat and drink more.
Breakfasts presented fresh fruit compotes and juices,
porridge, home-made bread, home-made sausage,
black and white puddings, and marmalade. Dinner
during our stay brought nettle and mushroom
soups, asparagus flan, grilled salmon hollandaise,
roast lamb, sauté veal in creole rice, and home-grown
vegetables from the garden.' Seafood pancakes, light
flaky pastry for flans, and 'colourful and
attractive' soufflés, tarts, and roulades on the trolley
are also mentioned by others. It is true that if
Mrs O'Callaghan or her assistant are out of the
hotel for any reason it inevitably shows. The wines
improve steadily from Ch. de Longueville '72 red or
English Chilsdom '75 at £3·30, to runs of Ch.
Pichon-Longueville-Baron itself (even the '61, c.b.,
is a comparatively modest £12). There are good
Rhônes and Loires, and reasonably priced but
mostly only moderate burgundies. No music. No
pipes. No children under 12. Wear a jacket and tie.

App: by too many members to list

430

MOYARD Co Galway   Map 10

Crocnaraw
5 m N of Clifden
Moyard 9

Closed Sun D; Nov–Mar
Must book D
Meals 1–2.15, 8–9.45

Tdh L £4·15 (meal £5·90),
D £6·75 (meal £8·75)

Service 10%
Seats 36
♿ rest
Car park
Am Ex card
10 rooms (6 with bath)
B&B £8·90
D, B&B £14·10 (min
3 days)

Mrs Fretwell continues to run this country house hotel by the sea to the satisfaction of her regular summer visitors. Her aim is comfort, and informality without carelessness, and people find the atmosphere relaxing. Food comes direct from garden and orchard, and a home farm provides milk, butter and eggs, so not surprisingly a cream of green pea and lettuce soup (though, like some other dishes, it could have been hotter) was a 'taste sensation'. Fresh fish such as mackerel, brill, and dressed crab, are often on the menu. Sweets are mostly based on fresh fruit or ice-cream. The choice of wines on a list of 35 or so is above average for the area and shippers are shown; prices, too, are fair. No carafes or wines by the glass, but several half-bottles. Dogs allowed by arrangement only. No children under eight. No music. 'Delicious' afternoon teas can be taken outdoors in good weather. Smoking is admitted on occasion in kitchen as well as dining-room.

App: G. Wood, S.M., and others

NEWPORT Co Mayo   Map 10

Newport House
Newport (Mayo) 12 *and*
61

Closed Oct–Apr
Must book D
Meals 12.45–2.15,
7.30–9.30

Tdh L about £4·25
(meal £5·15), D about £7
(meal £7·90)

Service inc
Children's helpings
Seats 60 (parties 10)
♿ rest; w.c.
Car park
No dogs in public rooms
Am Ex, Barclay, Diners
24 rooms (20 with bath,
4 with shower)
B&B £10·25–£11·50

Two years of mixed accounts of Francis Mumford-Smith's Georgian house and park by the tidal Black Oak river leave some puzzles behind. It is clear that the house was on the chilly side in a disappointing May/June and not everyone found the flowers, good housekeeping and emotional warmth that would have made it easier to put up with, or for that matter mention, minor discomforts. The food, for which responsibility is shared between Gerard Morice's team and Rosaleen Moore (she makes the sweets) is 'normally excellent', especially 'fresh plaice with home-made tartare sauce', and naturally the sea-trout and salmon from their own fishery. But set meals offer no choice except of pudding, which means that there is no room for failure, and the July visitor who reports good terrine of duckling and minestrone, followed by 'most delicate' poached salmon and 'delicious rhubarb tarts and raspberry sorbet', has to be set against the May couple who found inferior versions of the first two items, and could admire baked brill and French lemon tart, but not the vegetables or the 'stringy, fatty' roast lamb. There are bar meals on request at lunch-time. Wine prices, with several clarets under £3, are gentlemanly, and though too many off-years are represented, £5·60 is not bad for château-bottled Ch. Léoville-Poyferré '73. No music.

*App: Dr & Mrs J. R. Norman, R.S.,
Henry Fawcett, and others*

New Ross Galley
New Ross 21723

Dick Fletcher points out that his dinners are the main attraction on his bateaux mouches sailing on the Barrow, Nore and Suir: 'Lunches and teas are more trippery.' And if an account of 'a midsummer night's dream' of a cruise holds good at other seasons – with hors d'oeuvre, salmon hollandaise, lamb, pork casserole and an almond and peach flan all pronounced excellent – 'an exceptional evening' can be expected, rain or shine. Carafino is £2·60 the litre. No music. Dress warmly.

Closed Sun; Oct–Easter
(exc Wexford Festival)
Must book
Meals 12.30, 7

Tdh L £5 (meal £6·30),
D £8·50 (meal £9·80)

Service inc

Children's helpings L
(under 9)
Seats 84 (parties 30)
No dogs

Currarevagh House

4 m N of Oughterard
on lake shore road
Galway 82313

Closed early Oct to Easter
Must book
Meals 1.15, 8

Tdh L £3 (meal £4·70),
D £6 (meal £8)

Service 10%
Seats 30
♿ rest (2 steps); w.c.
Car park
No dogs in d/r
Cheques by arrangement
15 rooms (5 with bath)
B&B from £10
Full board from £17 p.d.
(3 day min)

'East, west, Currarevagh's best' roughly sums up the response of the various nationalities who visit and revisit the Hodgsons' mid-Victorian house and wooded estate by Lough Corrib. Bridie Molloy and June Hodgson's cooking is only a part – though a vital part – of the unique, elsewhere mostly bygone, atmosphere which enables people to treat an Irish country house as home, and yet be efficiently fed and served. 'The gong drags you from the blazing turf fire to (choiceless) meals twice a day if you wish, and that is not counting the cold ham or tongue and porridge with cream on the sideboard at breakfast, and the home-made scones and cakes at tea.' Lunch may bring spicy spaghetti or cauliflower au gratin, various pâtés, egg dishes and salads, and a substantial syrup pudding or fluffy sweet omelette. At dinner there will be soup, then scallops, or brill, or tomato mousse with a traditional roast ('better than the mixed grill') as a centrepiece, and well-cooked – seasonally limited – vegetables. Lemon soufflé, oranges in caramel and baked Alaska are among sweet successes, and, as a 12-year-old writes, 'We were always offered seconds of main course and sometimes of hors d'oeuvre too.' The coffee is Kenya. The Mommessin ordinaire is £2·50; other wines are unremarkable but easily priced. Children – like non-resident visitors – are 'tolerated but not encouraged'. No music. No cigars till the coffee stage. Wear a tie at dinner.

*App: Emma Steafel, Freda & Godfrey Ridout,
N. & V.W., Elizabeth Foster, and others*

1979 prices are as estimated by restaurateurs in the autumn of 1978.

RATHFARNHAM Co Dublin   Map 10

Killakee House
Killakee Road
Dublin 906645

Closed L; Sun; mid-Jan
to mid-Feb
Must book
D only, 7–11

Alc £7·80 (meal £10·45)

Service 12½%
Seats 50 (parties 20)
Car park
No dogs
Am Ex, Barclay

Josef Frei has retired from the Pot Pourri in Dublin to this allegedly haunted dower house 'in the foothills, on the road to the pine forest'. His menu is unwisely long and therefore unnecessarily dear: one early visitor would have been prepared to overlook a stray ammoniac sweetbread, or 'messy' sole with shellfish, for the sake of the 'old world charm and good service', but for the high price of giving Mr Frei a second chance. Happily the Guide's system allows second chances, and other visitors, some already frequent, have found 'very subtle' scallop pâté, fine sole and salmon, tender rack of lamb, 'entrecôte Café de Paris superior to many Geneva versions', and a much better flavoured dish of sweetbreads (served with rösti potatoes). 'Swiss apple tart and café glacé Tia Maria are not to be missed either.' Wines from £2·90 in 1978 include some good Louis Latour burgundies and château-bottled clarets: Ch. de Pez '71, £5·20. Recorded music. Children 'not welcomed after 9 p.m.' More reports, please.

ROSSLARE Co Wexford   Map 10

Strand Hotel
Wexford 32114

Breda Kelly and her manager Austin Cody now run the late Billy Kelly's slap-up caravanserai. Set meals that sound impressive do not cost overmuch. But 'a solarium is no substitute for a decent sauce,' inspectors say, and a test meal yielded sad puddings, too. Happily, the consensus also includes some good soups, 'sweet scallops and bacon in vermouth and cream', brill, fried mussels, crab-meat au gratin, encouraging aubergine provençale, and lamb. Cherry strudel made with maraschino cherries was 'erotic', sweet soufflés 'blancmange-like'. As for the famous wines, in 1978 Ch. Brane-Cantenac '67 was £8·50 and Ch. Cos d'Estournel '70, £6, but the sight of Ch. Haut-Brion '74 already listed stirred doubts. No jeans. Wear a tie. Music 'in the ballroom, not the dining-room'. Bar snacks.

Closed mid-Dec to
mid-Feb
Must book
Meals 1–2.15, 7.30–9.15

Tdh L £4·25 (meal £5·95),
D £6·75 (meal £8·70)

Service 10%
Seats 200
♿ rest
Air-conditioning
Car park

No dogs
99 rooms (87 with bath,
12 with shower)
B&B £8·50–£10·50
Full board from £18 p.d.

Since each restaurant has a separate file in the Guide office, please use a separate form or sheet of paper for each report. Additional forms may be obtained free (no stamp required) from The Good Food Guide, Freepost, 14 Buckingham Street, London WC2N 6BR.

Mirabeau
Marine Parade
Dublin 809873

Closed L; Sun; public
hols
Must book
D only, 7–11.30

Alc £13·30 (meal £18·45)

Service 12½%
Seats 50 (parties 30)
& rest; w.c.
Air-conditioning
No dogs
Am Ex, Barclay, Diners

Behind the New Orleans wrought iron, Sean
Kinsella holds court, levying some of the highest
taxes in Ireland and chopping off the heads of
commoners bold enough to query them – 'You are
quite right about the mistake on the bill and the
whole meal will therefore be on the house, but don't
ever come here again.' No wonder Peter Ustinov
likes it. But barring accidents, one expects, after a
complimentary glass of less-than-regal fizzy wine in
front of the roaring fire, lavish helpings of very
well-cooked food: 'large fresh prawns in garlic
butter', minestrone with plenty of Parmesan cheese,
'duckling off the bone, tender and crisp on the
outside, served with good stuffing and orange sauce,
and red cabbage.' The shellfish platter is an aquarium
in itself, and prawns provençale as a main course
are also worth considering. Vegetables will be
properly done if you specify what you want, though
salad may be more appropriate. 'Most sweets are
the kind that arrive in hollowed-out pineapples.'
Coffee and service are both good, and people tend
to stay till the early hours. After all, with main dish
prices beginning at £8 and Mommessin carafe wine
at £4·50, *noblesse oblige*. Recorded music.

App: Terence O'Reilly, H.C., D.J.W.

Ballymaloe House

Cork 62531 *and* 62506

Closed 10 days winter
Must book
Meals 1 (buffet), 7–9.30

Tdh buffet L about £3
(meal £4·95), D about
£7·50 (meal £10)

Service 10%
Seats 80 (parties 30)
& rest (1 step)
Car park
No dogs in d/r
No cheques
23 rooms (15 with bath,
2 with shower)
B&B from £7

Twelve *Guide* years sit as lightly on the Allen family
as six centuries do on the Geraldine castle that
forms the core of their rambling mansion and park
where – if you are greeted at all – it may be by 'a
kitten tossing a ball of wool round the hall', or by
the children who abound in summer. The young are
'something we all need a rest from', in one crusted
Londoner's view, but he quickly found that the
outdoor amusements and the indoor high teas
removed them to a safe distance (they are not
encouraged at dinner). The cooking and service are
flawed but distinguished: 'the safest, least hotel-like
"tureen" hotel in Ireland, but with a large kitchen
team and two sittings on a Saturday night, it is not
consistent enough for a "pestle".' The breads –
both white and wholemeal – and the estate-churned
butter are as impressive in their way as the fruity
olive oil mayonnaise for fresh lobster. The best
dishes at test and other meals include 'very beefy'
cold consommé, 'a very woodsy, almost bitter
mushroom soup', cocktail of tomato and yoghourt
with herbs, potted crab, 'buttery and soft plaice en
coquille', fritto misto of fish (though apparently not
all of it was fried), Hungarian pork with peppers and
paprika, United Hunt turkey, and chicken in

tarragon cream. Comparative failures have included
'rather bland and bready' Danish pâté, spiced lamb,
and mashed potato. Cheeses are good, and so are the
sweets, especially pear and walnut meringue,
redcurrant meringue cake, and blackcurrant
ice-cream. The chocolate sauce for ice-cream also
deserves remark, as does the breakfast porridge
'with moist dark brown sugar and cream'. The
residents' lunchtime buffets are justly famous. The
service, though calm and smiling, has faltered on
occasion late in the evening, but the wine waiting
was good in 1978. The wines themselves are as good
as unchecked pipe and cigar smoke allows them to
be; tell the Allens if you would like them to banish
it from at least part of their dining-room (what has
it done over the years to the Jack Yeats pictures,
let alone you?). The white Nuits-St-Georges '72
(Clos de l'Arlot) at £7·50 delighted one member, and
the clarets include, for example, Ch. du Mirail '61
(a Graves) and Ch. Cos d'Estournel '67 at about £10.
There is also sound drinking under £4 still. No music,
apart from 'guitars and ballads some Saturdays'.
The rooms and to some extent their prices are
various and if you have not been before, explain as
much as you can of your needs and tastes when you
book. And expect to unwind, like that kitten's ball
of wool. Don't forget to visit the craft shop.

*App: James C. Doherty, Margaret-Anne Mackay,
D. J. Hogan, P.S., Joseph Gazdak, Rory F. Quirk,
and others*

SLANE Co Meath   Map 10

Slane Castle
Drogheda 24207 *and*
24163

Closed L (exc by
arrangement); Mon &
Tue; Aug 27; Dec 25,
26 & 31; Jan 1
Must book
D only, 7–10

Tdh from £3·50 (meal
£7·20)

Service 12½%
Seats 60 (parties 110)
♿ rest
Car park
No dogs
Am Ex card

The cachet of Irish peers may be greater in
Westchester than it is in Westminster, but so much
the better for the Earl of Mount Charles and
Tommy Fitzherbert (who cooks and helps to manage)
at this stately home, which is gradually being
upgraded to include a bigger bar and rooms for
private entertaining. Anyway, 'this is a well-run
place serving excellent food properly cooked, and
the vegetables in particular were far above the usual
Irish mush,' says a critical Dubliner after a dinner
of prawn quiche, wild duck with orange salad (£3·75
extra), and soufflé glacé Grand Marnier. Smoked
herring and pineapple mousse, prawns in
horseradish mayonnaise, 'fresh and generous turbot
with a correctly balanced mousseline', and 'crisp
but succulent' fillet of pork in peach and mushroom
sauce, are also praised. Baked sea trout jurassienne
is a speciality, though like most other dishes
mentioned, there is a supplement (£2·95) on the
table d'hôte. Lemon soufflé, apple tart, and black
grapes brûlée may perhaps be attributed to Mr
Fitzherbert's assistant Eileen Gough, and are liked.

Marqués de Riscal red or white '73, or Ockfener Bockstein '75, both at £3·75, were probably the best value in wine in 1978. Recorded music – and dancing sometimes at weekends.

App: G. M. Coburn, A.K. & L.C.J.

TRALEE Co Kerry   Map 10

Oyster Tavern
Spa
on Fenit Road
4½ m W of Tralee
Tralee 36102

Closed Sun L; Apr 13;
Dec 25
Meals 1–2.30, 7–10.30

Alc £5·25 (meal £6·65)

Service inc
Seats 120 (parties 40)
⑤ rest (1 step)
Car park

Very large, well-prepared helpings of fish draw crowds to Michael Lynch's country tavern. Midday food is not served till one, but Murphy, Guinness, Jamieson and other brand names must be well content with the time you spend in the large lounge bar. First courses (prawn cocktail, £1·50) are routine, and one couple divided a 'rather chewy' buttered lobster (£6) instead. As main courses at a test meal the 'firm, white juicy hake', and sole with garlic butter (both £3, with salad and brown bread) were ample and excellent. There are no sweets, and the coffee (25p) tastes instant – consider taking it doctored with whiskey and cream (80p). On Wednesday, Friday and Saturday nights a pianist plays. Carafe wines were £3·50 or £2·25 in 1978 for sizes unspecified (which is still legal in Ireland); on the wine list there are plenty of whites around £3–£4 and a Louis Latour Puligny-Montrachet '73 or '76 at £8·50, but if you prefer a red Rhône or a Beaujolais with your salmon, they too are there.

App: G. C. Hall, Henry Potts, P.S., R.M.F.

WICKLOW Co Wicklow   Map 10

Knockrobin House
Wicklow 2344

Herbert and Annemarie Bittel's Victorian country house is reached through a tunnel of greenery in the drive. The cooking is Germanic and normally good, though an August visitor whose party's meal began well with egg à la russe garnished with fresh prawns, and home-made soups of onion and oxtail, found both the roast venison with game sauce and the accompanying vegetables very poor, and except in the game season the house schnitzel may be a wiser choice. Finish with fruit ices or 'a Viennese iced coffee confection'. 'The taped music is a great irritant in the quiet dining-room.'

Closed L (exc Sun); Mon;
Sun D; Aug 27; Dec 24,
25 & 26
Must book
Meals 1–2, 7–9

Tdh Sun L £4 (meal
£5·60), D £9·50 (meal
£11·10)

Service inc
Seats 45 (parties 25)
⑤ rest (2 steps); w.c.

Air-conditioning
Car park
No dogs in d/r
Am Ex, Euro
4 rooms (all with bath)
B&B £8
D, B&B £15·50

YOUGHAL Co Cork   Map 10

Aherne's Seafood Bar
163 North Main Street
Youghal 2424

Closed Sun L; Mon D;
Apr 13; Oct 1–21;
Dec 24, 25 & 26
Must book D
Meals 12–2.30, 6.30–10
(9 Sun)

Alc £5·50 (meal £7·55)

Service 10%
Seats 50
♿ rest
Am Ex, Barclay

There is nowhere much to sit apart from the dark red restaurant, and you will have to wait while one of the FitzGibbons cooks your food. But they keep a vivier for lobsters and oysters, cook 'fresh and garlicky' mussels or prawns in butter as a first or main course, and may serve excellent mushrooms (also used for soup) with 'juicy and tasty' Dover soles on the bone as dishes of the day (£4·20 with vegetables). Mayonnaise, salads, and meringues are also creditable. Carafino is £2·20 for 45 cl, though Muscadet '76 at £3·80 sounds better value. Bar food all day. No children under 14. Car park. No dogs. Air-conditioning. More reports, please.

NORTHERN IRELAND

COMBER Co Down   Map 10

Old Crow
Glen Road
Comber 872255

A 'rather smart 1930s' pub-restaurant outside Belfast, with an ambitious menu, competent cooking and 'expeditious service'. Crab cocktail (£1·50), escalopes de veau Orloff (£3·75), rainbow trout amande (stuffed with prawns and herbs, coated with almonds and baked in butter, £4·40), and entrecôte chasseur (£4·20) are generously helped and invitingly presented. The sweets are 'a bit lush and creamy, but freshly made', and the coffee is good. Simpler and cheaper versions of the dinner dishes (rump steak chasseur, £2·30 including vegetables) have replaced the set lunches. Various wines; by the glass, 50p. Recorded music; supper dance on Saturdays. Soup and sandwiches in the lounge bar at lunch-time.

Closed Sun L; Dec 25
Must book D
Meals 12.30–2.30, 7–9.30
(10 Fri & Sat)

Alc L £3·30 (meal £4·40),
D £6·50 (meal £9·20)

Service inc

Children's helpings
Seats 65 (parties 120)
Air-conditioning
Car park
No dogs

GILFORD Co Armagh   Map 10

Pot Belly
7 m SE of Portadown
Gilford 404

Closed Mon; Sat L;
Apr 15 L; Dec 25, 26 &
31
Must book
Meals 12.30–3, 7.30–10

Tdh L £4·50 (meal £7·90)
Alc D £7·65 (meal £11·65)

Seats 48 (parties 30)
⑤ rest
Car park
No dogs

The Boyds' old linen mill (with pottery and leather workshops attached) lies 'on the edge of what locals call Red Indian country'. But it is a welcoming place, 'sympathetically converted', with open fires, and Helen Boyd varies what she cooks in a manner still unusual in Northern Ireland: you may begin, perhaps, with tomato and carrot soup, or peperonata with hot herb loaf (90p), or grilled kipper, and continue with lambs' kidneys with wine and herbs (£3·75), stuffed cabbage (with pork fillet and chicken livers, £3·95), chicken with aubergines, or plaice Véronique. 'They really try with their vegetables', as they should at £1·80 per person. Finish with peaches in brandy or biskotten-torte, perhaps. Spanish Garnacha red or Vivra white ordinaires are £3·50; the wine list lacks vintages, so Ch. Brane-Cantenac, say, may or may not be a bargain at £6·15. Recorded music. No children under eight for lunch – perhaps this is sacred to business deals, but we would still like more reports on both this set meal and the evening à la carte menu, please.

'Meal' indicates the cost of a meal for one, including food, coffee, half the cheapest bottle of wine, cover, service, and VAT (see 'How to use the Guide', p. 4).

SAINTFIELD Co Down   Map 10

The Barn
120 Monlough Road
off A7
1¾ m from Saintfield
Saintfield 510396

Closed L; Sun–Tue;
Thur; 2 weeks May &
Sept; public hols
Must book
D only, 7.30–9.30

Tdh from £7 (meal £9·40)

Seats 37
 ⌖ rest (1 step)

Little has been heard of the Misses McDonald and Jackson's elusive, gently converted barn since last time, but that is their guests' fault not theirs, for they are still providing the kind of natural, home-cooked food that Northern Ireland needs so badly and so seldom gets outside private houses. You may begin, for instance, with cream of celeriac soup or home-smoked trout or prawn mousseline, and thereafter look for stuffed plaice in cream, or spiced tongue in glazed sherry sauce, or roast venison with plum sauce. The vegetables have 'their own half-forgotten flavour'. Sweets are simple enough, but again materials are good. Wines (from £3) are sufficient: try one of the '76 moselles under £5, perhaps, or Ch. du Mirail '73 (a red Graves) at £5·50. Sometimes they play records if the country feels too quiet. Car park. No dogs. More reports, please.

PUBS

In his patronising *Song against Grocers*, G. K. Chesterton bewails the cans of poisoned meat which lead to people dying in hecatombs. His advice is to eat well down at the pub:

> God made the wicked Grocer
> For a mystery and a sign,
> That men might shun the awful shop
> And go to inns to dine.

Unfortunately, some of those inns are nowadays worse than the corner shop as a source of nourishment. It is the age of the short cut, the age of the instant mashed potato. Every year more and more comes in cans or packets: steak and kidney pie filling, stewed rhubarb, oven-ready pastry, frozen peas, powdered soup . . . the list grows longer as more and more pubs go in for food as a sideline. The publican, even more than the restaurateur, is tempted to take the easy way out, leaving himself more time to stocktake his cellar, supervise his staff and talk to the regulars about last night's darts match. The result is a morose girl dishing up shepherd's pie conceived out of a packet of white powder and a tin of meat, delivered on a hot-plate, and baptised with watery sprouts before being balanced awkwardly on the knee of a gentleman who would dearly like to be free of the entanglement. It is all apt to strengthen the resolve of those who believe that the pub is a place for drinking and that food there is at best a necessary evil.

Happily, as the *Good Food Guide* over the past five editions has shown, there are at least a few landlords and landladies who find room at the inn for food, not just blotting paper for the gallon of good ale that might follow, but also as a pleasure in itself, a quicker or less formal alternative to a meal in a restaurant. Pubs don't need to set aside a separate room as a restaurant to find a place in this section of the *Guide*; all the entries qualify on the food they serve in the bar, though some also have separate restaurants (which are not necessarily recommended). There is a refreshing variety in the kinds of food offered by the pubs on the following pages: from the humble cheese sandwich to intricate cold buffets; from home-made pasties to roast beef and Yorkshire pudding with all the trimmings. It is not quantity that counts, but quality. The publican whose staff or kitchen resources allow him to offer nothing more than home-made vegetable soup and a ploughman's lunch consisting of locally baked bread and cheese cut from the wedge gets the vote every time over his neighbour whose menu lists a variety of packet soups, a dozen Mother's Shame sandwiches and a choice of ten main courses which owe more to tin-openers and freezers than to butcher and greengrocer.

If the picture we present of pub food – a few hundred islands in a sea of mediocrity – is depressing, the news about beer is better than ever. The majority of the listed pubs now serve traditional draught beer, that is to say, beer brewed in the time-honoured way, without any of its goodness being removed by filtration or pasteurisation at the brewery, and stored and served in the pub without the use of carbon dioxide pressure. This is usually the measure of a good pub: whether the landlord is willing to give his time and skill to keep real ale, instead of opting for the gas bottle and spanner method, which has extinguished the cellarman's craft in many places. It is surely not coincidence that so many licensees who bother to serve good food also offer good ale.

Pub entries

The same abbreviations have been used in the pub section as in the rest of the *Guide* (see 'How to use the *Guide*', p. 4) but there are some differences:

The left-hand column of each entry gives the pub's name, its address or location (where necessary), telephone number and weekday opening hours (Sunday hours in England and Wales are universally 12–2, 7–10.30). When food is not served throughout licensing hours, separate times are shown in the text.

Some pubs, particularly those off the beaten track, do not always serve food during the advertised hours; if in doubt, telephone to check.

Separate restaurants, where they exist, are mentioned only for information and not as recommendations. If pub restaurants are good enough, they are listed in the main section of the *Guide*, with a cross-reference in the pub section.

Beer dispense is described thus:

'from the cask' – drawn by gravity
'pump' – drawn by hand pump (beer engine) or electric pump
'pressurised' – served by, or stored under, carbon dioxide
    pressure
'air pressure' – served by air compressor

Cider, where listed, is stored and served without carbon dioxide from a cask or similar container.

'Wine' means wine by the glass.

'Children' means they are legally allowed inside the building, but not into a bar where alcohol is served. Children over 14 and under 18 can, at the licensee's discretion, go into any part of a pub but cannot drink alcohol.

The licensee's reply has been accepted without query in many cases, which means that words or phrases such as 'home-made' or 'pump' may not always be accurate: good-quality pies may have been bought in, for instance, and beer served through a hand pump may be pressurised in the cellar.

Michael Hardman

ENGLAND

ABBERLEY Hereford & Worcestershire   Map 2

Elms Hotel

See main *Guide*

ABBOTSBURY Dorset   Map 2

Ilchester Arms
Market Street (B3157)
Abbotsbury 243 *and* 225
10.30–2.30, 6–10.30
(11 Fri, Sat & summer)
Closed Dec 25 evening

An old stone pub in the market square, close to Chesil Beach and swannery. Bar snacks (12–2 only): hot cottage rolls with cheese 40p–50p, or ham 60p, mackerel pâté 60p–75p, cooked snacks, including 'old-fashioned' bubble-and-squeak. Dinner by arrangement only: steaks, pheasant, partridge, wild duck. Devenish bitter and best bitter (pump); others pressurised. Taunton cider from the cask. Wine. Children. Fruit machine; bar billiards; darts. Garden. Car park. B&B £5·50.

ALBURY Surrey   Map 3

Drummond Arms
on A248
4 m SE of Guildford
Shere 2039
10.30–2.30, 5.30–10.30
(11 Fri, Sat)

A village local 'with a lot of pink lights'. Bar food (30p–65p; exc Sun L, Mon D)'good value for money': plain and toasted sandwiches, rolls, salads, daily hot dish. Separate restaurant (exc Sun D, Mon). Large choice of pressurised beers. Wine. Juke-box; fruit machine; darts. Garden. Car park. B&B £5.

Some pubs off the beaten track do not always serve food at times notified. Phone to check.

Hours given are opening times. Food may not be served over the whole period.

Wine bars are represented by a wine glass on the maps, pubs by a tankard.

ALMONDSBURY (LOWER) Avon   Map 2

The Bowl
Church Road
off M4/M5 and second
left off A38 towards
Gloucester
Almondsbury 612757
11–2.30, 6.30–10.30
(11 Fri, Sat)

A solid old pub next to the church in a secluded
village, caught in a net of motorways. Popular with
locals and tourists. Bar snacks ('everything on paper
plates'): baps 40p, turkey pie salad £1, ploughman's
35p–60p, toasted sandwiches 40p, salads £1–£1·50.
Separate restaurant (L only) with hot meals.
Courage (Bristol) bitter and best bitter (pump);
others pressurised. Wine. Children. Juke-box;
fruit machine; pool table; darts; pinball; table
football. Garden. Car park.

AMERSHAM Buckinghamshire   Map 3

King's Arms
High Street,
Old Amersham
Amersham 6333
10.30–2.30, 6–10.30
(11 Fri, Sat)
Closed Dec 25 evening

'Delightful' timbered coaching-inn dating from 1450;
ingle-nook fireplace. Bar food 'better value than
expected' (until 9 Fri & Sat): a 'very full ramekin
of lovely, smooth smoked mackerel pâté' 50p,
ploughman's ('enormous hunk of very good Stilton')
50p–60p, sandwiches 35p–40p, salads £1·15, soup and
roll 40p, jacket potatoes 35p. Separate restaurant
(exc Sun D, Mon). Ind Coope bitter from the cask or
pump and Burton ale from pump. Wine. Large
garden. Car park.

ANSTY Dorset   Map 2

The Fox
9 m SW of Blandford
Milton Abbas 880328
11–2.30, 6.30–11
Closed Tue

Hospitable Victorian pub in own grounds 'with a
large car park' – 'almost everything a pub should
be, packed with people.' 'Well worth a detour for
the marvellous selection of cold foods (from 60p)':
choice of fifteen meats and thirty salads, Dorset
pâté, 'excellent' gateaux. Separate restaurant (from
£2·50). Hall & Woodhouse bitter, Bass (pump), Old
Ansty strong ale (air pressure). Dorset farmhouse
cider. Wine. Children. Large garden. Juke-box;
fruit machine; bar billiards; darts. B&B from £5·50.

ARDLEIGH Essex   Map 3

Wooden Fender
Harwich Road (A137)
Colchester 230466
12.45–2.30, 6–11
(Sat 11–2.30, 7–11)

An old coaching-inn with pewter mugs, antique guns
and a log fire. Lunchtime bar food only (Mon–Sat,
12–2); home-made soup 30p, gammon £1·30, scampi
£1·30, local sausages and chips 60p, daily dish about
£1, ploughman's 60p, sandwiches 30p. Cold food
only on Sat. Adnams' bitter, Greene King IPA and
Abbot (pump); others pressurised. Wine. Tables
outside. Car park.

ARNCLIFFE North Yorkshire   Map 8

Falcon
Arncliffe 205
11–3, 5.30–10.30
(11 Fri, Sat)

An ancient pub in a peaceful, isolated village. Bar
food (L only) includes sandwiches, ploughman's,
pork pies, cold ham and 'excellent' roast beef.
Separate restaurant. Younger's Scotch bitter from
the cask. Garden. B&B. No details from landlord.

ARUNDEL West Sussex Map 3

White Swan
Chichester Road (A27)
Arundel 882677
11–2.30, 6–10.30
(11 Fri, Sat & summer)

A 300-year-old free house with exposed beams in the three small bars. Bar snacks: pâté 75p, smoked mackerel 70p, ploughman's 55p, sandwiches 28p–80p. Pies and pasties only in the evening. Separate restaurant (12–2, 7.30–9.30, exc Sun D & Mon L). Ruddle's County and bitter, King & Barnes bitter, Courage Directors (pump); others pressurised. Wine. Fruit machine; darts. Garden. Car park.

ASH Kent Map 3

Lion
The Street
on A257
9 m E of Canterbury
Ash 812234
10.30–2.30, 6–10.30
(11 Fri, Sat & summer)

Friendly, convivial pub near Pegwell Bay hoverport; lounge bar has low beams and copper pans. 'Very large' bar menu (30p–£3·75): soup, 'jumbo' prawns, smoked mackerel, plaice, steaks, roast beef, cottage pie, game pâté, 'things on toast'. Separate dining-room with same menu. Whitbread (Faversham) bitter (pump); mild and others pressurised. Wine. Juke-box; darts. Patio. Car park. B&B £6·50.

ASHBURNHAM East Sussex Map 3

Ash Tree
Brown Bread Street
off B2204
Ninfield 892104
12–2.30, 7–10.30
(11 Fri, Sat)

A 17th-century, beamed pub backing on to open farmland. Elaborate snack menu ('shepherd's pie crowned with toasted cheese' 95p, gammon steak £1·75, cheese and onion flan 60p) with roll and butter and fresh vegetables charged extra. Separate restaurant. Ind Coope Burton ale and Charrington IPA (pump). Wine. Bar billiards; darts. Garden. Car park.

ASKWITH West Yorkshire Map 5

Black Horse
on back road between
Otley and Ilkley
Otley 2425
11–2.45, 6–10.30
(11 Fri, Sat)

'Large, old, beamed, roomy and well-run' pub with extensive views of Wharfedale and Ilkley Moor. Bar lunches (Mon–Sat, 12–2): help-yourself cold buffet 'amazing value' at £1·40, steak £1·40, ham and egg £1·50, daily special £1·30. Similar but higher-priced menu Sun. Evening menu (6.30–10.15): home-made chicken and ham or steak and kidney pie 60p, curried beef 50p, cottage pie 50p. Separate restaurant (12–2, 7–9.30). Pressurised Webster's beers. Wine. Fruit machine; darts. Patio. Car park.

AUSTWICK North Yorkshire Map 8

Game Cock

See main *Guide*

Please report to us on atmosphere, decor and – if you stayed – standard of accommodation, as well as on food, drink and prices (send bill if possible).

Pubs are represented on the maps by a tankard.

AXMOUTH Devon Map 2

Ship
S of A3052
5 m W of Lyme Regis
Seaton 21838
10.30–2.30, 5.30–11
(winter 11–2, 6–10.30;
11 Fri, Sat)

Comfortable, friendly inn – a sanctuary for sick
birds, particularly owls. Bar meals (12–2, 7–9.30):
soup 25p, 'highly delectable' prawns 75p, pizza 75p,
ploughman's 45p–55p, trout £1·70, chicken £1·10,
'excellent' salads £1·20–£1·50, toasted snacks 40p.
Dinners (exc Fri; 7.30–9) in Buttery Bar. Devenish
bitter and Wessex best bitter from the cask.
Taunton cider. Fruit machine; darts; shove ha'penny.
Garden. Car park.

BANBURY Oxfordshire Map 2

Unicorn
Market Place
Banbury 3396
10–2.30, 6–10.30
(11 Fri, Sat)

'Dickensian atmosphere engendered by the
collections of old helmets, armour and weapons.' Bar
food includes 'extremely good' ham and egg flan,
beef, ham or cheese rolls. Mitchells & Butlers bitter
and Bass (pump). Wine. Outside lavatories.

BARFORD Warwickshire Map 2

Glebe Hotel
Church Street
Barford 624218
10–2.30, 6–10.30
(11 Fri, Sat)

A Georgian rectory converted to a hotel in 1947.
Bar food (12.30–2, 7.30–10, exc Sun D): soup 35p,
home-made pâté 65p, ravioli 50p, smoked mackerel
80p, sandwiches 40p–£1, omelettes from 60p,
home-made steak and kidney pie with chips £1·35.
Private dinner parties by arrangement. Davenports'
bitter (pump); others pressurised. Wine. Children.
Garden. Car park. B&B from £7·25.

BARNSLEY Gloucestershire Map 2

The Village Pub
on A433
Bibury 421
11–2.30, 7–10.30
(11 Fri, Sat)

A 17th-century country pub, recently reopened
under new ownership – 'cosy, dark brown and pink
decor'. 'Reasonably priced' bar food (12–2, 7–9.30,
exc Sun evening): 'very hot, thick and substantial'
home-made soup 40p, hot daily dish £1·20, salads
£1·45–£1·75, home-made sweets ('too tempting to be
given the go-by') 40p–50p, sandwiches. Wadworth's
6X (from cask and pump); others pressurised. Wine.
Tables outside. Car park.

BASSENTHWAITE LAKE Cumbria Map 7

Pheasant
off A66
at N end of lake
Bassenthwaite Lake 234
11–3, 5.30–10.30
(11 Fri, Sat)
Closed Dec 25

Well-run and efficient inn below Thornthwaite
Forest and next to the early British fort of Castle
How. Friendly service of bar food (L only, until
1.45): soup 30p, smoked salmon £2, prawns with
lobster sauce £1, pâté 85p, smoked eel fillet £1·50,
sweet smoked chicken 85p, 'bulging' sandwiches
32p–35p. Separate restaurant (12.30–2, 7–8.15).
Theakston's bitter and Bass (pump); others
pressurised. Wine. Garden. B&B from £8.

In England and Wales, Sunday opening hours are 12–2, 7–10.30.

See p. 441 for 'How to use the pub section'.

BATTS CORNER Surrey   Map 3

Blue Bell
off A325
4 m SW of Farnham
Frensham 2801
10.30–2.30, 6–10.30
(11 Fri, Sat)

Remote and 'uncomfortably small' old pub, with
'splendid fires in winter'. Bar food includes
home-made quiche with 'outstanding' salad £1·50,
pâté 75p, lumpfish caviare and toast 80p, sandwiches
30p–67p (toasted cheese and kipper, 47p). Gibbs
Mew premium bitter and Bishop's Tipple, Courage
Directors and bitter from the cask; others
pressurised. Wine. Darts. Garden. Car park.

BEACON HILL Surrey   Map 3

Woodcock
Churt Road (A287)
Hindhead 4079
10.30–2.30, 5.30–10.30
(11 Fri, Sat)
Closed Dec 25

An inn with a prosperous air in a delightful setting
opposite Golden Valley. The main attraction is the
cold buffet, 'though the pricing is erratic'; other bar
food includes soup and roll 35p, hot smoked
mackerel 70p, scampi and chips £1·20, rainbow trout
and chips £1·50, daily dish (Mon–Sat L) £1, Sunday
roast lunch £1·80. Separate restaurant. Gale's HSB,
bitter and mild (pump); others pressurised. Wine.
Darts. Car park.

BEAULIEU Hampshire   Map 2

Montagu Arms
Beaulieu 612324
10–2.30, 6–10.30
(11 Fri, Sat)

Business people and holiday-makers eat the 'well
above average' lunches in the hotel's Spats Bar; the
younger set take over in the evenings when there is
no food. Help-yourself salad buffet (£1·40–£1·80):
beef £1·80, roast duck £1·70, chicken and ham pie
£1·60. Soup and jacket potatoes 25p–50p in winter.
Wadworth's 6X and IPA, Hall & Woodhouse best
bitter, Whitbread Pompey Royal (pump); others
pressurised. Wine. Juke-box; fruit machine; darts;
pool table. Car park. B&B £12.

BECCLES Suffolk   Map 6

Loaves and Fishes
Fen Lane
Beccles 713844
10–2.30, 6–11
(7–11 in winter)

Converted maltings in a picturesque position by the
river. Bar food (exc Mon D; Fri and Sat evenings
only in winter; 35p–£1·30): chicken curry, beefburger,
quiche, pâté, salads, ploughman's, basket meals.
Separate restaurant (12–1.45, 7.30–9.30, exc Mon D;
3 courses about £4·50). Greene King IPA and Abbot
(pump); others pressurised. Wine. Juke-box;
fruit machine; darts; cribbage; dice. Courtyard.
Car park.

BECKHAMPTON Wiltshire   Map 2

Waggon and Horses
at junction of A4 & A361
Avebury 262
11–2.30, 6–10.30
(11 Fri, Sat)
Closed Dec 25

A 16th-century thatch and stone pub, mentioned in
the Pickwick Papers, and near Silbury Hill, Avebury
Circle and Kennet Longbarrow. Bar food (11.30–1.45,
6.30–10, exc Mon): salads £1·60, steaks £2·50,
scampi £2·30, 'poorman's' (chicken, cheese, lettuce)
£1, 'fisherman's feast' £1. Wadworth's 6X, IPA and
Old Timer (pump); others pressurised. Wine. Fruit
machine. Tables outside. Car park.

BEGBROKE Oxfordshire   Map 2

Royal Sun
on A34
Kidlington 2231
10–2.30, 6–10.30
(11 Fri, Sat)

A small 17th-century country inn with good service.
Bar food (until 30 minutes before closing): soup 35p,
daily special lunch 80p, pizza 80p, ploughman's 55p,
filled jacket potatoes 70p, gooseberry tart; suppers
(40p–£1·80): gammon, scampi and sausages.
Pressurised Ind Coope beers. Wine. Children.
Fruit machine. Garden. Car park.

BENENDEN Kent   Map 3

King William IV
High Street
Benenden 636
10.30–2.30, 6–10.30
(11 Fri, Sat)

A welcoming old pub with ingle-nook and a
pleasant atmosphere. Bar snacks (12–2, 6–8.30;
18p–£1·10): pâté, ploughman's, quiche, pizza, rolls,
pasties; two hot daily dishes. Shepherd Neame
bitter and mild (pump), stock ale from the cask;
others pressurised. Juke-box; fruit machine; darts;
dominoes; cribbage; dice. Garden. Car park.

BENTLEY Hampshire   Map 3

Bull
on A31
E of village
Bentley 2156
10–2.30, 6–10.30
(11 Fri, Sat)

An attractive, old-world coaching-inn with
ingle-nooks. Bar food (until 30 min before closing;
50p–£1·45): smoked mackerel, sandwiches,
home-made daily special. Separate restaurant.
Courage bitter and Directors (pump); others
pressurised. Wine. Fruit machine; darts; shove
ha'penny. Patio. Car park.

BIDDENDEN Kent   Map 3

Three Chimneys
on A262
Biddenden 291472
11–2.30, 6–10.30
(11 Fri, Sat)
Closed Dec 25

Tiny, cosy pub with a smoky atmosphere, both from
the wood fire and cigarettes. Bar extensions
promised. Mrs Sayers, the landlord's wife, prepares
all the food: soup 45p, pâté 55p, salmon mousse 85p,
'huge portions' of black-waxed Cheddar with cottage
loaf 55p, beef curry £1·85, smoked haddock in
cheese and wine £1·90, 'super' sea food pie £1·85.
Whitbread (Faversham) bitter, Greene King Abbot
Adnams' bitter, Brakspear's bitter from the cask;
others pressurised. Weston's farm cider from the
cask. Wine. Darts. Garden. Car park.

BINFIELD HEATH Oxfordshire   Map 3

Bottle and Glass
3½ m SW of
Henley-on-Thames
on Harpsden road
Henley-on-Thames 5755
10–2.30, 6–10.30
(11 Fri, Sat)
Closed Dec 25 evening

Attractive old thatched pub, 'with the best log fire
for miles'. Bar food (exc Sun): home-made soup 25p,
pâté 60p, scampi 85p–£1·60, rainbow trout £1·20,
salmon steak £1·50, salads 80p–£1·20. Sandwiches
35p–50p. Brakspear's bitter, special bitter, mild and
old from the cask. Gaymer's cider. Wine. Garden.
Car park.

Hours given are opening times. Food may not be served over the whole period.

BIRDLIP Gloucestershire Map 2

Golden Heart
on A417
1 m E of village
Coberley 261
11.30–2.30, 6–10.30
(11 Fri, Sat)
Closed Dec 25

'A cosy pub with ancient settles, yawning fireplaces and low beams.' Bar food (L until 2.30, D until 9): stockpot soup 45p, home-made pâté 65p, ploughman's 60p–70p, French bread with ham 55p, cheese or salad 45p, sandwiches. Theakston's bitter and Old Peculier, Wadworth's 6X and Old Timer, and Bass (pump); others pressurised. Weston's cider. Wine. Darts. Garden. Car park.

BISHOP'S LYDEARD Somerset Map 2

Rose Cottage

See main *Guide*

BISHOP WILTON Humberside Map 6

Fleece Inn

See main *Guide*

BLEDINGTON Gloucestershire Map 2

King's Head
3½ m from Stow-on-the-Wold
Kingham 365
10–2.30, 6–10.30
(11 Fri, Sat)

Welcoming old pub in a beautiful setting. Help-yourself bar food: onion soup 45p, smoked mackerel 65p, pâté 65p, potted shrimps 75p, grilled gammon £1·95, steak and wine pie £1·90, rabbit pie £1·90, steaks £3·45–£3·95, trout £2·25. Separate restaurant. Hook Norton bitter, Whitbread bitter (pump); others pressurised. Weston's cider from the cask. Wine. Fruit machine; darts; Aunt Sally. Two gardens. Outside lavatories. Car park.

BLICKLING Norfolk Map 6

Buckinghamshire Arms
Aylsham 2133
10.30–2.30, 6–11

A pleasant old inn in a picturesque village at the gates of 'magnificent Blickling Hall'. Wide range of 'superior' bar meals, including home-made soup, smoked eel pâté, black pudding with salad, ploughman's, cottage pie. Separate restaurant (7.30–9.30 and Sun L). Greene King Abbot and Adnams' bitter (pump). Garden. Car park. B&B.

BLYTHBURGH Suffolk Map 6

White Hart
on A12
3½ m from Southwold
Blythburgh 217
10.30–2.30, 6–11
Closed Dec 25

A gabled country pub, built in 1248 as an ecclesiastical court house, with oak beams and ingle-nooks. Large choice of cold food (exc Tue D; 50p–£2): home-cooked meats, salads, pâté. Hot lunches and home-made pies in winter. Separate restaurant (Wed-Sat D only). Adnams' bitter, mild and old ale (pump). Wine. Children. Garden. Car park.

BODIAM East Sussex Map 3

Curlew

See main *Guide*

Some pubs off the beaten track do not always serve food at times notified. Phone to check.

BOLDRE Hampshire   Map 2

Red Lion
Rope Mill
2½ m N of Lymington
Lymington 73177
10.30–2.30, 6–10.30
(11 Fri, Sat)

An old pub in the New Forest, with oak beams, brasses, antiques and log fires. Bar food (exc Sun D): 'delicious, juicy' gammon £1·75, duckling £2·10, scampi £1·30, home-made soup 45p, pâté 60p, smoked salmon £1, salads 90p–£1·75, sandwiches 28p–60p. Eldridge Pope Dorchester bitter, IPA and Royal Oak (pump). Wine. Patio. Car park.

BOUGHTON Kent   Map 3

White Horse
The Street
Boughton 343
10.30–3, 6–11

A Tudor pub with industrial bellows used as tables, and beer pumps and barrels 'scattered throughout'. Bar food: scampi and chips £1·30, steak sandwich £1·20, other sandwiches 35p–50p, home-made pâté 55p, ploughman's 45p. Separate restaurant (closed D Sun & Tue). Shepherd Neame bitter and best bitter (pump). Wine. Bulmer's cider. Darts; fruit machine. Children on covered terrace. Car park. B&B from £4.

BRANDON Suffolk   Map 6

Great Eastern Hotel
next to the station
Thetford 810229
11.30–2, 6.30–11

An old hotel serving bar food at lunch-time and before 9 in the evening: soup 23p, pâté 55p, egg mayonnaise 50p, ploughman's 60p–70p, sandwiches 30p–40p, toasted sandwiches 33p–43p. Separate restaurant (12.30–2, 6.30–8, exc Sun D). Ind Coope bitter (pump). Wine. Fruit machine; darts; pool table. Car park. B&B from £7·55.

BRENDON Devon   Map 1

Stag Hunters
off A39
2¼ m E of Lynmouth
Brendon 222
11–2.30, 6–10.30
(11 Fri, Sat & summer)

Clean, comfortable and efficiently run free house beside the East Lyn River in Brendon Valley. Snacks (L only; evenings promised for summer 1979): ploughman's 60p, ham or beef ploughman's 75p ('very generous quantities'), soup and roll 35p, scampi and chips £1·20, pâté 75p, hot daily special 80p. Small separate restaurant (7–8.15 only). Whitbread (Tiverton) bitter, Courage (Plymouth) bitter (pump); others pressurised. Rich's cider from Highbridge. Children. Fruit machine; bar billiards; darts. Garden. Car park. B&B £5·75.

BRENTWOOD Essex   Map 3

Greyhound
Magpie Lane,
Little Warley
Brentwood 220385
10–2.30, 6–10.30
(11 Fri, Sat)

A warm welcome – except for 'riff-raff' – at this extensively renovated pub at the bottom of Childerditch Common. Home-made snacks (average 70p; L Mon–Sat, D Mon–Fri) include lasagne, sausage pie, steak and kidney pie, cheese and onion pie, ploughman's, sandwiches, omelettes. Ind Coope bitter and Burton ale (pump); others pressurised. Patio and gardens. Car park.

Wine bars are represented by a wine glass on the maps, pubs by a tankard.

BRIDEN'S CAMP Hertfordshire   Map 3

Crown and Sceptre
off A4146
near Water End
Hemel Hempstead 53250
11–2.30, 6–10.30
(11 Fri, Sat)

A pleasant, well-run country pub with log fires. Bar food (L Mon–Sat only; 25p–£1): home-made soup, salads, pâté, ploughman's, sandwiches, meat rolls. Greene King IPA and Abbot, Samuel Smith's bitter, Adnams' bitter, Courage bitter (pump); others pressurised. Wine. Darts. Garden. Car park.

BRIDGNORTH Salop   Map 5

Parlors Hall Hotel

See main *Guide*

BRIDPORT Dorset   Map 2

George
4 South Street
Bridport 23187
10–2.30, 6–10.30
(11 Fri, Sat & summer)
Closed Apr 13; Dec 25

'Unplasticised' and comfortable pub in the town centre. 'Plenty of choice' on the bar menu (12–2.15, 7–10.15 or 10.30, exc Sun L, Thurs D): home-made soup 25p, pâté 65p, grilled plaice £1·10, omelettes 50p, home-made pies 65p–£1, ploughman's 55p, sandwiches 35p–45p. Palmer's best bitter and IPA (pump). Wine. Children. Darts in winter. B&B £5.

BRIGHTON & HOVE East Sussex   Map 3

Cricketers
Black Lion Street
Brighton 29472
10–2.30, 6–11

'Aggressively Victorian – huge silvered mirrors, lots of mahogany, red lampshades, huge mahogany bar.' Bar snacks always available: home-made cottage pie 40p, chicken and ham pie 65p, 'excellent' quiche 35p, sandwiches 30p–35p. Separate Buttery Bar (12–2 Mon–Sat only). Watney's Fined Bitter (pump); others pressurised. Wine. Children allowed only in the Buttery. Fruit machine. Outside gents'.

BROMYARD Hereford & Worcester   Map 2

Hop Pole
The Square
Bromyard 2449
10.30–2.30, 6–10.30
(11 Fri, Sat)
Closed Dec 25 evening

A Georgian hotel in an ideal spot for exploring the Malvern Hills. Bar food (L only): steak and kidney pie 75p, home-made soup 25p, cottage pie 50p, pâté 45p, whitebait £1, and bobotie 75p. Separate restaurant (12.30–2, 7.30–9; closed D Sun & Mon). Marston's Burton bitter and Pedigree (pump); others pressurised. Wine. Tables outside in summer. Car park. B&B from £6·50.

BURGH ISLAND Devon   Map 1

Pilchard
Bigbury-on-Sea 344
10.30–2.30, 5.30–10.30
(11 Fri, Sat & summer)

Walk or cross by sea tractor from Bigbury-on-Sea to reach this cosy and friendly free house, a monk's rest-house in 1336 and later a smugglers' haunt and a home for local pilchard fishermen. In summer there are salads 75p–£1·75, ploughman's 50p, pâté 50p, meat and salad rolls 50p; in winter home-made soup 20p or ploughman's. Palmer's bitter from the cask; others pressurised. Taunton cider. Wine. Darts. Children. Seats on sea wall.

BURHAM Kent   Map 3

Toastmaster's Inn

See main *Guide*

BURNHAM MARKET Norfolk   Map 6

Hoste Arms

See main *Guide*

BURWASH East Sussex   Map 3

The Bell
High Street
Burwash 882304
10–2.30, 6–10.30
(11 Fri, Sat)

A pretty pub, partly dating from the 15th century, in an attractive village. Bar snacks: soup 35p, ploughman's 65p, sandwiches 30p–40p, ham salad £2·30, plaice and chips £1·30, sausage, egg and chips 70p. Separate restaurant (12–2, 7–9; closed Tue from Oct to May). Harvey's BB, PA, mild (pump) and XXXX from the cask in winter. Mulled ale. Wine. Fruit machine; darts. Garden. Car park. B&B from £4.

CALLINGTON Cornwall   Map 1

Coachmakers Arms
N of A390 at junction
with A338
Callington 2567
11–2.30, 6–11

Comfortable free house with an 'olde village pubbe' atmosphere. Bar food (12–2, 7–10, exc Sun L, Mon D): soup, 'delicious' mushroom omelette, duck, chicken, steaks. Separate restaurant (Wed–Sat D only; must book Sat 2 weeks in advance). Range of pressurised beers, but 'we are considering St Austell real ale'. Wine. B&B from £5·50.

CAMBRIDGE Cambridgeshire   Map 3

Fort St George
Midsummer Common
Cambridge 54327
11–2.30, 6–10.30
(11 Fri, Sat)

On the banks of the river Cam, one of Cambridgeshire's oldest pubs, with roses round the door. Bar food (12–2, 6.30–10): Granary bread with cheese 50p–55p, Scotch eggs 30p, pâté 60p–65p, chicken 60p, smoked mackerel 75p, quiche 45p. Greene King IPA and Abbot (pump). Bulmer's cider. Wine. Children. Juke-box; fruit machine; ringing the bull. Garden.

CAREY Hereford & Worcester   Map 2

Cottage of Content
6 m NW of Ross-on-Wye
(Ballingham road)
Carey 242
11.30–2.30, 6.30–11
(summer); 12–2.30, 7–11
(winter)
Closed Dec 25 evening

Picturesque 15th-century free house hidden in beautiful Wye valley. 'Appetising display' of bar food (12.30–1.45, 7–9.30; Sun 12–1.30, 7–9.15): home-made soup 45p, pâté 80p, chicken with chips or salad £1·20, lasagne £1, trout with chips or salad £1·25, sandwiches 35p, ploughman's 55p–65p. Separate restaurant (D only; not Tue or Sun). Hook Norton bitter and mild, Whitbread (Cheltenham) bitter (pump); others pressurised. Wine. Fruit machine; darts. Garden. Car park. B&B £7·50.

CARTMEL Cumbria   Map 7

King's Arms
The Square
Cartmel 220
10.30–3, 6–10.30
(11 Fri, Sat)

A down-to-earth eating and drinking house near the Priory church and racecourse. Bar food (L only; last orders 2, 1.30 Sun): soup 20p, sandwiches 40p–69p, ploughman's 65p, salads 70p–£1·75, savoury quiche 70p, asparagus quiche 75p. Hartleys' XB bitter (pump); others pressurised. Wine. Children. Darts; dominoes; cards; children's games. Tables on forecourt.

CAVENDISH Suffolk   Map 3

Bull Hotel
High Street
Glemsford 280245
11–2, 6–11

'Very helpful service' in a pub built around 1530 but 'mucked about' by the Victorians. Home-cooked bar meals (L and 6.30–9.30; not Mon D): steak and kidney pie £1·10, Dunmow ham £1·20, cottage pie 65p; roasts on Sunday £1·20; spaghetti and curries occasionally. Pressurised Bass Charrington beers. Wine. Children. Juke-box; fruit machine; darts; shove ha'penny; dominoes. Garden and patio. Car park. B&B £4·50.

CHAPEL AMBLE Cornwall   Map 1

Maltsters Arms
Wadebridge 2473
10.30–2.30, 5.30–10.30
(11 Fri, Sat & summer)

Attractive village pub, which draws people from miles around. Bar food: soup 25p, scampi £1·40, plaice 95p, ploughman's 65p, salads 85p–£1·40, country hot-pot 65p. Separate restaurant (Sun 12.30–1; Mon–Sat 7.30–9.30). Wide range of pressurised beers. Wine. Children. Darts in winter. Car park.

CHENIES Buckinghamshire   Map 3

Bedford Arms

See main *Guide*

CHICKSGROVE Wiltshire   Map 2

Compasses
2 m NE of Tisbury
Fovant 318
12–2.30, 7–10.30
(11 Fri, Sat; closed
Tue L)

Thatched free house which 'doesn't look as though it's changed much since the Middle Ages'; easily reached from the A30. Extensive bar menu: soup 35p, smoked mackerel 60p, plaice and chips 90p, trout and chips £1·75, mushroom omelette 85p, sandwiches 25p–65p, 'really good ploughman's' 50p; cold Sunday buffet £1. Wadworth's 6X and Old Timer from the cask, Ind Coope bitter and Burton ale (pump); others pressurised. Bulmer's cider. Wine. Children. Fruit machine; darts; skittles; shove ha'penny. Garden. Car park. B&B £4.

CHIDDINGSTONE Kent   Map 3

Castle
Penshurst 247
10–2.30, 6–10.30
(11 Fri, Sat)
Closed Dec 25 evening

Part of a lovely greystone building dating from 1420, and a pub since 1730, set in a corner of a National Trust village. Comprehensive bar menu: scampi and chips £1·50, locally made pork sausage 15p, prawn cocktail 75p, smoked trout £1·25, home-made pâté 75p, salads £1·75, sandwiches 45p–95p. Separate restaurant (12.30–2·15, 7.30–9.30, exc Wed L, Tue). Shepherd Neame bitter, Young's special, Whitbread (Faversham) bitter (pump); Young's Winter Warmer, Shepherd Neame stock ale and Bob Luck's cider from the cask. Wine. Darts; shove ha'penny; cribbage. Garden.

In England and Wales, Sunday opening hours are 12–2, 7–10.30.

CHIPPING Hertfordshire   Map 3

Countryman
on A10
Royston 72616
11–2.30, 5.30–10.30
(11 Fri, Sat)

Friendly old pub with beams and ingle-nook.
'Attractively presented' bar food (from 6 p.m.;
50p–£1·50): fish, meat, home-made pizza, pâté, pies.
Separate restaurant (12–2, 7–9.30). Adnams' bitter,
Marston's Burton bitter and Ind Coope Burton ale
(pump); others pressurised. Wine. Children (L only).
Cribbage; dominoes. Garden. Car park.

CHURCH KNOWLE Dorset   Map 2

New Inn
Corfe Castle 357
10.30–2.30, 6–10.30
(11 Fri, Sat; 11.30 most
public hol weekends &
Chr; supper licence until
midnight)

Popular and cosy old pub in a pretty village. Cold
bar food: pâté and toast 70p, 'fresh and tasty'
sandwiches 40p–45p, rolls 45p–50p, ploughman's 45p.
Hot snacks (evenings only): scampi £1·50, chicken
£1·10, cod, plaice, sausages 80p, all with chips.
Separate restaurant (7–10.30, Tue–Sat). Devenish
beers (pressurised). Taunton cider. Wine. Children.
Fruit machine; darts; shove ha'penny. Garden. Car
park.

CLEOBURY MORTIMER Salop   Map 5

Old Lion
High Street
Cleobury Mortimer 395
10.30–2.30, 6–10.30
(11 Fri, Sat)

An Elizabethan inn near the Wye Forest. Bar snacks:
basket meals 60p–90p, sandwiches 18p–30p, 'steak
on a board' £1·60, ploughman's 50p, soup 20p.
Wider choice (Mon–Fri L) includes steak cutlet 75p,
Cleobury pie 95p, pâté 55p, cold table £1·20.
Separate restaurant (7.30–9.30 only). Banks's bitter
and mild (pump). Bulmer's cider. Wine. Juke-box;
fruit machine; darts. Car park. B&B £7–£8·50.

COCKERMOUTH Cumbria   Map 7

Old Court House

See main *Guide*

COCKWOOD Devon   Map 1

The Ship
off A379
6 m S of Exeter
Starcross 373
11–2.30, 6–10.30
(11 Fri, Sat & summer)

An old riverside pub near a picturesque harbour.
Bar food: soup 30p, scallops 85p, mussels in wine
85p, lobster salad from £5, grilled local salmon £2·60,
smoked local salmon £3, mackerel £1·95, cheese and
biscuits 45p, sandwiches 55p–85p. Separate
restaurant (12–2, 7–10). Pressurised Courage beers.
Taunton cider. Children. Fruit machine. Three
gardens. Outside gents'. Car park.

CODICOTE Hertfordshire   Map 3

The Goat
High Street
Stevenage 820475
11–2.30, 6–10.30
(11 Fri, Sat)

Lovely old village pub – 'attractive outside and in'.
Well-presented bar food (not Sun): pâté 60p,
ploughman's 50p, 'plentiful, well-presented salads
90p–£1; daily specials, including roast lamb £1·10,
curry 80p, quiche 80p; sandwiches only in the
evening. Ind Coope bitter and mild (pump); others
pressurised. Wine. Darts; dominoes; shove ha'penny;
cribbage. Garden. Car park.

COLTISHALL Norfolk   Map 6

Rising Sun
River Green
Norwich 737440
10.30–2.30, 6–11

An old inn in 'a superb position on the River Bure'.
Bar food (12–2, 7–10; Sun 12–1.45, 7–10):
sandwiches 30p–70p, salads 80p–£1·80, soup 30p,
basket meals 80p–£1·40, grills £2–2·90, pâté and
hot bread 75p ('the recollection is mouth-watering').
Selection of Watney's beers. Bulmer's cider. Wine.
Children. Garden. Car park.

COMBE HAY Avon   Map 2

Wheatsheaf
3½ m SW of Bath
Combe Down 833504
10.30–2.30, 6–10.30
(11 Sat)
Closed Dec 25 evening

'A gem of a pub' in a 'pretty, slightly urban village'.
The food 'was absolutely staggering': smoked salmon
£2·75–£5, home-pressed tongue £2·50, fresh salmon
mayonnaise in season £4, chicken £2·50, veal, ham
and egg pie £2·40, all with salad; rolls and
sandwiches 35p–80p; soup in winter. Courage
(Bristol) bitter and best bitter from the cask; others
pressurised. Wine. Garden and forecourt. Car park.

COMPTON Surrey   Map 3

Withies Inn

See main *Guide*

COWTHORPE North Yorkshire   Map 5

Old Oak
off A1
3 m N of Wetherby
Tockwith 272
12–2.30, 6.45–10.30
(11 Fri, Sat)

Attractive, warm and comfortable pub with 'masses
of flowers' and a wide range of snacks and meals
(55p–£1·40): 'delicious' beef sandwiches, rolls,
cottage pie, coq au vin, lasagne, curried chicken,
smoked trout, home-made soup. Tetley's mild and
bitter, Theakston's bitter and Old Peculier,
Younger's bitter (pump). Wine. Children. Garden
and patio. Car park.

CRACKINGTON HAVEN Cornwall   Map 1

Coombe Barton Hotel

See main *Guide*

CRAWLEY Hampshire   Map 2

Fox and Hounds

See main *Guide*

CROSSBUSH West Sussex   Map 3

Plough and Sail
on A27
½ m E of Arundel
Arundel 883118
10.30–2.30, 6–10.30
(11 Fri, Sat)

'First-class atmosphere and cheerful, attractive
service' in 200-year-old former stables. 'Excellent
range' of bar meals (until 30 min before closing;
£1·20–£1·90): gammon, scampi, chicken, seafood,
sausages. Snacks (from 35p): sandwiches, pâté,
home-made pies. Separate restaurant (11.45–2,
6.45–9.45; £6–£6·50). Pressurised Watney and
Truman beers. Wine. Children. Patio and gardens.
Car park.

Some pubs off the beaten track do not always
serve food at times notified. Phone to check.

CROSTHWAITE Cumbria   Map 7

Hare and Hounds
Bowland Bridge
Crosthwaite 33
11–3, 6–11

Immensely popular coaching-inn with oak beams, log fires and brass. Bar food (12–1.45, 7–10): home-made pâté 70p, ploughman's 70p, home-made steak and kidney pie and chips 95p, scampi £1·20, salads £1·20. Separate restaurant (12–1.45, 7–8.30). Greenall Whitley pressurised beers. Blackthorn cider. Wine. Juke-box; darts; dominoes. Children. Garden. Car park. B&B £5·50–£7·50.

CULLERCOATS Tyne & Wear   Map 8

Piper
Farringdon Road
Whitley Bay 522513
11–3, 6–10.30
(11 Fri & Sat in summer)

A modern pub, five minutes' walk from the station and a few hundred yards from the sea. Bar lunches (Tue–Fri, 12–2): haddock 70p, 'mini grill' 75p, scampi and chips 93p, curried hamburger 68p, stottie cakes (Tyneside buns) 23p–30p, sandwiches 22p–30p; home-made steak and kidney pie (Wed only); sole (Thur). Toasted sandwiches only in the evening and Sun L. Soup and toasted sandwiches Sat L. Bass (pump); others pressurised. Wine. Fruit machine; dominoes. Tables outside in summer. Car park.

DEDHAM Essex   Map 3

Marlborough Head
Mill Lane
Colchester 323124
11–2.30, 6–11

Friendly service in an old pub whose 'beautiful carved beams and fireplaces' have recently been restored. Bar food (40p–£1·50) includes Suffolk Slice (mixture of pork, stuffing and apple invented by the landlady), crab salad, ham salad and sandwiches. Ind Coope bitter. Wine. Garden. Car park. B&B from £6·60.

DEDDINGTON Oxfordshire   Map 2

Holcombe Hotel

See main *Guide*

DENVER Norfolk   Map 6

Jenyns Arms
at Denver Sluice
Downham Market 3366
11–2.30, 6–11
Closed Dec 25 evening

A friendly welcome at this free house overlooking the Great Ouse at a key point in the Fens drainage system; Jenyns was the maiden name of the first Duke of Marlborough's wife. Bar food (until 10.30): sandwiches 34p–40p, salads £1·60–£2·30, 'enormous' ploughman's 70p, basket meals 80p–£1·50. Separate restaurant (12–2, 7–10.30). Theakston's Old Peculier from the cask; others pressurised. Wine. Children. Juke-box; fruit machine; dice. Garden with peacocks. Car park.

DERBY Derbyshire   Map 5

Blessington Carriage

See main *Guide* (Ben Bowers)

DEREHAM (EAST) Norfolk   Map 6

Phoenix Hotel

See main *Guide*

DORCHESTER Dorset Map 2

Royal Oak
High West Street
Dorchester 2423
10–2.30, 6–10.30
(11 Fri, Sat)

Popular old inn opposite the Council offices. Good
selection of quickly served bar food: hot daily dish
65p–95p, sandwiches (prawn and asparagus 'highly
recommended') 35p, gammon £1·50, steak £1·95.
Separate restaurant (12–2, 6.30–10). Eldridge Pope
Royal Oak and Dorset Original bitter (pump);
others pressurised. Wine. Gaming machine. Patio.
Car park.

DRAGONS GREEN West Sussex Map 3

George & Dragon
on A272
E of Billingshurst
Coolham 320
10.30–2.30, 6–10.30
(11 Fri, Sat)

The staff in this small, rural pub 'seem positively
to enjoy running around with trays, locating
hungry customers'. Hot lunches Mon–Fri: roast
beef and Yorkshire pudding, roast lamb or pork,
all £1·20. Snacks at all times: ploughman's 55p,
sausages, pasties, savoury flan. King & Barnes
bitter, mild and old (pump). Fruit machine; bar
billiards; darts; dominoes; shove ha'penny. Garden.
Car park.

DRIFFIELD Gloucestershire Map 2

Horse and Groom
Cricklade Road
on A419
South Cerney 236
11–2.30, 6.30–10.30
(11 Fri, Sat)

An old toll-house – now a crowded but efficiently run
pub. 'Delicious, imaginative' bar food (exc Mon D):
soup 40p, seafood cocktail 40p, haddock £1·55,
ham salad £2·75, rump steak £3·25, ploughman's
90p, 'fisherman's net' (seafood salad with chips)
£1·10. Separate restaurant (exc Mon D) serves
similar food. Pressurised Courage beers. Wine.
Children in restaurant. Juke-box; fruit machine.
Garden. Car park.

DROXFORD Hampshire Map 2

White Horse
on A32
Droxford 490
10.30–2.30, 6–10.30
(11 Fri, Sat & summer)

A warm welcome at this popular pub, built in 1580
and an inn since 1620. Bar snacks (12–2, 7–10; not
Sun evening): home-made soup 45p, ploughman's
45p, quiche 65p, prawns and cheese on toast 75p,
chicken and chips £1, pâté 65p–75p, 'excellent'
stuffed baked potatoes 45p. Separate restaurant
(Sun L, Tue–Sat D only). Variety of traditional
beers, including Courage Directors, Hall &
Woodhouse best bitter, Bass, and Ringwood bitter
(pump). Wine. Juke-box; darts; table football.
Patio and garden. Car park. B&B £6·50–£7·50.

DURHAM Durham Map 8

Travellers Rest
72/3 Claypath
Durham 65370
11–3, 6–10.30

A 250-year-old half-timbered pub, 'full of students
and soldiers relaxing'. Pleasant service of bar food
(Mon–Sat L only): home-made soup 35p, cheese pâté
65p, Norwegian mushrooms 75p, beef curry 80p.
Separate restaurant (Mon–Fri, 7.30–9.30 only).
Variety of pressurised beers. Wine.

EASTBOURNE East Sussex   Map 3

Porthole

See main *Guide*

EAST CLANDON Surrey   Map 3

Queen's Head
The Street
3 m N of Guildford
Guildford 222332
11.30–2.30, 6.30–10.30
(11 Fri, Sat)

People 'come from miles around' to this small,
16th-century country inn in a scenic village. Bar
food (12–2.15, 7–10.15 or 10.45): soup 50p, mushroom
casserole 60p, prawn cocktail £1, scampi £3·85,
beef and Yorkshire pudding £3·75, home-made steak,
kidney and mushroom pie £3·25. Separate
restaurant (12.30–1.45, 7.30–9.30; closed Sun). Ind
Coope bitter and Burton ale (pump); others
pressurised. Wine. Garden. Car park.

EAST COKER Somerset   Map 2

Helyar Arms
West Coker 2332
11–2.30, 6–10.30
(11 Fri, Sat & summer)

Old pub on the site of a monastery. Good
selection of bar food (not Sun L; 40p–£1·95):
home-made soup, pizza, pies, salads, daily special.
Separate restaurant (Mon–Sat 12–1.45; Tue–Sat
7.30–9.45). Pressurised Devenish beers. Taunton
cider. Wine. Fruit machine; darts; skittle alley.
Garden. Car park.

EAST MARTON North Yorkshire   Map 5

Cross Keys
on A59
3 m W of Skipton
Earby 3485
11–3, 5.30–10.30
(11 Fri, Sat)

An old inn by the Leeds–Liverpool Canal, offering
an excellent welcome and warm, happy atmosphere.
Bar food (30p–£1·50): 'generous' sandwiches
40p–80p, soup 30p, pâté 60p, basket meals
70p–£1·20, salads £1·40–£1·50. Theakston's bitter
and Old Peculier from the cask or pump; others
pressurised. Wine. Separate restaurant (12–2, 7–10).
Children. Juke-box; fruit machine; darts. Drinking
on forecourt. Car park.

EAST SUTTON Kent   Map 3

Prince of Wales
off A274
3¼ m N of Headcorn
Sutton Valence 2235
11–2.30, 6.30–11

Clean, pleasant country pub, now part of the Shant
Hotel, which has its own airstrip and swimming-pool.
Bar food (no prices stated): home-made soup, steak
and kidney pudding, rabbit and pork pie, spiced
turkey and rice, 'very pleasant' pâté, baked
potatoes. Separate restaurant (12.30–2.30, 7–10.30).
Young's special and Bass (pump); others pressurised.
Wine. Drinking outside in summer. B&B £9·75.

EGGLESTONE Durham   Map 8

Three Tuns
Cotherstone 289
11–3, 6.30–10.30 (11 Sat)
Closed Mon (exc public
holidays)

An old free house on the village green, with flagged
floors and beams. Bar food (12–1.45, 7.30–9.45; Sun
12–1.30 only): home-made soup and bread 25p,
ploughman's 75p, home-made pâté 75p. Wider
choice in the evening, including home-made pie and
chips £1·40. Separate restaurant (Sun L, Tue–Sat
D). Pressurised Whitbread beers. Wine. Children
(L only). Dominoes. Patio and garden. Car park.

ELSWORTH Cambridgeshire Map 3

George and Dragon
41 Boxworth Road
Elsworth 236
10.30–2.30, 7–10.30
(11 Fri, Sat)
Closed Dec 25 evening

An old building, painted in 'very pale apricot'; cosy and chintzy inside. Bar food (until 30 min before closing): soup 30p, pâté 65p, sirloin steak £2·95, 'light and well-flavoured' pizza £1·25, various chicken dishes £1·10–£1·25, gammon Hawaii £1·60, omelettes 75p, sandwiches 35p (toasted 38p). Pressurised beers, mainly Tolly Cobbold. Wine. Children. Darts. Garden and patio. Car park.

EWHURST Surrey Map 3

Windmill
Pitch Hill
on road from Ewhurst to
Shere
Ewhurst 566
10.30–2.30, 6–10.30
(11 Fri, Sat)

Friendly free house with log fires in winter and magnificent views of the South Downs. Bar snacks (from 12 and 7) are 'very good value': home-made soup 30p, pâté 60p, turkey or prawn curry 75p, scampi and chips £1·35, sausages and mash 55p, salads £1–£1·50, sandwiches 50p. Pressurised Whitbread beers; King & Barnes bitter promised. Wine. Fruit machine; darts. Children. Porch and garden. Car park.

EWHURST GREEN East Sussex Map 3

White Dog
6½ m NE of Battle
Staplecross 264
12–3, 6.30–11
(11.30 Fri, 12 Sat)

A 'most unusual pub' in a beautiful village. All the food is home-made, most of the vegetables come from the pub's own market garden and all poultry is raised on site; 'splendid' seafood pie; 3 courses £1·80–£4·70. Bass and Whitbread Trophy (pump); others pressurised. Bob Luck's cider from the cask. Wine. Darts. Children. Seats outside. Car park. B&B £6·25.

EWYAS HAROLD Hereford & Worcester Map 2

Temple Bar
off A465
between Hereford
and Abergavenny
Pontrilas 423
10.30–2.30, 7–10.30
(11 Mon, Fri, Sat)

A 'splendid' stone-built pub close to the Black Mountains and Golden Valley. Bar food (not Mon, Tue D; 50p–£1·50): 'really excellent' ploughman's, pâté, rolls, toasted sandwiches, Temple Special ('bacon sandwich with a difference'), home-made soup, steak butties. Separate restaurant (Wed–Sat D only). Bass, Hook Norton mild (pump); others pressurised. Wine. Fruit machine; darts; table skittles; skittle alley; cards; dominoes. Patio and garden. Car park.

EXETER Devon Map 1

White Hart
South Street
Exeter 79897
11–2.30, 5–10.30
(11 Fri, Sat)

A 14th-century coaching-inn on the edge of the city centre. Bar food (not Sun D): pâté 55p, prawns 70p, soup 20p, steak and oyster pie £2·05, turkey pie £1·20; daily hot dish chalked on blackboard. Separate restaurant (12.15–2, 7–10; L £3, D £3·95, or alc). Choice of pressurised beers. Wine. Children. Garden and barbecue area. Car park. B&B from £8·70.

EXMINSTER Devon   Map 1

Swan's Nest
Station Road (A379)
Kennford 832371
11–2.30, 5.30–10.30
(11 Fri, Sat)

Well-appointed, efficiently run free house converted from a 200-year-old farmhouse. 'The best cold buffet for miles around' (12–2, 6.15–10): salad and roll with everything; choice of meats, seafood or pies 98p–£1·74, pâté 88p, baps with salad 89p–96p, sandwiches 50p–58p. Wide range of pressurised beers. Wine. Fruit machine. Car park.

FADMOOR North Yorkshire   Map 8

Plough Inn

See main *Guide*

FALMOUTH Cornwall   Map 1

King's Head
Church Corner
Falmouth 315273
11–2.30, 6–10.30
(11 Fri, Sat & summer)

A rambling old building in the centre of town, decorated with old pub signs. Bar food (Mon–Sat, L only): home-made cheese and potato pie, pizza, ham, mackerel, cheese, crab sandwiches. Devenish bitter and Cornish best bitter (pump); others pressurised. Wine. Children allowed at landlord's discretion. Fruit machine.

FARLEIGH HUNGERFORD Somerset   Map 2

Hungerford Arms
Trowbridge 2411
11–2.30, 6.30–10.30
(11 Fri, Sat)

Friendly service in a beamed pub with views across a beautiful valley. Bar food (not Sun D): soup 35p, ploughman's 50p, pâté 65p, turkey and ham pie 85p, smoked salmon £2, sandwiches 30p–60p; help-yourself cold table £1–£2. Restricted snacks Sat, Sun L. Separate restaurant (3 courses, £4; closed Sun D). Usher's bitter and best bitter (pump), Thos Usher 1060 (winter) from the cask. Wine. Children. Patio and garden. Car park.

FAR SAWREY Cumbria   Map 7

Sawrey Hotel
on B5285
Windermere 3425
11–3, 5.30–10.30
(11 Fri, Sat & public hols)

Quick and mostly friendly service in this attractive coaching-inn with the public bar in the old stables. Bar food (L only; 25p–£1·25): 'ample and excellent' home-made soup, 'generous' ploughman's, pâté, salads, fisherman's platter, scampi, sandwiches. Separate restaurant (12.30–2, 7.30–8.45). Theakston's bitter and Old Peculier, Younger's Scotch bitter (pump); others pressurised. Wine. Fruit machine; darts. Children. Garden. Car park. B&B £4·75–£5·50.

FAUGH Cumbria   Map 8

String of Horses
4 m E of M6, exit 43
3 m S of A69
Hayton 297 *and* 425
11.30–3, 5.30–11.30
(midnight Fri, Sat)

A 'super little pub' with friendly staff. Bar food (35p–£2·95) includes sandwiches, daily dish, grills, seafood, curries; 'as much as you want' from cold table (L only). Separate restaurant (7.30–10.30 only). Selection of pressurised beers. Wine. Children. Fruit machine. Patio. Car park. B&B from £8.

FIDDLEFORD Dorset   Map 2

Fiddleford Inn
on A357
Sturminster Newton
72489
11–2.30, 6.30–10.30
(11 Fri, Sat)

'Deservedly popular with both locals and visitors':
a pleasant old pub with a creeper-covered façade.
Bar food (12–2, 7.30–9.30): carrot soup 50p, mussels
70p, pâté 75p, ploughman's 55p–75p, chicken and
mushrooms in cider £1·25, steak £2·65, salads
£1·25–£1·65. Separate restaurant for private bookings.
Wadworth's 6X (pump) and Old Timer from the
cask; others pressurised. Children. Bar billiards;
darts. Terrace. B&B from £7.

FINGEST Buckinghamshire   Map 3

Chequers Inn

See main *Guide*

FINGLE BRIDGE Devon   Map 1

Anglers' Rest
off A30 & A382
Drewsteignton 287
10.30–2.30, 7–11
Closed Nov–Easter
(exc Sun)

A long, low building in a superb riverside position.
Bar food (12–2, 7–10; no hot food Sun): home-made
soup 25p, home-made pâté 55p, prawn cocktail 75p,
fisherman's bite (cheese with roll or bread) 50p,
'real' Cornish pasty 30p, steak and kidney pie £1·20,
seafood platter £1·45, salads £1–£1·95, sandwiches
40p–70p. Separate restaurant (12.30–2, 7–10).
Courage (Plymouth) best bitter and Bass (pump);
others pressurised. Bromell's farm cider. Wine.
Children. Tables on terrace. Car park.

FLITTON Bedfordshire   Map 3

White Hart

See main *Guide*

FORD Gloucestershire   Map 2

Plough
on B4077
Stanton 215
10–2, 5.30–10.30

A stone-built pub with three low-beamed rooms
around a central bar. Well-presented bar food:
home-made vegetable soup, trout, venison stew,
sandwiches. Donnington bitter and special bitter.
Garden. Car park. B&B £4.

FORDCOMBE Kent   Map 3

Chafford Arms
4 m W of Tunbridge Wells
N of A264
Fordcombe 267
10.30–2.30, 6–10.30
(11 Fri, Sat)
Closed Dec 25 evening

Attractive red-brick pub with friendly and helpful
staff. Bar snacks (12.30–1.45, 7.30–9.15) include
pasties, flans (45p), salads (from £1·10), home-made
pies (steak and kidney or chicken and ham, 60p),
things in baskets. Whitbread Trophy on hand
pump; pressurised Trophy and best bitter. Bob
Luck's cider. Fruit machine; darts. Garden. Car park.

FORDWICH Kent   Map 3

George and Dragon
on A28
Canterbury 710661
10–2.30, 6–10.30
(11 Fri, Sat)

A rambling old inn by the River Stour, with low
rooms and winding passages. Bar food (L only):
help-yourself cold buffet £3·15, home-made duck pie,
pâté, ploughman's. Separate restaurant (Mon–Sat,
D only). Whitbread (Faversham) bitter (pump);
others pressurised. Children. Garden. Car park.
B&B from £8·15.

FORTY GREEN Buckinghamshire   Map 3

Royal Standard of England
N of A40 & M40
Beaconsfield 3382
10.30–2.30, 6–10.30
(11 Fri, Sat)

'Almost too good to be true' – a beautifully kept and famous old inn at the foot of the Chilterns. 'Good value' bar food (exc Sun; no prices stated): 'dozens of different cheeses', Scotch eggs, sausages, pork pies, ham, salads, bread baked locally to the pub's own recipe. Marston's Pedigree and Owd Roger (which originated here), Samuel Smith's bitter (pump); others pressurised. Wine. Gardens. Car park.

FOWEY Cornwall   Map 1

Safe Harbour
Lostwithiel Street
Fowey 3379
11–2.30, 5.30–10.30
(11 Fri, Sat & summer)

Clean and cosy old coaching-inn. Bar food (until 2 and 8.30): home-made pasties 35p, ploughman's 55p, steak and chips £1·40, salads 75p–£1·25, sandwiches 30p–45p. Pressurised St Austell beers. Bulmer's cider. Wine. Children. Fruit machine; darts. Seats outside. Car park. B&B £4·50–£5·50.

FRAMFIELD East Sussex   Map 3

Hare and Hounds
The Street (B2102)
Framfield 327
10–2.30, 6–10.30
(11 Fri, Sat)

Pleasant, comfortable pub, tastefully modernised. 'Outstandingly good' bar food (12–2, 7–9.45): daily special (coq au vin was £1·10 in 1978), ham, egg and chips £1·30, fresh prawns wrapped in smoked salmon £2·45, steaks, salads, ploughman's, sandwiches and rolls. Pressurised Watney's and Truman's beer. Wine. Fruit machine; bar billiards; darts; shove ha'penny. Large garden. Car park. B&B £5·40.

FROME Somerset   Map 2

George Hotel
4 Market Place
Frome 2584
10.30–2.30 (4 Wed),
6–10.30 (11 Fri, Sat)

A pleasant hotel with one of the bars – the Riot Bar – near where the Riot Act was read in 1832. Bar food: ploughman's 55p, sandwiches 35p, toasted sandwiches 40p, scampi or chicken with chips £1·10, cottage pie 55p, curry 70p, soup 35p. Separate restaurant (12–2, 7–10). Wadworth's 6X (pump); others pressurised. Wine. Children. Juke-box; fruit machine; bar billiards; darts; pinball. Car park. B&B from £8·50.

Mendip Lodge

See main *Guide*

GEORGEHAM Devon   Map 1

Rock Inn
Rock Hill
Croyde 890322
Summer: 11–2.30, 5.30–11
Winter: 11.30–2.30,
6.30–10.30
(Sat 11–2.30, 6–11)

Simply decorated with natural pine furniture. Georgeham has twice won best-kept-village competitions. Bar food (12–2, 7–10): summer – smoked mackerel, cheese, tomato and onion flan 65p, chicken pie 90p, home-made pâté 55p, ploughman's 50p–55p, roast beef sandwich 40p; winter – home-made soup 35p, pasty 32p, rabbit pie 80p. No chips. Usher's best bitter (pump) and 1060 strong ale from the cask; others pressurised. Children. Darts in winter; skittles. Garden. Car park.

GIBRALTAR Buckinghamshire Map 3

Bottle and Glass
on A418
Stone 488
10–2.30, 6–10.30

Attractive thatched building with low ceilings but a modern appearance. Friendly and efficient service of bar food, including sandwiches from 30p, pâté 68p, trout £1·85, salads. Ind Coope Burton ale (pump); others pressurised. Wine. Car park.

GITTISHAM Devon Map 2

Combe House

See main *Guide*

GLYNDE East Sussex Map 3

Trevor Arms
off A27
Glynde 208
10–2.30, 6–10.30
(11 Fri, Sat)

A fine pub in a picturesque village, frequented by Glyndebourne musicians in summer. Bar food includes home-made steak and kidney pie 65p, minced beef and carrot pie 45p, quiche, sandwiches, ploughman's. Curried chicken £1·20, steak £2·95, and other grills in the evening. Harvey's best bitter (pump). Darts. Garden. Car park.

GODALMING Surrey Map 3

Star
Church Street
Godalming 7717
11–2.30, 6–10.30
(11 Fri, Sat)

An attractive, old-world pub in a quiet side street. Bar food (not Sun; L 35p–£1·20, D 85p–£4) includes pâté, sandwiches, grills, fish, steak, and salads. Courage bitter and Directors (pump); others pressurised. Wine. Fruit machine; juke-box.

GOOSTREY Cheshire Map 5

Crown
111 Main Road
off A535 & A54
Holmes Chapel 32128
11.30–3, 5.30–10.30
(11 Fri, Sat)

Pleasant service in this 16th-century inn, half a mile from Jodrell Bank and 5 miles from the M6, junction 18. Bar food (exc Mon): scampi £1·15, chicken 95p, pizza 70p, daily special 95p, 'excellent' steak sandwiches 55p, soup 25p, rolls with a 'large choice of fillings'. Separate restaurant (8–11, Wed–Sat only). Marston's Burton bitter, Pedigree and mild (pump); others pressurised. Wine. Fruit machine; darts. Children. Garden. Car park.

GOSFORTH Cumbria Map 7

Gosforth Hall

See main *Guide*

GREAT BARRINGTON Gloucestershire Map 2

Inn for all Seasons
on A40
Windrush 324
11–2.30, 6–10.30
(11 Fri, Sat)
Closed Chr

Stone-built Georgian coaching-inn, with the remains of old stone-mines at the bottom of the garden. Sandwiches only at the bar, but meals in the buttery (minimum charge £1·50): 'excellent' home-made soup, home-made steak and kidney pie with 'delicious' pastry, 'tasty' pâté, cold meats, 'very superior' lemon meringue pie. Separate restaurant for residents only. Wadworth's 6X (pump); others pressurised. Wine. Car park. B&B from £7·40.

GREAT BROUGHTON North Yorkshire   Map 8

Bay Horse
88 High Street
Wainstones 319
11–3, 6–10.30

'The staff are delightful' in this local country pub.
Bar food (L and D menus vary): soup, pâté, chicken,
trout, scampi, seafood selection, kebabs, curries,
moussaka, salads, sandwiches. Separate restaurant
(12.15–2, 7–10). Pressurised John Smith's and
Courage beers. Wine. Garden. Car park.

GREAT DUNMOW Essex   Map 3

Queen Victoria
on A120
Great Dunmow 3330
10–2.30, 6–10.30
(11 Fri, Sat)

Attractive, clean and well-run thatched pub, with
low ceilings. Bar food: ravioli 75p, pâté 95p, soup
50p, lasagne £1·30, chicken and chips £1·20, plaice
and chips £1·50, ploughman's 50p, sandwiches 40p;
daily special lunch (exc weekends) £1·20. Separate
restaurant (exc D Sun & Tue, Sat L). Tolly
Cobbold Cantab (pressurised). Wine. Children.
Garden. Car park.

GREAT YELDHAM Essex   Map 3

White Hart

See main *Guide*

GRINTON North Yorkshire   Map 8

Bridge Hotel
on B6270
Reeth 224
10.30–3, 6–10.30
(12–2, 7–10.30 Sun;
11 Fri, Sat & summer)

A 17th-century inn serving bar food until an hour
before closing (no prices given): sandwiches, pâté,
ploughman's, pies, beefburgers, sausages, fish.
Separate restaurant (from 7; 4 courses £3·50).
Pressurised Theakston's bitter and others. Wine.
Fruit machine; darts; dominoes. Tables outside. Car
park. B&B £5·50–£6.

GROOMBRIDGE Kent   Map 3

Crown
3½ m SW of Tunbridge
Wells
Groombridge 361 *and* 742
10.30–2.30, 6–10.30
(11 Fri, Sat)

A 'perfect English pub', built in the 16th century,
with beams and open log fires. Limited bar menu
written on a blackboard (L 50p–£1·50, D £3·50–£5·50):
'incredibly generous helpings of sliced cold meats'
with salads, 'huge portions of pâté' and hot bread.
Separate restaurant (D only, closed Sun). Harvey's
bitter and old ale, Whitbread (Faversham) bitter
(pump). Wine. Darts. Children. Car park. B&B £5.

GUILDFORD Surrey   Map 3

Duke of Normandy
Guildford Road,
Normandy
on A323
Normandy 2157
10.30–2.30, 6–10.30
(11 Fri, Sat)

'Delightful' pub with quiet, efficient service of bar
lunches (Mon–Sat; 50p–95p): home-made flan,
spare ribs, sausages, plaice. Toasted sandwiches,
sausage rolls, pasties always available. Pressurised
Ind Coope beer. Wine. Juke-box; fruit machine;
darts; pool table. Garden. Car park.

Wine bars are represented by a wine glass on the maps, pubs by a tankard.

In England and Wales, Sunday opening hours are 12–2, 7–10.30.

GUILDFORD Surrey   Map 3

Jolly Farmer
Millbrook
(on Guildford-Horsham
road)
Guildford 75386
10.30–2.30, 5.30–10.30
(11 Fri, Sat)

A pleasant, friendly pub in a splendid position, with three terraces overlooking the river. A 'good selection' of bar snacks: soup 18p, smoked salmon £1·80, grills 55p–£1·35, choice of stuffed baked potatoes 35p–75p, salads 42p–£1·45, sandwiches 26p–80p. Ind Coope bitter and Burton ale (pump); others pressurised. Wine. Children. Seats outside. Car park.

HALLAND East Sussex   Map 3

Halland Motel

See main *Guide*

HALLATON Leicestershire   Map 5

Bewick Arms
1 Eastgate
Hallaton 217
12–2.30, 7–11

This 400-year-old thatched pub on the green in a quaint village has a large variety of bar food, all freshly prepared to order: soup 25p, pâté 65p; plaice £1·20, scampi £1·60, chicken £1·80, steak £2·75, all with salad and chips; ploughman's 60p–75p, sandwiches 40p–£1·15. Ruddle's County ale and bitter, Marston's Pedigree (pump); others pressurised. Wine. Fruit machine; bar billiards; darts. Children. Patio and garden. Car park.

HARPENDEN Hertfordshire   Map 3

Silver Cup
St Albans Road (A6)
Harpenden 3095
10.30–2.30, 5.30–10.30
(11 Fri, Sat)

Efficiently run old coaching-inn, named after a prize for horse races on the common in days of yore. 'Good value' bar food (L only, exc Sun; 30p–£2·50): 'excellent' home-made soup and steak pie, sandwiches, pâté, 'plate snacks', four-course meals. Charles Wells bitter and Fargo (pressurised). Wine. Fruit machine; darts. Car park.

HARTOFT END North Yorkshire   Map 8

Blacksmiths Arms
Lastingham 331
10.30–2.30, 5.30–10.30
(11 Fri, Sat)

An old moorland inn with settles, wooden tables, and stuffed fish on the wall. Bar food: soup 30p, sandwiches 50p, basket meals £1–£1·25. Separate restaurant (Mon–Sat, 7–8 only; tdh £5). Choice of pressurised beers. Wine. Children. Fruit machine. Car park. B&B £6–£8·50.

HATHERLEIGH Devon   Map 1

George Hotel

See main *Guide*

HAZELEY HEATH Hampshire   Map 2

Shoulder of Mutton
on B3011
2 m NW of Hartley
Wintney
Heckfield 272
10.30–2.30, 6–10.30
(11 Fri, Sat)

Busy but comfortable and pleasant country pub, serving 'nicely presented' bar snacks (no prices stated): three types of curry, chicken, basket meals; more than 20 types of sandwich (L only). Separate restaurant (until 1.45 and 10). Courage (Reading) bitter and Directors (pump); others pressurised. Wine. Live music on Sun evenings in autumn and winter. Garden. Car park.

HELFORD Cornwall   Map 1

Shipwright's Arms
Manaccan 235
11–2.30, 6–10.30
(10.30–2.30, 6–11 in
summer; 12–2, 7–10.30
Sun)

Unspoilt thatched house in a picturesque village,
looking over the creek. A table just off the bar is
laden with snacks (35p–£2·25): salads, cooked meats,
four types of ploughman's and hot pasties.
Pressurised Devenish beers. Wine. Darts. Tables
outside. Three patios. Outdoor lavatories. Car park.

HEMEL HEMPSTEAD Hertfordshire   Map 3

White Hart

See main *Guide*

See also **BRIDEN'S CAMP** in this section

HENLEY-ON-THAMES Oxfordshire   Map 2

The Angel
(on the Bridge)
Thameside
Henley-on-Thames 4977
11–2.30, 6–10.30
(11 Fri, Sat)

'As good as ever' – a lovely old pub by the river.
Bar food (until 30 min before lunchtime closing and
until 9.30; no prices given): soup, home-made pâté,
ploughman's, steaks; better selection of grills in the
evening. Brakspear's bitter and special bitter
(pump), old ale from the cask. Wine. Fruit machine;
backgammon. Riverside terrace.

HENNOCK Devon   Map 1

Palk Arms
off B3193
Bovey Tracey 833027
11–2.30, 6–10.30
(11 Fri, Sat)

Small village pub 'with glorious views over the Teign
valley' from lounge bar. Bar food: home-made soup
25p, pâté 60p, 'wonderful choice' of salads with cold
meats £1·90–£2·25, steaks £2·50–£3·10, toasted
sandwiches 65p–95p, ploughman's 50p–70p.
Pressurised Whitbread beers. Local cider. Wine.
Darts. Garden.

HILLINGTON Norfolk   Map 6

ffolkes Arms
on A147
Hillington 210
10.30–2.30, 6–11

Excellent old flintstone pub with 'adventurous' bar
food, thought value for money: home-made soup
55p and pâté 95p, scallops and prawns in cheese
sauce £1·85, hot daily dish £1·50, pigeon casserole
£1·50, 'enormous plate' of venison stew £1·50.
Separate restaurant (12–2, 7–9.45). Tolly Cobbold
bitter and Cantab (pump); others pressurised. Wine.
Children. Garden. Car park.

HINDON Wiltshire   Map 2

The Lamb
2 m S of A303
Hindon 225
10–2.30, 6–10.30
(11 Fri, Sat)

Flourishing old coaching-inn in a lovely countryside
setting. Bar food (12–2, 7–10): sandwiches from 30p,
salads £1, hot dishes from £1, bread and cheese 40p,
sweets from 30p. Separate restaurant (12.30–1.30,
7.30–9; 3 courses £2·75 L, £3·85 D). Wadworth's
6X, IPA and Old Timer (pump); others pressurised.
Wine. Garden. Car park. B&B £7·85.

Hours given are opening times. Food may not be served over the whole period.

HINTON CHARTERHOUSE Avon   Map 2

Stag
on B3110
5½ m S of Bath
Limpley Stoke 3456
11–2.30, 6–10.30
(11 Fri & Sat in summer)

A 'splendid place' with a clean, single room, a former bakehouse. Well-presented bar food (12–2, 7.30–10): pizza 75p, veal cutlet 80p, snails 90p for six, ravioli 50p, home-made cottage pie 65p, beef curry 75p, scampi £1·10, whitebait 60p, salads from 70p, ploughman's 50p. Whitbread (Cheltenham) PA (pump); Marston's Pedigree in the offing; others pressurised. Wine. Fruit machine. Garden. Car park.

HOLT Dorset   Map 2

Old Inn
1 m from Wimborne
Wimborne 883029
11.30–2.30, 6.30–10.30
(11 Fri, Sat & summer)

'Admirable' country pub run by the same family for more than 70 years. Bar food: salads £1·50–£2, sandwiches 30p–50p, chicken 65p, soup 27p, smoked salmon £1·10, steaks £1·80–£2·15, and 'very good steak, kidney and mushroom pie' £1·25. Hall & Woodhouse pressurised beers. Strongbow cider from the cask. Wine. Garden. Car park.

HOLYWELL Cambridgeshire   Map 6

Old Ferry Boat
on A1123
St Ives (Cambs) 63227
11–2.30, 6–10.30
(11 Fri, Sat)

Old, country inn on the banks of the Ouse, thatched and haunted, and reputed to date from 968 A.D. Bar food is simple and good value for money (L only): soup and bread 35p, daily special 95p, omelettes 95p–£1·25, pizza £1, seafood platter £1·55, cold buffet £1·75, pâté 85p, sandwiches 40p. Separate restaurant (12.30–1.30, 7.30–9.30). Greene King Abbot from the cask; others pressurised. Wine. Terrace and garden. Car park. B&B £6.

HORTON Dorset   Map 2

Horton Inn
off B3078
Witchampton 252
11–2.30, 6–10.30
(11 Fri, Sat)

A modernised old inn, with a friendly welcome, in a pleasant location. Bar food (until 30 min before closing): home-made soup 60p, Dorset pâté 85p, rolls and sandwiches 45p–85p, salads £1·60–£1·90, ploughman's 65p–75p, daily hot dishes – shepherd's pie, curry or omelettes. Separate restaurant (not Sun). Ind Coope Burton ale, Whitbread (Romsey) Trophy, Eldridge Pope Royal Oak (pump); others pressurised. Patio. Car park. B&B from £9·25.

HOUGHTON West Sussex   Map 3

George and Dragon
on B2139
Bury 225
10.30–2.30, 6–10.30
(11 Fri, Sat & summer)

A popular 13th-century pub, enlarged without losing its old atmosphere. Bar food: soup 40p, chicken and chips, scampi, pâté 70p, potted shrimps on toast 90p, sandwiches 35p–80p, ploughman's 60p–70p, salads from £1·50. Separate restaurant (D only, closed Sun). Young's bitter, King & Barnes bitter (pump); others pressurised. Wine. Garden. Car park.

See p. 441 for 'How to use the pub section'.

HOUGHTON-ON-THE-HILL Leicestershire   Map 5

Rose and Crown
69 Uppingham Road
(A47)
Leicester 412044
10–2, 6–10.30
(11 Fri, Sat)

A comfortable lounge bar with friendly service. Bar food (Mon–Fri, 12–1.45): meat salads (generous meat, self-service salad) £1·40, rolls 24p, sandwiches 33p, cheese and biscuits 25p. Bass and Mitchells & Butlers mild (pump); others pressurised. Wine. Car park.

HOVINGHAM North Yorkshire   Map 8

Worsley Arms

See main *Guide*

HUNTINGDON Cambridgeshire   Map 6

Old Bridge Hotel

See main *Guide*

HURLEY Berkshire   Map 3

Dewdrop
Batts Green
Littlewick Green 4327
11–2.30, 6.30–10.30
(11 Fri, Sat)

A 'lovely, cosy' 16th-century country pub with beams and log fires. Bar food (until 15 min before closing; none Sun D): soup 25p, pâté 55p, whitebait 75p, ploughman's 50p–55p, scampi in the basket £1·50, salads £1·35. Brakspear's bitter and old (pump). Garden. Darts; shove ha'penny. Car park.

IDDESLEIGH Devon   Map 1

Duke of York

See main *Guide*

IDEN GREEN Kent   Map 3

Royal Oak
3¼ m SE of Cranbrook
Benenden 585
10.30–2.30, 6–10.30
(11 Fri, Sat)

'Rather anonymous' free house but 'making a rare effort to please'. 'The landlord's early-morning market trips to London are reflected in excellent – and good-value – steaks and seafood': home-made steak pies, crab, lobster, sole, rainbow trout; sausages too. Separate restaurant (L & D; exc Sun & Mon). Large range of pressurised beers. Wine. Fruit machine. Garden. Car park.

ILCHESTER Somerset   Map 2

The Bull
The Square (A37)
Ilchester 318
11–2.30, 6–10.30
(11 Fri, Sat & summer)

A pleasant pub, dating in part from the 11th century. Cold buffet: 'very generous' salads with home-cooked meats 70p–£1·40, sandwiches 30p–45p, ploughman's 45p. Hot snacks (L exc Tue & Sun): scampi £1, cod £1, sausages 65p. Pressurised Bass Charrington beers. Wine. Children. Pool table; skittles. Patio. Car park.

IRON ACTON Avon   Map 2

White Hart
5 m SE of Thornbury
Rangeworthy 228
10–2.30, 6–10.30
(11 Fri, Sat)

'Ladies in clean pinnies' do the cooking and serving at this 'ornamental' pub. Wide range of bar food (limited on Sun) includes lasagne 70p, spaghetti 60p, home-made goulash 75p, moussaka £1, prawn salad £2·50. Courage (Bristol) bitter and best bitter (pump); others pressurised. Wine. Tables outside. Juke-box; fruit machine. Car park.

ISFIELD East Sussex   Map 3

Laughing Fish
off A26 between Lewes
and Uckfield
Isfield 349
10.30–2.30, 6–10.30
(11 Fri, Sat)

An Easter Monday beer race is organised annually at
this pleasant pub. Hot bar food (Wed–Sat): ham,
egg and chips 90p, plaice £1·70, scampi £1·60, rump
steak £3. Cold food at all times: ploughman's 60p,
pâté 65p, sandwiches from 35p. Harvey's bitter
(pump), mild and old from the cask. Fruit machine;
darts. Garden. Car park. B&B from £5.

ISLE OF WIGHT   Map 2

Clarendon
Newport Road,
Chale
Niton 730431
11–3, 6.30–11

An old coaching-inn, renamed in 1836 after a ship
which sank off Blackgang. 'An array of outstanding
snacks' (12–2.30; Sun 12–1.30) includes 'superb'
cockles 30p, taramosalata ('must be eaten to be
believed') 85p, 'gorgeous' steak and kidney pie, steak
sandwiches £1.40, scampi and chips £1·70,
ploughman's 40p. Separate restaurant (Fri & Sat
only, 7.30–10). Whitbread (Portsmouth) Pompey
Royal from the cask; others pressurised. Wine.
Children. Fruit machine; bar billiards; darts; pool
table. Garden and courtyard. Car park. B&B from
£6–£60.

KELBROOK Lancashire   Map 5

Stone Trough
Colne Road (A56)
Earby 3432
11–3, 7–11

'Fast, friendly, efficient service' in this early
19th-century inn. Bar food (until 30 min before
closing, exc Mon D): soup 35p, sausage and chips
85p, scampi and chips £1·90, home-made steak pie
£1·50, pâté 85p, salads £1·20, ploughman's 60p,
sandwiches. Separate restaurant (12–2.15; 7–10, exc
Mon). Lees bitter (pump); others pressurised. Wine.
Car park.

KINGSTON NEAR LEWES East Sussex   Map 3

The Juggs
Little Orchard
Lewes 2523
10–2.30, 6–10.30
(11 Fri, Sat)

Beams and a log fire make the Juggs a cosy inn.
Bar food (11–2.15, 6–9.30; 50p–£2) includes 'real'
sausages, hot and cold snacks, and sandwiches.
Pressurised beers only 'until cellar is rebuilt'. Wine.
Children. Darts; shove ha'penny; skittles. Garden.
Car park.

KINGTON ST MICHAEL Wiltshire   Map 2

Jolly Huntsman
2 m from M4, junction 17
Kington Langley 305
10.30–2.30, 6–10.30
(11 Fri, Sat)

A Cotswold-stone building with ingle-nook and
brasses; converted from an old brewery fifty years
ago. Bar food (12–1.30, 7–10): home-made soup 30p,
home-made kipper pâté 50p, basket meals 55p–£1·20,
chicken vindaloo £1, gammon £1·20–£1·60; daily
special 65p (Mon–Fri L). Usher's best bitter,
Whitbread (Cheltenham) PA, Wadworth's 6X
(pump), Old Timer from the cask; others
pressurised. Wine. Fruit machine; skittles; cribbage;
backgammon. Music on Thursday evenings. Patio.
Car park.

KINTBURY Berkshire   Map 2

Dundas Arms

See main *Guide*

KIRKBY LONSDALE Cumbria   Map 8

Snooty Fox
Main Street
Kirkby Lonsdale 71308
10.30–3 (3.30 Thur, Fri &
Sat), 6–10.30 (11 Thur,
Fri & Sat)

A pleasantly down-to-earth pub with tables made
from old treadle sewing-machines and a collection
of stuffed animals around the walls. Bar food (until
30 min before closing; 30p–£1): sandwiches,
'excellent' moussaka, home-made steak and kidney
pie, shepherd's pie, braised liver and bacon.
Separate restaurant. Hartleys' bitter, Tetley
(Warrington) bitter and mild (pump); others
pressurised. Wine. Children (summer only).
Juke-box; fruit machine; darts; pool table; video
machines. Seats outside in summer. Car park.

KIRKBY OVERBLOW North Yorkshire   Map 5

Shoulder of Mutton
1½ m off A61
Harrogate 871205
11–3, 5.30–10.30
(11 Fri, Sat; 11.30
public hols)

An old stone-built pub with antique furniture in a
pretty village. Bar food (last orders 30 min before
closing time): fresh rolls with beef, turkey, tongue,
ham, cheese 17p–32p, pâté 48p, 'superb' pork pie
and pickles 31p, smoked salmon sandwiches 85p,
sausage rolls 12p. Tetley (Leeds) bitter and mild
(pump); others pressurised. Wine. Fruit machine;
bar billiards; darts; dominoes; shove ha'penny.
Garden. Car park. Caravan site.

LANCASTER Lancashire   Map 7

Brown Cow
44 Penny Street
Lancaster 66474
10.45–3, 5.45–10.30
(11 Fri, Sat)

A quaint, old-fashioned pub, first licensed in 1810.
'Comprehensive choice' of bar snacks (L only, 12–2;
Sun 12.30–1.30): home-baked chicken and mushroom
or steak and kidney pie 70p, farmhouse grill 75p,
pizza 70p, all served with peas and chips or jacket
potato; salads 60p–95p, sandwiches 25p–35p. Less
choice Sun; buns and sandwiches only, every
evening. Yates & Jackson bitter and mild (pump);
others pressurised. Wine. Juke-box: fruit machines;
darts; dominoes; cards. Live music on Mon & Thur
evenings.

LANGLEY MARSH Somerset   Map 2

Three Horseshoes
off A361
Wiveliscombe 23763
10.30–2.30, 6–11

'Relaxing and simple – just as a real village pub
used to be years ago.' Wide range of 'ambitious and
unusual' bar food (exc Thur D; last orders 30 min
before closing): soup 30p, mushrooms in garlic
butter 60p, mussels in white wine and parsley 85p,
fishy flan 45p, Bridport beef pie 75p, quiche 45p,
toasted steak sandwich 90p, potted prawns 85p,
ploughman's 50p. Hall & Woodhouse bitter and best
bitter (pump), Palmer's IPA and Tally Ho! from the
cask; others pressurised. Perry's farmhouse cider
from the cask. Wine. Fruit machine; darts; shove
ha'penny; table skittles, and other games. Children.
Garden and yard. Outside gents'. Car park.

LANGTON HERRING Dorset Map 2

Elm Tree
on B3157
Abbotsbury 257
11–2.30, 6–10.30
(11 Sat & summer)

A crowded 16th-century inn with original
ingle-nook, exposed beams and a wealth of brass
and copper. Bar menu (11.30–2, 7–10; Sun 12–1.30,
7–10) under revision: soup 20p, pâté 65p,
ploughman's 55p–60p, whitebait 70p, scampi £1,
corn-on-the-cob 65p. Devenish Wessex IPA (pump);
others pressurised. Wine. Garden. Car park.

LAPWORTH West Midlands Map 5

Boot Inn
Old Warwick Road
Lapworth 2464
11–2.30, 6–10.30
(11 Fri, Sat)

A cheerful old pub on the canalside. Bar food (exc
Mon D): pâté 55p, soup 33p, smoked salmon £2,
scampi £1·75, steak £2·30, omelettes £1·35, cold
buffet £1·60–£2·45. Separate restaurant (Sat & Sun,
D only). Whitbread bitter (pump). Wine. Children.
Fruit machine; darts. Garden. Car park.

LAVENHAM Suffolk Map 3

Angel
Market Place
Lavenham 388
10.30–2, 5–11
(6–11 Sat)

'Warm and helpful atmosphere' in a 600-year-old
pub surrounded by the 'largest collection of Tudor
houses in the country'. Bar snacks (not Sun):
hamburger 25p, cheeseburger 30p, sandwiches from
30p, ploughman's 40p, farmer's platter 60p, pâté
platter 60p. Separate restaurant (12.30–1.30, 7.30–9;
closed Sat L, Sun D). Pressurised Truman beers;
Tap promised from the pump. Wine. Fruit machine;
bar billiards; darts; shove ha'penny; bar skittles;
dominoes. Car park. B&B £5·50.

Timbers

See main *Guide*

LEDBURY Hereford & Worcester Map 2

Old Talbot
New Street
Ledbury 2963 *and* 2602
10.30–2.30, 6–10.30
(11 Fri, Sat)

A half-timbered building dating from 1596, the scene
of a Royalist/Cromwellian encounter in the Civil
War. Fine oak panelling and Jacobean overmantel.
Bar snacks (12–2, 7–9.30; not Sun D): soup 30p,
gammon £1·40, cod 95p, steak £1·80, curries £1·15,
toasted sandwiches 35p–90p, pizza 35p–45p.
(Separate restaurant 12–2, 7–9.30; not Sun D).
Ansells' bitter, Aston ale and mild (pump). Weston's
cider. Wine. Fruit machine; darts; cards; dominoes.
B&B from £4·50.

LEWES East Sussex Map 3

Pelham Arms

See main *Guide*

LICKFOLD West Sussex Map 3

Lickfold Inn
2 m N of Lodsworth
Lodsworth 285
11–2.30, 6–10.30
(11 Fri, Sat & summer)

Built in 1460 and renovated in 1972 – 'your typical
olde worlde country pub.' Bar food includes
Lickfolder (home-made beefburger) 75p, scampi 75p,
whitebait 60p, chicken £1, sandwiches 40p–65p.
Separate restaurant. Ruddle's County, Fuller's ESB
and London Pride, Bass, Whitbread Pompey Royal
(pump). Wine. Tables outside. Car park.

LINCOLN Lincolnshire   Map 6

Wig and Mitre
29 Steep Hill
Lincoln 35190
11–3, 5.30–10.30
(11 Fri, Sat)

A 14th-century timber-framed building 'like a tea shoppe'; associated with the Cornhill vaults. Bar menu (until 30 min before closing) changes daily: salads 85p–95p, ploughman's 55p–65p, six pâtés 60p, toasted sandwiches 30p–35p, fresh sandwiches 25p–35p. Ruddle's County, Samuel Smith's bitter (pump). Wine. Fruit machine. Seats outside.

LITLINGTON East Sussex   Map 3

Plough and Harrow
off B2108, near Alfriston
Alfriston 870632
11–2.30, 6.30–10.30
(11 Fri, Sat & summer)

An 'admirable and popular place on a quiet road in wonderful country'; parts of the pub are 600 years old. Bar food: ploughman's 65p, pâté 80p, sandwiches 30p–70p, plate of prawns with brown bread £1·15, salads 90p–£5, including salmon and lobster. Ind Coope bitter and Burton ale, Watney's Tamplins bitter (pump); others pressurised. Merrydown cider. Wine. Fruit machine; darts in winter. Garden. Car park.

LITTLE CHART Kent   Map 3

Swan
off B2077
Ashford 23250
10.30–2.30, 6–10.30
(11 Fri, Sat)

An old pub in a pretty village with Roman ruins nearby. Three-course meals in the evening but any item can be had as a snack: pâté, prawn cocktail, and chicken, scampi, rump steak, beefburger – all with chips. Whitbread Trophy and mild. Car park.

LITTLE HAMPDEN Buckinghamshire   Map 3

Rising Sun
off Butlers Cross–Great
Missenden road
Hampden Row 393
12–2.30, 6–10.30
(11 Fri, Sat)

Large, comfortable bars in an old pub of character, set among beechwoods. Bar food (until 30 min before closing; 28p–£1): 'excellent' pâté, home-made quiche, scampi and chips, salad rolls with crab or prawns. Restricted choice at weekends. Marston's Pedigree, Adnams' bitter, Samuel Smith's bitter, Greene King Abbot (pump). Wine. Darts; cribbage; dominoes. 'Enormous lawn.' Car park.

LITTLE LANGDALE Cumbria   Map 7

Three Shires Inn

See main *Guide*

LITTLE MARLOW Buckinghamshire   Map 3

Crooked Billet
Sheepridge Lane
Bourne End 21216
10–2.30, 6–10.30
(11 Fri, Sat)

Cosy old-world pub. Lunchtime micro-waved snacks include cottage pie 60p, steak and kidney pie 70p, pizza 60p–75p; 'farmhouse-style' sandwiches from 30p. No food Sat evening or Sun L. Wethered's bitter and special bitter (pump).

Pubs are represented on the maps by a tankard.

Some pubs off the beaten track do not always serve food at times notified. Phone to check.

LITTLE WASHBOURNE Gloucestershire   Map 2

Hobnails Inn
on A438
4 m from M5, junction 9
Alderton 237 *and* 458
10.30–2.30, 6–10.30
(11 Fri, Sat)

Built in 1474 and run by the same family for well over 200 years. Bar food: 'generously filled' baps 30p–85p, and 'substantial' snacks. Home-made puddings with cream 60p–70p, but 'diabetics, weight-watchers, low cholesterol types, vegetarians, babies, and dogs catered for on request.' Separate restaurant (D only; closed Sun & Mon). Pressurised Whitbread beers. Bulmer's cider. Wine. Darts; skittles. Children allowed in the dining-room or on the patio. Car park.

LIVERPOOL Merseyside   Map 5

Everyman Bistro

See main *Guide*

LONG HANBOROUGH Oxfordshire   Map 2

The Bell
on A4095
Freeland 881324
10.30–2.30, 6–10.30
(11 Fri, Sat)

A Morrell's house serving 'good-value' bar food (Mon–Fri L): Berkshire broth 30p, home-made pâté 40p, stuffed pepper 45p, savoury pancake 45p, seafood cocktail 50p, smoked mackerel 50p, grilled mullet 45p. Separate restaurant (7–9.30). Morrell's bitter from the cask. Wine. Fruit machine and electronic games. Patio. Car park.

LONG MELFORD Suffolk   Map 3

Crown Inn
Hall Street
Long Melford 366
11–2, 6–11

A small hotel, redesigned and redecorated 'to good advantage'; under new ownership. Bar food 'beautifully cooked, presented and served' (12–1.30, 7–9.15): pâté 55p, omelettes £1, quiche 80p, steak sandwich 95p, 'most delicious' home-made game pie with chips £1, toasted sandwiches 45p–65p, plain sandwiches 45p–£1·10. Separate restaurant (12–1.30, 7–9.30). Adnams' bitter, Greene King IPA and Abbot, Courage Directors (pump); others pressurised. Wine. Fruit machine. Garden. Car park. B&B £6·50.

LONGPARISH Hampshire   Map 2

Plough
Longparish 358
10.30–2.30, 6–10.30
(11 Fri, Sat)

'Just what a village pub should be.' Bar food (exc Mon D; pâté only Sun L); three kinds of home-made pâté, home-made soup, smoked salmon, salads, savouries on toast. Separate restaurant. Whitbread Pompey Royal and others. Wine. Fruit machine. Patio and lawn. Car park.

LONG PRESTON North Yorkshire   Map 5

Boar's Head
on A65
Long Preston 217
11–3, 6–10.30
(11 Fri, Sat)

Originally a farm, and a pub since 1725; now clean, well decorated and well run. Home-cooked bar food (until 30 min before closing): soup 26p, quiche with chips and peas £1·35, steak and kidney pie £1·40, fried chicken £1·15, salads £1·60, ploughman's 75p, sandwiches 45p; two daily set meals – 'bargains' at £2·25. Wide range of beers, mainly pressurised. Wine. Children. Fruit machine; darts. Car park. B&B £5·50.

LONGSTOCK Hampshire   Map 2

Peat Spade
off A30
1½ m from Longstock
Stockbridge 612
11–2.30, 6–10.30
(11 Fri, Sat)

An old inn off the beaten track; popular with trout
fishermen, golfers and beaglers. Bar food (until 30
min before closing): 'excellent' sandwiches 25p–42p,
ploughman's 40p, cheese 28p, soup, hot pies. Gale's
HSB and light mild (pump); winter brew from the
cask. Old English wines, including raisin. Fruit
machine; bar billiards; darts; shove ha'penny.
Garden with swings. Car park. B&B £5.

LUDLOW Salop   Map 5

Wheatsheaf
Lower Broad Street
Ludlow 2980
10.30–2.30, 6–10.30
(11 Fri, Sat)

Ancient and unspoilt pub with fine wood and
stone-work, and a 'funny old African idol' on the
wall. Bar food (12–2, 7–9.30; 25p–£1·30):
home-made soup 25p, pâté 55p, trout and chips £2,
hot sausages with French bread 45p, steak butty
50p, sandwiches 30p–70p. Separate restaurant (12–2,
7–9.30). Robinson's bitter (pump); others
pressurised. Wine. B&B £6·50.

LYMPSTONE Devon   Map 1

Globe
The Strand
Exmouth 3166
10.30–2.30, 5.30–10.30
(11 Fri, Sat)

'The service is unusually quick, courteous and
helpful' in this old pub on the edge of the Exe
estuary. Bar food (12–1.30, 7–10.15; Sun 12–1.15,
7–10.15): 'excellent crab salad in very ample
quantities' £1·80, other salads 80p–£1·90, sandwiches
50p, ploughman's 45p. Separate restaurant (L only).
Wide range of pressurised beers. Wine. Hill's cider.
Fruit machine; darts; cards; dominoes.

MAIDENSGROVE Oxfordshire   Map 2

Five Horseshoes
4½ m NW of Henley
Nettlebed 641282
11–2.30, 6–10.30
(11 Fri, Sat)

Brick-and-flint pub 'in the wilds' on the edge of
Russell's Water common, popular for its simple
home-cooking (12–2, 7.30–10 exc Mon; menu changes
daily): country meat pie, sea food pie, chicken and
mushroom pie, smoked salmon and prawn quiche,
curries, jacket potatoes, home-cooked ham and beef
salads, £1–£1·50. Snacks too (exc Mon): pâté, soup,
sandwiches 45p–70p. Candlelit suppers in winter
(Tue, Wed & Thur only; must book): including
steak and kidney pudding and casseroles (£2·50).
Brakspear's bitter and special bitter (pump); old ale
from the cask in winter. Gaymer's cider. Wine.
Darts. Garden. Car park.

MANACCAN Cornwall   Map 1

New Inn
off B3293
S of Helford
Manaccan 323
11–2.30, 6–10.30
(11 Fri, Sat & summer)

A pleasant, unimproved pub – small, old and
thatched – in an unspoilt village. 'Superb' bar
snacks (12–2, 7.30–10; Sun till 1.30): home-made
soup 25p, crab soup 40p, liver pâté 50p, ham and
onion pie 40p, fish pie 85p, toasted sandwiches
38p–44p. Devenish Cornish bitter and mild from the
cask; others pressurised. Taunton cider. Wine.
Darts; shove ha'penny; dominoes; cards. Garden.

MANCHESTER   Map 5

Royal Oak
729 Wilmslow Road,
Didsbury
061-445 3152
11–3, 5.30–10.30
(11 Fri, Sat)

'A victim of its own success, now overflowing with students' but 'still the best range of cheeses and pâtés' in the area, served with locally baked bread (Mon–Fri L only). Marston's Burton bitter, Pedigree and mild (pump); others pressurised. Wine.

MARLOW Buckinghamshire   Map 3

Hare and Hounds
Henley Road
Marlow 3343
10.30–2.30, 6–10.30
(11 Fri, Sat)
Closed Dec 25 evening

A 15th-century posthouse with 'not much style or comfort but excellent food'. Home-made bar lunches (Mon–Sat, 12.30–2) include a daily special such as jugged hare, moussaka, steak and kidney pie, game hot-pot, beef stew with dumplings, stuffed cabbage. Separate restaurant (12.30–1.30, 7.30–9; exc Sun). Wethered's special, Trophy and Winter Royal (pump). Wine. Car park.

MARNHULL Dorset   Map 2

Crown
Crown Road
Marnhull 224
10–2.30, 6–10.30
(11 Fri, Sat)

Attractive, friendly country pub with simple public bar and 'smoother' saloon. Bar food (no prices stated) includes sandwiches, pâté, steak and chips. Separate restaurant (12–2, 7–9.30). Hall & Woodhouse best bitter (pump); others pressurised. Wine. Fruit machine; darts; skittles. Outdoor gents'. Seats outside. Car park. B&B from £5·50.

MARSTON TRUSSELL Northamptonshire   Map 5

Sun Inn

See main *Guide*

MAYFIELD East Sussex   Map 3

Rose and Crown
Fletching Street
Mayfield 2200
10.30–2.30, 6–10.30
(11 Fri, Sat)

A pretty, low-beamed old coaching-house, with working ingle-nook, 'and flowers virtually everywhere'. Bar menu (Mon–Sat L only) changes regularly (55p–£1·10): seafood curry mayonnaise, marinated kipper fillets, crab mousse, squid and prawn vinaigrette, pâté, ploughman's. Separate restaurant (L Tue–Fri, D Wed–Sat). Courage Directors, Charrington IPA, Bass from the pump; others pressurised. Wine. Darts; shove ha'penny. Garden. Car park.

MICHELDEVER Hampshire   Map 2

Lunways Inn
on A33
Micheldever 258
10.30–2.30, 6–10.30
(11 Fri, Sat)

'The only pub for miles along a piece of dual carriageway' linking the M3 and the M27. 'Excellent' choice of bar snacks: help-yourself cold buffet (priced according to how much you take), home-made soup, steak and kidney pie, game, jacket potatoes. Pressurised Marston's beers. Wine. Children. Fruit machine; darts. Garden. Car park. B&B.

Hours given are opening times. Food may not be served over the whole period.

MIDDLEHAM North Yorkshire   Map 8

Millers House Hotel

See main *Guide*

MIDDLE WALLOP Hampshire   Map 2

Fifehead Manor

See main *Guide*

MILBORNE PORT Dorset   Map 2

Queens Head
on A30
2 m E of Sherborne
Milborne Port 314
11.30–2.30, 6.30–10.30
(11 Fri, Sat & summer)

A Georgian stone-built country pub with log fires – 'traditionally a cider house.' All snacks (L only) home-made and under £1: pizza, quiche, 'very tasty' pâté, ploughman's, sandwiches; hot food from November, including lasagne, stuffed baked potatoes, Somerset smokies and 'others depending on the whims of the cook'. 'No chips.' Separate restaurant 'coming shortly'. Large range of traditional beers, including Wadworth's 6X, Hall & Woodhouse best bitter, Courage Directors (pump) and Wadworth's Old Timer from the cask. Choice of cider. Wine. Fruit machine; darts; table skittles. Enclosed courtyard. Car park. B&B £5.

MILTON STREET East Sussex   Map 3

Sussex Ox
off A27
Alfriston 870840
10.30–2.30, 7–10.30
(11 Fri, Sat;
6–11 summer)

An 'enterprising place' in an out-of-the-way hamlet, in the heart of the Downs. The pub's van boasts: 'For all the family.' 'Excellent and varied' home-produced bar food (all under £1): salads and home-made bread with pies, flans or quiche served on wooden platters; home-made soups and hot dishes in winter. Harvey's best bitter, mild and old (pump). Wine. Darts; shove ha'penny; devil among the tailors; dominoes. Children. Car park.

MODBURY Devon Map 1

Exeter Inn
Modbury 239
11–2.30, 6–10.30
(11 Fri, Sat)

'Genuinely ancient, up-market, a bit pleased with itself' – but an unspoilt, popular pub. 'Generous helpings' of first-class bar food (until 30 min before closing; no prices stated): home-made soup, spaghetti, omelettes, curry, ploughman's, mackerel, duck pie with orange salad, sandwiches. Usher's bitter from the cask; others pressurised. Taunton cider. Wine. Children. Garden. B&B £12.

MORETON-IN-MARSH Gloucestershire   Map 2

Lamb's

See main *Guide*

MORPETH Northumberland   Map 8

Gourmet

See main *Guide*

In England and Wales, Sunday opening hours are 12–2, 7–10.30.

See p. 441 for 'How to use the pub section'.

MOULTON North Yorkshire   Map 8

Black Bull

See main *Guide*

NEEDHAM MARKET Suffolk   Map 3

The Swan
9 High Street
Needham Market 720280
11–2.30, 6.30–11

A welcoming pub, built around 1520. Bar food (not
Sun D) all cooked on the premises: soup 30p, cold
platter 95p, daily dish (including rabbit pie) 88p,
omelettes 55p, ploughman's 45p. Separate
restaurant (12–2, 7.15–9.30). Tolly Cobbold bitter
(pump); others pressurised. Strongbow cider. Wine.
Children. Fruit machine. Car park.

NEWBOLD-ON-AVON Warwickshire   Map 5

Barley Mow
64 Main Street (B4112)
Rugby 4174
11–2.30, 6–10.30
(7–11 Fri, Sat)

'Cheerful and informal' service in a 150-year-old
canalside pub undergoing modernisation. Bar food
(Mon–Sat 12.30–2.30; evenings promised): home-made
soup 26p, pâté 50p, home-made pie 95p,
ploughman's 60p, rolls 21p. Bass, Mitchells &
Butlers bitter and mild (pump); others pressurised.
Wine. Children. Fruit machine; darts; dominoes;
cards. Patio and garden. Car park.

NEWTON Cambridgeshire   Map 3

Queen's Head
on B1368
1¼ m off A10 at Harston
Cambridge 870436
11.30–2.30, 6–10.30
(11 Fri, Sat)

An Elizabethan saloon and Victorian public bar in
this delightful pub on the green. Bar food (not
Sun L): home-made soup, sandwiches made from
locally baked bread 35p, stuffed baked potatoes 28p,
pâté 65p, ploughman's 50p, smoked mackerel 65p.
Adnams' bitter and old from the cask. Bulmer's
cider. Wine. Fruit machine; darts; skittles. Seats
outside. Car park.

NEWTOWN-IN-ST-MARTIN Cornwall   Map 1

Prince of Wales
Manaccan 247
11–2.30, 6–10.30
(11 Fri, Sat & summer)

A rambling old pub in a quiet village close to
Frenchman's Creek. Bar food (L, and 7.30
onwards): scampi £1·40, ham and egg £1·10, sausage
and egg 85p, salads £1·20–£2, sandwiches 28p–45p,
home-made pâté 60p, local smoked mackerel 60p.
Separate restaurant (11.30–2, 7.30–10; not Wed,
Sun in winter). Pressurised Devenish beers. Wine.
Children. Fruit machine; darts; dominoes; euchre
(American card game). Tables on forecourt.
Car park.

NORTHLEACH Gloucestershire   Map 2

Sherborne Arms
The Square
Northleach 241
10.30–2.30, 6–10.30
(11 Fri, Sat)
Closed Dec 25 evening

Locals say this pub has the best snacks in the area.
Try the soup, ham, cheese or beef rolls, 'good'
pâté 50p, or ploughman's 70p. Separate grill-room.
Whitbread Trophy. Wine. Juke-box.

NORTON ST PHILIP Somerset   Map 2

The George
on B3110
6 m S of Bath
Faulkland 224
10–2.30, 6–10.30
(11 Fri, Sat)

A 'nice, cosy' pub with open fires – built in 1223,
visited by the Duke of Monmouth and mentioned
by Pepys. 'Tempting' bar food (30p–£1·25) includes
ham and baked potatoes, sandwiches and cottage
pie. Separate restaurant (12.30–2, 7–9; 3 courses £5).
Wadworth's PA, 6X and Old Timer (winter), Bass
(all on pump). Wine. Children. Courtyard and
garden. Car park.

NOTTINGHAM Nottinghamshire   Map 5

Punch Bowl
214 Porchester Road
Nottingham 55293
10.30–2.30, 5.30–10.30
(11 Fri, Sat)

Small pub with a maritime flavour and fine views of
the city. Wide choice of cold food (exc Sun):
sandwiches 30p, ploughman's, three kinds of pâté,
'enormous helpings' of meat with salad. Separate
restaurant in the offing. Bass (pump); others
pressurised. Wine. Terrace. Car park.

ODELL Bedfordshire   Map 3

The Bell
Bedford 720254
10.30–2.30, 6–10.30
(11 Fri, Sat)

Attractive 17th-century pub in a pretty village near
the River Ouse. Basket meals (65p–£1·15) in the
evening (exc Sun, Mon); sandwiches with 'real
bread' (25p) and 'excellent' ploughman's (45p) at all
times (exc Mon D, Sun). Facilities for private
parties. Greene King IPA and Abbot (pump). Fruit
machine. Garden. Car park.

OLDBURY-UPON-SEVERN Avon   Map 2

Anchor
Thornbury 413331
11.30–2.30, 6.30–10.30
(11 Fri, Sat)

'Keep places like this in the *Guide*' – 'plain, decent
but (unselfconsciously) picturesque pub.' Cold bar
snacks (exc Sun L): 'handsome portions' of cheese
28p–40p, roast beef 96p, baked ham 50p, home-made
pâté 44p, home-made turkey pie 58p, smoked spare
ribs 48p. Theakston's bitter, Marston's Pedigree
(pump); Robinson's bitter, Bass and Theakston's Old
Peculier from the cask. Bulmer's and local village
cider. Wine. Fruit machine; darts. Garden. Car park.

OLD HEATHFIELD East Sussex   Map 3

Star
Church Street
Heathfield 3570
10–2.30, 6–10.30
(11 Fri, Sat)

Large, ivy-clad pub with an attractive garden; in an
idyllic setting next to the church. 'Good choice' of
home-made bar food (12–2, 7–10, not Mon D; Sun
12–1.30): soup 30p, egg mayonnaise 45p, pâté 50p,
salads £1·60–£1·95, ploughman's 60p, turkey and
ham pie £1·10, bubble and squeak £1·10. Pressurised
Watney's beers. Wine. Children. Fruit machine;
darts. Garden. Outside gents'. Car park.

Towns shown in black on our maps contain at least one recommended
restaurant or pub (see map key). The dot denotes the location of the
town or village, not the restaurant. Where necessary, we give
directions to the restaurant in the entry. If you can, help us to
improve them.

PATTISWICK Essex Map 3

Compasses
off A120 between
Braintree and Coggeshall
Coggeshall 61322
10.30–2.30, 6–11

Dimly lit and tightly packed little pub in pleasant surroundings. Bar food always available: pâté 55p, chicken and chips 80p, scampi and chips 90p, sandwiches; grills at lunch-time. Greene King IPA and Abbot, Adnams' bitter, Courage Directors (pump); eighteen keg beers. Wine. Fruit machine; darts. Garden. Car park.

PELYNT Cornwall Map 1

Jubilee Inn
on B3359
Lanreath 312
10.30–2.30, 6–11

A modernised old pub with 'many relics of royalty, mainly Victoriana'. Bar food (L only): soup, pâté, fisherman's lunch, ploughman's 70p, sandwiches, mixed grill £1·50, seafood salad £1·60, hot daily dish. Separate restaurant. Bass (pump); others pressurised. Wine. Children in summer. Juke-box; fruit machine; darts. Garden. Car park. B&B.

PETER TAVY Devon Map 1

Peter Tavy Inn
3 m NE of Tavistock
Mary Tavy 348
11.30–2.30, 5.30–10.30
(11 Fri, Sat & summer)

Delightful little pub with the original slate floor in a small, picturesque village on Dartmoor. Bar menu chalked on a slate in the fireplace: broth with brown bread 40p, cottage pie 95p, quiche 50p, pasty 25p, pâté 75p, trout £2·25, steak £3·25, sandwiches 45p–60p. Incredible range of beers from the cask, including Courage, Bass, Gibbs Mew, Wells, Fuller's and Theakston's. Taunton and Lancaster's cider. Wine. Garden. Car park.

PETWORTH West Sussex Map 3

Angel
Angel Street (A283)
Petworth 42153
10–2.30, 6–10.30
(11 Fri, Sat & summer)

A small old inn with plenty of character, log fires and two ghosts. Bar food (until 15 min before closing; no prices given) includes home-made curries, 'delicious' sandwiches, prawns, smoked salmon, ploughman's. Separate restaurant (closed Tue & Sun in summer; open Fri & Sat only in winter). Pressurised Whitbread beers. Wine. Bar billiards; darts; shove ha'penny. Children. Garden. Car park. B&B £5·50.

Welldigger's Arms
on A283 to Pulborough
Petworth 42287
10–2.30, 6–10.30
(11 Fri, Sat)

Popular pub with Victorian photographs and farm implements on the walls. Friendly, efficient service of bar food: 'generous platters of well-cooked grills', seafood platter £3, prawns, smoked mackerel, smoked salmon, whitebait. Pressurised Watney's beer. Wine. Garden. Car park.

PIDDLEHINTON Dorset Map 2

Thimble
Piddletrenthide 270
10.30–2.30, 6–10.30
(11 Fri, Sat)

'Nothing is too much trouble' at this popular, thatched pub with 'excellent' bar snacks, some of them home-made: sandwiches 45p, scampi and chips £1·25, egg mayonnaise and prawns 86p. Separate restaurant (D only, Wed–Sat). Pressurised Hall & Woodhouse beers. Wine. Garden. Car park. B&B £5·50.

PIDDLETRENTHIDE Dorset   Map 2

Poachers Inn
on B3143
Piddletrenthide 358 *and*
420
10.30–2.30, 6.30–11

William Pearson, landlord of this 15th-century inn,
'recognises and chats with customers and
remembers their foibles.' Lunches (12–2) in the
lounge; dinners (7–10) in the restaurant. Bar food:
cheeses, chicken, scampi, plaice, pâté. Barbecue in
the garden for kebabs and steaks. Choice of beers,
including Eldridge Pope Royal Oak and Dorchester
bitter (pump). Taunton cider. Wine. Children. Car
park. B&B £6.

PLUSH Dorset   Map 2

Brace of Pheasants

See main *Guide*

POLKERRIS Cornwall   Map 1

Rashleigh Inn
off A3082 between
Par and Fowey
Par 3991
11–2.30, 6–10.30
(11 Fri, Sat)

Comfortable, friendly pub on the beach in a hamlet
of 28 people, some of whom take part in occasional
sing-songs round the piano. 'Excellent' bar food
(12–1.30, 6–10): roast ham, pâté, terrine, local
smoked mackerel, salami, pies. Separate restaurant
(Mon–Sat, D only). St Austell, Whitbread and other
pressurised beers. Bulmer's cider. Wine. Outside
terraces.

POLPERRO Cornwall   Map 1

Noughts and Crosses
Lansallos Street
Polperro 72239
10.30–2.30, 6–10.30
(11 Fri, Sat)

Named after the habit of a 'little old lady' who
owned the place when it was a bakery: because she
was illiterate, she used noughts to signify orders and
crosses for payments. Bar food (12–2, 7–9, not Mon
D): ploughman's 65p, sandwiches 35p–50p, scampi
£1·50, chicken £1·30. Pressurised Courage beers.
Wine. Juke-box; fruit machine; darts; pool table in
winter. B&B £5.

PORLOCK WEIR Somerset   Map 1

Ship Inn

See main *Guide*

PRINCES RISBOROUGH Buckinghamshire   Map 3

George and Dragon
High Street
Princes Risborough 3087
10.30–2.30, 6–10.30
(11 Fri, Sat)

Attractive 300-year-old coaching-inn on the
Ridgeway walk in the Chilterns. Wide selection of
bar food (no prices stated): home-made soup,
chicken, herrings, home-made brawn, bread and
cheese, pâté, rib of beef, omelettes; choice of three
daily dishes £1–£1·35. No bar food Sun L; limited
snacks Sat, Sun D. Separate restaurant (12–2, 7–9;
9.30 Sat; not Sun D). Ind Coope Burton ale (pump);
others pressurised. Bulmer's cider. Wine. Car park.
B&B from £5·50.

PRIORS HARDWICK Warwickshire   Map 2

Butchers Arms

See main *Guide*

PUCKERIDGE Hertfordshire   Map 3

White Hart
1 Braughing Lane
Ware 821309
10.30–2.30, 5.30–10.30
(11 Fri, Sat)

A 16th-century coaching inn with a 'very good selection of food': home-made soup 40p, meat balls 75p, lasagne 75p, home-made smoked salmon pâté £1·75, prawns and crayfish £2·85, seafood quiche £1·65, baked ham £1·60, home-made turkey and mushroom pie £1·30. Separate restaurant (12.30–2, 7.30–9.30; exc Sun L; must book). McMullen's bitter and mild (pump). Wine. Fruit machine. Seats outside. Car park.

PUTTENHAM Surrey   Map 3

Jolly Farmer
Guildford 810374
10.30–2.30, 6–10.30
(11 Fri, Sat)

Pleasant inn, established in 1673, though considerably modernised. On Pilgrims Way, four miles from Guildford along the Hog's Back. Bar food: sandwiches from 35p, ploughman's 50p, home-made pâté 50p, soup 30p, chicken £1·15, 'first-class' cold roast beef and salad £1·75. Separate restaurant (L Tue–Fri, D Tue–Sat). Young's special bitter, Hall & Woodhouse best bitter from the cask; others pressurised. Wine. Seats outside in summer. Car park.

RATTERY Devon   Map 1

Church House Inn
N of A385
4 m W of Totnes
Buckfastleigh 2220
11–2.30, 6–10.30
(11 Fri, Sat & summer)

Attractive, up-market building with a spiral stone staircase, log fires and many antiquities. Bar food (11.30–2, 6.30–10): ploughman's 55p, toasted sandwiches 55p–90p, soup 30p, smoked salmon £1·45, grills 95p–£2·55, salads £1·40–£2. Separate restaurant (D Tue–Sat; L by arrangement only). Pressurised beers. Wine. Darts. Patio. Car park.

RAVENGLASS Cumbria   Map 7

Ratty Arms
Ravenglass 676
11–3, 6–11

Converted from a station booking-office and still on the Ravenglass-Eskdale miniature steam railway, known locally as La'al Ratty. 'Excellent' snacks (12–2, 7–9): ploughman's 50p, baked potato 45p, mackerel 90p, 'recommended' Cumberland sausage £1·10, home-baked ham £1·60, scampi £1·85, sandwiches 35p–40p. Pressurised Scottish & Newcastle beers. Wine. Children. Fruit machine; darts; bar billiards in winter. Tables on forecourt. Car park.

REMENHAM Berkshire   Map 3

Little Angel
Henley-on-Thames 4165
10–2.30, 6–10.30
(11 Fri, Sat)

An attractive pub across the bridge from the Angel in Henley (q.v.). 'Reasonably priced' bar snacks: soup, pâté, cottage pie, pasties, smoked mackerel, beef Wellington £3·95. Separate dining-room (closed Sun; Mon D). Brakspear's bitter and old (pump). Wine. Children. Garden. Car park.

Hours given are opening times. Food may not be served over the whole period.

RIPLEY Surrey   Map 3

Anchor
High Street
Ripley 2120
11–2.30, 6–10.30
(11 Fri, Sat)

An old low-gabled building in a pretty village; open fireplace and low beams. Home-made bar food (Mon–Sat L only): steak and kidney, and turkey and ham pies 55p each, quiche 40p, beef curry 65p, pâté 50p, turkey salad 85p. Ind Coope Burton ale (pump); others pressurised. Wine. Children. Darts. Patio. Car park.

ROMALDKIRK Durham   Map 8

Rose and Crown
on B6277
Cotherstone 213
11–3, 6–10.30
(11 Sat)

A warm welcome at this comfortable coaching house where 'the atmosphere is cheerfully permissive'. Bar food: soup, pâté, casseroles, scampi, steak, salads, sandwiches. Separate restaurant (Mon–Sat D; Sun L). Theakston's bitter and Old Peculier (pump); others pressurised. Wine. Children. Tables outside. Car park. B&B.

ROSTHWAITE Cumbria   Map 7

Riverside Bar
Scafell Hotel
on B5289
Borrowdale 208
11–3, 6–10.30
(11 Fri, Sat)

A basic bar attached to a hotel in idyllic surroundings. Bar food: soup 30p, ploughman's 80p, duck casserole 80p. Separate restaurant. Samuel Smith's bitter (pump); others pressurised. Children. Garden. B&B.

ROTHBURY Northumberland   Map 8

Anglers Arms
Weldon Bridge
Longframlington 655
11–3, 6–10.30

A traditional Northumbrian inn beside the River Coquet; popular with fishermen. Bar lunches (12–2.30): home-made soup 35p, home-made steak and kidney pie £1.25, fish and chips £1. Basket meals (6–10.30) £1. Sandwiches 35p–45p. Separate restaurant (12–2.30, 7–10.30). Pressurised Scottish & Newcastle beers. Wine. Children. Fruit machine; darts; dominoes. Garden. Car park. B&B from £6.

ROWSLEY Derbyshire   Map 5

Peacock Hotel

See main *Guide*

RYE East Sussex   Map 3

Union
East Street
Rye 2334
10.30–2.30, 6–10.30
(11 Fri, Sat)

A quaint, beamed pub with antiques. Bar food (Mon–Sat, L only; hot food 12–2): plaice £1·45, hot-pot £1·10, steak and kidney pudding £1·05, fish platter £1·45, curries £1·20, home-made soup, 'excellent' chips and jacket potatoes. Young's bitter and special bitter, Worthington best bitter (pump). Wine. Fruit machine; poker dice. B&B.

In England and Wales, Sunday opening hours are 12–2, 7–10.30.

Some pubs off the beaten track do not always serve food at times notified. Phone to check.

SAFFRON WALDEN Essex   Map 3

Eight Bells
18 Bridge Street (A130)
Saffron Walden 22790
11–2.30, 6–10.30
(11 Fri, Sat)

Enterprising and popular old pub with a wealth of oak beams and a separate restaurant in a 15th-century barn. Bar food (until 30 min before closing; 40p–£2): 'delicious' duck pâté, 'very good' home-made steak pie, 'super' quiche, mackerel, devilled crab. Ind Coope Burton ale (pump), bitter (pump or pressurised). Wine. Fruit machine; bar billiards; darts. Car park.

ST IVES Cambridgeshire   Map 6

Slepe Hall

See main *Guide*

ST JUST IN PENWITH Cornwall   Map 1

Star Inn
1 Fore Street (B3306)
St Just 788 767
10.30–2.30, 6–10.30
(11 Fri, Sat & summer)

A 'simple' old pub with 'entertainment by local characters'. Bar food always available: soup 30p, sandwiches 28p–30p, fisherman's lunch with mackerel 70p, ploughman's 50p, pâté 70p, salads 90p–£1·20. St Austell BB, Hicks special and mild from the cask. Coates' cider. Wine. Children. Fruit machine; darts; skittles; cards. Garden. B&B £4.

SALHOUSE Norfolk   Map 6

The Lodge
Vicarage Road
Wroxham 2828
10.30–2.30, 6–11

A former vicarage with 'the ambience of a posh wedding reception'. Home-made daily hot lunch £1·10 or help-yourself buffet £1·35–£2·50: gammon, pâté, beef, prawns, trout, fresh salmon. Sandwiches (from 35p) only in evening and at Sun L. Adnams' bitter, Greene King IPA, Abbot and mild, Courage Directors (pump); others pressurised. Wine. Fruit machine; darts in winter. Garden. Car park.

SALISBURY Wiltshire   Map 2

Haunch of Venison

See main *Guide*

SCOLE Norfolk   Map 6

Crossways Restaurant

See main *Guide*

SEAVINGTON ST MARY Somerset   Map 2

The Pheasant

See main *Guide*

SEDBERGH Cumbria   Map 8

Bull
Main Street
Sedbergh 20264
11–3, 6–10.30
(11 Fri, Sat)

A small, comfortable hotel with two bars – 'all a bit clinical, but very satisfactory.' Bar food is taken into the dining-room to be eaten (12–2, 6.30–8.15): chicken and chips £1·35, 'good northern' roast ham salad £1·40, soup 25p, meat and potato pie 85p, salads £1·15–£1·65, pâté 55p. No snacks Sun L, but choice of four roasts (£2·95). Plain and toasted sandwiches always available. Pressurised Whitbread beers. Bulmer's cider. Wine. Children (L only). Fruit machine; darts; pool table. Car park. B&B £5·50.

SEIGHFORD Staffordshire   Map 5

Holly Bush
near M6, exit 14
Seighford 280
12–2.30, 7–10.30
(11 Fri, Sat)

According to a sign on the door of this 'charming old inn', men with eccentric clothing or hair-styles will not be served. But the bar food (exc Sun; 40p–£2·40) is 'excellent': soup, sandwiches, seafood, whitebait and 'sophisticated' meals such as kidneys in Madeira. Separate restaurant. Pressurised Ansells' beers. Wine. Children. Fruit machine; darts; cribbage; dominoes. Garden. Car park.

SELBORNE Hampshire   Map 3

Selborne Arms
High Street (B3006)
Selborne 247
10–2.30, 6–10.30
(11 Fri, Sat)

Traditional village pub with friendly service; surrounded by beautiful countryside. Bar food (not Sun evening): two daily hot lunch dishes 60p–80p, home-made pâté 56p, ploughman's 45p, pot au feu cooked on open fire 50p, sandwiches; grills and fry-ups (£1·40–£2·50) in evenings. Courage Directors, bitter and mild from the cask. Wine. Fruit machine; darts. Garden. Car park.

SEMLEY Wiltshire   Map 2

Benett Arms
The Green
East Knoyle 221
11–2.30, 6–10.30
(11 Fri, Sat)

Built 200 years ago by the local squire for his workers and now a 'pub for the gentry'. Bar food (until 30 min before closing): soup 30p, steak and kidney pie 85p, pâté 70p, steak £2·40, savoury flan 80p, omelettes 80p–£1, trout £1·50, salads £1·25–£1·50, sandwiches 30p–45p. Separate restaurant (7.30–9.15). Gibbs Mew premium bitter (pump); others pressurised. Wine. Children. Fruit machine; darts; skittles. Garden. Car park. B&B £5.

SHAFTESBURY Dorset   Map 2

Ship
Bleke Street
(opposite main car park)
Shaftesbury 3219
10.30–2.30, 6.30–10.30
(11 Fri, Sat)

Built in 1605 and a doctor's surgery until 1932 – now a pub with a 'mellow, friendly atmosphere'. Bar food (until 45 min before closing): sandwiches 25p, hot meals (such as roast beef and Yorkshire) about £1, 'well-presented, help-yourself' salads with cold buffet £1·25–£1·75. Hall & Woodhouse bitter and best bitter (pump); others pressurised. Wine. Fruit machine; darts; dominoes and other games. Tables outside. 'Quieter under previous owners, and they kept real cider too.'

SHAVE CROSS Dorset   Map 2

Shave Cross Inn
off B3162
Broadwindsor 358
11–2.30, 7–10.30
(11 Fri, Sat & summer)
Closed Mon (exc public hols)

A 14th-century lodging place for travelling monks, now a free house. Bar food (12–1.30, 7–9.30): ploughman's ('very generous portion of excellent Cheddar'), Dorset farmer's lunch 65p, monk's lunch (ham with hot roll) 70p, pâté 65p, soup 15p; basket meals in the evening 65p–£1·05. Bass, Eldridge Pope IPA and Royal Oak, Devenish Wessex best bitter (pump); others pressurised. Taunton cider. Wine. Skittle alley. Garden. Car park.

SHEPERDINE Avon   Map 2

Windbound Inn
Thornbury 414343
10.30–2.30, 6–11

Hospitable old pub on the bank of the Severn, with flower beds and hanging baskets. Bar food (until 30 min before closing): soup 22p, cockles or mussels 46p, gammon £1·90, steak £2·15, plaice £1·20, salads 60p–98p, ploughman's 36p. Whitbread and Theakston's bitter from the cask; others pressurised. Bulmer's cider. Wine. Children at lunch-time. Fruit machine; darts. Garden. Car park.

SHEPTON MONTAGUE Somerset   Map 2

Montague Inn
2 m S of Bruton
Bruton 3213
10.30–2.30, 5.30–10.30
(11 Fri, Sat & summer)
Closed Mon (Nov–Feb)

Old black-and-white country pub in a small village. Bar food (12–1.45, 6–9.30): steaks £1·70–£2, omelettes 50p–55p, home-made soup 25p (winter only), sandwiches 25p–30p, ploughman's 50p; salads in summer. Wadworth's IPA, 6X and Old Timer (winter) from the cask; others pressurised. Wine. Fruit machine; darts; shove ha'penny. Garden. Car park.

SHIPTON-UNDER-WYCHWOOD Oxfordshire   Map 2

Lamb
High Street
Shipton-under-
Wychwood 830465
10.30–2.30, 6–10.30
(11 Fri, Sat)

A 17th-century inn with well-served bar food in friendly surroundings (exc Sat D, Sun L): ploughman's 65p, beef salad £2, daily hot dish £1·75. Separate restaurant (Sun L and Tue–Sat D only). Hook Norton bitter, Usher's bitter (pump). Weston's cider. Wine. Children. Garden. Car park. B&B £8.

SHOREHAM Kent   Map 3

Two Brewers
High Street
Otford 2800
10.30–2.30, 6–10.30
(11 Fri, Sat)

An old, beamed pub with three bars, one with a piano. Bar food includes steak sandwich 65p, ploughman's 55p, chicken and chips £1, scampi £1·25, pâté 55p, steaks from £2·35. Pressurised Courage beers. Wine. Fruit machine; bar billiards; darts. Outside lavatories. Patio and lawn. Car park.

SIDMOUTH Devon   Map 2

Bowd Inn
on A3052
2 m N of the town
Sidmouth 3328
11–2.30, 6–10.30
(11 Fri, Sat)

Popular thatched pub with log fire, brass and copper. Bar food (12–2, 7–10): soup 24p, home-made pâté 50p, chicken £1, scampi £1·30, curry 95p, home-made bacon and mushroom flan 95p, and steak and kidney pie 95p; hot daily dishes £1–£1·15. Separate restaurant undergoing alterations. Devenish bitter and Wessex best bitter (pump); others pressurised. Taunton cider. Wine. Garden. Car park. B&B £8.

Hours given are opening times. Food may not be served over the whole period.

See p. 441 for 'How to use the pub section'.

Pubs are represented on the maps by a tankard.

SINGLETON West Sussex   Map 3

Fox and Hounds
just off A286
Singleton 251
10.30–2.30, 6–10.30
(11 Fri, Sat & summer)

A 'splendid' old pub with ingle-nook and beams; close to Goodwood racecourse. Bar food (until 30 min before closing): choice of nine salads 65p–£1·50, sandwiches 25p–50p, ploughman's 35p; hot food (not public holidays, race days and height of summer) includes home-made pies 80p, plaice and chips £1, mixed grill £1·75. Separate restaurant (Mon, Tue, Fri, Sat 7.30–9.30). Pressurised Watney and Truman beers. Bulmer's cider. Wine. Cribbage; chess; dominoes. Garden. Car park.

SIZEWELL Suffolk   Map 3

Vulcan
6 m E of Saxmundham
Leiston 830748
10.30–2.30, 6–11

Cheery old inn with beams and log fire; two minutes from the sea and close to an atomic power station. 'Generous portions' of bar food: ploughman's 40p, soup 25p, home-made steak and kidney pie 35p (with vegetables and potatoes 90p), home-made chicken pie 35p, omelettes 80p–90p, sandwiches 28p. Adnams' bitter and mild (pump), old ale from the cask. Wine. Darts. Garden. Car park.

SMARDEN Kent   Map 3

The Bell
¾ m NW of Smarden
Smarden 283
11–2.30, 6–10.30
(11 Fri, Sat)

'Nice atmosphere and friendly bar staff' at this country pub with beams, ingle-nooks, and chickens scratching about in the garden. 'Good value' bar food (cooked food until 30 min before closing): basket meals 75p–£1·20, home-made soup 40p, grills £1·80–£3·75, plain and toasted sandwiches 29p–£1·35, ploughman's 45p. Variety of hand-pumped beer, including Bass, Whitbread (Faversham) bitter and Shepherd Neame bitter; Theakston's Old Peculier from the cask. Bob Luck's cider. Juke-box; fruit machine; bar billiards; darts. Garden. Car park.

SNAPE Suffolk   Map 3

Crown
Snape 324
10.30–2.30, 5.30–11

'Friendly and helpful service in cosy but unusual surroundings' – an old smugglers' inn with log fires. 'Some form of food always available': stockpot soup 35p, mixed meat curry 85p, turkey casserole £1·25, garlic sausage with bread 50p, salads £1·75–£4·50. Adnams' bitter, mild and old (pump); others pressurised. Wine. Children. Garden. B&B £6·60.

SOUTHILL Bedfordshire   Map 3

White Horse
Hitchin 813364
11–2.30, 6–10.30
(11 Fri, Sat)

A modernised pub surrounded by farmland in a remote village. It began as a farm and slaughterhouse more than 200 years ago. Bar food (12–1.45, 7.30–9; not Sun): prawns £1·25, pâté 65p, soup 40p, grills £1·75–£3·50, salads £1·30–£2·35, home-made steak and kidney pie or chicken, ham and egg pie £1·30; smaller choice Sat. Separate restaurant. Wethered's bitter (pump); others pressurised. Wine. Children. Fruit machine; darts. Garden. Car park.

485

SOUTHSEA Hampshire Map 2

Eldon Arms
13–17 Eldon Street
Portsmouth 24140
10–2.30, 6–10.30
(11 Fri, Sat)

A pleasant, friendly pub with a Victorian façade.
Bar food always available: 'huge portion' of pâté
75p, meat platter £1·50, seafood salads £1·50–£2·85,
meat salads £1–£1·15, ploughman's 55p–75p,
sandwiches 40p–50p. Separate restaurant (12–2,
7.30–10). Eldridge Pope Royal Oak, IPA and
Dorchester bitter (pump); others pressurised. Wine.
Juke-box; fruit machine; darts. Garden.

SOUTHWOLD Suffolk Map 6

King's Head
High Street
Southwold 723829
10.30–2.30, 6–11

300-year-old hotel which has 'kept the basic
characteristics of a village pub'. Bar snacks are
'substantial and excellent value', and always
available: shepherd's pie 65p, hamburger 65p, pizza
65p, omelettes 60p, toasted sandwiches 25p–50p,
ploughman's 40p. Grills (11.45–2.15, 6–9; Sun
12–1.45 only): scampi £1·30, fresh fish from 80p,
sole £1·80, steaks £2·45–£2·90, Wiener schnitzel
£1·70. Adnams' bitter, mild and old (pump).
Juke-box; fruit machine; darts; pool table. B&B £4.

Red Lion
South Green
Southwold 722385
10.30–2.30, 6–11

A 'clean place, nicer inside than you expect' – in a
'delightful spot near the sea'. Bar food (12–2; Sun
12–1.45): salads 95p–£1·10, garlic pâté 90p, rollmop
95p, mackerel £1, savoury flans 95p. Adnams' bitter,
mild and old (pump); others pressurised. Wine.
Children. Tables outside. Car park. B&B £5.

SOUTH ZEAL Devon Map 1

Oxenham Arms
off A30 in centre of
village
Sticklepath 244
11–2.30, 6–10.30
(11 Fri, Sat)

'Beautiful snacks in a glorious pub' – built in the
12th century by monks. Bar food: home-made steak,
kidney and mushroom pie 95p, seafood platter £1·25,
home-made pâté 60p, ploughman's 60p, sandwiches
from 45p, soup 35p. Separate restaurant
(12.30–1.45, 7.30–9; 3 courses £4·50). Courage
(Plymouth) bitter from the cask; others pressurised.
Inch's cider. Wine. Children. Garden. Car park.
B&B from £7.

SPELDHURST Kent Map 3

George and Dragon
Langton 3125
10–2.30, 6–10.30
(11 Fri, Sat)

'Lots of well-arranged flowers and beams everywhere'
in this handsome, 13th-century pub. Bar food at all
times: 'excellent choice of cold meats' with salad
£1·30–£1·50, prawns £1·65, salmon £1·75,
home-made chicken and ham pie 50p, home-made
pâté 65p, ploughman's 60p, sandwiches from 40p,
local sausage 20p, soup 25p, daily hot dish
(Mon–Sat) 95p. Separate restaurant (12–2, 7–9.30,
exc Mon, Sat L, Sun D). Harvey's bitter, best bitter,
mild and old (winter), King & Barnes bitter (pump).
Bob Luck's cider. Wine. Darts. Lawn. Car park.

Wine bars are represented by a wine glass on the maps, pubs by a tankard.

SPYWAY Dorset Map 2

Spyway Inn
near Askerswell
Powerstock 250
10–2.30, 6–10.30
(11 Fri, Sat & summer)

An old country inn on the western slope of Eggardon Hill. Bar food (25p–95p): home-made soup, steak and kidney pie, game pie (in season), ploughman's, pâté, sandwiches. Separate restaurant. Whitbread (Tiverton) bitter, Eldridge Pope bitter and Bass (pump). Wine. More than forty whiskies. Darts; dominoes. Garden. Car park. B&B £5–£6·50.

STAMFORD Lincolnshire Map 6

George of Stamford
St Martins
Stamford 2101
10.30–2.30, 6–11

'Delightful' 16th-century hotel in the centre of town. Bar food available at all times: home-made minestrone 65p, lasagne £1·25, trout and salad £1·90, turkey and mushroom pie £1·45, home-made pâté £1·15, spare ribs £1·30. Cold buffet at lunch-time – 'eat as much as you want'. Food from separate restaurant served in all bars on request (12.30–2.15, 7–10.30; 3 courses £5). Pressurised Ruddle's and Tolly Cobbold beers. Wine. Children. Garden and covered patio. Car park. B&B from £10.

STAPLE FITZPAINE Somerset Map 2

Greyhound
4½ m SE of Taunton
Hatch Beauchamp 480227
10.30–2.30, 5.30–11
(6 Fri & Sat)

A charming pub ('but could be sprucer') with 'an excellent display of salads', home-made soup, whitebait, pâté, shepherd's pie, venison and rabbit casserole, seafood. Barbecues on Sun evening in summer. Separate restaurant (12–2.15, 7.30–10). Theakston's bitter and Old Peculier, Eldridge Pope Royal Oak from the cask; Eldridge Pope Dorchester bitter (pump). Draught cider. Wine. Children. Fruit machine; darts; skittles; shove ha'penny. Tables in courtyard. Car park.

STARBOTTON North Yorkshire Map 8

Fox and Hounds
2 m N of Kettlewell
Kettlewell 269
11–3, 6–10.30
(11 Fri, Sat & summer)

Small country inn 'beautifully done up, very simply and in excellent taste'. Bar food (12–2, 7–9; 9.30 in summer; none Mon in winter): soup 30p, pâté 75p, gammon, egg and chips £1·25, scampi £1·30, omelettes 80p, salads 80p–£1·15, sandwiches 35p. Winter weekdays only: steak £1·85, trout £1·60, prawn salad £1·40. Theakston's bitter and Old Peculier (pump); others pressurised. Wine. Children. Darts; dominoes. Garden. Car park. B&B £5·50.

STEEP Hampshire Map 3

Harrow
off A272
1½ m NW of Petersfield
Petersfield 2685
10.30–2.30, 6–10.30
(11 Fri, Sat)

Magnificent old pub – almost impossible to find, but one visitor suggests you go 'past Bedales School, past the church, continue half a mile and it is on your left'. 'Extremely generous' quantities of bar food: 'excellent' soup 40p, ploughman's 60p, Scotch eggs 27p, salads £1·40–£1·80. Whitbread (Portsmouth) bitter, Pompey Royal and mild from the cask. Cider. Garden. Loos over the road. Car park.

STEEPLE ASTON Oxfordshire   Map 2

Red Lion

See main *Guide*

STOCKBRIDGE Hampshire   Map 2

Vine Inn
High Street
Stockbridge 652
10–2.30, 6–10.30
(11 Fri, Sat)

'Marvellous value' at this 18th-century pub with a
spacious lounge and a trout stream running through
the garden. 'Pleasant presentation' of home-made
bar food (exc Sat D, Sun): soup 40p, beef Stroganoff
£2·25, spiced liver hot-pot £1·50, hot game pie £1·50,
chicken curry £1·25, pâté 85p, ploughman's 60p,
sandwiches 40p. Whitbread Trophy and Pompey
Royal (pump); others pressurised. Wine. Fruit
machine; darts. Car park. B&B from £5·50.

STODMARSH Kent   Map 3

Red Lion
Littlebourne 339
11.30–2.30, 7–10.30
(11 Fri, Sat)

Free house with open fires and pleasant service of
'good value for money' bar snacks (until 9.30):
cheese 60p, ham 70p, home-made pâté 70p, all with
hot roll and pickles. Whitbread (Faversham) Trophy
from the cask; others pressurised. Wine. Bar
billiards; darts. Garden. Car park.

STOKESLEY North Yorkshire   Map 8

Golden Lion

See main *Guide*

STONE Kent   Map 3

Crown
Appledore 267
11–2.30, 6–10.30
(11 Fri, Sat)

Julian and Pauline Rouse are 'trying very hard and
succeeding' in their restored old pub, with
ingle-nook and antiques. Bar food (until 2; evenings
by request or booking, exc Tue, Wed): hot dog 20p,
pasty 25p, rolls from 25p, 'excellent' pâté 60p,
choice of one or two home-cooked dishes 80p–£1·50.
Shepherd Neame bitter and stock ale, Ind Coope
Burton ale, Whitbread (Faversham) bitter (pump);
others pressurised. Bob Luck's cider. Wine. Fruit
machine; darts; cribbage; Patio; garden. Car park.

STOULTON Hereford & Worcester   Map 2

Bird in Hand
Worcester 840647
11–2.30, 7–10.30
(11 Fri, Sat)

Come early to this pub for an 'exceptional' cold
buffet (not Sun D; £1·10) and snacks (30p–£1·10),
including soup, pies and hot dishes. Separate
restaurant (Tue–Sat D only). Mitchells & Butlers
beers. Wine. Juke-box; fruit machine; darts; pool
table. Drinking outside. Car park.

STRATFORD-UPON-AVON Warwickshire   Map 2

Old Tramway
91 Shipston Road
Stratford-on-Avon 3933
11–2.30, 6–10.30
(11 Fri, Sat)

Massive changes in the past couple of years –
unrecognisable as the old-fashioned inn it used to
be. Bar food (Mon–Sat L only): scampi £1, mackerel
75p, beef and kidney pie 50p, all with chips and
peas; ploughman's 50p, cold meat salad 75p, rolls
25p. Extra winter menu promised. Davenports'
bitter (pump). Fruit machine. Garden. Car park.

STUDHAM Bedfordshire   Map 3

The Bell
4 m S of Dunstable
Whipsnade 872460
11–2.30, 6.30–10.30
(11 Fri, Sat)

Small, attractive country pub in a quaint village.
Bar food: soup 35p, whitebait 75p, pâté 70p, hot
smoked mackerel 75p, fish dishes £1·25–£2·60,
chicken in the basket £1·20, steaks £2·20–£2·95,
seven types of sausage 55p–80p. Ind Coope bitter
and Burton ale (pump). Wine. Fruit machine; darts;
dominoes. Garden. Car park.

SUTTON BANK North Yorkshire   Map 8

Hambleton Inn
on A170
7 m from Thirsk
Sutton 202
Summer: 10.30–2.30, 6–11
Winter: 11–2.30, 7–10.30
(11 Fri, Sat)

A pleasant, log-fired 300-year-old pub sandwiched
between racing stables. Wide variety of bar food
(different menus in summer and winter): soup 20p,
home-made pâté 65p, ploughman's 60p, beef curry
75p, omelettes 50p–75p, salads 85p–£1·35. Dinners
to order in separate dining room. Cameron's bitter
(pump). Children. Fruit machine; darts; quoits;
dominoes. Terrace. Car park. B&B £4.

SUTTON-UNDER-WHITESTONECLIFFE

see **SUTTON BANK**

SWERFORD Oxfordshire   Map 2

Mason's Arms
on A361
Great Tew 212
11–2.30, 6.30–10.30
(11 Fri, Sat)

Cotswold-stone pub with beams and old farm tools.
'Obliging' service of bar food (12–2, 7–10; 10.30 Fri,
Sat): soup 25p, pâté 50p, salmon steak or trout
£1·95, mixed grill £2·65, curried chicken £1·15,
salads 95p–£1·90, ploughman's, sandwiches.
Mitchells & Butlers bitter and mild (pump). Fruit
machine; darts; dominoes; Aunt Sally. Garden.
Car park.

TENTERDEN Kent   Map 3

The Vine
76 High Street (A28)
Tenterden 2922
10–2.30, 6–10.30
(11 Fri, Sat)

A modernised pub on the site of an old brewery and
near the Kent and East Sussex Steam Railway. Cold
buffet at all times: salads with home-made turkey
pie £1, quiche £1, beef £1·65, sandwiches 28p–38p,
ploughman's 40p. Hot lunches (Wed–Sat): soup 25p,
scampi 98p, beefburger 65p. Dinners (Wed–Sat) in
separate restaurant; must book. Shepherd Neame
best bitter, mild and stock ale (pump). Wine.
Children. Juke-box; fruit machine; darts. B&B £4.

THAMES DITTON Surrey   Map 3

Crown
Summer Road
01-398 2376
10.30–2.30, 5.30–10.30
(11 Fri, Sat)

Friendly and comfortable pub, built in 1925. Bar
food 'from lengthy menu' (12–2, 7–9.45; 55p–£2·75):
steak, scampi, lamb chop, ploughman's. Sun L: soup
and ploughman's only. Watney's London bitter and
fined bitter (air pressure). Wine. Children. Juke-box;
fruit machine; darts. Drinking outside in summer.
Car park.

THETFORD Norfolk   Map 6

Anchor

See main *Guide*

TIPTOE Hampshire   Map 2

Plough
Sway Road (B3055)
New Milton 610185
10.30–2.30, 6–10.30
(11 Fri, Sat)

A lovely old pub with pleasant service and bar food
(12–2, 7–10; 75p–£3): home-made soup, steak and
kidney pie, fish; cold buffet, including 'interesting'
salads. Separate restaurant (Sun 12–1.45; Tue–Fri
7–10). Whitbread Pompey Royal from the cask;
others pressurised. Bulmer's cider. Wine. Fruit
machine. Garden. Car park.

TIPTON ST JOHN Devon   Map 2

Golden Lion
Ottery St Mary 2881
10.30–2.30, 6–10.30
(11 Fri, Sat; opens
7 p.m. Nov–Feb)

Clean and friendly pub, just off the main road to
Sidmouth. 'No place to drop into for a quick snack',
as they prepare each order freshly. 'Excellent
food on wooden platters' (until 2 Mon–Sat, 1.15
Sun; 7–9.45 Sun–Thur, 7–10 Fri, Sat): soup 20p–38p,
pâté 52p, ploughman's 60p–69p, sandwiches 38p–67p,
salads £1·10–£2. Bass and Whitbread Trophy
(pump); others pressurised. Inch's cider. Fruit
machine; darts; shove ha'penny; dominoes. Garden.
Car park. B&B from £4·50.

TOCKHOLES Lancashire   Map 5

Victoria
Blackburn 71622
12–2, 7–11

Believed originally to have been a mill; in an area
of great scenic beauty. Bar food (12–2, 8–10):
soup 12p, steak and kidney pie 45p, chicken pie 45p,
steak 95p, plaice 75p. Separate restaurant (Tue–Sat
8–10 only; must book). Variety of pressurised beers.
Wine. Fruit machine. Car park.

TORMARTON Avon   Map 2

Compass
first right from
M4, junction 18
Badminton 242
10–2.30, 6–10.30
(11 Fri, Sat)

Congenial surroundings in a Cotswold-stone pub
with several small bars. All food is cooked in the
Vittles Bar, away from the drinks, but can be eaten
anywhere (till 20 mins before closing): soup 35p,
pâté 75p, salads 80p–£1·75, home-made cheese flan
50p, savoury pastries 50p, sandwiches and rolls
18p–80p. Choice limited Sat, Sun D. Wadworth's
6X and Worthington E (pump); Wadworth's Old
Timer from the cask; others pressurised. Wine.
Children (L only). Fruit machine; darts; dominoes.
Car park. B&B from £5·60.

TOWN ROW East Sussex   Map 3

Harvest Moon
off B2100
1 m E of Rotherfield
Rotherfield 2516
10.30–2.30, 6–10.30
(11 Fri, Sat)

A square Victorian pub with a good atmosphere.
Bar food: soup 13p, sausage and chips 45p, scampi,
'out of this world' bacon sandwiches 28p.
Charrington IPA (pump). Wine. Garden. Car park.

TREGREHAN Cornwall Map 1

Britannia
on A390
Par 2889
11–2.30, 6–10.30
(11 Fri, Sat & summer)

An 18th-century pub now rebuilt as a free house after a fire. Bar food: seafood platter £1·20, plaice and chips £1·35; chicken, scampi, sausages from 65p; cold buffet at lunch-time. Separate restaurant. Bass from the cask; others pressurised. Wine. Juke-box; fruit machine; darts. Garden with swings. Car park.

TROTTON West Sussex Map 3

Keepers Arms
on A272
Midhurst 3724
10.30–2.30, 6–10.30
(11 Fri, Sat & summer)
Closed Mon

A former blacksmith's forge, with views over the fields to the Downs. 'Friendly and efficient service' of bar snacks (not Mon): salads £1–£2·75, ploughman's 60p, home-made pâté 80p, onion soup 65p, basket meals 80p–£1·40, sandwiches 30p–90p. Separate restaurant (12–2, 7.30–10; closed Sun D, Mon). Hall & Woodhouse bitter and King & Barnes bitter (pump); others pressurised. Wine. Terrace. Car park.

TUNBRIDGE WELLS Kent Map 3

Hole in the Wall
9 High Street
(opposite Central station)
Tunbridge Wells 26550
10.30–2.30, 6–10.30
(11 Fri, Sat)
Closed Sun

Victorian decor in a pub first licensed by Charles II 'to stay open during his royal pleasure'. Home-made bar food (no prices stated): lasagne, cannelloni, steak and kidney pie, hot-pot, pâté, ploughman's, salads. Separate restaurant (12–2, 7–10; 3 courses £3). Young's special bitter, Samuel Smith's bitter, Whitbread (Faversham) Trophy (pump). Wine. Walled garden.

Royal Wells Inn

See main *Guide*

UPPER DICKER East Sussex Map 3

Plough
on B2108
2½ m W of Hailsham
Hailsham 844859
10.30–2.30, 6–10.30
(11 Fri, Sat & summer)

A 17th-century pub with ingle-nook and 'most hospitable people'. Bar food (from noon and 7 p.m.): soup 25p, ploughman's 40p, sandwiches from 30p, salads 85p–95p, scampi £1·55, home-made steak and kidney pie £1·25, turkey kebabs £1, home-made pizza 80p. Pressurised Watney and Truman beers. Wine. Darts; dominoes. Outside gents'. Garden with swings. Car park.

UPTON NOBLE Somerset Map 2

As we went to press, the pub recommended here changed hands.

Towns shown in black on our maps contain at least one recommended restaurant or pub (see map key). The dot denotes the location of the town or village, not the restaurant. Where necessary, we give directions to the restaurant in the entry.

Swan
Upton-upon-Severn 2601
10.30–2.30, 6–10.30
(11 Fri, Sat)

Small, beamed pub by the river. 'Excellent, imaginative' bar food (exc Sun, Mon; 45p–£2·85): home-made mackerel pâté, potted shrimps, duckling, crab, smoked salmon, prawns, salads; daily hot dish. Wadworth's 6X from the cask. Wine.

WADDINGTON Lancashire Map 5

Moorcock
Waddington Fell
Clitheroe 22333
11–3, 6–11

Black-and-white moorland hotel with views over Pendle Hill. Bar food always available: steak and kidney pie £1·25, plaice 85p, beefburger 85p, all with chips; toasted steak sandwiches £1, other sandwiches from 40p. Separate restaurant (12.15–2, 7–10; 3 courses £5·50). Robinson's bitter, Theakston's bitter (pump); Theakston's Old Peculier from the cask; others pressurised. Wine. Children. Juke-box; fruit machine; pool table; darts. Garden. Car park. B&B £10·50.

WANSFORD Cambridgeshire Map 6

Haycock Inn

See main *Guide*

WARWICK Warwickshire Map 2

Roebuck
Smith Street
Warwick 41072
10.30–2.30, 6–10.30
(11 Fri, Sat)

'A superior kind of pub' with 'old furnishings and a welter of horse brass'. Bar food (12–2, 7–10; 30p–£1·50) includes 'outstanding' sandwiches 'made from meat cut before your eyes', soup, cheeses, salads with roast meats, pork pie, pâté or salami. Separate restaurant (until 2 and 9.45). Pressurised Watney Mann & Truman beers. Wine. Fruit machine. B&B £4.

Zetland Arms
11 Church Street
Warwick 41974
10–2.30, 6–10.30
(11 Fri, Sat)

A 400-year-old pub in the centre of town, with a wide range of bar snacks: home-made steak and kidney pie, chicken pie, cottage pie 70p; hot dogs, beefburgers, home-made faggots, rolls, salads, ploughman's. (Rolls only, Sat.) Davenports' bitter (pump); others pressurised. Garden. B&B from £5·50.

WATFORD GAP Northamptonshire Map 5

Stag's Head
Daventry 3621
10–2, 6–10.30
(11 Fri, Sat)

A pleasant, beamed pub, accessible on foot from the M1 service area over the canal. ('Gentlemen in dirty clothes aren't allowed in' says a notice on the door.) 'Imaginative' snacks: soup 30p, home-made pâté 55p, whitebait 75p, steak £2·20, chicken £1, home-made steak and kidney pie £1·25, scampi £1·35. Separate restaurant (12.30–1.45, 7–9.45). Variety of pressurised beers. Wine. Children. Fruit machine. Canalside gardens. Car park.

Some pubs off the beaten track do not always serve food at times notified. Phone to check.

WELLESBOURNE Warwickshire Map 2

King's Head
5 m E of
Stratford-upon-Avon
Stratford-on-Avon 840206
10.30–2.30, 6–10.30
(11 Fri, Sat)

A fine-looking red-brick hotel with a pleasant atmosphere. 'Superb array' of bar snacks (12–2, 6–10): soup 30p, 'very good' home-made pâté 70p, daily hot dish £1·20, 'attractive selection' of cold meats with 'enterprising' salads £1·20, ploughman's 55p–60p, sandwiches from 40p. Separate restaurant (12–2, 7.30–9). Mitchells & Butlers bitter and Bass (pump); others pressurised. Wine. Children. Juke-box; fruit machine; darts. Garden. Car park. B&B £7·25–£11.

WEOBLEY Hereford & Worcester Map 2

Red Lion
off A4112
Weobley 220
10.30–2.30, 6–10.30
(11 Fri, Sat)
Closed Dec 25 evening

A friendly old coaching inn in a medieval village. Bar food (L only; not Sun): curried prawns £1·20, soup 30p, pâté 75p, ploughman's 55p, sandwiches 25p–30p. Separate restaurant (7–10 only; tdh £3·25). Whitbread bitter (pump); others pressurised. Bulmer's Strongbow cider. Wine. Children. Fruit machine; darts. Garden. Car park. B&B from £8.

WEST HOATHLY West Sussex Map 3

Cat Inn
Sharpthorne 810369
10.30–2.30, 6–10.30
(11 Fri, Sat)

Roses around the door and beams, brass and log fire inside this 16th-century pub. Bar food (11.30–2, 7–10): soup 35p, toasted sandwiches 45p, pâté 75p, ploughman's, salads. Separate restaurant (Thur–Sat 7.30–9.30 only). Beard's bitter and best bitter (pump). Wine. Children. Fruit machine; bar billiards; darts; dominoes. Patio and terrace. Car park.

WESTON Northamptonshire Map 2

Crown
Sulgrave 328
11–2.30, 6–10.30
(11 Fri, Sat)

Three log fires in this old free house keep the customers warm while they eat the 'enterprising' home-made food: soup 35p, pâté 80p, lasagne £1, steak and kidney pie £1·25, beef curry £1, toasted sandwiches 35p, steak £2·60. Separate restaurant (Thur–Sat 7.30–10.30 only). Hook Norton bitter, Marston's Pedigree and Merrie Monk, Fuller's ESB and guest beers (pump); Marston's Owd Roger from the cask. Bulmer's cider. Children. Juke-box; darts; trestle skittles; shove ha'penny. Outside gents'. Garden. B&B £6.

WEYBOURNE Norfolk Map 6

Maltings
Weybourne 275
11–2.30, 6–11

As the name suggests, an old maltings, dating in parts from 200 years ago; now a complex of hotel buildings in the middle of the village. Food is served in the Buttery in summer and in the bar from October to March (until 2 and 10): ploughman's 65p, prawns 75p, salads £1·35–£2·40, scampi and chips £1·65, steak £2·95, soup 30p. Adnams' bitter (pump); others pressurised. Wine. Car park. Garden and courtyard. B&B £7·50–£9.

WHISTON South Yorkshire   Map 5

Sitwell Arms
Pleasley Road
on A618
Rotherham 77003
10.30–3, 6–10.30

'We got lost trying to find it', but the bar food makes the search worthwhile: ploughman's 55p, soup 35p, prawn cocktail £1·10, salads £1·50–£2·25, sandwiches. Limited snacks in the evening (exc Sun). Separate restaurant (closed Sun D). Pressurised Tetley's beers. Wine. Garden. Car park.

WILLIAN Hertfordshire   Map 3

Three Horseshoes
off A1(M) at Letchworth
Letchworth 5713
10.30–2.30, 5.30–10.30
(11 Fri, Sat)

Comfortable village pub with beams, antique weapons, old prints and 'always a friendly greeting'. 'Excellent' bar lunches (Mon–Sat): home-made pâté 50p, home-cooked ham 90p, smoked mackerel 55p, ploughman's 32p, smoked salmon £1·20, sandwiches 25p–45p, rolls 18p–20p. Greene King IPA and Abbot (pump). Wine. Seats outside.

WINCHELSEA East Sussex   Map 3

New Inn
on A259
Winchelsea 252
10–2.30, 6–10.30
(11 Fri, Sat)

An attractive pub in a 'perfect' village. Bar food includes soup 40p, pâté 60p, spaghetti 80p, smoked mackerel 65p, smoked eel 70p. Separate restaurant. Pressurised Courage beer. Wine. Car park. B&B. No details from landlord.

WINCHESTER Hampshire   Map 2

Splinters

See main *Guide*

WINDSOR Berkshire   Map 3

Two Brewers
Park Street
Windsor 61593
10.30–2.30, 5.30–10.30
(11 Fri, Sat)

A 17th-century pub at the entrance to Long Walk. Bar food at all times: salads with home-made beef and ham pie £1·40, ham £2, turkey £2, rib of beef £2. Courage bitter and Directors (pump); others pressurised. Darts; dominoes; cribbage. Benches outside.

WINKLEIGH Devon   Map 1

King's Arms
in village square
Winkleigh 384
10–2.30, 6–10.30
(11 Fri, Sat & summer)

'Everyone here is concerned in making your visit an enjoyable one.' A 400-year-old thatched pub with scrubbed whitewood tables. Cold buffet at all times, plus bar lunches (Mon–Sat): soup 30p, daily dish £1·35, 'superbly seasoned' home-made steak and kidney pie. Three-course Sunday lunch £2. Separate restaurant (Tue–Sat from 8.15 only). Pressurised Truman and Courage beers. Inch's cider. Wine. Children (L only). Patio. Holiday flat to let.

WINTON Cumbria   Map 8

Bay Horse Inn
1½ m NE of Kirkby
Stephen
Kirkby Stephen 71451
11.30–2.30, 7–10.30
(11 Fri, Sat)

Friendly and cosy little pub in a tiny village, off A683. Bar food (Tue–Sun L only; no prices given): home-made soup, rolls, sandwiches, home-made pâté and pasties. Younger's bitter and Theakston's bitter (pump). Bulmer's cider. Wine. Children. Darts; dominoes. Garden.

WITLEY Surrey Map 3

Star
Petworth Road
Wormley 2287
10.30–2.30, 5.30–10.30
(11 Fri, Sat)

Quiet, relaxed atmosphere in a charming but modernised pub built around 1500. Bar food (30p–£1·20): sandwiches, gammon or beef salad, home-cooked cottage pie, curries. Ind Coope bitter and Burton ale (pump); others pressurised. Coates' cider. Wine. Juke-box; fruit machine; bar billiards; darts; cribbage; shove ha'penny. Garden. Car park.

WOODS CORNER East Sussex Map 3

Swan
on B2096
Brightling 242
11–2.30, 6–10.30

'Efficient and pleasant bar staff' in an old inn with a superb view towards the coast. Bar food (11–2 – 'very prompt') includes turkey and ham pie with chips £1·50, meat pie £1·50, mackerel £1·50, lasagne £1, soup, pâté. Beard's bitter and mild (pressurised). Wine. Bar billiards; fruit machine. Garden. Car park.

WOODSTOCK Oxfordshire Map 2

Punch Bowl
12 Oxford Street (A34)
Woodstock 811218
10–2.30, 6–10.30
(11 Fri, Sat)

Clean and bright old pub with 'delightful' service of bar food: whitebait, pâté, ploughman's, salads. Separate restaurant. Wadworth's 6X and Old Timer from the cask; others pressurised. Wine. Patio. Car park. No details from landlord.

Star
22 Market Place
Woodstock 811209
10–2.30, 6–10.30
(11 Fri, Sat)

This pleasant, friendly pub – the nearest to Blenheim Palace – offers a wide choice of 'straightforward' bar lunches (70p–£1·40): steak and kidney pie, egg and mushroom pie, home-cooked ham, curry, salads, 'real' puddings and 'really first-rate' cheese. Pressurised Ind Coope beers. Wine. Darts; table skittles; shove ha'penny; dominoes. Garden. B&B £6.

WORMINGFORD Essex Map 3

Crown
on B1508
Bures 227 *and* 405
10.30–2.30, 6–11

A 14th-century timbered inn on the road between Colchester and Sudbury. Wide range of bar snacks and basket meals every lunch-time (25p–£1). On Friday, Grandma makes steak and kidney pie with chips (50p) – 'it has to be tasted to be believed.' Separate dining-room (L & D, about £5). Greene King IPA and Abbot from the cask; others pressurised. Wine. Juke-box; fruit machine; darts. Garden. Car park.

WRECCLESHAM Surrey Map 3

Bear and Ragged Staff
on A325
Farnham 716389
10.30–2.30, 6–10.30
(11 Fri, Sat)

An attractive pub 'of obviously genuine antiquity'. Bar food (limited on Sun): plaice and chips £1·20, pizza 75p, ploughman's 40p, pâté 70p, chicken curry 90p, scampi £1·40, soup 35p, jacket potatoes with choice of fillings 28p–60p, sandwiches 28p–50p. Courage bitter and Directors (pump); others pressurised. Wine. Fruit machine. Tables on forecourt. Car park.

WRELTON North Yorkshire   Map 8

Huntsman

See main *Guide*

WYE Kent   Map 3

New Flying Horse
Upper Bridge Street
off A28
Wye 812297
10–2.30, 6–10.30
(11 Fri, Sat)

A well-run, pleasant old pub with oak beams and an ingle-nook fireplace. 'Attractively presented' bar food. Lunch (12–2): hot daily dish £1·20, sandwiches 35p–85p, pâté 60p, ploughman's 50p. Evening (6–10): bacon and eggs £1·20, omelettes £1·20–£1·60, salads £1·40–£3·30, steaks £2·75. Separate restaurant (12–2, 6.30–9.30). Shepherd Neame bitter, best bitter, mild and stock ale (pump); others pressurised. Wine. Children at lunch-time. Darts. Patio. Car park. B&B from £6.

YORK North Yorkshire   Map 5

Lew's Place

See main *Guide*

Olde Starre
Stonegate
York 23063
11–3, 5.30–11

Believed to be the longest-running pub in the city; several small bars. Bar snacks (Mon–Sat 12–2.30; Sun 12–1.30): soup 20p, shepherd's pie 60p, sandwiches made with York bread cakes 24p–26p, ploughman's 45p, salads 70p–£1. Cameron's bitter (pump); others pressurised. Wine. Juke-box, dominoes and darts in the evening; fruit machine. Courtyard.

ZEALS Wiltshire   Map 2

Bell and Crown
on A303
Bourton (Dorset) 227
11–2.30, 6–10.30
(11 Fri, Sat)

An old pub which used to be Hartgill's brewery. Bar food at all times (30p–£1·95): 'excellent' pâté, salads, including cold trout ('a superb meal for an out-of-the-way pub'); home-made soup, hot pies and pasties in winter. Usher's best bitter (pump); others pressurised. Wine. Children. Juke-box; fruit machine; bar billiards; darts. Three lawns. Car park.

WALES

BODFARI Clwyd   Map 4

Dinorben Arms
on A541
4 m from Denbigh
Bodfari 309
12–3, 6–10.30
(11 Fri, Sat & summer)

Once a small, half-timbered local, but now 'more like a miniature holiday camp'. There's a Carvery (8 p.m. onwards), a Badger Suite (exc Mon, Tue, Thur, Sun evenings, when it can be hired) and 'informal evening meals' and in the midst of all that there are 'some very palatable salads . . . as well as fresh meats and salami to go with them'. 'One may eat oneself to a standstill without hindrance.' Bass (pump); others pressurised. Wine. Children. Garden and terraces. Four car parks.

Within parts of these old county boundaries, alcohol is not served on Sunday, except to hotel residents: Anglesey, Cardigan, Carmarthen, Merioneth.

BRECON Powys Map 4

Wellington
The Bulwark
Brecon 2506
11–3, 6–11
(open all day Fri)

'Rather decaying' but comfortable small hotel in the centre of town. Bar food (L only; 50p–£1·20): salads, ploughman's, sandwiches, chicken, meat and potato pie, curry, faggot and peas. Separate restaurant (12.30–2.15, 7–8.45; L from £2·50, D from £3·50). Marston's Pedigree, Felinfoel Double Dragon (pump); others pressurised. Wine. Children. Juke-box; fruit machine; bar billiards. Car park. B&B £7·25.

BROAD HAVEN Dyfed Map 4

Druidstone Hotel

See main *Guide*

CARMARTHEN Dyfed Map 4

Welsh Guardsman
Heol Penlanffos, Tanerdy
Carmarthen 31891
11–3, 5–10.30
(11 Fri; 5.30–11 Sat)
Closed Sun

Pleasant, friendly, clean and modern pub near the junction of the A40 and A484 on the outskirts of town. Bar food always available: soup 35p, pâté 50p; chicken £1·20, plaice £1, scampi £1·35, all with chips; salads £1·10. Buckley's bitter and mild by air pressure. Wine. Dominoes. Garden. Car park.

CRICKHOWELL Powys Map 4

Nantyffin Cider Mill

See main *Guide*

CROSS INN Dyfed Map 4

Rhos-yr-Hafod Inn

See main *Guide*

DINAS Dyfed Map 4

Glan Hotel
on A487
4 m E of Fishguard
Dinas Cross 309
11–3, 5.30–11

A quiet and cosy little pub. Bar food includes ploughman's 55p, chicken and chips £1, steaks, sandwiches. Separate restaurant (12–2 or 2.30, 6.30–10.30). Wide range of pressurised beers. Wine. Children. Fruit machine; darts; pool table. Garden. Car park. B&B £3·50–£4.

Ship Aground
Dinas Cross
off A487
Dinas Cross 261
11–3, 5.30–10.30
(11 Fri, Sat; open all day
public hols)

Built in 1735 and extended over the years, this nautical free house is on a minor road leading to the small bay at Pwllgwaulod. Bar lunches (12–2.30): soup 30p, 'fresh and delicious' crab salad £1·50, salmon steaks £1·75, 'generous and tasty' ploughman's 75p, pizza £1·10, pâté 75p. Grills (£1–£2·60) and salads in the evening (7–10). Cold buffet Sun (12–2). No food Sun D. Felinfoel bitter and Welsh Brewers' bitter (pump); others pressurised. Wine. Children. Fruit machine; darts. Seats outside. Car park.

GLASBURY-ON-WYE Powys Map 4

Maesllwch Arms

See main *Guide*

See p. 441 for 'How to use the pub section'.

LITTLE HAVEN Dyfed   Map 4

Swan
6 m SW of Haverfordwest
Broad Haven 256

A wide range of customers in this pub on the sea-wall. Bar food (12–2) includes 'excellent and decidedly filling' Provencal soup and mackerel pâté. Separate restaurant (D only; 7–9.30). Bass and Worthington best bitter. Wine.

LLANCARFAN South Glamorgan   Map 4

Fox and Hounds
Bonvilston 287
11.30–3, 6–10.30
(11.30–3.30, 5.30–11
in summer)

A large, popular old pub on the banks of the River Whitton in a secluded village. Bar food: soup 25p, sausage and mash 95p, beef curry 90p, baked ham £1·25, salads £1·30–£1·60, ploughman's 60p, sandwiches from 30p. Separate restaurant (Mon–Sat 7.30–9.30 only). Samuel Smith's bitter, Marston's Pedigree, Welsh Brewers' HB (pump); others pressurised. Wine. Fruit machine. Patio. Car park.

LLANDEWI SKIRRID Gwent   Map 4

Walnut Tree Inn

See main *Guide*

LLANDUDNO Gwynedd   Map 4

King's Head
Old Road
Llandudno 77993
11–3, 5.30–10.30
(11 in summer)

Well-organised, friendly and informal old pub near the bottom terminal of the Great Orme tramway. A brisk trade with an emphasis on food which can also be eaten in a curtained-off bar: ploughman's 65p, salads £1–£1·30, rolls 25p–40p, 'beautifully cooked' Conwy mussels in garlic and cheese, baked potato with cheese 35p, spaghetti £1. Ind Coope bitter (pump). Wine. Car park. No children under 12. No details from landlord.

LLANDYSILIO Dyfed   Map 4

Bush Inn
on A478
Clunderwen 239
11–3, 5.30–10.30
(11 in summer)

'Excellent cats' at this comfortable free house, serving chicken and chips, ham and poultry. Worthington best bitter from the cask, kept cool by an underground stream. Garden. Car park. No details from landlord.

LLANGYNIDR Powys   Map 4

Red Lion Hotel

See main *Guide*

LLANWDDYN Powys   Map 4

Lake Vyrnwy Hotel

See main *Guide*

LLOWES Powys   Map 4

Radnor Arms

See main *Guide*

NEWPORT Dyfed   Map 4

Pantry

See main *Guide*

PEMBROKE FERRY Dyfed Map 4

Ferry Inn
off A477 at S end of
Cleddau Bridge
Pembroke 2947
11.30–2.30, 6–11 (7–10.30
winter; 11 Fri & Sat)

'Nothing pseudo or arty-crafty' about this old riverside pub which began life as a ferry house. Bar food (not Sun, D Mon & Tue): soup 30p, prawns 75p, home-made pâté 60p, scampi £1·75, rump steak £2·10; three daily specials, such as 'outstanding' local scallop and crawfish Mornay. Must book for self-service carvery Sun L, £2·20: 'as much as you can eat' ('50p surcharge if anything edible is left on your plate'). Felinfoel Double Dragon and bitter (pump); others pressurised. Wine. Patio. Car park. Cottage to let next door.

PENMAENPOOL Gwynedd Map 4

George III Hotel

See main *Guide*

PORTFIELD GATE Dyfed Map 4

Penry Arms
Broadhaven Road
(B4341)
Haverfordwest 2128
11.30–3, 6.30–10.30
(11 Fri, Sat & summer)

Open fires in both bars, with the lounge 'very much the hunting scene'. 'Obviously geared to food' (20p–£1): rolls, savoury pancakes, chicken, scampi, ploughman's, salads, daily special (exc mid-season). Pressurised Ind Coope beers. Fruit machine; darts; dominoes; cards. Garden. Car park.

ST DAVID'S Dyfed Map 4

St Non's Hotel

See main *Guide*

SARN MELLTEYRN Gwynedd Map 4

Penrhyn Arms
Botwnnog 218
11–3, 6–10.30
Closed Sun

An old free house between Pwllheli and Aberdaron – 'clearly for a family on holiday; child-detesters will find the turmoil penitential.' Food is served in the Oak Bar downstairs (25p–£2·20): steak, gammon, scampi, chicken, cold meats, lasagne, moussaka; soup, ploughman's and sandwiches L only. Wide choice of pressurised beers. Wine. Juke-box; fruit machine; darts and other games. Garden. Car park.

THREE COCKS Powys Map 4

Three Cocks Hotel

See main *Guide*

WHITEBROOK Gwent Map 4

Crown Inn

See main *Guide*

WOLF'S CASTLE Dyfed Map 4

Wolfe Inn
on A40
7 m N of Haverfordwest
Treffgarne 662
11–3, 6–10.30
(11 Fri, Sat & summer)

An old stone building by the River Cleddau – thoroughly modernised but 'splendidly run'. Bar food (not Mon): soup 30p, pâté 60p, ploughman's 60p, scampi and chips £1·75, salads 85p–£1·65, sandwiches from 30p. Separate restaurant (12–2, 7–10, exc Sun L, Mon; must book). Wide choice of pressurised beers. Wine. Fruit machine; darts. Patio and garden. Car park.

SCOTLAND

ALYTH Perthshire (Tayside) Map 9

Lands of Loyal Hotel   See main *Guide*

ARDENTINNY Argyll (Strathclyde) Map 9

Ardentinny Hotel   See main *Guide*

ARDUAINE Argyll (Strathclyde) Map 9

Loch Melfort Hotel   See main *Guide*

AUCHTERARDER Perthshire (Tayside) Map 9

Gleneagles Hotel   See main *Guide*

BALLATER Aberdeenshire (Grampian) Map 9

Tullich Lodge   See main *Guide*

BEATTOCK Dumfriesshire (Dumfries & Galloway) Map 7

Old Brig Inn   See main *Guide*

CLEISH Kinross-shire (Tayside) Map 9

Nivingston House   See main *Guide*

CRINAN Argyll (Strathclyde) Map 9

Crinan Hotel   See main *Guide*

DALBEATTIE Kirkcudbrightshire (Dumfries & Galloway) Map 7

Granary   See main *Guide*

DIRLETON East Lothian (Lothian) Map 9

Open Arms   See main *Guide*

EDINBURGH Map 9

Silver Buckle
16–18 Hamilton Place
031-225 6084
11–2.30, 5–11

Clean and comfortable pub near the Stockbridge clock. Bar food (Mon–Sat, 12–2 only): 'delicious' savoury meat roll 58p, macaroni cheese 59p, home-made soup, haggis, pizza, tripe and onions. Pressurised Scottish & Newcastle beers. Wine. Juke-box; fruit machine.

Town and Country   See main *Guide*

GLASGOW Map 9

Beacons Hotel   See main *Guide*

Scottish public holidays do not all coincide with English ones.

Hours given are opening times. Food may not be served over the whole period.

HAWICK Roxburghshire (Borders)   Map 8

Kirklands
West Stewart Place (A7)
Hawick 2263
11–2.30, 5–11
(Sun 12–2, 7–11)
Closed Dec 25

A small hotel with a popular bar trade. Bar lunch (Mon–Sat L only; 75p–£1·95): trout, savoury pancakes, pâté, scampi, omelettes, soup, sandwiches. Separate restaurant (12–2, 7–9, exc Sun). Pressurised McEwan's beer. Wine. Children. Garden. Car park. B&B from £7.

ISLE ORNSAY Skye Inverness-shire (Highland)
Map 9

Kinloch Lodge Hotel   See main *Guide*

KINGSKETTLE Fife   Map 9

Annfield House   See main *Guide*

LEVEN Fife   Map 9

Star Hotel
5 North Street
Leven 26179 *and* 26450
11–2.30, 5–11
(Sun 12.30–2.30, 6.30–11)

It's worth tolerating the loud juke-box for 'superb' chips at lunch-time (12–2), served with a choice of meats (from 50p) and salads. Separate functions room available in the evenings (3 courses £2·25). Pressurised Tennent's beers. Wine. Fruit machine; darts. Car park. B&B £3·25.

LINLITHGOW West Lothian (Lothian)   Map 9

Champany   See main *Guide*

LOCHGAIR Argyll (Strathclyde)   Map 9

Lochgair Hotel   See main *Guide*

LOCHMADDY North Uist, Inverness-shire
(Highland)   Map 9

Lochmaddy Hotel   See main *Guide*

MARYCULTER Kincardineshire (Grampian)   Map 9

Maryculter House   See main *Guide*

MELROSE Roxburghshire (Borders)   Map 9

Burts Hotel
Market Square
Melrose 2285
11–2.30, 5–11
(Sun 12.30–2.30, 6.30–11)

Welcoming and comfortable country-town hotel, popular with the locals. Efficient service of 'good value' bar food (12–2, 6.30–9.30; 10.30 Fri, Sat): soup 25p, chicken in the basket £1, scampi £1·25, daily choice of cooked dishes 80p–90p, sandwiches from 30p. Separate restaurant (12.30–2, 7–8.30). Choice of pressurised beers. Wine. Children. Car park. B&B £7·50–£9.

NAIRN Nairnshire (Highland)   Map 9

Clifton Hotel   See main *Guide*

OVERSCAIG Sutherland (Highland)   Map 9

Overscaig Hotel   See main *Guide*

	PEAT INN Fife Map 9
Peat Inn	See main *Guide*
	PORTPATRICK Wigtownshire
	(Dumfries & Galloway) Map 7
Knockinaam Lodge	See main *Guide*
	SEIL Argyll (Strathclyde) Map 9
Dunmor House	See main *Guide*
	SKEABOST BRIDGE Skye, Inverness-shire
	(Highland) Map 9
Skeabost House Hotel	See main *Guide*
	TOBERMORY Mull, Argyll (Strathclyde) Map 9
Western Isles Hotel	See main *Guide*
	ULLAPOOL Ross & Cromarty (Highland) Map 9
The Ceilidh Place	See main *Guide*
	WEEM Perthshire (Tayside) Map 9
Ailean Chraggan Hotel	See main *Guide*
	WESTER HOWGATE Midlothian (Lothian) Map 9
Old Howgate Inn	See main *Guide*

CHANNEL ISLANDS

ALDERNEY   Map 1

Old Barn
Loney Bay
Alderney 2537
10 a.m.–1 a.m.
(Sun 12–2, 8–12)

Just what it says – a converted barn, with a
corrugated roof – but it is attractive and friendly
inside. Bar food (Tue–Sun L; Tue–Sat D): soup
50p, sausage and chips or mash 50p, 'Barnburger'
and chips 75p, omelettes 75p, spare ribs £1·50,
crab claws and garlic butter £1·50. Separate
restaurant. Guernsey bitter (air pressure). Wine.
Garden and patio. Car park.

SARK   Map 1

Dixcart Hotel   See main *Guide*

ISLE OF MAN

DOUGLAS   Map 7

Villiers Hotel
Clarendon Grill

See main *Guide*

VAT is not levied in the Channel Islands.

IRELAND

CLARINBRIDGE Co Galway   Map 10

Paddy Burke's
11 m S of Galway
on Limerick road
Galway 86107
10.30 a.m.–11 p.m.
(11.30 p.m. in summer)

Alcoves and small rooms give 'Ireland's most famous oyster tavern' a good atmosphere. 'Excellent range of bar food': oysters in season; home-made pâté £1·25, soup 40p–60p, salmon mayonnaise £2·75, roast beef or chicken £2·75, lasagne £1, Irish stew £1·35, smoked cod casserole £1·25. Separate restaurant (D only, until 10; 3 courses £6). Guinness, Murphy's, Bass, Smithwick's and Harp (pressurised). Wine. Children. Garden. Car park.

CORK Co Cork   Map 10

Arbutus Lodge

See main *Guide*

Rearden's Cellar Bar
26 Washington Street
Cork 22097 *and* 20032
10.30–2.30, 3.30–11

A 19th-century bar with gas lighting – 'a reliable, relatively inexpensive place to eat.' Bar food (12.30–2.30, 4.30–10; exc Sun): turkey and ham salad £1·40, prawns £2, smoked salmon £2·45, fresh salmon (in season) £3, seafood platter £2·20, smoked mackerel 90p. Separate restaurant (12.30–2.30, 4–10; exc Sun). Murphy's, Guinness and Beamish & Crawford stouts, and other pressurised beers. Wine.

CURRAGH Co Kildare   Map 10

Jockey Hall

See main *Guide*

DUBLIN   Map 10

Royal Hibernian Hotel

See main *Guide*

GLENBEIGH Co Kerry   Map 10

Towers Hotel

See main *Guide*

GOREY Co Wexford   Map 10

Marlfield House

See main *Guide*

KILLINEY Co Dublin   Map 10

Fitzpatrick Castle Hotel

See main *Guide*

LETTERFRACK Co Galway   Map 10

Rosleague Manor

See main *Guide*

MALLOW Co Cork   Map 10

Longueville House

See main *Guide*

ROSSLARE Co Wexford   Map 10

Strand Hotel

See main *Guide*

	SHANAGARRY Co Cork Map 10
Ballymaloe House	See main *Guide*
	TRALEE Co Kerry Map 10
Oyster Tavern	See main *Guide*
	YOUGHAL Co Cork Map 10
Aherne's Pub	See main *Guide*

NORTHERN IRELAND

| | COMBER Co Down   Map 10 |
| Old Crow | See main *Guide* |

WINE BARS

ENGLAND

AMERSHAM-ON-THE-HILL Buckinghamshire
Map 3

Annie's
16 Hill Avenue
Amersham 22713
10.30–2.30, 6–10.30
(11 Fri, Sat; 7–10.30 Sun)
Closed Sun L; L public
hols

A lively place, run by the Robinsons and their daughters. They – and their customers – seem to thrive on constant change, so don't expect to find the same food, wines, music or 'theme' on two successive visits. But there are generally two hot dishes (chicken Marengo £1·65, stuffed peppers £1·70, goulash £1·90) as well as snacks (soup, cold meats and salad, jacket potatoes with cheese, toasted sandwiches), home-made gateaux and pies, and three kinds of coffee. All wine is sold at a flat-rate mark-up; all by glass or half-bottle with free 'tasters' before you buy. Australian Arrowfield red (£2·90), Spanna '74 (£3·50); Argentine house wine, £4·20 the litre, 50p the glass. Also various beers including Belgian Chimay (75p). 'Live' musicians play anything from folk to Hawaiian. Smoking 'jokily discouraged'.

AYLSHAM Norfolk   Map 6

D'Accord
Bank Street
Aylsham 3582
9–5 (9–2.30 Wed),
7.30–11
Closed Sun; Dec 25

Robin Barnes is a cheese-importer, and in this little wine bar near the market square you can try some of the eighty varieties he stocks in his delicatessen next door. The menu predictably stresses pâtés, sausages and ham, but soup, steaks (with baked potato and vegetables, from £2·18) and gateau or cheesecake also appear. (Note the opening hours: morning coffee and afternoon tea are also served.) French house wine is £2·20 the bottle, 35p the glass; Ch. Modésir Gazin '71 (French-bottled) is £4·70, and Marburg Laski Riesling £2·30. Taped music.

BATH Avon   Map 2

Clarets
6–7 Kingsmead Square
Bath 66688
10–2.30, 6.30–11
Closed Sun L

A delightfully light, wood-panelled cellar, with slate floors and pine furniture, run by the Tearles (who have sold their Limpley Stoke restaurant). Their casseroles are popular (pork and prune, beef noodle, fish and garlic, about £1·50) and there are also cold dishes, salads and pâtés, with chocolate St Emilion (55p) or bread-and-butter pudding to finish. House wines are French, £2·40 the bottle, 40p the glass. Others (mainly Averys) include Ronsac (£2·95), Pilton Manor '76 (£3·85), and Australian Robinvale Lexia (£3·95). Too few vintages listed. Taped music. A few tables in the square under the plane tree.

BATH Avon Map 2

La Vendange
11 Margaret's Buildings,
Brock Street
Bath 21251
10.30–2.30, 5.30–10.30
(11 Sat)
Closed Sun; most public
hols

A 'cheerful and cosy place', between the Circus and
Royal Crescent. It is crowded, but there is a room
off the bar with separate tables 'to make serious
conversation possible'. (In summer you can also
escape to the pedestrian precinct outside.)
Home-made soups, pâtés, quiches (85p), casseroles,
cold meats and salad, continental cheeses and local
Cheddar, 'wholesome' bread, 'mouth-watering'
brandy-cake and Carolyn's syllabub. (Food is
served from 12 and 7.30.) French house wine,
£2·80 the litre, 38p the glass. Others by the glass
include local Dunkerton wine (Roughton's) at 54p
and Rosé d'Anjou, 48p. Bottles from Bouchard
Aîné and Averys. No vintages listed. 'Quiet'
background music.

BILLINGSHURST West Sussex Map 3

Badger's
87 High Street
Billingshurst 3547
11.30–2.30, 7–10.30
(11 Sat)
Closed Sat L; Sun; Mon D

A friendly beamed cottage with open fire and 'keen
young proprietor'. Snacks at lunch-time ('delicious'
moussaka £1·10, toad-in-the-hole 90p, liver and
onions £1); full meals lunch and evening (chicken
Kiev £2·70, steaks from £3·20, veal with cream and
mushrooms, 'real' apple pie or gooseberry crumble).
Wines by the glass (Rioja 55p, house claret 50p);
various bottles (Côtes du Rhône '76, £3). No music.
Two outside tables.

BRISTOL Avon Map 2

Arnolfini Gallery
Narrow Quay
Bristol 299191
12–2.30, 5.30–10.30
(Tue–Sat), 7–10.30 (Sun)
Closed Mon; public hols

A nicely situated Victorian warehouse on the docks,
opposite the Trade Centre. Before, after – or
instead of – viewing exhibitions, plays and films
in the complex, visit the plain but attractive
self-service wine bar. Rather bland but healthy
food (taramosalata, corn chowder, stuffed marrow,
80p) with some interesting salads, based on broad
beans, mushrooms, rice or fresh fruit. Separate
wine counter reveals good selection of Spanish
house wines by the glass (40p), several modestly
priced bottles (many from Harvey's 'bin-ends'),
Wadworth's ale on hand-pump, and some unusual
bottled beers. Casual service; tables are crowded,
and might be cleared more often.

CHELTENHAM Gloucestershire Map 2

Forrest's Wine House
Imperial Lane
Cheltenham 38001
10.30–2.30, 6–10.30
(11 Fri, Sat)
Closed Sun; Dec 25; Jan 1

It may be too crowded or too smoky for comfort
here, and is 'rather bare and dark', but the
waitresses are clothed and sunny, and 'they still
count prices in pence.' Hearty soups (25p) with
good French bread, aubergine caviare with pitta
(70p), boeuf bourguignonne with cabbage and
potatoes (£1·90), grilled rump steak with chips and
salad (£2·50), bratwurst and red cabbage (£1·05), pies,
pâtés and 'continental ploughman's' (sausages with

rye bread, 65p). Cheeses are not always at their peak, nor coffee strong, but sweets are good. Over twenty wines by the glass (Tres Torres 53p, Wachenheimer Mandelgarten '75, 59p) with a wide choice of sherries, madeiras and ports. No animals.

CHIPPING CAMPDEN Gloucestershire   Map 2

Badger's
The Square
Evesham 840520
12–2.30, 7–10.30
(11 Sat)
Closed Sun D;
Mon (exc public hols);
2 weeks Jan

'Spick-and-span' little place with well-spaced pine tables, chintzy curtains, natural stone walls and an open fire. The food is 'endearingly home-made' – quiches and salads (£1·30), baked stuffed potato (50p), ratatouille (85p), cottage pie. The cheesecake came as a breath of fresh air to an inspector tired of packet mixes. Good choice of wines by the glass – Australian, even English. House claret 50p. About eighty bottles, very reasonably priced. Slowish but pleasant service. Walled patio. Live music sometimes.

COLCHESTER Essex   Map 3

Wm. Scragg's

See main *Guide*

CONISTON Cumbria   Map 7

Wine Shop and Restaurant
Lake Road
Coniston 256 *and* 426
12–2, 6.45–9.30
(10 Sat)
Closed Tue; Feb to
mid-Mar

A substantial stone building on the corner of the main street and the harbour, run in 'traditional Lakeland style: meats off the bone, plain vegetables, light sauces, and as much home-made as possible.' Set dinner and Sunday lunch in the ground-floor restaurant, snacks in the basement lounge. Goujons of codling (£1·10) were fresh-tasting and good when tried ('not packet crumbs'), though the salad was plopped underneath them in the basket. Try also the Cumberland sausage (95p), crab or prawn salads, braised beef with fresh vegetables, and 'warm and crumbly' bilberry pie (45p). Chips (20p) are crisp, coffee (25p) 'excellent'. French wine by the glass 45p; Chianti £2·90, Ch. La Tour St Bonnet '70, £5·50. Various beers on tap. Helpful service. Their licence requires you to eat if you have a drink.)

DERBY Derbyshire   Map 5

Ben Bowers

See main *Guide*

EXETER Devon   Map 1

White Hart

See pub section

FARNHAM Surrey   Map 3

Seven's Wine Bar and Bistro
7 The Borough
Farnham 5345
12–2.30, 6.30–10.30
(11 Fri, Sat)
Closed Sun; public hols

Fine old building in the town centre, handy for the Redgrave Theatre. Soup, cold table (£1·40) with good salads, pizzas, two or three hot dishes (around £1) at lunch-time. Evening menu changed daily. Reasonably priced blackboard wine list. About seven wines by the glass, around 45p; thirty or so bottles, from £2·10. Pleasant service. Walled garden, floodlit at night. No dogs. Taped and live music.

GLOUCESTER Gloucestershire Map 2

Tasters
22 London Road
Gloucester 417556
12–2.30, 7–10.30
Closed Sun; Dec 25–
Jan 3; public hols

A comfortable place, agreeably served – 'it feels almost like a vegetarian restaurant, what with the unusual salads and the concern for your digestion.' The food, mainly cold, is imaginative and carefully prepared: quiches (60p, or as a main course with salad, £1·20), Snaffles mousse (50p), cider-baked gammon ('with a crust of sugar and a fresh, sweet-sour taste', £2), blackcurrant and mint pie (70p), treacle tart (60p). 'Fresh and crisp' salads may contain pasta, apple, peanuts, curried rice, raisins, cabbage . . . Granary or French breads are 'worth special mention'. Ten wines, besides the ordinaires, at 50p the glass (Soave, sweet Bordeaux); English Three Choirs, £2·90 the bottle, 65p the glass; and many fine wines by the bottle at reasonable prices: Ch. Terrefort-Quancard '71, c.b., £7·99 the magnum. No smoking at the food counters, and no cigarettes on sale. Taped music.

GUILDFORD Surrey Map 3

Rowley's
Tunsgate,
124 Fish Street
Guildford 63277
12–2.30, 6.30–10.30
(11 Fri, Sat)
Closed Sun; Mon eve;
public hols

'Meet me opposite the clock' could mean this 400-year-old building with its beams and open fire. Cold meats and salads (game pie £2, quiche Lorraine £1·25, chicken pie £1·75), and pâté or cheese with bread (from 50p) are the thing. 'Excellent mushroom salad and cole-slaw.' A few sweets. In winter, they add soup, lasagne (£1·40), and boeuf bourguignonne (£1·75). Various wines by the glass (from 42p); Buck's Fizz (55p, but sparkling wine not champagne); Ch. Calon '70, £4·75. Background music at weekends, when Hedley Kaye of BBC2 entertains.

HARTLEY WINTNEY Hampshire Map 3

Tullio

See main *Guide*

HERTFORD Hertfordshire Map 3

Bottles
11 Old Cross
Hertford 50405
11.30–2.30, 6.30–10.30
(11 Fri, Sat)
Closed Sun

Behind its own health-food shop, Bottles has two faces – one 'all red, with a coal fire and church pews', the other 'green and leafy'. Unpriced food and desultory staff mar 'on the day' cooking, with 'real' mayonnaise and salad dressing for a start. The cold table offers about a dozen salads: gazpacho salad (35p), courgette (25p), leek (25p), and mushroom; chicken quarters or ribs of beef; pâtés and quiches; and one hot dish, served with brown rice, pasta, potato or salad: boeuf niçoise, ham with courgettes in cheese and wine sauce, moussaka; gateaux, raisin pie, fruit flans; and cheeses. (Soup in winter, 40p.) Italian Soave and Chianti, £2·15 the bottle, 40p the glass, and some other routine wines (12 by the glass). Wells bitter and Fargo. Pianist or flamenco guitarist most evenings, and Saturday lunch-time.

HUNGERFORD Berkshire   Map 2

Thompson's   See main *Guide*

KINGSBRIDGE Devon   Map 1

Woosters
The Quay
Kingsbridge 3434
12–2.30, 7–1.30
(Sun L 12.30–1.30)

Freedom to 'eat without drinking or drink without eating' in this wine bar, 'nicely situated at the head of the river and away from the traffic main stream'. Service can be neglectful or peppery, but there is compensation in 'ample and good prawn salad' (£1·95), locally smoked Tamar or Dart salmon (£1·95), steaks in various ways (from £2·90), local scallops or crab, a daily hot-pot and other specials, sweets or cheese. A few wines by the glass (from 42p), others in bottle: Mâcon-Viré '77, £4·10. Weekday music and dancing licence. No food after 11 p.m. 'Accompanied children of all ages welcome.'

LAVENHAM Suffolk   Map 3

Timbers   See main *Guide*

LIVERPOOL Merseyside   Map 5

Everyman Bistro   See main *Guide*

LUDLOW Salop   Map 5

Penny Anthony   See main *Guide*

MANCHESTER   Map 5

Goblet
Midland Hotel,
Peter Street
(entrance in Mount
Street)
061-236 3333
12–3, 5.30–10.30
(11 Fri, Sat)
Closed Sun; Sat L;
public hols

Squander your Luncheon Vouchers in style at this efficiently run appendage to the Midland Hotel (*q.v.*). Praise still for the 'egg, bacon, cheese and pimento flan' (65p) with its good pastry and light and tasty filling, the cold meats ('especially the rare beef', £2·15 with salad), the chef-made rolls and the coffee. Other choices are soup, hors d'oeuvre, pâté, cold fried plaice (£1·40) and various sandwiches and sweets. In the evening there is a limited cold menu. Nine wines by carafe and glass (Minervois '75, £2 for 20 fl oz, 40p for 4 fl oz); other samplings from the BTH list: Ch. Guionne '71, £4·50; Pouilly-Vinzelles '75/'76, £4·50, £2·30 the half. The bin-end list often has bargains, especially in halves. Taped music.

NORWICH Norfolk   Map 6

Wine Press
Woburn Court,
8 Guildhall Hill
Norwich 612874
10.30–2.30, 7–10.30
Closed Sun; Mon–
Wed eve; public hols

Norfolk Vintners run this 'solidly furnished' cellar, roomy, with two bars – one for wine, one for food. Lunchtime buffet is appetising, with well-laid-out cold table – pâtés (45p), ham (£1), sausage pie, freshly made salads (60p), and a daily hot dish (95p). Puddings, at a separate counter, are very rich. Evening hot meals (post-theatre by request). André Simon wines 40p the glass; about thirty bottles. Taped music.

Ben Bowers

See main *Guide*

OXFORD Oxfordshire   Map 2

Emperors'
22 Broad Street
Oxford 42253
10.30–2.30, 6–10.30
(11 Fri, Sat; Sun 12–2)

'Fine wines by the glass or bottle and good food to fortify the drinker' at Mr Maguire's three-tier bar opposite Trinity. Coffee and croissants from 10.30 a.m. At lunch or supper, pâtés, quiches (90p – not always approved), hot dishes, cheese (about 45p) accompany wines from a far-ranging list. By the glass you might try a rosé from Hérault (40p), a French-bottled Saumur Blanc (47p) and a Ste-Croix-du-Mont (53p) with the apple pie. Bishop (mulled port to an 18th-century recipe, 50p) and Sangria (50p) are specialities. Sunday evening opening possible in term. No music. Garden. No dogs.

PLYMOUTH Devon   Map 1

Wine Lodge
5 The Quay,
Barbican
Plymouth 60875
11–2.30, 6–10.30
(Sat 11; Sun 12–2,
7–10.30)
Closed Sun L (Oct–
June); 3 days Chr

Four-hundred-year-old building overlooking the busy fish quay; eat upstairs, drink below. Lunchtime cold buffet with two hot dishes (pasta, goulash, cottage pie). Casseroles, pork fillet, fish dishes (£1·50–£3·30) at night. House red is Estancia (Argentine) 40p the glass, £2·30 the bottle. Over a dozen other wines by the glass, around 47p; sherry, tawny port, Kir 46p. Live music – 'various' on Sunday and Monday, jazz on Tuesday, folk on Thursday.

ST AUSTELL Cornwall   Map 1

Hicks Wine Bar
Church Street
St Austell 4833
11–2.30, 7–10.30
(11 Fri, Sat)
Closed Sun; Dec 25; Jan 1

Despite a new manager, 'Cornwall's first wine bar' remains unchanged, 'even to the lovely old dear behind the bar'. 'Proper' quiches of various flavours (50p), pâté (55p), local smoked mackerel (50p), and a daily hot dish (70p) all come with 'fresh and crisp' salad. Spanish house wine, £3 the litre, 35p the glass. About twenty others, from £2·75. (The list is changed monthly.) Taped music.

WESTERHAM Kent   Map 3

Henry Wilkinson
22 Market Square
Westerham 64245
11.30–2.30, 6.30–11
(Sat 7–12)
Closed Sun; Apr 13;
Dec 25

A family-run place on two levels, with Mr Ormonde in the ground-floor bar, and his wife and daughter downstairs in a neat and tiny galley (pies and cakes are made by a 'treasure' elsewhere). Sandwiches and filled baked potatoes at lunch-time; casserole or steak in the evening. The blackboard may also offer good hot vichyssoise 'with a few stray peas' (40p), chicken liver pâté (70p with toast, £1·25 with salad), turkey and ham pie (£2) with 'rather relentless' pastry, omelettes (from 75p), and meringues or 'nicely tart' blackcurrant pie (50p). Cona coffee (25p). About a dozen wines by the glass (⅛ or ¼ of a bottle); Bourgogne Aligoté 54p and 80p; Gamay d'Anjou 75p and £1. Many more by bottle: Loire Pinot Noir '76, £3·50; Alsace Pinot Blanc (Trimbach), n.v., £3·75. Wide range of spirits, beers, aperitifs. No dogs in the eating area. Music 'on quiet evenings'. Henry Wilkinson prints – and others – for sale.

WOBURN Bedfordshire   Map 3

Woburn Wine Lodge
13 Bedford Street
Woburn 439
11–2.30, 6–10.30 (11 Fri, Sat; Sun 12–2, 7–10.30)
Closed Dec 25 & 26

Main-street bar near the Abbey, 'worth a short detour from the lions or the M1'. Attractive cold buffet – salami, roast beef, salads (from 30p). Soups good. Daily hot dish around £1·75. Blackboard wine list – 42p–50p by the glass according to region. No details about names of wines – or brandies – offered. No bookings. No music.

WOKINGHAM Berkshire   Map 3

Setters
49 Peach Street
Wokingham 788893
12–2.30, 7–10.30
Closed Sun; public hols

Bistro-bar, named after a family pet, and run by cheerful young people. Daily menu on blackboard. The printed one offers pâté (75p), home-made soup (40p), chicken and ham or pork pie, roast beef with salad, quiches. Four wines only by the glass (35p–45p). About twenty in bottle, from £2·55 (Valpolicella, Soave). Recorded music, classical at lunch, pop at night. 'No animals.'

WALES

LLANGOLLEN Clwyd   Map 4

Gales
18 Bridge Street
Llangollen 860089
12–2, 6–10.30
(11 Sat)
Closed Sun (Nov–Easter);
2 weeks Nov;
2 weeks Feb

Simple family affair with chapel pews and bare wooden tables: 'a haven', think several locals (but hard to find – take the main street from the bridge, then first left). Almost everything is home-made – excellent soups (40p), daily hot dish (£1–£1·50), ham and salads, a few sweets. House ordinaire is 40p the glass, and among the eight offered is a Chenin Saumur at 45p. The very long list of 'fine wines' (Ch. Talbot '67, £7) is knowledgeably served. Taped music. Harpist two nights a week. B&B.

SCOTLAND

EDINBURGH   Map 9

Henderson's Salad Table   See main *Guide*

Towns shown in black on our maps contain at least on recommended restaurant or pub (see map key). The dot denotes the location of the town or village, not the restaurant. Where necessary, we give directions to the restaurant in the entry. If you can, help us to improve them.

JERSEY

ST HELIER   Map 1

La Bastille Taverne
4 Wharf Street
Jersey Central 74059
10–8 (10–2 Sat)
Closed Sun; Feb; public
hols

'Jersey's first wine bar', but more formal than
mainland versions, with waitress service and a
business clientele (book on weekdays). Pâté, smoked
mackerel, shrimps (all around 85p), oysters (£1·20
for six), chicken and ham pie (£1·20), salads,
cheeses, are accompanied by glasses of Berligou at
35p or Muscadet Château de la Cassemichère '76/7
at 50p. About forty wines by the bottle. Taped
music. Note that food is served only between noon
and 6.30 p.m.

IRELAND

DUBLIN   Map 10

Shrimps
1 St Anne's Lane
Dublin 713143
Noon–11
Closed Sun; public hols
Service 10%

A pretty and comfortable little place, relaxing for
weekday shoppers, and popular with chess and
backgammon players – 'the atmosphere encourages
it.' Limited 'but sensible' range of food: pizza
('nice taste, but do we blame the microwave for
texture?'); wild rabbit and prune terrine (£1·20);
curried chicken mousse (£1·20); turkey loaf (£1·60);
whisky or cheesecake. Good fresh brown bread (15p)
and coffee. Many things by the glass, from soda
water at 20p, through Kir at 55p and Gomes
Sercial madeira at 50p, to house Corbières at 50p.
Others by bottle. Pleasant service, 'though rather
gormless at Saturday lunch'. 'Background' music.

KINSALE Co Cork   Map 10

Max's
Main Street
Kinsale 72443
12.30–2.30, 7.30–11
Closed Tue; Nov & Feb

Max is a Dobermann Pinscher and Main Street runs
parallel with the main street. This popular
bar/restaurant is useful in these cloud-cuckoo parts
for passable soups, good lasagne, salads and
home-made fruit pies. Valpolicella or Soave are 45p
the glass, £2·05 the 'jug' (6 glasses). Taped music.
Tables outside.

Restaurants where smoking is restricted

Refer to the restaurant's entry to find out exactly what the restrictions are

London

Capital Hotel Restaurant, SW3
Chez Nico, SE22
Connaught, W1
Danwich Shop, Kingston-upon-Thames
Gay Hussar, W1
Justin de Blank, W1
Ma Cuisine, SW3
Salamis, SW10
Swiss Centre Restaurant, W1
Tate Gallery Restaurant, SW1

England

Aldborough, Norfolk
Old Red Lion

Ambleside, Cumbria
Rothay Manor

Bath, Avon
The Laden Table

Beaminster, Dorset
Pickwick's

Borrowdale, Cumbria
Leathes Head House

Bourton-on-the-Water, Glos
Rose Tree Restaurant

Brighton & Hove, E. Sussex
Bannister's
Eaton Restaurant

Bristol, Avon
Michael's

Burham, Kent
Toastmaster's Inn

Caldbeck, Cumbria
Parkend Restaurant

Cauldon Lowe, Staffs
Jean Pierre

Cawsand Bay, Cornwall
Criterion Hotel

Cheltenham, Glos
Food for Thought

Chesterton, Oxon
Kinchs

Chichester, W. Sussex
Little London Restaurant

Coatham Mundeville, Durham
Hall Garth Hotel

Colyton, Devon
Old Bakehouse

Dartington, Devon
Cranks

Drewsteignton, Devon
Castle Drogo

Eastbourne, E. Sussex
Bistro Byron
Porthole

East Grinstead, W. Sussex
Gravetye Manor

Exeter, Devon
Grael Wholefoods

Findon, W. Sussex
Findon Manor

Framfield, E. Sussex
Coach House

Frenchbeer, Devon
Teignworthy Hotel

Frome, Somerset
Mendip Lodge

Glastonbury, Somerset
No 3 Dining Rooms

Gloucester, Glos
Don Pasquale

Grasmere, Cumbria
Michael's Nook
White Moss House

Great Dunmow, Essex
The Starr

Guildford, Surrey
Cranks

Halesworth, Suffolk
Bassett's

Halland, E. Sussex
Halland Motel and Old Forge

Hertford, Herts
Maison Carton

Iddesleigh, Devon
Duke of York

Ipswich, Suffolk
Rosie's Place

Jevington, E. Sussex
Hungry Monk

513

Kersey, Suffolk
Quill's

Kintbury, Berks
Dundas Arms

Knutsford, Cheshire
David's Place

Lewes, E. Sussex
Nitchevo

Little Langdale, Cumbria
Three Shires Inn

Lower Swell, Glos
Old Farmhouse Hotel

Lustleigh, Devon
Moorwood Cottage

Manchester, Gtr Manchester
On the Eighth Day

Middleham, N. Yorks
Miller's House

Nantwich, Cheshire
Churche's Mansion

Northrepps, Norfolk
Church Barn

Ottery St Mary, Devon
The Lodge

Porlock Weir, Somerset
Ship Inn

Poundisford, Somerset
Well House

Ramsbury, Wilts
Bell Inn

St Dominick, Cornwall
Cotehele House

St Martin in Meneage, Cornwall
Boskenna

St Michaels-on-Wyre, Lancs
Rivermede Country House Hotel

Salisbury, Wilts
Crane's

Shepton Mallet, Somerset
Bowlish House

Shrewsbury, Salop
Penny Farthing

Stratford-upon-Avon, Warwicks
Ashburton House

Talkin, Cumbria
Tarn End Hotel

Tunbridge Wells, Kent
Mount Edgcumbe Hotel

Ullswater, Cumbria
Sharrow Bay Country House

West Stoughton, Somerset
Eethuys

Windermere, Cumbria
Miller Howe

Woodstock, Oxon
Luis

Wootton Bassett, Wilts
Loaves and Fishes

Wales

Cardiff, S. Glamorgan
Field's
Harvesters

Crickhowell, Powys
Gliffaes Country House Hotel

Llanwrtyd Wells, Powys
Llwynderw Hotel

Llanychaer Bridge, Dyfed
Penlan Oleu

Robeston Wathen, Dyfed
Robeston House

Scotland

Achiltibuie, Ross & Cromarty
Summer Isles Hotel

Arduaine, Argyll
Loch Melfort Hotel

Ballater, Aberdeenshire
Tullich Lodge

Eddleston, Peeblesshire
Cringletie House Hotel

Edinburgh
Henderson's Salad Table

Galashiels, Selkirkshire
Redgauntlet

Glasgow
Ubiquitous Chip

Gullane, E. Lothian
La Potinière

Inverness, Inverness-shire
Dunain Park

Isle Ornsay, Skye
Kinloch Lodge Hotel

Nairn, Nairnshire
Clifton Hotel

Peat Inn, Fife
Peat Inn

Port Appin, Argyll
Airds Hotel

Selkirk, Selkirkshire
Philipburn House Hotel

Uphall, W. Lothian
Houstoun House

Channel Islands

Sark
Aval du Creux
Hotel Petit Champ

Republic of Ireland

Annamoe, Co Wicklow
Armstrong's Barn

Bettystown, Co Meath
Coastguard Restaurant

Cork, Co Cork
Arbutus Lodge

Gorey, Co Wexford
Marlfield House

Mallow, Co Cork
Longueville House

Oughterard, Co Galway
Currarevagh House

Restaurants with air-conditioning

London

After Dark, N1
L'Amico, SW1
Arirang, W1
Arlecchino, W8
Il Barbino, W8
Beotys, WC2
Bewick's, SW3
Bloom's, E1
La Brasserie, SW7
La Bussola, WC2
Bumbles, SW1
Capital Hotel Restaurant, SW3
Carlo's Place, SW6
Carlton Tower, SW1
Carrier's, N1
Carroll's, W1
Chez Moi, W11
Daphne's, SW3
Drury Lane Hotel, Maudie's, WC2
Food For Thought, WC2
Gatamelata, W8
Gay Hussar, W1
Le Gourmet, SW3
Granary, W1
The Grange, WC2
La Grenouille, SW11
Guinea Grill, W1
Hathaways, SW11
Holy Cow, W8
Hostaria Romana, W1
Trattoria Imperia, WC2
Justin de Blank, W1
Kerzenstüberl, W1
Kew Rendezvous, Richmond
Langan's Brasserie, W1
Lebanese, W2

Leith's, W11
Little Akropolis, W1
Lockets, SW1
Maxim, W13
New Rasa Sayang, WC2
Oslo Court, NW8
I Paparazzi, W1
Pilgrim's, N6
Plummers, WC2
Poissonnerie de L'Avenue, SW3
Red Lion Chinese, Richmond
Richmond Rendezvous, Richmond
Rugantino, W1
San Frediano, SW3
Swiss Centre Restaurant, W1
Tarabya, SE13
Tate Gallery Restaurant, SW1
Throgmorton Restaurant, EC2
Uncle Pang, NW1
Upper Crust, SW1
Walton's, SW3
Wolfe's, W1

England

Ambleside, Cumbria
Rothay Manor

Bath, Avon
Lyons Bistro

Beaminster, Dorset
Pickwick's

Berkhamsted, Herts
Christl's

Blackpool, Lancs
Danish Kitchen

515

Bournemouth, Dorset
The Stable

Bridgnorth, Salop
Bambers

Brighton & Hove, E. Sussex
Athenian Steak and Kebab House
Bannister's
Eaton
Hove Manor Restaurant

Bristol, Avon
Restaurant du Gourmet

Burnham Market
Fishes'

Cambridge, Cambs
Peking

Cauldon Lowe, Staffs
Jean Pierre

Cheltenham, Glos
Food for Thought

Crackington Haven, Cornwall
Coombe Barton Hotel

Derby, Derbys
Ben Bowers

Eastbourne, E. Sussex
Porthole

Folkestone, Kent
Emilio's

Harrogate, N. Yorks
Apollo
Oliver

Heckfield, Hants
Andwell's

Henley-in-Arden, Warwicks
Filbert Cottage

Ivinghoe, Bucks
King's Head

Leeds, W. Yorks
Jumbo Chinese Restaurant
Shabab

Lewes, E. Sussex
Pelham Arms, Sussex Kitchen

Liverpool, Merseyside
Oriel

Luton, Beds
Acropolis Kebab House

Maidenhead, Berks
Maidenhead Chinese Restaurant

Malvern Wells, Hereford & Worcs
Cottage in the Wood
Croque-en-Bouche

Manchester
Danish Food Centre
Hotel Armenia Shish Kebab House
Kwok Man
Midland Hotel French Restaurant
Royal Exchange Restaurant
Woo Sang
Yang Sing

Newcastle-upon-Tyne, Tyne & Wear
Black Gate Restaurant

Oxford, Oxon
Opium Den
La Sorbonne

Pool-in-Wharfedale, W. Yorks
Pool Court (Regency)

Ramsbury, Wilts
Bell Inn

St Albans, Herts
Aspelia

St Mawes, Cornwall
Rising Sun

Salisbury, Wilts
Le Provençal (lower rest)

Shrewsbury, Salop
Penny Farthing

Southport, Merseyside
Squires

Stokeinteignhead, Devon
Harvest Barn

Tunbridge Wells, Kent
Mount Edgcumbe Hotel

Weymouth, Dorset
Sea Cow Bistro

Whitstable, Kent
Giovanni's

Windermere, Cumbria
Miller Howe

Wolverhampton, W. Midlands
Tandoor

Wrelton, N. Yorks
Huntsman

Wales

Cardiff, S. Glamorgan
Harvesters
Riverside

Llandewi Skirrid, Gwent
Walnut Tree Inn

Llangynidr, Powys
Red Lion

Swansea, W. Glamorgan
Drangway

Scotland

Auchterarder, Perthshire
Gleneagles Hotel

Edinburgh
Henderson's Salad Table
Madogs
North British Hotel, Cleikum

Wester Howgate, Midlothian
Old Howgate Inn

Channel Islands

Jersey, St Helier
La Capannina

Isle of Man

Douglas
Villiers Hotel, Clarendon Grill

Port St Mary
The Barn

Republic of Ireland

Cloon, Co Wicklow
Enniscree Lodge

Cork, Co Cork
Arbutus Lodge

Dublin
Le Coq Hardi
Kilkenny Kitchen
Tandoori Rooms

Glenbeigh, Co Kerry
Towers Hotel

Killiney, Co Dublin
Fitzpatrick Castle Hotel

Malahide, Co Dublin
Johnny's

Rosslare, Co Wexford
Strand Hotel

Sandycove, Co Dublin
Mirabeau

Wicklow, Co Wicklow
Knockrobin House

Youghal, Co Cork
Aherne's Sea Food Bar

Northern Ireland

Comber, Co Down
Old Crow

Where to dine and dance

London

La Bussola, WC2
Cervantes, Coulsdon
Kerzenstüberl, W1

England

Bridgnorth, Salop
Parlors Hall Hotel (occasionally)

Chittlehamholt, Devon
Highbullen Hotel (occasionally)

Dereham (East), Norfolk
Phoenix Hotel

Fingest, Bucks
Chequers Inn (occasionally)

Frilford, Oxon
Noah's Ark (once a month)

Frome, Somerset
Mendip Lodge (Sat in Dec & Jan)

Leeds, W. Yorks
Shabab (occasionally)

Scotland

Auchterarder, Perthshire
Gleneagles Hotel (nightly)

Aviemore, Inverness-shire
High Range Hotel (Fri)

Kirkcudbright, Kirkcudbrightshire
Ingle Restaurant (weekends)

Selkirk, Selkirkshire
Philipburn House Hotel (Sat)

Republic of Ireland

Glenbeigh, Co Kerry
Towers Hotel (Sat)

Rosslare, Co Wexford
Strand Hotel (Tue–Sat)

Slane, Co Meath
Slane Castle

Northern Ireland

Comber, Co Down
Old Crow (Sat)

Where to eat out of doors *(4 or more tables; meal not snack)*

London

La Brasserie, SW7
Le Chef, W2
Fingal's, SW6
Il Girasole, SW13
Hard Rock, W1
Maxwell's, NW3
Montpeliano, SW7
Oslo Court, NW8
Poissonnerie de l'Avenue, SW3
The Refectory, Richmond
Savvas Kebab House, W11

England

Abberley, Hereford & Worcs
The Elms

Ardingly, W. Sussex
Camelot

Birmingham, W. Midlands
Jonathans'
Michelle

Bishop's Lydeard, Somerset
Rose Cottage

Bleadon, Avon
La Casita

Bourton-on-the-Water, Glos
Rose Tree

Bridgnorth, Salop
Parlors Hall Hotel

Brighton & Hove, E. Sussex
Al Forno

Broadstairs, Kent
Marchesi Bros

Broadway, Hereford & Worcs
Hunter's Lodge

Caldbeck, Cumbria
Parkend Restaurant

Cheltenham, Glos
Aubergine

Chichester, W. Sussex
Little London Restaurant

Chittlehamholt, Devon
Highbullen Hotel

Claughton, Lancs
Old Rectory

Colchester, Essex
The Barn

Compton, Surrey
Withies Inn

Corse Lawn, Glos
Corse Lawn House

Dartington, Devon
Cranks

Ely, Cambs
Old Fire Engine House

Findon, W. Sussex
Findon Manor

Framfield, W. Sussex
Coach House

Glastonbury, Somerset
No 3 Dining Rooms

Great Yeldham, Essex
White Hart

Guist, Norfolk
Tollbridge Restaurant

Gulworthy, Devon
Horn of Plenty

Helford, Cornwall
Riverside

Herstmonceux, E. Sussex
The Sundial

Huntingdon, Cambs
Old Bridge Hotel

Iddesleigh, Devon
Duke of York

Knutsford, Cheshire
Le Belle Epoque

Lewdown, Devon
Lew Trenchard Manor

Lower Swell, Glos
Old Farmhouse Hotel

Malvern Wells, Hereford & Worcs
Cottage in the Wood

Moulton, N. Yorks
Black Bull

Nantwich, Cheshire
Churche's Mansion

Nayland, Suffolk
The Bear

Oundle, Northants
Tyrrells

Parkham, Devon
Foxdown Manor

Prior's Hardwick, Warwicks
Butcher's Arms

Redruth, Cornwall
Basset Count House

Rowsley, Derbys
Peacock Hotel

St Albans, Herts
Aspelia

St Ives, Cambs
Slepe Hall, Rugeley's Restaurant

Scole, Norfolk
Crossways Restaurant

Skipton, N. Yorks
Oats

South Petherton, Somerset
Oaklands

Stokeinteignhead, Devon
Harvest Barn

Sutton Bingham, Somerset
Sutton Bingham Manor

Tiverton, Devon
The Lowman

Torquay, Devon
Fanny's Dining Room

Underbarrow, Cumbria
Tullythwaite House

Wansford, Cambs
Haycock Inn

Wells, Somerset
Rugantino

Wootton Bassett, Wilts
Loaves and Fishes

Wales

Broadhaven, Dyfed
Druidstone Hotel

Colwyn Bay, Clwyd
Holland Arms

Crickhowell, Powys
Nantyffin Cider Mill

Llandewi Skirrid, Gwent
Walnut Tree Inn

Penmaenpool, Gwynedd
George III Hotel

Robeston Wathen, Dyfed
Robeston House

St David's, Dyfed
St Non's Hotel

Scotland

Ardentinny, Argyll
Ardentinny Hotel

Arduaine, Argyll
Loch Melfort Hotel

Crinan, Argyll
Crinan Hotel

Dirleton, E. Lothian
Open Arms

Kingskettle, Fife
Annfield House

Overscaig, Sutherland
Overscaig Hotel

Selkirk, Selkirkshire
Philipburn House

Weem, Perthshire
Ailean Chraggan Hotel

Channel Islands

Jersey, St Brelade
La Place Hotel, Cartwheel

Jersey, St Brelade
Greenhill Country Hotel

Sark
Dixcart Hotel

Republic of Ireland

Dunderry, Co Meath
Dunderry Lodge

Glenbeigh, Co Kerry
Towers Hotel

Knockferry, Co Galway
Knockferry Lodge

Mallow, Co Cork
Longueville House

Value for money

We list here restaurants and hotels whose prices are underlined in the text to indicate (in the *Guide*'s opinion) good value for money. Places where such a meal can be had for under £4·50 are starred. But please consult individual entries carefully: 'value' meals may not be offered every day, or at all times of day.

London

Alonso's, SW8 (tdh L)
Bloom's, E1
Carlo's Place, SW6
Le Chef, W2
Diwana Bhel Poori House, NW1 & W2*
Eatons, SW1
Efes Kebab House, W1
Gay Hussar, W1 (tdh L)
La Giralda, Pinner (tdh D)*
The Grange, WC2
Hathaways, SW11
Vasco and Piero's Pavilion, W1

England

Bourton-on-the-Water, Glos
Rose Tree Restaurant (tdh L & Sun L)

Brighton, E. Sussex
Lawrence Restaurant
Peking

Caldbeck, Cumbria
Parkend Restaurant

Chittlehamholt, Devon
Highbullen Hotel

Eastbourne, E. Sussex
Bistro Byron

East Horsley, Surrey
Tudor Rose (tdh L & Sun L)*

Fadmoor, N. Yorks
Plough

Folkestone, Kent
Emilio's

Great Dunmow, Essex
Starr (all exc Sat D)

Great Witley, Hereford & Worcs
Hundred House (tdh buffet L)*

Halesworth, Suffolk
Bassett's

Heald Green, Gtr Manchester
La Bonne Auberge (tdh L)*

High Easter, Essex
Punch Bowl

Horton, Northants
French Partridge

Husbands Bosworth, Leics
Fernie Lodge*

Knutsford, Cheshire
David's Place (tdh L)

Leeds, W. Yorks
Jumbo Chinese*

Liverpool, Merseyside
Oriel (tdh)
Peking and Shanghai*

Manchester, Gtr Manchester
Casa España*
Woo Sang

Nantwich, Cheshire
Churche's Mansion*

Newcastle upon Tyne, Tyne & Wear
Moti Mahal*

Newton Poppleford, Devon
Bridge End House (tdh)*

Northallerton, N. Yorks
Romanby Court (tdh L)*

Oxford, Oxon
Les Quat' Saisons (tdh L)

Porlock Weir, Somerset
Ship Inn (tdh L)

Poundisford, Somerset
Well House

Pulborough, W. Sussex
Stane Street Hollow*

Reeth, N. Yorks
Burgoyne Hotel*

Romiley, Gtr Manchester
Waterside (tdh L)

St Just in Penwith, Cornwall
Count House (tdh Sun L)

St Martin in Meneage, Cornwall
Boskenna

South Petherton, Somerset
Oaklands (tdh D & Sun L)

Southport, Merseyside
Le Coq Hardi

Stratford-upon-Avon, Warwicks
Ashburton House

Sway, Hants
Pine Trees

Talkin, Cumbria
Tarn End Hotel (tdh)

Teignmouth, Devon
Churchill's (tdh L)

Tonbridge, Kent
A La Bonne Franquette (tdh L)*

Tregony, Cornwall
Kea House

Underbarrow, Cumbria
Tullythwaite House

West Runton, Norfolk
Mirabelle (tdh)

Weybourne, Norfolk
Gasché's Swiss Restaurant (tdh)

Weybridge, Surrey
Casa Romana (tdh L)

Weymouth, Dorset
Sea Cow Bistro

Whitstable, Kent
Giovanni's (tdh L)

Worthing, W. Sussex
Paragon (tdh)

Wye, Kent
Wife of Bath

Wales

Llanwddyn, Powys
Lake Vyrnwy Hotel*

St David's, Dyfed
St Non's (tdh buffet L)*

Scotland

Eddleston, Peeblesshire
Cringletie (tdh L)

Edinburgh
Loon Fung*

Gullane, E. Lothian
La Potinière*

Channel Islands

Sark
Hotel Petit Champ*

Ireland

Oughterard, Co Galway
Currarevagh House

Shanagarry, Co Cork
Ballymaloe House

REPORT FORMS
for the use of members

Please use a separate report form (or sheet of paper
if you prefer) for each restaurant or hotel, so that
we can file each report separately in its own
restaurant file. Forms for reporting on restaurants,
pubs and wine bars follow.

Tell us, if you can, exactly what you ate and
drank, what it cost and whether or not it was
good, and what the service was like. Mention the
surroundings, the decor, the music. Was the place
friendly? Clean? Quiet? Was it good value for
money?

If you report on a hotel you have stayed at, tell
us also something about the standard of
accommodation – whether or not it was
comfortable and pleasant, and if it was good
value for money. But please: food first and
foremost; comfort and hotel facilities second.

Let us have your report as soon as you can after
your meal or stay, and in no case later than
September 30, 1979.

Write – and sign – as clearly as possible: we hate
misprinting names.

Ask us for more forms, which we will
send free, from Freepost, The Good Food Guide,
14 Buckingham Street, London WC2N 6BR

And above all, please do report to us. Do not
let the villain who half-poisoned you get away
unmarked; do not deprive the excellent people
who served you so well of the reputation and
custom they deserve.

The Good Food Guide REPORT FORM [I.79]

To the Editor, *The Good Food Guide*, Freepost,
14 Buckingham Street, London WC2N 6BR

From my personal experience I CONFIRM that _____

_____

on page _____ deserves its place in the list.

I stayed/had lunch/dined there on _____ 19_____

I am not connected directly or indirectly with management or proprietors.

You may/may not print my name.

Signed _____

Name and address (BLOCK CAPITALS) _____

_____

Report (please describe anything you think relevant – style, comfort,
accommodation, if any, sounds and smells, as well as food, drink and service.)

☐ *please tick if you would like
   this report acknowledged*

☐ *please tick if you would like
   more report forms*

please continue overleaf

My meal for . . . . people
cost: food £
drink £
VAT & service £
(if added on)
total £
Attach bill where possible

To the Editor, *The Good Food Guide*, Freepost,
14 Buckingham Street, London WC2N 6BR

From my personal experience I NOMINATE for inclusion in your list

_____

_____

Telephone: _____

I stayed/had lunch/dined there on _____ 19____

I am not connected directly or indirectly with management or proprietors.

You may/may not print my name.

Signed _____

Name and address (BLOCK CAPITALS) _____

_____

Report (please describe anything you think relevant – style, comfort,
accommodation, if any, sounds and smells, as well as food, drink and service.)

☐ *please tick if you would like
this report acknowledged*

☐ *please tick if you would like
more report forms*

please continue overleaf

| My meal for . . . . people |
| cost: food £ |
| drink £ |
| VAT & service £ |
| (if added on) |
| total £ |
| *Attack bill where possible* |

To the Editor, *The Good Food Guide*, Freepost,
14 Buckingham Street, London WC2N 6BR

From my personal experience I DO NOT/WOULD NOT APPROVE of the
inclusion in your list of the following establishment

_____

_____ on page _____
for the reasons given below.

I stayed/had lunch/dined there on _____ 19____

I am not connected directly or indirectly with management or proprietors.

This communication is confidential and my name is not to be disclosed.

Signed _____

Name and address (BLOCK CAPITALS) _____

_____

Report

☐ *please tick if you would like
this report acknowledged*

☐ *please tick if you would like
more report forms*

please continue overleaf

My meal for . . . . people
cost: food £
       drink £
VAT & service £
(if added on) · _____
     total £
Attach bill where possible

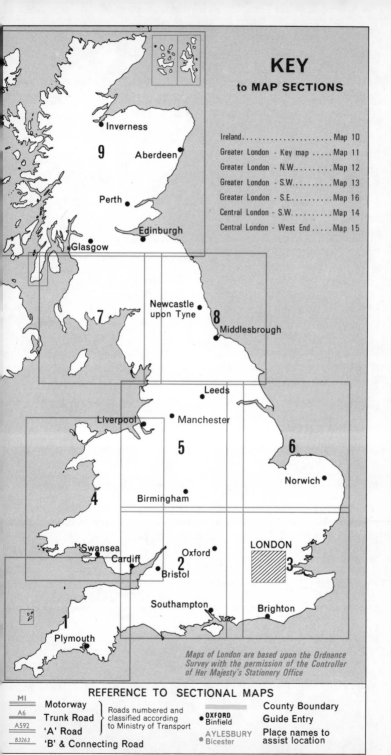

KEY
to MAP SECTIONS

Inverness

Aberdeen

9

Perth

Edinburgh

Glasgow

Newcastle upon Tyne

7   **8**

Middlesbrough

Leeds

Liverpool   Manchester

5   **6**

Norwich

4

Birmingham

Swansea
Cardiff   Oxford

2   LONDON   **3**

Bristol

Southampton   Brighton

*Maps of London are based upon the Ordnance
Survey with the permission of the Controller
of Her Majesty's Stationery Office*

1

Plymouth

REFERENCE TO SECTIONAL MAPS

MI	Motorway	Roads numbered and classified according to Ministry of Transport
A6	Trunk Road	
A592	'A' Road	
B3263	'B' & Connecting Road	

●OXFORD
Binfield   Guide Entry

AYLESBURY
●Bicester   Place names to assist location

▒▒▒▒▒   County Boundary

Cartographic Services (Cirencester) Ltd.

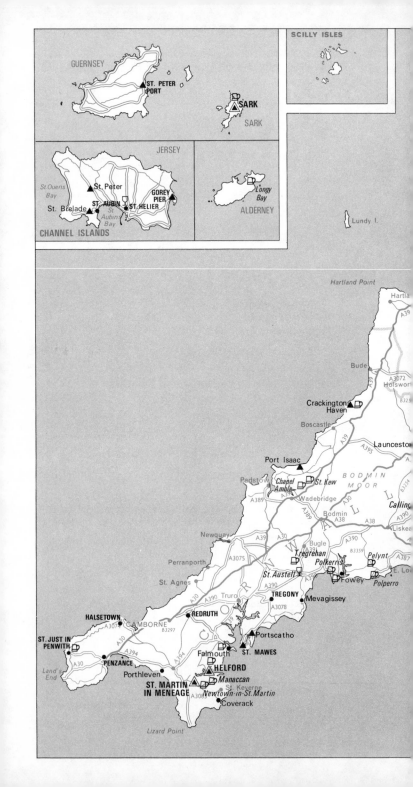

1

SOUTH-WEST ENGLAND

SCILLY ISLES

CHANNEL ISLANDS

Rooms   NoRooms
△ **BATH** ⊙   Recommendation with distinction
                (See How to Use the Guide)
▲ **LEEDS** ●   Recommendation with credit
▲ Melrose ●   Useful in the area or price range

🍺 *Brecon*   Public house
🍷 *Woburn*   Wine bar

BRISTOL   CHANNEL

Lynton
Ilfracombe
PORLOCK WEIR
🍺 *Brendon*
MINEHEAD
lacombe
Georgeham
EXMOOR
Watchet
BILBROOK ▲
▲ **WILLITON**
raunton
Wrafton
BARNSTAPLE
BISHOP'S LYDEARD 🍺
Langley Marsh
Bideford
Milverton
PARKHAM
Great Torrington
△ **CHITTLEHAMHOLT**
Bampton
2
Chulmleigh
IDDESLEIGH 🍺▲
🍺 *Winkleigh*
🍺▲ *Hatherleigh*
TIVERTON
Honiton
D   E   V   O   N
🍺
Crediton
GITTISHAM
Okehampton
South Zeal
▲ *Drewsteignton*
Exeter
OTTERY ST MARY
▲ Lewdown
CHAGFORD
🍺 *Fingle Bridge*
NEWTON POPPLEFORD ▲
St John
Tipton
Lydford
FRENCHBEER ▲
Exminster
Sidmouth
DARTMOOR
LUSTLEIGH *Hennock*
Mamhead
Lympstone
Budleigh Salterton
🍺 *Peter Tavy*
🍺
A380
🍺 *Cockwood*
Dawlish
vistock
⊙ **GULWORTHY**
Combeinteignhead
Newton Abbot
▲ **TEIGNMOUTH**
● **STOKEINTEIGNHEAD**
St. Dominick
Buckfastleigh
Rattery 🍺
Dartington
TORQUAY
Crown Hill
TOTNES
PAIGNTON
Plympton
Plymouth
▲ **BRIXHAM**
▲ *Cawsand Bay*
🍺 *Modbury*
Kingswear
DARTMOUTH
Burgh Island 🍺
Kingsbridge
Start Point

10   0   Miles   10   20

Cartographic Services (Cirencester) Ltd.

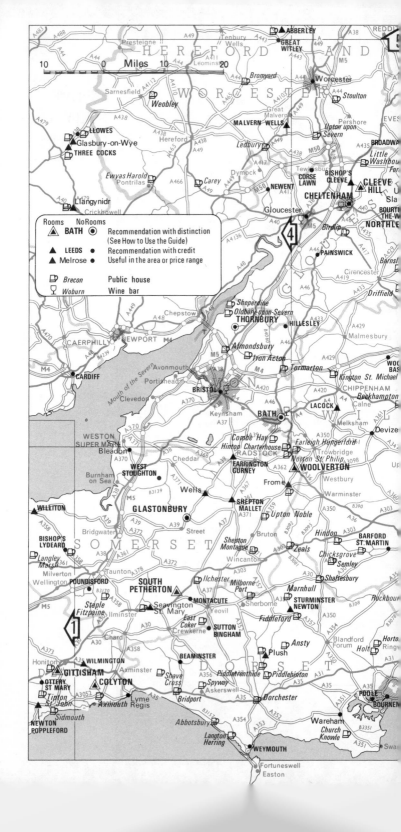

2

SOUTH-WEST ENGLAND

(see map 1 for Devon and Cornwall)

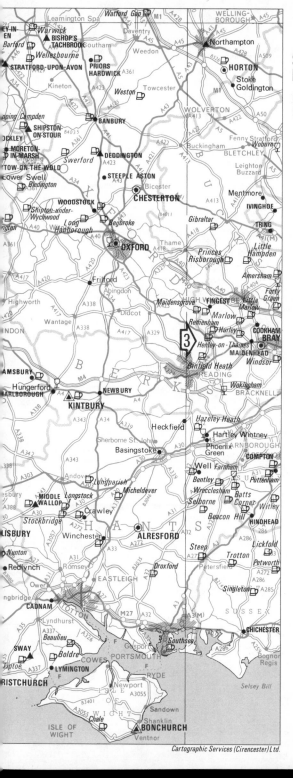

Cartographic Services (Cirencester) Ltd.

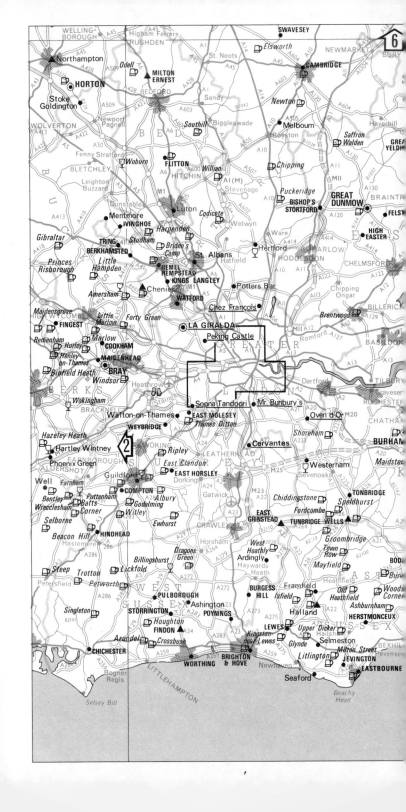

SOUTH-EAST ENGLAND and THE HOME COUNTIES

BADWELL ASH

Framlingham

Saxmundham

Sizewell
Leiston

Stowmarket

Snape

A45

A134

A1141

Needham Market
Bildeston

A140

ORFORD

avenham

Woodbridge

Orford Ness

Cavendish

Long Melford KERSEY

HADLEIGH
HINTLESHAM

IPSWICH

A137

A107

A12

NAYLAND

A14

FELIXSTOWE

Wormingford
Halstead

DEDHAM
Ardleigh

HARWICH

Earls Colne

COLCHESTER A136

The Naze

Pattiswick

Wivenhoe

Walton-on-the-Naze

Frinton

tham

West Mersea

CLACTON-ON-SEA

B1010

BURNHAM-ON-CROUCH

ayleigh

A127

SOUTHEND
Shoeburyness

NVEY

River Thames

SHEERNESS

Leysdown-on-Sea

MARGATE

North Foreland

NGHAM

A250

Herne Bay

Broadstairs

SITTINGBOURNE
FAVERSHAM

WHITSTABLE

Stodmarsh

RAMSGATE

Boughton

Fordwich

Ash

PAINTER'S
FORSTAL Chilham

CANTERBURY

A257

EASTRY

Deal

East Sutton

A256

Walmer

Little
Chart

WYE

A2

South Foreland

Biddenden

Dover

nenden

Tenterden

FOLKESTONE

en
een

Stone

Hythe

S T R A I T

ewhurst
reen

Rye

O F   D O V E R

Winchelsea

Lydd

Dungeness

ASTINGS

| 10 | 0 | Miles | 10 | | 20 |

Rooms	NoRooms	
▲ **BATH**	◉	Recommendation with distinction (See How to Use the Guide)
▲ **LEEDS**	●	Recommendation with credit
▲ Melrose	●	Useful in the area or price range
⌂ *Brecon*		Public house
♀ *Woburn*		Wine bar

Cartographic Services (Cirencester) Ltd.

WALES

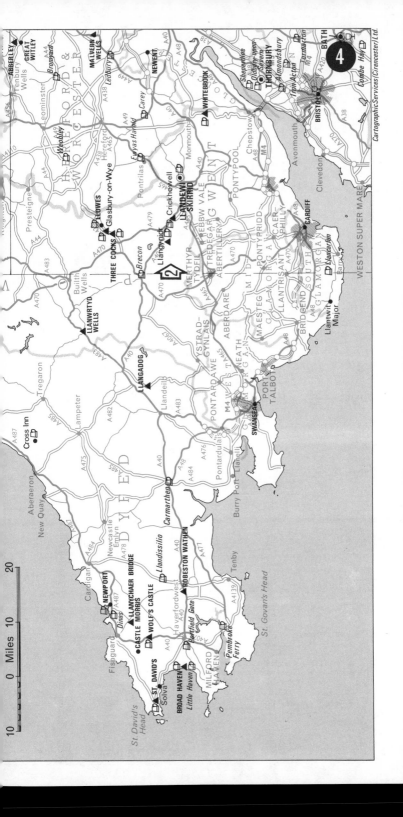

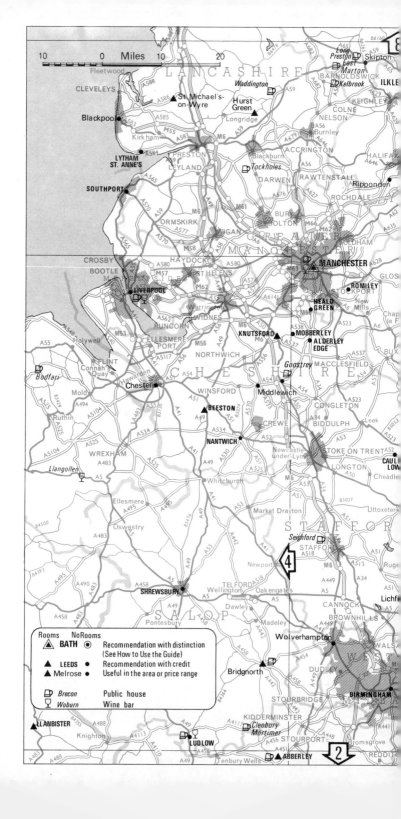

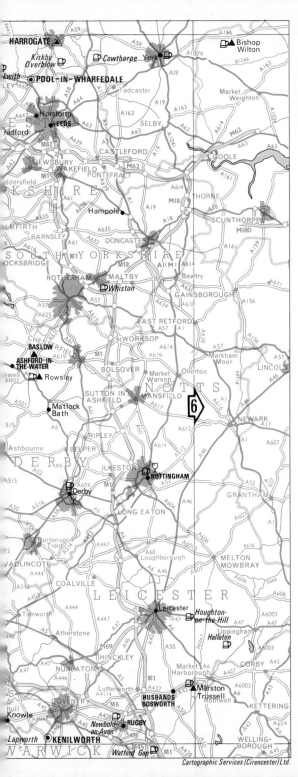

Cartographic Services (Cirencester) Ltd.

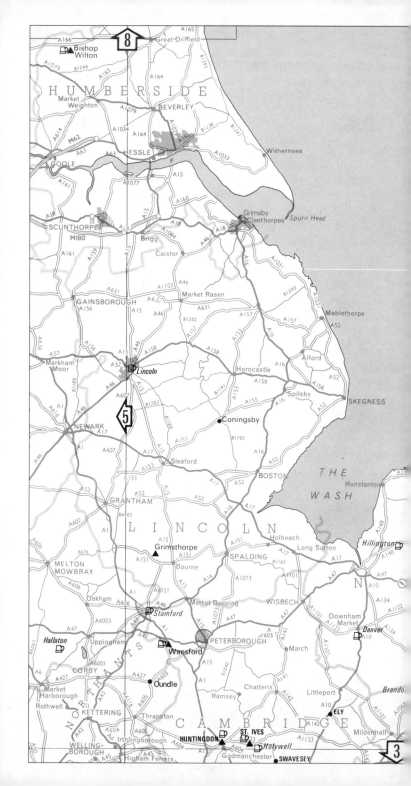

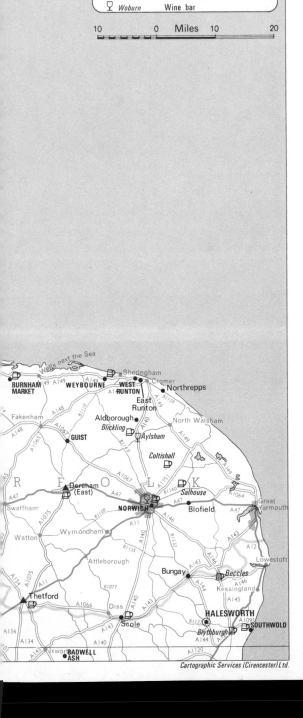

Rooms	NoRooms	
△ **BATH**	⊙	Recommendation with distinction (See How to Use the Guide)
▲ **LEEDS**	●	Recommendation with credit
▲ Melrose	●	Useful in the area or price range
🏠 *Brecon*		Public house
🍷 *Woburn*		Wine bar

10　　0　Miles　10　　20

Wells next the Sea
Sheringham
BURNHAM MARKET A149 A149 **WEYBOURNE** **WEST RUNTON** Cromer Northrepps
East Runton
Fakenham A148 Aldborough
Blickling Blickling 🏠 Aylsham North Walsham
GUIST
Coltishall 🏠
R F O L K
Dereham (East) A47 Salhouse
NORWICH Blofield Great Yarmouth
Swaffham Wymondham
Watton
Attleborough Lowestoft
Bungay Beccles 🏠
Thetford 🏠 Kessingland
Diss **HALESWORTH**
Scole Blythburgh 🏠 **SOUTHWOLD**
BADWELL ASH

Cartographic Services (Cirencester) Ltd.

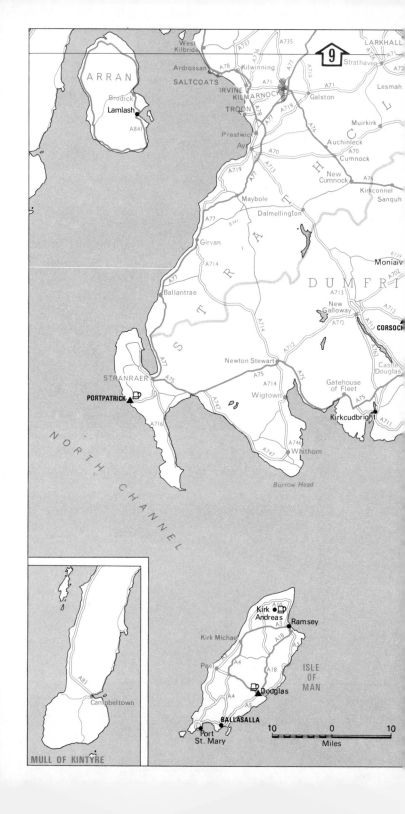

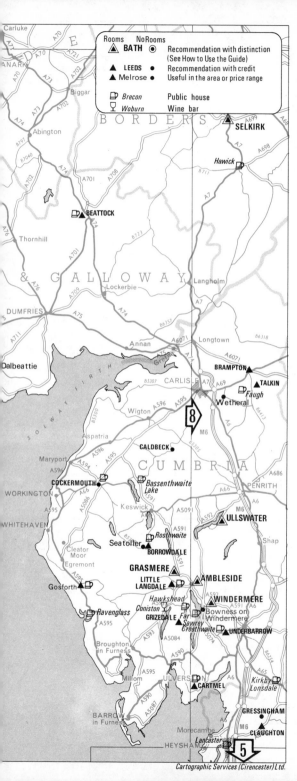

Rooms NoRooms
△ **BATH** ⊙ Recommendation with distinction
(See How to Use the Guide)
▲ **LEEDS** ● Recommendation with credit
▲ Melrose ● Useful in the area or price range

🏠 *Brecon* Public house
🍷 *Woburn* Wine bar

Cartographic Services (Cirencester) Ltd.

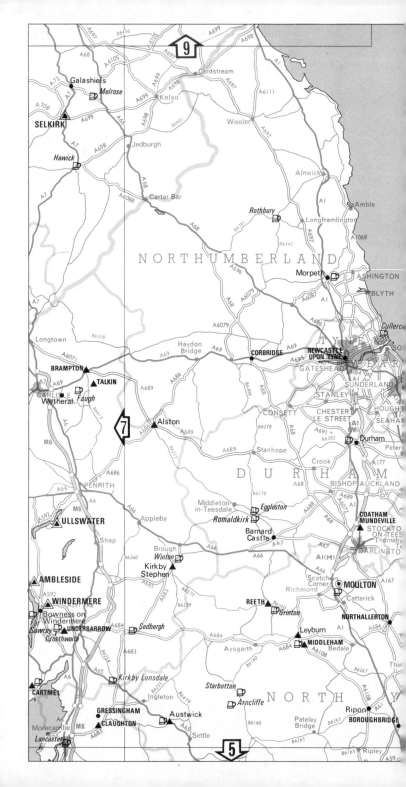

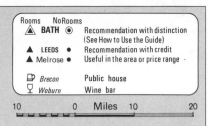

	Rooms	NoRooms	
△	**BATH**	◉	Recommendation with distinction (See How to Use the Guide)
▲	**LEEDS**	●	Recommendation with credit
▲	Melrose	●	Useful in the area or price range ·
⌂	*Brecon*		Public house
♀	*Woburn*		Wine bar

10   0   Miles   10   20

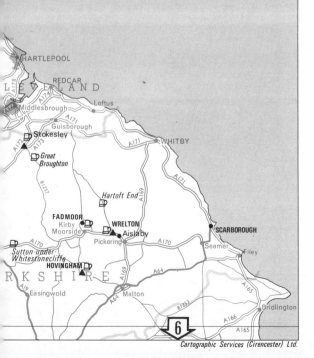

HIELDS

E SPRING

HARTLEPOOL

REDCAR

L E V E L A N D

Middlesbrough
Loftus

Guisborough

Stokesley   WHITBY

Great Broughton

Hartoft End

FADMOOR   **WRELTON**
Kirby Moorside   Aislaby
Pickering   **SCARBOROUGH**

Sutton-under-Whitestonecliffe   Seamer   Filey

HOVINGHAM

R K S H I R E

Easingwold   Malton

Bridlington

6

Cartographic Services (Cirencester) Ltd.

SCOTLAND (see also maps 7 & 8)

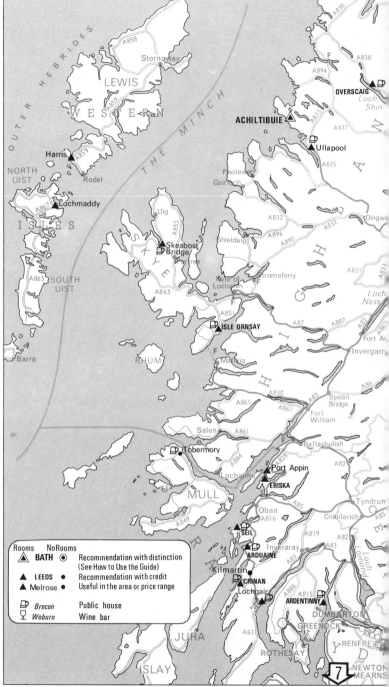

10   0   10   20 Miles

OUTER HEBRIDES

LEWIS

WESTERN

Stornoway

A858

A859

THE MINCH

Harris

NORTH UIST

Rodel

A859

Lochmaddy

A867

ISLES

SOUTH UIST

A865

Barra

Durness

A838

F

A894

A838

OVERSCAIG

Loch Shin

A837

ACHILTIBUIE

A835

Ullapool

A835

Poolewe

Gairloch

Dingwa

A832

A896

A832

Shieldaig

A890

A831

Uig

A855

Skeabost Bridge

Portree

Stromeferry

F F

A831

Loch Ness

Kyle of Lochalsh

A863

F

A851

ISLE ORNSAY

A87

A887

A82

Fort Au

Invergarry

F

RHUM

Mallaig

A861

A830

A861

Spean Bridge

A86

Fort William

Salen

A861

Ballachulish

A82

Tobermory

A884

Port Appin

A828

ERISKA

Lochaline

MULL

Oban

A85

Tyndrum

Crianlarich

A82

A849

A816

SEIL

A819

A82

Inveraray

ARDUAINE

A83

Kilmartin

A83

CRINAN

Lochgair

A886

A815

ARDENTINNY

Loch Lomond

DUMBARTON

GREENOCK

JURA

A83

RENFREW

ROTHESAY

ISLAY

NEWTON MEARNS

7

Rooms NoRooms

△ ▲ **BATH** ⊙ Recommendation with distinction (See How to Use the Guide)

▲ **LEEDS** ● Recommendation with credit

▲ Melrose ● Useful in the area or price range

🏠 *Brecon* Public house

🍷 *Woburn* Wine bar

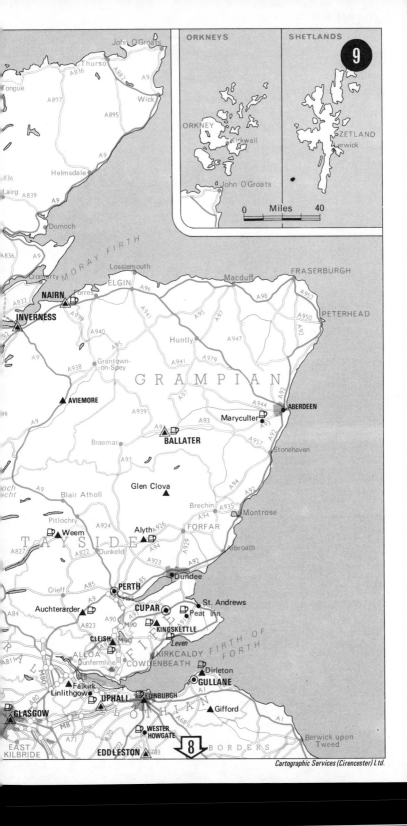

ORKNEYS

SHETLANDS

9

ORKNEY

Kirkwall

ZETLAND

Lerwick

John O'Groats

0   Miles   40

John O'Groats

Thurso   A882   A9   Wick

Tongue   A836

A897   A895

A9

Helmsdale

836

Lairg   A839   A9

Dornoch

A836   A9

MORAY FIRTH

Cromarty   Lossiemouth   Macduff   FRASERBURGH

NAIRN   Forres   ELGIN   A96   A98   A952   PETERHEAD

INVERNESS   A939   A941   A95   A97   A947   A950   A92

A832

A9   A940   Huntly   A979   A92

A938   Grantown-   A941

on-Spey   A95   G R A M P I A N

A9   AVIEMORE   A97   A944   ABERDEEN

is   A939   A93   Maryculter   A92

A9   A93   A957   Stonehaven

Braemar   BALLATER   A957

A93   A94

och   A9   Blair Atholl   Glen Clova

cht   Brechin   A935   Montrose

Pitlochry   A94   A94

Weem   A924   Alyth   A926   FORFAR   A929   Arbroath

T A Y S I D E   Dunkeld   A94   A92

A827   A822   A923

Crieff   A85   A85   Dundee

PERTH   St. Andrews

Auchterarder   A9   CUPAR   Peat Inn

A84   A823   A90   KINGSKETTLE

A90   M90   Leven

CLEISH   M90   F I F E   FIRTH OF

ALLOA   KIRKCALDY   FORTH

Dunfermline   COWDENBEATH   Dirleton

Falkirk   GULLANE

Linlithgow   UPHALL   EDINBURGH

GLASGOW   L O T H I A N   Gifford

M8   A68   A1   Berwick upon

A71   WESTER   Tweed

EAST   HOWGATE   8   B O R D E R S

KILBRIDE   EDDLESTON   A703

IRELAND

Rooms NoRooms

△MALLOW○   Recommendation with distinction (See How to Use the Guide)

▲ MOYARD :   Recommendation with credit

▲ Comber •   Useful in the area or price range

🏠 *Clarinbridge*   Public house

🍷 *Kinsale*   Wine bar

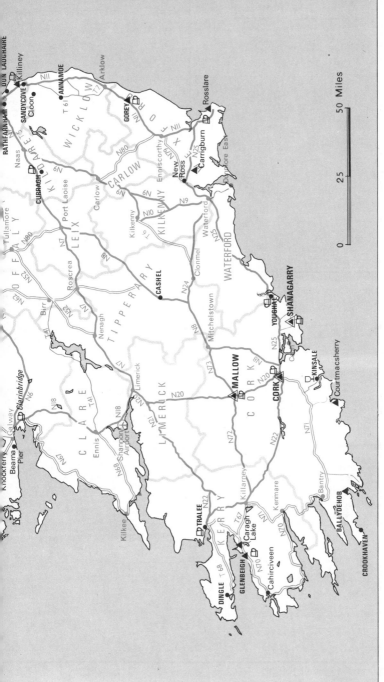

50 Miles

25

0   25   50

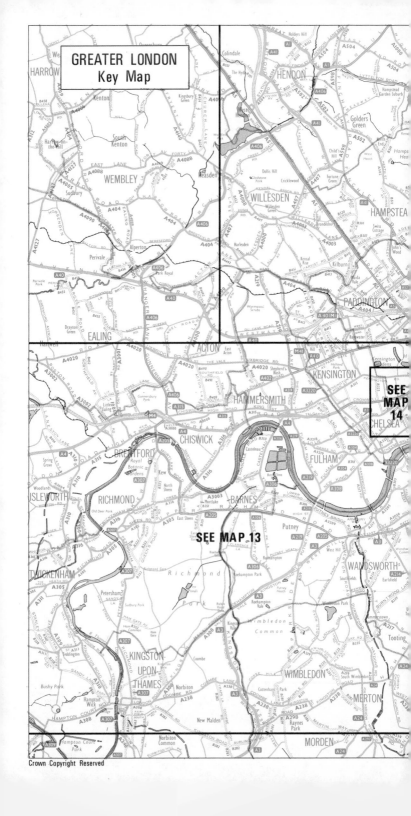

GREATER LONDON
Key Map

SEE MAP 14

SEE MAP 13

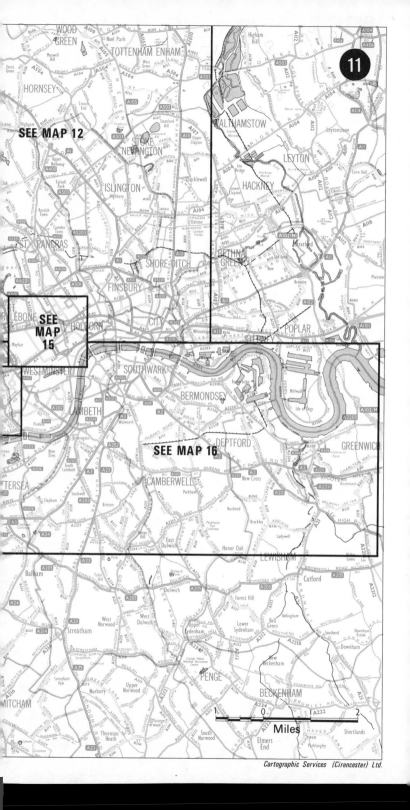

Rooms   No Rooms
△ CHEZ NICO ⊙   Recommendation with distinction
                (See How to Use the Guide)
▲ Bubb's   ●   Recommendation with credit
▲ Lockets   ●   Useful in the area or price range
🏠 Salisbury   Public house
🍷 Coates   Wine bar

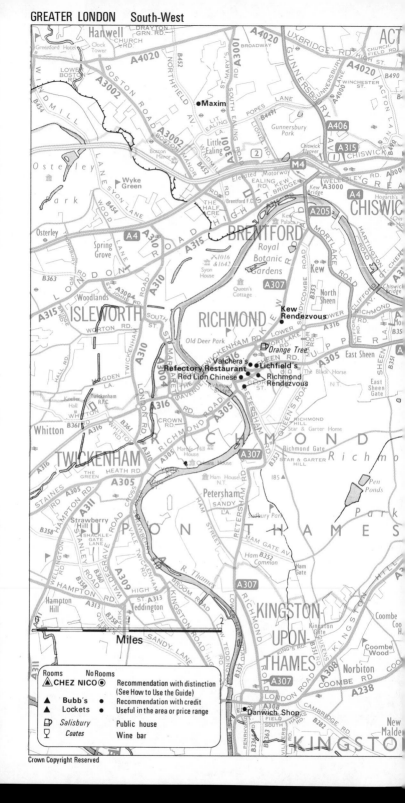

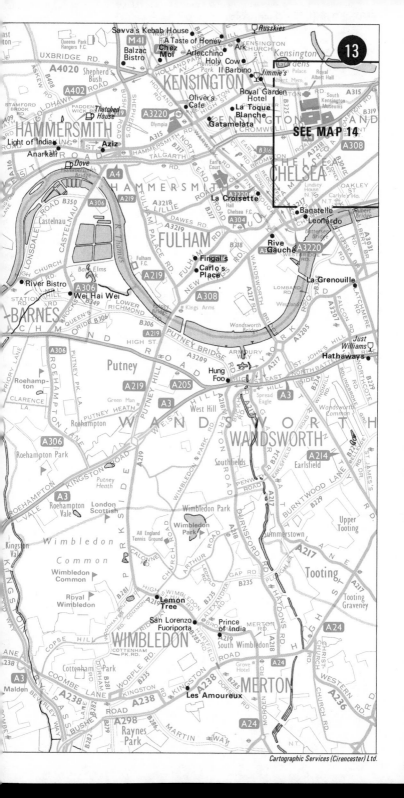

Rooms   No Rooms
△ **CHEZ NICO** ◉   Recommendation with distinction
                    (See How to Use the Guide)
▲ **Bubb's** ●   Recommendation with credit
▲ **Lockets** ●   Useful in the area or price range
🍺 *Salisbury*   Public house
🍷 *Coates*   Wine bar

Coalbrookdale Gate
Alexandra Gate
Prince of Wales Gate

Kensington Rd.
Princes Gate

Kensington Gore

Royal College of Art

Royal Albert Hall

Imperial College

Prince Consort Road

Royal College of Music

City & Guilds College

Princes Gardens
Ennismore Gdns.

Princes Gate Mews

Holy Trinity Church

Imperial Institute Rd.

Royal College of Science

Science Museum

Royal College of Art

Brompton Oratory

Geological Museum

Victoria and Albert Museum

Natural History Museum

Cromwell Gardens

La Brasserie ●

French University College

Thurloe Place

Thurloe St.

South Ter.

Walton

⊖ South Kensington

Pelham Street

Poissonner de l'Avent

Harrington Rd.
Bangkok ●

Crescent

Stanhope Gdns.

Onslow Sq.

Onslow

● Al Ben Accolto

San Frediano

Brompton Hospital

Royal Cancer Hospital

St. Luke's Hospital

Chelsea Hospital for Women

Il Girasole ●

Chelsea Polytechnic

● William F's Restaurant

🍷 *Brays Place*
● Salamis

Le Gourmet ●

● La Fringale

St. Stephen's Hospital

Crown Copyright Reserved

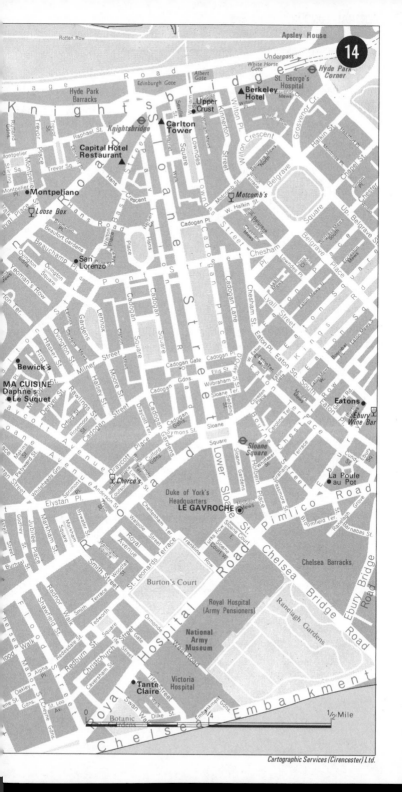

14

Rotten Row

Apsley House

Underpass
White Horse Gate
Albert Gate

Hyde Park Corner
St. George's Hospital

Edinburgh Gate

Hyde Park Barracks

Berkeley Hotel

Knightsbridge

Upper Crust

Carlton Tower

Belgrave Square

Capital Hotel Restaurant

●**Montpeliano**

♟*Loose Box*

Motcomb's

Chesham Pl

●**San Lorenzo**

Cadogan Pl.

Chesham St.

Cadogan Lane

Eaton Square

Cadogan Place

●**Bewick's**

MA CUISINE
Daphne's
●**Le Suquet**

Cadogan Gate Cadogan Pl.
Ellis St.
Wilbraham St.
Sloane Ter.

Eatons ●

Ebury Wine Bar

Cadogan Square

Sloane Square

♟*Charco's*

Sloane Square

La Poule au Pot ●

Duke of York's Headquarters
LE GAVROCHE ⊙

Pimlico Road

Elystan Pl.

Chelsea Barracks

Burton's Court

Royal Hospital (Army Pensioners)

Ranelagh Gardens

Ebury Bridge Road

Chelsea Bridge

National Army Museum

●**Tante Claire**

Victoria Hospital

Chelsea Embankment

0 ¼ ½ Mile

Botanic

Cartographic Services (Cirencester) Ltd.

CENTRAL LONDON West End

Diwan-I-Am

Madame Tussaud's Exhibition

Great Portland Street

Euston

Royal Academy of Music

Regent's Park

Crescent

Nottingham St.

Devonshire Place

Marylebone High Street

Moxon St.

St. Vincent

Manchester Street

Robert Adam

Fitzhardinge

Seymour

Orchard St.

Carburton St.

Clipstone St.

Post Office Tower

Howland

Portland Place

Broadcasting House

All Souls Church

Langham Place

Middlesex Hospital

Efes Kebab House

Wigmore Hall

Wigmore Street

Cavendish Square

Margaret

Arirang Korea

Singapore

Chaopraya

Kerzenstüberl

Oxford Circus

Vasco and Pieros Pavilion

Grahame's Sea Fare

Justin de Blank

Bond Street

New Bond Street

Hanover Square

Brook Street

Grosvenor Street

Conduit St.

Shamp

Grosvenor Square

Grosvenor Hill

Guinea Grill

Bruton

CONNAUGHT HOTEL

Berkeley Square

Royal Academy of Arts

Burlington House

Upper Grosvenor St.

Farm Street

Hill Street

Granary

Burlington

Old Bond St.

Vigo St.

South

Stanhope Gate

Curzon

Langan's Brasserie

Green Park

Wolfe's

Queen's Walk

Hard Rock Cafe

GREEN PARK

Crown Copyright Reserved